TEXTS AND TRANSMISSION

TEXTS AND TRANSMISSION

A Survey of the Latin Classics

EDITED BY

L. D. REYNOLDS

Contributors

P. K. MARSHALL

M. D. REEVE

L. D. REYNOLDS

R. H. ROUSE

R. J. TARRANT

M. WINTERBOTTOM

and others

CLARENDON PRESS · OXFORD
1983

Oxford University Press, Walton Street, Oxford OX2 6DP

London Glasgow New York Toronto
Delhi Bombay Calcutta Madras Karachi
Kuala Lumpur Singapore Hong Kong Tokyo
Nairobi Dar es Salaam Cape Town
Melbourne Auckland

and associated companies in
Beirut Berlin Ibadan Mexico City Nicosia

Oxford is a trade mark of Oxford University Press

Published in the United States by
Oxford University Press, New York

British Library Cataloguing in Publication Data
Reynolds, L.D.
    Texts and transmission.
    1. Latin literature – History and criticisms
    I. Title
    870.9'001   PA6003
ISBN 0-19-814456-3

Typeset by Oxford Verbatim Limited
and Printed in Great Britain
at the University Press, Oxford

This book
largely the work of friends and pupils
was planned as a tribute to

SIR ROGER MYNORS

Kennedy Professor of Latin
in the University of Cambridge 1944–53
Corpus Christi Professor of Latin
in the University of Oxford 1953–70

to be presented to him on the occasion of his
eightieth birthday

PREFACE

This book was conceived as a tribute to Sir Roger Mynors by a group of pupils and friends who wished to put together a volume of more practical use to readers than the traditional type of Festschrift. Our aim has been to present a series of concise and up-to-date accounts of the manuscript tradition and transmission of Latin texts. Although we have considerably changed the scale and emphasis, it was the need to revise the entries in a book remarkable for its time, F. W. Hall's *Companion to Classical Texts* (Oxford, 1913), that provided the original motive.

The book attempts to serve editors and palaeographers in so far as it provides under one cover information on the tradition of Latin authors which otherwise has to be laboriously extracted from numerous editions and articles. But it is intended more for classicists whose interests are not primarily textual or palaeographical but who do need concise and critically digested information on these matters, and in particular for students of other disciplines who desire short and readily accessible accounts in a modern language of the critical basis, historical transmission, or geographical availability of texts which form an essential part of the substructure of western European culture.

It was decided to include all authors and texts down to Apuleius which had their own independent transmission, and to add to these a generous selection of later authors who might be regarded for one reason or another as belonging to the classical tradition. In this latter category there are no firm criteria, decision is often arbitrary, and some will find omitted an author whom they would have wished to see included; we ourselves regret that more attention has not been paid, for example, to the *grammatici*. But time and space, among other considerations, dictated that a line had to be drawn somewhere, however difficult that line would be to draw and defend.

The task of writing up the accounts of the 134 separate traditions included in the alphabetical series was largely shared among the six main contributors, but scholars known to be working on specific texts were asked, and kindly agreed, to contribute articles based on their own research or to help in various ways. The main contributors have read and had the opportunity to comment upon all the articles included and are jointly responsible for the policy and the results of the project. Collaboration extended to individual articles: some were jointly written, either in the sense that different sections were written by different contributors, or that one revised or amplified the original draft submitted by another. The editor is responsible for the general organization, the Index of Manuscripts, and the map.

The articles differ in various ways. Some are original pieces of research containing unpublished material, others summarize and where necessary bring up to date traditions which are amply treated in existing publications, some simply reflect our present, often inadequate, knowledge of a text and attempt, where there are gaps in that knowledge, to indicate possible areas for further research. We have constantly tried to provide as accurate information as we could about the manuscripts we mention, their current shelf-marks, date, and, where possible, some indication of origin or provenance, details which are often lacking even in recent and authoritative editions. The articles necessarily vary somewhat in style and emphasis and reflect the interests of the individual contributors.

We are greatly indebted to those who have given their expert advice, particularly on palaeographical matters. Professor Bernhard Bischoff has responded with his customary generosity to queries, and his help in this, as in all similar ventures, is paramount. Professor Birger Munk Olsen kindly supplied information about a number of manuscripts from his forthcoming catalogue of Latin classical manuscripts down to the year 1200. Dr Virginia Brown allowed us access to the revised edition of *The Beneventan Script* while it was still in proof. Constant help and advice has been given by those whose eyrie is in the Bodleian Library. The late Dr Richard Hunt took a great interest in the project until we were suddenly and sadly bereft of his help. Dr Bruce Barker-Benfield has assisted at every stage with advice and criticism and also undertaken the heavy task of compiling the Index of Names. The constant help and advice we have received from Dr A. C. de la Mare is abundantly apparent from the notes. Among the many others to whom we are indebted particular mention must be made of Dr François Avril, Dr Christopher de Hamel, Miss Carlotta Dionisotti, Mr P. T. Eden, Professor Mirella Ferrari, Mme Jeannine Fohlen, Professor F. R. D. Goodyear, Mr N. R. Ker, Dr Konrad Müller, Mr M. B. Parkes, M. Pierre Petitmengin, Dr Jørgen Raasted, Professor Silvia Rizzo, and Dr Danuta Shanzer. We also wish to thank the Institut de Recherche et d'Histoire des Textes for invaluable help, the many librarians who have supplied essential information about manuscripts in their collections, and the staff of the Oxford University Press.

August 1982

P. K. M.

M. D. R.

L. D. R.

R. H. R.

R. J. T.

M. W.

CONTENTS

LIST OF CONTRIBUTORS

B. C. B.-B.	B. C. Barker-Benfield
L. H.	L. Håkanson
J. B. H.	J. B. Hall
H. M. H.	H. M. Hine
P. K. M.	P. K. Marshall
J. G. F. P.	J. G. F. Powell
M. D. R.	M. D. Reeve
L. D. R.	L. D. Reynolds
R. H. R.	R. H. Rouse
R. J. T.	R. J. Tarrant
R. M. T.	R. M. Thomson
S. J. T.	S. J. Tibbetts
S. F. W.	S. F. Weiskittel
M. W.	M. Winterbottom

ABBREVIATIONS

Abbreviations for periodicals normally follow those used in *Année philologique*. As the Index of Manuscripts lists the libraries to which all the manuscripts mentioned in the text belong, the name of the library is not always specified if it can be readily inferred from that of the town.

Becker	G. Becker, *Catalogi bibliothecarum antiqui*, Bonn, 1885
Beneventan Script[2]	E. A. Loew, *The Beneventan Script: a History of the South Italian Minuscule*, 2nd edn., prepared and enlarged by V. Brown (Sussidi Eruditi, 33–4), 2 vols., Rome, 1980
Bischoff, *Lorsch*	B. Bischoff, *Lorsch im Spiegel seiner Handschriften*, Munich, 1974
Bischoff, *Mitt. Stud.*	B. Bischoff, *Mittelalterliche Studien. Ausgewählte Aufsätze zur Schriftkunde und Literaturgeschichte*, 3 vols., Stuttgart, 1966–81
Bollettino	*Bollettino del comitato per la preparazione dell' edizione nazionale dei classici greci e latini*, Accademia Nazionale dei Lincei, Nuova Serie, Rome, 1945–
Chatelain	É. Chatelain, *La Paléographie des classiques latins*, parts i–ii, Paris, 1884–1900
CLA	E. A. Lowe, *Codices Latini Antiquiores*, 11 vols. and Supplement, Oxford, 1934–71
Cosenza	M. E. Cosenza, *Biographical and Bibliographical Dictionary of the Italian Humanists and of the World of Classical Scholarship*, 6 vols., Boston, 1962–7
CTC	*Catalogus Translationum et Commentariorum: Mediaeval and Renaissance Latin Translations and Commentaries*, ed. P. O. Kristeller and others, Washington, DC, 1960–
de la Mare, *Handwriting*	A. C. de la Mare, *The Handwriting of Italian Humanists*, i. 1, Oxford, 1973
Delisle	L. Delisle, *Le Cabinet des manuscrits de la Bibliothèque Nationale*, 4 vols., Paris, 1868–81
Flodr	M. Flodr, *Incunabula classicorum. Wiegendrucke der griechischen und römischen Literatur*, Amsterdam, 1973
Karl der Grosse	*Karl der Grosse, Lebenswerk und Nachleben*, Band ii, *Das geistige Leben*, ed. B. Bischoff, Düsseldorf, 1965
Ker[2]	N. R. Ker, *Medieval Libraries of Great Britain*, 2nd edn., London, 1964
Lowe, *Pal. Papers*	E. A. Lowe, *Palaeographical Papers 1907–1965*, ed. L. Bieler, 2 vols., Oxford, 1972

Manitius, *Geschichte*	M. Manitius, *Geschichte der lateinischen Literatur des Mittelalters,* 3 vols., Munich, 1911–31
Manitius, *Handschriften*	M. Manitius, *Handschriften antiker Autoren in mittelalterlichen Bibliothekskatalogen, Zentralblatt für Bibliothekswesen,* Suppl. 67, Leipzig, 1935
Medieval Learning	*Medieval Learning and Literature. Essays presented to Richard William Hunt* (eds. J. J. G. Alexander and M. T. Gibson), Oxford, 1976
MGH	*Monumenta Germaniae Historica*
Pellegrin, *Manuscrits*	É. Pellegrin and others, *Les Manuscrits classiques latins de la Bibliothèque Vaticane,* Paris, 1975–
PL	J.-P. Migne, *Patrologia Latina*
Sabbadini, *Scoperte*	R. Sabbadini, *Le scoperte dei codici latini e greci ne' secoli XIV e XV,* Florence, 1905–14 (reprinted in 2 vols. with the author's additions and corrections by E. Garin, Florence, 1967)
Sabbadini, *Storia e critica*[2]	R. Sabbadini, *Storia e critica di testi latini,* 2nd edn., with Indexes and Bibliography of the author by E. and M. Billanovich, Padua, 1971 (Medioevo e Umanesimo, 11; 1st edn., Catania, 1914)
Settimane	*Settimane di studio del Centro italiano di studi sull'Alto Medioevo,* Spoleto, 1954–
Survival	R. W. Hunt and others, *The Survival of Ancient Literature,* Exhibition Catalogue, BodleianLibrary, Oxford, 1975
Ullman, *Salutati*	B. L. Ullman, *The Humanism of Coluccio Salutati* (Medioevo e Umanesimo, 4), Padua, 1963
Ullman, *Humanistic Script*	B. L. Ullman, *The Origin and Development of Humanistic Script,* Rome, 1960

INTRODUCTION

The contributors to this volume have tried to present as concisely as possible the essential facts of the transmission of each of the texts discussed. The major events in the history of western Europe, whether political or economic, religious or cultural, have inevitably created the framework in which the handing down of the Latin classics has taken place; but within the boundaries imposed by history the paths by which individual authors and texts have travelled from ancient to modern times are many and various. The character and appeal of each text as it interacts with the shifting and uneven patterns of European culture, the powerful intervention of individuals, and above all the hand of fortune which determined whether or not a book would be in the right place at the right time have produced considerable diversity of result. This is immediately apparent to anyone who consults a sample of the textual histories in this book. It seems appropriate in this Introduction to see how the information provided by these detailed investigations can be related to any general pattern of transmission.

It is probably true to say that the classical tradition as it expands and contracts in its course from Antiquity to the end of the Renaissance does conform to a basic pattern. In its crude and essential form it appears to the imagination to follow the traditional lines of the hourglass, which funnels down to a narrow middle and then bellies out again, or the simplified shape in which the female form is often represented – broad shoulders, tiny waist, full skirt. The vital statistics of the figure will vary considerably from text to text; but these diverse patterns, when super-imposed one upon the other, should still produce a dominant shape. The slender waist is the most permanent feature, for the Dark Ages so constricted the flow of classical learning that for a time it was universally reduced to a trickle.

In one respect, at least, our hourglass figure belongs more to the world of the Platonic forms than to the realm of demonstrable pheno-mena. Our knowledge of the transmission of texts in Antiquity is very patchy. It is difficult to trace the circulation of individual works through the quotations and echoes from them in other authors, because of the likely use in ancient times of lost intermediaries; and such ancient traditions as we do have are often fragmentary and disappointingly unrelated to those which emerged in the Middle Ages. Thus the top half of our figure is sketched in hazily or not at all; it disappears thinly into the mists of time, a ghost from the waist up. We are left with the bottom half, often expressed in the traditional form of a stemma. This gradually fans out, as texts emerge from the constriction of the Dark Ages, build up layer upon layer as the tradition unfolds, and finally billow out into the Renaissance.

The way in which the classical tradition expands from about the year 800, growing in richness and volume with each succeeding century, is illustrated again and again by the articles in this book. What they illustrate less graphically, since they are naturally more concerned with matter than with void, is the decline in classical culture which preceded the revival of the late eighth century. Before asking what they tell us about the rising fortunes of the classics, we might pause for a moment and make some attempt to ink in the shadowy outline of their decline.

An enormous amount of Latin literature was lost in ancient times,[1] much of it through natural selection and changes in taste, some through the limited efficiency of the ancient book trade or the hazards of fire and war. The renewed interest in Republican authors which was a feature of the age of Fronto and Gellius, like the pagan revival of the late fourth century, must have helped to save some authors from oblivion, but changes in the literary language, the narrowing of the educational curriculum, and increased reliance on epitomes and secondary sources took their toll. However complex and ambivalent the attitude of the Christian Church to pagan learning may have been, the triumph of Christianity and the degree to which it gradually and surely absorbed more and more of the intellectual drive and emotional commitment of the West could only have been at the expense of pagan literature and values. Much will have perished before the parchment codex emerged as the vital instrument of survival, and the very transference of literature from roll to codex involved an element of selection which could in some cases have been fatal. Finally, pagan literature, if it was to survive, had not only to withstand the battering which the private and public libraries of the Empire must have suffered during the centuries of collapse but also succeed in finding a refuge within the walls of the monasteries and cathedrals which were to carry forward the tradition of learning.

The evidence we have suggests that the decline was gradual and that the real crash did not come until the end. Indeed, the classics shared in the resurgence of intellectual activity which began in the late fourth and extended to the early sixth century. The classical manuscripts which survive from this period, some of them very splendid, are evidence of this, as are the subscriptions transmitted in the manuscripts of some texts, which record, sometimes with information about date, place, and circumstances, that a work had been duly corrected. This period of cultural vigour saw the culmination of the advances in book-production

---

[1] See H. Bardon, *La Littérature latine inconnue* (2 vols., Paris, 1952–6).

and handwriting which regularly accompany such revivals. By the fifth
century the roll had given way to the codex, a form of book which has
never been superseded. Although the change of format had not necessarily entailed a change of material, papyrus had by now yielded to
parchment, which was much more durable and not subject to the
monopoly of the Middle East; it could be manufactured wherever there
were cows and sheep and goats. The beautiful uncial script was firmly
established, as was the first minuscule book-hand, half-uncial. All the
arts essential to the making of books as the Middle Ages knew them
were fully developed.

Among the Republican works which Nonius Marcellus was still able
to excerpt at first hand in the fourth century were Varro's *Menippean
Satires*[2] and some tragedies of Ennius.[3] In the fifth century or later a
reader of Orosius' *Historiae* was able to gloss his text with lines from the
seventh book of Ennius' *Annales*.[4] As late as the sixth century Johannes
Lydus at Constantinople had more complete texts than we have of
Seneca's *Natural Questions*[5] and Suetonius' *De vita Caesarum*,[6] in Africa
Fulgentius could cite passages of Petronius which have not come down
to us,[7] and in Spain Martin of Braga could plagiarize one of Seneca's
lost works.[8] It is difficult not to believe that there were still plenty of
classical texts in the early decades of the sixth century, in Italy and the
provinces, and that more could have survived, had conditions been
favourable. But by the time the sixth century had reached its mid-
course the Dark Ages had come, and they seem to have come with a
vengeance.

Now that *Codices Latini Antiquiores* is complete, with its massive and
magisterial survey of all surviving Latin books written before the year
800, we can form some idea of what happened to books during this
crucial period of transition from classical Antiquity to the Middle Ages.
In particular we can see how the Latin classics fared in comparison with
Christian texts. The comparative figures are so decisive, and so consistent from one volume of *CLA* to another, that they tell a story which
we have to believe.

The manuscripts which have survived from the period covered in
CLA are dominated by those of the Latin Fathers; at their head, in order
of popularity, stand Augustine, Jerome, and Gregory. These patristic
texts are by far the largest class, and they are followed by a formidable
array of biblical and liturgical books. When we come to secular works,

---

[2] On the transmission of Varro see, most recently, L. Alfonsi, *ANRW* i. 3, 41.

[3] H. D. Jocelyn, *The Tragedies of Ennius* (Cambridge, 1967), 56.

[4] E. Norden, *Ennius und Vergilius. Kriegsbilder aus Roms grosser Zeit* (Leipzig and Berlin, 1915),
78–86.   [5] p. 376, below.

[6] p. 399, below.   [7] p. 298, below.

[8] Martin's *Formula vitae honestae*, written between 570 and 579, is quarried from a lost work by
Seneca, probably the *De officiis* (cf. E. Bickel, *RhM* 60 (1905), 505–51).

we find that they form a small proportion of the whole, and only a fraction of these is made up of literary texts of the classical age.

A quick analysis of samples of the manuscripts which survive from this period will make the point. If we are right to assume that the years from c.550 to c.750 may with justification be called the Dark Ages, then it seems reasonable to regard the seventh century as the trough of this cultural recession. This will be the darkest time for polite studies, the point of greatest constriction in the flow of pagan culture. How far this is true may be seen from a rough and ready calculation based on *CLA*, which will give us an idea of the types of text being copied in the seventh century and how the classics fared in comparison with Christian writings. From this period 264 books (or fragments of books) survive.[9] Of these 264 only a tenth (26) are secular works, and most of these are of a technical nature. Eight of them are legal texts, 8 are medical, 6 are works of grammar, 1 is a gromatic text. It is clear from the historical evidence that the basic arts of life went on; education, law, medicine, and the surveying necessary to administration and the levying of taxes still required manuals and works of reference, and these needs are duly reflected in the pattern of manuscript survival. Two of the remaining 3 manuscripts of our 26 are likewise of a practical character. The first contains extracts from Vegetius' *Epitoma rei militaris*[10] which had been superimposed, along with Jerome's *De viris illustribus* and other Christian texts, upon a work which clearly catered less for the needs of the time, a fifth-century copy of Cicero's *Verrines*.[11] The other is a Spanish manuscript which contains, along with Isidore and other texts of local origin, Rufius Festus' *Breviarium* and the *Antonini itinerarium*.[12] Finally, we have a fragment of Lucan.[13]

Lucan was probably lucky to have been copied at this time, to judge from the fate of authors like Virgil and Cicero. These will provide us with samples of a different sort. Of the 16 manuscripts of Rome's national poet to have survived from late Antiquity and the early Middle Ages,[14] 6 are attributed to the fourth century, 5 to the fifth, 3 to c.500; then we have nothing until the late eighth century. Cicero tells a similar story:[15] 3 manuscripts survive from c.400, 9 from the fifth century, 2 from c.500, then again nothing until the late eighth century. The pattern is so consistent that it must reflect the truth, even allowing for the later destruction of such seventh-century manuscripts as were

---

[9] I have allowed a generous margin by counting those manuscripts attributed in *CLA* to s. VI/VII, s. VII, s. VII/VIII.

[10] I have counted the *Epitoma* as a secular work, though Vegetius was of course a professed Christian.   [11] Vatican, Reg. lat. 2077 (*CLA* I. 114–15).

[12] Escorial R. II. 18 (*CLA* XI. 1631).

[13] Vatican lat. 5755 (*CLA* I. 33); three other ancient manuscripts of Lucan survive in fragmentary form, dated respectively to s. IV, s. IV/V, s. V ex. (see LUCAN, n. 3).

[14] pp. 433–5, below.   [15] pp. 55–7, below.

written. The copying of classical texts tapered off to such an extent during the Dark Ages that the continuity of pagan culture came close to being severed; our model has the waist of a wasp.

The constriction of classical culture in the Dark Ages throws into greater relief the prolific expansion of the Carolingian Revival. The movement which saved for us so much of the heritage of Rome proceeded with such impetus and vigour that by the end of the ninth century the classical tradition had been securely re-established. This phenomenon is in some ways still so mysterious that we are often reduced to describing the mechanics of the process in the vaguest of terms: manuscripts 'come to light', authors 'reappear', texts 'emerge', like streams from underground chambers or animals from hibernation, as if part of nature's process. But such a prodigious rebirth must have been massively induced: texts came to light because men were looking for them, finding them, and transcribing them. So few classical authors were actually copied during the Dark Ages that the foundations of such a revival must largely have been ancient codices which had survived the collapse of the Roman Empire. Great as the upheavals and disasters had been, it would have taken a holocaust of nuclear proportions to wipe out a culture which had extended from Spain to the Middle East, from the Danube to North Africa. Deposits of books must have survived, some of them destined to become vital links in the chain of transmission when reactivated by the new and expanding orbit of Latin culture.

The beginnings of the Carolingian Revival, the point at which classical culture stopped contracting and began to expand again, is such a crucial stage in the history of Latin texts that it is worth asking where the architects of the revival actually found the manuscripts which played such a large part in it.[16] The natural and obvious answer is Italy. But what, it has been asked, about the cultivated aristocracy of Roman Gaul and the books which had been at Arles or Vienne? Had not manuscripts percolated to the Carolingian centres from far-flung areas where Latin culture had flourished in late Antiquity, from Spain or North Africa or Constantinople? What about Ireland and England, which had succeeded in bypassing the Dark Ages and had manifestly made a significant contribution to the revival of learning on the Continent?

In fact very few of our texts appear to depend on manuscripts written or preserved from ancient times in Gaul. One candidate is worth putting forward, the corpus of *Panegyrici latini*. Except for Pliny's speech in honour of Trajan, which had served as a model for such encomia and

---

[16] On this question, with special reference to the *Hofbibliothek*, see now B. Bischoff, 'Das benediktinische Mönchtum und die Überlieferung der klassischen Literatur', *Studien und Mitteilungen zur Geschichte des Benediktiner-Ordens und seiner Zweige*, 92 (1981), 165–90, particularly 170 ff.

was given pride of place in the corpus, most of the speeches were delivered in Gaul – the majority of them at Trier – all the orators were Gauls, and the collection itself was put together in the province. The manuscript on which we ultimately depend was found at Mainz, not far from Trier, and what appears to have been a twin manuscript – both are now lost – was at Saint-Omer.[17] Pliny's speech had circulated widely in Antiquity, but had it not been put at the head of these Gallic orations all that we would have had of it are the fragments preserved in a manuscript palimpsested at Bobbio.[18] It is reasonable to suppose that our manuscript tradition of the *Panegyrici* remained on this side of the Alps and that Italy played no part in its transmission.

Further to the south, attention naturally focuses on Lyon, which had formed an unbroken link between Roman Gaul and Merovingian France and was famed for its early scriptoria.[19] It dominated the Rhône valley and was an important centre for the political and ecclesiastical organization of Gaul. Its connections with other administrative centres such as Constantinople,[20] and its links with Spain, also made it a potential home for imported books. But even before the collapse of the Empire its scriptoria were specializing in Christian texts, and the only secular works which we appear to owe with any certainty to its early scriptoria are legal texts.[21] The only literary manuscripts of Gaulish origin which come to mind are a palimpsest of Fronto's *Letters*,[22] the important collection of poetry in Vienna 277,[23] and a Visigothic manuscript to be discussed in a moment.

One might expect Spain to have been a fruitful source of books, at least until it was overrun by the Arabs in 711; and the phenomenal way in which the works of Isidore were diffused all over Europe[24] shows what might have happened to its stores of classical texts. It was also a bridge by which the literature of North Africa could pass to northern Europe. Spain is the source of at least part of an important collection of poetry that includes Dracontius, Ausonius, and poems from the *Latin*

---

[17] See *PANEGYRICI LATINI*.

[18] Milan, Ambros. E. 147 sup. + Vatican lat. 5750 (*CLA* I. 29, III, p. 20, s. VI).

[19] Lowe, *CLA* VI, xiii–xiv; *Codices Lugdunenses Antiquissimi* (Lyons, 1924). A papyrus codex of Avitus survives from the sixth century, probably written in Burgundy, and in Lyon by s. XVI (Paris lat. 8913 + 8914; *CLA* V. 573); and Lupus knew of a papyrus codex of Boethius in Tours (p. 130 n. 31, below). This suggests that there may have been some continuity with the ancient book trade in Gaul, and that a certain class of evidence may not have survived.

[20] Lowe, *Pal. Papers*. ii. 466–74.

[21] e.g. Paris lat. 9643 (*CLA* V. 591, s. VI), *Codex Theodosianus*; Berlin (East), Phill. 1761 (*CLA* VIII. 1064, s. VI²), *Lex Romana Visigothorum*; Berlin (East), Phill. 1745 + Leningrad, Lat. F. v. II. 3 (*CLA* VIII. 1061, XI, p. 8, s. VII), *Concilia Galliae, Notitia Galliarum*, etc.

[22] Paris lat. 12161, pp. 133/4 (*CLA* V. 629, s. VI); see FRONTO.

[23] *CLA* X. 1474, s. VIII ex.; see pp. 10 ff., below.

[24] Bischoff, 'Die europäische Verbreitung der Werke Isidors von Sevilla', *Isidoriana. Estudios sobre San Isidoro de Sevilla en el XIV centenario de su nacimiento* (León, 1961), 317–44 = *Mitt. Stud.* i. 171–94.

Anthology. This manuscript[25] was copied early in the ninth century by Visigothic scribes, probably working at Lyon.[26] The works of Dracontius which it transmits (*De laudibus Dei* 1, *Satisfactio*) are in the version made at the behest of the Visigothic king Chindasvinth (641–52) by Eugenius of Toledo;[27] the other and better copy of the archetype remained in Spain.[28] It also contains the *In laudem* of Corippus and is consequently a prime exhibit for the transmission through Spain of the literature of the Vandal kingdom. Spain was also the centre for the diffusion of Pompeius' popular commentary on Donatus, composed in Africa in the fifth century; from Spain it spread to Italy and, via Ireland, to the north of continental Europe.[29] But there was more than one route out of Africa. The other works of Dracontius[30] and Corippus did not travel via Spain, and the main manuscript of the *Latin Anthology*[31] has now been firmly located in central Italy. The same is true of another work of North African origin which had an enormous influence in the Middle Ages, the *De nuptiis* of Martianus Capella. The subscription preserved in many early manuscripts testifies that our text descends from a recension made at Rome in 534 by the rhetor Securus Melior Felix.[32] The 'mendosissima exempla' which he claims to have used may have been brought to Rome from Carthage after its liberation by Belisarius in September of the previous year. At all events, the *De nuptiis* reached us via Italy; it was corrected in such a homely spot as the Porta Capena and passed through the hands of the same Felix who in 527 had been working on the *Epodes* of Horace.

On the whole there is not much evidence for the successful passage of classical texts through Spain,[33] and there are some grounds for caution. Martin of Braga must have had a copy of Seneca's *De ira* to hand when he adapted it for his own homily on anger,[34] but there is nothing to connect Martin with the live tradition of the *Dialogues* preserved at Montecassino, and his own epitome of Seneca did not cross the Spanish

[25] Paris lat. 8093 + Leiden, Voss. Lat. F. 111; see pp. 26–7, below.

[26] Bischoff, *Mitt. Stud.* i. 292.

[27] Schanz-Hosius, *Geschichte der römischen Literatur*, iv. 2 (Munich, 1920), 60–1.

[28] Madrid 10029, s. X, in Visigothic script.

[29] L. Holtz, 'Tradition et diffusion de l'oeuvre grammaticale de Pompée, commentateur de Donat', *RPh* 45 (1971), 48–83.

[30] F. Corsaro, *Blossi Aemilii Dracontii De laudibus Dei libri tres* (Catania, 1962), 12–15.

[31] Paris lat. 10318 (*CLA* V. 593, *codex Salmasianus*); see p. 9 n. 4, below.

[32] J. Préaux, 'Securus Melior Felix, l'ultime Orator Urbis Romae', *Corona Gratiarum. Miscellanea patristica, historica et liturgica Eligio Dekkers O.S.B. XII lustra complenti oblata* (Brugge-Gravenhage, 1975), i. 101–21; p. 245, below.

[33] Two extant manuscripts of possibily Spanish origin which reached the north are both of a technical nature: Reims 132 (*CLA* VI. 823, s. VI/VII), a fragment of a treatise on surveying, and the medical corpus in Paris lat. 10233 + Berne F. 219.3 (*CLA* V. 592 + VII, p. 7, s. VII ex.); the latter has *probationes pennae* in a Beneventan hand of s. XI. For the possibility that the *Disticha Catonis* were transmitted through Spain, see Bischoff, 'Das benediktinische Mönchtum', 170–1.

[34] Edited by C. W. Barlow, *Martini Episcopi Bracarensis Opera Omnia* (New Haven, 1950), 145–58.

border.[35] His *Formula honestae vitae*,[36] on the other hand, did enjoy a wide medieval circulation, but the treatise of Seneca on which it was based (*De officiis?*) was never heard of again. The Spanish manuscript of Festus which has been mentioned did not produce any surviving copies.[37] The contribution from a country which had been able to produce Isidore of Seville is ultimately rather disappointing.

The strength of Irish and English scholarship during the Dark Ages, the importance of the foundations which missionaries from these islands established on the Continent, and the crucial role played in the Carolingian revival by Alcuin and the *Scotti peregrini* made Britain an obvious place to which Carolingian scholars might turn for books. The insular contribution to the transmission of classical texts has been so thoroughly studied[38] that nothing need be stated here except the basic facts. It is unlikely that Ireland possessed much in the way of classical literature, and there is no evidence that the Irish actually carried literary texts from their homeland to the Continent. Their strength lay in exegesis, computus, and grammar, and the few extant manuscripts which can be said to have reached the Continent from Ireland reflect these interests. One example is a manuscript of the *Ars de verbo* of the late grammarian Eutyches, written in an Irish minuscule of s. VIII/IX and apparently in Ireland; it must have soon reached the Continent, for it now contains a ninth-century Corbie charter.[39] Another is a computistical manuscript now in Vienna[40] which contains excerpts from Macrobius' *Saturnalia*, Solinus, and Gregory of Tours's *De cursu stellarum*; it was written in the late eighth century at Salzburg, but seems to have been copied from an Irish exemplar.

The attraction of texts from the more distant parts of a cultural orbit to its centre is as clearly illustrated in the case of England by the manuscripts of Bede as it was in the case of Spain by those of Isidore. The Moore Bede[41] was written in Northumbria soon after 737; it had

---

[35] It survives in only one medieval manuscript, Escorial M. III. 3, s. X, in a Visigothic hand.

[36] Barlow, 204–50.

[37] J. W. Eadie, *The Breviarium of Festus* (London, 1967), 22.

[38] In particular by T. J. Brown, 'An Historical Introduction to the Use of Classical Latin Authors in the British Isles from the Fifth to the Eleventh Century', *Settimane*, 22. 1 (Spoleto, 1975), 237–99. See too H. Gneuss, 'A Preliminary List of Manuscripts written or owned in England up to 1100', *Anglo-Saxon England*, 9 (1981), 1–60; *Survival*, 46–8.

[39] Paris lat. 10400 (ff. 109–10) + lat. 11411 (ff. 124–5) (*CLA* V. 599), attributed to Ireland with some confidence, despite the difficulty of knowing whether an insular scribe was working at home or on the Continent. Two early Irish manuscripts of another late grammarian, Consentius, have a similar history: Paris lat. 11411 (f. 123) (*CLA* V. 610); Basle F III 15d (*CLA* VII. 847). It was also the insular tradition of Pompeius, as mentioned above, which circulated in Carolingian Europe. It is worth noting in this context that Eutyches subsequently had to be reimported into England: the first part of Oxford, Bodl. Auct. F. 4. 32, probably put together by St. Dunstan (p. 261 n. 12, below), is a fragment from a ninth-century Breton copy of the *Ars de verbo*.

[40] Vienna 15269 + ser. nov. 37 (*CLA* X. 1510); cf. *Survival*, 46–7, no. 93.

[41] Cambridge, University Library Kk. 5. 16 (*CLA* II. 139), known as the Moore MS because it had belonged to John Moore, Bishop of Ely.

reached the Carolingian court by about 800,[42] and its surviving copies show how the *Ecclesiastical History* spread through France in the course of the ninth century.[43] None of our traditions has such a nicely drawn pedigree, though one family of Justinus' manuscripts has points of similarity. The only classical authors to survive in early English manuscripts are the well-known trio of the Elder Pliny, Justinus, and Servius,[44] and all three of these manuscripts may have reached the Continent at an early date. It should be observed that all three are essentially utilitarian works, and evidence for the flow of texts across the Channel can easily be increased if we turn again to those late authors who nobly provided the lifeline of Latin learning, the *grammatici*. A volume[45] which now contains Pompeius' *Commentum in Artem Donati* and two other commentaries on Donatus, all three written in Anglo-Saxon minuscule of s. VIII and all apparently of English origin, seems to have been put together on the Continent, possibly at Murbach and some time before 800. A copy of Priscian's *De nominibus*[46] may similarly have moved from Northumbria to Reichenau. An example of a different sort is offered by Oxford, Bodl. Add. C. 144:[47] this collection of grammatical treatises was written in Italy in the early eleventh century, but it still preserves Anglo-Saxon glosses which indicate a Mercian origin early in the eighth century. When we move from such tangible evidence to the positing of insular ancestry for continental traditions we are on less sure ground, but among the texts in whose early history England may possibly have played some part are the Fifth Decade of Livy,[48] Vitruvius,[49] and the *carmina figurata* of the late writer Optatianus Porfyrius.[50]

If we turn to Italy, the results are much more positive; the movement of books northwards over the Alps can be amply documented. It began long before the Carolingian period, as books were attracted to the powerful monastic foundations of northern Europe. There were some bad casualties among the early migrants, for they had arrived at a time when some of them would find that their parchment presented a greater attraction than their contents. The unique manuscript of Sallust's

[42] Bischoff, *Karl der Grosse*, 56–7 (= *Mitt. Stud.* iii. 160–1).

[43] B. Colgrave, R. A. B. Mynors, *Bede's Ecclesiastical History of the English People* (Oxford, 1969), lxii–lxiv.   [44] See pp. 309, 197–8, 385, below.

[45] St. Paul in Carinthia 2. 1 (25. 2. 16) (*CLA* x. 1451–3); Bischoff, *Mitt. Stud.* i. 97.

[46] Karlsruhe Fragm. Aug. 122 + Aug. CXVI (binding) + Zürich, Staatsarchiv A. G. 19, No. XIII (*CLA* VII. 1009, VIII, p. 30).

[47] *Survival*, 47–8 and plate XIV; C. Jeudy, *Viator*, 5 (1974), 120–3.

[48] See p. 214 n. 38, below.   [49] See p. 441, below.

[50] Brown, 259–60; C. Nordenfalk, 'A Note on the Stockholm Codex Aureus', *Nordisk Tidskrift för Bok- och Biblioteksväsen*, 38 (1951), 145–55. For the popularity of Porfyrius at the Carolingian court see Bischoff in *Karl der Grosse, Werk und Wirkung* (Aachen, 1965), 201, pl. 37 (on Berne 212 II); on the manuscript tradition in general, G. Polara, *Ricerche sulla tradizione manoscritta di Publilio Porfirio* (Salerno, 1971), and the editions of E. Kluge (Teubner, Leipzig, 1926) and Polara (Paravia, Turin, 1973).

Histories[51] had reached Fleury by the seventh century only to be reduced to tatters. The remarkable *codex Moneus* of the Elder Pliny,[52] our only ancient manuscript of Ovid,[53] and the Veronensis[54] of Livy's First Decade were all palimpsested at Luxeuil, and another early Pliny[55] perished somewhere in the south of France. Such accidents could happen at any time as books were rewritten or carved up for bindings, but they became less likely, or at least were less calamitous, when the classical revival had taken hold and the copying of pagan authors was a regular activity: there was less danger that an old book would be discarded before it had been copied.

When we come to the Carolingian period and manuscript traditions begin to blossom forth in profusion, the chances are that many of their archetypes were books imported from Italy. This is of course often impossible to prove; but it is not unreasonable to assume that many texts had indeed travelled by the prevailing wind. The richness of the Italian deposits of classical books is demonstrated above all by the fact that Italy continued to be the prime source for new texts in the centuries which followed the Carolingian revival, texts which had never been known, as far as we can tell, north of the Alps. That the prevailing wind was now blowing from Italy is amply illustrated by the movement of extant manuscripts. Those of Virgil provide a clear example. Our text is based on 7 ancient codices, all apparently of Italian origin: at least 4 of these 7 found homes in Carolingian monasteries, the *Romanus* and *Augusteus* at Saint-Denis, the *Palatinus* at Lorsch, the *Sangallensis* at St. Gall.[56] If we wish to look to a specific monastery for our evidence, Lorsch, which enjoyed the special patronage of Charlemagne and built up much of its fine collection during the Carolingian period, comes immediately to mind.[57] Its library acquired some very impressive books with which Italy had been persuaded to part, the Palatine Virgil already mentioned, our unique manuscript of Livy's Fifth Decade,[58] and the archetype of Seneca's *De beneficiis* and *De clementia*.[59] The claim that our prime source for the *Historia Augusta* (Vatican, Pal. lat. 899) belonged to Lorsch has collapsed, but this manuscript, written in Italy in the early decades of the ninth century, generated copies at Fulda, Lorsch, and Murbach.[60] Other celebrated manuscripts which joined

---

[51] Orléans 192 + Vatican Reg. lat. 1283B + Berlin (East) lat. 4° 364 (*CLA* VI. 809, I, p. 34, VIII, p. 10).   [52] St. Paul in Carinthia 3. 1 (25. 2. 36) (*CLA* X. 1455).

[53] Wolfenbüttel Aug. 4° 13. 11 (*CLA* IX. 1377), containing a fragment of the *Ex Ponto* (q.v.).

[54] Verona XL (38) (*CLA* IV. 499).

[55] Autun 24 + Paris n. a. lat. 1629 (*CLA* VI. 726).

[56] See VIRGIL; the date at which these manuscripts arrived at their northern homes is of course sometimes a matter of conjecture.

[57] Largely thanks to Bischoff, *Lorsch*.

[58] Vienna 15 (*CLA* X. 1472).

[59] Vatican, Pal. lat. 1547.

[60] See pp. 354–6, below; Bischoff, *Lorsch*, 66, 77, 81; *Mitt. Stud.* iii. 60–1.

this drift to the north, to confine ourselves for the moment to ancient codices, include the Morgan manuscript of the Younger Pliny which is the source of the ten-book tradition,[61] the *Puteanus* of Livy's Third Decade[62] – actually the archetype of Books 21–5 – and the unique manuscript of Cledonius' *Ars grammatica*.[63]

When it comes to asking from which regions and places in Italy these manuscripts mainly came, not much can be added to what has already been said.[64] The subscriptions which have been transmitted in the manuscripts of some authors often name the precise place where an ancestor of that tradition had been corrected, and these places range from Spain to Constantinople. Some of the subscriptions are as late as the sixth century, but even then we cannot be certain where the carriers of these traditions were when the Carolingian book-hunters were seeking their quarry. A subscription can tell us little in this context unless a very close link can be established between the manuscript which carried the original subscription and its Carolingian descendants. Rome, still the centre of western Christendom and containing the stores of books into which popes would dip to meet the obligations of patronage and diplomacy, must have been one of the major sources, but there is no classical manuscript or text to which one can point and say that it had reached the north from Rome itself.[65] There is some evidence for Campania: the fifth-century *Puteanus* of Livy's Third Decade which was copied at Tours about 800 had itself been corrected at Avellino, near Naples. Paul the Deacon sent his own abridgement of Festus to Charlemagne specifically as a gift for his library,[66] and there was clearly an interchange of books between Montecassino and the north, as there must have been in the case of other major ecclesiastical centres in Italy. There is good evidence that Ravenna was an important, if not the prime source for books.[67] It had remained as a seat of imperial power and cultural life well into the sixth century, and its recapture, after a period of Byzantine and Lombard dominion, by the forces of Charlemagne provided the perfect opportunity; columns of stone and the statue of Theoderic cannot have been the only objects transported to Aachen. The Ravenna origin of the miscellany of texts in Vatican lat. 4929 – Julius Paris, Pomponius Mela, and others – is well known;[68] the signifi-

---

[61] New York, Morgan Library M. 462.

[62] Paris lat. 5730.

[63] Berne 380 (*CLA* VII. 864); for Cledonius, see Keil, *Grammatici Latini*, v. 9–79.

[64] Most recently by Bischoff, 'Das benediktinische Mönchtum', 170–2.

[65] It has been suggested that some of the imposing and de luxe copies of Virgil were produced for the Roman aristocracy, and they would have made impressive presents: see R. Seider in *Studien zum antiken Epos*, ed. H. Görgemanns and E. A. Schmidt (Meisenheim am Glan, 1976), 138, 140, 143, 146, 149, 151. The *codex Arcerianus* of the *Agrimensores* may have been written in Rome (p. 1, below), but it remained in Italy for centuries. [66] p. 163, below.

[67] Suggested by Bischoff, e.g. *Mitt. Stud.* ii. 318 f., iii. 155, 'Das benediktinische Mönchtum', 171 f. [68] p. 290, below.

cant fact is that our archetype, written at Auxerre within the circle of Lupus and Heiric, reproduces with photographic fidelity what must have been the original subscription, executed in small, elegant rustic capitals and neatly inserted, as the subscriber would himself have inserted it, between the *explicit* of one work and the *incipit* of the next.[69] In a ninth-century manuscript of Macrobius' *Commentary* a member of the same circle, if not Heiric himself, has added the Ravenna subscription which is transmitted in some manuscripts of this text, again transcribing it directly, it would appear, from an ancient copy.[70] Here we have another direct link between the ancients working on their texts in Ravenna and their Carolingian successors in the valley of the Yonne. To this evidence may now be added that of the *Notitia dignitatum*, the grand roll of imperial posts, with its lists of officers province by province, their titles, functions, and the staff or units under their command. The version of the *Notitia* which we have is derived from a copy used in the *officium* of the *magister utriusque militiae*, the virtual ruler of the West for a large part of the fifth century; and the continued use of this *officium* by Theoderic as his administrative organ in Italy would have ensured its survival at Ravenna.[71] Such a manuscript, illustrated for each entry with pictures of insignia, shields, and forts and offering a vast and imposing panorama of power, would have an obvious appeal for the builders of the new empire in the West. Evidence for a knowledge of the *Notitia* at the Carolingian court, and perhaps on the part of Charlemagne himself,[72] together with its survival via a manuscript preserved at Speyer, makes it difficult not to believe that Ravenna was the source of the *Notitia* and its attendant texts.

The fundamental function of the Carolingian revival in the transmission of our texts was to gather in what could be found of the literature and learning of the past and generate from it the new medieval traditions which would carry the classics through the centuries. The extant manuscripts of the eighth century taken as a whole reveal the same concentration on the basic essentials of learning as was characteristic of the Dark Ages. We have a great deal of grammar, often assembled into large corpuses, such as Paris lat. 7530,[73] Paris lat. 7502 + Berne

---

[69] See, for instance, the plate of f. 188 in C. W. Barlow, 'Codex Vaticanus Latinus 4929', *MAAR* 15 (1939), 87–124, pl. 17.

[70] pp. 224–5, 227, below.

[71] J. C. Mann, in *Aspects of the* Notitia Dignitatum, ed. R. Goodburn and P. Bartholomew, *BAR* Supplementary Series 15 (Oxford, 1976), 8; A. H. M. Jones, 'The Constitutional Position of Odoacer and Theoderic', *JRS* 52 (1962), 126–33.

[72] J. J. G. Alexander, *Aspects of the* Notitia, 19; pp. 256–7, below.

[73] *CLA* v. 569, AD 779–97, Montecassino. Among the contents of this remarkable manuscript are two curious survivals, the *didascaliae* to the lost *Thyestes* of the Augustan poet Varius and the *Anecdoton Parisinum*, which contains material from a lost work of Suetonius; for a full account of the manuscript see L. Holtz, 'Le Parisinus Latinus 7530, synthèse cassinienne des arts libéraux', *Stud. Med.*³ 16 (1975), 97–152.

207,[74] Berlin (West) Diez. B Sant. 66,[75] Cologne 166,[76] Naples IV.A.8.[77] There are computistical miscellanies like Vienna 15269 + ser. nov. 37,[78] medical and botanical writings,[79] and works which had won a place in the educational system, such as Martianus Capella[80] and the *Disticha Catonis*.[81] The manuscript which contains the latter work, written in Verona, also provides us with our earliest copy of the *carmina minora* of Claudian. The first author of the classical period to appear is Virgil, towards the end of the century.[82]

The discriminating bibliophile who browsed through the contents of the Palace library about 790 and jotted down the titles of the pagan works which caught his eye thus becomes one of the most arresting figures in the whole story and his scrappy little list one of the most important documents in the transmission of classical texts.[83] Within a decade the copying of classical texts had begun in earnest. The upturn, to judge from the extant manuscripts, came about 800, and the evidence which has been, and is still being, accumulated by Professor Bischoff has put beyond doubt the fact that the Carolingian court and the monasteries closely associated with it were the prime agents of the whole movement. Among the classical manuscripts of *c*.800 which he has attributed to the court scriptorium or its milieu are copies of Lucretius,[84] Vitruvius,[85] Justinus,[86] a Latin Euclid,[87] texts of the *Agrimensores*,[88] the Elder Pliny,[89] the Elder Seneca,[90] and Calcidius.[91] The anthology of poetry in Vienna 277, written at this time somewhere in France, includes rare texts known to the circle of the court. At Tours, under the abbacy of Alcuin (796–804), were copied the *Reginensis* of Livy,[92] our most important manuscript of Nonius Marcellus,[93] and one of the earliest copies of Donatus' commentary on Virgil.[94] From Fleury

[74] *CLA* V. 568 + VII, p. 6, *c*.797, Fleury.

[75] *CLA* VIII. 1044, *c*.790, probably at the court of Charlemagne.

[76] *CLA* VIII. 1160, s. VIII².

[77] *CLA* III. 400, s. VIII, Bobbio.

[78] *CLA* X. 1510, s. VIII ex., Salzburg.

[79] Paris n. a. lat. 1619 (*CLA* V. 688, s. VIII, northern France: Oribasius); Erlangen 2112, 21 + Göttingen, Hist. Nat. 91 (*CLA* VIII. 1191 + Suppl., p. 20, s. VIII², north-eastern France?: Dioscorides latinus).

[80] Karlsruhe, Fragm. Aug. 136 (*CLA* VIII. 1129), s. VIII ex.

[81] Verona CLXIII (150) (*CLA* IV. 516), s. VIII².

[82] p. 435, below.

[83] For the book-list and Bischoff's convincing account of it see *Karl der Grosse*, 42–56 (= *Mitt. Stud*. iii. 149–69, with plates V–X); *Sammelhandschrift Diez. B Sant. 66. Grammatici Latini et Catalogus librorum* (Codices selecti phototypice impressi, 42) (Graz, 1973).

[84] Leiden, Voss. Lat. F. 30.

[85] British Library, Harley 2767.

[86] Paris lat. 4950.

[87] Munich, Universitätsbibl. 2° 757.   [88] Florence, Laur. 29. 32.

[89] Leiden, Voss. Lat. F. 61 + Vatican lat. 3861 (*CLA* X. 1580, Suppl., p. 28).

[90] Bamberg Msc. Class. 45ᵐ.   [91] Paris lat. 2164.

[92] Vatican, Reg. lat. 762.   [93] Leiden, Voss. Lat. F. 73.

[94] Florence, Laur. 45. 15, from a Luxeuil exemplar; p. 157, below.

we have the grammatical corpus in Berne 207, which contains *inter alia* some Porfyrius and verses from Petronius, and our earliest medieval manuscript of Vegetius;[95] from Lyon the poetic miscellany in Leiden, Voss. Lat. F. 111;[96] from St. Gall a body of technical material containing some interesting excerpts from the Elder Pliny.[97] From south of the Alps we have the *codex Salmasianus* of the *Latin Anthology*, the archetype of Seneca's *De beneficiis* and *De clementia*, and a manuscript of the Elder Pliny copied at Lucca.[98]

This assortment of Latin texts, all written about 800 or shortly afterwards, gives one a fair idea of the first crucial stage in the *renovatio* of Latin literature. The emphasis is still perhaps more on learning than on literature, but the range of books is comprehensive, extending from technology to history and poetry. From now on there is a continuous if irregular growth in the number of classical manuscripts in circulation, an increase in the range of authors available, and an extension of the geographical areas in which they could be found. That this *épanouisse-ment* took place is obvious; how to illustrate some of its stages from the contents of this book is less clear. It is impossible to assess the growth in the volume of books in circulation without a complete catalogue of all surviving classical manuscripts.[99] Accurate figures are sometimes available for individual authors; but each of these will have its own pattern and tempo,[100] and it is not easy to explain why some texts take off and others just bump along the bottom. For instance, there are only two Carolingian manuscripts of Sallust's *Catiline* and *Jugurtha*, only two of Valerius Maximus; but while Sallust surged forward in the eleventh century, Valerius, who was perfectly well suited to the taste of the Middle Ages if not to ours, had a surprisingly modest medieval tradition and did not come into his own until the Renaissance.[101] The steady growth in the number of manuscripts of a popular author like Sallust,

---

[95] Berne 280, apparently copied from an uncial exemplar.

[96] pp. xviii–xix, above; 26–7, below.

[97] Leiden, Voss. Lat. Q. 69.

[98] Lucca 490 (*CLA* III. 303e).

[99] The publication by Professor B. Munk Olsen of a catalogue of some 3,000 manuscripts of the Latin classics from s. IX to s. XII is an enormous step forward. The first volume has just appeared: *L'Étude des auteurs classiques latins aux XIe et XIIe siècles*. Tome I. *Catalogue des manuscrits classiques latins copiés du IXe au XIIe siècle: APICIUS – JUVENAL* (Paris, 1982).

[100] For an analysis of the relative popularity of Latin historians, including some ancient historians, see B. Guenée, *Histoire et culture historique dans l'Occident médiéval* (Paris, 1980), 248 ff. The comparative figures for Macrobius' *Commentary* and *Saturnalia* are given below, pp. 223–4. Lucretius and Nonius Marcellus almost disappeared from sight between the ninth century and the Renaissance. For some other examples of irregular distribution, see pp. 32 (Avianus), 36 n. 9 (Caesar), 383, 385 (Q. Serenus).

[101] Figures may be extracted from D. M. Schullian, 'A Revised List of Manuscripts of Valerius Maximus', *Miscellanea Augusto Campana* (Padua, 1981), 695–728: no manuscript of s. X, 1 of s. XI, only 5 (excluding excerpts) of s. XII, 14 of s. XIII, then some 500 from s. XIV–XV.

for whom approximate figures are to hand, will, for all that, give some
idea of the way in which such a tradition might develop:[102]

s. IX	s. X	s. XI	s. XII	s. XIII	s. XIV	s. XV
2	4	33	58	39	46	330

The present volume, with its list of some 1700 manuscripts, is no
substitute for a complete catalogue, but it does offer something else: the
manuscripts which we mention are by and large those on which our
critical texts are based, they are the bones and sinews of the classical
tradition. Their distribution over the centuries may therefore be of some
interest:[103]

s. IX	s. X	s. XI	s. XII	s. XIII	s. XIV	s. XV
290	150	230	280	140	90	420

The peaking in the twelfth and fifteenth centuries, which predictably
reflects the increased interest in the classics characteristic of these
periods, will be a constant feature of most sets of figures.

What we can readily learn from these 1700 manuscripts – or in some
cases printed books – is when an author or text first appears in an extant
witness. I hasten to point out the obvious, that this chance event should
not imply that the texts in question did not circulate earlier: quotations
and library catalogues often demonstrate that they did, and any work
which has come down to us must have reposed somewhere, on a shelf or
in a chest. Nor of course do texts necessarily become available, in any
real sense, after what may have been just one act of copying. But the
first appearance of a text in a witness which we can see and touch is a
datum of some importance, and often provides the baseline from which
investigation starts. Such 'first appearances' will at least provide a
convenient, if crude, yardstick for measuring the expansion of the
classical tradition as the limited stock of texts initially in use grew until
it comprised almost the whole range of Latin literature which has come
down to us.

We have been able to form some picture of what had been achieved
by the early years of the ninth century. The full measure of the achievement of the Carolingian period can easily be appreciated if one moves
forward a century, to the year 900, and takes stock of how much Latin
literature had by then, on the evidence of our extant manuscripts, been
copied. The picture has changed dramatically. By the end of the ninth
century the major part of Latin literature had indeed been copied and
was enjoying some degree of circulation, however limited, localized, or

[102] I count manuscripts dated to the turn of a century as belonging to the later century; the
figures are incomplete, especially for the later period.

[103] Rounded to the nearest ten. It is worth adding, as an indication that the manuscript book
did not become redundant with the age of printing, that we have occasion to cite 27 manuscripts of
s. XVI, 2 of s. XVII, 1 of s. XVIII, and 1 of s. XIX.

precarious it may in some cases have been. The list of texts for which we have ninth-century manuscripts, however fragmentary some of them have now become, will speak for itself:[104]

Agrimensores, Ammianus Marcellinus, *Anthologia latina*, Apicius, Apuleius (philosophical works), *Aratea* (all three versions), Ausonius (in part), Avianus, Caelius Aurelianus (*Responsiones, Tardae passiones*), Caesar, Celsus, Censorinus, Charisius, a large part of Cicero,[105] Claudian (*carmina minora*), Columella, Curtius Rufus, Ti. Claudius Donatus, Eutropius, Faventinus, Florus, Frontinus (*Strategemata*), Gellius (Books 9–20), Grattius, *Historia Augusta*, Horace, Hyginus, Justinus, Juvenal, Livy (First and Third Decades), Lucan, Lucretius, Macrobius, Martial, Martianus Capella, Pomponius Mela, Nemesianus (*Cynegetica*), Nonius Marcellus, *Notitia dignitatum*, Ovid (*Amores, Ars, Remedia, Ex Ponto, Heroides, Metamorphoses*), Palladius (Books 1–13), Julius Paris, Persius, Petronius (the O excerpts), Phaedrus, Elder Pliny, Younger Pliny, Publilius, *Querolus*, Quintilian (*Institutio oratoria* and the dubious *Declamationes minores*), *Rhetores latini minores*, *Rhetorica ad Herennium*, Sallust (*Catilina, Jugurtha*, excerpts from the *Historiae*, the dubious *Epistulae ad Caesarem*), Elder Seneca, Younger Seneca (*Apocolocyntosis, De beneficiis, De clementia, Letters*), Q. Serenus, Servius, Solinus, Statius (*Achilleid, Thebaid*), Suetonius (*De vita Caesarum*), Tacitus (*Annals* 1–6, *Agricola*), Terence, Valerius Flaccus, Valerius Maximus, Vibius Sequester, Virgil, *Appendix Vergiliana*, Vitruvius.

Some of these works were circulating widely by the end of the century, but many were still confined to certain areas, and some were so rare that you could only find a text if you happened to know where to go for it. For all that, it is a singularly impressive list: a large part of the classical heritage had been safely gathered up and in most cases transcribed into a script which was new and elegant and a pleasure to read. The comparative illegibility of the 'national' hands might help to account for the relatively modest contribution of Ireland and Spain and the slowness with which texts written in Beneventan percolated from their base in the south of Italy; the adoption of Caroline minuscule had been of fundamental importance for the success of the revival. Very little which had survived into the Carolingian age was subsequently lost.[106]

---

[104] I have not included Catullus and Statius' *Silvae*, although in both cases one poem does survive in a ninth-century manuscript, and many of the texts rediscovered by the humanists will of course have been Carolingian books which were subsequently lost.

[105] Speeches: *Post reditum ad senatum, Post reditum ad populum, De Domo, Pro Sestio, In Vatinium, De provinciis consularibus. De haruspicum responso, Pro Balbo, Pro Caelio, In Catilinam, 1–4, Pro Marcello, Pro Ligario, Pro rege Deiotaro, In Verrem, I, II.1–5, In Pisonem, Pro Flacco, Pro Fonteio, Philippics, 1–14.* Rhetorical Works: *De inventione, De oratore, Orator* (the last two *mutili*), *Brutus.* Philosophical Works: *Cato Maior de senectute, Laelius de amicitia, De natura deorum, De divinatione, Timaeus, De fato, Topica, Paradoxa Stoicorum, Academica priora, De legibus, De officiis, Tusculan Disputations.* Letters: *Epistulae ad familiares.*

[106] Among the works which have been lost are Septimius Serenus' *Opuscula ruralia* and the 'Bucolicon Olibrii' (Olybrius, *cos.* 395?), which are listed in the ninth-century catalogues of Bobbio (Becker 32. 446–7, pp. 69–70) and Murbach (no. 327, p. 48 Milde) respectively. It was

When the manuscripts which carry this array of texts have been mustered on parade, we are able to observe, thanks to the palaeographical expertise so generously put at our disposal, from which geographical regions the various contingents come. Two-thirds of the ninth-century manuscripts mentioned in this book were written in what we now know as France. They come mainly from the north and centre, from the abbeys and cathedrals so generously scattered over that ample landscape. The names which occur most frequently are those which one would expect: Corbie, Reims, Tours, Fleury, Auxerre. Certain groups of manuscripts stand out, such as those written in the abbeys strung along the valleys of the Loire and the Yonne, from the books copied early in the century at Tours to those associated with Lupus and Heiric, or the block of classical texts copied at Corbie in the time of its librarian Hadoard;[107] again and again these recur in our ninth-century traditions. The manuscripts from the Germanic area, smaller in number but not necessarily in importance, are predictably dominated by those of Fulda, Lorsch, and the monasteries of Lake Constance. Some local patterns of circulation become apparent, as texts move through the valley of the Loire or along the Rhine, and it is interesting to observe how geographical proximity or the special relationships which bind one institution to another affect the movement of manuscripts. But any elaborate attempt to plot the routes by which texts travelled in the Middle Ages seems likely to remain a complex and difficult task; we are sometimes at a loss to know whether a text moved from A to B or from B to A, and it has to be borne in mind that whole libraries which may have played a key part in the tradition of some authors have disappeared without trace. But amid all this flux and reflux it is perhaps not too fanciful to sense a general drift towards the south and west, as the deposits of texts built up at the Carolingian court and in the abbeys of western Germany and north-eastern France were carried to other regions, where, sooner or later, they would help to stimulate fresh revivals of classical learning.

Italy made a significant contribution to the revival, even if in a comparatively minor key. It was nourished to some extent by an overflow of manuscripts from the north, but also by the emergence in Italy of indigenous Italian traditions. A good example of the latter is the

apparently still possible to read the *Controversiae*(?) of Alcimus at the Carolingian court *c.*790, for it is described in the book-list in Diez. B Sant. 66 (Bischoff, *Mitt. Stud.* iii. 166). There were at one time fuller texts of Petronius and Festus. For lost texts known to the humanists, see Sabbadini, *Storia e critica*², 144.

[107] Bischoff, 'Hadoardus and the Manuscripts of Classical Authors from Corbie', *Didascaliae, Studies in honor of Anselm M. Albareda* (ed. S. Prete, New York, 1961), 41–57 (= *Mitt. Stud.* i. 49–63 (in German)). It is noticeable that a number of Hadoard's manuscripts appear to have been copied from German exemplars.

De medicina of Celsus, which belongs to Italy alone.[108] A group of medical treatises in Milan, Ambros. G. 108 inf., which comes from the same milieu as Celsus, leads back once again to a corpus of texts compiled in Ravenna in the sixth century.[109] In two cases Italy appears to have preserved complete texts which were known north of the Alps only in a mutilated form: to Italy we owe the source of the complete tradition of Quintilian,[110] and the Italian manuscript of Cicero's *Brutus*,[111] which has survived in fragmentary form, probably belonged to the complete tradition of his rhetorical works which later came to light at the cathedral of Lodi. Of Italian origin too are the archetype of the *Historia Augusta*,[112] our earliest manuscript of Porphyrio's commentary on Horace,[113] the important *Basilicanus* of Cicero's *Speeches*,[114] the corpus of texts in Berne 363,[115] and a great body of historical material compiled at Verona.[116] From the turn of the century we have the poetic miscellany in Paris lat. 7900A[117] and the earliest manuscript of Seneca's *Letters* to contain the whole extant collection.[118]

The revival largely took place within the Carolingian sphere of influence. Little happened in Spain. But on the Celtic fringe a Welshman was moved to copy Book I of Ovid's manual of seduction, the *Ars amatoria*.[119] This book, together with a Cambridge manuscript of Martianus Capella,[120] is a sign that the Welsh, using continental exemplars, were helping to prepare the way for an insular revival of

---

[108] See CELSUS; G. Billanovich, 'Milano, Nonantola, Brescia', *Settimane*, 22 (Spoleto, 1975), 321–52. The two extant ninth-century manuscripts are Vatican lat. 5951 (s. IX¹, Nonantola) and Florence, Laur. 73. 1 (s. IX², Milan); in addition to Celsus the latter has unique medical items.

[109] A. Beccaria, 'Sulle tracce di un antico canone latino di Ippocrate e di Galeno, II', *IMU* 4 (1961), 1–75; 'Sulle tracce . . ., III', *IMU* 14 (1971), 1–23; *I codici di medicina del periodo presalernitano* (Rome, 1956), 288–91.   [110] Milan, Ambros. E. 153 sup.

[111] Cremona, Archivio Storico Comunale S. N.

[112] Vatican, Pal. lat. 899, s. IX¹, northern Italy.

[113] Vatican lat. 3314, s. IX in., central Italy; p. 186, below.

[114] Vatican, Arch. S. Pietro H. 25, s. IX²/₄ northern Italy; pp. 73–4, below.

[115] Written in an Irish hand; on the Irish colony at Milan, see M. Ferrari, *Settimane*, 22 (Spoleto, 1975), 312–13.   [116] pp. 160–1, 198, below.

[117] s. IX/X, Milan; it includes Lucan, Terence, Horace, Juvenal.

[118] s. IX/X, Milan; it includes Lucan, Terence, Horace, Juvenal.

[118] Brescia, Biblioteca Queriniana B. II. 6, written at Brescia. It is perhaps worth listing the other Italian manuscripts of this period mentioned in this book: Bamberg, Class, 34 (M. IV. 8), s. IX² (Livy, First Decade); Berlin (West) lat. 2° 641, s. IX/X, northern Italy (*Agrimensores*); The Hague 135. G. 8, s. IX¾, northern Italy (Cicero, *De divinatione*); Karlsruhe Aug. CXX, s. IX med., area of Verona (Caelius Aurelianus, *Responsiones*); Munich Clm 6437 + Erzbischöfl. Ordinariatsarchiv 934, c.900, in Beneventan (Hyginus, *Fabulae*); Oxford, Bodl. Laud Lat. 29*, s. IX, Verona (Cicero, *Tusculans*); Paris lat. 7972, s. IX/X, Milan (Horace); Rome, Casanat. 641, s. IX ex., in Beneventan (some poems from the *Latin Anthology*); Rome, Casanat. 1086, s. IX, in Beneventan (Aquila Romanus); St. Gall 44, part II, s. IX²/₄, northern Italy (Q. Serenus); Vatican, Reg. lat. 1529, s. IX²/₄ (Seneca, *De beneficiis, De clementia*); Vatican lat. 3246, s. IX²/₃ (Cicero, *Tusculans*). It should be noted that a fair number of these Italian manuscripts had crossed the Alps by the end of the century.   [119] Oxford, Bodl. Auct. F. 4. 32, part IV.

[120] Corpus Christi College 153, s. IX ex. or X in.; see T. A. M. Bishop, 'The Corpus Martianus Capella', *Tr. Camb. Bibliog. Soc.* 4 (1964–8), 257–75.

learning while their English neighbours were still reeling from the Viking raids which had devastated their stocks of classical texts.

On any statistics the tenth century will appear as something of a trough, and the process of redating to the ninth century manuscripts once attributed to the tenth has not worked its way through to all the literature. The tenth century added comparatively little to the large stock of classical works available at the end of the ninth. Those texts which appear for the first time in tenth-century manuscripts are:

> *Carmina Einsidlensia*, more Cicero (*Partitiones oratoriae*; *Pro lege Manilia, Pro Milone, Pro Sulla, Pro Plancio, Pro Caecina*), pseudo-Cicero and pseudo-Sallust (*Invectivae*), more Ovid (*Fasti, Tristia*), Plautus, pseudo-Quintilian (*Declamationes maiores*).

The pattern of activity seems to be rather different. The French centres continue to add to the general stock of classical books, and Fleury, particularly under Abbo, maintains its importance. But under the Ottonian dynasty Germany is holding its own, and the monasteries of Bavaria and the south-west are becoming very active. The five new speeches of Cicero came to light in Germany,[121] and it was there that the *Invectivae* began to circulate. The *Carmina Einsidlensia* emerge in a unique copy at Fulda,[122] and the earliest surviving manuscripts of Plautus, which begin to appear at the end of the century, are all of German origin. Italy continues to produce valuable books, both new works and superior texts of works already known. To Italy we owe our earliest copy of the *Declamationes maiores*,[123] Cicero's *Partitiones oratoriae*,[124] the *Commentum Monacense* on Terence,[125] and two valuable witnesses to the Latin historians. The first is an excellent manuscript of Florus, Festus, and Eutropius,[126] the other the great copy of Livy's First Decade which was written at Verona on the instructions of Rather.[127]

England must have had to start building up its stock of classical books again almost from scratch, and it naturally has nothing new to offer; but it begins once again to play its part in the business of transmission. It is evident that considerable collections of books had been established by the end of the century, particularly at Canterbury and Winchester, some of them imported from such centres as Fleury and Corbie, others copies made on English soil.

The network of religious houses which covered Europe and the movements along it of men and books made it possible for classical texts

---

[121] Munich Clm 18787, s. x², western Germany (belonged to Tegernsee).
[122] Einsiedeln 266.
[123] Bamberg Class. 44 (M. IV. 13).
[124] Cologny-Geneva, Bodmer lat. 146.
[125] Munich Clm 14420; pp. 202 n. 15, 419–20, below.
[126] Bamberg Class. 31 (E. III.22).
[127] Florence, Laur. 63. 19.

to surmount eventually all natural barriers. But crossing the English Channel is always something of a bore, and the gradual restocking of English libraries is one indication of the vigour and success with which classical learning was able to expand its orbit. To judge from the surviving books, a fair range of poetry was available in English houses in the tenth century: Virgil,[128] Statius,[129] Persius and Juvenal,[130] Cicero's *Aratea*,[131] Nemesianus' *Cynegetica*,[132] Q. Serenus,[133] the *Appendix Vergiliana*,[134] and some Ausonius.[135] One of the early copies of the *Aratea* also contains Hyginus' *Astronomica*.[136] Prose does not appear to have been so well served. Copies of Martianus Capella continued to multiply.[137] Otherwise the extant manuscripts offer only Censorinus and the *Agrimensores*,[138] but some of the texts which were well established by the eleventh century very probably crossed the Channel at this time.[139] Although the classical texts which appear in England before the Conquest reflect in some measure the tastes of earlier generations of English scholars, they are recent offshoots of continental traditions rather than descendants of the books used by Aldhelm or Bede.

As we move into the eleventh century the manuscripts which we have had occasion to cite in these articles will inevitably form a significantly smaller proportion of the extant total, and increasingly so with the passage of time; as manuscripts multiply, editors can afford to be more selective. There is thus more concentration on the 'nerves and sinews' of the classical tradition, on the manuscripts which are valuable or at least serviceable witnesses to the texts they carry. Judged by this narrow criterion, the contribution of France in the eleventh century is less impressive than that of Germany or Italy. Germany owed a great deal to the cultural interests of its emperor, Otto III, whose library, much of

---

[128] Vatican, Reg. lat. 1671 (s. x^2, Worcester?); London, College of Arms, Arundel 30 (s. x, Bury); Oxford, Bodl. Lat. class. c. 2, f. 18 (s. x/xi).

[129] London, Royal 15. C. x (s. x ex., Canterbury?); Worcester, Cathedral Library Q. 8 + Add. 7 (s. x/xi, Worcester).

[130] Cambridge, Trinity College 1241 (O. 4. 10) (s. x, Juvenal and Persius); 1242 (O. 4. 11) (s. x, St. Augustine's Canterbury, Juvenal); B. L. Royal 15. B. xix (s. x, Persius); Oxford, Bodl. Auct. F. 1. 15 (s. x^2, St. Augustine's Canterbury, Persius).

[131] pp. 22–4, below.

[132] Paris lat. 4839 (s. x).

[133] Ibid.

[134] Cambridge, U. L. Kk. 5. 34 (s. x ex., Winchester).

[135] Ibid.

[136] Cambridge, Trinity College 945 (R. 15. 32) (*c.*1000, New Minster Winchester).

[137] Cambridge, Corpus Christi College 206 (s. x); B. L. Harley 3826 (s. x/xi, Abingdon?).

[138] Both are found in Cambridge, Trinity College 939 (R. 15. 14) (s. x, St. Augustine's Canterbury). The same gromatic text ('Boethius'; see pp. 4–5, below) appears in Oxford, Bodl. Douce 125 (s. x/xi, St. Swithun's Winchester).

[139] For example, some of the texts in B. L. Cleo. D. 1 (s. xi, St. Augustine's Canterbury): Vitruvius, Vegetius, Solinus. For the overall picture, see Gneuss, 'A Preliminary List' (n. 38, above), to which this paragraph is much indebted.

it now at Bamberg, is a worthy successor to the line of imperial libraries extending back to Charlemagne. Germany also owed much to its fruitful contacts with Italy, and to the industry of such monasteries as Freising, St. Emmeram, and Tegernsee. The contribution of Italy was much enhanced by the spectacular revival in the copying of classical authors at Montecassino.

The texts which first appear in manuscripts of the eleventh century, crudely lumped together, are:

Apuleius (*Apologia, Metamorphoses, Florida*), more Cicero (*Pro Archia, Pro Cluentio, De optimo genere oratorum, De finibus, Epistulae ad Atticum*[140]), more Claudian (*Claudianus maior*), Donatus (*Commentary on Terence*), Festus (*De verborum significatu*), *Ilias latina*,[141] more Livy (Fourth Decade), Manilius, more Ovid (*Medicamina faciei femineae*), pseudo-Ovid (*Nux*), more Seneca (*Dialogues, Tragedies*), Tacitus (*Annals*, 11–16, *Histories*), Varro (*De lingua latina*).

The most remarkable phenomenon is of course the copying at Montecassino within the course of a few decades of a whole clutch of hitherto totally unknown texts. These are Apuleius (*Apologia, Metamorphoses, Florida*), Seneca (*Dialogues*), Tacitus (*Annals*, 11–16, *Histories*), Varro (*De lingua latina*); Frontinus' *De aquis*, although it was not copied until the next century, is another work whose survival is due to this great Cassinese revival. The manuscript which gives us Varro also contains the first extant copy of Cicero's *Pro Cluentio*, which also has a northern tradition.[142] Other Beneventan manuscripts of this period contain important texts of Cicero,[143] Ovid,[144] Justinus,[145] and Juvenal.[146]

To Italy we also owe the unique manuscript of Festus,[147] written in the area of Rome, the earliest manuscript of Seneca's *Tragedies*,[148] copied at Pomposa, perhaps from a Cassinese exemplar, and the earliest witness of the *Medicamina*.[149] The main stream of Livy's Fourth Decade descends from an uncial codex which had survived at Piacenza. This

---

[140] The corpus of the *Ad Atticum* makes a formal appearance here because of the existence of a few leaves of a manuscript written in Germany in s. XI which is part of the rare northern or 'transalpine' tradition. Four leaves still survive in Würzburg (Univ., Fragm. S. N.; Chatelain, plate XXXVI a); four in Munich (Clm 29220 (8, *olim* 29001). All our complete manuscripts belong to the Italian family, which did not emerge until s. XIV.

[141] It must be fortuitous that our earliest manuscripts of the *Ilias latina*, which had been a school text since the Carolingian period, are as late as s. XI.　　　　　　[142] pp. 88 ff., below.

[143] Leiden. B. P. L. 118 (the Leiden corpus of philosophical works); Vatican, Ottob. lat. 1406 (*Topica*).

[144] Eton College 150 (*Remedia, Heroides*); Naples IV. F. 3 (*Met.*); Vatican lat. 3262 (*Fasti*), Urb. lat. 341 (*Met.*).　　　　　　　　　　　　　　　　　[145] Florence, Laur. 66. 21.

[146] Oxford, Bodl. Canon. Class. Lat. 41 (containing the unique 'Oxford fragment').

[147] Naples IV. A. 3.

[148] Florence, Laur. 37. 13.

[149] Laur. S. Marco 223, which also contains *Nux*. But *Nux* appears, a little earlier, in an English manuscript, Oxford, Bodl. Auct. F. 2. 14 (s. XI², Sherborne?).

venerable book, taken off to Germany by Otto III and donated to Bamberg Cathedral by Henry II, is now reduced to fragments; but the eleventh-century copy which was made at Bamberg survives intact.[150] Two other important witnesses to this tradition, now lost but at one time respectively at the cathedrals of Chartres and Speyer, were themselves also of Italian origin.[151]

The other texts which emerged at this time look more like late outcrops of the bedrock of the Carolingian age. The pseudo-Ciceronian *De optimo genere* appears in two German manuscripts, one of them written at St. Gall,[152] and the authentic *De finibus* first comes to light in western Germany.[153] A whole group of texts begin to circulate in the area of Liège, and these we appear to owe to the impulse of Olbert, Abbot of Gembloux and St. James's Liège. The earliest witness of the *Pro Archia*, which was later rediscovered by Petrarch at Liège, is a Gembloux manuscript;[154] the two oldest extant manuscripts of Manilius are also from this area, one from Gembloux itself;[155] the new poems of Claudian are first found in a Gembloux manuscript which is clearly connected with a book at one time in the palace library;[156] Gembloux has preserved the unique manuscript of Favonius Eulogius.[157] The monasteries of this area are obviously beneficiaries of its Carolingian patrimony.[158]

The importing of classical literature to England continued. The arrival of the Norman conquerors must have facilitated and intensified this process, and the effects of the Conquest are reflected in the rapid expansion of classical learning in England in the following century. But it is of course impossible to draw a sharp line between those texts which reached these shores before 1066 and those which came after, and the flow of classical learning to England must in any case have by now generated some momentum of its own. The movement in reverse of English scribes to the Continent is a further sign of the growing cultural continuum, which makes it difficult to say whether a Norman scribe at this time was writing on this or that side of the Channel. The works of poets already recorded in England went on being multiplied,[159] and more poetic texts

---

[150] Bamberg Class. 35 (M. IV. 9).

[151] p. 211, below.

[152] St. Gall 818.

[153] Vatican, Pal. lat. 1513.

[154] Brussels 5348–52; pp. 85–6, below.

[155] Brussels 10012.

[156] Brussels 5381; p. 143, below.

[157] Brussels 10078–95; p. 131 n. 1, below.

[158] The monastery of Lobbes, not far from Gembloux, had a similar Claudian, and copies – all unfortunately lost – of such rare texts at Lucretius, Cicero's *De oratore*, Tibullus, Valerius Flaccus, and probably Manilius; for its library see F. Dolbeau, 'Un nouveau catalogue des manuscrits de Lobbes aux XIᵉ et XIIᵉ siècles', *Recherches Augustiniennes*, 13 (1978), 3–36, 14 (1979), 191–248.

[159] Virgil (B. L. Royal 8. F. XIV, s. XI in., Bury?); Statius (Cambridge, St. John's College 87 (D. 12), s. XI, Oxford, Bodl. Auct. F. 2. 14, s. XI², Sherborne?); Persius (Edinburgh. Adv. 18. 6. 12, s. XI ex., Thorney Abbey).

were added to those already available, namely the *Fables* of Avianus and the *Ilias latina*.[160] Of greater interest is the number of prose works which had reached England by the end of the century, Cicero's *De officiis*[161] and *In Catilinam*,[162] Macrobius' *Commentary on the Somnium Scipionis* with the *Somnium* itself,[163] the pseudo-Cicero/Sallust *Invectivae*,[164] Suetonius' *Lives of the Caesars*,[165] Vitruvius,[166] Vegetius,[167] Solinus.[168]

With the beginning of the twelfth-century renaissance there is a very substantial increase in the volume of books in circulation. Editors do not necessarily look upon the manuscripts of the later Middle Ages with any great enthusiasm. In the case of some authors they will have had a long copying tradition behind them, with its inevitable accumulation and compounding of error and conjecture, and there is now a marked propensity towards arbitrary alteration. But they are of course vital witnesses for texts which are just emerging from hibernation, and are often of great service in other cases where areas of the tradition are thinly represented, if at all, by earlier witnesses. A large part of the manuscripts of this period which have been exploited by editors – and there is no reason to suppose that this is not a representative sample – were written in France, though there is strenuous competition from the monasteries of Bavaria and Austria. Many of these books come, as one would have expected, from Normandy and the Île de France, and there are significant contributions from new foundations, such as Clairvaux and Pontigny. The new monastic orders were creating whole networks of new foundations, and the need to stock their libraries explains part of the great surge in book production which took place in the twelfth century. The Cistercians were a vigorous order and their scriptoria were particularly busy.

Amid the exploitation and consolidation of existing traditions a considerable number of new works do come to light:

Calpurnius Siculus (*Eclogae*, 1–4.12), Cato (*De agri cultura*), Cicero (*De lege agraria, Academica posteriora*), Claudian (*Panegyric on Probinus and Olybrius, De raptu Proserpinae*), Frontinus (*De aquis*), Aulus Gellius (Books 1–7), Cornelius Nepos, Ovid (*Ibis*), Propertius, Seneca (*Natural Questions*), Varro (*Res rusticae*).

Italy is still bit by bit uncovering its treasures: Frontinus' *De aquis*, mentioned above, some new poems of Claudian,[169] the agricultural works

---

[160] Both texts are found in Bodl. Rawlinson G. 57 + G. 111 (s. XI ex.) and Auct. F. 2. 14 (see n. 159, above), Avianus in Adv. 18. 6. 12 (n. 159, above).

[161] Cambridge, Trinity College 982 (R. 16. 34), s. XI ex., Salisbury.

[162] Adv. 18. 7. 8, s. XI/XII, Thorney.

[163] Bodl. Auct. F. 2. 20, s. XI².

[164] Adv. 18. 7. 8 (see n. 162, above).

[165] Durham C. III. 18, s. XI ex.

[166] B. L. Cotton Cleo. D. I, s. XI, St. Augustine's Canterbury.

[167] Ibid.

[168] Ibid.; also Cambridge, Clare College S. N., s. XI, Bury.

[169] p. 143, below.

of Cato and Varro.[170] The other novelties we owe to northern Europe. The now fashionable habit of assembling the works of an author into a corpus encourages the rounding up of stragglers. The large omnibus Cicero which was put together for Wibald of Corvey contains the three speeches *De lege agraria*,[171] which do not appear to have circulated previously. Seneca's *Natural Questions* first circulates in northern France, the oldest manuscript of Calpurnius' *Eclogae* comes from the Loire,[172] the tradition of Nepos seems to have originated in the Low Countries or Rhineland. The part of Gellius which has not been in circulation before, Books 1–7, first appears in French manuscripts, the two earliest extant copies of the *Academica posteriora* were written at Pontigny.[173] Other texts which emerged from their hiding places towards the end of the century, again in France, are Ovid's *Ibis* and the poems of Propertius; in both cases there is no extant witness before *c.* 1200.[174]

The rising level of English classical culture in the century after the Conquest is apparent from the surviving library catalogues[175] and from the breadth of reading of such a writer as William of Malmesbury,[176] who was totally dependent on the books which he could obtain in England. The stocking of the libraries of the post-Conquest foundations was largely responsible for this upturn. A fair number of the manuscripts which were written in England or brought there in the twelfth century do find a place in this volume, and it is perhaps worth quoting them, for they have all been fitted into the transmission of their respective authors and a glance at the articles will illustrate the interlocking of the British and continental traditions:

Apuleius (*Opera philosophica*),[177] Cicero (*Philippics*,[178] *Partitiones oratoriae*,[179] *De amicitia* and *De senectute*,[180] part of the Leiden corpus[181]), Eutropius,[182]

---

[170] Paris lat. 6842A.

[171] Berlin (West) lat. 2° 252; p. 83, below.

[172] Paris lat. 8049. The scribe went no further than 4.12, but he may well have been drawing on the complete tradition which later emerged in Italy.

[173] Paris lat. 6331; Amsterdam 77.

[174] The oldest manuscript of Propertius is Wolfenbüttel, Gud. lat. 224; the earliest of the miscellanies to contain *Ibis* appears to be Tours 879.

[175] For a survey of English libraries in general see R. A. B. Mynors, 'The Latin Classics known to Boston of Bury', in *Fritz Saxl, 1890–1948: a Volume of Memorial Essays from his Friends in England* (ed. D. J. Gordon, Edinburgh, 1957), 199–217.

[176] Examined by R. M. T., in a series of articles: *Rev. bén.* 85 (1975), 362–402; 86 (1976), 327–35; *Journal of Ecclesiastical History*, 29 (1978), 387–413.

[177] Cambridge, U. L., Ff. 3. 5 (Bury), which also contains Macrobius, *Sat.*, and Corpus Christi College 71 (St. Albans).

[178] Oxford, Merton College 311; for earlier manuscripts with English connections, see p. 75, below.

[179] Oxford. Bodl. Rawl. G. 139 (William of Malmesbury); London, Lambeth Palace 425, part II (?England).

[180] Eton College 90 (s. XII/XIII, Haverfordwest); Lambeth Palace 425, part I (s. XII/XIII, Llanthony).   [181] Merton College 311.

[182] Oxford, Lincoln College Lat. 100 (William of Malmesbury).

Frontinus (*Strategemata*),[183] Aulus Gellius,[184] Livy (Third Decade),[185] Ovid (*Fasti*),[186] Plautus (plays 1–8),[187] the Elder Pliny,[188] Seneca (*De clementia*,[189] *Letters*[190]), Terence,[191] Valerius Maximus.[192]

These manuscripts form an interesting group and their existence helps to give substance to the general picture which can be pieced together from other sources of the deposits of classical books in England at this time. But of course many other texts were demonstrably available for which no contemporary English witnesses survive, and in the case of popular authors no one has taken the trouble to dip into the ruck and fish out the first English manuscript.

The volume of classical manuscripts which survive from the later Middle Ages and Renaissance is so large that it would be incautious to draw many general conclusions from the small sample which has proved to be of interest to classical scholars. But the material which we have assembled does suggest a few observations, and in particular allows the simple record to be completed of when classical works first appear in extant manuscripts. The twelfth century had marked a turning-point in the development of literacy, which had hitherto been largely confined to the clergy and the families of those in power. The putting into circulation of newly discovered works of Latin literature could have a wider impact on taste and culture now that books were coming within the reach of a reading public.

If one asks which of the texts we have included in this volume first surfaced in a thirteenth-century manuscript, one asks an embarrassing question. The answer is a work which would hardly have set the world on fire even in this feminist age, the *Gynaecia* of Caelius Aurelianus. That this crude fact distorts the contribution of this period to classical learning goes without saying, because it takes no account, for instance, of the Latin translations from Greek and Arabic which were making the philosophy and science of Aristotle and others accessible to the West and exerting a powerful influence on the very shape of university education. But the large number of thirteenth-century manuscripts which we do cite, some 140 drawn from widely divergent areas, shows that the consolidation and

[183] Ibid.; Cambridge, Peterhouse 252, part III (?England).

[184] Paris lat. 13038 (Thomas Becket?); excerpts in Cambridge, Trinity College 982 (R. 16. 34) (Salisbury), Oxford, Bodl. Lat. class. d. 39, Rawl. G. 139 (see n. 179, above).

[185] Cambridge, Trinity College 637 (R. 4. 4), brought from France by Thomas Becket in 1170.

[186] Cambridge, Pembroke College 280 (Dover).

[187] B. L., Royal 15. C. XI.

[188] B. L., Arundel 98; Le Mans 263.

[189] Leiden, Lips. 49.

[190] Leiden, Lips. 49: B. L., Harley 2659 (St. Peter's, Gloucester); Oxford, Magdalen College Lat. 22 (Abbey of B. V. M. and St. Egwin, Evesham).

[191] Oxford. Bodl. Auct. F. 2. 13 (St. Albans); if Oxford, Brasenose College 18 is an English book, it would take back the arrival of Terence in England to the eleventh century.

[192] Cambridge, U. L., Kk. 3. 23.

organization of learning which is characteristic of the age was still firming up our traditions of the classics. Manuscripts of Ovid and Seneca are so common as to be almost a feature of the period, and it is obvious that the dissemination in northern Europe of such texts as the *Dialogues* and *Tragedies* of Seneca was of immeasurably greater cultural significance than their isolated appearances in Italy at an earlier date. An increasing quantity of Latin literature is now circulating in the more easily digested form of the florilegium. As many as seventy different classical florilegia have now been catalogued for the period up to 1200.[193] The majority were compiled in the twelfth century and the florilegists were particularly active in the second half of the century. The industry seems to have gained rather than lost momentum after 1200: existing florilegia, such as the *Florilegium Gallicum* and *Angelicum*, are multiplied and enlarged, and new compilations come on to the market.[194] Rare authors and texts, including some which did not fully emerge until later, like Tibullus and the *Laus Pisonis,* are fleetingly glimpsed in this rather twilight world, as the classics are processed to provide material for the schoolroom, ammunition for the growing fraternity of preachers, and interest and stimulation for a wider public of amateurs.[195] Thus among the phenomena of the age which stand out in the memory after scanning these pages are the encyclopaedic compilation of Vincent of Beauvais, the breadth of reading of the annotator of Berne 276, and the rich and elaborate library of the first great private collector, Richard de Fournival.

What this book does not provide to any degree is a sense of the *largior aether* as the main focal points of classical studies move from the rather cloistered world of medieval learning to the more limpid atmosphere of the Italian Renaissance. Our main occupation is naturally with the nuts and bolts of classical philology, with assessing the stemmatic value of Renaissance manuscripts, with trying to decide whether an interesting reading came from the 'vetustissimus codex' which a humanist claimed to have seen or merely from the top of his head. So the emphasis is more on the complexity of humanist scholarship, on the lifetime's laborious effort which may have gone into assembling texts as good and as complete as they could be made, and on the corresponding effort which is required to unravel the labyrinthine history of even one text, as manuscripts pass from hand to hand and city to city, are borrowed and

---

[193] B. Munk Olsen, 'Les Classiques latins dans les florilèges mediévaux antérieurs au XIIIe siècle', *RHT* 9 (1979), 47–121; 10 (1980), 115–64.

[194] R. H. R., 'Florilegia and Latin Classical Authors in Twelfth- and Thirteenth-Century Orléans', *Viator,* 10 (1979), 131–60.

[195] The compiler of the *Florilegium Duacense* sees himself catering for a remarkably varied readership: 'Habeat ergo hinc rudis animus quo se erudiat, prudens quo se exerceat, tepidus quo se inflammet, pusillus quo se confortet; sumat hinc etiam eger quo curetur, sanus quo custodiatur, fessus quo recreetur, esuriens quo pascatur; legat studiosus, legat fastidiosus, iste ut incitetur, ille ut delectetur; legat simplex quod per se intellegat, habeat pauper quod scribere valeat (Troyes, Bibl. Mun. 215, f. 71^r, quoted by Munk Olsen, 'Les Classiques latins', 56).

borrowed again, corrected and collated with a feverish enthusiasm that is not easily paralleled in an earlier age. The close links between cultural renaissance and palaeographical changes are seen once again in the invention of the new and elegant humanistic scripts.

The vitality and intensity of the revival of learning may be readily seen from its effect upon our manuscript traditions. Completely new traditions sprout from what had been a single manuscript, as with Asconius, Silius Italicus, and Statius' *Silvae*. Sometimes a new source is discovered in Italy for a work which had hitherto rested on an exclusively northern base, and the result may be one of those texts, like Cicero's *Ad Atticum*, which majestically straddle the Alps and demonstrate how deeply that range of mountains can so often bisect our manuscript traditions. Often, however, the humanists seized upon a very ordinary manuscript; given a role disproportionate to its merit, it blossoms into one of those complex and textually useless growths which are glumly designated as *recc.* or *dett.* or *Itali*. But these too, when patiently dissected, are revealing an enormous amount of valuable information about individual humanists, their scholarly circles, and their methods of work.

The milestones in the progress of the rediscovery of the classics in the Renaissance are already familiar, and there is no point in taking that road again. It may be more appropriate to end this somewhat geographical survey by reminding oneself where the humanists found, sitting forlorn on a shelf or locked in what they liked to regard as the dungeons of the north,[196] the new and exciting books which helped to maintain the verve of their movement.

The distribution of classical manuscripts over Europe was to change once again, as books inevitably migrated to the new centres of power and intellectual ferment. There had been a gradual percolation of texts from north to south since early times, though this is not easily charted, and most texts which freely circulated in the Middle Ages had established offshoots in Italy in the twelfth and thirteenth centuries. These, together with what was already there, provided the humanists with their basic stock of classical books. This they were able to improve and expand by bringing to bear the new and superior traditions which they discovered further afield. The imports were sometimes copies of manuscripts which had remained in the north, not infrequently the old manuscripts themselves; a number of books which had crept over the Alps in Carolingian times came tumbling back, like a film put into reverse, and in time many of our prime witnesses found their way into the great Renaissance libraries; the number of old and valuable manu-

---

[196] For some rich elaborations on this theme see the accounts by Poggio and Cencio Rustici of their finds at St. Gall, conveniently quoted by A. C. Clark in his OCT of Asconius (Oxford, 1907), xi–xiii; cf. pp. 6 n. 1, 91, below.

scripts which Politian could himself consult is a striking indication of this.

The first great batch of discoveries made by Petrarch, during his stay at Avignon, came from French libraries. Seneca's *Tragedies*[197] and the texts associated with Pomponius Mela[198] he may have found at Avignon, his Livy came from Chartres;[199] his other finds were the result of a foray to Paris (Propertius)[200] and Liège (Cicero's *Pro Archia*).[201] In Italy he was able to draw on the rich resources of the Chapter Library at Verona. Over the centuries it had been adding to the stock of books which it had preserved from Antiquity, fortunate to be one of the comparatively small number of libraries to enjoy such a measure of stability; it had already been, with Pomposa, an important source of classical texts for the pre-humanists. Here Petrarch found a collection of Ausonius' poems,[202] Cicero's *Letters to Atticus*,[203] the *Eclogues* of Calpurnius and Nemesianus,[204] and the *Historia Augusta*.[205] Two of his texts, Varro's *De lingua latina* and Cicero's *Pro Cluentio*, he owed to Montecassino.[206] For these he was indebted to the good offices of Boccaccio, who was instrumental in making other Cassinese texts, Tacitus and Apuleius, available to the humanists. For some other works, like the large corpus of Cicero in Troyes 552,[207] he was dependent on the resources already available in northern Italy.

To some extent Salutati, the most influential of the next generation of humanists, took his cue from Petrarch. He had obtained a copy of Petrarch's Propertius shortly after Petrarch's death.[208] His manuscript of Tibullus is our oldest complete witness;[209] it must have descended ultimately from a French exemplar, and Petrarch may have been the link.[210] It was Petrarch's possession of Cicero's *Letters to Atticus* that prompted Salutati to write to the Chancellor of Milan and ask him to root out a copy for himself. He did eventually get an *Ad Atticum* from Milan,[211] but not before he had been sent by mistake a copy of the splendid Carolingian manuscript of the *Ad familiares*[212] which had in all probability been executed in the scriptorium of Louis the Pious and had reached Vercelli by the time of Bishop Leo.[213] His copy of Pliny's *Letters*

---

[197] p. 380, below.   [198] p. 292, below.

[199] pp. 212–13, below.

[200] pp. 324–5, below.   [201] pp. 85–6, below.

[202] Paris lat. 8500; p. 27, below.

[203] Petrarch, *Fam.* XXI. 10, *Var.* 25.   [204] p. 37, below.

[205] Vatican, Pal. lat. 899.

[206] pp. 86–7, 430, below.   [207] p. 67, below.

[208] Florence, Laur. 38. 49.

[209] Milan, Ambros. R. 26 sup.

[210] p. 423, below.   [211] Laur. 49. 18.

[212] Laur. 49. 9; Salutati's copy is Laur. 49. 7. The letter which Salutati wrote to Pasquino de' Capelli on receipt of the *Ad familiares* is a remarkable expression of the excitement of humanist discovery: F. Novati, *Epistolario di Coluccio Salutati*, ii (Rome, 1893), 386 ff.

[213] Bischoff, in *Medieval Learning*, 21.

had found its way from the valley of the Loire,[214] and he was able to supplement its truncated text by drawing upon an independent tradition of the *Letters* which had survived at Verona. From Verona too came his Catullus.

So far the great monasteries and cathedrals of the Rhineland and Lake Constance had not been called upon to further by a direct levy the progress of Italian humanism. This was to change when in 1414 the papal curia moved to Constance and the opportunity was given for a more systematic and at times ruthless search of Carolingian libraries. The prime mover in this was the Papal Secretary, Poggio Bracciolini. Some of the texts which he discovered came from France, from Burgundy and Champagne, and to these his attention had no doubt been directed by the French humanists who had been there before him. A whole batch of Cicero's speeches was found at Cluny,[215] the *Pro Caecina* at Langres.[216] But the bulk of his discoveries were made in Switzerland and Germany. Asconius, a complete Quintilian, and Valerius Flaccus came to light at St. Gall, while unspecified libraries in the area of Constance provided Poggio and his band of humanist searchers with their first sight of Silius Italicus, Manilius, and Statius' *Silvae*. Trips further afield were hardly less fruitful. Cologne yielded another important corpus of Cicero's orations,[217] and also the *Cena Trimalchionis*; Fulda produced Ammianus Marcellinus and Columella. His journey to England, however, was something of a disappointment.[218] The 'barbari et suspiciosi' who presided over the booky prisons of the Germanic area did not always succumb with alacrity to the requests of their Italian visitors, and decades were to pass before all of the many books which eventually reached the humanist circles of Florence or Rome arrived in Italy. But the resources of this region were so rich that important texts remained to be found by the scholars of the sixteenth century.[219]

These expeditions had been remarkably fruitful, despite the concentration on certain areas, and it is tempting to reflect how drastically the history of some texts would have changed if the humanists had penetrated to other richly endowed regions of Europe. The concentration on the hunting grounds of the north did not deflect from further discoveries in Italy. Some came sooner, like that of Cicero's rhetorical works at Lodi in 1421, some later, such as the block of new texts found at Bobbio in 1493.[220] Others remain shrouded in mystery. The missing parts of

---

[214] Laur. S. Marco 284; pp. 318–9, below.

[215] pp. 88–91, below.

[216] p. 91, below.

[217] pp. 83–4, 91, below.

[218] The O excerpts of Petronius and a manuscript of Calpurnius.

[219] For example, the fine codices of Livy later found at Worms, Speyer, Mainz, and Lorsch, Velleius Paterculus (Murbach), the *Laus Pisonis* (Lorsch).

[220] Rutilius Namatianus, Sulpicia, the *Epigrammata Bobiensia, grammatica*.

Palladius first turn up in an Italian book of s. XIII/XIV, the *Priapea* in a manuscript written by Boccaccio. Cicero's *Pro Quinctio* and new works of Ausonius quietly begin to circulate in the late fourteenth century. Bits of Gellius which are lacking in all earlier witnesses duly appear in manuscripts of s. XV. The *Consolatio ad Liviam* first shows its face in a manuscript dated 1469. Such texts, for all we know, might have dropped from the sky.

Some of the works of Latin literature which came to light again in the Renaissance had enjoyed some degree of circulation in earlier times, others were to all intents and purposes quite new. We may conclude with a simple tally of texts which first appear in extant witnesses of s. XIV–XVI, whether manuscript or printed:

s. XIV   Ausonius (family (2), including, e.g., *Gratiarum actio* and *Cento nuptialis*), Calpurnius and Nemesianus (*Eclogae*, 4.13 to 11 end), Catullus, Cicero (*Pro Quinctio*), Palladius (Book 14, *Carmen de insitione*), *Priapea*, Tibullus;[221]

s. XV Asconius, Cicero (*Pro Murena, Pro Roscio Amerino; Pro Rabirio Postumo, Pro Rabirio perduellionis reo, Pro Roscio comoedo*), *Consolatio ad Liviam, De viris illustribus*,[222] *Panegyrici latini,* Petronius (*Cena Trimalchionis*), Silius Italicus, Statius (*Silvae*), Suetonius (*De grammaticis*), Sulpicia, Tacitus (*Opera minora*);

s. XVI   Caelius Aurelianus (*Acutae passiones*), Julius Obsequens, *Laus Pisonis*,[223] Petronius (L excerpts), Rutilius Namatianus,[224] Scribonius Largus, Velleius Paterculus.

The process of transmission is essentially that of finding, preserving, and renewing the legacy of past ages. The humanists were not always as careful as we would have wished in physically preserving what they had found, so that we are often forced to reconstruct the manuscript we want from its tangle of progeny, but the enthusiasm and determination with which they revived and fostered the tradition of classical learning had an incalculable effect on our texts. The finding of new texts and important manuscripts did not cease when the heroic age of discovery came to an end; and the recent publication of a valuable text of Cicero's *In Catilinam* and fragments of the poetry of Gallus suggests that papyri, at least, will continue to provide moments of excitement even for Latin texts. The later humanists lived into the age of the printed book, the most momentous development in the transmission of learning since the substitution of the codex for the roll and parchment for papyrus. Although the change was gradual – some of our late manuscripts are copies of printed editions – most Latin authors were available in print

[221] Earlier only in florilegia.
[222] A shorter version of this corpus of texts was in circulation in s. XIV.
[223] Excerpts had appeared in the *Florilegium Gallicum* (s. XII).
[224] Discovered in 1493, but the earliest witness, apart from fragments, is a manuscript of 1501.

by the end of the fifteenth century. For a few texts we are dependent entirely on printed sources.[225] The vast majority of these *editiones principes* were produced in Italy, with Rome and Venice accounting for the lion's share.[226] With the advent of printing the survival of the classics was no longer hazardous, and the type of degeneration which had been inherent in scribal transmission was brought to an end. Books were multiplied in standardized copies on an unprecedented scale; but the text immortalized by such an *imprimatur* was often nothing more than a humanist manuscript which had been rushed to the press from the end of the line of transmission. A new process had now to begin, that of ensuring that our critical editions make the best possible use of the material which has been accumulating century by century since Antiquity. That process, as the articles in this volume make clear, is still far from complete.

L. D. R.

---

[225] Among them are Julius Obsequens and the *Acutae passiones* of Caelius Aurelianus, also five of Cicero's letters to Brutus and most of Pliny's correspondence with Trajan.

[226] A chronological table of the *editiones principes* of Latin authors may be found in J. E. Sandys, *A History of Classical Scholarship*, ii (Cambridge, 1908), 103, which, despite its shortcomings, gives a quick visual impression of the progress made in the printing of classical texts.

LIST OF AUTHORS AND TEXTS

TEXTS AND TRANSMISSION

Every schoolboy knows that the Romans were a practical people, but not every schoolboy knows what they did with a *groma*. They surveyed with it. How and why they surveyed may be read in the words of the *Gromatici* or *Agrimensores*, writers of treatises on surveying and related subjects from the reign of Domitian to the third century. What survives of their treatises can appeal to few readers now, but so diverse are the manuscripts that preserve it, so many the names associated with its preservation, that no text opens the window wider on the transmission of Latin literature from Antiquity to print.

The earliest book that can be glimpsed behind the extant manuscripts was a compilation of the later fifth century. Besides extracts from technical treatises it contained the *lex Mamilia* and a *liber coloniarum*, and it had illustrations, which always make a manual more useful. Its exact contents are uncertain, because the extant manuscripts have suffered losses since they were written. In general, the later a manuscript, the more it differs from the original compilation; but the additions that constitute the main differences introduce later material, not earlier material that bypassed the original compilation.[1]

The earliest manuscript extant, Wolfenbüttel, Aug. 2° 36. 23 (*CLA* IX. 1374), was written within half a century of the original compilation, perhaps at Rome.[2] It has two parts, one illustrated and the other not, and experts date the illustrated one, A, somewhat later than the other, B; but it seems unlikely that A ever led a separate existence. One of its scribes annotated B, to which it was probably intended as a continuation; their overlap in contents, which might seem to rule this out, was a

---

[1] Mommsen, 'Die Interpolationen des gromatischen Corpus', *Gesammelte Schriften*, vii (Berlin, 1909), 464–82. He wrote in 1895, before F. Blume's study of the manuscripts in *Die Schriften der römischen Feldmesser*, ii (Berlin, 1852), 1–78, had been overtaken by N. Bubnov's in *Gerberti opera mathematica* (Berlin, 1899) and C. Thulin's in three articles: 'Die Handschriften des Corpus agrimensorum Romanorum', *Abh. der preuss. Akad.* 1911, Anh. ii. 1–102; 'Zur Überlieferungsgeschichte des Corpus agrimensorum: Exzerptenhandschriften und Kompendien', *Göteborgs Kungl. Vetenskaps- och Vitterhets-Samhälles Handlingar*, 4, 14–15 (1911–12); and 'Humanistische Handschriften des Corpus agrimensorum Romanorum', *RhM* 66 (1911), 417–51.

Thulin's edition of the corpus stopped at vol. i.1 (Teubner, Leipzig, 1913), and for most of the other texts K. Lachmann's, *Die Schriften der römischen Feldmesser*, i (Berlin, 1848), must still be used. Bubnov, 494–553, supplied the mathematical texts omitted by Lachmann, and two other texts have been published separately: *Casae litterarum* by Å. Josephson (Uppsala, 1950); *De munitionibus castrorum* most recently by A. Grillone (Teubner, Leipzig, 1977) and M. Lenoir (Budé, Paris, 1979).

O. A. W. Dilke, *The Roman Land Surveyors* (Newton Abbot, 1971), offers a readable introduction to the subject. See especially ch. 9, 'Roman Surveying Manuals', and app. A, 'Contents of the Corpus'.

[2] A. Petrucci, *Studi Medievali*,[3] 12 (1971), 107–9; cf. Bischoff, *Gnomon*, 46 (1974), 567, where he reviews the facsimile cited in the next footnote.

small price to pay for including the illustrations omitted by B.[3] Still in
the order BA, the manuscript is recognizable in the list of Galbiato's
discoveries at Bobbio in 1493: 'Agenius Urbecus de controversiis
agrorum, Higinus de limitibus agrorum et metatione castrorum,
Balbus de nominibus mensurarum [= B], Vitruvius de exagonis
heptagonis et id genus, Frontinus de qualitate agrorum, Caesarum
leges agrariae et coloniarum iura [= A]'.[4] The two parts changed places
before Vatican lat. 3132 was copied from the manuscript in s. XVI
(another copy, Jena fol. 156, has an order of its own[5]), and three sets of
foliation bear witness to minor displacements. Where it was when all
this happened is a puzzle; by s. XVI other old manuscripts too were in
use, and it is not easy to pick out BA or AB in the tangle of references
and quotations.[6] Its first owner north of the Alps was quite distinguished enough for so distinguished a manuscript – Erasmus.[7] Since
Scriverius acquired it from Joannes Arcerius and first used it for an
edition (Leiden, 1607), it has been known as the Arcerianus. For all its
distinction, its sixteenth-century copies are not to be sneezed at,
because it went on losing leaves.

About the middle of s. VI someone produced a new compilation for
the schoolroom by omitting 'Higinus de metatione castrorum' and
'Vitruvius', condensing and rearranging the rest, and adding extracts
from laws and from a body of gromatic material ascribed to a range of
very suspicious 'auctores'. A century or more later, this compilation in
turn was augmented with extracts from Isidore and elsewhere.[8] The
result, with its Latinity polished as the revival of classical learning
demanded,[9] can be seen in Vatican, Pal. lat. 1564 (P, s. IX ¼). A copy of
a copy of P, Wolfenbüttel, Gud. lat. 105 (G), was written at Corbie
under Hadoard (s. IX ¾)[10] before migrating to Saint-Bertin, but P itself,
probably written in western Germany, was at Fulda when found by
Sichardus in 1526/7.[11] Like the Arcerianus, P has lost leaves, but it is
helped out by G and two later descendants, Brussels 10615–729 (s. XII)

---

[3] Thulin, 'Die Handschriften', 31–2. A facsimile of A has been published (Leiden, 1970) with
an introduction by H. Butzmann.

[4] See, e.g., M. Ferrari, *IMU* 13 (1970), 140–1.

[5] For an illustration of this manuscript see Thulin, 'Humanistische Handschriften', 428.

[6] On these see G. Mercati, *M. Tulli Ciceronis De re publica libri e codice rescripto Vaticano Latino 5757
phototypice expressi: Prolegomena* (Vatican, 1934), 94–108. Josephson, 74 n. 1, and Ullman, op. cit.
(n. 20, below), 265 n. 1, say that Mercati contested the identification of BA with the Bobiensis, but
that is not how I read him; Ullman's summary of his views is inaccurate in other respects too.

[7] f. 2ʳ: 'Et hinc [invariably misread as *hic*] ex bibliotheca Erasmi', written by a later owner
whose name appears on the adventitious f. 1ʳ. He must have meant that when Erasmus owned it it
began with f. 2.   [8] Thulin, 'Die Handschriften', 69–72, in the footsteps of Mommsen.

[9] Thulin, 'Die Handschriften', 59.   [10] Bischoff, *Mitt. Stud.* i. 60.

[11] P. Lehmann, *Erforschung des Mittelalters*, iii (Stuttgart, 1960), 162 and *Johannes Sichardus und die
von ihm benutzten Bibliotheken und Handschriften* (Munich, 1912), 115; Bischoff in *Medieval Learning*,
20–1. For an illustration see Ullman, op. cit. (n. 20, below), opposite p. 280. More illustrations
and fuller discussion in F. Mütherich, *Aachener Kunstblätter*, 45 (1974), 59–74.

and Sichardus's edition of the *Codex Theodosianus* (Basle, 1528). Turnebus made fuller use of G in the first recognizable edition of the *Agrimensores* (Paris, 1554) than Sichardus had done of P.

P begins 'Iulius Frontinus Celso', and a 'Iulii Frontini de geometrica' recorded at Murbach in s. IX[12] could well be P or a close relative; but there is something else it could be. A third compilation that survives in three far from perfect copies – Florence, Laur. 29.32 (F, s. IX[1], written in western Germany[13]), Erfurt, Amplon. Q. 362 (E, s. XI[1]), and (fuller than either) British Library, Add. 47679 (H, s. XII, from western Germany or France[14]) – consisted of two books, the first of which began in the same way as P and the second in the same way as A. In fact the compiler seems to have come by two manuscripts, one like P and the other like A, and to have produced his two books without much shunting from one to the other.[15] The value of his work is that his P-like manuscript was less corrupt in places than P and his A-like manuscript less corrupt than A (and less lacunose than A has become). His successors, however, have let him down: the source of FEH suffered from dislocations and serious corruptions, which the source of FE compounded. Amongst other defects E lacks the beginning, where it might have had 'Iulius Frontinus Celso'; F has no title; but H, despite omitting the first four texts in FE, mentions 'Iulius Frontinus Siculus' in its opening title. Whether from the neighbourhood of Murbach or not, F by the end of s. XV had reached Florence, where it was frequently copied or inspected; Politian, for instance, collated its text of Stat. *Silv.* 2.7, which antedates all others by 500 years. H was first used by Scriverius, E by Lachmann.[16]

Similar to FEH in the combination of texts from different sources is a curious fragment of unknown provenance, Berlin (West) lat. 2° 641, ff. 1–14 (C), acquired in 1889 from a collector in Milan. At first sight its rustic capitals suggest s. V/VI, but it is actually a later imitation, of s. X if the texts bound with it are any guide;[17] blank pages at beginning and end show that its ancient exemplar was itself a fragment. Although it contains nothing more than two versions of *Casae litterarum*, it has clear affinities with A in one and with P in the other.

[12] W. Milde, *Der Bibliothekskatalog des Klosters Murbach aus dem 9. Jahrhundert* (Heidelberg, 1968), 48 no. 319.

[13] Date and provenance kindly supplied by Professor Bernhard Bischoff; for illustrations see Thulin, 'Die Handschriften', plate VII. Bischoff has now found the same scribe at work in F and in Brussels II. 2572 (*CLA* X. 1553), a manuscript written c.800 'ex autentico Petri archidiaconi'; see *Stud. und Mitt. zur Gesch. des Ben.* 92 (1981), 170.

[14] Bischoff ap. M. Folkerts, p. 54 of 'Zur Überlieferung der Agrimensoren: Schrijvers bisher verschollener "codex Nansianus" ', *RhM* 112 (1969), 53–70. I call it H because Folkerts's N already belongs to Naples V.A.13, on which see below.

[15] Thulin, 'Die Handschriften', 95–101.

[16] Thulin, ibid. 78, identified it with Scriverius's Nansianus, which has turned out to be H.

[17] S. IX ex./X, wohl Oberitalien' according to Professor Bischoff.

Almost everything that an editor will want to print in a *Corpus agrimensorum* occurs in BA, P, or FEH, though only Hyginus Gromaticus in all three. Until Euclid was translated from Arabic in s. XII[1], however, scholars and teachers for whom geometry was a quarter of the quadrivium had only two sources of it: Boethius's partial translation of Euclid, and the *Agrimensores*. Accordingly, at an unknown date (s. VIII/IX ?), someone put together mainly from these sources an *Ars geometriae* in five books that goes under Boethius's name, and it enjoyed a wider circulation than the *Agrimensores* ever did in their own right. Combined in varying proportions with further extracts from the *Agrimensores* and occasionally from Cassiodorus, or later (s. XI) recast into the two books of the first Latin work to use Arabic numerals,[18] it accounts for the medieval transmission of what escaped the principal manuscripts of the *Agrimensores*. Editors therefore supplement BA, P, and FEH, from the following groups of manuscripts:

X (18 MSS): 'Vitruvius' from a manuscript like A[19], 'Boethius', other gromatic extracts ultimately from P.
Y (4 MSS): 'Vitruvius' from the same manuscript, extracts from 'Boethius' combined with extracts from Cassiodorus, gromatic extracts from a manuscript like P but independent.
Z (2 MSS): extracts from 'Boethius', gromatic extracts from a manuscript like FEH.

'Boethius' itself includes gromatic material from a manuscript like FEH. The home of 'Boethius' may have been Corbie; but if not, certainly Corbie played such an active part in copying it and combining it with extracts from the *Agrimensores* as to have been called 'the gromatic and geometric capital of the mediaeval world'[20]. No fewer than four members of X, and those among the earliest, were written at Corbie under Hadoard (s. IX¾), and Hadoard actually wrote part of

---

[18] M. Folkerts has edited this version, *'Boethius' Geometrie* II (Wiesbaden, 1970). He includes a partial edition of the five-book version (pp. 173–218).

[19] Thulin, *Exzerptenhandschriften*, 4–5, does not exclude A itself. The question should be pursued, not least because the whereabouts of BA before 1493 are unknown.

[20] Ullman, p. 283 of 'Geometry in the mediaeval quadrivium', *Studi di bibliografia e di storia in onore di T. de Marinis* (Verona, 1964), iv. 263–85. On the use of the *Agrimensores* as a geometrical source Ullman was anticipated by Bubnov, 395–6, and M. Cantor, *Die römischen Agrimensoren und ihre Stellung in der Geschichte der Feldmesskunst* (Leipzig, 1875), 185 ('dass überhaupt irgend etwas von Geometrie in die wissenschaftliche Barbarei des frühsten Mittelalters hinüber sich retten konnte, das ist das unschuldige Verdienst der römischen Agrimensoren'), but his important conclusions about Corbie were new. Neither point has been taken up in recent studies of the liberal arts or medieval mathematics, such as G. Beaujouan, 'L'Enseignement du "Quadrivium" ', *Settimane*, 19.2 (1972), 639–67, or A. Murray, 'The Dark Age of European Mathematics', *Reason and Society in the Middle Ages* (Oxford, 1978), 141–61. Ullman himself missed the extract in 'Boethius' from Columella, who was available only at Corbie and Fulda; see Thulin, *Exzerptenhandschriften*, 36, and P.-P. Corsetti, *RHT* 7 (1977), 128 n. 5.

one, Naples v.A.13(N)[21]; we have already seen that G was written at Corbie in the same period, and an eleventh-century catalogue from Corbie includes a manuscript that, if not identical with G, was a relative of PG. In its diffusion from Corbie X had reached England by the end of s. x: Cambridge, Trinity College 939 (R.15.14) belonged to St. Augustine's Canterbury, Oxford, Bodl. Douce 125 to St. Swithun's Winchester.[22] The main member of Y, perhaps its archetype, is Munich Clm 13084 (s. IX ¾, from Freising or therabouts[23]), also an important witness to the text of Hyginus' *Astronomica*. From the archetype of Z, compiled in Spain apparently by one Gisemundus, derives a fascinating miscellany from Ripoll, Barcelona, Archivo de la Corona de Aragón 106 (s. IX/X),[24] and Paris lat. 8812 (s. IX[25]). Perhaps men like Gisemundus, in copying out texts on surveying, had in mind the interests of landowning monasteries.[26]

In the later Middle Ages the *Agrimensores* bow out to Euclid. Antiquarians of the Renaissance gave them a new lease of life by discovering and copying F, BA, P, and G.

In following the fortunes of the *Agrimensores* we have visited four monasteries vital for the transmission of Latin literature, Bobbio in Italy, Corbie in France, Murbach in Alsace, and Fulda in Germany, with brief excursions to England and Catalonia. We have met an uncial manuscript, Carolingian manuscripts, an archaizing fragment, sixteenth-century manuscripts, manuscripts no less important for other works, and manuscripts that may be a mere entry in a monastic catalogue. We have seen scholars through the ages not slavishly copying the text but adapting it to their different requirements and inevitably corrupting it; and at the end of the road we found two of the greatest figures in Renaissance humanism, Politian and Erasmus. A more leisurely tour would have introduced us to Richard of Fournival, whose diligently catalogued manuscripts turn up in Italy and elsewhere

---

[21] Bischoff, *Mitt. Stud.* i. 59. Bubnov, 472–6, followed by Thulin, *Exzerptenhandschriften*, 5–6, supposed for poor reasons that Gerbert used the source of N (not N itself as Ullman says, p. 278) at Bobbio in 983/4; Bubnov assigned N to s. XI, Thulin to s. X. Bischoff's attribution of N, which appeared too late to help Ullman or Folkerts, calls for a proper appraisal of its place in the stemma of X. Folkerts, *'Boethius'*, 104, 105 n. 1, saw something of its importance.

[22] H. Gneuss, 'A Preliminary List of Manuscripts written or owned in England up to 1100', *Anglo-Saxon England*, 9 (1981), 15, 39.

[23] Bischoff, *Die südostdeutschen Schreibschulen und Bibliotheken in der Karolingerzeit*, i (Wiesbaden, 1974³), 119–20. For illustrations see *Notices et Extraits*, 35.2 (1897), after p. 550.

[24] R. Beer, *SAWW* 155.3 (1907), 59–67 with plates 4–9; Z. Garcia, ibid. 169.2 (1915), 56–8; another illustration in Thulin, *Exzerptenhandschriften*, opposite p. 64.

[25] Date and origin supplied by Professor Bischoff; cf. *Mitt. Stud.* ii. 71.

[26] Beer, 66. Henry Mayr-Harting kindly draws my attention to the following sentences of A. Mayhew, *Rural Settlement and Farming in Germany* (London, 1973), 47: 'A certain amount of regularity in the form of the settlements [in medieval Germany] was assured through the use of settlement planners by the landowners. These planners (the *Reutmeister* or *Lokatoren*) were responsible for the design of the settlement. . . . Occasionally these skills were sought from the experienced ecclesiastical circles.' Were the *Agrimensores* involved?

like ringed pigeons; to Petrarch, who owned a mysterious 'librum M. Varronis de mensuris orbis terre, librum quidem magnum in antiquissima littera, in quo sunt quedam geometrice figure'; to Nicholas of Cues, who owned Brussels 10615–729; to Poggio, who knew that P was at Fulda but never laid hands on it; and to Angelo Colocci, who when his estate at Rome was ravaged in 1527 may have lost a manuscript quite as venerable as BA, P, and F. Perhaps we should go off and read the *Agrimensores* after all.

M. D. R.

AMMIANUS MARCELLINUS

Of the original thirty-one books of the *Res Gestae* of Ammianus only Books 14–31 survive. The text of these books rests on sixteen manuscripts, two of the ninth and fourteen of the fifteenth century. The two Carolingian manuscripts are:

V Vatican lat. 1873, s. IX[1], Fulda.
M Fragmenta Marburgensia, six surviving leaves of a manuscript once at Hersfeld which were rediscovered at Marburg in 1875 and are now at Kassel, Landesbibliothek Philol. 2° 27, s. IX[1].

V appears to have been discovered by Poggio in 1417,[1] but the means by which it was winkled out of Fulda are not clear; it was already in

The fundamental work on the manuscript tradition was done by C. U. Clark, *The Text Tradition of Ammianus Marcellinus* (New Haven, 1904). The standard modern editions are those of Clark (Berlin, 1910–15); the Budé edition, of which two volumes have so far appeared (Livres xiv–xvi, by E. Galletier and J. Fontaine, 1968; Livres xvii-xix, by G. Sabbah, 1970); W. Seyfarth, Ammianus Marcellinus, *Römische Geschichte*, Teil i–iv (Berlin, 1968–71), and his Teubner text (Leipzig, 1978).

[1] Poggio reports his discovery with typical flamboyance in a letter written much later (1448–9) to Francesco d'Arezzo: 'Ammianum Marcellinum ego Latinis Musis restitui, cum illum eruissem e bibliothecis, ne dicam ergastulis, Germanorum. Cardinalis de Columna habet illum codicem, quem portavi, litteris antiquis, sed ita mendosum ut nil corruptius esse possit.' (*Epist.* IX. 12, p. 375 de Tonellis.) V belonged first to Odo Colonna (after the Council of Constance Pope Martin V) and then to his nephew Prospero. Poggio was interested in obtaining the Hersfeld manuscript too (*Epist.* III. 12, p. 208), which featured in the famous inventory of Heinrich von Grebenstein, but in Hersfeld it remained.

Italy and in Niccolò Niccoli's hands in 1423.[2] All the fifteenth-century manuscripts are derived from V.[3] Four of these are direct copies: Vatican lat. 1874 (D), Vatican lat. 2969 (E, written in Rome in 1445), Paris lat. 6120 (N), and Florence, Bibl. Naz. Conv. Soppr. J. v. 43 (F). F is the copy which Niccoli himself made of V in 1423, and from it, directly or through intermediaries, descend the other ten manuscripts.

When M was lent by the Abbot of Hersfeld to Froben in 1533, it already lacked the last chapter of Book 30 and the whole of 31. About 1584–5 it was taken apart at the village of Friedewald, some seven miles from Hersfeld, to provide covers for account-books, and it remained unknown until 1875.[4] The comparative dates of V and M and their precise relationship were long disputed, but in 1936 Robinson demonstrated as cogently as it can be demonstrated that V was copied from M.[5] M is thus a fragment of the archetype; symptoms of an insular pre-archetype are evident.[6]

Ammianus did not fare well at the hands of the early printers. The *editio princeps,* by Angelus Sabinus, was printed in Rome in 1474 by two German clerics, Georg Sachsel and Bartholomaeus Golsch. It was based on Vatican, Reg. lat. 1994 (R), the worst of the *recentiores,* and, like R, it broke off at the end of Book 26. The next edition (Bologna, 1517) suffered from the attention of Petrus Castellus, who disfigured the already poor and truncated text with his own monstrously bad conjectures. The first Froben edition (Basle, 1518), in which Ammianus was included with Suetonius, the *Historia Augusta,* and other historical works, appeared under the aegis of Erasmus, but for Ammianus it did little more than pirate Castellus's unfortunate text. Two editions which marked considerable advances both came out in 1533. The first, printed in Augsburg, in May of that year, by Silvanus Otmar and edited by Mariangelus Accursius, benefited from the use of copies of both E and V and became the *editio princeps* of the last five books. Then in June

[2] *Epist.* II. 7, p. 97; Ullman, *Humanistic Script,* 63. V has notes and corrections in Niccoli's hand: see de la Mare, *Handwriting,* 47 n. 4, 52, 65 n. 2, plate XIf; and, for a detailed study of his annotations and corrections in V, R. Cappelletto, 'Niccolò Niccoli e il codice di Ammiano Vat. Lat. 1873', *Bollettino,* 26 (1978), 57–84, Tav. I-II. For Poggio's part in the tradition see Cappelletto's recent article, 'Marginalia di Poggio in due codici di Ammiano Marcellino (Vat. Lat. 1873 e Vat. Lat. 2969)', *Miscellanea Augusto Campana* (Medioevo e Umanesimo 44–5; Padua, 1981), 189–211. ·

[3] The notion that E may have been influenced by an independent tradition was demolished by W. Seyfarth, 'Der Codex Fuldensis und der Codex E des Ammianus Marcellinus', *ADAW* 1962.2.

[4] It was discovered by G. Könneke in the Staatsarchiv and published by H. Nissen, *Fragmenta Marburgensia* (Berlin, 1876).

[5] R. P. Robinson, 'The Hersfeldensis and the Fuldensis of Ammianus Marcellinus', *University of Missouri Studies,* 11 (1936), 118–40. Arguments about date are inconclusive: Professor Bernhard Bischoff would date them both to about the second quarter of the ninth century. Robinson has complete photographs of M; facsimiles of MVE may be found in Clark, *The Text Tradition,* and also in his edition of the text; Chatelain has a photograph of V (Plate CXCV) and Ullman of F (fig. 30); and see n. 2, above.

[6] Robinson, 120. For a highly suspect report of a majuscule manuscript at Lorsch, see Mommsen, *Hermes,* 7 (1873), 172 n. 1; Bischoff, *Lorsch,* 64, 69.

appeared the second Froben edition, edited by Sigismundus Gelenius. Gelenius was able to make use of M, which had been lent to Hieronymus Froben by the Abbot of Hersfeld. What he appears to have done in practice was to base his text of books 14 to 26 on the 1518 Froben edition, using M as a control, and to use M directly only for the later books;[7] his text stopped short, as did M at this time, at 30.9.6. The subsequent loss of most of M means that Gelenius's edition (G) is an important witness to the text.

The late manuscripts are only of use where a leaf of V is now lacking,[8] or as a repository of humanist conjectures. Since so little of M survives, the text rests in practice on V and G. But Gelenius had the disquieting habit of simply omitting corrupt words,[9] and he failed to distinguish in his edition between those readings which he had taken from or based on M and his own often arbitrary and audacious conjectures; so he bequeathed to his successors a delicate and not uncommon editorial problem.

L. D. R.

[7] See R. I. Ireland, in his edition of the *De rebus bellicis*, *BAR International Series*, 63 (Oxford, 1979), n. 13 on pp. 68–9.

[8] 31.8.5 *paulatim* – 31.10.18 *incredibile dictu*.

[9] For an account of Gelenius's critical methods, see Ireland, 44 ff.

L. AMPELIUS

Lucius Ampelius' *Liber Memorialis,* allegedly of the second or third century AD, a handbook of knowledge geographical, mythological, and historical, was first printed, along with Florus, by Salmasius (Claude de Saumaise), Leiden, 1638. Salmasius's later edition (1655) was relied upon by subsequent editors, and it was not until 1853 that E. Woelfflin returned to a seventeenth-century manuscript known to Sirmond and P. Pithoeus and used by Salmasius, Munich Clm 10383a. Its original, thought by Ampelius' most recent editor, E. Assmann (Teubner, 1935), to have been French and of the tenth century, belonged to the Benedictine abbey of Saint-Bénigne at Dijon.

M. W.

ANTHOLOGIA LATINA

The collection of verse printed under this title[1] in modern editions does not wholly correspond to any single anthology known or likely to have been put together before the end of Antiquity. The core of the collection comprises a body of material probably assembled in north Africa not before nor long after AD 534[2] and preserved in a single manuscript, the famous Codex Salmasianus (Paris lat. 10318, *CLA* v. 593 = A in Riese's edition), so called because it was owned by Claude de Saumaise before passing to the Bibliothèque Nationale.[3] The manuscript was written in uncials towards the end of the eighth century;[4] its whereabouts from that time until 1615 are unknown. The first eleven quires have been lost, perhaps along with the original title of the collection: the words *epigrammaton liber* are found at several points in the manuscript, but Riese's use of *epigrammaton libri* as a title for the entire codex is purely speculative.[5]

The Teubner edition of A. Riese (2nd edn., Leipzig, 1894) has long been the standard critical text of the material in the Codex Salmasianus. (Riese's two volumes also contain hundreds of ancient and medieval poems not in ABV and with no link to any medieval anthology.) A new Teubner text of much of the material in Riese's first volume has been produced by D. R. Shackleton Bailey (Stuttgart, 1982); see also his *Towards a Text of 'Anthologia Latina'*, PCPS Suppl. Vol. 5 (1979). Several parts of Riese's collection have been separately edited: *Pervigilium Veneris* by C. Clementi (Oxford, 1936), I. Cazzaniga (Paravia, 1959), and L. Catlow (Brussels, 1980); Luxorius by M. Rosenblum (New York, 1961) and H. Happ (diss. Tübingen, 1958); the epigrams attributed to Seneca by C. Prato (Rome, 1964); Reposianus' *De concubitu Martis et Veneris* (253) by U. Zuccarelli (Naples, 1972); Symphosius' *Aenigmata* by Fr. Glorie (Turnhout, 1968); the *Medea* of Hosidius Geta by G. Salanitro (Rome, 1981).

[1] Derived from the title *Anthologia Veterum Latinorum Epigrammatum et Poematum sive Catalecta Poetarum Latinorum* used by the younger Burman in his Amsterdam edition of 1759–73. References in what follows are to the Teubner edition of A. Riese.

[2] H. Happ, *Gnomon*, 34 (1962), 696 and n. 6: *Anth. Lat.* 341 gives a *terminus post quem* of 533, and the collection is not likely to have been put together long after the overthrow of the Vandal kingdom in 534. For a more precise calculation of the later *terminus* see the Preface of Shackleton Bailey's edition, iv.

[3] Saumaise received it between April and August 1615 from Jean Lacurne, cf. H. Omont, *RPh* 19 (1895), 182 ff. A complete facsimile was published by Omont (*Anthologie de poètes dite de Saumaise*, Paris, 1903); descriptions in Clementi, 30–8 (with plates of pp. 108–12 on pp. 167–71), Rosenblum, *Luxorius: A Poet Among the Vandals* (New York, 1961), 97–101 (with plate of p. 156 facing p. 108). There are plates of all the manuscripts of the *Pervigilium* in R. Merkelbach/H. van Thiel, *Lateinisches Leseheft* (Göttingen, 1969), 3 A-C.

[4] L. Traube (*Philologus*, 54 (1895), 125 ff. = *Vorlesungen und Abhandlungen*, iii (Munich, 1921), 51 ff.; *Nomina Sacra* (1907), 223) had thought A to be a Spanish manuscript of the seventh century; Lowe tentatively (and rather improbably) suggested northern Italy or southern France; most recently B. Bischoff (*Karl der Grosse*, 249 = *Mitt. Stud.* iii. 29) has described A as a product of central Italy written near 800.

[5] *Liber (epi)grammaton* occurs in the colophon of the section preceding the *Pervigilium Veneris* (200), in the *titulus* to the poems of Luxorius (287), and in the colophon to item 379.

The Codex Salmasianus incorporates several smaller groupings of related material, in which the principle of affiliation is either that of form (e.g. Virgilian centos make up items 7–18) or of common authorship (e.g. 287–375 are poems of Luxorius); some components retain their original preface (19, 20, 286, 287). Marginal numbers attached to eight items have been plausibly interpreted as referring to books or sections of the collection, offering another clue to the process of compilation; Riese has conjecturally reconstructed an original anthology of twenty-four sections, of which the first five and part of the sixth have been lost.[6]

The manuscript contains much that is remote from sixth-century Africa either in time or place of composition, e.g. the *Medea* of Hosidius Geta (17, cf. Tert. *Praescr. Her.* 39), epigrams attributed to Seneca (232, 236–8), and the famous *Pervigilium Veneris* (200), a work probably of the late third or early fourth century AD. It has not yet been determined whether all of this material formed part of a single anthology compiled in Africa around 534, or whether some of it was added to a smaller African anthology in the approximately 250 years separating the latest poems in the collection from the copying of A itself.

A is the only surviving witness to many of the items it contains, but several miscellanies of the ninth or tenth centuries overlap with it to a greater or lesser extent. The most interesting of these is Paris lat. 8071 (s. IX, central France), owned by Jacques de Thou and hence called the Codex Thuaneus or *florilegium Thuaneum* (Riese's B). Together with Juvenal and poems of Eugenius of Toledo the manuscript contains a number of rare texts: the pseudo-Ovidian *Halieutica* and Grattius' *Cynegetica*, excerpts from Catullus (62) and from Seneca's *Troades*, *Medea*, and *Oedipus*, and seventy-three items found also in the Codex Salmasianus.[7] Behind this manuscript lies a contemporary of A, Vienna, Österreichische Nationalbibliothek 277 (s. VIII ex., France (possibly Lyon) = *CLA* x. 1474).[8] Only nineteen folios (two quaternions and three leaves) of Vienna 277 survive; in the texts still extant in it and Paris 8071 (*Halieutica* and Grattius) it seems clear that the *florilegium Thuaneum* is a direct descendant of Vienna 277,[9] and it is a plausible assumption that this is also true of the texts now preserved in Paris 8071 alone. This hypothesis can be verified for part of the material shared

---

[6] Riese, *praef.* xx ff. A further sign of the subdivisions of the collection is the appearance of phrases like *sunt uero uersus* (= *carmina*) *CLXXII* (before 20) at several points (also before 200, 223, 254, 287, 383).

[7] Details in Riese, *praef.* xxxiv f. Plate showing f. 52[r-v] in Clementi, 172–3. Fleury was suggested as B's place of origin by U. Knoche, *D. Iunii Iuvenalis Saturae* (Munich, 1950), xxv–xxvi.

[8] Chatelain, plate cl. 1 reproduces f. 55[v]–56[r], *CLA* f. 58[v] and 72[v] (partial).

[9] H. Schenkl, 'Zur Kritik und Überlieferungsgeschichte des Grattius und anderer lateinischer Dichter', *Jahrb. für class. Philol.* Suppl. 24 (1898), 383–480; B. L. Ullman, *Studi Castiglioni* (Florence, 1960), 1028 f.; J. A. Richmond, *The Halieutica Ascribed to Ovid* (London, 1962), 6–9; E. J. Kenney, *CR* 15 (1965), 51; 25 (1975), 218 f.

with the Codex Salmasianus. Vienna 9401*, ff. 28–43, written by the poet-scholar Jacopo Sannazaro, contains the *Pervigilium Veneris* and some of the epigrams common to A and B.[10] The selection and order of items coincide exactly with that in B, including a significant departure from the order in A. Comparison of readings confirms the close relationship of B and Sannazaro's manuscript, while also showing that B was not the source of Sannazaro's text.[11] Since Sannazaro is known to have discovered Vienna 277 in France in the years 1501–3,[12] one may confidently conclude that Vienna 9401* is a partial transcription of Vienna 277 when that manuscript was more nearly complete, and that for the *Pervigilium* and the epigrams they both contain, B and Vienna 9401* can be used to reconstruct part of the material now lost in Vienna 277. (Sannazaro's copy is more useful for this purpose than B; B is highly corrupt, while Sannazaro seems both to have copied Vienna 277 with care and also to have kept at least some of his emendations separate from his transcription.[13])

The poems found in B (and thus presumably in Vienna 277) do not derive from A itself, but might come from an ancestor of A: B, like A, contains a mixture of African and other material, generally presents its selections in A's order, and agrees with A in many corruptions, which implies descent from a common source some distance removed from the originals. B therefore derives from an anthology similar to the source of A in many respects; for the sake of economy this may be identified with the source of A. Since A and Vienna 277 were both written near the end

---

[10] A partial list in Clementi, 39; photographs of ff. 32ʳ–34ᵛ on pp. 175–80.

[11] E. Valgiglio, 'Sulla tradizione manoscritta del *Pervigilium Veneris*', *Bollettino*, 15 (1967), 15–20. I. Cazzaniga (*SCO* 3 (1955), 93 f., Paravia edition (Turin, 1959), p. vii) wrongly attempted to derive Vienna 9401* from B.

[12] Sannazaro's discovery was known to Pontano by February of 1503 and was described by Pietro Summonte in a letter published in 1507; cf. Clementi, 8 f.

[13] In Vienna 9401* several readings (listed in Cazzaniga, 91 f.) are entered in the margin with the siglum *f* attached; this has been most often interpreted as = *forte, fortasse* and as signalling a conjecture, cf. Clementi, 46, Valgiglio, 118.

B seems the ultimate source of the copy of the *Pervigilium* shown to Erasmus by Aldus in or shortly before 1508: 'Meminit de Amyclarum silentio . . . et Catullus nisi fallit inscriptio carminis DE VERE, quod nuper nobis Aldus Manutius meus exhibuit, in antiquissima quadam Galliae bibliotheca repertum, *Sic Amyclas, dum tacebant, perdidit silentium*' (*Adagiorum Chiliades tres ac Centuriae fere totidem* (Aldus, 1508), f. 94, line 820). For *dum tacebant* AB and Vienna 9401* give *cum tacere(n)t*; the variant could be due to Erasmus himself. The title *De Vere* may have appeared in Aldus's copy or may have been inferred from the opening lines; B, it may be noted, has no *titulus*. The attribution to Catullus has no basis in any of the three extant MSS, but in an incomplete transcription of the poem based on B (as shown by the omission of line 40, present in Vienna 9401*) and made in the latter part of the sixteenth century for Giovanni Vincenzo Pinelli, the *Pervigilium* follows an epigram entitled *Catulli de Ichtyde;* in B this epigram is headed simply *De Tetide*. The transcription is in Milan, Ambros. S. 81 sup., f. 233ʳ⁻ᵛ; it breaks off after *congreges* in line 43; cf. Cazzaniga, 87 ff. (who wrongly states that the Catullian attribution of the epigram is found in B), Valgiglio, 119, 123 ff. (who implausibly makes the Ambrosian manuscript an independent copy of B's exemplar). The close relationship of Ambros. S. 81 sup. to B holds true for the text of Grattius and the *Halieutica*. Pinelli's manuscript thus derives from B via a copy in which an ascription to Catullus had been added; such a copy – perhaps even the same one – was presumably what Aldus showed Erasmus.

of the eighth century in areas of France or Italy not entirely remote from each other, it is not implausible that both might derive from the same anthology. A is clearly a more faithful witness than B to the extent of this anthology, but A is defective at both beginning and end, and the possibility cannot be excluded that some texts in B that are not in A formed part of this lost anthology.[14]

It must also remain for the moment an open question whether this anthology or another is the source for the poems preserved only in Leiden, Voss. Lat. Q. 86 (Riese's V), written *c*.850 in central France.[15] The most notable of these are a body of epigrams often attributed (though not in the manuscript) to Seneca and Petronius and printed as items 396–479 in Riese's edition.[16] V also includes poems found in AB, and here it displays a close affiliation with B: all but two of the thirty-nine items are present in B; BV agree fairly often in error against A; V contains a set of excerpts from Martial with a spurious poem (26 Riese, inc. *rure morans*) in the same place and preceded by the same *titulus* ('incipit ex sexto') as in B. For this material V may have drawn on the same source as B, namely Vienna 277.

Individual items from the anthology represented by ABV are found in a number of other manuscripts, but there is no reason to believe that this anthology was the only or even the primary source of these scattered survivals. The manuscripts in question include (among others) Paris lat. 8069, s. X/XI (twenty-three items with a Virgilian emphasis, Riese, *praef.* xlii), Leipzig, Rep. I. 4°.74, s. IX/X (nine items, Riese, *praef.* xxxvii), Berlin (West), Diez. B Sant. 66, s. VIII/IX (186–8, Riese, *praef.* xlii), and Rome, Bibl. Casanatense 641, s. IX (232, 224, 318, Riese, *praef.* xlii).[17] One item of the anthology, the *Aenigmata* of Symphosius (286),

---

[14] A prefaces item 383 with the words 'sunt uersus LXX', but only six selections are preserved (this material begins on p. 273 in A, and is separated from the rest of the anthology by a body of unrelated prose). Some of the excerpts in B not present in A also turn up in other manuscripts, e.g. 389 (inc. *Dum mundum*) in Leipzig, Rep. I. 4°.74, the 'Eucheriae versus' (390) extant in Vienna 277 and six other manuscripts, the even more popular 392 (inc. *Ut belli sonuere tubae*) and 393 (inc. *Almo Theon Thyrsis*), and two of the *aenigmata* comprising 481, found in Berne 611, the Leipzig manuscript mentioned above, and others.

[15] Thorough description in K. A. de Meyier, *Codices Vossiani Latini*, ii (Leiden, 1975), 197–204. The Leiden manuscript is the second part of a larger book, of which the opening section is now Vat. Reg. lat. 330. De Meyier tentatively assigns the manuscript to Fleury, but A. Wilmart presented arguments for a Tours origin in *Codices Reginenses Vaticani*, ii (Vatican City, 1945), 245. The manuscript also contains several popular moralizing poems (Arator, Avianus, Avitus, the *Disticha Catonis*) and was probably used for teaching, cf. G. Glauche, *Schullektüre im Mittelalter* (Munich, 1970), 33 ff. Three items of the *Anth. Lat.* contained in it (405, 418–19 Riese) were cited by Hrabanus Maurus, cf. Manitius, *Geschichte*, 330.

[16] The *titulus* of 430 reads 'Liber IIII', which Riese once took to refer to section IV of the anthology represented by A, which has lost its first five sections. He later withdrew the suggestion (*praef.* xl), proposing instead that 430 began the fourth book of another anthology, which may have contained item 480 as well (also headed 'Liber IIII' in V).

[17] This group also includes the lost Beauvais manuscript (Riese's S) from which Claude Binet printed 218, 364, 348, 347, 349, 346, 233, and 232 in his 1579 edition of Petronius (Riese, *praef.* xxxiii f.). These poems seem to have been interspersed with a group printed by Riese as 690–715, and with

shows a rich manuscript tradition independent of A; Riese divided his seventeen manuscripts into two recensions and regarded the text of A, which agrees with neither consistently, as a conflation of both.[18]

R. J. T.

414 (attributed to Varro of Atax, cf. *Schol. Pers.* 2. 36, an attribution not present in V). Binet also printed nine poems from V itself.

[18] Riese chose Leiden, Voss. Lat. Q. 106 (d) and St. Gall 273 (a) as the primary witnesses to the generally better recension (D), and St. Gall 196 (β) as the best representative of the other (B). The recent edition of the *Aenigmata* by Fr. Glorie, *Corpus Christianorum*, ser. lat. 133A (Turnhout, 1968), 611–723, provides fuller reports of the manuscripts and incorporates the translation of R. T. Ohl (diss. Pennsylvania, 1928), but does not attempt a new recension. Work towards this has been done by C. E. Finch: 'The Bern Riddles in Codex Vat. Reg. Lat. 1553', *TAPA* 92 (1961), 145–55; 'Codex Vat. Barb. Lat. 721 as a source for the Riddles of Symphosius', *TAPA* 98 (1967), 173–9; 'Symphosius in Codices Pal. lat. 1719, 1753, and Reg. lat. 329, 2078', *Manuscripta*, 13 (1969), 3–11.

APICIUS

The text of Apicius *De re coquinaria*[1] is based on two manuscripts, Vatican, Urb. lat. 1146 (s. IX[1], Tours = V) and New York, Academy of Medicine, MS Safe (*olim* Phillipps 275, s. IX[1], Fulda = E).

V is a very handsome book written at Tours towards the middle of the ninth century as a present for Charles the Bald.[2] There is no evidence as to when it first entered Italy, but it appears in the catalogue of the

The above account is based on two articles, from which further information can be sought: M. E. Milham, 'Towards a Stemma and *Fortuna* of Apicius', *IMU* 10 (1967), 259–320; A. Campana, 'Contributi alla biblioteca del Poliziano, IV: L'Apicio del Poliziano', in *Il Poliziano e il suo tempo: Atti del IV Convegno internazionale di studi sul Rinascimento* (Florence, 1957), 198–217. The recension was first put on a firm basis by C. Giarratano, *I codici dei libri de re coquinaria di Celio* (Naples, 1912), and F. Vollmer, *Studien zu dem römischen Kochbuche von Apicius, SBAW*, 1920. 6. The text was edited for Teubner by Giarratano and Vollmer in 1922, more recently by M. E. Milham (1969). There is a Budé edition by J. André (Paris, 1965).

[1] M. Gavius Apicius was a gourmet of the age of Tiberius. The work attributed to him is a compilation made from various sources in the late fourth or early fifth century, and the core of recipes more properly ascribed to Apicius have themselves been reworked and augmented from time to time. The *Excerpta* of the Ostrogoth Vinidarius, who belongs to the fifth or sixth century, are taken from a similar compilation; these are preserved in the eighth-century Codex Salmasianus (Paris lat. 10318, *CLA* V. 593) and are usually appended to texts of the *De re coquinaria* in modern editions. On the composite nature of these collections, see S. Brandt, *Untersuchungen zum römischen Kochbuch* (*Philologus*, Suppl. 19.3), Leipzig, 1927.

[2] E. K. Rand, *Studies in the Script of Tours, I: A Survey of the Manuscripts of Tours* (Cambridge, Mass., 1929), i. 144, no. 90; ii, plate CXII; W. Köhler, *Die Karolingischen Miniaturen*, i: *Die Schule von Tours* (Berlin, 1930), 288–9, 409, plates 114 d-f.

library of the Duke of Urbino compiled between 1482 and 1487. The oldest dated humanist manuscript is Florence, Bibl. Riccardiana 662, written at Bologna in 1464. All the sixteen extant manuscripts of the humanist period are derived from V via an intermediate lost copy (ζ), with some contamination from E in parts of the tradition; ζ seems to have reached the Medici family about 1458.[3]

E is written partly in Caroline minuscule and partly in Anglo-Saxon script of the Fulda type.[4] It was known to Poggio in 1417, but remained at Fulda until brought to Rome by Enoch of Ascoli in 1455.[5] It subsequently had a long series of Italian owners, beginning with Cardinal Bessarion, and had sojourned in France and England before it emigrated to the United States in 1929.

The fifteenth-century manuscripts have considerable importance for the history of Italian humanism. Of particular interest is a fragmentary manuscript at Leningrad (Library of the Academy of Sciences 627/1, known as P or Pol), which contains the collations of both E and V which Politian made at Florence in 1490 and 1493 respectively. The *editio princeps* was printed at Milan in 1498 by Guillermus Le Signerre and exists in two issues, with identical text but different preliminaries.[6] It shares a common parent with a manuscript now at Oxford, Bodleian Library, Canon. Class. Lat. 168, written at Bologna in 1490 by Pierantonio Sallando of Reggio for Mino Rossi, senator of Bologna.[7] There is some evidence that the text was edited for the printer by Giovanni Battista Pio (1460–1540).[8]

L. D. R.

[3] Milham, 'Towards a Stemma', 265 ff.

[4] E. A. Lowe, 'Die Haupt-Handschriften des Apicius', *BPhW* 40 (1920), 1174–6. There is a photograph in B. L. Ullman, *Ancient Writing and its Influence* (London, 1932), plate IX c.

[5] Sabbadini, *Scoperte*, ii. 201; *Storia e critica*[2], 8, 208–11; Campana, 211.

[6] For the early printed editions of Apicius, cf. Milham, 'Towards a Stemma', 275 ff.; B. Flower and E. Rosenbaum, *The Roman Cookery Book* (London, 1958), 10–11.

[7] A. J. Fairbank and R. W. Hunt, *Humanistic Script of the Fifteenth and Sixteenth Centuries* (Bodleian Picture Book 12) (Oxford, 1960), no. 10, fig. 10.

[8] Milham, 'Towards a Stemma', 275–6.

APULEIUS

Apologia, Metamorphoses, Florida
Opera philosophica

Apologia, Metamorphoses, Florida

Our knowledge[1] of the *Apologia, Metamorphoses,* and *Florida* (transmitted in that order) is derived solely from F (Florence, Laur. 68.2), written at Montecassino, s. XI[2], and containing (like φ and C) the hand of the fourteenth-century scholar Zanobi da Strada.[2] This text goes back ultimately, as is shown by the subscription to *Met.* Book 9, to a double revision made at Rome in AD 395 and Constantinople in 397 by one Sallustius: 'Ego Sallustius Legi et Emendavi Romae Felix Olibrio et Probino V. C. Cons. [i.e. 395] in Foro Martis Controversiam Declamans Oratori Endelechio. Rursus Constantinopoli Recognovi Caesario et Attico Cons. [i.e. 397].'

This simple picture of the tradition is confused, however, by the fact that numerous passages in F are now illegible (from wear or heavy correction), and that f. 160 (containing *Met.* 8. 7–9) has been badly torn. In order to re-create the original readings in F, editors must look to two other sources. The first is φ (Florence, Laur. 29.2), probably also from Montecassino, s. XII/XIII, copied[3] directly from F *after* the damage to f. 160. A strange feature of φ is the so-called *spurcum additamentum* at *Met.* 10. 21, a scurrilous passage written in the margin in the hand of Zanobi da Strada.

The Teubner text was edited by R. Helm, *Met.* 1931[3], *Apol.* 1972[5], *Flor.* 1910[1]; this last volume contains the *Praefatio* on the manuscripts. *Apol.* and *Flor.* were edited for the Budé series by P. Vallette (1924); *Met.* by D. S. Robertson (1940–5). Robertson's is by far the most authoritative critical text; it includes a *stemma codicum* at the end of the Introduction. There is a separate edition (text and commentary) of the *Apol.* by H. E. Butler and A. S. Owen (Oxford, 1914). See too E. H. Haight, *Apuleius and his Influence* (London, 1927).

[1] See the full account of the manuscripts (excluding U) given by D. S. Robertson, *CQ* 18 (1924), 27–42, 85–99. It seems to be the case that no one has examined the illegible passages in F with a modern aid such as an ultraviolet lamp. Note that F is bound with the celebrated manuscript of Tacitus, *Annals*, 11–16 and *Histories*, 1–5. Confirmation of the primacy of F is given by K. Dowden, 'Eleven notes on the text of Apuleius' *Metamorphoses*', *CQ* (1980), 218–26.

[2] For the identification see G. Billanovich, *I primi umanisti e le tradizioni dei classici latini* (Fribourg, 1953), 31–3, who suggests that Zanobi, not Boccaccio, was responsible for bringing most of the discoveries at Montecassino to Florence. On Zanobi (died 1361) see Cosenza, 3743–5.

[3] On this manuscript see E. A Lowe, *CQ* 14 (1920), 150–5. On the authorship of the *spurcum additamentum* see E. Fraenkel, 'A sham Sisenna', *Eranos*, 51 (1953), 151–4.

The second is a group of manuscripts all deriving from a lost copy of F made *before* the damage to f. 160. The most valuable of these are:

A   Milan, Ambros. N. 180 sup., s. XIV[1].
U   Illinois 7,[4] written at Rome by Holt de Heke of Osnabrück, and dated 31 August 1389.
E   Eton College 147, s. XV[1], Italian, containing only *Met.* and *Flor.*
S   Saint-Omer 653, s. XV[1].

Of some interest historically (but not textually) is Florence, Laur. 54.32 written in the hand of Boccaccio.

Hopes of an independent witness were raised in 1942 by the discovery by G. Muzzioli[5] of C (Assisi 706), ten leaves of a Beneventan manuscript containing parts of *Apol.*, probably s. XI[2]. Of interest are notes in the hand of Zanobi da Strada, the same fourteenth-century scholar whose work was seen in F and φ. The latest investigation, however, shows that C is derived from F, and has nothing new to offer.

Only *Met.* has been edited (by Robertson) in full accordance with the principles given above. Whether *Apol.* and *Flor.* would profit substantially from the application of these discoveries remains to be seen.

P. K. M.

---

[4] See S. de Ricci, *Census of Medieval and Renaissance Manuscripts in the United States and Canada*, i (1935), 699.

[5] See D. S. Robertson, 'The Assisi Fragments of the *Apologia* of Apuleius', *CQ* 6 (1956), 68–80. It is worth observing that C demonstrably was *not* the source of AUES.

Opera philosophica

While Apuleius' other works had survived at Montecassino and had an Italian tradition, his philosophical writings emerged and initially circulated in northern Europe, so that the two groups did not combine to form a corpus until the fourteenth century.

Only one of the philosophical works which circulate under his name, the *De deo Socratis*, is certainly by Apuleius, but the *De Platone et eius dogmate* and *De mundo*, of disputed authenticity, are included for the purpose of this article. The *Asclepius*[1] has basically the same tradition as these three works, but really belongs to the corpus of *Hermetica*. The spurious Περὶ ἑρμηνείας has its own tradition.[2]

The text of the *De deo Socratis*, *De Platone*, and *De mundo* depends on a single archetype of very indifferent quality. The following stemma, a

---

[1] Edited by Nock in A. D. Nock and A.-J. Festugière, *Hermès Trismégiste*, ii (Paris, 1945).

[2] The most recent edition is that of P. Thomas, *Apulei opera quae supersunt*, iii (Leipzig, 1908).

simplified version of the one drawn by J. Beaujeu in his recent edition,[3] will serve to give a general picture of the tradition, but some of the details have not been rigorously demonstrated.[4]

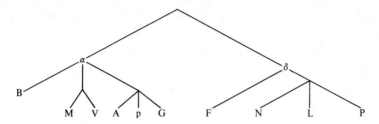

An account of the manuscript tradition of Apuleius' *Opera philosophica* must begin with Brussels 10054–6 (B), which editors have dated nearly two hundred years too late. By far the earliest and best manuscript, this beautifully written book belongs to the third decade of the ninth century. Although Bischoff no longer closely associates it with the group of manuscripts which he attributed to the court library of Louis the Pious,[5] it clearly has an excellent pedigree and the *a* family to which it belongs must have sprung from the heart of the Carolingian revival. Munich Clm 621 (s. XI/XII = M) and Vatican lat. 3385 (s. X/XI = V) are textually very close to B[6] and of German origin. The third group of *a* manuscripts is later and appears to form a French branch of the tradition: Paris lat. 8624 (s. XII², French = A), Paris lat. 6286 (s. XIII ex., French = p), and Wolfenbüttel, Gud. lat. 168 (s. XIII = G).[7]

The *δ* branch of the tradition is inferior to *a*; it appears to have its roots in France. Florence, Laur. S. Marco 284 (F), written in France at the end of the eleventh century, is more celebrated as a representative of the Ten-Book tradition of Pliny's *Letters* (q.v.). Its two oldest copies, Berne 136 (s. XII²) and Laur. S. Marco 341 (s. XII²), are both French,[8] and the two manuscripts of Apuleius recorded in twelfth-century French catalogues presumably belong to this group too, for they contained *inter alia* both Apuleius and Pliny; one was given to Bec by Philip of Bayeux in 1164, the other was at Saint-Martial, Limoges. F itself was taken to

---

[3] *Apulée, Opuscules philosophiques* (Paris, 1973). The fundamental work on the tradition was done by A. Goldbacher (Vienna, 1876), though he was unfortunately unaware of the existence of the manuscript B, first brought into prominence by E. Rohde (*RhM* 37 (1882), 146–51). Still important are P. Thomas's edition (see n. 2) and his article 'Etude sur la tradition manuscrite des œuvres philosophiques d'Apulée', *Bull. Acad. Royale de Belgique*, Classe des Lettres, 1907, 103–47.

[4] As Beaujeu himself makes clear (p. xlv). He is the first modern editor to make use of N.

[5] Bischoff, in *Medieval Learning*, 21 (= *Mitt. Stud.* iii 185–6).

[6] Thomas held that they were derived from a corrected copy of B; contra Nock, 263.

[7] Contaminated with *δ*, at least for *Asclepius* (Nock, 263 f.). There are of course a number of mixed manuscripts, of which the earliest are Cambridge, Corpus Christi College 71 (s. XII, St. Albans), Wolfenbüttel, Aug. 8° 82. 10 (s. XIII), and Paris lat. 15449 (s. XIII).

[8] R. H. and M. A. Rouse, in *Medieval Learning*, 74–6, 78–80, locate Berne 136 at Orléans.

Italy[9] and one of its Italian descendants has the whole of Apuleius, Florence, Laur. 54.32 (s. XIV). Leiden, Voss. Lat. Q. 10 (s. XI[1] = N), Laur. 76.36 (s. XII = L), and Paris lat. 6634 (s. XII, from Saint-Victor = P) are all probably of French origin. A copy of N, Cambridge, U. L. Ff. 3. 5 (s. XII), has the pressmark of Bury St. Edmunds.[10]

L. D. R.

[9] See THE YOUNGER PLINY, n. 7.
[10] Ker[2], 17.

ARATEA

What the Middle Ages knew of Greek astronomy they knew mainly through the Latin *Aratea*. 'Le grand travail sur la tradition médiévale de tous ces textes astronomiques latins reste à écrire,'[1] and it will have to embrace not just the three poems more or less modelled on Aratus' but also the partly independent tradition of the scholia and illustrations that accompany two of them. In fact, more is said about the origin of manuscripts in Saxl–Meier–McGurk, *Verzeichnis astrologischer und mythologischer illustrierter Handschriften des lateinischen Mittelalters*,[2] than in the editions, even editions as recent as those of Cicero by J. Soubiran (Budé, Paris, 1972) and of Germanicus by A. Le Boeuffle (Budé, Paris, 1975) and D. B. Gain (London, 1976). On the transmission P. von Winterfeld's informative but carelessly argued piece 'De Germanici codicibus', in *Festschrift Johannes Vahlen* (Berlin, 1900), 391–408, remains the only work of any scope.[3]

Aratus' original falls into two parts, *Phaenomena* (1–732) and *Prognostica* (733–1154). The surviving fragment of CICERO'S translation covers 229–700; quotations from the rest occur almost exclusively in his other works and in Priscian. GERMANICUS adapted the *Phaenomena* in 725

[1] J. Soubiran, *RPh* 49 (1975), 226.
[2] i, *Sitzungsber. der Heidelberger Akad.* 1915, nos. 6–7; ii, ibid., 1925–6, no. 2; iii, London, 1953; iv, London, 1966. See especially the introduction to iii, and also McGurk, *Nat. Lib. of Wales Journal*, 18 (1973–4), 197–216, and 'Carolingian Astrological Manuscripts', in *Charles the Bald*, ed. M. Gibson and J. Nelson (*BAR International Series*, 101, Oxford, 1981), 317–32.
[3] Gain seems almost defiantly silent on the subject. In Cicero Soubiran leans heavily on the important edition of V. Buescu (Paris & Bucharest, 1941), which leaves him in the lurch here.

verses, and another 207 verses of a continuation survive. RUFIUS FESTUS AVIENIUS (s. IV[2]) expanded the whole poem into 1878 verses. These three versions, which have distinct but connected traditions, were printed together at Venice in 1488, and Avienius' other poems were included: a preface (31 hexameters), *Orbis terrae* (1393 hexameters), and *Ora maritima* (713 iambics, incomplete).[4]

First the simplest tradition, that of AVIENIUS:

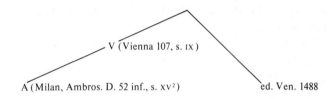

V (Vienna 107, s. IX)

A (Milan, Ambros. D. 52 inf., s. XV[2])   ed. Ven. 1488

V contains only *Aratea*, 1–1581, followed in A by 1750–end, *Orbis terrae*, and 1582–1749. The ed. Ven. contains the whole of both poems in the right order; before them it puts the preface, after them *Ora maritima*. V does not match the ed. Ven. for accuracy and more often betrays their common descent from an insular source.[5] The three witnesses were first used together in A. Holder's edition (Innsbruck, 1887);[6] but by collating V and A at an interval of eleven years Holder missed several indications that A is not merely a copy of V, as Winterfeld maintained in *De Rufi Festi Avieni metaphrasi Arateorum recensenda et emendanda* (Berlin, 1895), 3–7, but a direct copy, as Soubiran proved in a crisp and instructive article, *RPh* 49 (1975), 217–26. The disorder in A after *Aratea*, 1581, where V now ends at the end of a gathering, must reflect a transposition of leaves in the next gathering of V, since lost; but whether V then or ever contained the preface and *Ora maritima* cannot be determined, and its history is also obscure.[7] A was written not later than 1477 by the Milanese scholar Boninus Mombritius.[8] The ed. Ven. seems to have been printed from a manuscript scrupulously written out by Giorgio Valla; it was doubtless before he left Milan for Venice in 1486 that he discovered both Avienius and 'Probus Vallae' on Juvenal.[9]

---

[4] The ed. Ven. calls the author Avienius, the form that Alan Cameron argues for in *CQ* 61 (1967), 392–3.

[5] Winterfeld, 402 n. 4.

[6] *Orbis terrae* and *Ora maritima* have since been edited separately, and D. Stichtenoth's posthumous edition of the latter (Darmstadt, 1968) includes a facsimile of the relevant pages in the ed. Ven., which his publishers wrongly believed to be very rare: *Gesamtkatalog der Wiegendrucke*, iii (Leipzig, 1925–   ), 3131 lists numerous copies.

[7] No photograph, no discussion. It is bound with the *schedae Vindobonenses* of Lucretius and Juvenal. I am obliged to Dr O. Mazal for the date of Avienius; editors say s. X.

[8] It has his *ex libris*, and Mirella Ferrari kindly writes that it is in his hand. For an illustration see A. Traglia, *Ciceronis poetica fragmenta*, ii (Rome, 1952), opposite p. 48 (Cic. *Arat.* 55–82).

[9] Gius. Billanovich, *IMU* 17 (1974), 43–60, especially 56–8.

As V and Valla's manuscript contained more of Avienius than *Orbis terrae,* neither can readily be identified with or derived from a manuscript of 'Priscianus . . . de terra mari fluminibus et montibus . . . Festi Ruffi descriptio orbis terrarum in versu' rescued 'e quodam teterrimo et fedissimo carcere' in 1423 by Bart. Capra, Archbishop of Milan.[10] The title that the ed. Ven. gives to the *Aratea* recurs purely as a title in Vatican, Urb. lat. 674 (s. x)[11] and Wolfenbüttel, Gud. lat. 132 (s. x, from Corvey[12]), and somehow a manuscript of Avianus' *Fables,* Oxford, Bodl. Auct. F. 2. 14 (s. xi², Sherborne?), came to call the author Avianus Festus (f. 58ᵛ).

Interpolations from Avienius characterize the lost manuscript Z of GERMANICUS.

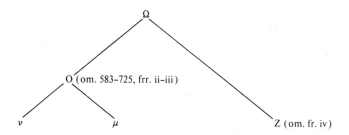

A firm home for Z would therefore be useful. Its surviving descendants are these:

L   Leiden, Voss. Lat. Q. 79 (s. ix¹, written in rustic capitals).
E   Einsiedeln 338 (s. x).
      Boulogne 188 (not before 905), allegedly from Saint-Bertin; copied from L.[13]
      Berne 88 (s. x), presented to St. Mary's Strasbourg by Werinhar, bishop 1001–28;[14] copied from Boulogne 188.

The home of L is unknown,[15] and published works reveal nothing about E.[16]

---

[10] Sabbadini, *Scoperte,* i. 101–2, 104. No manuscript of Priscian's *Periegesis* described in the edition of P. van de Woestijne (Bruges, 1953) has this title, but Marina Passalacqua, *I codici di Prisciano* (Rome, 1978), 382–5, lists several that he does not mention, including one in the Biblioteca Ambrosiana (Z. 157 sup.).

[11] P. van de Woestijne, *Classical Mediaeval and Renaissance Studies in honor of Berthold Louis Ullman* (Rome, 1964), ii. 433–4.

[12] Passalacqua, no. 756, presumably on the authority of some discussion buried away in her mass of references.

[13] See M. D. R., *CQ* 74 (1980), 518.

[14] According to B. L. Ullman, *Studi di bibliografia e di storia in onore di T. de Marinis* (Verona, 1964), iv, 268, Werinhar intended this and other surviving manuscripts to foster the study of the liberal arts in the cathedral school.

[15] Bischoff, *Mitt. Stud.* ii. 44. See now C. L. Verkerk, *Journ. of Med. Hist.* 6 (1980), 245–87.

[16] Professor B. Munk Olsen assigns it to Germany or Switzerland.

Guided by the layout of L, Gain holds that Ω of Germanicus lost a quire before O was copied from it. If that is so, the omission common to ν and μ does not guarantee the existence of O; but other errors do. ν is reconstructed from:

B   Basle AN IV 18 (s. IX), from Fulda.[17]
P   Paris lat. 7886 (s. IX¾), from Corbie;[18] full of conjectures.[19]
Ab   Aberystwyth 735 C (s. XI), from Limoges (?).[20]
π   the lost source of:

>   Berlin (East) Phill. 1832 (s. IX¾), from Laon by way of Saint-Vincent, Metz.[21]
>   Paris lat. 5239 (s. X).
>   Strasbourg 326 (lat. 275) (s. X).

Perhaps before 800 μ or an ancestor migrated to Montecassino, where it aroused much interest in s. XII–XIII.[22]

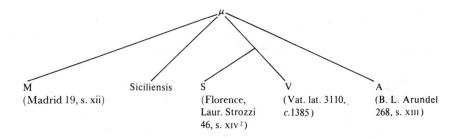

M	Siciliensis	S	V	A
(Madrid 19, s. xii)		(Florence, Laur. Strozzi 46, s. XIV²)	(Vat. lat. 3110, c.1385)	(B. L. Arundel 268, s. XIII)

M comes from southern Italy or Sicily. The illustrations in a similar manuscript have long been recognized as an important influence on the work of Michael Scot, astrologer to the court of Frederick II at Palermo c.1227–35, and his activity would account for the presence in Sicily of an illustrated manuscript that had suffered loss and damage by the time that Poggio reported its discovery to Niccoli in 1429 or shortly before; the Siciliensis has left twenty-five mainly calligraphic descendants, of which twenty-one belong to a Florentine and four to a Neapolitan family. Salutati, who owned S and himself wrote V, does not say where

---

[17] Winterfeld, 393–5.
[18] Bischoff, *Mitt. Stud.* i. 59.
[19] Gain, 8.
[20] McGurk, op. cit. (n. 2 above). His reasons for regarding it as hybrid (p. 197 and n. 10) are bad.
[21] J. J. Contreni, *The Cathedral School of Laon from 850 to 950* (Münchener Beiträge zur Mediävistik und Renaissance-Forschung, 29, 1978), 125.
[22] For more details about μ and its descendants, with reservations not expressed here, see M. D. R., *CQ* 74 (1980), 511–17, which would have benefited from knowledge of P. Meyvaert, *Anal. Boll.* 84 (1966), 350–6. I have since inspected M, which has on f. 1ʳ an erased and smudged *ex libris* of s. XIII/XIV: 'Liber Sancte Marie . . .'. Someone better at using ultra-violet might decipher more. Vernacular jottings on f. 54ʳ may also hold some clue.

he discovered their source. A, perhaps the earliest *chartaceus* of a classical Latin text, must have been produced in the kingdom of Sicily. A alone contains fr. v, whose genuineness has been disputed.

Finally Soubiran's stemma of CICERO, with one addition, G.

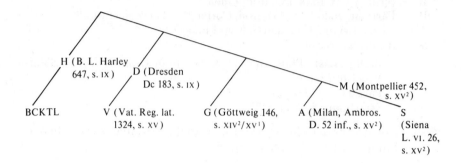

H (B. L. Harley 647, s. IX)   D (Dresden Dc 183, s. IX)   M (Montpellier 452, s. XV²)

BCKTL   V (Vat. Reg. lat. 1324, s. XV)   G (Göttweig 146, s. XIV²/XV¹)   A (Milan, Ambros. D. 52 inf., s. XV²)   S (Siena L. VI. 26, s. XV²)

As AMS also contain Germanicus, where they derive from the Siciliensis, Soubiran supposes that Cicero too was recovered from the Siciliensis; but the lowly position of AMS in the Florentine family of Germanicus is only one among many objections. The scribe of A, Boninus Mombritius, worked at Milan, and it can hardly be a coincidence that in Cicero an error of AMS recurs in the eleven lines noted by Cyriac of Ancona in 1442 from a 'liber antiquissimus' at Vercelli. Being free of this error, G cannot derive from the Vercellensis unless Cyriac was quoting from a corrupt copy, but its north-Italian origin and its abundant signs of descent from a ninth-century ancestor suggest that it does and he was.[23] The nearest relative of the Vercellensis, D, left France after 1573;[24] its precise home has not been determined. H, assigned by Bischoff to Lotharingia,[25] was at St. Augustine's Canterbury[26] by the end of s. X. L (Leiden, Voss. Lat. F. 121, s. XII) derives from B, BCKT from a lost copy of H that incorporated most of its corrections;[27] C (British Library, Cotton Tib. B. V, *c*.1000), K (Cambridge, Trinity College 945, s. XI¹), and T (Cotton Tib. C. I, s. XII¼) are all English,[28] but B (Harley 2506, *c*.1000), though partly produced by English hands, probably comes

[23] On G and the Vercellensis see M. D. R. (n. 22), 508–11. G. Kauffmann, 'De Hygini memoria scholiis in Ciceronis Aratum Harleianis servata', *Breslauer philologische Abhandlungen*, 3.4 (1888), 24–36, offers much the fullest treatment of the Vercellensis.

[24] Buescu, 108–9 and more fully in *Problèmes de critique et d'histoire textuelles* (Bucharest and Paris, 1942, repr. Hildesheim, 1973), 93–132. For a reproduction see ibid. plate II.

[25] *Karl der Grosse, Werk und Wirkung* (Aachen, 1965), 303.

[26] Saxl–Meier, iii. 1. 149–51; T. A. M. Bishop, *Aethici Istrici Cosmographia: codex Leidensis Scaligeranus 69* (Umbrae Codicum Occidentalium, 10), Amsterdam, 1966, p. xix.

[27] V. H. King, 'An Investigation of some Astronomical Excerpts from Pliny's *Natural History* found in Manuscripts of the earlier Middle Ages' (B. Litt. thesis, Oxford, 1969), 83–91, especially 90; Soubiran (Budé, 1972), 125–32.

[28] Saxl–Meier, ii. 1. 119–34; T. A. M. Bishop, *English Caroline Minuscule* (Oxford, 1971), 23.

from Fleury.[29] However the origin of B is to be reconciled with the migration of H, the background of HBCKTL is traffic between Fleury and English abbeys in s. x[2], and it may be significant that a scholar much interested in mathematics and astronomy, Abbo of Fleury, spent the years 986–8 at Ramsey Abbey in Huntingdonshire.[30] Corrections in H have even been attributed to Abbo, but wrongly.[31] Saxl attributed them to a scholar of the previous century, Lupus of Ferrières, but again wrongly.[32] Nevertheless, a letter written by Lupus in 847 to Ansbald of Prüm shows that both Ferrières and Prüm had the text: 'Tu autem huic nostro cursori Tullium in Arato trade, ut ex eo quem me impetraturum credo quae deesse illi Egil noster aperuit suppleantur.'[33] At about the same time Mico of Saint-Riquier put four lines into his *Florilegium*,[34] and rather earlier, perhaps in the time of Bede, someone had used 320–31 in a small astronomical anthology.[35] Whether medieval or older, the archetype of HDGAM poses a problem inasmuch as quotations in *De natura deorum* and Hyginus, *Fab.* 14 disagree with it;[36] Hyginus at any rate is unlikely to be quoting from memory.

Despite differences and uncertainties, then, the impression created by the surviving manuscripts of the three poems is that the tradition of each took root in north-eastern France during s. VIII[2]–IX and very soon put out an offshoot in Italy. Cicero alone spread to England (unless the Germanicus at Aberystwyth crossed the Channel in the Middle Ages), and Germany can show only one manuscript of Germanicus (at Fulda) and perhaps one of Avienius (at Corvey ?).

Avienius has neither scholia nor illustrations. The scholia on Cicero in H and the Vercellensis derive from a text of Hyginus' *Astronomica* less corrupt in places than the extant manuscripts.[37] O of Germanicus had the *scholia Basiliensia*, which go back at least to the time of Lactantius; while *ν* simply took them over, *μ* conflated them with the *scholia Sangermanensia*, themselves adapted from the prose *Aratus latinus* of s. VII.[38] The

---

[29] F. Wormald, *English Drawings of the Tenth and Eleventh Centuries* (London, 1952), 70–4 nos. 35, 36, 45; Bishop, *English Caroline*, 18.

[30] See most recently J. Vezin, 'Leofnoth – un scribe anglais à Saint-Bénoît-sur-Loire', *Codices Manuscripti*, 3 (1977), 109–20.

[31] A. van de Vyver, *Rev. ben.* 47 (1935), 143; but B. C. B.-B. tells me that the script does not suit Fleury in Abbo's time, and see É. Pellegrin, *BEC* 17 (1959), 15–16.

[32] iii. 1. xv–xvi, contested by É. Pellegrin, *BEC* 115 (1957), 19 n. 1.

[33] L. Levillain, *Loup de Ferrières: correspondance*, ii (Paris, 1935), 4–6. 'Metrum Tulli Ciceronis' in the ninth-century catalogue from Lorsch (Manitius, *Handschriften*, 20) probably conceals not the *Aratea* but 'Marci Tulli Ciceronis . . .'; cf. CICERO, *Speeches*, n. 170.

[34] It also includes two lines of Germanicus; see *PLMA* 3.781–2.

[35] Baehrens, *PLM* i (Leipzig, 1879), 1–2. In 326 it shares with D an error that could perhaps have occurred more than once.

[36] Soubiran (Budé edn.), 138–42.

[37] Kauffmann, 2.

[38] Cf. J. Martin, *Histoire du texte des Phénomènes d'Aratos* (Paris, 1956), 38–51. *Aratus latinus* makes even harder the identification of such entries as 'Aratus' and 'liber astrologiae Arati' in medieval catalogues; see Manitius, *Handschriften*, 80–2.

great glory of the *Aratea,* however, is the illustrations in many of the
manuscripts, above all in H and G of Cicero and in L and M of
Germanicus.[39] In H, for instance, Cicero's verses in minuscule occupy
the foot of each page and the rest is given over to the appropriate
illustration, painted only at the extremities and filled out to the requisite
shape with scholia in small capitals; except that arranging prose in such
a way is just a matter of layout and not of composition, the result
resembles the patterned poems of Antiquity. Some manuscripts lower
in the stemma treat their heritage very freely; the illustrations in B of
Cicero, Harley 2506 (Winchester school, *c.*1000), are fine works of art.

M. D. R.

[39] For reproductions of L see G. Thiele, *Antike Himmelsbilder* (Berlin, 1898); of G, H. Tietze,
Österreichische Kunsttopographie 1: *die Denkmale des politischen Bezirkes Krems* (Vienna, 1907), figs.
388–9, and Saxl-Meier, iii. 1. xxi; of H, Buescu, plate I, Saxl-Meier iii. 1. xiii, 2, plates 57, 60–1,
63–4, 66–7, A. Grabar and C. Nordenfalk, *Early Medieval Painting* (1957), 91 (colour); of M,
Inventario general de manuscritos de la Biblioteca Nacional, i (Madrid, 1953), Saxl-Meier iii. 1. xxxvi,
xxxix.

ASCONIUS

How many of Cicero's speeches Asconius expounded is not known, but
more, certainly, than the five covered by the commentary that appears
under his name in roughly thirty manuscripts of s. XV. As it happens,
only one of the five, *Pro Milone,* is fully preserved.

The manuscripts all derive from a damaged one (s. IX *ut vid.*) found at
St. Gall in the summer of 1416 by Poggio and Bartolomeo da Monte-
pulciano; both copied it in that year, Sozomeno of Pistoia in the next.
Sozomeno's copy (S) survives in Pistoia, Bibl. Forteguerr. A. 37.
Bartolomeo's is lost but generated Florence, Laur. 54. 5 (M). Poggio's
(P) follows the Chronicle of Sigebertus Gemblacensis, which he found
in England during 1419–22, and precedes Valerius Flaccus, which he
found at St. Gall on the same visit as Asconius, in Madrid 8514 (x. 81).[1]
The edition of Kiessling and Schöll (Berlin, 1875) was the first to use S
and M, A. C. Clark's (Oxford, 1907) the first to use P. M has undergone
the influence of corrections to P, but there is little to choose between P

[1] On all three see de la Mare, *Handwriting,* 78 no. 14 and pl. XIVc (P), 89 no. 1 (M), 104 no. 38
and pl. XXe (S). A facsimile of P can be consulted in the Bodleian Library (MS facs. e. 24).

and S. From P derive all the other manuscripts listed by Clark except Paris lat. 7833, a descendant of S;[2] 'scilicet prae fama Poggii exemplaria ab aliis confecta parvi habebantur,' Clark surmises (p. xv).

That at any rate is Clark's story; but it needs checking for three reasons given away by Clark himself. Paris lat. 7833, though it largely agrees with S, (1) does not share all its faults, and (2) has much the same subscription as M (p. xiv n. 4); furthermore, (3) agreements with S against PM do not immediately prove anything if M has undergone the influence of P (pp. xxxi–xxxii). Another manuscript like the Parisinus, Vatican, Ottob. lat. 1322, came to light recently.[3] The next editor must therefore establish his own stemma from scratch. It would not be surprising to discover that the busy explorers contented themselves with fewer than three direct copies of the Sangallensis.

In all the manuscripts and in all editions from the first (Venice, 1477) to the nineteenth century, Asconius' commentary is followed by a largely grammatical one on part of the *Verrines*. Madvig, *De Q. Asconii Pediani et aliorum veterum interpretum in Ciceronis orationes commentariis* (Copenhagen, 1828), showed that it belongs to s. v or thereabouts, P. Schmiedeberg, *De Asconi codicibus et de Ciceronis scholiis Sangallensibus* (Breslau, 1905), 30–52, that it was compiled from more than one set of annotations. Next to Asconius the most important part of the material collected by Th. Stangl, *Ciceronis orationum scholiastae,* ii (Leipzig, 1912), is the *Scholia Bobiensia,* one of the original texts in Milan, Ambros. E. 147 sup. (now S. P. 9/1–6, 11) + Vatican lat. 5750 (*CLA* iii. 28, uncial, s. v); the *Scholia* may have drawn directly or indirectly on Asconius' commentary, which Quintilian and Gellius also cite.

M. D. R.

[2] 'Vindobonensis 26' (Vienna 152) is now Budapest 427. Other progeny of P: Bologna 2785, Holkham Hall 392, B. L. Add. 24894, Vatican, Barb. lat. 131, Vatican lat. 5983. For readings of Add. 24894 and other *descripti* see J. F. Lockwood, *CQ* 33 (1939), 154–6, and the works he refers to on p. 155.

[3] Pellegrin, *Manuscrits,* i. 517–8. I have collated enough of both to say that neither derives from the other. Though I saw them nine months apart, let me record the impression that they are in the same hand.

AUSONIUS

The extant works of Ausonius occur in overlapping collections, two large and one small. All three overlap only in the twelve *Monosticha de aerumnis Herculis,* in sixty-five lines of the *Caesares,* and in one epigram; no two agree anywhere in error against the third, but editors emend their common text. Where the large collections overlap, their texts sometimes diverge widely enough to have suggested that they go back to different editions issued by Ausonius himself or from his papers; but though Ausonian scholarship in the last ninety years has been devoted almost entirely to this question, no one has yet tried to defend their independence of each other by dethroning the emendations with which editors supplant a number of shared readings. The theory of different editions must therefore be left in suspense and investigation of the tradition begin again from the point to which R. Peiper and K. Schenkl brought it in the 1880s. The only edition since published that rests on further study of manuscripts, the Teubner of S. Prete (Leipzig, 1978), achieves little beyond the amassing of material.[1]

First, then, the three collections:

(1) is the orderly collection mainly represented by V, Leiden, Voss. Lat. F. 111, written about 800 in Visigothic script and discovered by Jacopo Sannazaro shortly after 1500 on the Île Barbe at Lyon.[2] S. Tafel, after establishing that ff. 1–38 of Paris lat. 8093 were originally the beginning of V, associated the production of the manuscript with Theodulf of Orléans, who was on close terms with the church at Lyon and paid at least one visit.[3] Another member of the same family, Paris lat. 2772 (s. IX), is in the style of manuscripts from the chapter library at Lyon, and a monastery closely connected with Lyon, Saint-Oyan, had 'libri carminum Ausonii consulis' in s. XI. Though many of the texts in

---

[1] For *recensio* Schenkl's apparatus is more use than Peiper's; for *emendatio* both record too many trifling variants and too few conjectures. Prete gives more conjectures, but buries these and the variants that matter under a heap of eliminable variants from unimportant manuscripts; see M. D. R., *Gnomon,* 52 (1980), 444–51. Most of what follows can be found in Peiper's article 'Die handschriftliche Ueberlieferung des Ausonius', *Jahrb. für class. Phil.* Suppl. 11 (1880), 189–354, and the prefaces to the editions of Schenkl and Peiper; for modifications see M. D. R., 'Some Manuscripts of Ausonius', *Prometheus,* 3 (1977), 112–20, and 'The Tilianus of Ausonius', *RhM* 121 (1978), 350–66. On the question of different editions in Antiquity see most recently D. Nardo, *Atti dell'Ist. Ven.* 125 (1966–7), 321–82. In *CTC* iv (Washington, D.C., 1980), 193–222, Prete and H. L. Felber survey commentaries of s. XVI.

[2] A facsimile was published as an adjunct to H. de la Ville de Mirmont, *Le Manuscrit de l'Île Barbe* (Bordeaux and Paris, 1917–19).

[3] 'Die vordere, bisher verloren geglaubte Hälfte des vossianischen Ausonius-Kodex', *RhM* 69 (1914), 630–41. F. Della Corte, *RCCM* 2 (1960), 21, has actually attributed the hand to Theodulf.

V + Paris lat. 8093 came to Lyon from Spain, the evidence that Ausonius was one of them is confined to two alleged echoes at Toledo in s. VII, of which the one in Eugenius (Vollmer, edn., p. 269) is uncertain and the one in Julian (Peiper edn., p. xxxii), albeit certain, may have come through an anthology (cf. Peiper, ibid., on Paris lat. 8071).

Omissions and other errors bind to V the surviving descendants of a manuscript written 'longobardo charactere' and brought to light about 1300 in the chapter library at Verona. They contain fewer works than V but make one or two additions to what it offers. The best known, Paris lat. 8500 (P), was written for Petrarch. The Veronensis probably had some connection with one of two manuscripts catalogued at Bobbio in s. IX.

To this collection alone belong, for example, the *Parentalia, Professores,* and *Ordo urbium nobilium;* none of it was printed before 1490 and some of it for the first time in 1558.

(2) is the untidy collection most fully represented by over twenty Italian witnesses of s. XIV–XV, including the *editio princeps* (Venice, 1472). The earliest of them, Florence, Bibl. Naz. Conv. Soppr. J. VI. 29, was written for Coluccio Salutati soon after 1385; this and three others of *c.*1465–75 stand out from the herd. To (2) alone belong, for example, the *Gratiarum actio* and *Cento nuptialis,* and it contains far more Greek than (1). Excerpts from it appear in Paris lat. 18275 (s. XIII, French), and some peculiarities of its text go back even further: most notably, Cambridge, U.L. Kk. 5. 34 (s. X), which was at New Minster Winchester about AD 1000, conflates the texts of (2) and (1) in the two works that it contains.

(3), like the whole corpus, occurs in overlapping collections, and neither its content nor even its existence is altogether certain. The main witnesses from which Peiper reconstructed it, namely St. Gall 899 (G, s. IX ex., from St. Gall[4]) and Brussels 5369–73 (B, s. XI[1], from Gembloux), introduce their contribution with the title 'incipiunt excerpta de opusculis Decimi Magni Ausonii'. (3) would be of little consequence but for two things: it circulated more widely than (1) and (2), and it alone of the three, despite its preponderantly edifying character, has preserved *Mosella*. In s. XII *Mosella* could be read at St. Eucharius Trier, and Trier would make a good home for a collection that includes it. Earlier evidence, however, points to Reichenau and St. Gall; Walahfrid, Abbot of Reichenau (†849), probably knew *Mosella* (*PLMA* 2.355, nn. 11–12), and Ermenricus, who spent time at both Reichenau and St. Gall in the middle of s. IX, certainly did. An acquaintance of Walahfrid's was Agobard, Archbishop of Lyon (†840), but the source could equally well have been Bobbio.

---

[4] Precise information on date and origin was provided by Professor Bischoff.

Odd works from the three collections, especially short poems, crop up in miscellanies, often with a different ascription or none. Letters exchanged with Symmachus and Paulinus appear among their works too; the manuscripts of Paulinus and Ausonius diverge even more than (1) and (2), and Paris lat. 7558 (s. IX²/₄, probably from central France[5]), which contains little more of either author, used both traditions, that of Ausonius in a manuscript like V (works by Florus of Lyon point once more to Lyon). From (3) the beginning of the *Caesares* passed into the tradition of Suetonius, *Vir bonus* and *Est et non* into the *iuvenalis ludi libellus* of the *Appendix Vergiliana* (L, s. IX *ut vid.*). It may be relevant that in s. XII there was an ancestor of the *iuvenalis ludi libellus* at Trier.[6]

Peiper, observing that (3) and the descendants of the lost Veronensis in (1) nowhere overlap, conjectured that they originated as complementary parts of a fuller collection. This conjecture came near to confirmation when R. Weiss published a list of Ausonius' works drawn up at Verona in the 1320s[7]; besides those contained in the descendants of the Veronensis it includes most of those contained in (3), but not *Mosella*. (3) and (1) must therefore stay separate in default of fresh evidence, though they share so many corruptions in the *Eclogues* that if (2) transmitted the *Eclogues* as well, it would prove that either (1) and (3) or all three collections derive from a corrupt ancestor.

Weiss's list also includes works not contained in (1), (2), or (3), such as a poem *De imperatoribus res novas molitis a Decio usque ad Dioclecianum*. Although the list was doubtless taken, as Weiss believed, from the Veronensis, there are reasons for thinking that it was merely transcribed from the front of the Veronensis without regard to the contents of the Veronensis at the time. How long the lost works survived is an open question. Unidentifiable quotations from Ausonius also occur in the treatise *De dubiis nominibus* (s. VII), compiled in Spain or southern France.

Much work remains to be done on the text and origin of the numerous manuscripts that contain small parts of the three collections. The nature of the tradition also makes it likely that further witnesses will turn up as hastily catalogued manuscripts are examined more thoroughly.

M. D. R

[5] See n. 4, above.
[6] Cf. E. Courtney, *BICS* 15 (1968), 139.
[7] 'Ausonius in the fourteenth century', in *Classical Influences on European Culture A.D. 500–1500*, ed. R. R. Bolgar (Cambridge, 1971), 62–72.

AVIANUS

Fabulae

Already in s. IX–X catalogues attest Avianus' forty-two *Fables* at Saint-Riquier, Fleury, Nevers, Murbach, Reichenau, St. Gall, Lorsch, Regensburg, Passau, and Cremona,[1] and the relationships of the manuscripts that survive from the same period are complex enough to suggest busy collation and emendation. Such popularity cannot wholly be due either to exposition by Alcuin and Remigius, of which few traces remain,[2] or to association with the *Disticha Catonis,* which though seen in some of the earliest manuscripts does not become constant until the heyday of the *Liber Catonis* in the thirteenth-century schools.[3] So edifying a work could stand on its own feet. Medieval interpolators made it more edifying still by adding an explicit moral to many fables, and other medieval readers turned their hand to paraphrase or imitation.[4]

The list of 114 manuscripts set out in the introduction to A. Guaglianone's edition (Turin, 1958)[5] was built up by L. Hervieux[6] and W. A. Oldfather.[7] Oldfather ventured the first stemma, albeit without citing evidence (the dates and ascriptions are his, the symbols Guaglianone's):[8]

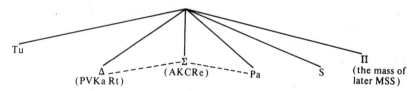

[1] Manitius, *Philologus,* 51 (1892), 533–5, together with medieval quotations; *Handschriften,* 234–7.

[2] Manitius, *Geschichte,* i. 512 n. 2; W. A. Oldfather, *TAPA* 42 (1911), 115–17.

[3] M. Boas, 'De librorum Catonianorum historia atque compositione', *Mnem.* 42 (1914), 17–46; cf. G. Glauche, *Schullektüre im Mittelalter* (Munich, 1970), index s. v. Avian.

[4] L. Hervieux, *Les Fabulistes latins III: Avianus et ses anciens imitateurs* (Paris, 1894). 'Hoc opere [all four volumes] materia immensa fusius quam scitius tractata est,' in the words of G. Thiele, *De antiquorum libris pictis capita quattuor* (Marburg, 1897), 38 n. 4.

[5] His article in *Rend. Accad. arch. lett. e belle arti,* 32 (1957, pub. 1958), 5–30, is slightly fuller in some respects. Nothing new in the Budé edition of F. Gaide (Paris, 1980).

[6] Ch. II.

[7] Op. cit. (n. 2, above). Thanks to Oldfather, the University Library at Urbana, Ill., has a large collection of photographs, but his work seems to have petered out in four unpublished dissertations by pupils. I have seen abstracts of W. R. Jones, 'The Text Tradition of Avianus' (1940), and Edith C. Jones, 'Avianus in the Middle Ages: Manuscripts and other Evidence of *Nachleben*' (1944). The former lists 115 manuscripts; Guaglianone passes over four and adds three of his own.

[8] *Philol. Quart.* 5 (1926), 20–8.

Tu   Zürich C 68 (s. VIII–IX, St. Gall).
P   Paris lat. 13026 (s. IX, from Saint-Germain).
V   Leiden, Voss. Lat. Q. 86 (s. IX, Fleury).
Ka   Karlsruhe, Aug. LXXIII (s. IX, Reichenau).
Rt   Vatican, Reg. lat. 208 (s. IX¾, Fleury).
A   Paris lat. 8093 (s. IX/X).
K   Karlsruhe 339 (s. IX).
C   Paris lat. 5570 (s. X, Fleury).
Re   Vatican, Reg. lat. 1424 (s. XI, 'the Orléans district').
Pa   Paris, n. a. lat. 1132 (s. IX/X, France).
S   St.Gall 1396 (s. XI).

The archetype, he surmised, was an illustrated manuscript that had
come to rest at St. Gall, the home of the two fragments Tu and S. S
leaves gaps that can only have been meant for illustrations, and Pa
actually has illustrations; Alemannic glosses that Pa took over from its
exemplar would suit the region of St. Gall. Δ, 'a faithful but unintelli-
gent copy', dispensed not only with the illustrations but also with titles.
Σ, 'carefully edited', gave titles. Π looks like a distortion of Σ but may
have had a more respectable origin.

W. R. Jones presented a comprehensive and diachronic stemma that
differs from Oldfather's in not giving Pa independent access to the
archetype.[9] A suspicious feature is that dotted lines lead to eight of the
twenty manuscripts written before s. XII[1] but to none of the multitude
written later; it also seems unlikely that the later manuscripts all derive
from one lost source (Oldfather's Π) independent of seventeen early
manuscripts that survive. Guaglianone differs from Oldfather and
Jones in regarding Tu, S, and Π as conflations of Δ and Σ. Manuscripts
that Jones and Guaglianone alike treat with respect are:

W   Leiden, Voss. Lat. O. 15 (s. XI[1], Limoges).
Vo   Leiden, Voss. Lat. O. 89 (s. XI, northern France).
B   Florence, Laur. Ashb. 1813 (s. XI/XII).
L   Florence, Laur. 68. 24 (s. XI, France).
Vl   Vatican lat. 3799 (s. X).

Guaglianone has the merit of offering evidence,[10] but he so often
contradicts himself in reporting the manuscripts that even when his
stemmatic arguments are valid,[11] their premises cannot be trusted.[12] A
more reliable foundation for stemmatic inferences is the Budé edition of
F. Gaide (Paris, 1980), which reports PVWRtLAKCRe.[13] A. Holder

---

[9] 'The Text Tradition'.   [10] Presumably Jones offers evidence in his dissertation.
[11] Against Oldfather's view of Tu and S, for instance, they are not.
[12] At 4.14, for instance, he variously gives *seposita* as the reading of V, Ka, and Δ; at 22.7 he
credits Δ with *rogaverit, speraverit,* and *speravit;* at 11.12 his apparatus reports *de-* from C and nothing
from Re, his article *de-* from Re and *dis-* from C. As no reviewer noticed these shortcomings, the
edition enjoys higher esteem than it deserves. See also nn. 14–15, below.
[13] I reviewed it in *CR* 31 (1981), 209–11.

published a collation of Ka,[14] and photographs of Pa have been printed.[15] Two things emerge very clearly: KCRe share numerous errors,[16] and so do PVKa. While the errors of KCRe are unremarkable, however, those of PVKa are mostly too absurd to have gone un-emended in more than a few manuscripts. PVKa differ most markedly from the other manuscripts in reading *defuncti* and not *Gaetuli* at 5.5, but both readings have had supporters.

Further work on the stemma must be accompanied by palaeo-graphical study of the older manuscripts, whose dates and origins need to be narrowed down. Meanwhile nothing should be taken on trust; catalogues published since Oldfather's articles, for instance, do not always bear out his dates and ascriptions.[17] Only when the movements of the text have been charted shall we know, amongst other things, whether the author's name reached the archetype as Avianus or Avienus.[18]

Re and a small group of English manuscripts interpolate between the preface and the first fable *Anth. Lat.* 26, *Rure morans*, preceded by a line of introduction.[19] It was obviously incorporated by someone who had found it ascribed to 'Avienus', as it is in two miscellanies from Reims, Vatican, Reg. lat. 2078 (s. IX¼) and British Library, Royal 15. B. XIX (s. X), and two others, one of which happens to be A of the *Fables*.[20]

The illustrations in Pa are thought to have originated in late Anti-quity (probably s. VI).[21] In 1560 Pa belonged to an abbot of St. Peter's Vienne, but as it seems to come from north-eastern France, connecting it with the treasures of seventh-century Vienne is a very long shot. Next to Pa the most important illustrated manuscript of fables is Leiden,

---

[14]   *Philologus*, 65 (1906), 91–6. Guaglianone cites Ka irregularly without explaining why.

[15]   A. Goldschmidt, *An Early Manuscript of the Aesop Fables of Avianus and Related Manuscripts* (Studies in Manuscript Illumination, 1, Princeton, 1947), plates I–X. Guaglianone frequently misreports it.

[16]   I have found no reason why Re should not be a copy of C; it often agrees with C². Guaglianone's arguments (op. cit. (n. 5 above), 11) do not square with either Gaide's apparatus or his own.

[17]   On Tu see L. C. Mohlberg, *Katalog der Handschriften der Zentral-Bibliothek Zürich i: Mittelalterliche Handschriften* (Zürich, 1952), 39 (s. IX/X); on V, A. Wilmart, *Codices Reginenses Latini*, ii (Vatican, 1945), 245 (Tours); on Rt, ibid. i (1937), 494 (s. XI, Micy). Bischoff, in *Medieval Learning*, 21, assigns Ka to s. IX⅓ and western Germany, and he has kindly communicated that K is of s. X²/₄ and French. C. Jeudy, *Mélanges E.-R. Labande* (Poitiers, 1974), 432, says of P: 'Copié par plusieurs scribes dans la région de Paris, le manuscrit a appartenu à l'abbaye Saint-Pierre de Corbie, dont l'ex-libris du XVIᵉ s. est au fol. 1'.

[18]   Oldfather, op. cit. (n. 8, above), 26 n. 16; Alan Cameron, *CQ* 61 (1967), 389–96; J. Küppers, *Die Fabeln Avians* (Bonn, 1977), 10–25.

[19]   Guaglianone, op. cit. (n. 5, above), 13, cites Cambridge, Trinity College 1229 (0. 3. 57) (s. XII), and Oxford, Bodl. Auct. F. 2. 14 (s. XI², Sherborne?) and Rawl. G. 111 (s. XI), to which may be added a fourth English manuscript, Edinburgh, Adv. 18. 6. 12 (s. XI², Thorney Abbey); see I. C. Cunningham, *Scriptorium*, 27 (1973), 84. On Re see Pellegrin, *Manuscrits*, ii. 1. 201–2.

[20]   G. Kölblinger, *Mittellat. Jahrb.* 8 (1973), 17–27, discusses the tradition of the poem but misses the manuscripts of Avianus that contain it.

[21]   On the contents of this paragraph see Goldschmidt, *An Early Manuscript*.

Voss. Lat. O. 15, part XIV, a prose paraphrase of Phaedrus written and illustrated by Adémar of Chabannes (†1034; part II of the manuscript, also written by Adémar, includes W of Avianus).[22] Abbot Arnoldus of Fleury (1030–2) decorated the refectory with frescoes illustrating fables, and scenes from fables appear in the Bayeux Tapestry.

A curiosity of the tradition is the almost total absence of Italian manuscripts even in s. XV;[23] and if there was an Italian edition before 1507, no one has mentioned it. In the *editio princeps* (Ulm, *c.*1476–7), a Latin-German 'Loeb', a selection of twenty-seven fables consorts with other *Aesopica;* the collection in its entirety came out on its own (Cologne, 1494). H. Cannegieter published the fullest edition with commentary (Amsterdam, 1731). Though Lachmann surprised even his contemporaries by accepting an Antonine date for Avianus and improving his language and metre accordingly, his ghost haunted the editions until Guaglianone laid it in 1958 by publishing an almost unemended text.[24] Needless to say, he went too far; but if ever a conservative edition was called for, Avianus at the time called for one. When Gaide published her otherwise useful and judicious Budé in 1980, there was less call for another.

M. D. R.

[22] Thiele, *Der illustrierte lateinische Aesop* (Leiden, 1905), 25–end, with plates.

[23] Considerable interest therefore attaches to Perotti's manuscript, Naples IV. F. 58, especially since it includes fables of Phaedrus' that occur nowhere else. The library at Murbach had 'fabula Aviani Esopi et Phedri' in s. IX; cf. n. 1, above.

[24] It would have been laid sooner if due attention had been paid to O. Unrein's dissertation *De Aviani aetate* (Jena, 1885).

CAELIUS AURELIANUS

The work of the Greek physician Soranus of Ephesus, a prominent representative of the Methodist school of medicine and the best ancient writer on gynaecology, survives in both Greek and Latin, and indeed more is extant in translation than in the original. This is largely due to the efforts of Caelius Aurelianus, a Methodist of African birth who put Soranus' treatises into Latin dress, probably in the fifth century AD, and so made them available to the Middle Ages.

Caelius' works were scarce at all times. Two were available at Lorsch in the ninth century.[1] One was the *Medicinales Responsiones,* a sort of medical catechism; the other was the *Tardae passiones,* a translation in five books of part of Soranus' great treatise *On Acute and Chronic Diseases* (Περὶ ὀξέων καὶ χρονίων παθῶν). The *Responsiones* has perished except for two substantial fragments rescued by Valentin Rose from two manuscripts, Karlsruhe, Aug. cxx (s. ix med. or ix¾; written in the area of Verona, it quickly found its way to Germany) and British Library, Sloane 1122 (s. xi).[2] But the *Tardae passiones* did survive into the age of printing and was edited in 1529[3] by Johann Sichart from a manuscript then apparently in the possession of Philipp Fürstenberger, the Bürgermeister of Frankfurt. The discovery in 1921 and 1922[4] of three leaves of a manuscript of Lorsch provenance[5] in the Ratsschulbibliothek at Zwickau leaves little doubt that Sichart's manuscript had come ultimately from Lorsch and that these leaves are remnants of it.[6] A comparison of the text of the manuscript with the relevant part of the *editio princeps* reveals that Sichart was a careful and cautious editor.

While the *Tardae passiones* has a German tradition, the *Acutae passiones* and the *Gynaecia* appear to have been more suited to the needs of the French. Saint-Amand is a central link in the chain. It certainly possessed a copy of the *Gynaecia* in the twelfth century, and item 207 in the same catalogue looks suspiciously like the *Acute Diseases* in disguise: 'liber Oxipate id est intelligentia ex qua omnes egritudines generantur. liber vetustissimus'.[7] No manuscript of this work survives and we are dependent on the *editio princeps,* edited by Johannes Guinterius Andernacus (Winter von Andernach) and published in Paris in 1533. He used a manuscript in the possession of Jean Brayllon, 'medicorum apud Luteciam facile princeps', and there may of course be a connection between his manuscript and the *liber vetustissimus* of Saint-Amand.

The *Gynaecia*[8] survives in one manuscript of the early thirteenth

---

[1] Becker, 37.388: 'Caelii Aureliani methodici Siccensis medicinalium responsionum libri III in uno codice'. 389: 'liber Caelii Aureliani Siccensis χρονίων in uno codice'.

[2] *Anecdota Graeca et Graecolatina,* ii (Berlin, 1870), 161–240.

[3] J. Sichardus, *Caeli Aureliani Siccensis tardarum passionum libri V* (Basle, 1529). For a modern edition of both the major works, see I. E. Drabkin, *Caelius Aurelianus. On Acute and on Chronic Diseases* (Chicago, 1950). On Sichart's edition, see P. Lehmann, *Iohannes Sichardus und die von ihm benutzten Bibliotheken und Handschriften,* Quellen und Untersuchungen zur lateinischen Philologie des Mittelalters, iv. 1 (Munich, 1911), 62–3, 139–41.

[4] J. Ilberg, *SPAW* 1921, 819–29; 1922, 282–4.   [5] Bischoff, *Lorsch,* 32, 34, 120–1.

[6] For the provenance and history of the Zwickau leaves, see Ilberg (1921), 820 ff. Janus Cornarius, a doctor and Greek scholar who helped Sichart with his edition, moved from Basle to Zwickau.

[7] Delisle, ii. 455. It is listed as a Caelian manuscript by Manitius, *Handschriften,* 252.

[8] Edited by M. F. and I. E. Drabkin, *Caelius Aurelianus,* Gynaecia (Supplements to the *Bulletin of the History of Medicine,* 13), Baltimore, 1951; for an account of the history of the manuscript, see pp. v–viii.

century, which appeared in 1948 in the hands of a Swiss rare-book firm, L'Art Ancien, Zurich,[9] and was acquired by Dr Elliott Hague of Buffalo, New York; he sold it in 1960 to the New York dealer I. Schumann, from whom it was acquired in 1962 for the New York Academy of Medicine, where it is now MS Safe.

The manuscript contains two units of material, the first veterinary, relating to horses, the second gynaecological. It was acquired by, if not written for, Richard de Fournival, physician, poet, and chancellor of Amiens, in the second quarter of the thirteenth century, and is no. 161 in the *Biblionomia*, a catalogue of Fournival's library at Amiens compiled *c*.1250.[10] Fournival's library passed, on his death in 1260, to Gerard of Abbeville, canon of Amiens. At Gerard's death the bulk of the books passed to the Sorbonne; but, according to his will, the medical books were to have been sold. The subsequent history of Fournival's medical books is not known, and this is the first of them to be identified. Happily, something of its later history is known. By the fifteenth century, Fournival's gynaecological manuscript belonged to St. Augustine's Canterbury, and can be identified on the basis of the second folio reference with no. 1274 in the late fifteenth-century catalogue of the abbey.[11] How and when the manuscript came to St. Augustine's is unknown; however, there must have been others like William of Clare, who, upon becoming a monk in 1277, gave the abbey some dozen books primarily acquired when he was a student in Paris, among them a manuscript containing Cicero's *De natura deorum* and excerpts from the *Ad familiares* (q.v.) The library was dispersed at the Dissolution. About 1836 the manuscript was given by G. Aspinall to his brother-in-law Thomas Dawson, according to the latter's book-plate. At a later date it became part of the Penzance library in Cornwall. The recent history before its re-emergence in Switzerland is unknown.[12]

The gynaecological corpus in Richard de Fournival's manuscript is in all probability a descendant, if not a copy, of the manuscript recorded in the twelfth-century catalogue of the abbey of Saint-Amand, not far from Amiens: '211. Liber febrium Constantini. Commentum super Ysagogas Johannitii. Liber pronosticorum Ypocratis. *Liber genetiae Aureliani Siccensis. Liber Cleopatrae de genetiis. Liber Muscionis de pessariis.* Microtegni. In uno volumine'.[13] The portions in italics reappear in Fournival's manuscript. It is likely that the Saint-Amand cataloguer recorded only the longer treatises in his description; the entry may well

---

[9] Catalogue 36, no. 4.   [10] Delisle, ii. 535.

[11] M. R. James, *The Ancient Libraries of Canterbury and Dover* (Cambridge, 1903), 347.

[12] Two short excerpts on conception from Muscio and Caelius Aurelianus (some dozen lines each), written in a German(?) hand of the thirteenth century, exist in Leiden, Voss. Lat. Q. 9, f. 82, a collection of medical manuscripts of disparate origin assembled by Melchior Goldast (1576–1635).   [13] Delisle, ii. 455.

conceal the whole of this small body of gynaecological texts. Saint-Amand 211 was very probably a Carolingian book; and from there the source might go straight back to a late antique codex.

L. D. R.

R. H. R.

CAESAR

In 1847 Karl Nipperdey[1] established the (largely valid)[2] distinction between two classes of Caesar manuscripts, those (a) containing only the *Bellum Gallicum* and notable for allusions in colophons to late antique *correctores* (Iulius Celsus Constantinus, Flavius Licerius Firminus Lupicinus), and those (β) containing the whole corpus (*Bellum Gallicum, Bellum Civile, Bellum Alexandrinum, Bellum Africum,* and *Bellum Hispaniense,* almost always in that order). In the *B. G.,* where the classes overlap, their readings are markedly different.[3]

The century after Nipperdey saw, for both a and β, the discovery of further early witnesses; but since the Second World War the tendency has been towards elimination. Thus in the a class A. Klotz (1921) worked with six manuscripts, two going back to a lost χ (Amsterdam 73, s. $IX^2/4$, written at Fleury = A; Paris lat. 5056, s. XI/XII, written at Moissac = Q) and four to a lost φ (Paris lat. 5763, s. $IX^1/4$, French, later at Fleury = B; Vatican lat. 3864, s. $IX^3/4$, written at Corbie = M;[4] Florence, Laur. Ashb. 33, s. X, French (?) = S; British Library, Add. 10084, s. XI/XII, from Gembloux (?) = L). Wolfgang Hering (1963) thought only A and B primary. Virginia Brown has listed seventy-five

---

[1] *C. Julii Caesaris Commentarii cum supplementis A. Hirtii et aliorum* (Leipzig, 1847). For a sketch of the work on Caesar since the *editio princeps* of Giovanni Andrea Bussi (Sweynheym and Pannartz, Rome, 1469), see W. Hering, *Die Recensio der Caesarhandschriften* (Berlin, 1963), 3–6; V. Brown, *The Textual Transmission of Caesar's Civil War* (*Mnem.* Suppl. 23, 1972), 1–9. From these pages further bibliography may be gleaned. The standard texts, marked by remarkable indifference to what the manuscripts actually read, are those of A. Klotz (Teubner, Leipzig, 3 vols.: *B. G.* 1948⁴; *B. C.* 1950²; *B. A.* etc. 1927) and O. Seel (Teubner, Leipzig, 1 vol. only, *B. G.* 1970³). For photographs of folios from BQTWVLS, see Chatelain, plates XLVI–LA; from BMSTVU, Hering, *ad fin.*).

[2] But, e.g., S (see below) has an a text of *B. G.,* though containing the whole corpus.

[3] Nipperdey thought β distinctly inferior. Opinion has swung to regarding a as better, but not overwhelmingly better, than β.

[4] Not to be confused with W (see below), which Brown calls M. Hering, viii, has a useful list of divergent sigla. I owe some revised datings to Dr Brown.

manuscripts later than the ninth century, and suggested tentative groupings.[5]

Similarly with the β class: Klotz (1950) used eight manuscripts, at least three of which are now thought to be *descripti*.[6] The other five are Florence, Laur. 68.8, basically s. X/XI, Italian (?), once owned by Niccolò Niccoli = W; Vatican lat. 3324, s. XI/XII, French (?) = U; Paris lat. 5764, s. XI², French = T; Vienna 95, s. XII¹, from Trier (?) = V; and S (see above). The interrelations of these are still disputed. Hering has argued for a bipartite stemma, with STV opposed to UW. Virginia Brown prefers a tripartite tradition S/TV/UW.[7] Her forthcoming edition of the *B. C.* will help to show if this view is correct.[8] Meanwhile her examination and elimination of no less than 162 *recentiores* marks a notable advance.[9]

The history of the transmission between the *correctores* and the earliest manuscripts is obscure.[10] Brown argues for a minuscule archetype.[11] It is a striking fact that such medieval authors, mostly French and German, as were acquainted with Caesar appear to know only the *B. G.*[12]

M. W.

[5] See her contribution to *Palaeographica diplomatica et archivistica. Studi in onore di Giulio Battelli* (Rome, 1979), 105–57.

[6] Both Hering and Brown eliminate Naples IV. C. 11, s. XI, French = N, together with L (see above) and Florence, Ricc. 541, s. XII¹, French (?) = R. Hering further eliminates V. I use throughout Brown's conclusions on date and provenance.

[7] Nor are her conclusions invalidated by Hering's criticisms in his review in *Gnomon*, 45 (1973), 763–6. The lack of *Trennfehler* separating TVUW from S actually supports Brown's view.

[8] But Hering (ibid.) was right to say that the evidence of the other *Bella* (including the *B. G.*) should have been taken into account.

[9] Dr Brown adds three more in her new article (n. 5, above), n. 3. It is strange that there seem to be almost no manuscripts between 1200 and 1397.

[10] Extensive interpolation, especially of geographical passages in *B. G.*, has been suspected by many editors; cf. G. Jachmann, *RhM* 89 (1940), 161–88 and *WS* 60 (1942), 71–8. Whether the *correctores* could themselves be responsible for any of it is probably an unanswerable question.

[11] 36–41. Contrast Hering, 87–111.

[12] Brown, *Transmission*, 14 n. 2.

CALPURNIUS AND NEMESIANUS

Eclogae

Calpurnius and Nemesianus reappeared in Italy at a time propitious to pastoral: a manuscript at Verona came to the notice of Petrarch about 1360, after the composition of his own *Bucolicum Carmen* but not too late to influence Boccaccio's. Its two descendants form a well-defined family:

N Naples V. A. 8.
G Florence, Laur. Gadd. 90 inf. 12.

Both date from the last third of the century, and G was written by Domenico Silvestri, a friend of Boccaccio and himself the author of *Eclogues*. Some *notabilia* dotted about the margins of N may be in the hand of Panormita.[1]

NG ascribe the first seven of the eleven *Eclogues* here concerned to Calpurnius and the other four to Nemesianus. In s. XII separate manuscripts at Prüfening (Regensburg) contained 'bucolica Aureliani' (NG call him Aurelianus Nemesianus) and 'IIII paria bucolica Calpurnii'.[2]

The other complete manuscripts, about thirty in number, date from s. XV or later and form another well-defined family, V, which ascribes all eleven *Eclogues* to Calpurnius. Its source can be adequately reconstructed from six manuscripts; the larger and earlier group within it is mostly north Italian (Paduan in origin?), the smaller and later Florentine and Roman. The *editio princeps* (Rome, 1471) belongs to the smaller, while its successor (Venice, 1472) derives from an extant member of the larger, Vatican lat. 5123. Some members of the larger call the poet Theocritus Calpurnius, and 'bucolica Theocriti' were catalogued in 1155 at Pfäffers (eastern Switzerland).

Nemesianus' title to the last four *Eclogues* was vindicated by M. Haupt.[3] The ascription of all eleven to Calpurnius therefore serves as a *Bindefehler*, and it connects with V the source of the citations in the margins of Berne 276 (s. XIII) and in the *Florilegium Gallicum* (s. XII),

---

[1] There are more in Cato and Varro than in Calpurnius. Note especially f. 88ʳ: 'Varro sub Cassino', f. 89ʳ: 'villae Varronis descriptio sub Cassino monte', f. 101ʳ: 'L. Lucullus apud Neapolim'.

[2] See most recently H.-G. Schmitz, *Kloster Prüfening im 12. Jahrhundert* (Munich, 1975), 103, 105.

[3] *De carminibus bucolicis Calpurnii et Nemesiani* (Berlin and Leipzig, 1854), reprinted in his *Opuscula*, i (Leipzig, 1875), 358–406. The question of whose accession Calpurnius celebrates, which appeared resolved in favour of Nero, has been reopened by E. Champlin, *JRS* 68 (1978), 95–110, who argues for Severus Alexander; but see G. B. Townend and R. Mayer, *JRS* 70 (1980), 166–76. Nemesianus in any case remains distinct.

which must have been a manuscript at Orléans or near by. Probably from the same area comes the earliest manuscript of Calpurnius, owned according to Pithoeus by Jean Duc de Berry (1340–1416):

P   Paris lat. 8049 (s. XII, Chatelain, plate CL).

As P never went further than 4.12, its connection with this family must be established otherwise, and agreement has not yet been reached about whether any readings shared by PV against NG are significant errors. If the conjunction of Calpurnius with Petronius is significant, however, it connects P with a manuscript sent to Florence from England by Poggio about 1420, which seems to have contained both; and V, none of whose members can be shown to antedate 1420, almost certainly derives from this manuscript of Poggio's. Nothing is known about the circulation of the *Eclogues* before 1420 that would bridge the Channel; the only clear imitations in the Middle Ages occur in two poets associated with Charlemagne, Paulus Diaconus (*c*.785) and Modoinus (*c*.810), and in one cited like Calpurnius by the annotator of Berne 276 and presumably to be placed in the same region, M. Valerius (s. XII).[4]

In the early 1490s Thadeus Ugoletus, 'Pannoniae regis bibliothecae praefectus', brought to Florence 'e Germania', which is usually taken to mean from the library of 'Pannoniae regis' Matthaeus Corvinus, a manuscript of which a collation by Nic. Angelius survives in a member of V, Florence Ricc. 636; a few other readings also seem to have found their way independently into editions of the early sixteenth century. As Angelius collated at least two other witnesses in his manuscript, the readings of Ugoletus's manuscript cannot be made out with complete certainty, but it undoubtedly had lines omitted by V and agreed with NG in ascribing the last four *Eclogues* to Nemesianus. Errors shared with G against NV suggest that it was of Italian origin and less important than has been thought.

Fundamental for the classification of the manuscripts and the history . of the text is an article by H. Schenkl, *WS* 5 (1883), 281–98 and 6 (1884), 73–97. See also, especially on V, L. Castagna, *I bucolici latini minori: una ricerca di critica testuale* (Florence, 1976), and M. D. R., 'The Textual Tradition of Calpurnius and Nemesianus', *CQ* 72 (1978), 223–38. For both critical and codicological purposes much the best edition is that of C. Giarratano (Naples, 1910¹, Turin, 1924², Turin, 1943³); but all editors of the last 100 years unduly favour NG and Ugoletus's manuscript, and none has sorted the wheat from the chaff in V.

M. D. R.

---

[4] f. 135ʳ: '*Mens* · | · ratio, unde Marcus Valerius consuli (?) in bucolicis: Hinc canit ad placitum cunctis ut nomina rebus mens dedit absentes oculis ut cernere formas possit' (4. 46–8; Munari's manuscript gives *hic*, which he left, and corrupts each *ut* to *ubi*, which he emended correctly).

CARMINA EINSIDLENSIA

Chr. Browerus, head of the Jesuit college at Fulda and author of *Fuldensium antiquitatum libri IIII* (Antwerp, 1612), found in the monastic library there a damaged manuscript that contained a collection of poems by Hrabanus Maurus, which he appended to his second edition of Venantius Fortunatus (Mainz, 1617). Part of the manuscript is now pp. 177–224 of Einsiedeln 266 (s. x),[1] and Browerus turns out to have left the distinction of publishing two pastoral poems of Neronian date on pp. 206–7 to H. Hagen, *Philologus*, 28 (1869), 338–41. As in the poems of Hrabanus, two lines of verse are generally squeezed into one of script, and over-enthusiastic trimming of the margins has carried off most of l. 42–3 at the top of p. 207.

No trace of these *Carmina Einsidlensia* has been found elsewhere. If they passed through the hands of Hrabanus, as their association with poems of his in the surviving manuscript might suggest, they presumably did so either at Fulda itself, where he was Abbot from 822 to 842, or at Tours, where he had studied. A textual analysis of the scientific and philosophical matter on pp. 177–205 may yield some clue.

A photograph of the whole text appears in S. Lösch, *Die Einsiedler Gedichte* (Tübingen, 1909), before p. 1, and in R. Merkelbach and H. van Thiel, *Lateinisches Leseheft* (Göttingen, 1969), no. 10. The most recent edition is that of D. Korzeniewski, *Hirtengedichte aus neronischer Zeit* (Darmstadt, 1971), 75–85, who joins the ranks of those who ascribe the poems to different authors.[2] Whether by different authors or not, they were both miserable productions even before the tradition played havoc with them.

M. D. R.

---

[1] E. Dümmler, *Neues Arch. für deutsche Gesch.* 4 (1878), 288–92, *PLAC* ii (Berlin, 1884), 157–8.
[2] More fully in *Hermes*, 94 (1966), 358–60.

CATO AND VARRO

De agri cultura; Res rusticae

Politian in 1482 and Vettori in the late 1530s[1] collated at S. Marco, Florence, an old manuscript of Cato and Varro that has since vanished. It had once contained Gargilius Martialis and Columella as well,[2] but it already broke off at Varro 3.17.4 when Florence, Laur. 51.4 was written *c*.1405.[3] All fifteenth-century manuscripts that break off at the same point or were supplemented beyond that point obviously derive from it, but so too, in the view of almost everyone since 1846,[4] do all the other manuscripts, whether of the fifteenth century or earlier.

The oldest manuscript, Paris lat. 6842A (A), was written in Italy not later than s. XII[5] and in 1426 belonged to the Visconti library at Pavia. Next in antiquity editors put a French manuscript, Florence, Laur. 30.10 (m), which they assign to s. XIV; but as it includes Vitruvius, it must have some connection with a manuscript that Jean de Montreuil (1354–1418) received from Italy together with a Vitruvius, and expert opinion favours s. XV¼.[6] It therefore yields precedence to Naples V.A.8 (n), a Varro of s. XIV³/₃ followed by Calpurnius and Nemesianus in the same hand and preceded by Cato in a later hand; the older texts owe their conjunction to a successful request made simultaneously for both by Petrarch.[7] Anm in Cato and Am in Varro, where n has not been collated, allegedly share readings absent from the other manuscripts;[8]

---

[1] V. Fanelli, *Rinascimento*, 10 (1959), 112 (Colocci to Vettori, 3 Feb. 1538).

[2] Gargilius survived the Middle Ages only in excerpts, an Arabic translation of other excerpts, and a palimpsest from Bobbio that is also the main witness to the text of Charisius, namely Naples IV.A.8 (ff. 40–7, s. VI, uncial, written over in s. VII; *CLA* III. 403); see S. Condorelli, *Gargilii Martialis quae exstant* (Rome, 1978). For a conjecture about the missing Columella see COLUMELLA, n. 6.

[3] On this manuscript see A. C. de la Mare in *Das Verhältnis der Humanisten zum Buch*, ed. F. Krafft and D. Wuttke (Boppard, 1977), 97 with fig. 4. Virginia Brown, *CTC* iv (Washington, DC, 1980), 227, 458, wrongly says that the lost Marcianus was intact when Politian saw it.

[4] A. Schleicher, *Meletematon Varronianorum specimen I* (Bonn, 1846). I have not seen this, and if S. Timpanaro had seen it he could have suggested more confidently in *La genesi del metodo del Lachmann* (new edn., Padua, 1981), 83–4, that the genealogy of manuscripts led Schleicher to the genealogy of languages.

[5] A. C. de la Mare from the plates in Mazzarino's Cato; cf. D. Petitjean, *Annuaire de l'École Pratique des Hautes Études*, IVᵉ section, 105 (1972–3), 824. Editors say s. XII ex. or s. XIII in. and give no place of origin.

[6] Gius. Billanovich, *IMU* 7 (1964), 346; A. C. de la Mare in *Cultural Aspects of the Italian Renaissance: Essays in honour of P. O. Kristeller*, ed. C. H. Clough (Manchester, 1976), 178.

[7] H. Schenkl, *WS* 6 (1884), 86 (missed by editors of Cato and Varro). For the possibility that n later belonged to Panormita see CALPURNIUS, n. 1.

[8] Keil, *ed. maior*, xi, xvi; Mazzarino, lxxxiv n. 2. I say 'allegedly' because in Cato Mazzarino's apparatus reveals only two agreements of Anm (3.4, 7.2) and in Varro Keil reports only five

if, therefore, any truth survives in A that was not in the Marcianus,[9] it should also survive in nm, which it appears not to do. Anm all contain the whole of Varro; whether one of them (A or n) supplied 3.17.4 – end to later manuscripts such as Paris lat. 6149 + 6830F, written in 1414,[10] no one has tried to determine.

Editors treat Politian's collation (Paris, B. N. Rés. S 439, *ed. princ.* Ven. 1472)[11] as the weightiest witness to the Marcianus. Why, with twenty manuscripts to choose from?[12] The answer lies in Politian's note on Cato 84: 'In marginibus vetustissimi codicis cum quo hunc nostrum conferebamus haec erant ascripta verba hic eiusdem librarii manu qui et ipsum descripserat codicem: *Huc usque de duobus emendavi, hinc de uno exemplario tantum.*' Not one of the manuscripts preserves the variants of these *exemplaria* with anything like the conscientiousness of Politian. Nevertheless, editors might have done more to establish the relationship of the manuscripts and set it alongside the external evidence, which after a yawning gap between Nonius and s. XIV[13] returns in abundance. About 1305 Petrus Crescentius of Bologna used Cato and Varro in his *Ruralia commoda.*[14] Extracts from Varro appear in the Verona *Flores* of 1329,[15] and it was from Guglielmo da Pastrengo in Verona that Petrarch expected his manuscript. At some date not far from 1400 another agricultural writer, Corneolus Corneus of Perugia,

witnesses. On the other hand Mazzarino's apparatus puts few obstacles in the way of deriving m from n; note several innovations of n^2m.

[9] Mazzarino, lxxiii–lxxv (unconvincing).

[10] C. Samaran and R. Marichal, *Catalogue des manuscrits en écriture latine portant des indications de date, de lieu ou de copiste,* ii (Paris, 1962), pl. lxxxii. Dr A. C. de la Mare wonders whether the hand is Francesco Barbaro's; if so, the manuscript could be one used by Vettori.

[11] A plate of the last page appears in R. Merkelbach and H. van Thiel, *Lateinisches Leseheft* (Göttingen, 1969), no. 22.

[12] To the lists given by Keil, *Observationes criticae in Catonis et Varronis de re rustica libros* (Halle, 1849), 5–12, 99–100, and Mazzarino, lxxvii–lxxviii, add two manuscripts of Cato and Varro mentioned by P.-P. Corsetti, *RHT* 8 (1978), 289–90, and Florence, Laur. Conv. Soppr. 285 (Varro to 1.2.9), B.L. Harl. 2579 (Cato), Lyon 331/264 (Varro, probably copied from the Oxoniensis below), Milan, Trivulz. 773 (Cato, Varro), Oxford, Bodl. Lat. class. d.2 (Varro, written 'apud clarissimum virum Guarinum Veronensem Ferrariae MCCCCLIIII° Idibus Augustis' and presumably identical with a manuscript used by Vettori), Sandaniele del Friuli 104 (Varro), Vatican lat. 6801 (Cato, Varro). Mazzarino's no. 6 should read v.A.5.

[13] Second-hand quotations are a trap. For Cato see Mazzarino, ix–xv; for Varro, G. Goetz, *Festschrift Walther Judeich* (Weimar, 1929), 48–67, and on Nonius' quotations, which improve the text, G. Heidrich, *Programm des k. k. Staats-Gymnasiums in Pola,* 3 (Pola, 1893), 33–46. 'Cato' on f. 43^r of Berne 363 (s. IX med.) need not refer to *De agri cultura* (Mazzarino, xv) any more than it does elsewhere in the manuscript; see Hagen's preface to the facsimile (Leiden, 1897), xliv–xlv. For the circulation in s. XIV–XV Mazzarino, xv–xx, xxx–xxxi, must be augmented from Sabbadini, *Scoperte,* and in what follows I add more and hazard connections made by neither. Virginia Brown, *CTC* iv. 226, jumps from s. XIV[1] to s. XV[2].

[14] Goetz, *Festschrift,* 62–7, refuses to draw conclusions about his text of Varro.

[15] The text of these has not been published. On the extant manuscript, written not before 1334, see G. Turrini, 'L'origine veronese del cod. CLXVIII (155) "Flores moralium auctoritatum" della Bibl. Capit. di Verona', *Atti e mem. dell' Accad. di agr. sc. e lett. di Verona,* ser. VI, 11 (1959–60, publ. 1961), 49–65.

used Cato, 'cui adeo est obsecutus ut nonnulla praeciperet a XIV saeculi moribus sane abhorrentia'.[16] Salutati, with whom Jean de Montreuil corresponded,[17] knew Cato, and his acquaintance Domenico di Bandino knew Varro. In 1407 one Giovenazzi of Siena owned Varro.[18] About 1412 a correspondent informed Niccoli that Giovanni Corvini owned both; as Corvini entered the service of the Visconti, his manuscript may have been A. In 1418 Cosimo de' Medici owned Cato, and in 1426 the Visconti owned not only A but a separate Varro.[19] Also in 1426 Poggio asked Niccoli for Cato and Varro, and in 1432 Niccoli himself wanted to borrow from Francesco Piendibeni 'uno libro anti- quissimo' of Cato 'di lettera longobarda' because a manuscript he already possessed was 'molto corropto'; Piendibeni, then at Monte- pulciano, had known Salutati and been chancellor of Perugia.[20] There- after references decrease in interest but not in frequency. A little work on the manuscripts and the external evidence should be enough to track the Marcianus through this maze.[21] The more can be deduced about it, the better: unless its scribe copied the note on Cato 84 from his exemplar, he had two other manuscripts at his disposal in this very narrow tradition, and one would like to know when and where he worked.

A stage of the tradition earlier than the Marcianus emerges from two incorporated variants in Cato 160 (*in alio s(ic)f(ertur) . . .*). The view that alien matter had already accumulated round Cato's book goes back to J. M. Gesner's edition (Leipzig, 1735) and was forcefully put by Leo.[22]

The most informative edition of either author is the Teubner Cato of A. Mazzarino (Leipzig, 1962; a second edition is announced), though trivialities clutter the apparatus and the text contains almost as many diacritical signs as words. The Teubner Varro of G. Goetz (Leipzig, 1929²) could hardly present a starker contrast, and for a proper apparatus recourse must be had to its archetype, Keil's *editio maior* (Leipzig, 1884); J. Heurgon has published the first volume of an edition for Budé (Paris, 1978).

M. D. R.

[16] Mazzarino, xvi.

[17] Gius. Billanovich and G. Ouy, *IMU* 7 (1964), 337–74.

[18] H. Baron, *Leonardo Bruni Aretino: humanistisch-philosophische Schriften* (Leipzig and Berlin, 1928), 110 (Bruni to Niccoli, 17 Dec. 1407: 'A Iuvenacio percontatus de M. Varronis libris, tres dumtaxat reperio apud ipsum de re rustica, illos ipsos quos Florentiae habetis').

[19] F. Pintor, *IMU* 3 (1960), 199 (reprint); E. Pellegrin, *La Bibliothèque des Visconti et des Sforza* (Paris, 1955), 169 no. 426.

[20] De la Mare, *Handwriting*, 59–61.

[21] For his thesis on book 2 of Varro D. Petitjean contented himself with collating Laur. 51.4 of the fifteenth-century manuscripts; cf. loc. cit. (n. 5, above).

[22] *Geschichte der römischen Literatur*, i (Berlin, 1913), 272 with n. 1. Others, e.g. A. E. Astin, *Cato the Censor* (Oxford, 1978), 191–203, blame the disorder and doublets on Cato himself.

CATULLUS

Catullus was virtually unknown during most of the Middle Ages, although intriguing echoes of his work have been noticed in several writers of the ninth through the twelfth centuries, including Heiric of Auxerre and William of Malmesbury.[1]

The main line of transmission begins appropriately in the poet's birthplace, Verona, where a manuscript (now lost) containing 113 of his poems came to light shortly after 1300.[2] The earlier history of this manuscript (called V by editors) is obscure. Bishop Rather could read Catullus in Verona in 966, but nothing securely connects the manuscript used by him with V. on the other hand, two of V's early descendants preserve an epigram by the Veronese Benvenuto Campesani in which Catullus is made to announce his return to Verona 'longis a finibus'; if the epigram is to be believed, its most probable meaning is that V was brought to Verona from the north.[3]

The text of V can be recovered in most places from three fourteenth-century descendants. The oldest and most faithful is Oxford, Bodl. Canon. Class. Lat. 30 (O), copied in Italy shortly before 1375;[4] O's exact place of origin is unknown, but it was in Lombardy by around 1430, to judge by the decoration of f. 1ʳ. The next oldest extant manuscript, Paris lat. 14137 (*olim Sangermanensis*, hence G), was written in Verona in 1375 by Antonio da Legnago;[5] it is closely related to Vatican, Ottob. lat. 1829 (called the *codex Romanus,* or R, by W. G. Hale, who discovered it in

The most widely used edition is that of R. A. B. Mynors (OCT, 1958). The recent edition of D. F. S. Thomson (Chapel Hill, NC, 1978) gives more detailed reports of the major manuscripts and a fuller introduction, on which the present sketch is largely based.

[1] B. L. Ullman, 'The Transmission of the Text of Catullus', *Studi Castiglioni* (Florence, 1960), 1027–57, especially 1028–38; R. G. M. Nisbet, *PCPS* NS 24 (1978), 106–7 (imitations of poem 68 in the *Epicedium Hathumodae* of Agius of Corvey, composed in 874). G. Billanovich, *IMU* 17 (1974), 46 ff., discerns an allusion to Catullus 67.34 (*Brixia Veronae mater amata meae*) in a verse epistle appended to the *Commentum Monacense* on Terence in Munich Clm 14420, f. 144ʳ. The manuscript was written in Brescia near the year 1000; Billanovich identifies the author of the verse letter as Hildemar of Corbie, who emigrated to Brescia in 841. Unfortunately, the leaf containing the letter is torn and a direct reference to Catullus cannot be proved.

[2] Three poems not transmitted with the corpus of Catullus' work were introduced by Muretus in 1554 as items 18–20: *Hunc lucum* (cited by several grammatical writers = *frag.* 1 Mynors), *Hunc ego*, and *Ego haec* (= *Priapea* 85–6 Bücheler, II–III in *Appendix Vergiliana*, ed. Richmond (OCT, 1966), 131–3). They were removed from the text of Catullus by Lachmann; most modern editions go directly from poem 17 to 21. Poems not in V are cited under Catullus' name by several ancient sources (*fragmenta* 2–5 Mynors).

[3] So, e.g., Ullman, 1036. Others, however, believe that V (or an ancestor) was the manuscript seen by Rather and that it never left Verona: Billanovich, 58–9.

[4] Complete reproduction in R. A. B. Mynors (ed.), *Catullus: Carmina. Codex Oxoniensis Bibliothecae Bodleianae Canonicianus Class. Lat. 30 (Codices Graeci et Latini Photographice Depicti*, XXI; Leiden, 1966); see also *Survival*, 80. Plates of OG in Chatelain, XIV–XVA, of R in *AJA* 1 (1897), pl. 1.

[5] G. Billanovich, *IMU* 2 (1959), 160–9.

1896), produced in Florence shortly after 1375 for Coluccio Salutati.[6] G and R derive from a lost copy of V, usually called X. All other surviving manuscripts so far investigated are either demonstrably or arguably dependent on OGR.[7]

The outlines of the transmission are thus tolerably clear, but the reconstruction of X (and so of V) is complicated by the presence of variant readings in both G and R;[8] G contains near the beginning a few variant readings in the hand of the scribe (G^1), probably transferred from the exemplar (X), and a larger number of variants in a later hand (G^2). R was corrected and emended over a span of years by Salutati himself. An important clue to the sorting of these GR variants is provided by Venice, Marc. Lat. xii. 80 (4167), or m, written by Poggio in an early form of humanistic script between 1400 and 1403.[9] Poggio used R as his exemplar, and transcribed as well the marginal variants present in R at that time. The variants subsequently added to R by Salutati before his death in 1406 appear in m in a later version of Poggio's hand (designated m' by the most recent editor), presumably as a result of a second collation of R. The distinction between m and m' is therefore useful in separating two phases of Salutati's additions to R; since m (and more precisely m') was in turn the source of G^2's variants, Poggio's MS also assists in distinguishing the variants of G^1 from those of G^2.

With the distinction between early and late R^2 variants established, the different character of the readings in each phase can be clearly seen. The early variants may well have been Salutati's own conjectures, while at least some of the later ones must have come from another manuscript, not yet securely identified. There are several striking agreements with O in wrong or even impossible readings, and also agreements with G.[10] The simplest explanation might be that Salutati had secured X and had found in it variants neglected by the scribes of G and R.[11] (R^2 agreements with O against GR might then point to pairs of variants in V.[12])

Much remains to be discovered about the remaining late manuscripts,

[6] Ullman, *Salutati*, 192–3, no. 96.

[7] 'Quod ad ceteros codices attinet, ... omnes a codicibus *OGR* originem aut duxerunt aut, quod nobis idem ualet, duxisse possunt,' Mynors (OCT), viii; cf. Ullman, 1052, Thomson, 3. The question, however, is far from settled and the current view may prove to be over-simplified; cf. M. D. R., *Phoenix*, 34 (1980), 179–80.

[8] Study of the question was long hampered by the successive failures of Hale and Ullman to publish Hale's material relating to R; cf. Ullman, 1054 and Mynors (OCT), vii: '[R] correxerunt plures manus, quas hic omnes praeter recentissimas inuitus *r* appello, dum spero quendam de Colucii eiusque amicorum studiis peritissimum nos tandem aliquando plenius esse docturum.' For what follows see Thomson, 13–35, *YCS* 23 (1973), 113–29.

[9] A. C. de la Mare and D. F. S. Thomson, *IMU* 16 (1973), 179–95.

[10] Thomson, 19–20(R^2O), 26–7 (R^2G).

[11] Some R^2 variants correspond with those of G^1, and are thus almost certainly derived from X (Thomson, 22–3).

[12] Thomson (25–9) proposes that X acquired some O readings between the copying of R and the later inspection of X by Salutati that produced the R^2 variants; following Ullman, 1043–4, he

approximately 150 in number,[13] but on the present showing their value to an editor is as *fontes coniecturarum*. The latest editors have adopted Mynors's compendious form of citing their readings, using the sigla α through θ to designate the source or group of sources in which a conjecture first appears.[14]

One poem only (62) is preserved in a manuscript independent of V, Paris lat. 8071 (s. ix, France), a miscellany often called the *florilegium Thuaneum* (T);[15] most of T was copied from a French manuscript of the late eighth century, Vienna 277 (*CLA* x.1474), which has now lost Catullus along with most of its other contents. T and V derive independently from a common source containing lacunae (after lines 32, 58b) and corruptions; this source may not have been much older than Vienna 277 (TV agree in *cura* for *cara* in 58, an error perhaps due to misreading the *cc* form of *a* frequent in early Caroline minuscule.[16] The date of V is disputed (the ninth and thirteenth centuries having both been recently proposed[17]), but comparison with T – itself carelessly written – shows clearly that V is more often and more deeply corrupt. Even when V has been adequately reconstructed, therefore, it offers a text that often requires (and often baffles) emendation.[18] There is also reason to think that the tradition ultimately descends from a posthumous edition of Catullus' works in which the order and divisions of poems were at times those of the editor rather than the author.[19]

R. J. T.

suggests that some variants in X are the work of Petrarch and advances the hypothesis that X was Petrarch's own copy of Catullus, compared with O in Petrarch's last years.

[13] Handlist in Thomson, 44–63, partial stemma, 69; cf. M. Zicàri, 'Il codice pesarese di Catullo e i suoi affini', *Studia Oliveriana*, 1 (1953), 5–23, 'Il "Cavrianeus" antaldino e i codici Catulliani affini al Bononiensis 2621', 4 (1956), 145–62, 'Ricerche sulla tradizione manoscritta di Catullo', *Bollettino*, 6 (1958), 79–99 (= *Studi Catulliani* (Urbino, 1978), 43–60, 61–77, 79–104 respectively).

[14] Mynors (OCT), ix–xi; Thomson, 43 (with two deletions, one addition, and one substitution).

[15] Plate in Robinson Ellis's edition of Catullus (Oxford, 1878), facing p. 100; Chatelain, xva. See *ANTHOLOGIA LATINA*.

[16] The ancient book from which Vienna 277 and V ultimately derive may have been preserved in a French library: Ullman, 1029, notes an echo of Catullus 68 in Venantius Fortunatus.

[17] W. V. Clausen, *CP* 71 (1976), 42–3 (ninth); Thomson, 11 (second half of the thirteenth century). Clausen rejects the examples of OGR errors induced by Gothic script alleged by Ullman, and Thomson's appeal to 64.11 (following *Survival*, 80) as an additional instance is problematical. The correct reading *prima* is found in β; GR (= X) have *primam* and O gives *posteam* (p̄eā) in the text with *proram* (O¹) in the margin. If O's exemplar really read *proram*, that exemplar can hardly have been V, since X's *primam* would then be a remarkably acute conjecture. But if O is not a direct copy of V, then its peculiar errors reveal nothing about the date of V. (It seems more likely that O's *posteam* is a misreading of *primam* abbreviated p̄mā, a form possible in Caroline as well as in Gothic.)

[18] Debate over what Catullus actually wrote is still vigorous; see, for example, the provocative edition 'lectorum in usum' of G. P. Goold (Groton, Mass., 1973) and the emendations published by R. G. M. Nisbet, *PCPS* NS 24 (1978), 91 ff.

[19] Clausen, 37–41, suggesting 1–50 as the *libellus* dedicated to Cornelius Nepos. On the division of poems in V (often defective), cf. Mynors (OCT), xiv–xv.

CELSUS

De medicina, the lone survivor of Celsus' four *Artes,* is mentioned only twice between Quintilian and s. XV, *c.* 990 by Gerbert of Reims (Pope Silvester II)[1] and *c.*1300 by Simon of Genoa (physician to Pope Nicholas IV). Two of the three manuscripts that antedate s. XV may account for both mentions: Paris lat. 7028 (P) was written by 'sacer Johannes', probably Johannes Philagathus (abbot of Nonantola from 982, later bishop of Piacenza, and in 997–8 Antipope John XVI), who taught Gerbert's master Otto III; and Florence, Laur. 73.1 (F, s. IX) proclaims itself 'liber monasterii Sancti Ambrosii Mediolanensis',[2] where Simon of Genoa could have seen it. P, which in s. XV belonged to St. Hilary Poitiers, was copied from the other medieval manuscript, Vatican lat. 5951 (V, s. IX[1], northern Italy[3]), before it lost a gathering and the last leaf.

F came to light in 1427, and V too was copied in s. XV;[4] but most of the fifteenth-century manuscripts, which number more than twenty, owe the staple of their text to a lost manuscript (S) first heard of at Siena in 1426, when Panormita described its appearance as 'prae vetustate venerabilis'.[5] S had leaves missing when Niccoli copied from it, before the end of 1427, Florence, Laur. 73.7 (J); in 1431 he filled from F as many of the gaps as he could. The last editor, F. Marx, maintained for reasons of varying weight that the other descendants of S all derive from J;[6] Sabbadini, who laid the foundations on which Marx built,[7] made no such claim but equally made none to the contrary beyond assuming that Battista Pallavicini corrected F from S itself in 1465.[8]

[1] F. Weigle, *Die Briefsammlung Gerberts von Reims* (Weimar, 1966), *Ep.* 169, written, according to Weigle, at Reims early in 990.

[2] The second word was deciphered by G. Billanovich, whose account of the tradition in *Settimane,* 22.1 (1975), 321–42, not only contributes valuable details, especially about the history of F, but also makes easier and livelier reading than the latest editor's preface (*Corpus medicorum latinorum,* i, Leipzig, 1915), where the wood cannot be seen for the trees.

[3] Information on date and provenance kindly supplied by Bernhard Bischoff.

[4] Vatican lat. 5951–63 all entered the Vatican Library from the same collection, and 5953 has annotations by Pietro Leoni, physician to Lorenzo de' Medici; see J. Ruysschaert, *Bull. Acad. Roy. Belg.* sér. v, 46 (1960), 37–65, esp. 56. Did he own V?

[5] Nothing known about S or any other manuscript bears out Vespasiano's assertion that Poggio found Celsus during the Council of Constance. Manitius, *Handschriften,* 90, reports a manuscript at Montecassino from a fifteenth-century catalogue, but it need not have been old.

[6] Some of his reasons carry no weight at all. The manuscripts that most need investigating are Perugia D.57 and Munich Clm 5328.

[7] *SIFC* 8 (1900), 1–32 = *Storia e critica*[2], 215–37. When Sabbadini had called the lost manuscript S and Niccoli's copy N, it was churlish and foolish of Marx to use one symbol, and J at that, for both, to say nothing of substituting F for L.

[8] The corrections actually came from Vatican lat. 2371, written by Pallavicini before 1447 (Sabbadini, 7–8 = 220–1). Marx's attempt to dissociate this manuscript from Pallavicini (pp.

By coincidence FV and J have overlapping lacunae in book 4. The lacuna common to FVJ was diagnosed by Egnatius in 1528, its content divined by Morgagni in 1721, and its length calculated by Marx from transpositions in FV and Niccoli's statements about S; Marx also observed that part of the missing passage lay behind an interpolation in two manuscripts of Muscio, F (the very same) and Brussels 3701–15 (s. IX/X). The whole passage has now turned up in a hitherto unexamined manuscript, Toledo 97.12 (T), written in s. XV²/₄ by Jacobus de Hollandia; its discovery was announced independently by D. Ollero and U. Capitani.[9] According to Capitani, the end of T derives from F, the rest from S by a route independent of J.[10]

Marx showed that an ancestor of J was a relative of FV into which readings had been imported from a manuscript in many respects superior; the most alarming of the numerous misunderstandings that the interlinear variants later gave rise to occurs at 8.2.6, where

ad ossi
pernicissimum est

(i.e. ad perniciossissimum est) has become per alias os si in J (Marx, p. lx). The stemma is therefore uncertain,[11] but for editorial purposes it amounts to FV/J. Critics before and after Marx who have thought FV more honest than J win support from an indirect tradition already attested in s. VII by Paris lat. 10233 + Berne F 219.3 (CLA v.592).[12]

The editio princeps (Florence, 1478) was prepared by Bartolomeo Fonzio from Florence, Laur. 73.4, which his brother Niccolò wrote and he himself corrected from F.[13] Marx has no competitor, but both Baader and Capitani promise editions.

M. D. R.

lvi–lvii) is perverse and futile: the words at first omitted by 'F man. rec.' at p. 239.26–7 (Marx) form a single line in Vatican lat. 2371.

[9] Emerita, 41 (1973), 99–108; Maia, 26 (1974), 161–205. On the scribe and his date see Silvia Rizzo, RFIC 104 (1976), 117–20.

[10] 166 nn. 15, 18–20. Ollero, Emerita, 45 (1977), 65–72, says little of moment where he agrees with Capitani and nothing where he disagrees.

[11] Marx puts J near F on p. lxii but not in his stemma on p. 16.

[12] On this see M. Niedermann, RPh 59 (1933), 18–20. Literature on the relative merits of FV and J is cited by G. Baader, 'Überlieferungsprobleme des A. Cornelius Celsus', Forschungen und Fortschritte, 34 (1960), 215–18.

[13] A. C. de la Mare, 'The library of Francesco Sassetti', Cultural Aspects of the Italian Renaissance: Essays in honour of P. O. Kristeller, ed. C. H. Clough (Manchester, 1976), 188 no. 78.

CENSORINUS

The text of Censorinus, *De die natali* as it has come down to us is actually parts of two works: chapters 1–24 of *De die natali*, with the remainder of the work missing, followed without a break by fifteen chapters of another work by a different author (numbered as Frag. 1–15 in the editions). This conflation may be at least as old as the sixth century. The text is based on a single manuscript of the eighth century from which the rest of the tradition stems, Cologne, Dombibl. 166 (Darmst. 2191) (*CLA* VIII.1160) (D), containing Fortunatianus, *De arte rhetorica*, Augustine, *De rhetorica* and *De principiis dialecticae*, Victorinus, *In rhetoricam M. T. Ciceronis*, Censorinus, *De die natali*. It was written, according to Lowe, 'in a Continental centre under insular influence' and bears a ninth-century *ex libris* of Cologne Cathedral. D was carefully corrected at an early date. For the texts of Fortunatianus and Augustine, D is closely related to, if not the parent of, the great ninth-century collection of rhetorical texts now in the Bodmer Library.[1]

Two important early texts of Censorinus are thought to descend, directly or at one remove, from D. Vatican, Pal. lat. 1588 (P), s. IX[1], written at Lorsch, is a direct copy of the whole of D, containing the five works in the same order. P itself does not appear to have been copied. The second, Vatican lat. 4929 (V), s. IX[2], containing Censorinus, a unique epitome of Augustine, *De musica*, four anonymous sermons, Ps.-Plautus, *Aulularia sive Querolus*, Julius Paris' *Epitome* of Valerius Maximus, *Septem mira*, Pomponius Mela, *De chorographia*, and Vibius Sequester, *De fluminibus*, was written in France and belonged to Heiric of Auxerre, who was probably responsible for assembling the collection.[2] Of the works contained in V, only for Censorinus does an ancestor survive. There is some disagreement over whether or not V is a direct copy of D; Billanovich has suggested quite plausibly that Heiric was using a copy of D rather than D itself. This matter cannot be resolved until we have a detailed comparison of the texts of Censorinus in V, D, and P. V itself was corrected twice, once by Heiric, probably from the exemplar, and a second time by an unknown grammar master of the late eleventh or early twelfth century in Orléans, whose corrections do not represent a manuscript source.

The standard editions are those of O. Jahn (Berlin, 1845) and F. Hultsch (Leipzig, 1867). R. M. T. has recently published a survey of the medieval transmission and use of Censorinus: 'The Reception of Censorinus' *De Die Natali* in Pre-Renaissance Europe', *Antichthon*, 14 (1980), 177–84.

[1] G. Billanovich, 'Il Petrarca e i retori latini minori', *IMU* 5 (1962), 103–64.
[2] C. W. Barlow, 'Codex Vaticanus latinus 4929', *MAAR* 15 (1939), 87–124; G. Billanovich, 'Dall' antica Ravenna alle biblioteche umanistiche', *Aevum*, 30 (1956), 319–62.

V had passed to Orléans by the tenth century; it was used there by the compiler of the *Florilegium Angelicum* for Julius Paris, the *Querolus*, and Censorinus. The brief excerpt from Censorinus which concludes the *Florilegium Angelicum* in several manuscripts is the source of some confusion. Richard de Fournival, describing (in his *Biblionomia*, no. 84) his copy of the *Florilegium Angelicum*, seems to attribute it to Censorinus. And Manitius, Beeson, and Ullman, attempting to identify the Censorinus mentioned in Hadoard's ninth-century florilegium, equated his Censorinus with Fournival's and made of him a ninth-century ghost compiler of a proverb collection and a florilegium.[3] Nevertheless, Censorinus' name was given some currency in the later Middle Ages through the ten or more manuscripts of the *Florilegium Angelicum* that carried his name.[4]

V and the Censorinus in it were used in Orléans by the thirteenth-century annotator of Berne 276 (see ff. 89ᵛ, 142 for Censorinus). By the beginning of the fourteenth century a text of Censorinus descended from V was available in England. British Library, Harley 3969 contains numerous classical and late antique texts, including the florilegium of William of Malmesbury (the *Polyhistor*), William's collection of grammatical manuals, and works by Apuleius, as well as Censorinus. Censorinus appears again in England, in the early fourteenth-century catalogue of Lanthony Priory (Glos.): 'Censorius de natali die, liber mediocris in rubeo corio', presumably also a descendant of V.

V, or a copy of it, came into Petrarch's hands by 1335. But, although we know that Petrarch had the geographical corpus contained in Vat. lat. 4929, it is not certain whether his copy contained Censorinus or not. Censorinus does not circulate in Italy until the early fifteenth century, by which date V itself is in Italy.

In addition to P and V, a third line of descent from D exists for chapter 13 only, which was inserted into an anonymous ninth-century German treatise on geometry. The treatise survives in five manuscripts of German origin, four of which contain the excerpt: Munich Clm 13084 (s. IX ex., Freising); Clm 6406 (c.1000), at Freising in the eleventh century and perhaps written there; Clm 14836 (s. XII in., Würzburg?): and Vienna 51 (s. XII in.), German, of unknown origin.[5] A thorough study of the other sources used in this treatise might serve to localize more precisely its place of composition.

Finally, there are brief extracts from Censorinus in three early manuscripts. Leiden, Voss. Lat. O.79 (s. IX ex.), written perhaps around Reims and later belonging to Fleury, contains Cicero, *De senect.*, untitled

---

[3] R. H. and M. A. Rouse, 'The Florilegium Angelicum', in *Medieval Learning*, 66–114.

[4] One might note also that Adam of Petit Pont's *Ars disserendi* (a. 1132) reflects a passage from Censorinus chap. 23, though not verbatim; ed. L. Minio-Paluello (Rome, 1956), 109–10.

[5] The fifth, Sélestat 17 (s. X in., St. Gall), does not contain the chapter from Censorinus.

excerpts from Augustine, (ff. 30–1) Censorinus 13.1–5 (untitled), anon. *De supinis verbis,* Marius Plotius Sacerdos, *De metris,* brief patristic excerpts, and Servius, *De centum metris.* This excerpt from Censorinus derives from the lost exemplar of V, a copy of D. Berne 87 (a. 1004), written by Constantius, priest of St. Peter's abbey church in Luxeuil, contains Boethius, *De geometria* and a series of late antique and Carolingian works on geometry and land-measurement; both the Boethius and some of the gromatic works were used by the author of the treatise on geometry discussed above. After Constantius' colophon, but still in his hand, is Frag. 5–8 entitled 'Ex libro Censorini de geo-metrica'. The same excerpt is found in another manuscript with much the same contents, Cambridge, Trinity College 939 (R. 15.14), s. x, written probably in the region of the Loire, but at St. Augustine's Canterbury by the fifteenth century. This excerpt may derive from a text of Censorinus anterior to D.

The text of Censorinus, *De die natali* was first printed at Bologna in 1497; its modern history begins with the discovery and use of Cologne 166 (D) by L. Carrio in his editions of 1583 and 1593, and the reports of readings from the Cologne manuscript at about this same time by Franz Modius.

R. H. R.
R. M. T.

CHARISIUS

The text of Charisius' *Ars grammatica,* completed in the late fourth century, rests on a manuscript written on reused parchment at Bobbio in the early eighth century (N), a copy of this manuscript made in the early sixteenth century after it had been rediscovered, and a handful of fragments and excerpts descended from a lost congener of the Bobbio manuscript. Because of its haphazard transmission, the first book is lacking its introduction, the fourth has lacunae, and the fifth is largely lacking.[1]

[1] Ed. H. Keil, *Grammatici latini,* i (Leipzig, 1857), and C. Barwick (Leipzig, 1925), annotated by F. Kühnert (Leipzig, 1964). The fullest account of Charisius' transmission is provided by C. Barwick, 'Zur Geschichte und Rekonstruktion des Charisius-Textes', *Hermes,* 59 (1924), 322–55, 420–9; see also A. C. Dionisotti, 'On Bede, Grammars, and Greek', *Rev. bén.* 92 (1982), 111–41. N preserves part of the first chapter of book 5; but Barwick was surely wrong in assuming that most of the rest of N's contents also belonged to book 5.

Naples IV.A.8 (*CLA* III.400) (N) was written presumably at Bobbio in the early eighth century, on parchment from a group of sixth-century uncial manuscripts that once contained Chronicles, the *Digest,* and Gargilius Martialis, *De re rustica,* reused to make up a codex of more immediate necessity containing ancient grammar: Charisius, Servius, *De centum metris,* and the patristic *Liber pontificalis.* The manuscript evidently remained at Bobbio through the Middle Ages. Bypassed there, N was not copied until it was discovered and removed to Naples, by G. Merula in 1493.[2] From him it passed to Antonio Seripando (d. 1531), and then to the latter's brother Girolamo, Archbishop of Naples (d. 1563), who left it with the rest of his library to the Augustinians of S. Giovanni a Carbonara in Naples.

Extracts from Charisius appear in one other Bobbio manuscript: Milan, Ambros. L.22 sup., which was written at Bobbio in the tenth century. The tenth-century inventory of Bobbio books refers to yet another copy: '[434] librum Sosipatris I. [i.e. Charisius] in quo continetur liber differentiarum Plinii' (Becker, 69.32).

The surviving Bobbio text (N) is both difficult to read and deficient in places. Fortunately, it was copied for Parrhasius probably in Milan by G. Galbiato between 1493 and 1497[3] before it began to fall to pieces, to produce Naples IV.A.10 (n), which according to Barwick contains Parrhasius's hand in its margins. And, again according to Barwick, it was a copy of n, Naples IV.A.9, written for Parrhasius in Rome between 1514 and 1522, that was used by Johannes Pierius Cyminus, the first editor of the *Ars grammatica* (Naples, 1532).[4]

That the *Ars grammatica* survives in only one medieval manuscript would, on the surface, suggest that Charisius was not read in the Middle Ages, outside of Bobbio. But this is true only for the period after 1100, when the interests of grammarians had begun to change and the body of ancient grammar to be replaced. In the early Middle Ages, as long as medieval grammatical endeavour rested on the corpus of ancient grammarians, Charisius was known, copied, and read. Evidence of the circulation of his work must be reconstructed from the surviving fragments of codices no longer extant, and from excerpts taken from the texts.

At the head of the medieval dissemination of Charisius stood a single manuscript copied probably at Bobbio and brought north shortly thereafter to a Carolingian house in either France or Germany. Fragments of or extracts from at least four descendants of this manuscript are known. (i) One of these manuscripts must have been at Saint-Benoît of Fleury; extracts from it are seen in two collections of ancient

---

[2] M. Ferrari, *IMU* 13 (1970), 139–162, and D. Gutiérrez, *Analecta Augustiniana,* 29 (1966), 60–2, 76–7.

[3] Ferrari, 150.   [4] Ibid. 164.

and medieval grammar associated with the abbey, Leiden, Voss. Lat.
0.37, written according to Bischoff in the area of the Loire at the end of
the ninth century and bearing what appear to be the remnants of a
Fleury *ex libris*, and Berne 123, written at Fleury in the tenth century.
(ii) Another manuscript was at Reichenau, where it was cut up and
used in late medieval bindings. Parts of three folios survive (*CLA* VIII.
1124 + x, p. 13) from a book written in the late eighth century at some
Anglo-Saxon centre on the Continent. These folios may belong to a
group of fragments of ancient grammatical texts (*CLA* VIII.1125–7,
1129) found in the bindings of Reichenau manuscripts, which according to Lowe may, on the basis of their dimensions and palaeographical
features, come from the same scriptorium, possibly Murbach. (iii)
Another in this group of manuscripts is known only in a mutilated
bifolium, now Jena, Nachlass G. Goetz, Mappe 1 (*CLA* VIII.1227),
written in the late eighth century by the same Irish scribe who wrote the
grammatical fragments now in Würzburg Mp.j.f.5 (*CLA* IX.1399); this
latter, it is thought, may have been taken to Würzburg from the Palace
School by the Irish grammarian Clement. The Jena fragment of
Charisius was brought to Barwick's attention after his edition was
finished, and was only published in his introduction. Lowe suggests
that this fragment may come from the same codex as the fragment once
in Giessen, Univ. 808, reported briefly in 1842. The present location of
the Giessen fragment is not known, and to my knowledge there is no
evidence either of its date or of its association with *CLA* VIII.1227. (iv)
Finally, there is the lost manuscript of Charisius that belonged to the
little-known Dutch scholar Johannes Cuyck, who also owned two
manuscripts of Lucretius and may have owned the only manuscript of
Cornelius Nepos (q.v.) that survived the Middle Ages. Some time
before 1551 Cuyck collated his manuscript with the first printed edition,
entering the variants in his copy, which is now in Heidelberg. Because of
his careful work we know far more about the text of this manuscript
than we do about the other 'lost codices'. The manuscript passed to Fr.
Dousa, and was also used by L. Carrio, Putschius, and A. Schott;
Carrio appears to have seen the old book in Cologne. Unfortunately,
nothing is known about its date or physical appearance.

Two other extensive excerpts from the *Ars grammatica* are known. The
one is found in Paris lat. 7560, a collection of ancient grammar appar
ently written by a woman, Eugenia; according to Bischoff, it was
probably written in France, at some institution under insular influence,
in the third quarter of the ninth century. It was already in the south of
France or Catalonia by the end of that century.[5] The other excerpt is
found in Paris lat. 7530 (*CLA* V.569), a collection of ancient grammar

[5] The manuscript is described by C. Jeudy, 'L'*Ars de nomine et verbo* de Phocas: manuscrits et
commentaires médiévaux', *Viator*, 5 (1974), 129–30.

written at Montecassino between 779 and 797, i.e. during the lifetime of Paul the Deacon. In the fifteenth century it belonged to the church of Benevento. Perhaps a whole text of Charisius was also to be found at Montecassino in the late eighth century.

Further light will be shed on the transmission of Charisius when we have a clearer knowledge of the sources used by early medieval and Carolingian grammarians. Charisius was clearly known to these scholars; but to what degree, and in which instances this was a firsthand knowledge, is not yet established.

R. H. R.

CICERO

Speeches

De inventione, and *Ad Herennium*
De optimo genere oratorum
De oratore, Orator, Brutus
Partitiones oratoriae

Academica posteriora and *De finibus bonorum et malorum*
Cato Maior de senectute
Laelius de amicitia
De natura deorum, De divinatione, Timaeus, De fato, Topica,
 Paradoxa Stoicorum, Academica priora, De legibus
De officiis
De republica
Tusculan Disputations

Epistulae ad Atticum, ad Brutum, ad Quintum fratrem
Epistulae ad familiares

Speeches

1

Of the hundred-odd speeches that Cicero is known to have delivered
between 81 BC and his death in 43, not all have travelled the long road
from the forum to the libraries of the present day. Some never appeared
before the reading public at all. Others, including one that began its
journey without Cicero's blessing (*Ad Att.* 3.12.2, 15.3), reached the
fifth century but not the Middle Ages.[1] We might know why not if
we knew what company they had been keeping, but information is
meagre.[2]

True, scholars soon set out to establish the chronological order of the
speeches: Asconius in his commentary, compiled between AD 54 and 57,

---

[1] Towards AD 400 Arusianus Messius, whose *exempla elocutionum* come only from Virgil, Sallust,
Terence, and Cicero, cites most of the extant speeches and also *Pro Cornelio, Pro Oppio, Cum quaestor
Lilybaeo decederet,* and *Cum a ludis contionem avocavit.* Fragments and titles are collected by F. Schoell
in vol. viii of the Teubner Cicero (1918) and by G. Puccioni in the Mondadori Cicero (1963).

[2] Furthermore, as J. E. G. Zetzel says in *HSCP* 77 (1973), 230 n. 21, 'the composition of the
various collections of Cicero's speeches in antiquity is a problem that has not been adequately
studied'. We have found nothing on the subject except P. Hildebrandt, *De scholiis Ciceronis
Bobiensibus* (Berlin, 1894), 10–32.

treats the speeches in order of delivery and already has one false dating to contend with (*In Pisonianam*, 1); the first or second of the surviving speeches *De lege agraria* was dated and numbered 24 by Statilius Maximus (s. II²) or a predecessor;³ and the grammarian Diomedes cites an expression from 'causarum decimo tertio' (*GLK* 1.368.28–9).⁴ As long as chronological schemes remained available, therefore, anyone might assemble a chronological collection of speeches. None is recorded, however, let alone any anterior to the chronological schemes. The much canvassed edition of Cicero's secretary Tiro is a modern figment,⁵ and without Asconius' preface we cannot tell what he was doing (if it was he and not a later reader) when he referred to passages of a speech 'circa vers. LXXX' or 'cir(ca) ver(sum) a nov(issimo) DCLX'.

The evidence that we have suggests collections of much more modest scope. In 60 BC Cicero departed from his amply attested practice of publishing speeches singly, and arranged for a collected edition of his consular speeches (*Ad Att.* 2.1.3); Pliny the Elder may have used it (*NH* 7.116–17), but four of the twelve have perished, and another four, as will emerge in a moment, often circulated on their own. What we call the *Second Philippic* was already the *Second Philippic* to Juvenal (10.125–6), and other writers refer to the set as *Antonianae*. Grammarians cite the four *Catilinarians* (included in the edition of 60 BC) as *invectivae*, and *Pro Marcello, Pro Ligario,* and *Pro rege Deiotaro* as *Caesarianae*.

Papyri cannot be expected to shed much light on the matter, because fragments seldom represent enough of a volume. It does not look like coincidence, however, that of the seven papyri so far discovered (one of s. I² BC/AD I¹, the rest of s. IV–VI) three have part of the *Catilinarians*, three part of the *Verrines*.⁶ Two of the former and one of the latter were used in teaching Latin to speakers of Greek, and there are other indications that the *Catilinarians* were a school text;⁷ the *Verrines* are so long anyway that they cannot often have shared a volume with other speeches. Only

³ 'Acta ipso Cicerone et Antonio coss. oratio xxiiii. Statilius Maximus rursum emendavi . . .': Vatican lat. 11458, f. 56ᵛ. On the whole subscription see Zetzel, 225–43.

⁴ Aldhelm must be using a lost grammarian when he cites 'Cicero in libro XV' (= *Verr.* II.5) and 'Cicero in libro XIII' (= *Verr.* II.4). See M. Manitius, *SAWW* 112 (1886), 601.

⁵ Its origin lies in Gellius' remarks about Tironian copies of Cicero (1.7.1, 13.21.16). Zetzel rightly takes these remarks with a pinch of salt.

⁶ As all the papyri of Cicero have been listed, discussed, and illustrated by R. Seider, 'Beiträge zur Geschichte und Paläographie der antiken Cicerohandschriften', *Bibl. und Wiss.* 13 (1979), 101–49, it would be superfluous to say more about them here than that the Giessen fragment of the *Verrines*, P. Iand. 90, which Seider dates to s. AD I¹ and others half a century earlier, is the oldest witness to any Latin text preserved in medieval manuscripts (see GALLUS for an even older witness to one that is not).

⁷ They are used in the Latin–Greek glossary of 'Philoxenus', edited by M. L. W. Laistner in *Glossaria Latina*, ii (Paris, 1926); see his remarks on p. 133. The bronze of a Gallic schoolmaster (s. III/IV?) described and illustrated by M. Passelac, *Rev. arch. de Narbonnaise*, 5 (1972), 185–90, has the opening of *Catil.* 1 engraved on it. R. M. Ogilvie, *The Library of Lactantius* (Oxford, 1978), 71–2, shows that the 'Christian Cicero' knew *Catil.* and *Verr.* but otherwise only *Pro Marcello.* Jerome's reading was not so narrow; see H. Hagendahl, *Latin Fathers and the Classics* (Göteborg, 1958), 285.

British Library, P. Lit. Lond. 143 (s. v; *CLA* ii.210) has parts of unrelated speeches: *Pro lege Manilia,* the *Verrines,* and *Pro Caelio,* an odd assortment.

All the papyri except the earliest come from a codex, not from a roll. The codex was tailor-made for collections, and since parchment, if it survives at all, tends to survive more substantially than in the scraps to which papyrologists are inured, it is not surprising that three of the seven parchment manuscripts preserved from Antiquity should contain parts of unrelated speeches. All three are palimpsest.[8]

(1) A. Mai discovered in a seventh-century manuscript of Sedulius from Bobbio, Milan, Ambros. R. 57 sup. (now S. P. 11.66), 11½ reused leaves of a fifth-century Cicero in rustic capitals (*CLA* iii.362–3): 6 leaves of *Pro Scauro,* 3½ of *Pro Tullio,* 1 of *Pro Flacco,* and 1 of *Pro Caelio.* He published a text of the first three speeches and a collation of the fourth (Milan and Rome, 1814).

(2) In 1773 P. J. Bruns discovered in a manuscript of the Old Testament, Vatican, Pal. lat. 24 (s. vii/viii, at Lorsch by s. ix), palimpsest fragments of ten ancient books, eight of them classical. With the aid of *'hydrosulphureum* (quod vocant) *potassae'* B. G. Niebuhr deciphered fr. 10, which contains parts of *Pro Rabirio perduellionis reo*[9] and *Pro Roscio Amerino* (s. v, uncial; *CLA* i.77). Like Mai, he published a text of the new material and a collation of the old (Rome, 1820).

(3) In 1820 A. Peyron discovered 56 palimpsest leaves in Turin D.iv.22, a seventh-century manuscript of Augustine from Bobbio. By a chemical process apparently more complicated than Niebuhr's he brought out the text underneath, which turned out to include passages from ten of Cicero's speeches: 5 leaves of *Pro Caecina,* 8½ of *Pro Tullio,* 4½ of *Pro Scauro,* 3 of *Pro Quinctio,* 6½ of *In Pisonem,* 1 of *Pro lege Manilia,* 12 of *Pro Cluentio,* 5 of *Pro Milone,* 3½ of *Pro Caelio,* and 1 of *In Clodium,* all from the same book (s. v, rustic capitals; renumbered A.ii.2*; *CLA* iv.442). Again, he published a text of the new material and a collation of the old (Stuttgart and Tübingen, 1824). Some photographs were taken before the manuscript was destroyed in the fire of 1904.

None of these as it survives presents a chronological group of speeches, and the Turin palimpsest could only have done so if it was a complete corpus, because it ranges from 81 BC (*Pro Quinctio*) to 52 (*Pro Milone*). Of the other four parchment fragments, one is a leaf of *Pro Plancio* (Berlin (East), Aegyptisches Museum P. 13229 A + B, s. v, uncial; *CLA* viii.1043), the second a palimpsest leaf of *Pro Fonteio* (Vatican, Pal. lat.

[8] Seider's article (n. 6, above) embraces palimpsests too. On (3) see especially C. Cipolla, *Codici Bobbiesi della Biblioteca Nazionale Universitaria di Torino* (Milan, 1907), 18–22, 36–45, plates ii–v.

[9] Seider, 112, misses *Rab. perd.* 16–19, also part of this manuscript. For a detailed description see J. Fohlen, *Scrittura e civiltà* 3 (1979), 195–222, esp. 218–20.

24, fr. 9, s. V, uncial; *CLA* I.76), the third a palimpsest leaf of the *Verrines* (Turin A.II. 2*, s. V/VI, rustic capitals; *CLA* IV.445), and the fourth a more substantial palimpsest of the *Verrines* (Vatican, Reg. lat. 2077, s. V, rustic capitals; *CLA* I.115).

The parchment fragments demand a brief but important digression. Unlike the papyri, they supply texts missing from the medieval manuscripts: they reduce gaps in *Pro Fonteio* (§ 4, below) and *Pro Flacco* (§§ 4, 9, below), together with Asconius' commentary they provide us with what we have of *Pro Scauro*, in *Pro Tullio* they stand alone, and the *Scholia Bobiensia* add little to the one leaf of *In Clodium* in the Turin palimpsest.[10] A few more palimpsests, of course, and there would have been no medieval manuscripts of any speeches at all. Four of the palimpsests are also extensive enough to be valuable witnesses to the text of speeches preserved in medieval manuscripts: (1) – (3) and the Vatican palimpsest of the *Verrines*. Apart perhaps from the last (§ 3, below), none of them can be associated with any family of medieval manuscripts that editors have defined.

To resume, some of the manuscripts that survived the Dark Ages seem likely to have presented a random or apparently random collection of speeches, and their contents no doubt overlapped. Though Carolingian scholars may have produced new combinations, however, they will scarcely have had the means to establish a chronological arrangement, and so if such an arrangement appears in medieval manuscripts it may be supposed to have come down from Antiquity. Appear it does, in one of the earliest manuscripts extant; and with that manuscript our survey of the medieval tradition may begin.

2

Paris lat. 7794 (P, s. IX[1]; Chatelain, plate XXIII) contains the spurious *Pridie quam in exilium iret*[11] and then *Post reditum ad senatum, Post reditum ad populum, De domo, Pro Sestio, In Vatinium, De provinciis consularibus, De haruspicum responso, Pro Balbo,* and *Pro Caelio.* All nine speeches belong to

---

[10] A. C. Clark edited both *Tull.* and *Scaur.* in OCT vi (1911); for *Tull.* see also F. Schoell in vol. iv of the Teubner (1923), H. de la Ville de Mirmont in vol. ii of the Budé *Discours* (1922), and G. Garuti in the Mondadori Cicero (1965); and for *Scaur.* Schoell in vol. vii of the Teubner (1919), P. Grimal in vol. xvi.2 of the Budé *Discours* (1976), and A. Ghiselli in the Mondadori Cicero (1975). Fragments of *In Clodium*: Schoell, Teubner viii. 447–8. On the *Scholia Bobiensia* see ASCONIUS.

[11] Billanovich, *Studi e testi,* 124 (1946), 99 n. 41, comes near to suggesting that Petrarch saw through it, which if he knew it (cf. n. 20, below) may well be so: its authenticity is questioned by contemporary annotators of two manuscripts written in the region of Padua within forty years of his death, Vatican, Pal. lat. 1476, f. 70ᵛ 'mentitur qui dicit huius orationis autorem fuisse Ciceronem' and 1478, f. 135ᵛ (Sicco Polenton) 'sunt tamen qui hanc orationem a Cicerone non emanasse quod Tullianam eloquentiam non sapiat suspicentur' (We owe this information to Silvia Rizzo's unpublished descriptions of manuscripts that contain *Pro Cluentio*). Naugerius

the years 57–56. This fact and the pattern of the transmission strongly
suggest that one manuscript of the same content as P survived the Dark
Ages.[12]

P is written in several good Tours hands,[13] but its whereabouts in the
Middle Ages are unknown until it was given to the Collège de Montagu
in Paris by Joachim Perion (1497–1559), a monk of Cormery and
student of classical literature.[14] It bears two sets of corrections, one
roughly contemporary and the other of s. XV/XVI. Berne 136 was copied
from it in s. XII med. and shortly thereafter used by the compiler of the
Florilegium Angelicum, a collection of extracts from ancient and patristic
letters and speeches made at Orléans;[15] at the end of s. XIV the speeches
in Berne 136 were copied for Nicholas de Clamanges (*c.*1355–1437) into
Paris lat. 14749, which was given by Simon de Plumetot (1371–1443) to
the abbey of Saint-Victor and there sired a number of French descendants.[16]

A second line of descent (Y) is reconstructed from two manuscripts
which derive from an insular parent.[17] Brussels 5345 (G), containing
Pridie, Sen., Pop., Cael., Dom., Sest., Vat., Balb., the *Caesarians, Prov., Har.,*
was probably written for Olbert, Abbot of Gembloux 1012–48, who
rebuilt the Gembloux library.[18] Berlin (West) lat. 2° 252 (E), containing
a large collection of Cicero, among which the speeches appear in the
same sequence as in P except that *Vat.* comes first,[19] was written for
Wibald, Abbot (1130–58) of Stavelot near Gembloux and later also
Abbot of Corvey (1146–58). Wibald and Olbert were in all probability

relegated it to the back of his edition (Venice, 1534) as 'oratio Ciceronis, si credendum est tam
inepte Ciceronem locutum' (p. 835), and Lambinus did the same (Paris, 1565) with the blunter
comment 'plane non est Ciceronis' (p. 849); it was last edited from manuscripts by Orelli–Baiter–
Halm, ii.2 (Zürich, 1856), 1412–20. Altogether it has aroused remarkably little curiosity; no
mention in W. Speyer, *Die literarische Fälschung im Altertum* (Munich, 1971).

[12] The speeches were edited by W. Peterson in vol. v of the OCT (1911, without *Cael.*) and by
A. Klotz in vol. vii of the Teubner (1919); Peterson had already discussed the tradition in *CQ* 4
(1910), 167–71, Klotz in *RhM* 67 (1912), 358–90, and 68 (1913), 477–511. They are divided
among vols. xiii–xv of the Budé *Discours* (1952–66), edited by P. Wuilleumier, J. Cousin, and
A.-M. Tupet. For the Mondadori Cicero J. Guillén has edited *Sen.* (1967, badly), V. Cremona *Vat.*
(1970), and G. C. Giardina *Balb.* (1971). Tralatician and selective collations have hampered the
textual study of these speeches, and Giardina's *Balb.* may well give, as he claims, the first full and
reliable report of the main manuscripts. A new Teubner of *Sen., Pop., Dom.,* and *Har.* is announced,
edited by T. Maslowski; he might have included *Pridie* and reminded classical scholars of its
existence.   [13] We owe this ascription to Bernhard Bischoff.
[14] R. H. and M. A. Rouse, in *Medieval Learning,* 75 n. 3.
[15] Rouse and Rouse, 66–114, esp. 75–6, 96–7.
[16] On these descendants of P see Peterson, *CQ* 4 (1910), 168–9. His proof that Paris lat. 14749
derives from Berne 136 is of a kind that everyone who deals with manuscripts would like to
discover at least once in his life. For Simon de Plumetot see G. Ouy in *Miscellanea codicologica
F. Masai dicata* (Ghent, 1979), ii.353–81, esp. 378.
[17] Klotz, *RhM* 67 (1912), 369–70.
[18] On Olbert see A. Boutemy, *Ann. de la Soc. arch. de Namur,* 41 (1934), 43–85.
[19] *Dom.* and *Sest.* are now missing with the end of *Pop.* and the beginning of *Prov.,* but the table of
contents has them. Vatican, Pal. lat. 1525 (a. 1467, Heidelberg) can be used instead.

drawing on a manuscript at the old insular centre of Liège. It would therefore be interesting to know something about the text of *Pridie* that Petrarch took from a manuscript at Liège in 1333; his copy is lost, but descendants may survive.[20]

By some means, readings from the Y tradition are added in the margins of P by its first corrector.[21] In addition, four other rather corrupt witnesses to Y are known. Berne 395, which contains *Pridie*, *Sen.*, *Pop.*, and the *Caesarians*, was written in Germany in s. XIII[2]; its precise relationship to Y is not yet clear, because it has not been formally reported, but it does not descend from either G or E. Troyes 552, a large collection of Cicero's works once owned by Petrarch, contains *Pop.* 1–23 and *Sen.* 1–7 in an Italian hand of s. XIV[1].[22] Two closely related manuscripts written not far from Liège, Brussels 14492 (s. XIV[2]/XV[1], Le Parc) and Cambridge, Univ. Dd. 13. 2 (a. 1444, Cologne), took their text of *Cael.* from a descendant of Y.[23]

What may be a third line of descent is represented by another manuscript known to Petrarch, British Library, Harley 4927 (h[24]), which contains *Catil.*, pseudo-Sall./Cic. *Invect.*, *Pridie*, *Sen.*, *Pop.*, *Dom.*, *Paradoxa*, *Vat.*, *Cael.*, *Balb.*, *Har.*, *Prov.*, *Sest.*, the *Caesarians*, *De amicitia*, *De senectute* (opening words only). It was written in the area of the Loire in s. XII med., and after Petrarch jotted notes in its margins it became the parent of a sizeable family of *recentiores*.[25] Its text of the speeches that concern us here is not a straightforward transcript but has been pruned. Though the *recentiores* variously patch up this text from a source related to GE, some of the havoc wrought by h was not undone in print before the sixteenth century; *Vat.* suffered worst and longest.[26] Editors have

---

[20] That *Pridie* was the speech copied at Liège 'manu amici' is only Clark's conjecture, OCT vi (1911), v–vii; but no alternative suggests itself.

[21] Both the date and the readings of P[2] have been much discussed. H. Wrampelmeyer, *Librorum manuscriptorum qui Ciceronis orationes pro Sestio et pro Caelio continent ratio qualis sit demonstratur* (Detmold, 1868), first vindicated its authority against K. Halm, *RhM* 9 (1854), 321–50, but disagreement persists about its relationship to GE; J. Cousin even disagrees with himself (Budé xv. 93, 95).

[22] Curiously, Salutati knew only as much of *Pop.* as is in Troyes 552 but the whole of *Sen.*; see F. Novati, *Epistolario di Coluccio Salutati*, i (Rome, 1891), 332–3. Wolfenbüttel, Gud. lat. 2 (s. XIV, Italy), for many of its contents a close relative of Troyes 552, once contained *Sen.*: see P. L. Schmidt, *Die Überlieferung von Ciceros Schrift 'De legibus'* (Munich, 1974), 177–9.

[23] For more on these terrible twins see §5, below. The text of the spurious *Pridie* (1–14) in Rouen 1040 (s. XII med.) and Oxford, Bodl. Lat. class. e. 48 (s. XII[2]/XIII[1]) derives from Y; for the background of these two manuscripts see below on the *Caesarians* (§3). Paris lat. 5721 and 5755, French manuscripts of s. XIV[2]/XV[1], owe *Prid. Sen. Pop.* to Y.

[24] Editors call it H, but we take the liberty of reducing the letter so that H can be used later for a more important Harleianus.

[25] E. Pellegrin and G. Billanovich, *Scriptorium*, 8 (1954), 115–17; cf. Peterson (edn.), x, xi n. 1. Only the earlier annotator (s. XII ex.) alters the text.

[26] The circulation of these speeches in Italy and France after Petrarch, whether in the version of h or supplemented, has not been studied. One thing that needs explaining is why several manuscripts of *Sen.* break off at 12 *malum gemeretis nihil* (e.g. Paris lat. 6342, written in 1376); did Petrarch find this fragment of *Sen.* with *Pridie* at Liège in 1333?

disagreed as to whether the good readings in h represent an independent witness to the archetype or merely felicitous conjecture in a P text.[27]

Further argument about the relationship of PGEP[2] h will be a waste of ink if editors continue to ignore Leiden, Voss. Lat. F. 67, part I, ff. 1–2 (L), a single bifolium containing *Sest.* 88–99 which was written *c*.860 in the area of the Loire.[28] Since there is no evidence that *Sest.* circulated independently, L is presumably a fragment of a manuscript that like PGEh contained all nine speeches. It has roughly contemporary corrections and others of s. XVI/XVII. Without a close inspection of P, where the adjustments of P[2] may not all have been noticed, the most that can be said about the relationship of L to PGEh is that L[1] appears to share errors with G.[29]

When the relationship of PGEP[2]hL has been worked out, the text of the *Florilegium Gallicum* may fall into place. This large collection of extracts from ancient authors, compiled probably at Orléans in the middle of s. XII and preserved in at least six manuscripts, contains extracts from *Pridie, Sest., Cael., Pop., Vat., Dom., Prov., Har., Balb.*;[30] perhaps the compiler found nothing to his liking in *Sen.*, the only speech of the group missing. These extracts must descend from an old manuscript of the speeches in one of the Loire houses, quite possibly from L when it was still complete: the extract from *Sest.* 99 is marked as a *notabile* in L.

In summary, these speeches appear to have come to France, perhaps to the Carolingian court, in the late eighth or early ninth century, from an insular centre (probably on the Continent), since the main lines of descent show varying degrees of insular influence.[31] A copy of this manuscript went to Tours, where it produced P. Another copy went to Liège, where it was copied twice by scribes who had difficulty with insular abbreviations, to produce G and E. A third line, if it does not stem from the first family, emerges in the twelfth century in h. L remains to be placed in this pattern of diffusion.[32]

Independent traditions exist for two of the speeches that we have been considering. A German tradition first seen in s. XII supplies good

---

[27] Baehrens, *RPh* 8 (1884), 33–9, first pressed the claims of h. An article on it by T. Maslowski is forthcoming in *RhM* 125 (1982). Guillén in his edition of *Sen.* seriously misreports it.

[28] Bischoff ap. K. A. de Meyier, *Codices Vossiani Latini, I: codices in folio* (Leiden, 1973), 130. J. A. Bake, *Scholica hypomnemata*, i (Leiden, 1837), 191–2, published a collation. R. H. R. has a photograph.

[29] e.g. 89 *corroboratas* for *corroborata*, 91 *disputatos* for *dissupatos*, 94 *Numenium* for *Numerium, ne* for *nec*, 95 *diem* omitted. E is missing hereabouts, and recent editors do not report its relative Vatican, Pal. lat. 1525 (cf. n. 19, above).

[30] They have not yet been published.

[31] Attempts at working out the line-lengths of various ancestors were made by Klotz and by Clark, *The Descent of Manuscripts* (Oxford, 1918), 266–80.

[32] Radbertus borrows *Sest.* 15 *ex omnium scelerum colluvione* in his *Epitaphium Arsenii*, written at Corbie in the late 840s; see E. Dümmler's edition, *AKAWB* 1899–1900, II. 71.

readings in *Post reditum ad senatum* (§ 6, below), and some of these are confirmed by Paris lat. 18104, part III, a small anthology compiled in northern France, probably at Chartres, towards the end of s. XII.[33] *Pro Caelio* was one of five speeches in Poggio's Cluniacensis (§ 10, below), and there are two palimpsests and a papyrus (§ 1, above).

3

That the corpus of 57–56 BC passed through the Carolingian court is no more than a conjecture. What the court certainly possessed, if the catalogue in question is rightly assigned to the court,[34] was the following: 'In Catelena Ciceronis libri VII. Deiotaro rege. Incipit Verrem actio M. Tulli Ciceronis. Incipit Verrem libri VIII'. With few exceptions, the texts in the catalogue had been common in Antiquity and were to remain so. This list of Ciceronian speeches reflects in two of its three constituents, the *Catilinarians* and the *Verrines*, what we saw to have been the Ciceronian syllabus of provincial schools in the later Roman Empire. Precisely for that reason, however, no one in the Carolingian renaissance need have had a monopoly, and it is unsafe to assume that all extant manuscripts of the *Catilinarians*, the *Caesarians* (*Marc.*, *Lig.*, *Deiot.*), and the *Verrines* go back to the court. Furthermore, the three texts inaccurately described in the catalogue do not make a natural group in anything but popularity and may therefore have lain before the cataloguer in one, two, or three manuscripts.

The only extant manuscript that has all three texts in the same order is the oldest manuscript that has any of them, British Library, Add. 47678 (C, formerly Holkham Hall 387;[35] Chatelain, plate XXVIIA) + Geneva lat. 169 (one leaf[36]), written like P in a Tours script of s. IX[1].[37] At some later date C passed to Cluny, where it is described in the mid-twelfth-century catalogue of the abbey's books: 'Volumen in quo continetur Cicero in Catillina et idem pro Quinto Ligario et pro rege Deiotaro, et de publicis litteris et de actione, idemque in Verinis.'[38] An erased but legible *ex libris* confirms the identification: *De conventu Clun'*.

[33] T. Maslowski and R. H. Rouse, *IMU* 22 (1979), 97–122.

[34] Bischoff, *Sammelhandschrift Diez. B Sant. 66* (Graz, 1973), 21–3, 39, 219.

[35] It was still there when Peterson brought it to notice in *Anecd. Oxon.* ix (1901), which includes plates. The route by which it arrived there from Cluny has not been determined; ibid. and more confidently in *CL* 16 (1902), 403–5 and *J. Phil.* 30 (1907), 194 n. 1, Peterson identified it with three manuscripts used by northern-European scholars of s. XVI[2], but his case needs reappraisal.

[36] G. Vaucher, *Genava*, 9 (1931), 120–4, with a plate; Bischoff ap. Rouse and Rouse, 81 n. 3, confirms Vaucher's identification of the leaf as part of C. Despite its importance (see below on the *Verrines*), the leaf has remained unknown.

[37] E. K. Rand, *A Survey of the Manuscripts of Tours* (Cambridge, Mass., 1929), i. 104–5.

[38] Delisle, ii. 478, no. 498.

C now contains parts of the *Catilinarians,* parts of *Lig.* and *Deiot.,* and parts of *Verr.* II. 2 and 4, but examination of the quires suggests that it once contained the whole of the *Catilinarians* and *Caesarians*[39] and perhaps even the whole of the *Verrines.*[40]

The next step in assessing the importance of the manuscript or manuscripts recorded at the Carolingian court is to investigate the tradition of all three constituents and see whether any manuscripts maintain a constant relationship to C.

In Catilinam

Editors since H. Nohl (Prague, 1886) have distinguished three families of manuscripts, α, β, and γ.[41] C leads the field in α. Two other old members of α descend from a lost sister of C. The one, Milan, Ambros. C. 29 inf. (A; Chatelain, plate XXVIII), containing *De officiis, Catil.,* and the *Caesarians,* was written in France in s. X/XI[1]. The other, Leiden, Voss. Lat. O. 2, part II (V), containing *Catil.* and the *Caesarians,* was also written in France – possibly at Saint-Germain-d'Auxerre[42] – in s. X. British Library, Harley 2682 (H[43]), a large collection of Cicero's works written in Lotharingia in s. XI[2] and later owned by the cathedral of Cologne, belongs to α but has an overlay of readings from β and γ.[44] Nohl assigned to α Florence, Laur. 45.2 (a, s. XII[1], France or England ?), containing Sallust, *Catil.* and *Jug., De senectute, De amicitia, Catil.,* and pseudo-Sall./Cic. *Invect.,* which struck him as a good copy of a good exemplar; but like H it is by no means pure. Two manuscripts hitherto unreported, B. L. Add. 21242 (s. XII, England or France) and Harl. 6522 (a. 1469, Angers), are pure members of α despite their date; the former contains Vegetius, pseudo-Sall./Cic. *Invect.,* and *Catil.* 1–2.24, the latter *Catil.* amongst philosophical works of Cicero's.

The second or β family of manuscripts emerged and circulated in Germany. It stems almost certainly from a manuscript which also contained *De senectute,* and another characteristic may be the insertion

---

[39] Clark, *Descent,* 235–40; T. S. Pattie, *British Library Journal,* 1 (1975), 15–21. Peterson, *CR* 17 (1903), 263, had already come round to this opinion on general grounds.

[40] Cf. n. 79, below.

[41] See Clark, *CR* 16 (1902), 322–7, OCT i (1905), *Descent,* 309–23, and P. Reis in the Teubner (1933); H. Bornecque in vol. x of the Budé *Discours* (1926) offers nothing new. All editions of *Catil.* 1–2 are out of date; see the end of this piece (*In Catilinam*). The relationship of $\alpha\beta\gamma$ has not been sufficiently discussed, and even the latest discussion, G. B. Alberti's in *Problemi di critica testuale* (Florence, 1979), 61–7, is out of date for the same reason as editions of 1–2.

[42] F. M. Carey drew up a list of manuscripts that he believed to have been written at Auxerre. It was never published but may be consulted at the Institut de Recherche et d'Histoire des Textes in Paris.

[43] On the siglum cf. n. 24, above.

[44] Clark, *Anecd. Oxon.* vii (1892), xxvi. Together with *J. Phil.* 18 (1890), 69–87, this monograph offers a thorough study of the speeches in H; it includes a plate.

after *Catil.* 1 of the note 'Superiore libro Catilina circumventus . . .'.[45]
The existence of β is in part explained in terms of the intellectual
activity in Bavarian abbeys of the twelfth century. The β text is recon-
structed from the following: (i) British Library, Harley 2716 (L, s. X ex.;
Chatelain, plate XLB), containing *Catil.* (a β text with leaves missing to
4.1, completed by another hand from a γ source), pseudo-Sall./Cic.
Invect., the *Caesarians*, and fragments of *De senectute*, written in the upper
Rhineland and in the late seventeenth century acquired by J. G.
Graevius at Cologne; (ii) Munich Clm 15964 (s, s. XI²/XII¹; Chatelain,
plate XXVII), containing *De amic.*, *De senect.*, *Catil.*, which belonged to St.
Peter's in Salzburg, identifiable in the twelfth-century catalogue of the
abbey;[46] (iii) Munich Clm 4611, part II (b, s. XII²), containing *inter alia*
the same works as s and also pseudo-Sall./Cic. *Invect.*, which belonged
to Benedictbeuern; (iv) Munich Clm 7809 (i, s. XII), containing *Catil.*
and *De senect.*, which belonged to the Augustinians of Indersdorf and
appears to have been corrected from a manuscript of the α family; (v)
Zürich Rh. 127 (s. XII; Chatelain, plate XXVIII), containing *De amic.*
(frag.), *De senect.*, and *Catil.*, which belonged to the abbey of Rheinau.[47]

The third family, γ, emerges only shortly after the α family, probably
from somewhere in Lotharingia. Editors have used the following manuscripts: (i) Brussels 10060–2(u), containing *Catil.* and Sallust, *Catil.*
and *Jug.*, written for Egmond at the behest of Abbot Stephen (d. 1083)
and identifiable with no. 152 in the eleventh-century catalogue of the
abbey;[48] (ii) Florence, Laur. 50.45 (x, s. XI; Chatelain, plate XLII),
containing *De inventione* and Victorinus' commentary, *De amic.*, *De
senect.*, pseudo-Cic./Sall. *Invect.*, *Catil.*, *Marc.*, *Lig.* 1–32, probably
written in Germany but of unknown medieval provenance; (iii) Munich
Clm 19472 (t, s. XI), containing *Catil.*, pseudo-Sall./Cic. *Invect.*, Sall.
Catil. and *Jug.*, which belonged to the abbey of Tegernsee; (iv) British
Library, Harley 2716 (L, s. X ex.; see above, family β, no. i) from 4.1 to
the end; (v) Berlin (West) lat. 2° 252 (E), the large collection of Cicero
assembled by Wibald Abbot of Stavelot (1130–58) and Corvey (1146–
58), which has lost 1.1–4.2;[49] (vi) Oxford, Corpus Christi College 57

---

[45] Recent editors say nothing about this, but we can vouch for its presence in nos. (i) and (ii)
below and in Admont 363 (cf. n. 47, below), Florence, Laur. 48.21 (s. XV), Strozz. 49 (s. XII¹,
Beneventan; 1.1–3.11), Conv. Soppr. 79 (s. XIV/XV), S. Croce 23 sin. 3 (XIV²/XV¹), and Paris lat.
18525 (cf. n. 52, below). It also occurs in u, x, and o, of family γ (below).

[46] Becker, 115.41 (p. 234).

[47] Admont 363 (s. XII), apparently a local product, must also be a member of β; see on *De
senectute*, where it is connected closely with our nos. (ii)–(iv) and more loosely with our no. (v).

[48] Manitius, *Handschriften*, 20.

[49] 'Huic familiae adscribendus esse videtur' according to H. Nohl, *M. Tulli Ciceronis Orationes
selectae*, iii (Prague, 1886), viii; readings can be unearthed from the apparatus of Orelli–Baiter–
Halm, ii.1 (Zürich, 1854), 657–715, and J. Zinzerling, *Criticorum iuvenilium promulsis* (Leiden,
1610), 147–52, reports a few readings from the missing section. Clark (n. 44, above) argued that
the variants added to the γ text in E derive from H; he took the same view of E's extracts from the
Verrines (cf. n. 95, below).

(o, s. XII[1]), containing Juvenal, Persius, Prisc. *Perieg.*, Don. *De barb.*, and *Catil.*, which was written by an English hand and is therefore the only surviving manuscript of the γ family that apparently did not originate in Germany. One might note in this context that the *Catilinarians* were known, at least by reputation, to William of Malmesbury (d. about 1143).[50] Finally, on the basis of geography and contents it is likely that a manuscript of pseudo-Sall./Cic. *Invect.*, *Catil.*, the *Caesarians*, and *De amic.*, listed in the catalogue (*c*.1049–1160) of the Benedictines of Lobbes (dioc. Cambrai and Liège), belonged to the γ family.[51]

There are several manuscripts of French origin whose place in the stemma remains to be worked out; at present one can merely list them: (i) Paris lat. 18525 (s. XII[1]; Chatelain, plate XXVIII), a fragment of six leaves, contains parts of *Catil.* 1–2;[52] (ii) Laon 453 bis (s. XII), containing *De inv.*, *Ad Herenn.*, Boeth. *Topica*, *Catil.*, belonged to the cathedral library; (iii) British Library, Harley 4927, containing *Catil.*, pseudo-Sall./Cic. *Invect.*, the corpus of 57–56 (where it is h), the *Caesarians*, *De amic.*, and *De senect.*, was written in central France in s. XII med. and later belonged to Petrarch; (iv) extracts from *Catil.* appear in the *Florilegium Gallicum* (s. XII med.); (v) Paris lat. 6602, part II (s. XIII[2/4]), containing *Philippics*, 1–4 and *Catil.*, was written for Richard de Fournival.[53] Further knowledge of these manuscripts would shed considerable light on the transmission of the *Catilinarians*.[54]

Three references in French medieval book-lists flesh out the importance and dispersal of the *Catilinarians* in France: (i) a book-list of the tenth or early eleventh century (British Library, Harley 2790, f. 262[v]) belonging to the cathedral of Saint-Cyr (Nevers): 'Invectivarum'; (ii) a second codex, in addition to C, recorded in the Cluny catalogue: 'Volumen in quo continentur Cicero de amicitia, et controversia cuiusdam in Salustium, et Salustii in eum, et invective Ciceronis in Catilinam, et Marius Platius Sacerdos de veritate metrorum';[55] (iii) a codex which probably originated in the area of the Loire, given by Philip of Bayeux to Bec, where it is described in the catalogue of 1164: 'Tullius de partitionibus oratoriis et de amicitia et de senectute et invective in Catilinam et invective in Salustum et Salustus in Tullium . . .'.[56]

Three fragments and two other references in medieval book-lists

---

[50] R. M. T., *Rev. bén.* 85 (1975), 375.

[51] F. Dolbeau, *Recherches Augustiniennes*, 13 (1978), 32 no. 270 and 14 (1979), 226 no. 270. Heraclius, Bishop of Liège 959–71, echoes *Catil.* 4.18 with *studio* added after *voluntate* as in β and x (no. (ii), above); cf. H. Silvestre, *Le Moyen Âge*, 58 (1952), 5.

[52] Cf. n. 45, above. Chatelain's plate suggests that it is an impure member of α.

[53] R. H. R., *RHT* 3 (1973), 259–60 no. 31 with plate XX.

[54] More manuscripts (the first four mentioned by our colleagues on *De senect.* and *App. Sall.* 2): Edinburgh, Adv. 18. 7. 8 (s. XI/XII, from Thorney Abbey), Florence, Laur. Strozz. 49 (cf. n. 45, above), Vatican lat. 3251 (s. XI/XII, from northern Italy), Cambridge, Trin. 1381/0. 8. 6 (s. XII), Munich Clm 14781 (s. XII, 1.1–2.27) and 22281 (s. XII).   [55] Delisle, ii.478, no. 501.

[56] *Catalogue général*, 2 (1888), 398 no. 107 = Becker, 86.104 (p. 202).

should also be noted: (i) Vienna 295 (s. XII ex., France), *Catil.* 3.17–4.14; (ii) Zwettl 313 (s. XII ex., Austria or Italy), *Catil.* 1.1–14; (iii) Munich Clm 19474 (s. XII/XIII; Chatelain, plate XXVII), containing in part I pseudo-Sall./Cic. *Invect., Marc., Lig.* 1–6, *Catil.* 1–2.17, from Tegernsee and written in Germany; (iv) 'Invectiva in Catilinam' in the mid-twelfth-century inventory of Oberaltaich;[57] and (v) '24. Ciceronis de invectivis Catalline' in an eleventh-century list of disputed origin.[58]

All editions of *Catil.* 1–2 have been out of date since 1977, when R. Roca-Puig published the text of a papyrus in the Fundació Sant Lluc Evangelista, Barcelona (CLA Suppl. 1782; cf. XI 1650). After fragments of 1.6–29 follows an almost undamaged text of 1.30–33 and the whole of 2. There are two other papyrus scraps of *Catil.* 1–2 (§ 1, above).

Caesarianae (*Pro Marcello, Pro Ligario, Pro rege Deiotaro*)

Here we meet α again, and editors agree that it is the most reliable family.[59] C, A, and V stand in the same relationship as in the *Catilinarians*, and the only differences in α are that H is pure[60] and that a and Add. 21242 are absent.

A second family, β, circulated from the Carolingian heartland around Aachen and Liège. It comprises four manuscripts: L and E of family γ in the *Catilinarians* (L never went beyond *Lig.* 15); the manuscript that together with E constitutes the Y family in the corpus of 57–56 BC (§ 2, above), namely Brussels 5345 (B, s. XI¹, from Gembloux; called G in the corpus); and Oxford, Bodl. D'Orville 77 + 95 (D, s. X²/XI¹),[61] containing the *Caesarians, De amic., De senect.,* pseudo-Sall./Cic. *Invect., Somn. Scip.* and Macrobius' commentary, Hyg. *Astron.,* which was written in southern Germany but for *De senect.* and Macrobius has an immediate ancestor from somewhere in France, possibly Corbie. D often sides with

---

[57] *Mittelalterliche Bibliothekskataloge Deutschlands und der Schweiz,* iv.1 (1977), no. 17.39 (p. 84).

[58] The list (Munich Clm 14436, f. 61ᵛ) was thought by Bischoff, *Mitt. Stud.* ii.77–115, to be part of a codex that belonged to Hartwic of St. Emmeram, who studied at Chartres under Fulbert and at Reims; and he suggested one of these two cathedrals as home for the books on the list. H. P. Lattin, *Isis,* 38 (1948), 205–25, saw in it rather the programme of studies of Gerbert at Reims. B. C. B.-B., 'The Manuscripts of Macrobius' Commentary on the *Somnium Scipionis*' (D. Phil. thesis, Oxford, 1975), suggests that the part of the codex containing the book-list (ff. 34–61) was not connected to Hartwic's manuscript until perhaps the late fifteenth century and is of German, not French, origin (vol. ii, 409–16).

[59] Nohl was again the first editor to propound a stemma (Leipzig, 1888), but Clark, *CR* 14 (1900), 251–7, 400–2, made the most fundamental contribution; his OCT followed (vol. ii, 1901), and in *CR* 16 (1902), 322–7 he took stock of C. The debate was continued by H. Reeder, *De codicibus in Ciceronis orationibus Caesarianis recte aestimandis* (Jena, 1906); Clark, OCT (2nd edn., 1918) and *Descent,* 309–23; and Klotz, Teubner viii (1918). M. Lob in vol. xviii of the Budé *Discours* (1952) has nothing new.

[60] It contains two texts of the *Caesarians,* of which the second concerns us here. According to Clark, *CR* 16 (1902), 323, A and H 'are derived from *gemelli* of C'; Klotz, xi n. 3, makes CH and AV *gemelli* without argument.   [61] Illustrated in *Survival,* plate 16.

α against the other members of β, apparently not through contamina-tion.[62] For both the *Caesarians* and the corpus of 57–56 BC, E and B probably descend from a common parent that was located at Liège. *Marc.* was quoted by Heraclius, Bishop of Liège 959–71,[63] and two other possible witnesses to a β exemplar at Liège are the manuscript of the *Catilinarians* and *Caesarians* described in the catalogue of s. XI²/XII¹ from Lobbes,[64] and a manuscript cited in the late eleventh-century catalogue of Egmond as a gift of Abbot Stephen (d. 1083): 'Tullius de senectute. Tullius de locis [= *Topica*]. Tullius de amicitia. Orationes Tulli ad Gayum Cesarem. Commentum Tulli super diffinitiones [= *Paradoxa*]'.[65] Another manuscript, Munich Clm 19474 (s. XII²/XIII¹, German; Chatelain, plate XXVII), unclassified in the *Catilinarians*, may also belong to the β family.[66]

A third family, γ, is contaminated and interpolated, and its status has been debated. Editors have used five manuscripts:[67] (i) Wolfenbüttel, Gud. lat. 335 (g, s. X/XI), containing *De amic.*, *Deiot.* 1–26, pseudo-Sall./ Cic. *Invect.*, Fulgentius, *Glossae*, pseudo-Sen./Paul, *Epp.*, Sen. *Epp.*, and a sermon of Augustine, was written in southern Germany. It has been suggested that g may be the incomplete copy of *Deiot.* whose existence is implied by Gerbert in a letter of AD 983 to an unidentified abbot Gisalbertus: 'If you have it, let us have the beginning of this book [i.e. Demosthenes, *Ophthalmicus*] and likewise the end of Cicero *Pro rege Deiotaro*.'[68] (ii) A γ text of the *Caesarians* appears in Harl. 2682 (H of family α).[69] (iii) Florence, Laur. 50. 45 (m, s. XI), probably German, contains *De inv.* and Marius Victorinus' commentary, *De amic.*, *De senect.*, pseudo-Cic./Sall. *Invect.*, *Catil.*, *Marc.*, *Lig.* 1–32. (iv) British Library, Harley 4927 (a, s. XII med.) is the French manuscript with notes of Petrarch's.[70] (v) Oxford, Bodl. Rawl. G. 138 (σ, s. XV), contain-ing eight other speeches, was written in Italy.

At least one manuscript of s. XI and three of s. XII, as well as a florilegium of s. XII med., remain unreported. Munich Clm 18787 (s. X²,

---

[62] Clark, *CR* 14 (1900), 254.

[63] Silvestre, loc. cit. (n. 51, above). Variants show that Heraclius's manuscript was not a member of α.

[64] Dolbeau, locc. cit. (n. 51, above).   [65] Manitius, *Handschriften*, 20.

[66] 'In fragmento Ligarianae fere ad verbum conspirat cum Erfurtensi [E]', according to Halm, *Zur Handschriftenkunde der Ciceronischen Schriften* (Munich, 1850), 6. Chatelain's plate suggests that it belongs to β.

[67] Nos. (i)–(iii) are closely related in pseudo-Sall./Cic. *Invect.*, on which see APPENDIX SALLUSTIANA 2.

[68] H. P. Lattin, *The Letters of Gerbert* (New York, 1961), 55; F. Weigle, *Die Briefsammlung Gerberts von Reims* (*MGH*, *Briefe der deutschen Kaiserzeit*, 2, Weimar, 1966), 32, *Ep.* 9.

[69] Cf. n. 60, above. Like g, it breaks off at *Deiot.* 26 *ineunte aetate*, and so do Leiden, Voss. Lat. O. 26 (s. XII¹, north-eastern France), Troyes 552 (s. XIV¹, northern Italy), which belongs to β in *Marc.* but to γ in *Lig.* and *Deiot.*, Escorial R.I.2 (s. XIV², Italy), and Florence, Laur. 48. 10 (a. 1416, Florence). The complete members of γ may therefore be *suppleti* rather than *integri*.

[70] See § 2 and on the *Catilinarians*, above.

western Germany), a manuscript important for the text of other speeches (§§ 4, 5, below), has lost its last quires and breaks off at *Marc.* 15 *victor pacis.*[71] Admont 363 (s. XII, apparently a local product) contains *Marc.* 1–30.[72] Leiden, Voss. Lat. O.26 (s. XII[1]) contains the *Caesarians,*[73] Quint. *Inst.* (excerpts), *De oratore.* Its text of Quintilian is considered a copy of Florence, Laur. 46.7 (Chatelain, plate CLXXVII), which was brought to Strasbourg, perhaps from Reims, by Bishop Werinharius (1001–28). For *De oratore* it appears to be related to Erlangen 380 (s. X ex.; Chatelain, plate XIXa), probably written at Reims. The fourth manuscript, Rouen 1040 (s. XII med.), contains the *Caesarians, Pridie* 1–14, Symmachus *Epp., Paradoxa,* Apuleius *De fato,* Claudian, *opusc.*; it belonged to the abbey of Lyre in Normandy. To judge from its contents (as well as its location), it must be related to a manuscript given to Bec by Philip, Bishop of Bayeux, and described in the catalogue of 1164: 'Super Marcianum et liber Tullii de paradoxis et Tullius pro Marco Marcello et pro Quinto Ligario et pro Deiotaro et pro se ipso et epistole Dindimi ad Alexandrum et Alexandri ad Dindimum et Apuleus de fato et Claudius Claudianus et epistole Giraldi Eboracensis et vita Neronis et liber variarum Cassiodori et liber eiusdem de anima'.[74] Also, brief extracts from the *Caesarians* appear in the *Florilegium Gallicum,* which was the source for Vincent of Beauvais's knowledge of the *Caesarians* in the thirteenth century. Finally, the *Caesarians* are recorded in the *Biblionomia* or catalogue of the library of Richard de Fournival, whose books after his death in 1260 passed in large part to the Sorbonne: 'Eiusdem oratio pro Marco Marcello et oratio pro Q. Ligario et oratio pro rege Deiotaro. Item invectio Salustii in eumdem Tullium et respontio Tullii ad Salustium. Item eiusdem Tulli liber declamationum. Item commentarium Grillii super rhetoricos Tullii secundos. In uno volumine cuius signum est littera D'.[75]

The *Caesarians* were known in Italy before Petrarch used Harley 4927. His other copy, Troyes 552 (s. XIV[1]), is Italian but was not written for him; its origin must be sought in learned circles at Padua *c.*1300, which evidently knew *Catil.,* pseudo-Sall./Cic. *Invect.,* the *Caesarians,* and *Post reditum ad senatum.*[76] Even earlier Brunetto Latini (d. 1294) had translated the *Caesarians* and probably the first *Catilinarian.*[77]

---

[71] From the readings printed by Orelli–Baiter–Halm, ii.2. 1184–9 the manuscript seems related to m but not descended from it, which in any case it cannot be if they have been correctly dated.

[72] Cf. n. 47, above.   [73] Cf. n. 69, above.

[74] *Catalogue général,* 2. 397 no. 94 = Becker, 86.91 (p. 201). Oxford, Bodl. Lat. class. e. 48 (s. XII[2]/XIII[1]), which contains amongst other things the *Epistole Dindimi et Alexandri,* the *Caesarians* and *Pridie,* 1–14, and *Paradoxa,* must be related to Rouen 1040 and Philip's manuscript; in the *Caesarians* it belongs to β (we found it too late to incorporate these manuscripts in our account of β).

[75] Delisle, ii.526, no. 32.

[76] P. L. Schmidt (n. 22, above), 177–92, 195 n. 44.

[77] Ed. L. M. Rezzi (Milan, 1832).

In Verrem

The precise relationship of the manuscripts is hard to establish, because the older manuscripts each present different parts of the text; but it has long been clear that they fall into two families, one of which circulated basically in northern France and Germany and the other in Italy.[78]

C, the oldest manuscript of the northern family, now contains parts of II.2 and 4,[79] and so far as the evidence goes may once have contained the whole of the *Verrines*. Folio 34, which presents II.2.112–17, is the last leaf of a quire originally numbered XVI but after erasure now numbered X;[80] perhaps the number was changed after the loss or removal of the quires that contained *Caecil.* – II.1.

A second member of the northern family associated with Tours is Paris lat. 7774A, made up of two manuscripts: I *Verr.* II. 4–5 (R), II. *De inv., Ad Herenn.* frag. (Chatelain, plate XXXI), both written in Tours script in the mid-ninth century.[81] Part II belonged to Lupus of Ferrières and contains notes in his hand; and we know from other evidence that Lupus may have owned a copy of the *Verrines*. In 856–8 he requested a manuscript of the *Verrines* in a letter to an unidentified 'Reg.': '. . . Catilinarium et Iugurthinum Sallustii librosque Verrinarum et siquos alios vel corruptos nos habere vel penitus non habere cognoscitis . . .'.[82] There is good reason to believe that R once contained the whole of the *Verrines*, since its first quire was once no. XXVI and the remaining books would have fitted nicely into I–XXV.[83] As R and C overlap only in II.4.86–92, it is impossible to say more than that R could have been copied from C: in the two places where C and R[1] differ, C has the truth.[84]

A third member of the northern family, Paris lat. 7775 (S), was written in France in the mid-twelfth century. It may once have contained all seven books of the *Verrines* but now contains only II. 1.90–111 (two leaves) and II.4–5. For the fragment of II.1, S is the oldest surviving member of the northern family, and since it breaks off at II.1.111

---

[78] Madvig, *Ad virum celeberrimum Io. Casp. Orellium epistola critica* (Copenhagen, 1828), 7–10; Peterson, *J. Phil.* 30 (1907), 161–207, the fundamental discussion for all its inadequacies, and OCT iii (1907); Klotz, Teubner v (1923). No progress was made in Budé *Discours* ii–vi (1922–9) or in the Mondadori edition of II.4 by H. Bardon (1964) or II.5 by L. Piacente (1975). See also Clark, *Descent*, 212–65, for an attempt at working out the lineation of hypothetical manuscripts higher in the stemma.

[79] No edition reveals this, not even H. Bardon's of II.4. The single leaf of C that is now Geneva lat. 169 (cf. n. 36, above) has II.4.86–92; We are greatly obliged to Dr T. S. Pattie for a reproduction of it.

[80] Pattie (n. 39, above), 17, 18.   [81] Rand (n. 37, above), 140–1.

[82] L. Levillain, *Loup de Ferrières: correspondance*, 2 (Paris, 1935), 124.

[83] É. Thomas, *RPh* 9 (1885), 167–8, strangely misreported by Peterson, *J. Phil.* 30 (1907), 162.

[84] 86 *domi* C. *domo* R, 87 *ipsi se* C *ipse se* R[1] (nothing else in eighty lines of the OCT). Editors of this century report R less fully than Orelli–Baiter–Halm, ii.1.

either through loss of leaves or because the scribe never started on the next page, all other manuscripts that break off at the same point must derive from it.[85] Peterson believed it to descend from a sister of R and thus to be of independent value in II.4–5, but Klotz, writing after him, convincingly argues that it derives from R, because it faithfully reproduces unique readings of R's corrector.[86] In the first half of the thirteenth century S belonged to Richard de Fournival;[87] after his death in 1260, it passed with his other books via Gerard of Abbeville to the Sorbonne. In the early fifteenth century, when it was still at the Sorbonne and still contained everything up to II.1.111, a copy was made by Nicholas de Clamanges, Paris lat. 7823 (D).[88] D thus preserves the text of *Caecil.* – II.1.90, missing from S. It passed via Simon de Plumetot to Saint-Victor; the abbey was the focal point of northern French humanism and it was frequently copied, producing the *deteriores* of the northern family. Editors have prematurely abandoned the search for other copies of S made before it lost *Caecil.* – II.1.90,[89] but one surely survives in Escorial R. I. 2 (s. XIV²), which may have been written in response to a papal request in 1374 for copies of Cicero from the Sorbonne.[90]

There is no way of telling when R lost *Caecil.* – II.3 and S II.1.111 – II.3. During the fourteenth century, however, a northern text of II.2–3 appears in Italy. Petrarch quotes from this part of the *Verrines* but no other,[91] and Florence, Laur. Conv. Soppr. 79 (O) begins with II.2–3, where it has a markedly better text than in the five books added by a different hand (4–5, *Caecil.* – II.1). The virtues of O in II.2–3 led Peterson to believe that C once contained II.2–3 and O was copied from it; but we now know that C did not stop at II.3, and a more plausible source lies to hand – the missing part of S, which could have been found by Petrarch or another Italian visitor to France.[92]

From fragmentary manuscripts of the continuous text we pass to a reference and a set of extracts, both still French. Gerbert, writing to his former pupil Constantine at Fleury in 986 to request that he come to

---

[85] Peterson, *CR* 16 (1902), 405–6, and *J. Phil.* 30 (1907), 163–4, ignored by Klotz, praef. xii.

[86] Praef. viii–xii. Halm, who did not know S, had maintained that R was the archetype of the French family in II.4–5; cf. Nohl, *Hermes*, 20 (1885), 56–61.

[87] R. H. R., *RHT* 3 (1973), 259 no. 30.

[88] For the attribution to Nicholas de Clamanges see G. Ouy (n. 16, above), 377.

[89] 'Ceteri huius familiae codices, ex SD derivati . . ., abiciendi sunt omnes,' says Peterson, OCT iii. xi. Descendants of D, yes; but why descendants of S?

[90] Rouse and Rouse in *Medieval Scribes, Manuscripts and Libraries: Essays presented to N. R. Ker*, ed. M. B. Parkes and A. G. Watson (London, 1978), 363.

[91] Silvia Rizzo, *La tradizione manoscritta della* Pro Cluentio *di Cicerone* (Genoa, 1979), 37–8; cf. P. de Nolhac, *Pétrarque et l'humanisme* (Paris, 1892), 209, 403 = ed. 2 (Paris, 1907), I.252, II.282 (out of date on Paris lat. 6342: see n. 223, below).

[92] Clark, *CR* 16 (1902), 325–6, argued against Peterson that O was not copied directly from C; Peterson, ibid. 401–3, replied but did not refute him. The Ciceronian section of O, a composite part of a composite manuscript, was briefly described by J. G. Baiter, *Philologus*, 20 (1863), 350.

Reims, adds 'Comitentur iter tuum Tulliana opuscula vel de re publica vel in Verrem vel que pro defensione multorum plurima Romane eloquentie parens conscripsit'.[93] This may be a reference to R, especially if R was formerly Lupus's; at least three of Lupus's other manuscripts did move to Fleury. But it seems more likely that Gerbert was simply listing desiderata, without any specific knowledge of whether or not the works were available at Fleury. Extracts from II.4–5 appear in the *Florilegium Angelicum*, compiled at Orléans in the second half of the twelfth century.[94] While they are unquestionably taken from a manuscript of the northern family, it is impossible to determine if any of the surviving manuscripts served as the source, since the eighteen extracts do not fall on any significant variant. The existence of these extracts confirms that the *Verrines* owe their medieval circulation largely to the intellectual activity of the Loire valley abbeys and schools. The extracts account for the widest circulation that these speeches achieved in the Middle Ages, for the *Florilegium Angelicum* is known in at least twenty-three copies.

In addition to the cluster of French manuscripts, extracts from II.3–4 occur in two German manuscripts, H and E of the *Catilinarians* and *Caesarians*. E may here be a copy of H.[95] In II.3 HE closely resemble O, and in II.4 they resemble R without deriving from it.[96] Some light is shed on the circulation of the *Verrines* in Germany by a letter of Meinhard of Bamberg. Writing *c*.1057–67 to his former teacher Herman of Reims, Meinhard notes that one Benno (Bishop of Osnabrück?) has told him of difficulty in transcribing Meinhard's *Verrines* because of the 'foreign' script; and Meinhard offers to provide Herman with a more readable copy: 'Amicus noster Benno, homo vobis certe deditissimus, retulit mihi Verrinas illas subdifficiles ad transscribendum propter peregrinam illam litteram visas fuisse. Unde, si ita vobis videatur, eas nobis remittite, et ego vobis humanius exemplar providebo'.[97] An old manuscript of the *Verrines* was clearly at Bamberg, old enough to prove difficult to read in the eleventh century. Might the old manuscript from the Carolingian court have migrated to Bamberg, perhaps as a gift of Otto III or Henry II? It is conceivable that Meinhard's manuscript was the ultimate source of the extracts in HE; Meinhard is known to have supplied other texts to Cologne, and H in *De officiis* closely resembles Bamberg Class. 26/M.v.1 (B, s. x).[98] At any event, Meinhard appears to have sent the

[93] Weigle (n. 68, above), 114, *Ep*. 86.

[94] Rouse and Rouse in *Medieval Learning*, 66–114, esp. 80–2, 98.

[95] Clark, *J. Phil*. 18 (1890), 74–5; Peterson, *J. Phil*. 30 (1907), 194. Peterson, however, cites two recalcitrant readings, and in *Ad fam.*, where H and E are very close, L. Mendelssohn in his edition (Leipzig, 1893), xxii n. 1, gives reasons why E cannot be a copy of H; cf. L. Gurlitt, *Jahrb. für class. Phil*. Suppl. 22 (1895), 536–41. The whole question should be reopened; see also n. 141, below.

[96] Peterson, *J. Phil*. 30 (1907), 194.

[97] C. Erdmann and N. Fickermann, *Briefsammlungen der Zeit Heinrichs IV* (*MGH*, Berlin, 1950), 113, *Ep*. 65. [98] Clark, *Anecd. Oxon*. vii (1892), xiv–xv.

manuscript to Herman at Reims; for the Bamberg catalogue of 1112–3 does not list the *Verrines* among the works of Cicero then in the library.

Of the northern-European family, then, editors have at their disposal D (s. XV) and perhaps other copies of S as far as II.1.90, S (s. XII) from there to 111, nothing from there to the end of II.1, C (s. IX) and O (s. XIV) in II.2–3 (with help from HE in 3.1–10), and R (s. IX) in II.4–5 (with help from HE in a dozen passages of 4 and from C in 4.86–92).

The oldest member of the Italian family, perhaps a fragment of its archetype, is a bifolium containing a partly erased text of II.3.120–9 inserted in Montecassino 361, the archetype of Frontinus, *Aq.*, written by Peter the Deacon *c*.1133. It is from a book written in Caroline minuscule of the tenth century; it contains the portion of the *Verrines* dealing with lands in Sicily which later came into the possession of Montecassino.[99] The second manuscript, Paris lat. 7776 (p; Chatelain, plate XXXI), containing the whole of the *Verrines*, was written in Italy in the second half of the eleventh century; it belonged in the sixteenth century to the Cittadini family of Siena.[100] It abounds in corrections and interpolations, and is inferior to C and R of the northern family. Paris lat. 4588A (k), written in Italy early in the thirteenth century, is both difficult to read and of limited value. Otherwise recent editors have used only fifteenth-century members of the Italian family, above all Florence, Laur. 48. 29 (q) and British Library, Harley 2687 (r, written in Florence or Rome, s. XV², with the Strozzi arms).[101] Wherever the *Verrines* may have emerged in Italy, they did not become popular until the end of the fourteenth century,[102] and only with the fifteenth do texts multiply.[103]

Of the five antique fragments (§1, above) much the most important for the text is the Vatican palimpsest, which contains parts of II.1–5; editors have been inclined to associate it with the Italian family. The Giessen papyrus, however, is the oldest witness to any Latin text

---

[99] No editor has used it, but R. H. R. has photographs; Professor Bischoff would assign it to s. X² and more tentatively to Italy. The bifolium is pp. 219–22, which should be read in the order 221–2, 219–20; pp. 221 and 219 are almost entirely legible, pp. 222 and 220 almost entirely illegible.

[100] M. C. Di Franco Lilli, *Studi e testi*, 259 (1970), 82–3 no. 91 with plate XVII.

[101] Peterson derived q from p in his article, 190–1, but not in his edition, xii, and r from q in his edition but not in his article. Klotz, xiv–xv, made short work of showing that on the evidence available r was not a copy of q and q not a copy of p. No one has revealed what is so special about q and r.

[102] According to F. Torraca, *Arch. stor. prov. napol.* 39 (1914), 413, they were known at Naples to Paolo da Perugia (d. 1348) and through him to Boccaccio; cf. Antonia Mazza, *IMU* 9 (1966), 34. According to Claudia Villa, *IMU* 12 (1969), 38 n. 1, they were known to Albertano da Brescia (died not before 1235); but she kindly tells us that the quotation she had in mind comes through Caecilius Balbus (see PUBLILIUS).

[103] For example, Poggio's was a very early fifteenth-century copy, Florence, Laur. 48. 27. G. López and L. Piacente in *Atti e memorie dell'Arcadia*, ser. III,6.2 (1973), 83–95, list seventy-five manuscripts, sixty-six of which belong to s. XV.

preserved in medieval manuscripts; it was written within a century of the *Verrines* themselves.

We may now stand back from the details and attempt to view the tradition of *Catil. Caes. Verr.* broadly, as the entry in the catalogue of the court library invites us to do.

In *Catil.* and *Caes.* the oldest members of α, CAV, behave very tidily, and it would be excessive scepticism to deny that they go back to one manuscript of both works. Apart from C, however, the only member of α that shows any sign of having in its ancestry a manuscript of all three works is H. In this manuscript, one of the earliest Ciceronian miscellanies, the works are separated by others and the text of *Catil.* is impure, but nothing in the available evidence makes it impossible to believe that they all derive from one source. If they do, it becomes important to decide whether Clark or Klotz was right about the stemma of CHAV,[104] because Clark's tripartite stemma would entail that the archetype of α included the *Verrines*. Even then, however, nothing would follow about the precise relationship of α to what the catalogue of the court library describes, still less anything about the relationship of the other families to it.

As both γ of *Catil.* and β of *Caes.* include E and L, it might be thought that they are really the same family, so that not only α but this family too derives from one manuscript of both works; and in that case why should not the same manuscript of both works have given rise to α and this family? Unfortunately, in *Catil.* most of L belongs to another family and the fragment of E (a notorious miscellany anyway) has not been securely assigned to γ.

It must be concluded, then, that medieval scribes did their best to confuse modern scholars if all three works spread from the Carolingian court. In order to prove that they did not spread from the Carolingian court, it would be necessary to trace at least one family back into Antiquity. Scholars have indeed tried to do this for other purposes,[105] but they tend to forget that families are defined by errors, and they have not paid enough heed to a proverb wisely invoked by Clark:[106] one swallow does not make a summer. An error that can arise in an ancient manuscript can arise in a medieval one, and the same standards should be applied in arguments about *Bindefehler* between an ancient and a medieval manuscript as about *Bindefehler* between one medieval manuscript and another. If the ancient reading is attested by an author whose works survived into the Middle Ages, there is the further problem of contamination.[107] Nevertheless, papyri of *Catil.* and *Verr.* have steadily

---

[104] Cf. n. 60, above. CH are reported as omitting *munera* at *Deiot.* 42.

[105] e.g. Reeder (n. 59, above); cf. Clark, *Descent*, 310–12.   [106] OCT ii (2nd edn.), preface.

[107] Clark, *Descent*, 310, ignores it in discussing *Catil.* 2.27 *conivere possum* γ (with Probus, Sacerdos, and the *scholia Gronoviana*), *consulere sibi possunt* $\alpha\beta$. If contamination in γ from a

been accumulating, and since 1977 an antique copy of *Catil.* 2 in its entirety has been available for comparison. The time has surely come, therefore, for another review of the evidence.

4

The mutilation of C in the course of the centuries has not done serious damage to the text of its original contents. By contrast, the mutilation of an Italian contemporary is the biggest disaster that can be seen to have occurred in the medieval transmission of Cicero's speeches.

Vatican, Arch. S. Pietro H. 25 (V; *CLA* I.3, Chatelain, plate XXVI)[108] was written in northern Italy probably in the second quarter of the ninth century.[109] It is written in three columns, and the first work, *In Pisonem*, in uncials, both archaisms which are thought to indicate imitation of an early exemplar. The remaining portions are written in Caroline minuscule. Clark comments on 'the remarkable ignorance of the writer'; 'no glimmer of intelligence appears amid his errors, and, but for such a passage as [*Philippics*] xiii.6, where for *seiungamus tamen* he reads *seiungamus amen*, he shows no knowledge even of ecclesiastical Latin'.[110] Some time in the middle of the ninth century V moved north and was used by the Irish scholar Sedulius Scottus. Little is known of his life save that he was among the Franks between 840 and 851; he was in Liège at the time of Bishop Hartgar (d. 855) and is found in Cologne in 850 and then in Metz.[111] Sedulius made extracts from V in his florilegium, which survives in a manuscript of the twelfth century, Cues, Nikolaus Hospitalbibliothek 52, ff. 246–73 (possibly from St. James in Liège).[112] The medieval history of V and the circumstances of its rediscovery in the fifteenth century are not known, but Poggio collated it in 1428 and it appears in the library of Cardinal Giordano Orsini (d. 1439), with whose books it passed to the chapter library of St. Peter's.[113] Possibly V was discovered at Cologne by Nicholas of Cues,

grammatical source can be ruled out, the passage has a stemmatic significance (or may have, not to forget the proverb) that seems to have escaped even Clark. The Barcelona papyrus reads *conhibere possunt exeant nemo prohibet.*

[108] Pellegrin, *Manuscrits*, i. 51–2. See also R. G. M. Nisbet's edition of *In Pisonem* (Oxford, 1961), xxi–xxiii.

[109] Bischoff, *Mitt. Stud.* iii.30 n. 124. Mirella Ferrari kindly writes: 'In my opinion the manuscript was written in a centre with Irish connexions, s. IX[1], and corrected by at least two almost contemporary hands, the first using pure Irish script, the second Caroline script with Irish influence. Where this centre is to be located, Italy or France, I do not know. The manuscript was corrected in the tenth century by a non-Italian hand.' [110] *CR* 14 (1902), 39.

[111] F. Brunhölzl, *Geschichte der lateinischen Literatur des Mittelalters*, i (Munich, 1975), 449–50.

[112] L. Traube, *ABAW* 19 (1892), 364–9 (though he thought V itself was too late to have been Sedulius's source); S. Hellmann, *Quellen und Untersuchungen zur lateinischen Philologie des Mittelalters*, i (1906), 92–117. H. Sauppe, *GGA* 1866, 1581–2, had already derived the extracts from V without knowing of the connection with Sedulius. [113] Sabbadini, *Storia e critica*[2], 39.

who accompanied Orsini to Germany in 1425; Sedulius could have left it there in 850.

V now contains *In Pisonem* 33–74, *Pro Flacco* 39–54 and *Pro Fonteio* 11–49 (without a break and both under the title *Pro Fonteio*), and the *Philippics*. The fragmentary nature of the first three works is due principally to the loss of quires I and III–VI. Sedulius's florilegium contains, among other texts, extracts from all four works, including parts that must have occupied quires I and III–VI. Before its excerpts from the surviving parts of *Flacc.* and *Font.*, it presents ten excerpts from the first part of *Font.* and eight from the first part of *Flacc.*, suggesting in combination with the title in V that V sandwiched *Pro Flacco* in *Pro Fonteio*. The fifteenth-century copies of V all reproduce its present state.

V and Sedulius's excerpts from the lost quires of V are the only medieval authorities for *Pro Fonteio*.[114] Paragraphs 1–6 are made up of three fragments from the Vatican palimpsest (§ 1, above), and passages cited by other authors have traditionally been assigned numbers 7–10.[115]

Pro Flacco survives in no other manuscripts earlier than the end of s. XIV, when it turns up from nowhere in the company of *Pro Quinctio* (§ 9, below). The Milan palimpsest (§ 1, above) providentially fills part of a lacuna between paragraphs 5 and 6.

Parts of Asconius' commentary on *In Pisonem* survive, and besides the Turin palimpsest.(§ 1, above) it also has a German tradition first seen in s. XII (§ 6, below).

The fourth work in V had the widest circulation, and in exploring it we shall meet the only remaining manuscripts of Cicero's speeches that survive from before AD 1000. One of them will lead us to five speeches of which we have not yet seen anything in the Middle Ages.

Philippics

The grammarian Arusianus Messius (towards AD 400) quotes from *Philippics*, 16 and 17, and a quotation from '14' in Nonius (half a century earlier ?) nowhere occurs in our text. This comprises fourteen speeches, and though various manuscripts break off before the end, enough stop at what is obviously the end of 14 to make it unlikely that other speeches were lost through damage to one ancient copy.

V occupies one branch of the tradition in splendid isolation. Quire XV, the last that survives, ends at 13.10, and disturbance in an ancestor

---

[114] P. K. M., *Mediaeval Studies*, 41 (1979), 517–18, has suggested that Lupus of Ferrières may also echo a passage of *Pro Fonteio* now missing from V.

[115] Editions: OCT vi (1911) by Clark, Teubner iv (1923) by F. Schoell, Budé *Discours* vii (1929) by A. Boulanger, Mondadori (1967) by G. Garuti.

has brought about the loss of 11.22–12. 12 and 12.23 – end and the transposition of what survives beyond 12.12 into the middle of a word in 11.17.[116]

The manuscripts of the second family, which represents the form in which the Middle Ages knew the *Philippics*, descend from a mutilated ancestor, D, which no longer survives.[117] Clark demonstrated that D had lost single leaves at two places and two quires of four leaves each at another;[118] the resultant gaps are 2.93–6, 5.31–6.18, 10.8–10, the second of which led to a widespread belief that there were thirteen *Philippics* and not fourteen. Where D was is difficult to say, but its descendants can be found in Italy, France, and Germany.

Only one medieval Italian manuscript is known, Vatican lat. 3227 (v), written in Beneventan script in the early twelfth century, probably at Montecassino. Montecassino's interest in this text is explained by Cicero's reference to the 'fundum Casinatem' of Varro (2.103), which is noted in v by the contemporary marginal heading 'CASINVM' at f. 24^r.[119]

The *Philippics* appear in France somewhere on the Loire and spread rapidly.[120] Two groups of manuscripts are discernible. The first consists of two tenth-century manuscripts and their descendants. Leiden, Voss. Lat. O. 2 (n) contains I. *Phil.* 1–13.29, II. *Catil.*, *Caes.*; it may have been written at Saint-Germain, Auxerre.[121] It was in a prominent place, for at least two direct copies of it are known: Oxford, New College 252 (o, s. XII²/4), probably of French origin, which William Say (d. 1468) left to New College; and Leiden B. P. L. 148 (s. XIII), of unknown origin and provenance. The Vossianus has a sister, Vatican lat. 3228 (s), which was written by an Anglo-Saxon in the second half of the tenth century; unfortunately, nothing else is known of its early history.[122] Separated from s by at least two intermediate copies is British Library, Royal 15. A. XIV (s. XI²), which on the basis of its 2° fol. can be identified with the *Philippics* listed in the 1391 catalogue of Durham Cathedral.[123] Milan, Ambros. T. 56 sup. (s. XI/XII), written in France and containing *Phil.*, *Tusc.*, and pseudo-Sall./Cic. *Invect.*, perhaps also belongs to the ns family. The parent of n and s lay in the Loire abbeys, like Fleury, which had important contacts with England in the tenth century.

---

[116] On the ancestors of V see C. E. Finch, 'The Two Texts of Cicero, *Philippicae* 11.20.21 . . . 11.21.5, in Arch. S. Pietro H 25', *Manuscripta*, 21 (1977), 27–33.

[117] The symbol D was first used by Orelli–Baiter–Halm, ii.2. 1223–1411. On the tradition see above all Clark, *CR* 14 (1902), 39–48, 249–51, OCT ii (1901,[1] 1918[2]), and *Descent*, 162–211. F. Schoell edited the text in vol. viii of the Teubner (1918), A. Boulanger and P. Wuilleumier in vols. xix–xx of the Budé *Discours* (1959–60); a new Teubner by P. Fedeli appeared in 1982.

[118] *Descent*, 172.   [119] *Beneventan Script*,[2] i.72, ii.145.

[120] Marshall, loc. cit. (n. 114, above), finds an echo of 3.18 in Lupus of Ferrières.

[121] Cf. n. 42, above.

[122] Clark introduced s in his second edition (1918), too late for the Budé editors (1959–60).

[123] *Publ. of the Surtees Soc.* 1838, 1. 30.

The second French group also originated from the Loire. It has been known to editors since Girolamo Ferrari in his *Emendationes in Philippicas Ciceronis* (Venice, 1542) reported readings from a Colotianus, a manuscript at Rome in the library of Angelo Colocci (1467–1549). Its hallmark is that it contains speeches 1–4 only – a pity, because it is the most faithful witness to D. Clark identified four relatives of the Colotianus, all more or less incapable of coping with the insular abbreviation for *autem*: Paris lat. 5802, containing Suetonius, Florus, Frontinus, Eutropius, *Phil.* 1–4, *Tusc.*, written at Chartres in the middle of the twelfth century[124] and given to Bec by Philip of Bayeux before 1164;[125] Paris lat. 6602, part II, containing *Phil.* 1–4, *Catil.*, written in s. XIII²/₄ for Richard de Fournival;[126] a manuscript now divided in two, Berlin (East) Phill. 1794 + Paris lat. 8049, containing among other things *Phil.* 1–4, *De legibus*, Petronius, which was written in the mid-twelfth century possibly in the Orléanais and belonged to Jean de Berry in the fourteenth century;[127] and Oxford, Merton College 311 (s. XII², England), containing I. *De off.*, *De nat. deorum*, *De fato*, *Phil.* 1–4.15, II. Palladius, which has the Colotian text only for *Phil.* 1–2.118 and was completed from a different source.[128] For its text of *De nat. deorum* Merton 311 is descended from the text of Lupus of Ferrières, Vienna 189; its home before it emerged in the hands of Thomas Tryllek, Bishop of Rochester (d. 1372), is unknown.[129] To these four manuscripts can be added the extracts in the late twelfth-century florilegium, Paris lat. 18104, part III, probably compiled at Chartres, and Escorial V.III.6 (s. XIV²), probably from Verona.[130]

The *Philippics* appear in two eleventh-century book-lists that may both be French. The one ('Divina Philippica Ciceronis'[131]) is added to the Sherborne Pontifical, and came from a French church dedicated to the Virgin which had contacts with Saxon England.[132] The other ('Phylippicarum libros') is a list of school authors added to a manuscript owned by Hartwic of St. Emmeram, who studied at Chartres under Fulbert and at Reims.[133] The *Philippics* also existed at Corbie

---

[124] F. Avril ap. R. H. Rouse, *IMU* 22 (1979), 121 n. 2.

[125] *Catalogue général*, 2.397 no. 79 = Becker 86.76 (p. 201): 'In alio Suetonius et Iulius Frontinus et Eutropius et Tullius Tusculane et Philippica eiusdem'.

[126] Cf. n. 53, above. A probable copy of Fournival's manuscript is Escorial R.I.2 (s. XIV²); cf. n. 90, above.

[127] P. L. Schmidt (n. 22, above), 201–5.

[128] Lambeth Palace 425 (s. XIII¹, England or France; 1.1–2.76) may be similar. Early in *Phil.* 1, and doubtless beyond, it is Colotian, and in 1.1 it agrees with Merton 311 in reading *sedandis discordiis usa fuerat*; cf. Clark, *CR* 14 (1902), 41.

[129] See *Survival*, no. 130.   [130] P. L. Schmidt (n. 22, above), 229–32.

[131] Juvenal 10.125 bestows this compliment on *Phil.* 2, but so narrow a sense is unlikely here.

[132] Edited by Delisle, ii. 446–7; see N. R. Ker, *Catalogue of Manuscripts containing Anglo-Saxon* (Oxford, 1957), 437–9, and D. de Bruyne in *Rev. bén.* 29 (1912), 481–5, who attributes the list to Notre-Dame, Paris.

[133] Bischoff, *Mitt. Stud.* ii. 80–4; but see above, n. 58, for the problem of the list's origin.

*c.*1200[134] and at Chartres in 1303, since they were borrowed from the cathedral library on 16 December by Landolfo Colonna.[135]

The *Philippics* were known in Germany by the late tenth century. After the Colotian group the best witness to D is Munich Clm 18787 (T, s. X²; Chatelain, plate XXVII), containing Symmachus, *Relationes, Phil.* 1–14.25, five speeches that will be our next subject (§ 5, below), and a fragment of the *Caesarians* (*Marc.* 1–15), and written somewhere in western Germany.[136] In a letter to Notker Labeo at St. Gall shortly before 1022, Hugh, Bishop of Sitten, says that the Bishop of Reichenau has given a more than equal pledge in return for Notker's *Philippics* and commentary on the *Topica*.[137] Cologne, Dombibl. 198, written in Germany in the late tenth or early eleventh century, contains Boethius on the *Topica* and *Phil.* 1–2.77. Editors have not reported it, but it resembles a manuscript that they have reported, Wolfenbüttel, Gud. lat. 278 (g, s. XII; at Bordesholm in s. XIV and presumably German).[138] The *Philippics* are also found in another Cologne manuscript, now British Library, Harley 2682 (H of *Catil. Caes. Verr.*, s. XI²). Two later manuscripts closely related to each other may be witnesses to what lay in Cologne at an earlier date: Brussels 14492 (s. XIV²/XV¹, Le Parc) and Cambridge, Univ. Dd. 13. 2 (a. 1444, Cologne).[139] About 1149 Rainald of Dassel, Prior of Hildesheim, warily offered Wibald, Abbot of Stavelot and Corvey, manuscripts of *De lege agraria*, the *Philippics*, and letters.[140] While Wibald certainly received *De lege agraria* and part of *Ad fam.* from somewhere (§ 6, below), evidently he did not receive the *Philippics*; at least he did not include them in his Ciceronian collection, Berlin (West) lat. 2° 252.[141] Another pre-Renaissance German manuscript survives, Bamberg Class. 28/M.IV.5 (s. XIII¹), which is recorded in the thirteenth-century catalogue of the cathedral.[142] Other manuscripts were recorded in the thirteenth-century catalogues of Rolduc near Liège ('Philippica Tullii') and of St. Pancras in Hamersleven near Magdeburg ('Tullium Philippicarum'), and in the catalogue of 1347 from Prüfening near

[134] Delisle, ii.437, no. 193.   [135] *Catalogue général*, 11 (Paris, 1890), iii.

[136] C. E. Eder, *Stud. und Mitt. zur Gesch. des Ben.* 83 (1972), 138 no. 162 (with Bischoff's assent). Apart from the copy of T mentioned below (§ 5), the only other manuscript of Symm. *Rel.* is Metz 500 (s. X², from St. Arnulf); cf. O. Seeck's edition (*MGH, Auct. ant.* vi.1, Berlin, 1883), xix–xxii.

[137] J. Grimm, *Kleinere Schriften*, 5 (Berlin, 1871), 191: 'Libros vestros, id est Philippica et commentum in Topica Ciceronis, petiit a me abbas de Augia, pignore dato quod maioris pretii est'.

[138] Clark, OCT ii (2nd edn.), preface.

[139] R. M. T., *Rev. bén.* 85 (1975), 373–4, ascribes to William of Malmesbury the brief introduction to the *Philippics* in the Cambridge manuscript, but see below, § 5 and n. 157.

[140] Ph. Jaffé, *Bibl. rerum Germanicarum* I: *monumenta Corbeiensia* (Berlin, 1864), 326–7, quoted below in § 6.

[141] The absence of the *Philippics* from this collection is another reason for doubting whether any of it was taken directly from H, which includes them; cf. n. 95, above. On the other hand, Wibald may have thought that such a long text deserved a volume to itself, and in that form it may even survive unrecognized.

[142] *Mittelalterliche Bibliothekskataloge Deutschlands und der Schweiz*, iii.3 (1939), no. 343.12.

Regensburg ('VIII [probably a slip for XIII] libri Marci Tullii Cyceronis Phylippicarum . . .').[143]

In the course of a fictitious example in his *Rhetorimachia*, the Milanese Anselm of Besate, a member of the imperial chancery and chaplain to Henry III (1039–56), accuses the villain Rotiland of having stolen the *Philippics* and given them in payment to his mistress.[144] What we have seen of the transmission makes it more likely that Anselm knew the *Philippics* in Germany, where he was employed, than in Italy, where he composed the *Rhetorimachia*.

During the twelfth and thirteenth centuries copies of the *Philippics* multiplied, though one could never claim that the work circulated widely before the Renaissance. The medieval manuscripts not referred to above[145] might some day be reported, or, if already reported, geographically placed. The *Philippics* 'returned' to Italy in the fourteenth century: Paris lat. 5802 (speeches 1–4) was in Petrarch's hands before the middle of the century, and he also knew the full text.[146] Among the early Italian manuscripts (excluding the Montecassino copy mentioned above) are Amsterdam 74, Wolfenbüttel, Gud. lat. 2, and Escorial V.III.6 (noted above). By 1428 V was in Italy; Poggio used it to annotate his D manuscript, Florence, Laur. 48.22,[147] and the merger of the two textual streams was under way.

5

At this point France leaves the picture, to return only in the late fourteenth century when French scholars disturb the dust in old libraries. The German contribution to the transmission of the speeches, so far as manuscripts still extant bear witness to it, begins a century and a half later than the French: P (§ 2, above) and C (§ 3, above) were

---

[143] Manitius, *Handschriften*, 22; Becker, 56.74 (p. 141), redated from s. XI to s. XIII by Th. Gottlieb, *Über mittelalterliche Bibliotheken* (Leipzig, 1892), 36; *Mittelalterliche Bibliothekskataloge*, iv.1 (1977), no. 42.443 (p. 439).

[144] Ed. K. Manitius (*MGH, Deutsche Geschichtsquellen des Mittelalters 500–1500*, 2, Weimar 1958), 169; *Philippics* cited on p. 176 (cf. 99, 126).

[145] Amsterdam 74 (s. XIII, Italy), Berlin (East) Phill. 1732, part II (s. XIII, Reims), Berne 104 (s. XII), Dresden R 52 (s. XII¹, Germany), Florence, Laur. S. Marco 268 (s. XII, France), Jena, Bose q.5 (s. XIII), B. L. Royal 15. A. VIII (s. XIII), Lambeth Palace 425 (s. XIII¹, England; cf. n. 128, above), *Florilegium Gallicum* (s. XII med., Orléans), lexical extracts in Berne 276 (s. XIII med., central France).

[146] P. de Nolhac, *Pétrarque et l'humanisme*² (Paris, 1907) i. 246–8, 252–3, ii. 279–82; cf. nn. 218 and 223, below. Paris n. a. lat. 3070 (s. XIV), which contains Florus and *Phil.* 1–4 and has annotations by Salutati, should prove to be a copy of Paris lat. 5802 or at least a close relative; cf. Ullman, *Salutati*, 196–7, 224.

[147] For an interesting study of his work on V see Silvia Rizzo, *Il lessico filologico degli umanisti* (Rome, 1973), 327–38. He took the same view of it as Clark: 'Nulla est femella tam rudis, tam insulsa, quae non emendatius scripsisset' (*Ep.* 1.216).

written early in the ninth century, T of the *Philippics* late in the tenth. Nevertheless, Germany makes up for its slow start.

Between the *Philippics* and its fragment of the *Caesarians* T has five new speeches, *Pro lege Manilia* (*De imperio Pompeii*), *Pro Milone*, *Pro Sulla*, *Pro Plancio*, and *Pro Caecina*.[148] T has lost *Manil.* 1–46 together with the end of the *Philippics*, but luckily it is the one speech copied into Hildesheim, Bibl. des Gymnasium Josephinum 3 (t, 'liber S. Godehardi episc. in Hildenesheim') with the *Relationes* of Symmachus.[149] Whether the copying took place at Hildesheim may be doubted. T is not known to have been there before it reached Tegernsee,[150] and a piece of external evidence suggests that t may have come to Hildesheim from the south. The twelfth-century collection of letters from Reinhardsbrunn (near Gotha) refers to a manuscript 'in quo simul continebantur libri Ciceronis de rethorica ad Herentium, pars commentarii super Porfirium, Tullius de inperio geñ Pompeii, Boetius de cathegoricis sillogismis, atque epistole Simmachi prefecti Romane urbis';[151] four of these five texts, an unusual combination, recur in t, and the 'epistole Simmachi', if they are those from book 10 known as the *Relationes*, occur in only one extant manuscript besides t and T, a manuscript from Metz.[152] It therefore seems possible that T moved soon after it was written from western Germany to Tegernsee, where someone drew on it in putting together the collection attested by t and by the letter from Reinhardsbrunn. Much depends, however, on the date of t, variously given as s. XII, s. XIII, and s. XV. Dare one suggest without seeing t that 'liber S. Godehardi episc. in Hildensheim', though obviously not written on the flyleaf by Godehard himself, is true? He was bishop of Hildesheim from 1022 to 1038 and went there from Tegernsee.[153] If the *ex libris*

---

[148] No one has edited them all together, though Clark in the OCT edited them all. For *Manil.* see OCT i (1905), P. Reis in vol. vi.1 of the Teubner (1933), and A. Boulanger in vol. vii of the Budé *Discours* (1929); for *Mil.*, OCT ii (1918²), Klotz in vol. viii of the Teubner (1918), and Boulanger in vol. xvii of the Budé *Discours* (1949); for *Sull.*, OCT vi (1911), H. Kasten in the Teubner (1933¹, 1949², 1966³), Boulanger in vol. xi of the Budé *Discours* (1943), and J. Em. Pabón in the Mondadori Cicero (1964); for *Planc.*, OCT vi, Klotz in vol. vii of the Teubner (1919), and P. Grimal in vol. xvi.2 of the Budé *Discours* (1976); and for *Caec.*, OCT iv (1909), F. Schoell in vol. iv of the Teubner (1923), Boulanger in vol. vii of the Budé *Discours* (1929), and A. D'Ors in the Mondadori Cicero (1965). W. A. Schröder of Hamburg will soon publish an edition of *Caec.*; he has kindly allowed us to read his discussion of the manuscripts. A new Teubner of *Planc.* is announced, edited by E. Olechowska.

[149] Cf. H. Nohl, *Hermes*, 21 (1886), 193; t had been described by J. G. Müller, *Nachricht über die Bibliothek des Gymnasii Josephini und die auf derselben vorhandenen Handschriften und alten Drucke* (Hildesheim, 1876), 2–3.

[150] We saw that Rainald had the *Philippics* at Hildesheim (cf. n. 140, above), but by then they were no great rarity.

[151] F. Peeck, *Die Reinhardsbrunner Briefsammlung* (*MGH, Epp. sel.* 5, Weimar, 1952), 48, *Ep.* 51.

[152] Cf. n. 136, above. Müller (n. 149, above), 2, gives the contents of t as *Ad Herenn.*, Boeth. *De syll.*, *De diff. top.*, *De divis.*, Cic. *Manil.*, *Somn. Scip.*, Symm. 'epist. 22 bis 69'.

[153] L. Mendelssohn in his edition of *Ad fam.* (Leipzig, 1893), pp. ix–x, without mentioning the letter from Reinhardsbrunn, noted that the movements of Godehard connect Niederaltaich, Tegernsee, and Hildesheim, but editors of *Manil.* have not picked this up. Addendum (March,

means rather that t belonged to the Benedictine monastery of St. Godehard, founded in 1136, then 1136 is the *terminus post quem* for the *ex libris*.

Another four extant manuscripts, a lost one, and the lost source of numerous others, include two or more of *Manil. Mil. Sull. Planc. Caec.* and maintain throughout the same relationship to T:[154]

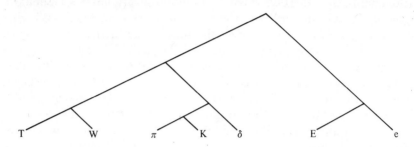

E is the Erfurtensis, now Berlin (West) lat. 2° 252 (s. XII med.), in which Wibald of Corvey assembled so many speeches that it has been mentioned several times already (§§ 2, 3, 4, above). Its sister e, Vatican, Pal. lat. 1525 (Chatelain, plate XXV), is another large collection of Cicero's works, written at Heidelberg in 1467.[155] Like T, E puts *Manil.* at the head of the five speeches, but it gives the other four in the order *Caec., Sull., Planc., Mil.*; it has lost *Caec.* 100 – *Sull.* 81.[156] The order of E doubtless recurred in the exemplar of e, but e contains only *Manil., Caec., Sull.* 1–43.

The only manuscript of the family besides TE that contains all five speeches is K, Cambridge, Univ. Dd. 13. 2, a Ciceronian collection even more ambitious than E and e if, as seems likely, it was copied partly from English and partly from Continental exemplars. The evidence for this comes from its contents. It opens with philosophical works (*De senect., De nat. deorum, De div., De fato, Lucull., Tim., Parad.*), and to *Lucullus* is appended a note of all the information that 'ego Willelmus Malmesburgensis' have collected about lost books of the *Academica*. William of Malmesbury (d. about 1143) took a great interest in Cicero,

1982): Dr W. Milde and Dr H. Härtel have kindly informed us that t is now Hildesheim, Dombibl. J. 70 and that the relevant part dates from s. XI[1].

[154] H. Kasten in his first edition of *Sull.*, p. xiii, gave this stemma, though without W and K; he needlessly modified it in his later editions. Grimal's stemma for *Planc.*, p. 41, has a serious misprint in it but will not work anyway.
[155] Pithou's copy of Lambinus's edition (Strasbourg, 1581) at Heidelberg (Hs. 222) contains a collation of a manuscript often supposed lost but identified with e by P. L. Schmidt (n. 22, above), 183.
[156] Before this accident befell it, J. Zinzerling reported a few readings from *Sull.* in his *Criticorum iuvenilium promulsis* (Leiden, 1610), 1–7 (cf. 179–80), and Gruter more in his edition (Hamburg, 1618) on the authority of Gulielmus's collation, for which see below, n. 160.

and presumably a manuscript that he annotated lies behind this part of K.[157] Then follow *Mil.* (with an introduction), *Planc.*, and a striking series of speeches presented in the same order and very much the same text by π: *Cael.*, *Sull.*, *Manil.* 1–51 and without a break *Caec.* 64–end, *Caes.*, *Caec.* 64–end again under the title *In Pisonem*,[158] *Catil.*, pseudo-Sall./Cic. *Invect.*, and the *Philippics*. K ends with *De officiis* and the *Tusculans*, and the subscription reads 'Per manus Theoderici Nycolai Werken de Abbenbroeck liber explicit anno domini M°CCCC°44 alias 1444'. Werken copied several manuscripts for William Gray, later Bishop of Ely, who in 1444 was studying at Cologne. If the whole manuscript was written at Cologne, including the works associated with William of Malmesbury, Gray must have brought at least one of his exemplars with him from England. William never travelled abroad, and it would be as surprising to find texts that he had worked on being read on the Continent with his annotations as it would be to find him using in England five speeches otherwise confined to Germany. Presumably, therefore, Werken discovered and copied the five speeches in the neighbourhood of Cologne.

It is to that region that π belongs. Now Brussels 14492, π was once at the abbey of Le Parc, near Louvain. Though it has usually been assigned to s. XIV, it may well be later, perhaps little earlier than K. It contains no other works beyond what it shares with K. The absence of *Mil.* and *Planc.*, unless they were once present, immediately suggests that it was not the exemplar of K, and readings do indeed show that K is a twin, not a copy.[159] Editors should therefore address to the exemplar of π and K the abuse that they have heaped on π for disfiguring the text.

W, the lost Werdensis, was brought from Saxony in the sixteenth century by Paulus Bruin, pastor of Werden (near Essen). F. Fabricius used it for his edition of *Mil.* (Düsseldorf, 1569), and J. Gulielmus (1555–84) collated it for *Mil.* and *Manil.* towards an edition that he did not live to complete; hitherto Gulielmus's collation has been known only from Gruter's edition (Hamburg, 1618), but it survives at Leiden.[160] Neither the full contents of W nor its exact place in the stemma will be determined until someone works through this collation and Fabricius's various editions of Cicero.[161]

[157] M. R. James, *Two Ancient English Scholars* (Glasgow, 1931), 21–5; R. A. B. Mynors, *Trans. Camb. Bibliog. Soc.* 1 (1949–53), 98 with plate VIIa and *Catalogue of the Manuscripts of Balliol College Oxford* (Oxford, 1963), xxix, 377; R. M. Thomson, *Rev. bén.* 85 (1975), 372–6. Clark, OCT vi.xii n. 2, mentions K as similar to π in *Pro Sulla*, but no other editor of any speech has acknowledged its existence.

[158] Whoever gave it this title was probably misled by the questions put to Piso in §§ 81, 89, 93.

[159] Thanks to W. A. Schröder (cf. n. 148, above) we have been able to compare photographs of π in both versions of *Caec.* with a microfilm of K. In the first version we found fifteen errors peculiar to π, singly not decisive but collectively too many for so slavish a scribe as Werken to have set right. That π was not copied from K is quite certain.   [160] P. L. Schmidt (n. 22, above), 219–20.

[161] They are all rare. The only copy that we have been able to trace of his *Pro Milone* is Graevius's, which Clark found at Heidelberg; cf. his *ed. maior* (Oxford, 1895) xxxvi. We have

The remaining witness, δ, is the lost parent of the *Itali*. Petrarch borrowed it in 1350 from his Florentine friend Lapo da Castiglionchio, but where or when Lapo acquired it is not known. One copy survives from Lapo's side of the transaction, Florence, Laur. S. Croce 23 sin. 3 (a, s. XIV²/XV¹),[162] and many from Petrarch's, including Vatican, Pal. lat. 1820, written at Padua in 1394,[163] and exports to the north such as Paris lat. 14749, the large collection of Cicero written about 1400 for Nicholas de Clamanges; a, free from Petrarch's emendations, more faithfully represents δ.[164] Missing from δ was *Pro Caecina*, which Poggio copied at Langres in 1417; his source, a relative of e, cannot have been very old and need not have spent much time at Langres.[165] The absence of δ makes πK useful in *Caec.* as arbitrators between T and Ee.

Some odds and ends of the family have yet to be placed in the stemma. Brussels 9755–63 of *Pro Sulla* (s. XV) is said to resemble π.[166] Berne 104 of *Pro Milone* resembles δ but may antedate Petrarch,[167] and Bonn S 140 of *Pro Milone*, written not far from Bonn in s. XV²/4, resembles K.[168]

All indications point to the preservation somewhere in western Germany of a manuscript that contained all five speeches. It is interesting, therefore, that in the ninth century the abbey of Lorsch possessed 'Metrum Tulli Ciceronis orationis pro Culentio, pro Melone, in Pisonem, pro Cornelio'.[169] Suitably emended, this entry attests two of the five speeches,[170] and it may not be an exhaustive enumeration.

associated W with T in the stemma because Gulielmus's collation of *Mil.*, which we have skimmed, records a number of errors shared with T against EKδ; his collation of *Manil.* we did not even have time to skim.

[162] Clark, OCT vi. v–ix; Billanovich, *Studi e testi*, 124 (1946), 99–100 and *Petrarca letterato*, i (Rome, 1947), 104–5, 107–8.

[163] Billanovich in *Studi e testi*, 88–97.

[164] For some emendations of Petrarch's in these speeches see Silvia Rizzo, *RFIC* 103 (1975), 5–15.

[165] Vatican lat. 11458 (Poggio's autograph), f. 49ᵛ: 'Hanc orationem antea culpa temporum deperditam Poggius Latinis viris restituit et in Italiam reduxit cum eam diligentia sua in Gallia reclusam in silvis Lingonum adinvenisset conscripsissetque ad Tullii memoriam et doctorum hominum utilitatem.' See J. Ruysschaert, *Codices Vaticani Latini 11414–11709* (Vatican, 1959), 94. Nicholas de Clamanges was treasurer of Langres and could have shown Poggio a manuscript acquired elsewhere; cf. G. Ouy, *The Library Chronicle*, 43.1 (1978), 20–1.

[166] Clark, OCT vi. xii n. 2.

[167] Ibid. viii. Pierre Petitmengin has kindly looked at it and reports that he would date it to s. XIII²/XIV¹. Lapo's manuscript of *Mil.* may have been distinct from his manuscript of *Manil. Planc. Sull.*; cf. A. Foresti, *Aneddoti della vita di Francesco Petrarca* (Padua, 1977²), 242–50, esp. 247–8.

[168] Halm, *Zur Handschriftenkunde der Ciceronischen Schriften* (Munich, 1850), 2, mentioned it and assigned it to s. XIV; T. W. Dougan in his edition of the *Tusculans*, i (Cambridge, 1905), xl, associated it with K. Professor O. Zwierlein has kindly confirmed that in *Mil.* it shares with K the brief introduction and the jumbled order (due to the transposition, in their source, of two bifolia in the middle of a quire); he has also furnished us with specimens of the hand.

[169] Becker, 37.445 (p. 111).

[170] *Marci Tulli Ciceronis orationes* etc.; see Bischoff, *Lorsch*, 72 n. 34. There were other speeches *Pro Cornelio* besides *Pro Sulla* (Teubner viii. 401–25), but no speech is known to have perished in the Middle Ages.

Pro Milone and *Pro lege Manilia* are also connected in a separate tradition, which will be treated when we come to Poggio's Cluniacensis (§ 10, below). The Turin palimpsest had parts of *Pro Caecina, Pro Milone*, and *Pro lege Manilia*, and there is a papyrus of *Pro lege Manilia* and a parchment leaf from Egypt of *Pro Plancio* (§ 1, above).

6

The lost manuscript at Lorsch included *In Pisonem*, of which we have already found a headless and tailless text in V (§ 4, above). German manuscripts restore the tail and at the same time supply three speeches *De lege agraria* and fresh evidence for the text of a speech that had long been in circulation.

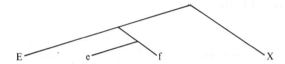

E (s. xii med.) and e (a. 1467) are the same as in *Pro lege Manilia* (§ 5, above). Their relative f, Erlangen 618, contains amid philosophical works two sequences of speeches, *Catil., In Pisonem*, pseudo-Sall./Cic. *Invect.*, and *De lege agraria, Pridie, Sen., Pop.*; it is dated 1466 and was bought in that year at Heidelberg, where it was doubtless written. Wibald when he put together E may well have received *De lege agraria* from Rainald of Dassel, Prior of Hildesheim, who in turn may have brought it from France:

Libros igitur qui apud nos sunt, Tullium de lege agraria et Philippica et epistolas eius, vobis transmisissemus, sed non est consuetudinis apud nos ut sine bonis monimentis aliqui alicui concedantur. Mittite igitur nobis Agellium Noctium Atticarum et Origenem super cantica canticorum; nostros autem, quos nunc adduximus de Francia, siqui vobis placent, vobis mittemus.[171]

Rainald moved from Hildesheim to the Archbishopric of Cologne, and it was probably at Cologne that Poggio found *Agr.* and *Pis.* in 1417. Certainly his friends and his son Jacopo believed that he had found speeches at Cologne,[172] and only one other group comes into question (§ 11, below). The copy that he made on the spot had to be laboriously and insecurely reconstructed from its descendants until A. Campana

---

[171] Jaffé, loc. cit. (n. 140, above), quoted by L. Mendelssohn (cf. n. 153, above) but missed by other editors of Cicero. W. Grebe, *Annalen des hist. Vereins für den Niederrhein*, 171 (1969), 11–12, = *Friedrich Barbarossa*, ed. G. Wolf (Darmstadt, 1975), 253–5, suggests that by 'nostros' Rainald means not 'our' manuscripts of *Agr., Phil.*, and *Epp.*, but 'my' manuscripts brought back from Reims in 1148.

[172] E. Walser, *Poggius Florentinus: Leben und Werke* (Berlin, 1914), 58–9; N. Rubinstein, *IMU* 1 (1958), 394, 399.

identified it in 1948: Vatican lat. 11458 (X).[173] Despite its late date among the authoritative witnesses to Cicero's speeches, X alone preserves explicit evidence of work on their text in Antiquity: 'In exemplari vetustissimo hoc erat in margine: Emendavi ad Tyronem et Laecanianum. Acta ipso Cicerone et Antonio coss. oratio xxiiii. In exemplo sic fuit: Statilius Maximus rursum emendavi ad Tyronem et Laecanianum et Dom. et alios veteres iii oratio eximia' (f. 56ᵛ, between *Agr.* I and II).[174] The 'exemplar vetustissimum' must have been the archetype, because it began at the same point as Eef through the loss of 'due charte in principio' (f. 53ʳ).

Agr. and *Pis.* stand next to each other in X and e but not in E or f. Furthermore, though both are headless, neither is tailless.[175] We also saw Rainald mentioning one without the other. It may be, therefore, that different manuscripts preserved them. If so, perhaps the same library possessed both.

Besides copying *Agr.* and *Pis.* in ff. 53–96 of X, Poggio noted the *incipit* and *explicit* of the four speeches towards the end of the quires that he used for copying *Caec.* (f. 51ʳ).[176] As the original order of quires is uncertain, it seems likely that after copying *Agr.* and *Pis.* at Cologne he found at Langres (§5, above) a relative of e. Both e and E include *Caec.*, *Agr.*, and *Pis.*, but nothing else that would have been new to him.[177] He therefore copied *Caec.* and noted the *incipit* and *explicit* of *Agr.* and *Pis.* for comparison later with what he had recently copied.[178]

In 1429 Poggio told Niccoli that Nicholas of Cues had many works of Cicero, including *De lege agraria* and *In Pisonem*.[179] For both speeches certain readings in descendants of X have been credited to this supposedly old manuscript of Nicholas's,[180] but not everyone is convinced that it was old,[181] and the attractive readings may have nothing to do

[173] *In Pisonem* has since been edited by R. G. M. Nisbet (Oxford, 1961) and in his footsteps by P. Grimal in vol. xvi.1 of the Budé *Discours* (1966), but for *De lege agraria* nothing has yet replaced the editions of Clark in OCT iv (1909), A. Boulanger in vol. ix of the Budé *Discours* (1932), and L. Fruechtel in vol. vi.1 of the Teubner (1933).

[174] Cf. J. E. G. Zetzel, *HSCP* 77 (1973), 227–43; plate II, opposite p. 228, illustrates the note.

[175] Poggio infers the headlessness of *Pis.* not from the state of the manuscript but from Asconius. See Ruysschaert (n. 165, above), 94–5.

[176] We are indebted to Silvia Rizzo for a reproduction of this page.

[177] Martin Davies kindly tells us that the snippets of text on f. 51ʳ twice agree with Ee against X: *Agr.* 2.1 *contionem* for *orationem*, 3.16 *coram* for *coram et*. These divergences certainly show that Poggio did not copy the snippets from X, but unless the readings of Ee are errors, which is not clear, he could have copied the snippets and X at different times from the archetype. Though the variants are perfectly consistent with our suggestion, therefore, we cannot argue that they support it.

[178] f. 51ʳ itself provides an analogy. At the top of the page he describes a *mutilus* of *De oratore*, mainly by *incipit* and *explicit* of the discernible sections; and he had copied *De oratore* at least once already, in Florence, Laur. S. Marco 262 (*c*.1403).   [179] *Ep.* I.266–7.

[180] Clark, *Anecd. Oxon.* xi (1909), 23–7, OCT, pp. xi–xii; G. Lieberg, *Hermes*, 97 (1969), 455–72; L. Coraluppi, *Scripta philologa*, 2 (1980), 17–49, a long-winded mixture of old evidence and new speculation.

[181] P. L. Schmidt (n. 22, above), 268–72, boldly identifies it with Paris lat. 17154, an enormous volume produced at Padua or Rome a few years before. See p. 269 for the text of Poggio's statement.

with it. Undeniably, however, a manuscript independent of X has left its mark on the Italian tradition of *Agr.* and *Pis.*: to restore so many words absent from X but present in Ee, and to introduce such striking variants in agreement with Ee, would otherwise have demanded nothing short of clairvoyance. The precise authority of the manuscript will not be determined without more work on the Italian tradition.[182]

Though Poggio says nothing about it, a third speech may once have been associated with *Agr.* or *Pis.* or both. Editors of *Post reditum ad senatum* have noticed good readings in contemporary marginalia of E (E²) and in ef, but they have only looked elsewhere in the same corpus (§ 2, above) for other traces of this valuable source.[183] As Ee have the whole corpus and f has *Pridie*, *Sen.*, and *Pop.*, perhaps the valuable source for *Sen.* was never copied out but merely collated. If other parts of it were copied out, the results seem most likely to survive in *Agr.* and *Pis.*, the only other speeches for which Eef have no French kin. In e *Sen.* does indeed follow *Agr.* and *Pis.* at some distance from the rest of the corpus; perhaps after all it was copied out and not merely collated.

In Pisonem is well served by the Turin palimpsest (§ 1, above), and parts of Asconius' commentary survive.

7

E and e now make their final appearance in the one speech of Cicero's that may not have reached the Middle Ages in the company of others, *Pro Archia*. They constitute a family by themselves.

In the oldest manuscript, Brussels 5348–52 (G; Chatelain, plate XXXIII) *Pro Archia* comes last, preceded by *Ad Herenn.*, *De inv.* and Grillius' commentary, and the *Tusculans*. G was probably written for Olbert, Abbot of Gembloux 1012–48 and of St. James's Liège 1020–48.[184]

This is not the first time that E has joined forces with a manuscript from Gembloux: it did so in the corpus of 57–56 BC (§ 2, above) and in the *Caesarians* (§ 3, above). Doubtless Wibald obtained all these texts from the same place. *Pro Archia* provides a more solid reason why that place should have been Liège. When Petrarch visited Liège in 1333, he found two speeches new to him, *Pro Archia* and the spurious *Pridie*.[185] His copy of *Pro Archia* has disappeared, but in the early 1350s he sent a

[182] On four manuscripts now at Naples see E. Scuotto, *Vichiana*, 7 (1978), 318–33.

[183] Halm, *RhM* 9 (1854), 323 n. 4; W. Stock, *Genethliacon Gottingense* (Halle, 1888), 106–11; Klotz, *RhM* 68 (1913), 479–505. J. Guillén in his Mondadori edition (1967) does not comment on the status of E² ef. E. Courtney, *BICS* 10 (1963), 15–16, sounds a warning against some of their readings.

[184] Cf. n. 18, above and T. Maslowski and R. H. Rouse, *IMU* 22 (1979), 99 n. 2.

[185] P. de Nolhac, *Pétrarque et l'humanisme* (Paris, 1892), 182–3 = ed. 2 (Paris, 1907) i. 221–2; Clark, OCT vi. iv–vii. Cf. n. 20, above.

text to Lapo da Castiglionchio in return for Lapo's loan of *Manil. Mil. Planc. Sull.*, and his copy can be reconstructed in the same way as δ of those speeches (§ 5, above).[186] The manuscript he found was plainly neither G nor a relative of Ee; it may have been the archetype.[187] It cannot have contained anything else unusual, or he would have snapped that up too.

Another witness has recently been identified in a florilegium, Paris lat. 18104, part III (s. XII²), f. 194, compiled probably at Chartres but certainly in northern France.[188] The text might easily have migrated from Liège to Chartres: at least six scholars from Liège, including Olbert, studied at Chartres in the eleventh century. Variants suffice only to dissociate the manuscript from Ee, but it differs from EeGδ in four readings that need not be errors.[189] Though the process of excerpting often inspires alterations that would not be ventured in a continuous copy, these readings may show that an old manuscript of *Pro Archia* survived in a second place besides Liège.

8

In 1355 another of Petrarch's Florentine friends, Boccaccio, gave him a copy of a new speech. Boccaccio had carried off from Montecassino earlier in the same year the archetype of Varro, *De lingua Latina*, Florence, Laur. 51. 10 (M, s. XI²), which also contains *Pro Cluentio*.[190]

Like other manuscripts written at Montecassino in the Desiderian revival, M was copied from a worn exemplar. The length of the five lacunae in M (102–7, 127–32, 149–54, 176–82, 192–end) suggests that its exemplar had lost four bifolia and the final quire.[191] How the length of these lacunae is known we shall see presently (§ 10, below).

[186] There is a puzzle in this that Petrarchan scholars have not noticed. Petrarch had had *Arch.* since 1333, and yet the text that he gave Lapo nearly twenty years later had none of his emendations.

[187] So H. Nohl (Vienna–Prague–Leipzig, 1889), xi–xii. Clark misguidedly separated the manuscripts into a German and a French family without offering a stemma. The stemma in the Teubner of P. Reis (1933¹, 1949²) reflects Clark's view of the tradition. H. Kasten's new Teubner (Leipzig, 1966) is a great improvement both in assessment of the manuscripts and in accuracy, but of the two readings that he regards as *Bindefehler* of Gδ (p. x), one, the gloss *Archia* in 1, is not in both branches of δ, and the other, 16 *profugium* for *perfugium*, is trivial. F. Gaffiot in vol. xii of the Budé *Discours* (1938) contributes nothing on the manuscripts.

[188] T. Maslowski and R. H. Rouse, *IMU* 22 (1979), 97–106, 118–22.

[189] 4 *his me*, 5 *ex illis*, 16 *et facultas* om., 31 *in illis* (references are by line to Maslowski-Rouse, 102–3).

[190] Clark, *The Reappearance of the Texts of the Classics* (London, 1921), 20–1; Billanovich (n. 162, above), 102–5. Chatelain's plates of M (XII, XVII) show that Varro and *Ad Herennium* are in different hands, and *Pro Cluentio* is in a third; the three texts were not designed for inclusion in the same volume.

[191] Silvia Rizzo, *La tradizione manoscritta della* Pro Cluentio *di Cicerone* (Genoa, 1979), 23–5.

Once in Petrarch's hands, *Pro Cluentio* spread quickly, not only in Italy but also in France.[192]

9

When a text that first appears in the fourteenth or fifteenth century appears simultaneously on both sides of the Alps, either external evidence or the shape of the tradition will usually reveal in which direction it travelled. *Pro Archia* (§ 7, above) travelled in both directions: Petrarch found it in the north, and descendants of Petrarch's copy returned to the north. *Pro Quinctio* and *Pro Flacco* likewise appear on both sides of the Alps towards 1400. Whether they too came to light in the north is unknown, but the shape of the tradition shows that in their diffusion they crossed with *Pro Archia* and *Pro Cluentio* from south to north.

Antonio Loschi, secretary to the Duke of Milan, composed between 1391 and 1405 an *Inquisitio* on eleven of Cicero's speeches, *Manil.*, *Mil.*, *Planc.*, *Sull.*, *Arch.*, *Caes.*, *Cluent.*, *Pro Quinctio*, and *Pro Flacco*. Many manuscripts from the late fourteenth century on, both Italian and French, have the same eleven speeches in the same order, and the likeliest reason for this uniformity is that a lost collection of Petrarch's lies behind them. We have seen how he acquired the first nine speeches, and in a marginal note he refers to *Pro Flacco*. Perhaps *Quinct.* and *Flacc.* stand last because he acquired them last.[193]

Editors of *Quinct.* and *Flacc.* may well not have used the best members of this populous family. To say which they have used would merely reinforce unsupported claims. Instead let Vatican lat. 9305 and Pal. lat. 1478 be mentioned.[194]

Some fifteenth-century manuscripts have been thought to incorporate readings from a second source. A later hand added unimpeachable variants and supplements to the margins of Florence, Bibl. Naz. Conv. Soppr. J. iv. 4 (*olim* S. Marco 255, b),[195] and the two streams of tradition rapidly merge.[196] What happened is surely that one old manuscript was

---

[192] Ibid. 30. Until she publishes her edition, the only serviceable one is P. Boyancé's in vol. viii of the Budé *Discours* (1953); cf. Rizzo, *La tradizione* 27.

[193] For the material in this paragraph see Sabbadini, *Scoperte*, ii. 172, and Billanovich (n. 163, above), 101–2.

[194] Rizzo, *RFIC* 103 (1975), 7 and *La tradizione*, 27–34. E. Ströbel, *Philologus*, 52 (1894), 491–5, gives information about some manuscripts of *Pro Flacco*.

[195] De la Mare, *Handwriting*, 130, identifies b² with the Florentine humanist G. A. Vespucci (*c.*1434–1514).

[196] Clark, OCT iv (1909) and *Anecd. Oxon.* xi (1909), 3–9. L. Fruechtel in vol. vi.2 of the Teubner (1933), xxii, followed by A. Boulanger in vol. xii of the Budé *Discours* (1938), 71, and F. Zucker in the Mondadori edition of *Flacc.* (1963), 3, asserts that b² derives from an old manuscript related to V (§ 4, above); but agreements with V in true readings prove nothing of the

discovered twice, once by Petrarch if Petrarch it was, then by whoever brought the readings of b² into circulation.[197] Often in the Renaissance, and no doubt at other periods, descendants of the same manuscript come in waves; we shall see another example in a moment.

The text recoverable from these manuscripts omits *Flacc.* 47–53 and 75–83 and an uncertain amount between 5 and 6. The first gap is filled by V (§ 4, above), the second by a manuscript that will conclude this survey of Cicero's speeches (§ 12, below), and the third only partially by the Milan palimpsest (§ 1, above), by excerpts taken from V when it was intact (§ 4, above), and by the *Scholia Bobiensia*.[198] Three leaves of the Turin palimpsest had parts of *Pro Quinctio* (§ 1, above).

10

Perhaps awakened by Petrarch to the treasures of their old libraries, French scholars towards the end of the fourteenth century began to make discoveries of their own. Jean de Montreuil and Nicholas de Clamanges deserve the credit for the one to which we now turn, but Poggio stole their thunder.

The abbey of Cluny possessed in the twelfth century two collections of Ciceronian speeches. As we have seen (§ 3, above), one survives, albeit hardly less of a ruin than the abbey itself. The other is described as follows: 'Volumen in quo continetur Cicero Pro Milone et Pro Avito [= Habito; Habitus was the *cognomen* of Cluentius] et Pro Murena et pro quibusdam aliis.'[199] The story of how Clark identified the *alii* with Roscius and Caelius and the manuscript with a Cluniacensis that Poggio sent to Florence in 1415 is best read in his own words.[200] He also accomplished much of the difficult task that its disappearance after Poggio's death imposes on editors: the recovery of its readings from manuscripts designed to offer good texts of Cicero, not facsimiles of semi-legible survivals from an age long past (s. VIII or earlier in this instance, to judge from spellings left unmodernized).

No one copied the whole manuscript. Poggio's companion Bartolomeo da Montepulciano took extracts from it, uncomprehendingly reproduced in Florence, Laur. 54. 5 (B), but no one else treated all five speeches alike. They concentrated on the novelties, which were of three kinds: *Pro Murena* and *Pro Roscio Amerino* were completely new, *Pro*

---

kind. Editions of *Quinct.*: OCT iv (1909) by Clark, Budé i by H. de la Ville de Mirmont (1921, rev. J. Humbert, 1934), Teubner iv (1923) by Klotz.

[197] Billanovich, *Studi e Testi*, 124 (1946), 106, wonders whether Boccaccio discovered the two speeches and sent Petrarch a copy from Florence, where the original (or Boccaccio's copy) could have remained.   [198] See ASCONIUS.

[199] Delisle, ii. 478, no. 496.   [200] *Anecd. Oxon.* x (1905).

Cluentio had five new passages, and *Pro Milone, Pro Caelio*, and the rest of *Pro Cluentio* had new readings.

Paris lat. 14749 (Σ) contains the oldest copy of *Pro Murena* and *Pro Roscio*. Someone other than the two scribes added the new passages of *Pro Cluentio* and variants in the rest of *Pro Cluentio*, in *Pro Milone*, and in *Pro Caelio*. He has recently been identified as Nicholas de Clamanges, whose part in the discovery of the Cluniacensis before Poggio used it had already been divined by Sabbadini.[201] As Clark saw, his work on Σ makes it much easier to tell which of the numerous Italian manuscripts carry readings from the Cluniacensis.

The oldest Italian copy of *Pro Murena* and *Pro Roscio* is probably the oldest dated copy, Florence, Laur. 48. 10 (A), finished by the Florentine scribe Giovanni Aretino on 9 February 1416. In *Pro Cluentio* it supplies only the most obvious of the new passages, the last. That is the extent of its debt to the Cluniacensis, and even so little it very likely took at second hand from a lost transcript of Niccoli's. Between February 1416 and August 1417, the date of Florence, Bibl. Naz. II. II. 65 (N), someone in Florence copied out the other four passages of *Pro Cluentio* and noted a few readings in the rest of the speech; the best witness to this phase of work on the Cluniacensis is Vatican, Rossi 957 (R). Only later did someone collate the Cluniacensis in as much detail as Nicholas de Clamanges; it was probably Poggio himself between 1425 and 1429. Four manuscripts reflect this collation in marginalia (Florence, Bibl. Naz. Conv. Soppr. J. IV. 4, Florence, Laur. 90 sup. 69. 1, Naples IV. B. 11, Turin E. II. 24) and two in their text (Munich Clm 15734, Florence, Laur. 48. 12); at least five of the six are Florentine.[202]

Editors of *Pro Murena* and *Pro Roscio* have been divided, apparently without noticing it, over the relationship of the Italian witnesses. Some derive them all from one lost copy of the Cluniacensis,[203] while others derive at least three of them directly from the Cluniacensis.[204] Neither camp has reckoned with the all too likely complication of corrections entered in the Cluniacensis by someone such as Niccoli, which might wrongly be treated as *Bindefehler*. Whoever tackles the problem will need to look at other manuscripts besides those that have been canonical since Clark's favour fell on them.

The Cluniacensis springs a surprise in *Pro Milone*. Outside the

---

[201] *RFIC* 39 (1911), 547–9 = *Storia e critica*[2], 16–18. G. Ouy has identified Nicholas's hand in Σ; cf. Rizzo, *La tradizione*, 52–3.

[202] For the material in this paragraph, and more, see Rizzo, *La tradizione*, 55–80.

[203] H. Nohl, ed. of *Mur.* (1889), v–ix; H. Kasten in the Teubner *Mur.* (1933[1], 1961[2], 1972[3]) and *Rosc.* (1968, a revision of Klotz's edition, 1923[1], 1949[2]).

[204] Clark, *Anecd. Oxon.* x (1905), xxxix–1, lvii–lviii, and OCT i (1905), iv–v; H. de la Ville de Mirmont in his edition of *Rosc.* in Budé *Discours*, i (1921, rev. J. Humbert, 1934), iv; P. J. Enk in the Mondadori *Rosc.* (1964), 9–10. A. Boulanger in his edition of *Mur.*, Budé xi (1943), 24, does not make himself clear.

German family that transmits it in company with four other speeches
(§ 5, above) Clark had already recognized a superior strain of text in a
single German manuscript, H (s. XI²) of *Catil. Caes. Verr.* (§ 3, above);
though superior, however, it omitted 18–37. The Cluniacensis turns
out to have had the same gap and the same kind of text. At first sight it
looks unlike a coincidence that H resembles one old Cluniacensis in
Catil. Caes. Verr. (§ 3, above) and another in *Pro Milone*, but unless it can
be shown to derive from both there is no simple explanation. Clark had
given good reasons why it should not derive from C of *Catil. Caes.
Verr.*,[205] and now proceeded to give an equally good reason why it
should not derive from Poggio's Cluniacensis in *Pro Milone*: though it
aims at being a Ciceronian corpus, it has none of the other four speeches
that the Cluniacensis still contained when Poggio used it. Instead,
between *Pro Milone* and an oddly placed introduction to *Pro Milone*, it
has *Pro lege Manilia*, where it stands in exactly the same relationship to
the large German family.[206] As no medieval catalogue mentions *Pro lege
Manilia*, it would be pure speculation to connect H with either of two
manuscripts besides Poggio's Cluniacensis that contained *Pro Milone*:

'Metrum Tulli Ciceronis orationis pro Culentio, pro Melone, in
Pisonem, pro Cornelio' (Lorsch, s. IX).[207]

'Volumen in quo continentur cantica canticorum glossata, defensio
Tullii pro Miloné, Catonis liber, et versus de xii lapidibus' (Cluny,
s. XII).[208]

These lost manuscripts are the greatest mysteries in the medieval
tradition of Cicero's speeches.

Five extracts from *Pro Cluentio* have recently been found in Paris lat.
18104, part III (s. XII²), f. 194, written probably at Chartres but
certainly in northern France. The relationship of this manuscript to the
Cluniacensis and the Casinensis (M, § 8, above) is problematical, but

---

[205] *CR* 16 (1902), 324–5.

[206] The *scholia Gronoviana* should be reconsidered in connection with H and the two
Cluniacenses. Leiden, Voss. Lat. Q. 130, from which Jac. Gronovius first published them in 1692
and Th. Stangl last published them in *Ciceronis orationum scholiastae*, ii (Vienna and Leipzig, 1912),
277–351, has recently been assigned to s. IX¹ and Tours by Bischoff ap. K. A. de Meyier, *Codices
Vossiani Latini II: codices in quarto* (Leiden, 1975), 281–3; he also ascribes some of its annotations to
Heiric of Auxerre. The speeches covered by the scholia are *Verr.*, *Catil.*, and *Caes.*, all of which are
in C (s. IX¹, Tours) and H, and *Rosc. Manil. Mil. Cael.*, of which three were in Poggio's Cluniacensis
and two are in H. It looks as though not only Cluny but the place where H was written had
acquired both groups of speeches from Tours. What the *scholia Gronoviana* are most likely to be is
notes collected from the margins of old manuscripts; why not from manuscripts that had found
their way to Tours? For an analysis of them see Stangl, *Der sogenannte Gronovscholiast zu elf
Ciceronischen Reden* (Prague and Leipzig, 1884); by 1912 he had changed his mind about where to
draw the line between 'scholiasta B' and 'scholiasta A', but ABC all comment on *Caecil.* – *Verr.* II.1
(B and C overlap in *Verr.* I), and *Catil.* – *Caes.* and *Rosc.* – *Cael.* are all the work of D.

[207] Becker, 37.445 (p. 111). On the text see n. 170, above.

[208] Delisle, ii.474, no. 412.

the last two extracts come from the end of the speech, missing in M, and so offer a useful check on the Cluniacensis.[209]

The Turin palimpsest had more of *Pro Cluentio* than of any other speech (§ 1, above), and the Vatican palimpsest has the beginning of *Pro Roscio* (§ 1, above). Ancient fragments of *Pro Caelio*, *Pro Milone*, and *Pro lege Manilia* have already been mentioned (§§ 2, 5, above).

11

If Poggio collated the Cluniacensis, the manuscript in which he entered the collation is lost. A manuscript survives, however, in which he copied out other speeches that he had discovered. Long given up for lost, it was identified by A. Campana in 1948: Vatican lat. 11458 (X), which contains in part I *Pro Rabirio Postumo*, *Pro Rabirio perduellionis reo*, *Pro Roscio comoedo*, Probus, *De notis* (frag.), Victorinus, *Ars gramm.* (excc.), *Pro Caecina*, descriptions of manuscripts that contained *De oratore*, *De lege agraria*, and *In Pisonem*, then *De lege agraria* and *In Pisonem*, and in part II *Pro Flacco* and *Pro Fonteio*. Part I has this subscription: 'Has septem M. Tullii orationes, que antea culpa temporum apud Italos deperdite erant, Poggius Florentinus, perquisitis plurimis Gallie Germanieque summo cum studio ac diligentia biblyothecis, cum latentes comperisset in squalore et sordibus, in lucem solus extulit ac in pristinam dignitatem decoremque restituens Latinis musis dicavit'.[210] *Pro Caecina* has its own subscription, which says that he found it at Langres.[211] The other seven speeches in part I (there are three *De lege agraria*) he apparently found at Cologne.[212] Like *Pro Caecina* (§ 5, above), *De lege agraria* and *In Pisonem* survive in manuscripts older than X (§ 6, above), but X is the sole authority for the first three speeches apart from the Vatican palimpsest of the middle one (§ 1, above). All three are very badly preserved: one loss of leaves in some ancestor of X has carried off the end of *Pro Rab. perd. reo* and the beginning of *Pro Rosc. com.*, another the end of *Pro Rosc. com.*, and for once the apparatus bristles with conjectures.[213] At least Campana's discovery of X will spare editors the additional headache of reconstructing it and pinning down Poggio's conjectures.

---

[209] T. Maslowski and R. H. Rouse, *IMU* 22 (1979), 97–9, 106–22; Rizzo, *La tradizione*, 83–90.
[210] Ruysschaert (n. 165, above), 95.   [211] Cf. n. 165, above.
[212] Cf. n. 172, above. What 'has septem orationes' refers to is disputed, because eight speeches precede the subscription as X is now bound; Campana, followed by Coraluppi, op. cit. (n. 180, above), 39, thinks that *Rosc. com.* is excluded because it lacks both beginning and end, but I have suggested above (§ 6 and nn. 177–8) that the subscription antedates the copying of *Pro Caecina*.
[213] All three have been edited since the discovery of X: in the Mondadori Cicero *Rab. Post.* by G. C. Giardina (1967) and *Rab. perd.* by Th. Guardi (1979), and for Teubner *Rosc. com.* by J. Axer (1976). A new Teubner of *Rab. Post.* is announced, edited by E. Olechowska.

12

Between Poggio's discoveries and the first decipherment of Ciceronian palimpsests 400 years later, only one event enlarged the corpus of speeches, and it did not give the world a new speech. Conrad Peutinger obtained from Hieronymus Rorarius of Friuli a text of *Pro Flacco*, 75–83 and printed it in Cratander's edition (Basle, 1528). It runs to the same length as the text of 47–53 in V (§ 4, above) and thereby shows that the source of the humanistic tradition (§ 9, above) had lost the same number of leaves at two points. No other traces of Rorarius's manuscript have been detected either in Cratander's edition or elsewhere.

In all, then, thirty-two speeches of Cicero's have come down in medieval manuscripts (to count as one the four *Catilinarians*, the seven *Verrines*, the fourteen *Philippics*, and the three speeches *De lege agraria*). Even if collectors in the Middle Ages had been given that target to aim at, it would have been hard not to fall a long way short. Nine speeches certainly reached the Middle Ages together in one copy (§ 2, above), but no other groups consisted of more than five (§§ 10, 5, perhaps 3, above). Impressive collections were nevertheless built up by men of enterprise and dedication; and even what seem to us small collections may in their day have been thought complete.

Whether the ninth century took the first steps is not clear (§ 3, above). Unquestionable progress had been made by the end of the next century: T (s. x^2) combines the *Philippics*, *Pro lege Manilia* and its four companions, and the *Caesarians* (§§ 4, 5, 3, above), G (s. xi^1) more modestly the *Caesarians* and the corpus of 57–56 BC (§§ 3, 2 above). The end of the eleventh century sees the first attempt at putting not just all the speeches but all of Cicero between two covers: H (§§ 3, 4, 10, above) contains *Ad fam.* 9–16, *De amic.*, *De senect.*, the *Philippics*, the *Catilinarians*, *Paradoxa*, the *Caesarians* (twice), *Pro Milone*, *Pro lege Manilia*, extracts from the *Verrines*, and *De officiis*.

Then, about 1150, comes something that puts all earlier and many later collections in the shade. Wibald of Corvey asks Rainald, Prior of Hildesheim, for manuscripts of Cicero, and the next two letters of their correspondence are preserved. Rainald begins: 'Quamvis Tullii libros habere desideres, scio tamen Christianum te esse, non Ciceronianum. Transis enim et in aliena castra non tamquam transfuga sed tamquam explorator [Sen. *Ep.* 2.5].' Wibald spots the quotation and confirms that he is a Christian first, a Ciceronian second: 'Nec vero . . . pati possumus quod illud nobile ingenium, illa splendida inventa, illa tanta rerum et verborum ornamenta, oblivione et negligentia depereant, sed ipsius opera universa, quantacumque inveniri poterunt, in unum volumen confici volumus.'[214] He achieved his aim. At the front of E his prostrate figure is depicted offering a book to the three patron saints of Corvey, and below this scene sits Marcus Tullius Cicero pointing to a scroll, which another figure helps him to hold open.[215] The book is E, and E contained *De off.*, *De orat.*, *De inv.*, *Ad Herenn.*, *Topica*, twenty-one of the thirty-two extant speeches and extracts from another (§§ 2, 3, 5, 6, 7, above), *Ad fam.* 9–16, *De senect.*, and *De amicitia*. The speeches alone Wibald collected from so many sources that it is surprising what he failed to include: the *Philippics*, which he must have come close to obtaining from Rainald and could have obtained from elsewhere in western Germany, and the Leiden corpus of philosophical works, at least part of which circulated in western Germany.[216]

In one sense, however, E must be adjudged a grand failure beside what contemporaries of Wibald achieved in central France. While E sat on its shelf at Corvey, never copied so far as we can tell, they were busy plucking the choicest morsels from all the ancient texts they could lay their hands on and capturing the market with compilations like the *Florilegium Angelicum* and the *Florilegium Gallicum*. The former, which survives in over twenty copies, includes excerpts from the corpus of 57–56 BC (§ 2, above), the *Tusculans*, and the *Verrines* (§ 3, above); the latter, not quite so popular, from *De inv.*, *Ad Herenn.*, *De off.*, *De amic.*, *De senect.*, *Parad.*, *De orat.*, the corpus of 57–56 BC (§ 2, above), *Catil.* and *Caes.* (§ 3, above), and the *Philippics* (§ 4, above).[217] Only one manuscript that survives from the same period and the same region, British Library, Harl. 4927 (h), contains a fair number of these works more or less intact; before its end came adrift, it had all the works used in the *Florilegium Gallicum* except the first three,[218] and whoever put it together obviously had the same resources at his disposal. Vincent of Beauvais (*c.*1190–1264) owned a manuscript of the *Florilegium Gallicum*, Paris lat.

---

[214] Jaffé (n. 140, above), 326–8.

[215] A. Ludorff, *Die Bau- und Kunstdenkmäler von Westfalen. Kreis Höxter* (Münster, 1914), plate 45. The donor was wrongly identified by the later hand that labelled the figures; see F. Philippi, *Abhandlungen über Corveyer Geschichtsschreibung* (Münster, 1906), x–xv. For a description of E see E. Wunder's book on it (Leipzig, 1827) and P. Lehmann, *ABAW* 30.5 (1919), 18–19, 35–6. On Wibald in general see F.-J. Jakobi, *Wibald von Stablo und Corvey (1098–1158), benediktinischer Abt in der frühen Stauferzeit* (Münster, 1979).

[216] See n. 141, above and *De natura deorum* etc., n. 13.

[217] On the *Florilegium Angelicum* see Rouse and Rouse in *Medieval Learning*, 66–114. The *Florilegium Gallicum* gives its excerpts from the speeches in the order *Caes.*, *Pridie Sest. Cael.*, *Catil.*, *Pop. Vat. Dom. Prov. Har. Balb.*, pseudo-Sall./Cic. *Invect.*, *Philippics*; see A. Gagnér, *Florilegium Gallicum* (Lund, 1936), 122.

[218] For the present contents of h see § 2, above. We had conjectured that the *Philippics* were missing with the rest of *De senect.* before Ezio Ornato kindly drew our attention to no. 829 in the papal catalogue from Peñiscola (1411 or later), which corresponds to h as far as *De senect.* and then finishes with *Phil.* and *De oratore*. See M. Faucon, *La Librairie des papes d'Avignon*, ii (Paris, 1887), 132. Dr Ornato hopes to publish further information on the history of h. We can add that B. L. Add. 19586, a Ciceronian collection of s. XIV ex./XV in. from northern Italy, owes all its speeches to h; on another feature of this interesting manuscript see Schmidt (n. 22, above), 182–3.

17903, and his canon of Ciceronian works partly reflects its contents, with the addition of *Tusc.*, *De fin.* + *Acad.* 1, *Partit.*, and most of the Leiden corpus, but no more speeches.[219] For speeches Wibald was streets ahead.

The earliest Italian collection is a lost one of the late thirteenth century that has been reconstructed principally from two similar manuscripts half a century later, Troyes 552 and Wolfenbüttel, Gud. lat. 2.[220] This lost collection, probably made at Padua, differed in three respects from Vincent's canon: it had the Leiden corpus in full, it had no *Partit.*, and of the speeches it had only the *Philippics*. So at least it has been argued; but both its copies include *Partit.* and *Catil.*, *Caes.*, pseudo-Sall./Cic. *Invect.*, and *Sen.* (1–7 in Troyes 552, lost from Gud.), and Troyes 552 includes *Pop.* (1–23). If these speeches were not in the original collection, therefore, they were easily enough found elsewhere.[221]

Two of the collections so far mentioned, Harley 4927 and Troyes 552, came into the hands of Petrarch, one in the early 1330s, the other perhaps twenty years later.[222] He also acquired a French text of *Phil.* 1–4, Paris lat. 5802. What first broke new ground in French and Italian knowledge of the speeches was his discovery of *Pro Archia* at Liège in 1333 (§ 7, above). He had to wait until the 1350s before Lapo introduced him to *Pro lege Manilia*, *Pro Milone*, *Pro Plancio*, and *Pro Sulla* (§5, above), and Boccaccio to *Pro Cluentio* (§8, above). When and how he added to his collection the rest of the *Philippics*[223] and *Pro Quinctio* and *Pro Flacco* (§ 9, above) is obscure, and the extent of his acquaintance with the *Verrines* also remains something of a mystery.

With Petrarch begins the practice of segregating the speeches from other works of Cicero's. A volume in which he united eleven speeches (§ 9, above) has not survived, but descendants of it swept through Italy and France; so did descendants of Harley 4927, easily recognized by their excisions in the corpus of 57–56 BC. Descendants of both can be seen nowadays in almost any library that has Latin manuscripts.

---

[219] *Spec. hist.* VII.6. By 'orationum libros XII' he means *Caes.* and the corpus of 57–56 BC as he found them in Paris lat. 17903. He seems to have seen other manuscripts of *Catil.* and the *Philippics*; cf. Ullman, *CPh* 27 (1932), 32–3.　　　　[220] Schmidt, ibid. 177–97.

[221] Paris lat. 7695, which the catalogue puts in s. XIV, has amongst rhetorical works pseudo-Sall./Cic. *Invect.*, *Catil.*, *Caes.*, *Sen.*, and the *Philippics*. Is it French or Italian?

[222] According to Schmidt, 182, the *terminus post quem* for a certain note in Troyes 552 is 1343 or 1345; he infers that 1343–5 is the *terminus ante quem* for its acquisition. I do not follow his logic. A. Petrucci, *Studi e testi*, 248 (1967), 129, dates the bulk of the annotations after 1355. Since P. de Nolhac wrote a chapter on Petrarch and Cicero in *Pétrarque et l'humanisme*[2] (Paris, 1907), i. 213–68, much information has accrued, mainly through the work of Billanovich; see Schmidt's bibliography.

[223] Paris lat. 6342 (a. 1376), which Nolhac ascribed to the Florentine Tedaldo della Casa and regarded as a copy of a manuscript from Petrarch's library (ii. 279–82), is assigned to northern Italy by Billanovich, *IMU* 8 (1965), 2; but the connection with Petrarch remains – if anything, stronger. Cf. also n. 218, above; and Silvia Rizzo points out that Petrarch borrowed a manuscript of the *Philippics* from Lapo (*Var.* 45, a. 1351).

Clark's work on the *vetus Cluniacensis* brought into the limelight a volume of speeches put together in France partly from local materials but entirely on Petrarchan principles, Paris lat. 14749, to which Nicholas de Clamanges put the finishing touches before 1415. Between 1415 and 1428 Poggio rescued another seven speeches from oblivion, and thereafter descendants of Petrarch's manuscripts are usually descendants of his too. When Giovanni Andrea Bussi printed the full corpus of thirty-two speeches at Rome in 1471, and when they went into vol. 2 of the first printed *Opera omnia* (Milan, 1498–9), neither Petrarch nor Poggio would have raised an eyebrow, still less the many booksellers and scribes who had been producing the heavy but handsome volumes that editors of Cicero ungratefully dub *deteriores*. On the present occasion one set of such volumes may be singled out for mention, because the task of describing it fell to Roger Mynors: Oxford, Balliol College 248 A (twenty-six speeches), B (*Philippics, Verrines*), C (*Epp.*), D (*Opp. philos.*), E (*Opp. rhet.*).[224] They were written at Florence for William Gray, later Bishop of Ely, by calligraphers in the employ of Vespasiano; E is dated 1445, B 1447.

A Cicero written for Gray in 1444 at Cologne and again described by Roger Mynors, Cambridge, Univ. Dd. 13. 2 (§ 5, above), is a large collection of a kind that Petrarch had made unfashionable in Italy and France: a mixture of speeches and philosophical works. The two important collections written at Heidelberg in the 1460s, e and f (§§ 5, 6, 7, above), are equally old-fashioned.

Once segregated, the corpus of speeches invited another improvement, which was slow to come. 'Ciceronis opera quae nobis benigniora fata reservarunt,' writes the Milan editor of 1498–9, 'in quatuor volumina digesta impressimus non eo ordine quem temporum ratio disponebat sed quem necessitas praescripsit dum vetustiora exemplaria ex diversis et longinquis locis accersita expectamus.' An odd excuse, and one that would have cut no ice with the reader who jotted the following note in a copy of Beroaldus's edition (Bologna, 1499): 'Vide quam ineptissimus fuerit Beroaldus, qui has orationes cunctas pervertit nec ullam in suo ordine posuit: primo loco ponit hanc de reditu [*Pop.*] quam alias que sunt ante exilium, et omnes ita sunt depravate ut sine summa indignatione legi non possint.'[225] He lived long enough to see the improvement made: Naugerius in the second volume of his edition (Venice, 1519) printed the speeches in chronological order.[226] The

---

[224] *Catalogue of the Manuscripts of Balliol College Oxford* (Oxford, 1963), xxxi, 270–3.

[225] Oxford, Bodl. Auct. N. 2. 30; he was Mario Maffei (1463–1537), for whom see J. Ruysschaert, *La Bibliofilia*, 60 (1958), 311, 329 fig. 2.

[226] For a clear account of the early editions see *Gesamtkatalog der Wiegendrucke*, vi (1934), 542–50, 514–15. Ernesti surveyed the relationship of previous editions in *Historia critica operum Ciceronis typographorum formulis editorum* (Leipzig, 1756) and *De editionibus orationum Ciceronis* (Leipzig, 1759).

Teubner and the Budé maintain this tradition, but the OCT largely allows the manuscripts to dictate the order.

From Statilius Maximus in the second century to the most recent editors it may be doubted whether many years have passed when no one has collated a manuscript of Cicero's speeches. Published statements about what manuscripts have what readings are another matter. Do they begin in 1542, when Hieronymus Ferrarius in his *Emendationes in Philippicas Ciceronis* consistently reports the readings of a 'liber Colotianus' (lost) and a 'liber Langobardicis litteris scriptus' (Vatican lat. 3227)?[227] Editions of the later sixteenth and early seventeenth century are explicit enough to show that of the older and more important manuscripts V, H, and E, were already in use; the oldest editions fullest in their report of manuscripts collated by various scholars are those of Gruter (Hamburg, 1618) and Graevius (Amsterdam, 1695–9). Since 1550 the busiest collators have probably been Janus Gulielmus (1555–84), who in a short life saw many manuscripts in Germany and France;[228] the Jesuit G. Lagomarsini, who between 1735 and 1744 minutely recorded the readings of countless manuscripts in Florence;[229] and A. C. Clark, who in preparing the OCT of the speeches 'esaminò un numero di manoscritti che tuttora stupisce per la sua ampiezza'.[230]

The first edition in which a reasonable number of respectable manuscripts are economically reported at the foot of the page is the revision of Orelli's by Baiter and Halm (vol. ii, Zürich, 1854–6). H. Nohl in his *Orationes selectae* (1884–91) gave the first set of stemmata, which often show a firmer grasp of the tradition than others more recent.[231] The six volumes of A. C. Clark and W. Peterson (1901–11) stand out not only among recent editions of the speeches but also among early OCTs for the variety and importance of their new material: Peterson's work on the family of P (§ 2, above) and on C and the French tradition of the *Verrines* (§ 3, above) is overshadowed only by Clark's on H, the *vetus Cluniacensis*, and the manuscripts of the *Catilinarians*, *Caesarians*, and *Philippics*. At his best, in his reconstruction of the *vetus Cluniacensis*, Clark combined textual and historical evidence in a way that has not been surpassed. He never gave a single stemma, however, and his views on the relationship of manuscripts are not always clear. The main merit of the Teubner edition (vols. iv–viii, 1918–33), especially the parts done

---

[227] 'Conductis in unum multis Philippicarum voluminibus, et his quidem perveteribus, operam dedi ut, quoniam inter ipsa conveniret interdum, saepe variaretur, hanc varietatem constantiamque ita diligenter notatam haberem ut ne littera quidem effugeret.' On Ferrarius's manuscripts see Clark, OCT ii (2nd ed., 1918), praef., and Ullman, *CPh* 30 (1935), 161–4.

[228] Cf. Schmidt (n. 22, above), 218–20.   [229] Cf. ibid. 421–3.

[230] Rizzo, *La tradizione*, 21.

[231] See, e.g., n. 187, above. Zumpt and Madvig in the early 1830s gave stemmata for the *Verrines* and *Sest. Vat.*, which are among the earliest given for any classical texts; see S. Timpanaro, *La genesi del metodo del Lachmann* (new edn., Padua, 1981), 50–1, 57–8.

by A. Klotz, is its analytical prefaces, which take account both of the OCT and of earlier work. Budé editors, with a translation to produce, have been content until recently to assume that their English and German predecessors devoted all the necessary effort and thought to the manuscripts.

How, then, does the editing of Cicero's speeches stand, and what prospect of improvement lay before Mondadori when they launched their series in 1963 and Teubner (Leipzig) when they began in 1961 to replace the edition of 1918–33?[232] First, Campana's discovery of X warranted a new edition of the speeches that Poggio copied at Cologne in 1417 (§§ 6, 11, above). Second, Peterson's contributions to the OCT (vols. iii and v) were not thorough enough.[233] Third, even Clark was not always accurate, and for the readings of at least one important manuscript, M of *Pro Cluentio* (§ 8, above), he relied ultimately on a collation made in 1740;[234] Peterson's vol. v has been described as 'a work of remarkable carelessness'.[235] Fourth, despite the arrangement of the OCT and the example set by Clark, much remains to be clarified about how and where the speeches circulated; Clark expressed surprise that the *Caesarians* had never been edited as a unit,[236] but even parts of the OCT disguise historical and stemmatic links. Mondadori and Teubner have responded in the same way to the first and the fourth of these points: they have acknowledged the first, but rather than confront the fourth they have issued the speeches singly, a policy that has nothing better to be said for it than that Cicero mostly did the same. The second, third, and fourth points are all ignored in J. Guillén's Mondadori edition of *Sen.* (1967). Besides Peterson's manuscripts he looked at only five others, all in the Escorial; he dates two of them to s. XIII/XIV, one to s. XIV, one to s. XIV/XV, and one to s. XV, when the catalogue correctly puts them all in s. XV and four of them contain speeches discovered by Poggio in 1417; and his apparatus is highly inaccurate.[237] Happily not all the new editions sink so low, but the mere fact that this one could be printed shows that the series was launched with no specific aim. Good editions of single speeches, such as R. G. M. Nisbet's of *In Pisonem* (Oxford, 1961) and Silvia Rizzo's of *Pro Cluentio* (forthcoming), are some compensation for the deficiencies of the new Teubner series and its Italian competitor.

After all this *recensio*, a final word about *emendatio*. Addressing Victorius in the preface to his edition of the *Philippics* and the other

---

[232] Cf. J. Irmscher, 'Die Cicero-Ausgabe der Bibliotheca Teubneriana', *Atti del I congresso internaz. di studi Ciceroniani* (Rome, 1961), ii. 287–91.

[233] See §2 and nn. 89, 101, above. [234] Rizzo, *La tradizione*, 26–7.

[235] E. Courtney, *BICS* 10 (1963), 14. We have noticed that GE often go unreported.

[236] *CR* 14 (1900), 252.

[237] It is especially dismaying that such an edition should have appeared in the city where Billanovich had been teaching since 1955.

speeches in V (Rome, 1563), Gabriel Faernus turns a compliment to his predecessor into a splendid lesson in editorial method:

Nolumus hic fraudare sua laude Ferrarium; praeter enim complura loca quae prius ab se ex ingenio emendata, postea exemplarium vetustorum auctoritate comprobata fuisse ipse commemorat, loca alia VII et XL contra omnium quos ipse vidisset librorum fidem emendavit ita ut in hoc nostro [V] postea inveni. Sed et tu nonnulla in his orationibus coniecisti, non pauca et ego, quorum nos hic antiquus liber veros coniectores probavit; ex quo re ipsa admonemur in emendandis auctoribus non esse perpetuo libris scriptis inhaerendum sed aliquid etiam hominum ingenio iudicioque tribuendum. Quod propterea libentius commemoramus quia superioribus litteris tuis mihi significasti esse istic nonnullos ad quos huius antiqui exemplaris nuper inventi fama pervenerit qui has orationes postulent edi ad eum prorsus modum ut in eo scriptae inveniuntur neque quicquam omnino variari. Qui si ipsi in hunc librum incidissent, sententiam mihi crede mutarent; non enim bene habet semper hic liber sed multis locis et ipse mendosus est, inque illis ipsis locis ubi melior est aliis non semper omnino sincerus aut rectus est sed alicubi vestigia tantum verae lectionis ostendit, quae si edere nullo adhibito iudicio voluissem pro correctore corruptor dici iure potuissem. Librum ergo antiquum sequuti quidem sumus sed ea cautione ne ea etiam quae in eo essent mendosa sequeremur.[238]

When Clark over 300 years later established the readings of his *vetus Cluniacensis* in *Pro Caelio*, he pointed out that they confirmed six conjectures made by Madvig.[239] Paris lat. 18104, a new witness to the end of *Pro Cluentio*, adds another,[240] and the Barcelona papyrus of *Catil.* 2 confirms one made by Clark himself.

R. H. R.

M. D. R.

[238] Carlotta Dionisotti kindly points out that from 'superioribus litteris tuis . . .' these remarks are almost a translation of what he had written to Victorius in 1558 (B. L. Add. 10266, f. 119ᵛ); he there adds a verdict on V similar to Poggio's and Clark's: 'questo libro non sta sempre bene, come quello che fu scritto da uno che non intendeva niente ma dipingeva'. Incidentally, do we detect Ciceronian clausulae in his Latin?

[239] *Anecd. Oxon.* x (1905), xxx–xxxi.   [240] Rizzo, *La tradizione*, 88–90.

De inventione, and Ad Herennium

Cicero's youthful rhetorical treatise *De inventione* is closely related to the anonymous *Ad Herennium*, which was indeed attributed to Cicero during the Middle Ages. The earliest manuscripts of both are mutilated; but complete manuscripts are known from as early as the tenth century, and the discovery in 1421 of the Laudensis, which seems to have contained both works complete, was therefore not so crucial for them as for the *De oratore*, *Orator*, and *Brutus* (q.v.). Still, it is hard to believe that the Laudensis was not exploited at all. Marx's assertion to this effect seems to reflect the lack of research on this topic. In the absence of such inquiry, we cannot know what relationship, if any, obtained between the Laudensis and the 'supplementing' manuscripts of earlier centuries.

For the *De inventione*, the early *mutili* lack at least 1.62–76 and 2.170–74.[1] The most valued are Würzburg, Mp. misc. f. 3, s. IX¾, written at Würzburg (H), and Paris lat. 7774A, s. IX (P: see *in Verrem*, above). Much less serviceable are St. Gall 820, s. X, written at St. Gall (S), Leiden, Voss. Lat. F. 70. IA, written at Fleury, s. X ex./XI in. (L), and Leningrad, Class. Lat. F. v. 8, s. IX/X, from Corbie (R). Contamination makes the construction of a stemma impracticable.[2] There are numerous complete manuscripts dating from the tenth century on, but hardly any attempt has been made[3] to answer the crucial question of the origin of the *integri* or to ascertain how homogeneous a group they form. Stroebel's use of the sigla J and i does not facilitate understanding even of the materials at his disposal. And there remains the related question, raised by R. Reitzenstein,[4] of the witness of Marius Victorinus.

Matters remain equally unsatisfactory for the *Ad Herennium*. Here again we have early *mutili*, beginning only at 1.6.9; another Würzburg book of local origin, Mp. misc. f. 2, s. IX¾ (H), and another Paris book, lat. 7714, s. IX¾, Corbie (P), are dominant, though Marx[5] also used the Leningrad manuscript, which he called C, together with Berne 433, s. IX²/₃ from the circle of Lupus (B) and Paris lat. 7231, s. XI (*Π*), to which should be added its twin Paris lat. 7696 (p. 110, below). There are innumerable (or at least unnumbered) complete manuscripts dating from the tenth century onwards. Marx knew only twelfth-century *integri*, using especially Bamberg Class. 22 (M.V.8), s. XII ex., Germany, Leiden, Gronov. 22, s. XII, and Darmstadt 2283 (s. XII², Germany?). But A. Stuckelberger has pointed out several earlier ones, including St.

---

[1] Convenient descriptions in R. Mattmann, *Studie zur handschriftlichen Überlieferung von Ciceros 'de inventione'* (Freiburg, 1975), 17–28. Mattmann's own work, restricted mainly to Swiss manuscripts, is in itself unhelpful, but his bibliography and handlist of manuscripts will be valuable to future researchers. H. Thurn, *Würzb. Jahrb.* 3 (1977), 227–30, discusses a new fragment at Würzburg (Mp. th. f. 185, s. IX², French). The ninth-century Vatican lat. 11506 (s. IX¾, Wissembourg, according to Bischoff) has not yet been employed by editors; C. E. Finch, *TAPA* 99 (1968), 178–9, claims that it is a *gemellus* of H.

[2] Though see Mattmann (opposite p. 112).

[3] One can hardly count the remarks of E. Stroebel in the preface to his standard text (Leipzig, 1915), xv. It is highly relevant that the lacunae of P are supplied by a hand thought to be that of Lupus of Ferrières (references in Mattmann, 18–19).

[4] *Gnomon*, 5 (1929), 606–10. A pupil of Reitzenstein's, Fr. Richter, worked on this matter for a Göttingen dissertation of 1923, but this was not available to Mattmann (14 n. 1) or to me. Reitzenstein, loc. cit., gives some details of his findings. For the fortunes of *De inv.* before the ninth century, see Stroebel, xviii–xix.

[5] See his *editio minor* (Leipzig, 1923, reissued with addenda by W. Trillitzsch in 1964). For the pre-medieval tradition see Marx's big edition (Leipzig, 1894), proleg. 1–9.

Gall, Vadianus 313 of the late tenth century.[6] His work has thrown open
a question that should never have been regarded as closed, that of the
nature and origin of the *integri*. For Marx they were *expleti*, the result of
the merging of a *mutilus* with a complete text discovered in the twelfth
century. We now know that this discovery, if it was that, was made
earlier; and the agreement of the Vadianus with many readings thought
to be proper to the *mutili* shows how deep is our ignorance[7] of this stage
(as indeed of all stages) of the tradition.[8]

M. W.

[6] *MH* 22 (1965), 217–28. His work is advanced by M. Spallone, *Bollettino dei classici*, serie terza,
1 (1980), 158–90. See also the earlier paper of K. Manitius, *Philologus*, 100 (1956), 62–6, with
valuable detail on use of the *Ad Herennium* in the eleventh century.

[7] It is to be expected that current work on the commentaries on the *Ad Her.* (as on those on the
De inv.) may advance knowledge of the main text itself. A new edition is a desideratum: Marx's,
besides various eccentricities of format, greatly undervalued the evidence of the *integri* (see W.
Kroll, *Philologus*, 89 (1934), 63–84).

[8] First edition of both treatises: 1470 (N. Jenson, Venice). Illustrations of manuscripts in
Chatelain, plates XVI (Paris lat. 7714, Berne 433); XVIIA (Würzburg, Mp. misc. f. 2 and 3); XVIII
(St. Gall 820 and Vadianus 313); XXII (Paris lat. 7696 and 7231); XXXI (Paris lat. 7774A).

De optimo genere oratorum

By saying that this short work 'Ciceronis nomine inscribitur de optimo
genere oratorum' (*In Milonianam*, init.) Asconius hints at its spuriousness, which A. Dihle has established.[1] Furthermore, though it purports
to introduce translations of Aeschines' speech against Ctesiphon and of
Demosthenes' reply, the only person who speaks as if he had read them,
Jerome in his famous letter on translation (*Ep.* 57.5.2), may well be
embroidering his acquaintance with *Opt. gen.*,[2] from which he not only
cites two passages (ibid. 3–4) but also borrows his own title, *De optimo
genere interpretandi.*

In 1412 Leonardo Bruni completed translations of the two speeches,[3]
and some manuscripts add his translations to *Opt. gen.*;[4] but if he
designed them to replace the missing translations of 'Cicero', he owed

[1] *Hermes*, 83 (1955), 303–14, not mentioned in the latest edition (Budé, Paris, 1964).

[2] G. L. Hendrickson, *AJP* 47 (1926), 110 n. 1a, contradicted but not answered by G. J. M.
Bartelink in his commentary (*Mnem.* Suppl. 61, 1980), 51.

[3] H. Baron, *Leonardo Bruni Aretino: humanistisch-philosophische Schriften* (Leipzig and Berlin, 1928),
162 (Demosthenes, 1407), 163 (Aeschines, 1412).

[4] So does the *ed. princ.* (Venice, 1485), the source of the note cited as 'inédit?' in Pellegrin,
Manuscrits, ii. 1. 324 n. 2. D. P. Lockwood, *Classical and Mediaeval Studies in Honor of E. K. Rand*, ed.
L. W. Jones (New York, 1938), 185, remarks that *Opt. gen.* was 'a very popular work in the XV
century, as being the prototype for *prooemia* to humanistic translations from the Greek'.

his knowledge of these to Jerome and not to *Opt. gen.* itself, which he does not list among Cicero's works in his *Cicero novus* of *c*.1415.[5] How surprising that is will not become clear until the Italian tradition has been investigated, but more of the thirty-odd Italian manuscripts seem to have been written before 1450 than after, and at least two of them are without much doubt earlier than 1415: Cesena S. XII. 6, which includes a letter dated 1406 and looks no later, and Oxford, Bodl. Lat. class. d. 37, written at Florence and dated 13 January 1412 (= 1413?) by the same hand at the end of the previous work.[6] Both have so corrupt a text that already a fair amount of copying had probably taken place.

However the work reached Italy, it was not from any of the three medieval manuscripts extant, which all have errors of their own.[7] The two hitherto used by editors are German: St. Gall 818 (G, s. XI, presumably written at St. Gall; Chatelain, plate XX), in which the work follows the *Topica*, and a quire (ff. 11–16) of Paris lat. 7347 (P, s. XI[2]; Chatelain, plate XXA), in which it is followed by an unlabelled extract from Martianus Capella (5.509–26).[8] The third, English or French, is the second part of Lambeth Palace 425 (L, s. XIII[1]), in which *Opt. gen.* under the title 'Tullius de Achademicis' is preceded by the *Partitiones* under the title 'Tullius de oratore' and followed by *Timaeus* with the subscription 'Tullius de Achademicis'.[9]

The Loeb editor, prevented by the war from collating manuscripts, declared himself 'embarrassed by the disagreement among previous editors as to the readings in several passages'.[10] The Budé of H. Bornecque (Paris, 1921) is not so shockingly inaccurate as the OCT of A. S. Wilkins (1903), but it still ascribes to GP, e.g., § 6 *in quorum* instead of *in quo summa*.[11] That no edition reports L, or any Italian manuscript in full, matters far less, because all manuscripts derive from the archetype of GP and GP are not only its oldest but its most reliable

---

[5] Baron, 116. The work 'de optimo genere dicendi ad M. Brutum' is *Orator* (cf. *Ad Att.* 14.20.3).

[6] Ullman illustrates it in *Humanistic script*, plate 44. His statement on p. 83 about the hands is wrong.

[7] One example from each: G omits § 21 *dixit*, P omits § 7 *si abiectum*, and L reads § 3 *bonorum sermonem* for *honorarium permovere*. After collating P and L, I was able to borrow microfilms of all three manuscripts from R. H. R., to whom I am most grateful.

[8] B. C. B.-B. kindly gave me his opinion on the date and origin of P. Its readings were first reported by E. Hedicke in an edition that I have not seen (Sorau, 1889); it is described by C. Leonardi, *Aevum*, 34 (1960), 433.

[9] See M. R. James and C. Jenkins, *A Descriptive Catalogue of the Manuscripts in the Library of Lambeth Palace*, iv (Cambridge, 1932), 585–8. A thirteenth-century hand entered on f. 58ᵛ a deed pertaining to land in Wycombe, Bucks., and there is something in Irish script on f. 70ʳ; the connections with Lanthony suggested in the catalogue for part II are tenuous.

[10] H. M. Hubbell (1949), 350.

[11] The more recent Budé of A. Yon (Paris, 1964) merely repeats Bornecque's apparatus in its entirety with one additional error (§ 8 *quaerant* GP not reported). Like Bornecque, Yon also misstates the extent of Jerome's first quotation, which begins forty-six words earlier at § 13 *putavi*. The conviction of editors since at least Orelli-Baiter (Zürich, 1845) that Jerome has *omne* in § 14 is not borne out by I. Hilberg's edition, *CSEL* 54 (1910), 509.

descendants.[12] Room might be found, however, for a German manuscript of 1466 scarcely inferior to GP, Vatican, Pal. lat. 1741, in which
Opt. gen. (ff. 260^r–262^v) is followed by an extract from Rufinus on
rhythm (*GLK* VI.567.30 ff.) and this by the same extract from Martianus
Capella as in P.[13] Other Ciceronian works (see *Speeches*, §§ 5–7) owe
even more to manuscripts written at this late date in the neighbourhood
of Heidelberg.

M. D. R.

[12] M. W. tells me that J. Raasted of Copenhagen is engaged in a thorough study of the tradition,
but a provisional sketch of its Italian branches may be useful. Three families can readily be
distinguished: § 9 *privatus ille plerasque aetates ipsas* and § 22 *concursum . . . factum* Cesena S. XII. 6,
Florence, Laur. 48. 15, 50. 1, Halle Yg 24, B. L. Arundel 124, Milan, Ambros. L. 86 sup., Naples
IV. G. 46, Paris lat. 7704, 7713, 11289, Vatican, Ottob. lat. 1996, Pal. lat. 1476, Reg. lat. 1841,
Wolfenbüttel, Gud. lat. 38 (kindly checked by Nigel Palmer); § 3 *eodem* [*genere*] and § 13 *magnum
errorem et quale* Florence, Laur. 90 sup. 88 (and its copy Vatican, Ottob. lat. 1449), Edili 207,
Genoa, Berio m. r. IX 2 13, Vatican lat. 3400; § 4 [*praeterea*] and § 15 *solvere* B. L. Add. 19586 (and
its copies Oxford, Linc. Coll. Lat. 38 and Rome, Casanat. 191), Munich Clm 812 (kindly checked
by R. H. R.), Oxford, Bodl. Lat. class. d. 37, Paris lat. 17154, Vatican, Ottob. lat. 2057, Pal. lat.
1493, Venice, Marc. lat. XI. 106 (4363; kindly checked by Carlotta Dionisotti), Vienna 3093, *ed.
princ.* Ven. 1485 (and its descendant Vatican, Reg. lat. 1622), Florence, Ricc. 671 (§ 19 *cum esset* –
fin.). Most members of the first family have no title, and only the third gives *De optimo genere
oratorum* with any consistency; all three repeatedly mistake *quom* for *quoniam* or *quomodo*. Vatican lat.
5137 does not belong to any of the three, has *De optimo genere orator*, and does not corrupt *quom*; it is
the only manuscript known to me that could with any plausibility be set against GPL and the rest
(§ 1 *cuique ius* for *quo ius*, § 6 *tolerabili* for *tolerabile*, § 19 *fieret* for *fecerit*). Florence, Laur. Ashb. 252, a
fragment hard to read, does not belong to any of the three families either (I am grateful to Luigi
Castagna for a collation). I have not seen a manuscript in the Alton collection at Dublin, Milan,
Ambros. L. 61 sup., Ravenna 349.

[13] For a description see C. Leonardi, *Aevum*, 34 (1960), 462–3. The manuscript shares three
errors with P (§ 12 *esse* om., § 17 *sepono, maximus*), but they may be coincidental. It regularly has *quo
in* for *quom* (cf. the previous note).

De oratore, Orator, Brutus

All surviving medieval manuscripts of *De oratore* and *Orator* are traditionally thought to descend from a mutilated manuscript of unknown
date; the only surviving medieval *Brutus* is a small ninth-century fragment.[1] In 1421 a manuscript containing all three texts was found in the
cathedral library of Lodi, between Milan and Piacenza. The thrust of
modern scholarship has been toward reconstructing the text of this lost
Laudensis from its fifteenth-century descendants. The history of the
mutilated family, the only history that any of the three texts had in the
Middle Ages, has aroused little interest.

Recent editors of *De oratore* have used four members of the mutilated

[1] Ed. K. Kumaniecki, *De orat.* (Teubner, Leipzig, 1969); P. Reis, *Orat.* (Teubner, Leipzig,
1932); R. Westman, *Orat.* (Teubner, Leipzig, 1980); E. Malcovati, *Brutus* (Teubner, Leipzig,
1965).

family: British Library, Harley 2736 (H, s. IX med.), Avranches 238 (A, s. IX), Erlangen 380 (E, s. X²), and a florilegium, Vatican, Reg. lat. 1762 (K, s. IX¾). When they were written, their archetype lacked 1.128–57, 1.193–2.13, 2.90–2, and 3.17–110, but a note by the scribe of H after 1.193, 'hic deest unus quaternio', makes it possible to work out that in the archetype 1.128–57 occupied one bifolium, 1.193–2.13 one quire, 2.13–3.17 four quires, and 3.17–110 one quire;[2] originally, therefore, the archetype lacked only 2.90–2 through some slip in copying,[3] but it lost a bifolium and two quires before the copying of HAEK.

HAEK are even more defective, in ways that editors have not fully grasped. The scribe of H left blank leaves for the passages missing from the archetype, and someone walked off with this wasted parchment and fourteen and a half words of 3.17 into the bargain;[4] otherwise H has what the archetype gave it. When A and E were first written, they lacked four passages present in the archetype and H but similarly absent from the exemplar of K: 1.157–93, 2.13–18, 2.234–87, and 3.149–71.[5] Neither, however, remained in that state. The fifteenth-century hand that supplemented E after the discovery of the Laudensis found it necessary to create space by obliterating 1.123–8. A was supplemented soon after being written; the supplements in what survives are 2.234–45 and 3.149–71, and the same hand added at the end most of *Orator* (91–191, 231–end), which is foreign to H and EK. Since then, however, A has lost everything before 2.19 and also the leaf that had on it 2.50–60. What editors have not realized about A is that 1.157–93 must have been among the supplements of the second hand, because it is present in later manuscripts that betray their descent from A not merely by joining mutilated texts of *De oratore* and *Orator* but by omitting 2.50–60.[6] It also seems likely that the second hand supplied 2.13–18 and 245–87,[7] but they have left no trace in descendants of A.

---

[2] C. H. Beeson, *Lupus of Ferrières as Scribe and Text Critic* (Cambridge, Mass., 1930), 8, strangely supposes that the note refers to a quire missing from H itself. Editors repeat the unrefutable but groundless assertion of E. Ströbel, *De Ciceronis de oratore librorum codicibus mutilis antiquioribus* (Erlangen, 1883), 37–8, 47, that H was not copied directly from the archetype.

[3] The occurrence of the words *ea diligentissime persequatur* in both 90 and 92 may somehow be responsible.

[4] See Beeson, loc. cit., for evidence that leaves are missing after 3.17 *inclinato iam in.*

[5] Neatly demonstrated by J. Stroux, *Handschriftliche Studien zu Cicero De oratore* (Basle, 1921), 162–5. As it is theoretically possible that the archetype deteriorated and A and E were copied from it after H, their content alone does not prove them related; see Ströbel, 34–8, for other evidence.

[6] At some stage ff. 1–3 of A must have been tucked in after f. 4 in the order 1, 3, 2, because its descendants have 2.60–9, 19–30, 39–50, 30–9; cf. W. Friedrich's edition (Leipzig, 1891), vi. F. Heerdegen in his edition of *Orator* (Leipzig, 1884), viii–xiv, lists and partly classifies thirty-seven descendants of A in *Orator*, thirty-six of which include *De oratore*.

[7] Cf. Friedrich, vi. On 2.245 Schneidewin's collation of 1842 (Oxford, Bodl. Lat. class. f. 8) has the note 'Bis hierher geht jene böse [?] Hand, die 2 volle Seiten geschrieben hat. Nun müssen Blätter ausgefallen sein: das folg. beginnt gleich mit *Colliguntur a graecis* § 288'. The operations of this hand in 1.1–2.19, laudable in themselves, may be to blame for the disintegration of the first two quires.

This unavoidably laborious account of what HAE once contained
and now contain prompts two observations. One is that recent editors
have been lax in not investigating descendants of A in Book 1, especially
in the parts absent from E as well, and *mutili* that include 2.13–18 and
245–87. The other, which may turn out to excuse neglect of the fuller
mutili, is that the presence of those fourteen and a half words in 3.17 will
not prove a manuscript independent of H.[8]

H was written by Lupus of Ferrières in the middle of the ninth
century.[9] Lupus asked Einhard in a letter written *c*.835 for the three
books of *De oratore*;[10] evidently Einhard complied, for *c*.856 Lupus wrote
to Pope Benedict III for a copy of *De oratore* against which to correct his
own copy.[11] Perhaps Lupus first encountered *De oratore* at Fulda, where
he had studied under Hrabanus Maurus and met Einhard in his youth.
It is noteworthy in this context that Rabanus quotes from *Orator*, 69.[12]
Moreover, the archetype of the mutilated family was an insular manuscript, or at least the tradition came through an insular centre, to judge
from the errors distributed through both branches of the *mutili*.[13] It
would be interesting to know if this centre was Fulda. H itself probably
went from Ferrières to nearby Cormery, a dependency of Tours.[14]

If *De oratore* emerged at Fulda and spread to France, it left very little
trace in medieval Germany. Wibald, Abbot of Corvey 1146–58,
included it in his large collection of Cicero's works, Berlin (West) lat. 2°
252; but to judge from the partial collation made by Wunder in 1827, his
text derives from H, because it adopts conjectures entered in H by
Lupus.[15] References to *De oratore* at Bamberg probably reflect a manuscript that came to Germany from France, as we shall see in following
the fortunes of E.

The oldest manuscript of the other family, A (Chatelain, plate XIX),
belonged to Mont-Saint-Michel, and was written by two scribes of the
middle third of the ninth century. The first (of Loire origin) wrote *De
oratore*; the second (origin unknown) wrote the supplements that we
mentioned earlier, including two passages of *Orator*.[16] Apart from the
hand, however, there is no indication that *Orator* was added from the
same codex; it is not with *De oratore* in H, K, or E.

  [8] Friedrich, *Jahrb. für class. Phil.* 135 (1887), 73, thought it would.

  [9] Beeson, *Lupus of Ferrières*, which includes a facsimile.

  [10] Ibid. 3; *Loup de Ferrières, Correspondance*, ed. L. Levillain, i (Paris, 1927), 8–9, *Ep.* 1.

  [11] Levillain, ii.122–3, *Ep.* 100.   [12] *PL* 107.408.

  [13] Kumaniecki, vii, falls into the old trap of inferring an archetype in capitals from shared errors
  due to confusion of capitals. In fact they show that an ancestor of the archetype was written in
  capitals.   [14] Beeson, 5; E. Pellegrin, *BEC* 115 (1957), 10–11.

  [15] E. Wunder, *Variae lectiones* (Leipzig, 1827), 6–16, reports it from 1.1 to 2.48. See also
  P. Lehmann, *Erforschung des Mittelalters* v (Stuttgart, 1962), 111–13, 131–3.

  [16] Since Professor Bischoff kindly gave us this opinion on the hands, he has assigned supplements in *De oratore* (the main ones, or others?) to Hadoard; see *Stud. und Mitt. zur Gesch. des Ben.* 92
  (1981), 176. It is not clear whether *Orat.* 1–91 has gone missing from A or was already missing
  from its exemplar; see J. E. Sandys's edition (Cambridge, 1885), lxxviii–lxxix.

How the A text spread is not known. The eleventh-century inventory of Saint-Gildas near Bourges contains *De oratore*[17] (whether *Orator* was included is impossible to say). Although located in central France, this house was founded in the tenth century by Saint-Gildas-des-Ruis in Brittany, only seventy-five miles from Mont-Saint-Michel; and Kohler, who edited the inventory of the daughter house, believed that the older items in it came from Mont-Saint-Michel. It is probable, hence, that the Saint-Gildas *De oratore* was related to A. A fragment of a mid-twelfth-century descendant of A, containing *De orat.* 3.110–21, 186–96, is found in the two flyleaves of Avranches 162, a bifolium in rather poor condition. So far we are still within the ambit of Mont-Saint-Michel. British Library, Harley 4927, written in central France in the mid- or late twelfth century, seems to have ended originally with *De oratore* and *Orator*,[18] and extracts from both works appear in a manuscript of the same date from Reims, Berlin (East), Phillipps 1732, which contains basically material relating to the *ars dictaminis*. By about 1300 the A text had reached northern Italy. It forms part of Troyes 552 (s. XIV[1]), the large collection of Cicero owned but not assembled by Petrarch,[19] and it was an A text, doubtless acquired at Avignon or on some excursion from there, that Simon of Arezzo left to the Dominicans at Arezzo in 1338 as part of another Ciceronian collection.[20] Also warranting further examination is Padua, Bibl. Capit. B 41, which contains *De oratore* and *Orator* written in the early fourteenth century in Italy. The later descendants of A are of interest only for their conjectures, some of which are the work of Gasparino Barzizza, who essayed the completion of both *De oratore* and *Orator* before the Laudensis was found.[21]

E and K descend from a sister of A; its location is not known. The older of the two, K, contains extracts from *De oratore*; it was shown by Bischoff to be the florilegium compiled by Hadoard, the mid-ninth-century librarian of Corbie, and is in fact his autograph.[22] E (Chatelain, plate XIXa) is a composite manuscript, the old part of which (containing *De oratore*, Remigius Favius, *De ponderibus*, and Priscian, *De figuris*

[17] C. Kohler, *BEC* 47 (1888), 103–12.
[18] See *Speeches*, n. 218.   [19] Ibid. n. 222.
[20] U. Pasqui, *Arch. stor. ital.*, ser. V, 4 (1889), 253. Ruth J. Dean, *Studies in Philol.* 45 (1948), 562–4, showed that Simon worked at Avignon; for more about him see L. Muttoni and C. Adami, *IMU* 22 (1979), 171–222, and the index in *IMU* 21 (1978), 155, under Simone di Benvenuto d'Arezzo. B. L. Egerton 2516 (s. XIV) is either Simon's manuscript or a close relative of it; it contains the same works of Cicero and Apuleius, but according to the catalogue is 'imperfect at the end', where Simon's manuscript had Pliny's *Letters*. Billanovich, *IMU* 2 (1959), 158 n. 4, identified Simon's Apuleius and Pliny with Florence, Laur. S. Marco 284 (s. XI[2]), but the inventory published by Pasqui shows quite plainly that Cicero, Apuleius, and Pliny, were 'in uno volumine'. Simon may of course have found S. Marco 284 and copied Apuleius and Pliny from it into Egerton 2516.
[21] D. Detlefsen, *Verhandlungen der 27. Versammlung deutscher Philologen und Schulmänner* (Leipzig, 1870), 94–6; Heerdegen, loc. cit. (n. 6, above); Sabbadini, *Storia e critica*[2], 80–4.
[22] Beeson, *CPh* 40 (1945), 201–22, and Bischoff, *Mitt. Stud.* i. 49–63.

numerorum) was written according to its colophon for Gerbert, Archbishop of Reims and later Pope Sylvester II, between 983 and 991 by the monk Ayrardus of Gerbert's former abbey Saint-Géraud of Aurillac in Aquitaine. In the fifteenth century E belonged to the abbey of St. Mary at Heilsbronn (O. Cist.), founded in 1132 by Otto, Bishop of Bamberg. It is highly probable that E was part of the group of manuscripts which came to St. Mary's from Bamberg: *De oratore* appears in Ruotger's catalogue (1172–1201) of St. Michael's, Bamberg, and in the list (*c*.1200) of books assembled by Master Richard for the cathedral library. If these are indeed references to E, then E may well be one of that distinguished group of manuscripts that came to Bamberg from Gerbert in Reims via his pupil Emperor Otto III (983–1002) and Otto's successor Henry II (1002–24), patron of Bamberg Cathedral.[23]

If Gerbert did give E to Otto III, then a copy must have remained at Reims, because E has at least one descendant (hitherto unreported) probably written there or not far away, Leiden, Voss. Lat. O. 26, which contains the *Caesarians*, Quintilian, *Inst.* (excerpts from Books 1–6), and *De oratore*. The manuscript is written by a single hand in an early twelfth-century French minuscule. The source of the excerpts from Quintilian was asserted by Winterbottom to be Florence, Laur. 46.7 (Chatelain, plate XXXVII), a manuscript brought to Strasbourg by Bishop Werinharius (1001–28), possibly from Reims.[24] Until the fire of 1870, there were in Strasbourg, Bibl. Univ. 3762 two folios from a tenth-century manuscript of *De oratore* (3.176 ff., 211 ff.).

Several other medieval manuscripts preserved or attested must be taken into account, to say nothing of later *mutili* not derived from A.[25] William of Malmesbury in the opening decades of the twelfth century is said to quote from *De oratore* in his *Polyhistor*.[26] *De oratore* is referred to in the newly discovered catalogue of Lobbes (1049–1160) and in the catalogue of Cluny (1158–61).[27] The *Florilegium Gallicum*, compiled in Orléans in the mid-twelfth century, contains long extracts from *De oratore* which derive from a manuscript outside the family of AE; they reappear in Vincent of Beauvais's *Speculum historiale* in the thirteenth

---

[23] H. Fischer, *Die lateinischen Pergamentschriften der Universitätsbibliothek Erlangen*, i (1928), 450–4.

[24] *Problems in Quintilian* (London, 1970), 20 n. 7. He dates the Leiden manuscript '?tenth to eleventh century'.

[25] e.g. Florence, Laur. 50. 33, Oxford, Lincoln College Lat. 38 (which has lost everything after 2.34); in some manuscripts, such as Milan, Ambros. E. 127 sup., 2.13–18 and 245–87 were added later. See Detlefsen, loc. cit. (n. 21, above), and Friedrich, op. cit. (n. 8, above), 73–4 (both missing from Kumaniecki's bibliography).

[26] R. M. T., *Rev. bén.* 85 (1975), 376–7. The evidence needs checking, because *Orator*, 132, which William quotes in his *Vita Dunstani*, came to him from Augustine's commentary on St. John (LVIII. 3, *CCSL* 36, p. 473); Thomson himself, *Rev. bén.* 89 (1979), 315, shows that William knew this work.

[27] F. Dolbeau, *Recherches Augustiniennes*, 13 (1978), 32, 14 (1979), 226; Delisle, ii. 478, no. 489.

century.[28] John of Salisbury used *De oratore* in Books 7–8 of the *Policraticus*, and upon his death in 1180 bequeathed a manuscript to Chartres.[29] Alexander Neckham (d. 1217) recommended *De oratore* as reading to schoolmen.[30] It was also known to the annotator of Berne 276, who worked in Orléans in the middle of the thirteenth century.[31] And it appears in the sixteenth-century catalogue of Fleury; but whether this is a medieval or a Renaissance manuscript cannot be told.[32] The *De oratore* in Paris lat. 7701, a collection of disparate texts brought together by Claude Dupuy, was written in France in the late twelfth century and is still unreported; it does not belong to the family of AE.[33] One would expect that H, because of its location in the area of the Loire schools, was the vehicle for the medieval dissemination of *De oratore* in that area, but the mobility of the A text complicates matters. In 1417, perhaps in the neighbourhood of Langres, Poggio found a *mutilus* of *De oratore* that included the parts never present in A; his unusually careful description will enable it to be identified if it survives.[34]

The second or 'complete' family of these texts emerged in 1421, when a text of the three works was discovered by Gerardo Landriani at the cathedral of Lodi near Milan, in an old manuscript difficult to read.[35] The codex contained *Inv., Ad Her., De orat., Orat., Brut.* The Laudensis (L) was lost by 1428; and because it was never copied as a whole, editors have had to find different ways of reconstructing its readings for the different texts that it contained.

For the *Brutus*[36] primacy is commonly given to Florence, Bibl. Naz. Conv. Soppr. J. 1. 14 (F), written *c.* 1423 by Niccolò Niccoli.[37] Another early book, Vatican, Ottob. lat. 1592 (B), in the hand of Flavio Biondo (1422), purports to be a transcript of L after paragraph 130; earlier, it displays corrections from L. Editors have also used Vatican, Ottob. lat. 2057 (O), with corrections made from L in 1425, and Naples IV. A. 44

---

[28] R. H. R., *Viator*, 10 (1979), 136. The extracts were published by J. Hamacher, *Florilegium Gallicum: Prolegomena und Edition der Exzerpte von Petron bis Cicero De oratore* (Frankfurt, 1975), 428–37. At 1.120 they read *pudendo* with the Laudensis (by conjecture?) where H[1] has a lacuna and H[2] (Lupus) a different supplement.

[29] C. C. J. Webb, ed. of *Policraticus*, 2 (Oxford, 1909), 482; *PL* 199.12; *Cartulaire de Notre-Dame de Chartres*, ed. De Lepinois and Marlet (1862–5), 3, 202.

[30] C. Haskins, *Studies in the History of Medieval Science* (Cambridge, 1924), 356–76.

[31] On this annotator see M. D. R. and R. H. R., *Viator*, 9 (1978), 235–49.

[32] Manitius, *Handschriften*, 31.

[33] Detlefsen (n. 21, above), 95.   [34] Cf. *Speeches*, n. 178.

[35] An account of this discovery is given in many places, e.g. by Stroux (n. 5, above), 7–12. Only Flavio Biondo gives the contents of the manuscript; for doubts see Stroux, 10 n. 2, and E. Malcovati, *Athenaeum*, 36 (1958), 33 n. 13.

[36] See especially Malcovati's introduction to her Teubner edition, summarizing previous articles in *Athenaeum*, 1958–60.

[37] Ullman, *Humanistic Script*, 61–3 and pl. 29.

(G). The hopes that Cornell Univ. Lib. B. 2 (U) would reproduce the wonderfully accurate text boasted of by Giovanni Lamola have hardly been realized.[38] Even greater excitement was caused in 1957 by the discovery at Cremona of a ninth-century fragment of Italian origin containing *Brutus*, 218–27, 265–74, but this seems not to be part of L, and it contributes nothing new to the text.[39] Other *recentiores* exist,[40] and it can hardly be said, here as elsewhere, that the progeny of the Laudensis has been properly sifted.

The *Orator*, though extant in part in the Middle Ages in A, had to await the Laudensis to be made complete. The text of the Laudensis was not only copied as a whole but was also used to correct and supplement the older *mutili*. F (cf. *Brutus*) seems to fall into the first category; while O (cf. *Brutus*) and Vatican, Pal. lat. 1469 (P) are used for their corrections from L. Again, there seems no doubt that much remains to be discovered about the use of L in the fifteenth-century copies of the *Orator*.

For the *De oratore*, L is reconstructed from Vatican lat. 2901 (V), which Stroux thought to be a copy of L made by a scribe who also had in front of him an already corrected *codex integer*; O (cf. *Brutus*) and P (cf. *Orat*.), thought to derive from a single 'corrected' apograph of L;[41] and especially specific reports of the readings of the 'vetus liber' in V, O, R (Vatican, Pal. lat. 1470), N (Naples IV. A. 43), B (Bologna 468) and now U (Cornell Univ. Lib. B. 2).[42] Stroux's work has been followed up by Kumaniecki's edition, but much probably remains to be discovered about the fortunes of the book in the fifteenth century.

Little attention has been given to the fact that all three of these texts are recorded in a thirteenth-century northern-European catalogue, the *Biblionomia* of Richard de Fournival: '[28.] Ejusdem de oratore libri tres, et quartus Brutus et quintus Orator, in uno uolumine cujus signum est littera O'.[43] This corpus leaves no trace. Fournival's books, with the exception of the medical works, passed to the Sorbonne after his death in 1260; but this codex is not recorded in the Sorbonne catalogues.[44]

---

[38] Malcovati, *Athenaeum*, 37 (1959), 174–83 with plates; Kumaniecki in his edition of *De orat.*, pp. xv–xvii.

[39] Malcovati, *Athenaeum*, 36 (1958), 40–7 and plate.

[40] See especially Malcovati, *Athenaeum*, 38 (1960), 328–40. Of particular interest is Florence, Laur. 50. 31, in the hand of Poggio. In *Emerita*, 28 (1960), 225–39, L. Rubio presses the claims of Barcelona, Bibl. Central 12; readings in the edition of A. Tovar and A. Bujaldón (Barcelona, 1967).

[41] G. Arrigoni, *Il De oratore e l'Orator nella tradizione del codice trivulziano 723* (Milan, 1969), argues that the manuscript of her title was copied from the same exemplar as O and P.

[42] Stroux (n. 5, above), esp. 118, 123. See also J. Martin, *Tulliana* (Paderborn, 1922), 73. Kumaniecki, xvii–xviii, argues for the occasional importance of the first hands of R and U. Stroux, 128–31, has a judicious discussion, important beyond *De oratore*, of the character of L and the *mutili*.

[43] Delisle, ii. 525, no. 28.   [44] Rouse, op. cit. (n. 28, above).

Very likely, however, Fournival composed the title in the *Biblionomia* straight out of *De divinatione*, 2.4: 'Ita tres erunt de oratore, quartus Brutus, quintus Orator'. Fournival seems frequently to have gone to the *De divinatione* for the 'authentic' titles of his Cicero works; and such a source would explain the inversion of *Brutus* and *Orator*, in comparison with their positions in the Lodi codex. In short, rather than an early copy of the Lodi codex, Fournival probably had nothing more than a *mutilus* of *De oratore* and *Orator*.

M. W.

R. H. R.

M. D. R.

Partitiones oratoriae

The text of the *Partitiones oratoriae* as presently edited is based on two manuscripts: Paris lat. 7696 (p), s. XI, and lat. 7231 (P), s. XI. It would benefit from a new edition based on a thorough study of the surviving manuscripts.

Little firm can be said about the transmission of this text until a new edition has been prepared. E. Ströbel laid the foundations for this in 1887, but neither Wilkins nor Bornecque built on them.[1] Ströbel clearly identified two families of manuscripts, A and J, and listed the readings by which they can be distinguished. On this basis, the transmission of the *Partitiones* can be tentatively reconstructed along the following lines.

The text apparently emerged in Italy. The *Partitiones* are noted in the tenth-century catalogue of Bobbio in north Italy: '[474] librum I Ciceronis in quo sunt topica et partitiones' (Becker, 32.474, p. 70). The A family, Pp in Wilkins, accounts in large part for the medieval circulation of the text. The oldest manuscript of the *Partitiones*, and probably the source of the A family, was discovered in 1962 by Billanovich at the Bodmer Library in Cologny-Geneva; Bodmer lat. 146 was written in the tenth century in northern Italy and contains Fortunatianus, *Ars rhetorica*; Augustine, *Principia rhetorices*; Julius Severianus, *Praecepta artis rhetoricae*; and Cicero, *Part*. ('M. Tulli Ciceronis Part[itiones] oratoriae incipiunt . . .'; Billanovich, plates V–VIII).[2]

Some time before the eleventh century a manuscript of the A text was brought to central France, probably Fleury, whence it spread in the course of the eleventh and twelfth centuries. This manuscript

---

[1] *Zur Handschriftenkunde und Kritik von Ciceros Partitiones Oratoriae* (Zweibrücken, 1887); ed. A. S. Wilkins (Oxford, 1903), H. Bornecque (Paris, 1921; 2nd edn., 1960).

[2] G. Billanovich, 'Il Petrarca e i retori latini minori', *IMU* 5 (1962), 103–64.

produced several descendants, primary among them the two manuscripts from which the text of the *Partitiones* has hitherto been reconstructed: Paris lat. 7696 (Chatelain, plate XXII. 1; Cicero, *Inv.*;
Victorinus; Cicero, *Part.* ('M. Tulli Ciceronis Partitiones oratoriae
incipiunt feliciter'); Julius Severianus, *Praecepta rhetorica*; Quintilian,
Inst. extracts 10, 12; *Ad Her.*), which was written in the late tenth or early
eleventh century at Fleury by several scribes, one of whom has been
identified as the Anglo-Saxon Leofnoth;[3] and Paris lat. 7231 (Chatelain,
plate XXII. 2; Vegetius; Solinus; *Ad Her.*; *Part.* ('M. Tulli Ciceronis
Partitiones oratoriae incipiunt feliciter. Dialogus Ciceronis cum filio
Cicerone'); Julius Severianus, *Praecepta rhetorica*; Quintilian, *Inst.*
extracts 10, 12; Augustine, *De musica*; Ps.-Cicero, *Synonyma*), which was
written, possibly at Fleury, in the eleventh century by Adémar of
Chabannes, monk of Saint-Martial of Limoges.[4] The Fleury exemplar
may well be that referred to, '[16] Cicero de partibus oratoriae' (Delisle,
ii. 445), in an eleventh-century book-list which appears at the end of
Paris lat. 7749, a manuscript of Victorinus, written in the eleventh
century somewhere on the Loire and owned by Richard de Fournival in
the first half of the thirteenth century.[5]

The Fleury exemplar doubtless also lies behind the twelfth-century
circulation of the *Partitiones* in France, centred around Chartres, and
one of the early English manuscripts. In France the *Partitiones* was
known to Thierry of Chartres, who included it in his *Heptatheucon*;
Chartres 497, '. . . ad Herennium, de partitione oratoria dialogus, Julius
Severianus . . .', was destroyed in 1944 but survives on microfilm at the
Institut de Recherche et d'Histoire des Textes, at Paris; and Philip,
Bishop of Bayeux, left to Bec two copies of the *Partitiones* along with 130
other books which are recorded in the Bec catalogue of 1164: '[64] in alio
Pomponius Mela de cosmographia et Tullius de fine boni et mali et de
academicis et Timaeus Platonis ab ipso Tullio translatus et Tullius de
particione oratoria' (Becker, 86.64, p. 201), and '[104] in alio Tullius de
partitionibus oratoriis et de amicitia et de senectute et invective in
Catilinam et invective in Salustum et Salustus in Tullium et Seneca de
causis et remediis fortuitorum et de naturalibus questionibus' (Becker,
86.104 p. 202). The one surviving manuscript known to have belonged
to Philip, now Paris lat. 5802, was written at Chartres in the middle of

---

[3] M.-Th. Vernet, 'Notes de dom André Wilmart sur quelques manuscrits latins anciens de la
Bibliothèque Nationale de Paris', *Bulletin d'information de l'Institut de recherche et d'histoire des textes*, 6
(1957), 32–3; J. Vezin, 'Leofnoth, un scribe anglais à Saint-Benoît-sur-Loire', *Codices manuscripti*, 4
(1977), 109–20.

[4] J. Vezin, 'Un nouveau manuscrit autographe d'Adémar de Chabannes (Paris, Bibl. nat. lat.
7231)', *Bulletin de la Société nationale des antiquaires de France*, (1965), 44–52. It is worth noting that the
extracts from Quintilian in these two manuscripts are *gemelli*; see M. Winterbottom, *Problems in
Quintilian*, BICS Suppl. 25 (1970) 31–3. Vezin, 'Leofnoth', notes that their texts of the *Ad
Herennium* also descend from a common parent.

[5] R. H. Rouse, 'Manuscripts Belonging to Richard de Fournival', *RHT* 3 (1973), 260, pl. XXII.

the twelfth century. Pomponius Mela and the Younger Pliny's letters in the Ten-Book family, other *rarae aves* owned by Philip, were disseminated from Fleury and Orléans. The A text of the *Partitiones* moved to England before the end of the twelfth century and is seen in Lambeth Palace 425, part II, s. XII², containing Cicero, *Parad.*, *Fat.*, *Part.* ('De oratore'), *Opt. gen.* ('De academicis'), *Tim.*, *Phil.* (see *De optimo genere oratorum*). This manuscript was known to Ströbel, but ignored by Wilkins and Bornecque.

The J family, whose readings are designated *vulg.* by Wilkins, had emerged in France by the early twelfth century, and moved to Italy by the end of the century. It accounts for most of the Renaissance circulation of the *Partitiones*. The oldest surviving member of the J family was written for William of Malmesbury[6] and is now Oxford, Bodl. Rawl. G. 139, s. XII¹, containing *Part.* ('M. T. Ciceronis ad filium suum Ciceronem de particionibus rethorice liber'), *Off.*, Ps.-Quintilian, *Decl.*, and added extracts from the early books of Aulus Gellius. Through what routes these texts came into William's hands is unknown. A second J manuscript, Poppi 39, s. XII, written in France, contains both the *Partitiones* ('M. T. Ciceronis ad filium suum de partitionibus rethorice liber') and the *De officiis*, as does William's manuscript. A third manuscript, Paris lat. 6333, s. XIII¹, containing I. *Tusc.*; II. *Tim.*, *Part.*, was written in the area of Poitiers and belonged to Guillaume Sacher (1522–81), canon of Poitiers.

The Italian branch of the J family is first seen in Vienna 157, which was written in northern Italy in the late twelfth or early thirteenth century; it contains Cicero, *Inv.*, *Ad Her.*, Leonine verses on rhetorical figures, *Part.*, *Top.* In the fifteenth century Vienna 157 belonged to Philippos Podokatharos of Cyprus, who bought it in 1452 from Thomas de Urbino. Later it passed to the Hungarian humanist Johannes Sambucus (1531–84). The other surviving J manuscript that antedates Petrarch, Vatican, Reg. lat. 1511, which contains the same sequence of works, was apparently copied from Vienna 157 in south Italy (Naples?) at the end of the thirteenth or early in the fourteenth century. It travelled north, and was given by the theologian Lawrence of Heilsberg (d. 1443) to the cathedral of Frauenburg.

The *Partitiones* appears to have had only a small readership in medieval Europe. It was not known to John of Salisbury; and Vincent of Beauvais, while he includes it in his list of Cicero's writings, '. . . de natura deorum, de divinatione, de fato, Timaeus, ad Hortensium [= Lucullus], partitiones oratoriae, de academicis, pro Marcello . . .',

---

[6] Regarding William's scribes see R. M. T., 'The "Scriptorium" of William of Malmesbury', in *Medieval Scribes, Manuscripts and Libraries: Essays Presented to N. R. Ker*, ed. M. B. Parkes and A. G. Watson (London, 1978), 117–42. The identity of Rawl. G. 139 was discovered in the process of assembling this synopsis.

quotes only a line, which may well have come from some intermediate source: 'Communia quinque lumina orationis sunt hec, dilucidum, breve, probabile, illustre, suave' (*Speculum historiale*, lib. 7, c. 6).

The fourteenth-century Italian emergence and circulation of the *Partitiones* were due to Petrarch and his circle. The tenth-century north Italian Bodmer manuscript came into Petrarch's hands *c*.1330. Petrarch also had a J text of the *Partitiones* in his collection of Cicero, now Troyes 552, containing as a group *De Orat.*, *Part.* ('Marci Tullii Ciceronis incipit liber rethorice sub compendio'), *Catil.*; and it most likely suggested the title, 'Marci Tullii Ciceronis de partitione [artis] rethorice sub dialogo incipit cum [filio]', which he added in the bottom margin of the Bodmer manuscript. The source of Petrarch's J text may well have been the codex described in Simon of Arezzo's bequest of 1338 to the Dominicans of Arezzo: '. . . pro Quinto Ligario, in topicis, de paradoxa, in rethorica sub compendio' – the same title for the *Partitiones* as is found in Troyes 552.[7] The further dissemination of the *Partitiones* through Petrarch's friends can be traced in the list of manuscripts given by Billanovich. It is possible that one of Philip of Bayeux's manuscripts may also have been brought south and copied in the fourteenth century. A codex in similar order, '[888] 4. M. T. Ciceronis de finibus bonorum et malorum, achademicorum, partitiones, de caelo et mundo, de fato . . .', of which only a few leaves survive, belonged to the library of San Marco in the fifteenth century.[8]

R. H. R.

[7] Ed. U. Pasqui, 'La biblioteca d'un notaro aretino del secolo XIV', *Archivio storico italiano*, ser. v, 4 (1889), 250–5.

[8] Ed. B. Ullman and P. Stadter, *The Public Library of Renaissance Florence, Medioevo e umanesimo*, 10 (Padua, 1972), 229.

Academica posteriora and *De finibus bonorum et malorum*

Cicero's second or 'posterior' edition of the *Academica* was originally published in four books, of which only the incomplete first book survives. It owes its survival to the fact that it became attached to the more substantial *De finibus*. The *De finibus* has an independent tradition as well; but one branch of the *De finibus*' descent is identical with the entire transmission of the 'Posterior Academics'.[1]

The *De finibus* survives in four eleventh- and twelfth-century manu-

[1] R. H. and M. A. Rouse, 'The Medieval Circulation of Cicero's "Posterior Academics" and the *De finibus bonorum et malorum*', in *Medieval Scribes, Manuscripts and Libraries: Essays Presented to N. R. Ker* (London, 1978), 333–67.

scripts, and a large number of fourteenth- and fifteenth-century manuscripts, primarily Italian. There is no adequate edition, or study of its medieval circulation. Previous editors, in particular T. Schiche (Teubner, 1915) and J. Martha (Budé, 1928), while they have not attempted a *stemma codicum*, agree that the manuscripts ultimately stem from a common archetype and appear to represent two families, the older of which circulated in Germany and the younger in France.

The oldest surviving manuscript, Vatican, Pal. lat. 1513 (A), containing the *De finibus* alone, was written according to Bischoff somewhere in western Germany in the eleventh century, and belonged to Lorsch in the fifteenth century. Two fifteenth-century copies of another manuscript, which was then at the Palatinate Library but has since disappeared, conclude the German family: Erlangen 618 (E), written by Bernard Groschedel and Conrad Haunolt at Heidelberg in 1466; and Vatican, Pal. lat. 1525 (B), written in Germany, doubtless also at Heidelberg, in 1467. Also, the *De finibus* was known at Bamberg, for it is referred to in the catalogue of Michaelsberg 1172–1201 (Becker, 80.82, 83) and that of the Cathedral Library, *c.*1200.

The French family survives from the twelfth century in two groups. The first group is distinguished by the inclusion of the 'Posterior Academics' as Book 6 of the *De finibus*. At some point after the German and French families divided, some scholar thought the argument of the *De finibus* was concluded by the refutation of Antiochus' doctrine in the first book of the 'Posterior Academics'. The transmission of the 'Posterior Academics' has been established by T. J. Hunt (MA thesis, Exeter, 1967), and it sheds considerable light on the French family of the *De finibus*. The oldest member of the French family stands at the head of the first group, Paris lat. 6331, s. XII (P = π for *Ac. post.*), containing *Fin.*, *Ac. post.* (as Bk. 6), Seneca, *Ben.*, *Clem.*, the *De remediis fortuitorum*, and a *Passio S. Albani*. Restored to its original order, it corresponds with an entry in the late twelfth-century catalogue of Pontigny. MS 6331 produced several descendants, the oldest being Amsterdam 77, s. XII, a direct copy of 6331 and of a codex of Seneca's letters whose description follows the entry for MS 6331 in the Pontigny catalogue. From Amsterdam 77 in turn descend Florence, Laur. Conv. Soppr. 131, finished probably in Florence on 30 May 1406, possibly for Antonio Corbinelli; and Paris lat. 14761, part II, written in Paris *c.*1457–63 by the hermit Girolamo da Matelica. After it left Pontigny, MS 6331 produced at least two other copies: Leiden, Periz. F. 25, written, according to Gilbert Ouy, for Pierre d'Ailly after 1409 and before his death in 1420; and Vatican, Pal. lat. 1511, thought to be a direct copy of MS 6331 after the latter had undergone careful correction.

The second group in the French family, considerably more nebulous, consists of a manuscript of the text, a collection of excerpts, notations of variant readings, and descriptions in two medieval book-lists. (1) Leiden, Gronov. 21 (R), s. XII ex./XIII in., found *c.*1650 by Bernard Rottendorf somewhere along the Rhine, contains *Fin.*, *Tim.*, Aulus Gellius, 1–7, *Theoretica geometria*, Hyginus, comm. on Boethius. R is closely related to (2) readings from 'an old manuscript' recorded in 1545 by the Parisian scholar-publisher Guillaume Morel. Morel's manuscript is not known, but a second witness to it may be (3) the extracts from the *De finibus* in Paris lat. 18104, s. XII ex., a florilegium compiled probably at Chartres. The extracts almost certainly share a common exemplar with (4) a manuscript given by Philip, Bishop of Bayeux, to Bec by 1164: 'In alio [volumine]: Pomponius Mela de cosmographia et Tullius de fine boni et mali et de academicis et Timaeus Platonis ab ipso Tullio translatus et Tullius de particione oratoria et liber Candidi Ariani ad Victorinum de generatione divina et Hilarius de sinodis et eiusdem liber contra Valentem et Auxencium.' Philip procured at least one other book from Chartres (Paris lat. 5802). It is possible also to assign to this second French group (5) the manuscript recorded in Richard de Fournival's *Biblionomia*, *c.*1250: '[75] Ejusdem [Ciceronis] liber Academicarum disputationum in quo ostendit quod genus phylozophizandi arbitrandum sit minime et arrogans maximeque et constans et elegans. Item ejusdem liber de universalitate qui vocatur Thimeus Tullii, in uno volumine.' Later descriptions of this manuscript, giving *incipit* and *explicit*, reveal the 'liber Academicarum' to have been in fact the *De finibus*. The common ancestor of this second French group must have contained the *De finibus*, followed by the 'Posterior Academics' with a colophon of its own. The source is in all probability to be sought in the Loire valley, perhaps Orléans. Paris lat. 18104 and Philip of Bayeux's text go back to Chartres, and portions of Richard de Fournival's library go back to Orléans. Noteworthy here is the appearance of extracts from the *De finibus* in the margins of an early thirteenth-century manuscript of Papias and Huguccio, Berne 276, whose copious marginalia depend on sources in Loire libraries, St. Columba's of Sens, Fleury, and especially Orléans cathedral.

If the composition of the second French group is largely speculative, the affiliations of the fourteenth- and fifteenth-century Italian manuscripts truly represent unmapped territory. It appears, however, that the German text of *De finibus* did not reach Italy in the Renaissance. Moreover, the progenitor of the Italian descendants of P, Florence, Laur. Conv. Soppr. 131, was written only in 1406, and its offspring have been identified.[2] Therefore it is a sensible assumption that the other Italian texts of *De finibus* derive, via means not always apparent, from a text or texts of the second French group. The *De finibus* and the

---

[2] T. J. Hunt, 'The Origin of the Deteriores of the "Academicus Primus"', *Scriptorium*, 27 (1973), 39–42.

'Posterior Academics' appear to have been in north Italy by *c.*1300. They are both paraphrased by Dante. In October or November 1343 Petrarch was given 'a small book of Cicero, at the end of which was the beginning, only, of the Academics' by his friend Barbato da Sulmona in Naples; the 'small book' was unquestionably *De finibus*, the inevitable companion of the *Ac. post.* until at least the beginning of the fifteenth century. Through Petrarch's friends the *De finibus* spread rapidly, but without the *Ac. post.*, which Petrarch apparently held back. It is also possible that Petrarch owned a second copy of the *De finibus* (one without the *Ac. post.*), and that it was this text that he circulated. If so, it is probable that he obtained the text from Avignon, where, in turn, the text derived from Fournival's copy, by then at the Sorbonne.

There are some nine fourteenth-century, principally Italian, manuscripts of the *De finibus*, as yet unclassified, that may well derive from Petrarch and his circle: Florence, Archivio di Stato, carte Strozziane, ser. 3 no. 46, ff. 11–36 (Salutati); Escorial V.III.6; Glasgow, Hunter T.2.14 (56), France; Milan, Ambros. E.15 inf. and S.64 sup.; Paris lat. 6375; Vatican, Arch. S. Pietro H.23; Venice, Marc. Lat. VI.81 (3036), France; and Wolfenbüttel, Gud. lat. 2.

In addition, there are five fourteenth- and fifteenth-century manuscripts of the *De finibus* that must belong to a single family; the affiliation of the *Ac. post.* (following the *De finibus* in this group, but with a separate rubric) in these manuscripts has been demonstrated, and that for *De finibus* will surely prove identical: Florence, Bibl. Naz. Magl. XXI.30; Gdansk 2388 (Florence, 1450–60); Madrid 9116; Modena Lat. 213 (*a.*Q.5.11); and Naples IV.G.43. Probably another member of this family was the fourteenth-century manuscript described in the fifteenth-century catalogue of the Medici library in Florence: '[888] M. T. Ciceronis de finibus bonorum et malorum, Achademicorum, partitiones, de caelo et mundo, de fato; item Francisci Petrarcae Florentini de vita solitaria . . .' (portions of this codex survive, but not the *De finibus*). The text of *De finibus* in this family, like the texts in the unclassified manuscripts, does not descend from P, and thus probably descends from the second French family; but this remains to be demonstrated, for both groups of manuscripts.

To reconstruct the text of the *De finibus*, an editor would need to use AEBPR and certain of the (non-P family) Italian manuscripts; the choice of these latter remains to be determined, through the establishment of lines of filiation for the unclassified manuscripts.

R. H. R.

Cato Maior de senectute

The *Cato Maior* survives in about 400 extant manuscripts:[1] this mostly
reflects Renaissance popularity, since all but about fifty of these are of
fourteenth or fifteenth century date. In the Renaissance, the *Cato*
usually appears with the *Laelius* and often with other Ciceronian works;
earlier, however, it keeps varied company, and the quite substantial
medieval circulation seems to denote genuine interest rather than mere
association with some other popular text.

The current text[2] is based on the six best ninth-century manuscripts,
which have been fairly well investigated. All of them are French; they
divide clearly into two groups, α (PV) and β (bLAD), which derive from
a single archetype. These manuscripts display 'insular symptoms' in
varying degrees;[3] these are more apparent in the β group, which has
received less scholarly editing in the course of production, but are not
entirely absent from α. It has therefore been reasonably thought that
the archetype was written in an insular hand. All except b are heavily
corrected by near-contemporary hands.

The best manuscripts have a number of descendants, but these do
not predominate in the later tradition. Relatives, not descendants, of P
appear in Germany in the eleventh century, and there are traces from
the tenth century onwards of a separate German group, which is in all
probability a branch of α, and is closest to V among the ninth-century
manuscripts, but which contains some correct readings not found in the
latter. The origin of these readings is unclear, but they may be remnants
of a tradition independent of the archetype of PVbLAD. In the twelfth
century this German tradition proliferates in a number of manuscripts,
whose detailed relationships are difficult to unravel owing to mutual
contamination. At the same time a similar tradition appears in northern
France and England. From then on, most manuscripts present a
roughly similar text, which became the vulgate of the early editions.
Readers had to be content with this text – which was not as bad as it
might have been from the point of view of the general sense – until the
nineteenth century, when more scientific reconstruction of the text
began. Several of the medieval manuscripts have remained uncollated
and neglected by editors until now.

---

[1] Cf. G. S. Vogel, *The Major Manuscripts of Cicero's* de Senectute (Chicago, 1939), 1. I have
located about 350 in an examination, certainly not exhaustive, of the catalogues available to me.

[2] As established by K. Simbeck (Teubner, 1912; 1917) and P. Wuilleumier (Budé, 3rd edn.,
Paris, 1961). Other modern editions generally follow the Teubner text; that of A. Barriera (Corpus
Paravianum) is eccentric, based on an overestimation of the value of D, discovered by Barriera in
1920 (cf. *Athenaeum*, 8 (1920), 174). All sigla used in the present article are Wuilleumier's except for
Ra = Vat. Reg. lat. 1414.   [3] Vogel, 6–14; Wuilleumier, 63.

The relationships of the principal manuscripts may be represented by the following stemma:

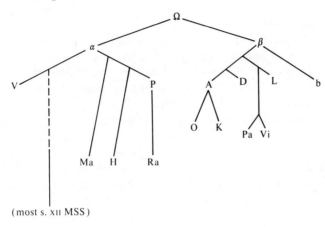

(most s. XII MSS)

P, Paris lat. 6332,[4] was written in the area of the Loire in the early ninth century; F. M. Carey assigned it to Saint-Germain-d'Auxerre. It has been thought that this manuscript and L (see below) may have belonged to Lupus of Ferrières, but neither contains any corrections or other marks by him, and there is no other evidence for the connection. P contains the *Tusculans* and the *Cato*, which breaks off at section 78. A singular feature of this manuscript is that it is written not in continuous prose but in verses in the biblical manner. The text of P has been highly regarded by all editors, and most have made it their principal witness. It should, however, be treated with caution, since it shows signs of editing in its ancestry, presenting in a number of places erroneous though plausible readings which depart from the main α tradition. It was corrected by a second hand from a manuscript of the β group, probably a close relative of L.

V, Leiden, Voss. Lat. O. 79,[5] is the other ninth-century representative of the α side of the tradition. It was written perhaps in the area of Reims, but moved later to Fleury, which may be where it was corrected from P or a manuscript of the same family. It contains the *Cato*, excerpts from Augustine, *Civ. Dei*, Censorinus, *De die natali*, and two metrical treatises.

The remaining ninth-century manuscripts belong to the β family. b, Brussels 9591, written in north-east France in the third quarter of the

---

[4] Cf. F. M. Carey, *Manuscripts from the Scriptorium of St. Germain d'Auxerre* (1956), 3; É. Pellegrin, 'Les Manuscripts de Loup de Ferrières', *BEC* 115 (1957), 5; R. J. Gariépy, *Mediaeval Studies*, 30 (1968), 94; E. von Severus, *Beiträge z. Gesch. d. alten Mönchtums*, Heft 21 (1940), 57; 65–7; 103; C. Graux, 'Nouvelles recherches sur la stichométrie', *RPh* 2 (1878), 126; Chatelain, plate XLIV. 1.

[5] Cf. K. A. de Meyier, *Codices Vossiani Latini III* (= *Codd. Mss. Bibl. Univ. Leid.* xv), 134–7; W. Gemoll, *Hermes*, 20 (1885), 331; C. Hofstede de Groot, *Hermes*, 25 (1890), 293; Chatelain, plate XLI.1.

ninth century,[6] contains in addition to the *Cato* the *Suasoriae* and *Controversiae* of the Elder Seneca and a number of works of Augustine, Alcuin, Cassiodorus, and others. The text is rather carelessly copied. There are a few corrections by the first hand.

L, Leiden, Voss. Lat. F. 12 β,[7] contains the *Cato* and fragments of Macrobius, *Comm. in Som. Scip.*, and was written either at or in the area of Fleury. It is corrected from a manuscript of P's family. Its text is closely related to two other ninth-century manuscripts which also contain the commentary of Macrobius: D, Vat. Reg. lat. 1587,[8] the most recently discovered of the major manuscripts, and A, Paris n.a.lat. 454,[9] which contains in addition the *Somnium* itself. (The Macrobius of D is detached and is now Paris lat. 16677.) D was also probably written at Fleury; A was written at Corbie, where a volume is recorded in the library catalogue (about 1200) containing 'arismetica – Tullius de senectute – Macrobius'; there are difficulties, however, in identifying this with A. The stemma would seem to indicate that the text travelled to Corbie from the Loire valley during the early ninth century, although this is not absolutely clear. Both D and A have corrections from a similar source to those of L, although almost certainly (in the case of A at least) not an identical one.

The seventh and last manuscript from the ninth century is K, Vat. Reg. lat. 1762,[10] which contains the Ciceronian florilegium of Hadoard, librarian of Corbie. The *Cato* excerpts are copied from A after the latter's correction, and hence are of virtually no use from the point of view of reconstructing the text.

The only complete manuscript from the tenth century is O, Oxford, Bodl. D'Orville 77,[11] which was written in south Germany. It contains, in addition to the *Cato*, the Caesarian orations, the *Laelius*, the pseudo-Sallustian invectives (all fairly regular companions of the *Cato* from now on), the *Somnium*, Macrobius, *Comm. in Som. Scip.*, and once contained Hyginus (detached in the eighteenth century). The text of the *Cato* (and of the *Somnium* and Macrobius) derives from A corrected. The most likely hypothesis is that a copy of A travelled to south Germany, where it not only became the exemplar of O but also infused a number of β readings into the local German tradition, which would account for their presence when that tradition emerges later on. The corrections of O

---

[6] Information kindly supplied by Professor Bernhard Bischoff.

[7] Cf. T. Mommsen, 'Über eine Leydener Handschrift von Ciceros Cato maior', *Monatsberichte Kön. Preuss. Akad. Wiss. zu Berlin*, 1863, 10–13; *Gesammelte Schriften*, vii, 6–8; Pellegrin, art. cit.; von Severus, 57–8; 102, pl. II; Lowe, *Pal. Papers*, i. 321; Chatelain, plate XLa; B. C. B.-B., 'A Ninth-century Manuscript from Fleury' in *Medieval Learning*, 157 ff.

[8] Pellegrin, *Manuscrits*, ii.1. 311–14; B. C. B.-B., 145 ff.; Barriera, art. cit.

[9] Bischoff, 'Hadoardus and the Manuscripts of Classical Authors from Corbie', in *Didaskaliae: Studies in Honor of Anselm M. Albareda*, ed. S. Prete (New York, 1961), 41–57, reprinted (in German) in *Mitt. Stud.* i. 49–63; Chatelain, plate XLb. 1; B. C. B.-B., 159 f.; L. Delisle, *Notices et extraits*, Bibl. Nat. Paris, xxxi, i (1884), 264.

[10] Bischoff, art. cit.   [11] Vogel, 46 ff.; B. C. B.-B., 160.

(hitherto not noticed by editors) provide the earliest evidence for the south German group which becomes prominent in the twelfth century.

Pa, Paris lat. 5752,[12] s. X/XI, France?, contains the *Cato* and *Laelius*, and is bound with a thirteenth-century copy of Sallust; the first part of the *Cato* (to section 19) is missing. The text cannot derive from L, as Wuilleumier thought; it is clearly related to that area of the tradition, but the non-β readings come from V or a relative of V, not from P. The only other manuscript of this period is British Library, Harley 2716 (s. X), written in the upper Rhineland and containing two separate fragments of the *Cato*, in addition to Cicero *in Catil.*, the Caesarian orations, part of the *De officiis*, and the pseudo-Sallustian invectives. One of the fragments is on the back of a leaf palimpsested on the other side to provide an extra page for the end of the *De off.*; the other is an isolated leaf which cannot have been part of a complete copy, as it breaks off in mid-paragraph halfway down the verso. Unfortunately these fragments are too short to enable them to be assigned definitely to a particular place in the stemma, or to be of much use in the constitution of the text, but there is nothing to suggest that they do not belong to the local German textual tradition, while the first-mentioned of them bears a clear affinity to other German manuscripts.

From the eleventh century we have the fragment in Vi, Paris lat. 14699 (Saint-Victor),[13] which contains sections 1–21 of the *Cato* together with Boethius, *in Topica Ciceronis*. The text of Vi derives from a similar source to that of Pa. Ma, Florence, Laur. 50.45,[14] is of unknown origin but perhaps German; it contains the *De inventione* with the commentary of Marius Victorinus, *Laelius*, *Cato*, the Sallustian invectives, the Catilinarians, and the Caesarians. A German origin might be supported by its textual affinity with H, Harley 2682,[15] a large collection of Ciceronian works written probably in the area of Cologne in the second half of the eleventh century. Ma and H form a well-defined group together with P, but H is considerably contaminated with β readings, derived almost certainly from O or one of its relatives, and both share readings with later German manuscripts. Ma has few corrections; H was corrected throughout by a second hand of distinctly south German affinities, containing also some β readings.

Ra, Vat. Reg. lat. 1414,[16] was written probably at Fleury by two eleventh-century scribes, and is a faithful copy of P as regards the *Cato*;

---

[12] Wuilleumier, 62, 64; B. Dahl, *Zur Handschriftenkunde u. Kritik des Ciceronischen Cato Maior, II. Codices Parisini*, Christiania Videnskabs-Selskabs Forhandlinger, 1886, no. 12.

[13] Cf. Pellegrin, 'Manuscrits de l'Abbaye de St.-Victor', *BEC* 103 (1942), 69 ff. Pellegrin shows that Vi was originally part of a larger MS, which contained another copy of the *Cato* whose description fits well with that of Pa: it could therefore be that Pa and Vi were at one time bound together. The script of the two MSS is certainly very similar.

[14] F. Ramorino, *RFIC* 15 (1886), 247 ff.; Chatelain, plate XLII.

[15] A. C. Clark, *Anecdota Oxoniensia*, Classical Series, 7 (Oxford, 1891), 20 ff.; H. Schwarz, *Philologus*, 8 (1895), 163 ff.; C. E. Wright, *Fontes Harleiani*, 109, 169.

[16] Pellegrin, *Manuscrits*, ii.1. 195–7; C. E. Finch, *TAPA* 91 (1960), 76–82.

it also contains parts of the *Tusculans* and the Catonian *Disticha*. First reported by C. E. Finch in 1960, too late to be used in any of the current editions, it would be of very limited interest were it not for the fact that the last few sections of the *Cato* are missing from P; it is therefore of considerable importance as a guide to the readings of P in those sections. Another eleventh-century Vatican manuscript, Reg. lat. 1424, also probably originating from the area of Fleury, contains a single page of excerpts from the *Cato*; it has not been reported, but is almost certainly of no critical value.

From south Germany in the twelfth century we find a group consisting of several related manuscripts: the two Rhenaugienses Q and R (Zürich Rh. 126 and 127); Munich Clm 15964 (Salisburgensis, = S), 7809 (Indersdorfensis, = I), and 4611 (Benedictoburanus, = B); and Admont 363 (a). To these may be added E (Berlin (West) lat. 2° 252, *olim* Erfurtensis), the Ciceronian collection from Corvey; also Florence, Laur. 76.31 (Mc), and Laur. Strozzi 36, both apparently Italian but closely related to the German group. These manuscripts all display a roughly similar text, and their detailed relationships with each other are difficult to determine. E has more β contamination than the others; in a number of places R and E agree with O^2, and sometimes also with QSB etc., in a correct reading absent from the rest of the tradition. It is likely that Wolfenbüttel, Aug. 4° 51.12 (Hildesheim), not as yet collated, is also a member of this group.

A text of very similar character appears at roughly the same time in northern France and England. No detailed collation is available of the three Paris manuscripts, Paris lat. 13340 (Saint-Germain-des-Prés, = Sg), 16588 (Sorbonne), and 18420 (Notre-Dame), but the readings provided by Dahl seem to confirm that they belong to this group; Voss. Lat. F. 104 (v), now considered to have been written in France in the twelfth century (De Meyier), seems not dissimilar; and my own collations of the British manuscripts, B. L. Egerton 654 (last part only, but containing some excellent readings), Lambeth Palace 425 (one complete text and one fragmentary), Eton College 90, and Cambridge, Trinity College 1381 (O.8.6), have shown their connections with the German manuscripts already mentioned.

As for the later manuscripts, from the thirteenth century onwards, very few have been collated, but those which have been do not show any significant variation from what had by then become the vulgate text. To collate many more of them would in all probability be a thankless task, and would not be likely to help in solving any textual problems that remain.

J. G. F. P.

Laelius de amicitia

The *Laelius de amicitia* appears at first to have been transmitted independently of the *Cato Maior*; but the two works, being natural companion pieces, were soon reunited by the anthologizing tendencies of the Middle Ages, and are found together very frequently from the twelfth century onwards. No doubt each contributed to the other's circulation. However, the earlier tradition of the *Laelius* is somewhat thin, indicating that the work was not, to begin with, as popular as the *Cato*.

For so well-known a text, the progress that has been made in the elucidation of its history is not great, and the current editions[1] are disappointingly vague on the subject. Further attention paid to some previously neglected manuscripts might help considerably. The following stemma contains only those manuscripts whose position has been definitely established.

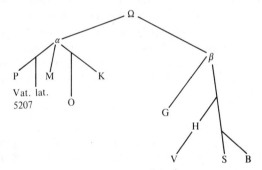

There are two families, α and β, which descend from a single archetype. The former is the one which emerges first, in the ninth century; it appears to be localized in south-west Germany, as far as can be seen at present, although it has French (Corbie) connections. The β family, which appears from the late tenth century onwards, is undoubtedly German, and overlaps to a considerable extent with the German group of *Cato* manuscripts. Thus the two branches of the tradition seem to have been moving in parallel in roughly the same area.

The only complete *Laelius* from the ninth century is or was the manuscript referred to by editors as P, Parisinus Didotianus. It was first brought to light by Mommsen, who found it in the private library of F. Didot at Paris.[2] It then passed into the hands of B. Quaritch, the London bookseller; the Bodleian missed the opportunity of buying it

---

[1] K. Simbeck, Teubner, 1917; L. Laurand, Budé, 1928; R. Combès, Budé, 1971.

[2] 'De Laelii Ciceroniani codice Didotiano narratio', *RhM* 18 (1863), 594; Laurand, xiv–xv; R. W. Hunt, 'An Opportunity Missed: the Didot Manuscript of Cicero, *De amicitia*', *Bodleian Library Record*, 7, no. 5 (July 1966), 275.

owing to lack of funds, and it was bought by the Deutsche Staatsbibliothek in 1893, where it was rediscovered (as MS lat. 4° 404) by L.
Laurand, editing the text for the Budé series. The latest Budé editor, R.
Combès, has reported that it is again missing, having been lost during
the war, and that only photographic records of it survive. As to its
provenance, Mommsen noted that it had a fifteenth-century *ex libris* of
the cathedral at Constance, and thought that it must have been written
in that area. This seems more plausible, given the proximity of related
manuscripts, than the attribution to Tours made by Rand[3] on the basis
of the script. P has been generally considered the best witness to the
text.

A text very similar to that of P is found in the fragment (§§ 1–28) in
Vat. lat. 5207, s. x[1], Italy, which also contains Macrobius, *Saturnalia*,
1–3. This manuscript is not mentioned by any of the editors, but a
collation was published in 1964 by C. E. Finch.[4]

Also from the ninth century is M, Munich Clm 15514, from the
Benedictine monastery at Rot-am-Inn (south-west Germany) and
probably written in that region. It contains §§ 44–end of the *Laelius*,
together with works of assorted other authors. The text of M is related to
that of P, but with considerably more errors and omissions.

The fourth and last ninth-century witness consists of Hadoard's
excerpts (K, Vat. Reg. lat. 1762), written at Corbie,[5] which are of much
more value for the *Laelius* than for the *Cato*, since in this case we do not
possess their exemplar. The text is midway between P and M, without
attaching itself strongly to either.

Further light is cast on Hadoard's lost exemplar by the tenth-century
south German manuscript, Oxford, Bodl. D'Orville 77 (O in the above
stemma). No modern editor of the *Laelius* seems to have been aware of
the existence of this manuscript, although it has been used for other
texts. It was seen in the case of the *Cato* to descend from the manuscript
used by Hadoard, and the same is true of its *Laelius* text. O agrees with
K in the great majority of the latter's readings, and, where K fails,
shows a similar relationship with P and M. It also incorporates some
readings that appear due to correction of its exemplar from the β group,
but these are few and do not obscure the manuscript's ancestry. Most
important, O contains two correct readings not found in any other
manuscript: § 9 *in pueris* and § 48 *diffundatur* and *contrahatur*. In view of
the former, it may be the book mentioned by Mommsen as having the
correct reading in that section ('Iacobi Susii liber'), although

---

[3] E. K. Rand, *Studies in the Script of Tours*, i. 114.

[4] *TAPA* 95 (1964), 66 ff. For date and origin we rely on information supplied by Professor
Bischoff.

[5] For further information about K, O, L, and H, see the *Cato* article. The information here given
about the text of O is the result of my own examination of the manuscript.

Mommsen himself thought that this was P. It is not clear whether, as in the case of the *Cato*, O was copied from a manuscript which originated at Corbie, or whether its text is native to south Germany, as the proximity of M and perhaps P would seem to indicate. In the latter case, the exemplar of K would have been a manuscript imported from Germany.

Another early manuscript which has so far escaped the notice of editors is Paris lat. 5752 (s. x/xi, France), which also contains part of the *Cato*. A cursory examination of the text has shown it to be nearer to the α family than to β, but it is contaminated and difficult to place exactly. More work is clearly needed on this area of the tradition.

The β family is headed by G, Wolfenbüttel, Gud. lat. 335, of the late tenth or eleventh century, written in south-west Germany. The remaining β manuscripts have long been supposed to descend from a lost *gemellus* of G, conventionally denoted by 'g'. Of these, the earliest is H, British Library, Harley 2682, containing a substantial collection of Ciceronian works, produced probably in the area of Cologne in the second half of the eleventh century.

Also from the eleventh century are L, Florence, Laur. 50.45, origin unknown (probably German), and p, Paris lat. 544, which was at one stage at Limoges and possibly originated in that area of France.[6] These two manuscripts are difficult to place; they are closely related to each other, but present a somewhat hybrid text. Combès thinks that they are contaminated members of α, while Venini (Ed. Paraviana) assigns them to β. Vienna 275 (s. xi, south Germany = V), which derives from H according to Clark and the editors, clearly belongs to the β family, as does the eleventh-century fragment in Munich Clm 29220 (6 (*olim* 29001,4) (m).

Passing to the twelfth century, one finds the tradition expanding considerably. The β family acquires more south German descendants; S (Munich Clm 15964, Salisburgensis), B (Munich Clm 4611, Benedictoburanus), and a (Admont 363) form a group, already familiar from the *Cato* tradition, whose *Laelius* text derives from the lost g. To these may be added the fragment at Sélestat, Bibl. Mun. 7 (s. x, written at St. Gall = s), which contains §§ 40–74 of the *Laelius*.[7] Also deriving from the β group is a second fragment in Munich, Clm 29220 (7 (n), and also the fragment in Angers 1898 (s. xii ex., France). The α family is also not without its descendants, although by this time it had undergone a considerable amount of contamination from the other branch of the tradition. These are: E, Berlin (West) lat. 2° 252, the manuscript written for Wibald of Corvey; b, Berne 514 (s. xii¹, France);

---

[6] Laurand, 'Le Manuscrit "Laurentianus L 45" du *de Amicitia*', *Musée Belge*, 30 (1926), 33; 'Le Texte du *de Amicitia* dans le "Parisinus 544" ', ibid. 131.

[7] Laurand, 'Le Fragment du *de Amicitia* contenu dans le "Selestadensis" ', *CPh* 21 (1926), 149.

e, Munich Clm 19473 (from Tegernsee); and F, the fragment belonging to the Collegium Stellae Matutinae at Feldkirch in Austria.[8] The rest of the twelfth-century manuscripts have not been used in editions. Of these, the following contain both the *Cato* and the *Laelius*: Wolfenbüttel, Aug. 4° 51.12; Leiden, Voss. Lat. F. 104; Florence, Laur. Strozzi 36; Paris lat. 18420; Cambridge, Trin. Coll. 1381 (O.8.6); Lambeth Palace 425; Eton College 90 (s. XII/XIII, England); Zürich Rh. 127 (fragment only of the *Laelius*). The *Laelius* is found without the *Cato* in Vatican, Reg. lat. 1439, of French origin; B. L. Harley 4927, also a French manuscript, which later belonged to Petrarch; Laur. Strozzi 49, written in Beneventan script of the Bari type;[9] Berlin (East), Diez. C. 8° 11 and Diez. C. 8° 12;[10] Glasgow, Hunter U.5.18 (278); and there are a number of other manuscripts of the twelfth century.

Some later manuscripts have achieved a rather undeserved prominence in editions; it is disputable whether they add anything to the information to be gained from those already described. They are all more or less contaminated, although the two families seem to have stayed more separate from each other, despite their geographical contiguity, than those of the *Cato* did; both sorts of text are to be found fairly evenly dispersed. The *Laelius* became very popular in the Renaissance and a large number of fifteenth-century copies are extant.

J. G. F. P.

[8] W. Fox, 'Bruchstücke einer bisher unbekannten Handschrift von Ciceros Laelius', *Neue philologische Rundschau*, 1904, 289.

[9] V. Brown, 'A Second New List of Beneventan Manuscripts', *Mediaeval Studies*, 40 (1978), 252; *Beneventan Script*[2], ii.45.

[10] Cf. P. Fedeli in *Hommages à M. Renard*, i, 339–49 (Coll. Latomus, 101, 1969) (also on Aug. 4° 51.12).

De natura deorum, De divinatione, Timaeus, De fato, Topica, Paradoxa Stoicorum, Academica priora, De legibus

The texts of eight of Cicero's philosophical works (*De natura deorum, De divinatione, Timaeus, De fato, Topica, Paradoxa Stoicorum, Lucullus* or *Academica priora*, and *De legibus*) are based on three Carolingian manuscripts from north-eastern and central France, and a late eleventh-century manuscript from Montecassino; two of the Carolingian codices containing at least partial texts of all eight works are in the Bibliotheek der Rijksuniversiteit at Leiden, hence the frequent designation of these works as the 'Leiden corpus'.[1]

The Leiden corpus survives in two families of manuscripts derived from a common archetype. The best of the manuscripts and head of one family is Leiden, Voss. Lat. F. 86 (B) (Chatelain, plate XXXIX), written in north-eastern France in the middle of the ninth century. At some time during the third quarter of the century a corrector at Corbie tried to rationalize the confused arrangement of B's texts.[2] It was also at Corbie that B served as partial exemplar for Florence, Laur. S. Marco 257 (F), discussed below, which had numerous progeny in fifteenth-century Italy. By the fifteenth century B was at Reims, where it can be identified from the opening words of its second folio with an entry in the catalogue (1456–7) of the chapter library.[3] B later belonged to P. Pithou (1539–96).

The second family, AVH, descends at one remove from the archetype and consists of two ninth-century Carolingian manuscripts and one eleventh-century manuscript from Montecassino. Leiden, Voss. Lat. F. 84 (A)[4] was written by several scribes in the middle of the ninth century in north-eastern France. In the third quarter of the century A was seen at Corbie by the corrector of B; in the tenth century it was given by a bishop Rodulfus to an unknown church; nothing of its later history is known until 1647, when it appears in the possession of A. Petau. The precise relationship of B and A with the Corbie products of this period has been worked out by Beeson and Bischoff.[5] Both B and A appear to have been at Corbie in the third quarter of the ninth century, when A was corrected against an emended version of B. After the work of emendation a copy was made which followed the text of B for the *De natura deorum* and the *De divinatione*, and the text of A for the rest of the corpus. This copy, Florence, Laur. S. Marco 257, s. IX¾ (F) (Chatelain, plate XXXVII),[6] then served as the source from which Hadoard, librarian of Corbie, took the philosophical portions of his excerpts contained in Vatican, Reg. lat. 1762, s. IX². At the beginning of the eleventh century

[1] Ed. O. Plasberg, *Parad., Ac. prior., Tim., D.N.D.* (Leipzig, 1908–11, *ed. maior*); W. Ax, *Div., Fat., Tim.* (Leipzig, 1938); K. Ziegler, *Leg.* (Leipzig, 1980³); A. S. Pease, *Div.* (Urbana, 1920–3, repr. Darmstadt, 1963); R. Badali, *Parad.* (Milan, 1968); M. van den Bruwaene, *D.N.D.* 1, in *Latomus*, 107 (Brussels, 1970). The richly informative study by P. L. Schmidt, *Die Überlieferung von Ciceros Schrift 'De legibus' in Mittelalter und Renaissance*, Studia et testimonia antiqua, 10 (Munich, 1974), though focused on *De legibus*, brings together material on many manuscripts in the tradition of Cicero's *philosophica*.

[2] C. H. Beeson, 'The Collectaneum of Hadoard', *CPh* 40 (1945), 201–22.

[3] Schmidt, 31–4.

[4] Chatelain, plate XXXVIIIa; a complete facsimile of A has been published by Plasberg, *Codices graeci et latini photographice depicti*, 19 (Leiden, 1915).

[5] Beeson, op. cit.; B. Bischoff, 'Hadoardus and the Manuscripts of Classical Authors from Corbie', in *Didaskaliae: Studies in Honor of Anselm M. Albareda*, ed. S. Prete (New York, 1961), 41–57, reprinted (in German) in *Mitt. Stud.* i, 49–63.

[6] Schmidt, 121–3.

F was given by Werinharius, bishop of Strasbourg (1001–28), to the cathedral library. Here, probably during his trip north in 1417, Poggio discovered F and brought it to Italy. F was probably among the books which Poggio left to his friend Niccolò Niccoli, before his journey to England (1418–22/3). Upon Niccoli's death, F passed to the library of S. Marco in Florence. The oldest direct descendant of F, Munich Clm 528 (M), s. XI[1], was probably written in Strasbourg.[7] M contains all the Leiden corpus save *Topica*; it has no known descendants. M belonged to the Bavarian humanist J. Aventinus, who may have acquired it during his study at Paris, 1504/5. The manuscript was in the library of the Benedictines at Biburg later in the sixteenth century.

The other Carolingian manuscript of the AVH family, Vienna 189 (V) (Chatelain, plate XXXVIII.1),[8] is its earliest member, written in the early part of the ninth century, possibly at Ferrières. V is the first manuscript to omit the *Topica*, which throughout its transmission in the Leiden corpus existed in a very mutilated condition. *De legibus*, which V originally contained, at some stage dropped from the manuscript. During the middle of the ninth century, Lupus, Abbot of Ferrières, corrected V against a Corbie manuscript. The fact that these corrections agree with the corrected version of B for the first two works of the corpus and with the corrected version of A for the remainder suggests that Lupus used F, and that F may have left Corbie at an early stage in its history.

V belonged in the fifteenth century to the Prieuré des Faucons at Antwerp and later to Theodor Poelman (1512–81), who gave it to Sambucus. From V descend the majority of late medieval and Renaissance manuscripts of Cicero's philosophical works. Three twelfth-century manuscripts are textually very similar to V: Paris lat. 17812 (N), s. XII, containing Cicero, *Ac. prior.*, *D.N.D.*, *Fat.*, *Fam.* 1–8, and Dares Phrygius, *Hist. Tro.*; Tours 688 (T), s. XII[2], containing Cicero, *Ac. prior.*, *D.N.D.*, *Fat.*, *Fam.*; and Oxford, Merton College 311 (O), s. XII[2], containing Cicero, *Off.*, epitaphs, *D.N.D.*, *Fat.*, *Phil.* 1–4, and (in a thirteenth-century hand) Palladius, *De re rust.*, written in England and owned by Thomas Trilleck, Bishop of Rochester (1364–72), and by William Reade, fellow of Merton and Bishop of Chichester (1368–85). N belonged to Antoine Loisel and came to Notre-Dame by way of Claude Joly. T, containing the texts in the same sequence, is probably a direct copy of N. Since T belonged to Saint-Martin-de-Marmoutier near Tours, N also may have circulated in that area. Two additional manuscripts, known only through medieval catalogues, probably witness the influence of V. Item 80 in the inventory of books which Philip of Bayeux bequeathed to Bec by 1164 contains *D.N.D.*,

---

[7] Ibid. 152–3.   [8] Van den Bruwaene, op. cit.

Div., *Tim.*, *Fat.*, *Ac. prior.*, *Leg.*[9] Nearly a century later the *Biblionomia* (*c.*1250) of Richard of Fournival contains a series of entries listing all the works of the Leiden corpus.[10] That V was the ultimate source of Fournival's manuscript is suggested by three French manuscripts of the first quarter of the fifteenth century which are important for reconstructing the *De legibus* missing from V.[11] These are Leiden, Periz. F. 25 (E) containing *Off.*, *Fin.*, *Ac. post.*, *Tusc.*, *D.N.D.*, *Div.*, *Fat.*, *Leg.*, and by a later hand *Senect.*, *Amic.*, *Parad.*; Paris lat. 15084 (S), containing *Leg.*, L. Bruni's translation of Plato's *Phaedo*, *Fat.*; and Rouen 1041 (O.47) (R), containing *Phil.*, *Leg.*, *Top.*, *D.N.D.* S and R were copied at Paris, S (after 1404/5) for Nicholas of Clamanges (later given to Saint-Victor), and R (*c.*1420) by and for the Sorbonne scholar, Guillaume Euvrie. The source of SR, at least for *De legibus*, was Fournival's manuscript (by then in the Sorbonne library), as Schmidt has shown. Textually, E does not appear to be a sister of SR but rather to have come directly from V.

The third member of the AVH family, Leiden B.P.L. 118 (H) (Chatelain, plate XXXVIII), was written at Montecassino during the abbacy of Desiderius (1058–87) and is the first extant copy of works of the Leiden corpus south of the Alps.[12] H contains *D.N.D.* and incomplete texts of *Div.* and *Leg.*, representing the first major breakup of the corpus. How these texts reached southern Italy is unknown; two relatives of H in *D.N.D.* and *Parad.*, British Library, Harley 2622 and 2682 (s. XI), belong to the neighbourhood of Cologne.[13] From Montecassino H went to Florence, where it is no. 27 in the catalogue of the library of Cosimo de' Medici (1418), 'Tulio de natura deorum de legibus et de divinatione lettera longobarda', and then to the library of the Dominican house of S. Marco at Florence. Heinsius probably acquired H during his trip to Italy (1651–3) in the service of Queen Christina of Sweden. A possible sister of H is B. L. Burney 148 (L), a southern Italian manuscript (perhaps from Montecassino) of the late thirteenth century containing *D.N.D.*, *Leg.*, and some anonymous *sententiae morales* appended in a later hand.[14] L soon moved north and was one of the sources for a manuscript, not extant, containing a great number of Cicero's works. Two fourteenth-century northern Italian descendants of L, via this manuscript, are Wolfenbüttel, Gud. lat. 2 (Gud.) and Troyes 552 (Trec.);[15] Gud. contains twenty-six works by Cicero or ascribed to him, while Trec. contains twenty. By the fifteenth century at the latest the Gudianus was in Paris. The Trecensis was owned by

---

[9] H. Omont, *Catalogue général des manuscrits des bibliothèques publiques de France: Départements*, ii (Paris, 1888), 397, no. 80.

[10] Delisle, ii. 525, 529, nos. 21, 26, 73–6, and 79.   [11] Schmidt, 57–61.

[12] Ibid. 37–41.   [13] Ibid. 175.

[14] Schmidt, 41–2. The extract from *D.N.D.* 1. 87 in B. L. Arundel 268 (s. XIII, southern Italy or Sicily), f. 95ᵛ, on which see *CQ* 30 (1980), 514, n. 36, presumably comes from a similar source.

[15] Schmidt, 177–82.

Petrarch and following his death in 1374 came into the hands of Pietro Malvezzi of Mantua and was copied at Padua. It was probably brought to France by François Pithou (1543–1621).[16]

Though B and A do not appear to have been copied, their influence endured in F, whose Renaissance Italian offspring were many. Direct descendants of F include three early fifteenth-century Florentine manuscripts: Vat. Chigi H.VIII.253 (Chis. 2) containing *Tusc., D.N.D., Div., Tim., Fat., Top., Leg.*; Florence, Laur. 76.11 (Laur. 2) containing *Luc., Leg.*; and Vat. Urb. lat. 319 (Urb.) containing *D.N.D., Div., Leg., Ac. post., Luc., Tim., Fat.*[17] But the most frequently copied descendant of F was Poggio's autograph of *Luc.* and *Leg.*, Vat. lat. 3245 (Vat. 4), written at the Council of Constance.[18] In addition to the numerous mid-fifteenth-century manuscripts copied from Vat. lat. 3245, two editions of Cicero, Rome 1471 and Venice 1472, drew their texts from it.

In terms of numbers, the most important disseminator of texts of these works proved to be the Ferrarese scholar, Guarino da Verona.[19] Textually, Guarino's version is very similar to Poggio's. From about 1430, following Guarino's lectures, copies of his text spread through north Italy.

R. H. R.

Topica

It can be seen all too plainly in editions of *D.N.D., Tim., Fat.*, and *Leg.* that the archetype of the Leiden corpus had a number of gaps, if not from the beginning, then certainly when the oldest of its surviving descendants was written.[20] Its text of *Topica* was also incomplete: in B and A § 3 *incredibili quadam* (B: § 4 *Non potui* B²A) follows the premature end of *Fat.* without title or gap, and §§ 28–72/3 *-tratuum more – possimus. Haec* is missing. Apart from descendants of A (F and its family), other manuscripts of the corpus omit *Topica* altogether.

Alone of the eight works in the corpus, however, Cicero's treatment of 'Aristotelis topica quaedam' has another line of transmission. The

---

[16] Other medieval manuscripts about which more information is needed include the following: The Hague 135.G.8, s. IX¾, probably north Italy, fragments of *Div.*; Paris lat. 6339 (*olim* Mazarin.), s. XIII, containing *D.N.D.* (beginning lost) and *Div.*; Escorial Q. I. 21, s. XIII, containing *D.N.D., Div., Fat., Off.*; Vatican lat. 2902, s. XIII.

[17] Schmidt, 155–9.   [18] Ibid. 279–82.   [19] Ibid. 344–90.

[20] M. T. Gibson, 'The Study of the *Timaeus* in the Eleventh and Twelfth Centuries', *Pensamiento*, 25 (1969), 183–94, does not mention the fragmentary state of Cicero's translation, which was never a complete translation anyway, as a reason why C(h)alcidius' was preferred when the work entered 'the main stream of scholarly thought' in s. XI. From s. IX–X scarcely more manuscripts of C(h)alcidius' survive than of Cicero's to judge from the list in J. H. Waszink's edition, *Plato Latinus*, iv (London and Leiden, 1962), cvii–cxxxi.

earliest witness to it is the text of §§ 1–3 and 28–72 added to B by a hand still of s. IX.[21] From nine complete witnesses of s. X-XII (there are several more[22]) W. Friedrich singled out a Beneventan manuscript written at Montecassino in s. XI[2], Vatican, Ottob. lat. 1406 (O);[23] with O, which he rated above all other manuscripts, he associated a Vitebergensis written at Rome in 1432 (f, now Halle Yg 24). Had he looked at other Italian manuscripts of s. XV, however, he would probably have found that they all resembled Of,[24] and had he not made light of agreements with Of that he noticed in northern-European manuscripts of s. XI–XII,[25] he might have gone on to establish something more solid about the tradition of *Topica* than he did.

The forensic slant that Cicero gave to his *Topica* for the benefit of the dedicatee, the lawyer Trebatius, explains its inclusion among his rhetorical works in modern editions, but whoever included it in the Leiden corpus must have perceived that *disciplina inveniendorum argu-*

Friedrich's edition (Teubner, Leipzig, 1891) and its twentieth-century descendants[26] have the same air of improvisation as the work itself, which Cicero wrote from memory on board ship. They do not even reveal that half the text is missing from BA, and they give an apparatus so lacunose and inaccurate that anyone who used them to affiliate a newly discovered manuscript would reach either erroneous conclusions or none whatsoever.[27]

---

[21] Bischoff ap. Schmidt, 30, 115 n. 14; in 1860 these additions were misguidedly transferred to A, and so they appear in the facsimile of A. Extracts from §§ 36–7 and 55 occur among the ninth-century marginalia in B. L. Harley 2735 (ff. 120^r, 24^r), some of which have been attributed by Bischoff, *Mitt. Stud.* iii. 66–7 nn. 47–8, to Heiric of Auxerre.

[22] e.g. Bamberg Class. 13 (M.IV.1) and 14 (M.V.13) (both s. XI), Chartres 71 (s. X) and 100 (s. X/XI), Oxford, Bodl. Laud. Lat. 49 (s. XI, south Germany), Paris Ars. 912 (s. XI), Valenciennes 406 (s. IX/X, given by Hucbald to Saint-Amand), Vatican, Reg. lat. 1405 (s. XI). Professor B. Munk Olsen adds four of s. X: Munich Clm 6367 (Freising), Paris lat. 7710 and 7711, Orléans 267 + Paris n.a. lat. 1611 (Fleury). Chatelain, plate XXI illustrates two of Friedrich's manuscripts, both Swiss; that five of his nine manuscripts were in Swiss libraries says less about the circulation of *Topica* than about his dependence on the edition of Orelli–Baiter (Zürich, 1845).

[23] *Jahrb. für class. Phil.* 139 (1889), 281–96. On O see *Beneventan Script*,[2] i.73, ii.166.

[24] There are four such manuscripts in Oxford and two in London, and like Of they all read, e.g., § 4 *cavisses* for *scripsisses*.   [25] Op. cit. 283.

[26] A. S. Wilkins in the OCT (1903), H. Bornecque in the Budé (1924), and H. M. Hubbell in the Loeb (1949) all rely on Friedrich's apparatus, which they often garble.

[27] For that reason C. E. Finch's article 'Codices Vat. Lat. 1701, 2110, and 8591 as Sources for Cicero's *Topica*', *CPh* 67 (1972), 112–17, serves only as a partial collation of these manuscripts (it also fills gaps in Friedrich's report of O). Many of the readings that he regards as peculiar to O and his three Vaticani occur in the so-called 'second family' (BA and everything else), as a glance at the facsimile of A suffices to show. The oldest of his manuscripts, Vatican lat. 8591 (s. XI[1]), had been described by E. M. Sanford, *TAPA* 55 (1924), 220, A. van de Vyver, 'Les Étapes du développement philosophique du Haut Moyen-Age', *RBPh* 8 (1929), 448, and G. Lacombe, *Aristoteles Latinus*, ii (Cambridge, 1955), 1240–1, no. 1897 and *Suppl.* (Bruges and Paris, 1961), 181–2, who agrees with G. F. Pagallo, *IMU* 1 (1958), 72, that it is largely a copy of Orléans 267 + Paris n.a. lat. 1611. Finch has also written about Chartres 498 (s. XII) and two excerpts in Vatican, Reg. lat. 1048 (s. XI[1]); see *Mediaeval Studies*, 40 (1978), 468–72 and *Illinois Class. Stud.* 3 (1978), 262–5.

mentorum (§ 2) was a broader and more philosophical subject than Cicero had made it appear. It recovered its Aristotelian breadth in the · hands of Boethius, who translated and commented on Aristotle's *Topica*, wrote a fuller commentary on Cicero's than Marius Victorinus had done in s. IV,[28] and finally produced a comprehensive treatise of his own *De topicis differentiis*.[29] The treatise but not the commentary on Cicero became a standard text in medieval schools: a recent estimate puts manuscripts of the one at 170 (s. X–XV), of the other at thirty (s. X–XV).[30] It remains to be established whether the commentary brought Cicero with it into the Middle Ages and created the line of transmission separate from the Leiden corpus.[31] Certainly many manuscripts contain both, usually side by side; and if manuscripts of Cicero out-number those of the commentary, they do so only in s. XV, when any work of Cicero might be copied *auctoris reverentia*.[32]

M. D. R.

[28] P. Hadot, *Marius Victorinus* (Paris, 1971), 115–41, 313–21.

[29] Eleonore Stump's translation of *De topicis differentiis* (Ithaca, NY, and London, 1978), 'with notes and essays on the text', offers a lucid and elegantly written introduction to the scope and purpose of classical and medieval *Topica*; on Cicero's see pp. 20–3, 211–12. She plans a similar treatment of the commentary (p. 23 n. 25); since Orelli included it in his Ciceronian corpus, v. i (Zürich, 1833), 269–388, only the first book has been edited, by A. Perdamo (diss. St. Louis, Mo., 1963; I have not seen it), but Th. Stangl, *Boethiana* (Gotha, 1882), 1–14, discussed eight manu-scripts.

[30] L. M. de Rijk, *Vivarium*, 2 (1964), 151 n. 2, 153 n. 1. Van de Vyver, 425–52, provides a context for the figures.

[31] That the text of the commentary influenced manuscripts of Cicero has been suspected but not proved. Two passages in point occur close together in § 24. For *quod* (AB) O has *quantum*, 'manifesto ex Boethio' say Orelli–Baiter; then follows '*tecto in eius* Boethius: *in tectum eius* codd.', where in fact A agrees with Boethius. In the 840s Lupus of Ferrières was interested in a papyrus manuscript of the commentary owned by St. Martin's Tours; see L. Levillain, *Loup de Ferrières: correspondance*, i (Paris, 1927), 214–7. Did it include the text of Cicero?

[32] B. L. Burney 156, f. 79[r]: 'Synonimas M. Tullii Ciceronis diu frustra quaesitas tandem inveni, quem libellum autoris reverentia potius quam alia causa exemplandum duxi.'Cf. Ullman, *Salutati*, 224.

De officiis

The *De officiis*, quarried over the centuries especially by Nonius and by Christian writers,[1] first emerges for us in a fragment, written in the first half of the ninth century at Tours (Q), containing 2.72 *necessaria* – 3.11 *non potest*, and now bound in the composite Paris lat. 6347. Other early and related books witness further to a hyparchetype surfacing in

[1] The earlier testimonia are to be found in C. Atzert's Teubner (Leipzig, 1963[4]), l; see also his discussion, v–xi. See generally N. E. Nelson, 'Cicero's *de officiis* in Christian Thought: 300–1300', *Univ. Michigan Public. Lang. and Lit.* 10 (1933); M. Testard's Budé, i (1965), 67–70 (this book is also valuable for its sketch of the history of work on the tradition, pp. 78–86; there is a stemma on p. 89).

Carolingian France: Paris lat. 6601 (P), s. IX[1], which belonged to Manno of Saint-Oyan (died 886) and may have been written in the Loire valley; close to this,[2] Berne 391 (b), s. IX, perhaps from Auxerre and containing corrections tentatively ascribed to Lupus of Ferrières;[3] and Leiden, Voss. Lat. Q. 71 (V), s. IX[2], written in France and at one time at Reims cathedral. V in turn is close to Würzburg, Mp. Misc. f. 1 (H), s. X[2], written in Switzerland;[4] of unknown provenance is Bamberg Class. 26 (M.v.1) (B), s. IX/X.

This group (Z) has for a century been regarded as much superior to a second family X, composed of British Library, Harley 2716 (L), s. X ex., from Germany and much mutilated, together with two later witnesses. Atzert distinguished a third family Y, among whose members Troyes 552 (T), s. XIV, is of interest for its annotations by Petrarch. But Fedeli dismisses Y as a mere conflation of Z and X.

There remain a host of *recentiores*,[5] not yet proved to deserve a grosser name, and much doubtless awaits discovery about the medieval and Renaissance fortunes of this text, whose popularity was fittingly marked by its being the first classical work to be printed (Mainz, 1465).

M. W.

[2] A copy, according to P. Fedeli's edition (Milan, 1965), 11. Fedeli also regards H as a copy of V.

[3] É. Pellegrin, *BEC* 115 (1957), 17 (opinion of F. M. Carey).

[4] I. Müller, B. Bischoff, *Vox Romanica*, 14 (1954), 137 ff.

[5] Atzert, xxxv–xlvi. Further information in Fedeli, 12; Testard, i. 71–7. There are plates of QbPV in Chatelain, XLIV–XLV.

De re publica

Cicero's answer to Plato's *Republic* bears the marks of a very rough passage to the modern world. The sublime conclusion, in which Scipio describes his vision of life after death, was much to the taste of later Antiquity and as a consequence has come down to us intact. Known as the *Somnium Scipionis*, it became the subject of a commentary by Macrobius and survived as an appendage to it.[1] A fine copy of all six

[1] Its manuscript tradition is therefore treated below, under MACROBIUS; see in particular pp. 230–1. The text of the *Somnium* which was appended to the *Commentary* is not that which Macrobius himself used; the fragments embedded in the commentary have a different, and in general superior, text. From the same period we have the more modest *Disputatio de somnio Scipionis* of Favonius Eulogius, a pupil of Augustine who describes himself in the title as *orator almae Carthaginis*. This survives in one manuscript only, Brussels 10078–95, of the eleventh century; it has the *ex libris* of Gembloux and may well be a product of the activity of Abbot Olbert. Favonius first appeared in print in 1612 (Antwerp, by Andreas Schott); recent editions are those of R.-E. van Weddingen (Brussels, 1957) and L. Scarpa (Padua, 1974), on which see *CR* 28 (1978), 161–2.

books of the *Republic* did outlive the collapse of the Roman world and found a refuge in the monastery of Bobbio, but there in the seventh century the text of Cicero was washed off to make way for Augustine's commentary on the Psalms. The lower script of this manuscript, now Vatican lat. 5757, is a beautiful uncial hand of the late fourth or early fifth century.[2] Fortunately the scrubbing which it received at Bobbio was not as vigorous as it might have been, and a great deal of Cicero can be recovered. Despite the passionate searching for Cicero's lost work in the Middle Ages and Renaissance, and the careful collecting by later scholars of such fragments as could be sifted from ancient authors,[3] the contents of the lower script of the Vaticanus lurked undetected until 1819, when Angelo Mai arrived in Rome, fresh from his series of palimpsest discoveries in the Ambrosiana, to be the new prefect of the Vatican Library; he published the *editio princeps* in 1822.[4] Our remains of the original manuscript contain large stretches of Books 1 and 2, some of 3, but little from the later books; for these we mainly depend on the *Somnium* and the considerable number of fragments which can be recovered from the indirect tradition.

L. D. R.

[2] *CLA* 1.35.
[3] The fragments were first edited by Robert Estienne (Stephanus), in his 1539 reprint of the 1536 Venice edition of Cicero by Vettori, iv 292–309. For the indirect tradition, see E. Heck, *Die Bezeugung von Ciceros Schrift De re publica* (Hildesheim, 1966).
[4] Another landmark in the editing of this text was the publication of a complete facsimile by G. Mercati, *M. Tulli Ciceronis De re publica libri e codice rescripto Vaticano 5757 phototypice expressi* (Vatican, 1934), with its famous *Prolegomena* on the dispersal of the Bobbio manuscripts and the fate of the Cicero manuscript in particular. Valuable work has been done on the text by K. Ziegler, who first discovered the importance of the correcting hand. His Teubner text, first edited in 1915, is now in its fifth edition (Leipzig, 1960). There are recent texts by P. Krarup (Milan, 1967), E. Bréguet (Budé, Paris, 1980).

Tusculan Disputations

The transmission of the *Tusculans* takes place largely in Carolingian Gaul. The older manuscripts are remarkably similar, and their filiation has been the subject of considerable discussion.[1] The addition of two or three manuscripts that have yet to be reported might conceivably alter the picture. Pohlenz suggests that the archetype was a manuscript of the sixth or early seventh century, written in uncials; Lundström

[1] Editors and students of the *Tusculans*, Ströbel (*Philologus*, 49 (1890), 49–64), Dougan (Cambridge, 1905) Pohlenz (Leipzig, 1909), and Fohlen (Paris, 1931), previously discerned two traditions: X, comprising the bulk of the surviving manuscripts, and Y, found in the ninth-century marginalia of Vatican lat. 3246 (V). More recently Drexler and Lundström, while markedly

believes that it could date from as late as the eighth or early ninth century. The early manuscripts indicate that the archetype was written in columns, with the initial letter of each passage set off in the left margin. The archetype came north probably in Charlemagne's lifetime, and its text was disseminated through the circle of court scholars. Charlemagne's biographer Einhard takes pains to refer to and to quote the *Tusculans* in the opening passage of the *Vita Karoli*, written shortly after 816.[2] During Einhard's lifetime the text of the *Tusculans*, still little known, was actively sought out. Lupus of Ferrières wrote (*c*.840) to his friend Adalgaudus, 'In fact you have not said whether the *Tusculan Disputations* have been copied for us, nor what happened to Agius, nor what books you have found.' Lupus does not quote from the *Tusculans*, and may never have received the copy he sought.[3]

A witness to the movement from Italy to the north – and perhaps, in a distant fashion, to the archetype – is seen in the leaf from a ninth-century manuscript of the *Tusculans*, written in three columns and, according to Bischoff, Veronese in origin. The leaf, now separately numbered as Oxford, Bodl. Laud Lat. 29*, was found by A. C. Clark in Archbishop Laud's binding of Laud Lat. 29, part I of which had belonged to the Carthusians of Mainz.[4] This Veronese fragment lies behind a group of manuscripts which appear to have dispersed from the Carolingian court.[5] Sometime between 840 and 857 Sedulius Scottus drew on a manuscript of the *Tusculans* for his florilegium. Among the surviving manuscripts, Sedulius's extracts relate most closely, as does the Verona fragment, to Brussels 5351–2, s. XI (B).[6] B, containing the *Tusculans* and *Pro Archia*, belonged to Gembloux in the Low Countries and was in all probability commissioned for the abbey by Abbot Olbert (d. 1048).[7] Olbert, builder of the Gembloux library, was also Abbot of

disagreeing on the details, have largely demolished Y by discounting the likelihood that V's marginalia represent a separate tradition: see H. Drexler, *Zu Überlieferung und Text der Tusculanen*, Collana di Studi Ciceroniani, 1 (Rome, 1961), the review by Lundström in *Gnomon*, 35 (1963), 168–71, and the response by Drexler in *Ciceroniana*, 1–2 (1964), 3–15; and S. Lundström, *Vermeintliche Glosseme in den Tusculanen*, Acta Universitatis Upsaliensis, 2 (Uppsala, 1964), the review by G. Williams in *Gnomon*, 37 (1965), 679–87, and those by Drexler in *Helikon*, 5 (1965), 500–8 and in *Miscellanea Teubner*, 2 (1964–5), 68–75.

[2] *Eginhard, Vie de Charlemagne*, ed. L. Halphen (Paris, 1923), 6–7.

[3] Ed. Levillain, i (Paris, 1927), 110–11, *ep.* 21. Adalgaudus has been identified by some as a monk of Tours and by others as Abbot of Fleury. Cf. p. 227, below.

[4] A. C. Clark, 'A Bodleian Fragment of Cicero, *Tusc. Quaest.*', *Mélanges Émile Chatelain* (Paris, 1910), 169–73, with fac.; *Survival*, p. 50 no. 99.

[5] Lundström (*Vermeintliche Glosseme*, 273 ff.) attempts to explain the transmission in terms of Fulda. The appearance of insular symbols particularly in K and H, noted by Lundström and by Beeson in *CPh* 40 (1945), 217, can be explained equally well in terms of Liège.

[6] S. Hellmann, *Sedulius Scottus*, Quellen und Untersuchungen zur lateinischen Philologie des Mittelalters, 1 (Munich, 1906), 106, 144 ff.

[7] On Olbert see A. Boutemy, 'Un grand abbé du XIe siècle: Olbert de Gembloux', *Annales de la Société archéologique de Namur*, 41 (1934), 43–85.

St. James and builder of St. Lawrence, both in Liège. Leiden, Lipsius 30, s. XI, which was given to the abbey of Egmond by Abbot Stephen (d. 1083), though unfortunately still unreported, may well also be a member of this group, as might have been the manuscript referred to in the recently discovered catalogue of Lobbes.[8]

A second group consists of at least four manuscripts, RKHP, descended from a text which moved from the Carolingian court to France probably in the early ninth century, and which may have been the one that belonged to Lupus's friend Adalgaudus. Paris lat. 6332, s. IX (R) (Chatelain, plate XLIV), containing the *Tusculans* and *De senectute*, may have originated at Saint-Germain-d'Auxerre, according to Carey. R bears an erased *ex libris* on f. 1, 'Hic est liber Sancti . . .'; all that can be said with any assurance is that it originated in the area of the Loire. It is the most faithful of the surviving witnesses to the text. Cambrai 842 (K) was written in the third quarter of the ninth century in north-east France, partially in the style of Soissons.[9] It contains the *Tusculans* alone, and belonged to the chapter library of Cambrai from an unknown date. K was written by several scribes and is, according to Pohlenz, very closely related to R. Vatican, Reg. lat. 1762, s. IX med. (H), is a florilegium compiled by Hadoard, librarian of Corbie.[10] The text of the *Tusculans* used by Hadoard, doubtless a manuscript then at Corbie and perhaps that quoted by Paschasius, was probably the volume referred to in the twelfth-century catalogue of the abbey (Becker, 79.104, p. 187). According to Pohlenz, H is closely related to R and K; and both H and K preserve numerous indications of an insular background. The fourth manuscript of this group, also closely related to R and K, is Vatican, Pal. lat. 1514, s. XI (P), containing the *Tusculans* only. In the mid-thirteenth century P belonged to the lexicographer who annotated Berne 276 and who worked at Orléans, Fleury, and St. Columba's in Sens.[11] P had moved to Italy by the fourteenth century; parts which it had lost by then were restored there. A fifth manuscript, Wolfenbüttel, Gud. lat. 294 (G), containing the *Tusculans* alone, was written in the third quarter of the ninth century at Reims, according to Bischoff; although textual filiation has not been demonstrated, one might expect on the basis of geography that G also belongs to this group. A sixth manuscript, as yet unreported in any detail, may also belong to this group, namely, Milan, Ambros. T. 56 sup., s. XI/XII (M), containing the *Philippics*, *Tusculans*, and pseudo-Cicero/pseudo-Sallust,

---

[8] Ed. F. Dolbeau, 'Un nouveau catalogue des manuscrits de Lobbes aux XIe et XIIe siècles', *Recherches Augustiniennes*, 13 (1978), 32 no. 273, 'Eiusdem [sc. Ciceronis] tusculanarum lib. V. Vol. I'.

[9] Information on date and origin was supplied by Professor Bischoff.

[10] On Hadoard see B. Bischoff, 'Hadoard und die Klassikerhandschriften aus Corbie', *Mitt. Stud.* i. 49–63.

[11] For the annotator of Berne 276 see M. D. R. and R. H. R., 'New Light on the Transmission of Donatus's *Commentum Terentii*', *Viator*, 9 (1978), 235–49.

Invectivae, written in France. A further witness to this group may possibly be seen in the eleventh-century book-list contained in a volume that belonged to Hartwic, a student of Fulbert of Chartres; Bischoff has ascribed the list to either Chartres or Reims.[12]

One remaining early manuscript, Vatican lat. 3246 (V), containing the *Tusculans* alone, was written in the middle third of the ninth century by an Italian scribe and corrected perhaps by French scribes, according to Bischoff; it belonged to Panormita in the fifteenth century. It has not yet been demonstrated whether V is filiated with B and the Veronese fragment, or with the group RKHP(G?), or with neither.

Predominantly a school text bearing on Platonic cosmology, the *Tusculans* were quoted in glosses on Macrobius' commentary on the *Dream of Scipio* from the tenth century. Though known in Bamberg, the *Tusculans* primarily circulated through the Loire houses. The role of this area in the dissemination of the text can be clearly seen in the library catalogues and surviving manuscripts of the late eleventh and twelfth centuries, by which time the *Tusculan Disputations* were well established and assured of survival.

R. H. R.

[12] Bischoff, *Mitt. Stud.* ii. 80–4. Concerning the possible origin of this book-list, see p. 65 n. 58, above.

Epistulae ad Atticum, ad Brutum, ad Quintum fratrem

The surviving witnesses to the text of Cicero's letters to Atticus, to Brutus, and to his brother Quintus[1] are divided into two families, *Y* and *Ω*, which descend from a common majuscule archetype X.

In contrast to the *Epistulae ad familiares*, there is no known use of the letters to Atticus by any medieval writer. Two medieval library catalogues contain entries thought to refer to these letters. First, the ninth-century catalogue of Lorsch contains the following: '49. Epistolarum Ciceronis lib. XVI in uno codice. 50. Epistolae Ciceronis in quaternionibus. [Inserted between the lines: 51. Epistolae Ciceronis diversae.] 52. Item epistolae Ciceronis diversae. 53. Item M. T. Ciceronis epistolarum lib. IIII in uno codice.' (Becker, 38, p. 122.)

[1] Recent critical editions are those of W. S. Watt in OCT (*Ad Atticum* 1965, *Ad Quintum fratrem, ad Brutum* 1958) and D. R. Shackleton Bailey in Cambridge Classical Texts and Commentaries (*Letters to Atticus*, 6 vols. and Index, 1965–70; *Epistulae ad Quintum fratrem et M. Brutum*, 1980); also in the Budé edition of *Cicéron, Correspondance*, by L.-A. Constans, J. Bayet, and J. Beaujeu, (7 vols., Paris, 1934–80). This account is largely based on Shackleton Bailey, *Letters to Atticus* i, pp. 77–101.

Although 49–52 probably refer to the *Fam.*, no. 53 may well refer to the three books *ad Quintum fratrem* and the 'one' book *ad Brutum* (*Brut.* 1 and 2). Second, the Cluny catalogue of 1158–61 contains a specific reference to the letters to Atticus: '492. Volumen in quo continentur libri epistolarum Ciceronis ad Atticum XVI' (Delisle, ii. 478). In addition to these, Petrarch in 1345 found and copied a manuscript of *Att.*, which had been used by others before him, at the Chapter Library in Verona. Both the Verona manuscript and Petrarch's copy of it have disappeared.

Of the surviving witnesses, the transalpine family (*Y*), which represents the older and better tradition, has three sources:

(1) Five double leaves, with fragments of a sixth, from a manuscript (W) written in the eleventh century; they were found in Würzburg, where they had been used to bind the account-books of the convent of St. Afra. (See (2), below; Introd., n. 140, above.)

(2) Readings in the margins of A. Cratander's Basle edition (*Opera omnia*, 1528), called C, and new readings in the text (c), which include the only text of *Brut.* 1–5. Apart from C and c, Cratander's edition is basically a copy of Ascensius's second edition (Paris, 1521–22). Shackleton Bailey has demonstrated the validity of the older view that Cratander's main manuscript source was W itself, before it was mutilated, and that C and (to a lesser extent) c derive from it. W was probably the manuscript which Niccolò Niccoli in 1431 ascribed to the library of Fulda: 'M. Tulli Ciceronis volumen epistolarum ad Atticum quod incipit: "Cum hec scribebam res existimatur etc."; finit: "Cicero Capitoni" ' (*Att.* 16.16).[2]

(3) Readings attributed in various sources to a lost manuscript which once belonged to the Lyon printer Jean de Tournes (d. 1564) and is hence known as the Tornesianus (Z). The manuscript, which did not contain *Q. fr.* and *Brut.*, disappeared after 1580, when Bosius used it in his edition. It has been suggested that Z is identical with no. 492 in the Cluny catalogue.[3]

The Italian family (*Ω*) falls into two groups, *Σ* and *Δ*, which comprise all extant manuscripts, apart from the fragments of W. *Σ* has been divided into three, E and the subgroups *Π* and *Φ*. The oldest surviving *Ω* manuscript is E, Milan, Ambros. E. 14 inf., s. XIV¹, an abridgement which contains about three-fifths of *Att.* and *Q. fr.* arranged in ten books, with *Brut.* 1 as an eleventh.

Π, characterized by texts which end in Book 6 or 7 (*Att.*), consists of three manuscripts: Paris lat. 16248 (G), s. XV, containing *Brut.* 1, *Q. fr.*,

   [2] Sabbadini, *Storia e critica*², 8.
   [3] A. C. Clark, in his Critical Introduction to W. W. How, *Cicero, Select Letters* (Oxford, 1926), ii, p. 20. The readings of Z have to be extracted from the notes of Lambinus, Bosius, and Turnebus; for the respective reliability of these various sources, see Shackleton Bailey, 93 ff.

and *Att.* to 6.1.8, where the hand changes and the text is then copied from a Δ manuscript; Piacenza 8 (H), s. xv, containing (with numerous lacunae) *Brut.* 1, *Q.fr.*, ps.-Cic. *Oct.*, *Att.* 1–7.22.2, and Caesar's letter to Cicero, *Att.* 10.8B; and Florence, Laur. Conv. Soppr. 49 (N), s. xv[1], written for Antonio Corbinelli and containing *Brut.* 1, *Q. fr.*, *Att.* 1–7.21.1. G, H, and N are thought to have derived from a manuscript discovered at Pistoia (Pavia?) *c*.1409 by Bartolomeo Capra, Bishop of Cremona.

Φ comprises five surviving manuscripts: Vatican, Pal. lat. 1510 (V), s. xv[2], containing *Att.* 1–3 and portions of 4, 5, and 9; Turin I.v.34 (O), s. xv[1], which was originally complete but lost the last four books (*Att.* 13–16) in the fire of 1904 (readings are preserved in Lehmann's collation); Ravenna 469 (Rav.), s. xv, a *gemellus* of V for which no complete collation has been published; Paris lat. 8536 (P), s. xv in., and 8538 (R), a. 1419, with Venetian decoration, both containing *Brut.* 1, *Q.fr.*, *Oct.*, and *Att.* 1–16; and two lost manuscripts, the codex Antonianus (Ant.) which was formerly in the Biblioteca Antoniana in Venice, and a codex (F) that belonged to Gabriel Faërnus of Cremona, both of which are cited in L. Malaespina's *Emendationes ac Suspiciones* of 1564.

The Δ branch of the Italian family (Ω), which is characterized by long lacunae in Books 1 and 16, is represented primarily by Florence, Laur. 49.18 (M), a. 1392/3, which contains *Brut.* 1, *Q.fr.*, *Oct.*, and *Att.* M was long thought to be Petrarch's copy of the Verona manuscript. Lehmann showed, however, not only that M was not the Veronensis or Petrarch's copy, but also that the Veronensis belonged to the Σ rather than the Δ branch. M was transcribed from a manuscript in Milan for Coluccio Salutati; and it abounds in corrections made by the original scribe and by three successive annotators, Salutati (1331–1406), Niccolò Niccoli (*c*. 1364–1437), and Leonardo Bruni (1370–1444). There are also a large number of fifteenth-century manuscripts in this family, so thoroughly contaminated with Σ readings that they cannot be accurately placed in the stemma. The best of these (δ, collectively), which serve primarily to corroborate M and thus establish Δ, are the following: Berlin (West), Hamilton 166 (m), copied from M in 1408 by Poggio, containing *Brut.* 1, *Q.fr.*, *Oct.*, *Att.* 1–14 (the conclusion of 14 is added); Hamilton 168 (b), s. xv¾, written by B. Fonzio, containing *Fam.* 1–16, *Brut.* 1, *Q. fr.*, *Att.* 4–16, *Oct.*; Vatican, Urb. lat. 322 (s), s. xv; and Florence, Laur. Edili 217 (d), s. xv med., written for Vespucci.

R. H. R.

Epistulae ad familiares

The text of Cicero's *Ad familiares* is reconstructed from a late antique palimpsest, a single manuscript of the ninth century containing all sixteen books, and two distinct groups of manuscripts: X, containing only Books 1–8, which circulated primarily in France; and Y, containing only Books 9–16, which circulated primarily in Germany.[1]

The earliest witness to the text, in the Turin palimpsest (see above, *Speeches* § 1), is a leaf (T) from a codex written in uncials of the fifth or sixth century containing an abridged version of *Fam.* 6.9.1–10.6 (*CLA* IV. 443; Chatelain, plate XXXVIa). In the seventh century the codex passed to Bobbio, where it was broken up and written over with works of St. Augustine.

Given the close relations between Lorsch and northern Italy, it is not surprising to find the earliest medieval reference to Cicero's letters in the ninth-century catalogue of Lorsch: '49. Epistolarum Ciceronis lib. XVI in uno codice. 50. Epistolae Ciceronis in quaternionibus. [Inserted between the lines: 51. Epistolae Ciceronis diversae.] 52. Item epistolae Ciceronis diversae. 53. Item M. T. Ciceronis epistolarum lib. IIII in uno codice.' (Becker, 38, p. 122.) There references have caused considerable speculation. However, at present, it appears that no. 49 refers to a full text of the *Ad familiares*, and that nos. 50 and 52 probably refer to manuscripts of Books 1–8 or of Books 9–16. (No. 53 may have contained the three books *Ad Quintum fratrem* and the *Ad Brutum*, both of which belong to the tradition of the *Ad Atticum* (see above).) It is likely, therefore, that Cicero's *Epistulae ad familiares* were dispersed from Lorsch.

Only one manuscript, Florence, Laur. 49.9 (M) (Chatelain, plate XXXIV.1) – along with its Renaissance descendants – contains all sixteen books. M was written in the first half of the ninth century by several hands, including a French hand perhaps from the Loire region, a hand schooled at Fulda, and one suggestive of Mainz. Bischoff suggests that the manuscript may have been written at a school associated with the court of Louis the Pious.[2] M belonged to Lorsch, and has been identified with the sixteen-book codex in the abbey's ninth-century catalogue (no. 49; see above);[3] and it contains numerous corrections by the scribes and by later readers. Early in its existence M came into the hands of Bishop Leo of Vercelli (*c.*988–1026). It was found there by

---

[1] Recent critical editions are those of L.-A. Constans, J. Bayet, and J. Beaujeu in the Budé series (7 vols., Paris, 1934–80) and D. R. Shackleton Bailey (Cambridge, 1977); an OCT edition by W. S. Watt appeared in 1982.

[2] 'Die Hofbibliothek unter Ludwig dem Frommen', in *Medieval Learning*, 21.

[3] Bischoff, *Lorsch*, 79, 94–5.

Pasquino de' Capelli, Chancellor of Milan, who had organized a search at the instigation of Coluccio Salutati. A copy of M, Florence, Laur. 49.7 (P) (Chatelain, plate XXXVI), was made for Salutati at Milan in 1392. M itself was transferred to Florence before Salutati's death in 1406; and Politian (1454–94) also saw the old codex there. However, the Italian Renaissance manuscripts of the *Ad familiares* evidently descend from M by way of P, Salutati's manuscript.

Two groups of manuscripts – X, containing Books 1–8, and Y, containing 9–16 – provide traditions independent of M. Since Book 9 in M is called *Liber I*, it appears that the tradition of dividing the letters into two volumes is older than M itself. Shackleton Bailey has shown that M's value is much greater for Books 1–8, where it is virtually the sole authority (X is a heavily interpolated tradition), than for Books 9–16, where the Y manuscripts preserve an independent tradition of high quality.

The text of Books 1–8 or X, probably available at Lorsch in the ninth century, left other traces in Carolingian Lotharingia. Ansbald, Abbot of Prüm, owned a manuscript of these early books which he sent, for collation, to Lupus of Ferrières in 847. While the eventual fate of Ansbald's manuscript is not known, the 'epistole Ciceronis' in the thirteenth-century catalogue of Rolduc (not far from Prüm) may be related to it.[4] Similarly, it is possible that one of the Lorsch manuscripts was used by Liutprand of Cremona (*c*.920–70) while writing the *Antapodosis* at Frankfurt and the *Liber de rebus gestis Ottonis*; Liutprand quotes frequently from Books 1–8.[5]

At much the same time, the text of Books 1–8 of the *Ad familiares*, brought most likely from a Lotharingian source, was beginning to circulate in the area of the Loire. Lupus of Ferrières already owned a manuscript himself, as he notes in *ep*. 69 when he received Ansbald's volume on loan: 'Tullianas epistolas, quas misisti, cum nostris conferri faciam ut ex utrisque, si possit fieri, veritas exculpatur.' Lupus's knowledge of *Fam*. 1.9.23 and 5.12.3 (in a letter of AD 829–30), and the citation of *Fam*. 5.16.5 by his pupil Heiric of Auxerre, confirm that the codices in question contained Books 1–8.[6] Subsequently, Lupus's books appear to have moved along the Loire, some to Fleury, others to Tours; and, hence, it is not particularly surprising that Books 1–8 of the *Ad familiares* appear at Tours and Cluny, both of which were closely associated with Fleury. The Cluny catalogue of 1158–61 contains two references to manuscripts of *Fam*. 1–8: '490. Volumen in quo continentur epistole Ciceronis ad Publicum Lentulum proconsulem et ad Curionem et ad Appium aliosque multos . . . 493. Volumen in quo

---

[4] Van Gils, *Handelingen van het 5e Nederlandsche Philologencongres* (1907), 1–29.

[5] F. Köhler, 'Beiträge zur Textkritik Liutprands von Cremona', *Neues Archiv*, 8 (1883), 49–89.

[6] K. Weyssenhof (n. 7, below); *MGH, Epp.* vi, p. 8; *MGH, Poetae lat. aev. Carol.* iii.431. 27.

continentur epistole Ciceronis ad Publicum Lentulum et ad alios multos ut supra.' (Delisle, ii.478.) Another manuscript of Books 1–8, probably of Loire origin, is recorded in the *Biblionomia* or catalogue of the library which Richard de Fournival collected in part at Orléans during the first half of the thirteenth century. The non-committal entry in the *Biblionomia*, '29. Eiusdem Ciceronis liber epistolarum', can be identified as *Fam.* 1–8 from the opening words of the second and penultimate folios, which are recorded in the 1338 catalogue of the Sorbonne, the eventual repository of much of Fournival's library. Unfortunately, the manuscript has left no further trace.[7] Also apparently lost is the manuscript of the letters referred to in the twelfth-century catalogue of the abbey of Saint-Victor in Marseilles. Finally, Nicholas of Clamanges cites *Fam.* 1.5.7 and perhaps 1.7.5 in a letter to Jean de Montreuil *c.*1407. Clamanges would probably have known the Cluny manuscripts of the early books, as well as Fournival's copy at the Sorbonne.

The X family is reconstructed from two medieval manuscripts that descend from an interpolated and emended sister of M – perhaps the manuscript which Lupus had worked over. The first of these, British Library, Harley 2773 (G), is a composite volume containing, part I, Servius, *Grammatica*, s. XII[1]; part II, Diomedes, *Grammatica*, s. XII[1]; part III, *Fam.* 1–8, *Johannis Diaconi Cena Cypriani*. Part III was written in France in the middle of the twelfth century. How long the parts have been together is not known. Parts II and III were purchased in Cologne by J. G. Graevius (1632–1703); H. Wanley acquired all three (together?) for Lord Harley. The second manuscript, Paris lat. 17812 (R) (Chatelain, plate XXXV), was also written in France in the mid-twelfth century and contains Cicero, *Ac. prior.*, *D.N.D.*, *Fat.*, *Fam.* 1–8; and Dares Phrygius, *De excidio Troiae*. It belonged to Antoine Loisel and passed via Claude Joly to Notre-Dame. A third medieval manuscript, Tours 688 (s. XII/XIII), containing the same sequence of texts as Paris lat. 17812, belonged to Saint-Martin-de-Marmoutier near Tours and is evidently a direct copy of R – suggesting that R was once in the area of Tours. For the other texts that it contains (apart from the *Ad familiares*), R descends from Vienna 189, s. IX, which belonged to Lupus of Ferrières.[8]

In addition to G and R, fragments of two twelfth-century codices are known: S, the outer bifolium of an eight-folio gathering, thirty-four lines per page, which belonged to Dr Freier of the Frankfurt an der Oder Gymnasium, reported by A. Golisch in *Philologus*, 26 (1867), 701–3, containing 2.1.1–2.17.4; and I, a single leaf of thirty-two lines from the late eleventh or early twelfth century, found in the binding of a printed

---

[7] K. Weyssenhof, 'Les Manuscrits des lettres de Cicéron dans les bibliothèques médiévales', *Eos*, 56 (1966), 281–7.

[8] M. van den Bruwaene, *Cicéron de natura deorum, Livre I*, Collection Latomus, 107 (Brussels, 1970), 37–8.

book *Mirabilia urbis Romae* at the Stadtbibliothek in Hamburg and reported by M. Isler in *Neue Jahrbücher für Philologie und Paedagogik*, 75 (1857), 289–91, containing 5.10.1–5.12.2. These two fragments do not apparently come from the X tradition, and represent a tradition now lost that circulated probably in Germany.

It is curious, in retrospect, that the letters were never seized upon by the dictaminal schools of Orléans in the twelfth and thirteenth centuries. They were unknown to the two great florilegists of these schools, the compilers of the *Florilegium Gallicum* and the *Florilegium Angelicum*, as well as to Vincent of Beauvais.

The manuscripts of the Y family, i.e. of *Fam.* 9–16, descend ultimately from a codex (χ: Shackleton Bailey) which was at the abbey of Lorsch in the Middle Ages and was brought to Italy in the Renaissance. How the text spread from Lorsch is still largely unclear, but it was in circulation at an early date. Sedulius Scottus appears to have known the later books; two lines from 15.6.1 and 16.26.1 are in his florilegium, as preserved in Cues, Nikolaus Hospitalbibliothek 52. Also to be noted is the reference to a manuscript of Books 9–16 in the sixteenth-century catalogue of Fulda.[9]

There are two medieval and two Renaissance witnesses, along with some excerpts and a fragment, from which the text of the lost Lorsch manuscript of *Fam.* 9–16 must be reconstructed. The fragment is a single leaf of thirty-two lines containing 12.19.1–12.23.1, from a manuscript written in Germany in the twelfth century. It was found in the binding of a printed book in the Heilbronn Gymnasialbibliothek and reported by C. E. Finckh in *Neue Jahrbucher für Philologie und Paedagogik*, 75 (1857), 725–7. The two medieval manuscripts descend from a common ancestor. The older, B. L. Harley 2682 (H) (Clark, *Anecdota Oxon.* 7, pl. I), the result of an effort to assemble a large corpus of Cicero between two covers, was written in Germany in the second half of the eleventh century. It belonged to Cologne Cathedral, and is called the 'codex Hittorpianus' by early modern editors, after the cathedral librarian. The *gemellus* of H appears in Berlin (West) lat. 2° 252 (F), the impressive collection of Cicero written for Wibald Abbot of Stavelot (1130–58) and Corvey (1146–58); it contains among other things *Fam.* 12.21, 12.29.2, and 13.78 to the end. Wibald's source for the letters in F is probably the manuscript at Hildesheim referred to by Rainald of Dassel, in a letter of 1149 to Wibald: 'Libros igitur, qui apud nos sunt, Tullium de lege agraria et Philippica et epistolas eius, vobis transmisissemus' (*Monumenta Corbeiensia*, ed. Jaffé (Berlin, 1864), *ep.* 207, pp. 326–7). The manuscript at Hildesheim may in fact be the same one that Godehard, Abbot of Tegernsee, requested from the monks of his former

[9] K. Christ, *Die Bibliothek des Klosters Fulda im 16. Jahrhundert*, ZBB Suppl. 64 (Leipzig, 1933), 149, 231.

house, Niederaltaich, in 1020: 'Mittite nobis librum Horatii et epistolas Tulli':[10] for Godehard became Bishop of Hildesheim in 1022 and remained there until his death in 1038. The fate of this Hildesheim manuscript is not known.

Books 9–16, or extracts from them, do appear to have been known further west in the Middle Ages in two instances. John of Salisbury quotes from *Fam.* 9, 15, and 16 in the *Policraticus* (1159). (Other echoes of the letters in the *Policraticus* come by way of Quintilian and Macrobius.) Extracts from books, 9, 10, and 13 appear in Oxford, Corpus Christi College 283, ff. 6–49ᵛ, a manuscript of disparate pieces brought together in Paris by William of Clare and given by him to St. Augustine's Canterbury in 1277 when he entered the abbey. The extracts were clearly copied in Paris in the second quarter of the thirteenth century.[11] Constans, the only recent editor to mention them, placed the extracts in the Y tradition and considered them of little value. No other trace of the later books has been found in medieval Europe west of the Rhine.

Two Renaissance manuscripts are of importance to the Y tradition. Vatican, Pal. lat. 598 (D), *gemellus* of the HF ancestor, was copied in Heidelberg in the fifteenth century, probably from a manuscript at the Palatinate Library, which may have been one of the manuscripts from Lorsch. D has later corrections which come from a corrupt copy of M. The other fifteenth-century manuscript of importance, Paris lat. 14761 (V), is a composite volume, part I of which contains all sixteen books of the *Ad familiares.*[12] For books 1–8, V is a copy of P (Salutati's manuscript). For the later books, Shackleton Bailey has shown V to be a descendant, via at least one intermediate, of χ. V was written in Italy by two (French?) scribes, and was given by an early owner to Saint-Victor in Paris.

R. H. R

---

[10] In a letter in the collection assembled by Froumund of Tegernsee; ed. K. Strecker, *MGH, Epp. selectae*, 3 (Berlin, 1925), 56, *ep.* 50.

[11] *Survival*, no. 137, pl. XXIV.

[12] Regarding part II see *Academica posteriora*, above.

CLAUDIAN

Claudian's poems survive in over three hundred manuscripts,[1] variously representative of a number of originally distinct lines of descent.[2] Earliest in evidence is the tradition of the *carmina minora*, which begins with Verona CLXIII (150) (*CLA* IV. 516), s. VIII[2], and St. Gall 273, s. IX[2]/4, Germany. In the middle of s. XI the tradition of *Claudianus maior*[3] is introduced by Brussels 5381, from Gembloux, which has a probable affinity to the (lost) Carolingian-court library copy (see TIBULLUS, p. 421), followed by Vat. lat. 2809, s. XII[1], probably of north French provenance according to B. Bischoff, in which *Claudianus maior* is found already combined with various *carmina minora*. At a somewhat later date begin the traditions of *De Raptu Proserpinae* (amongst the oldest manuscripts to offer this work are Berne 398 and Florence, Laur. S. Croce 24 sin. 12, both of s. XII and the latter written in Italy) and, already associated with *Claudianus maior*, of *Panegyricus dictus Probino et Olybrio consulibus* (the oldest manuscript to offer this panegyric is perhaps Florence, Laur. Acq. e Doni 672, an Italian manuscript of s. XII). Omnibus manuscripts in which all these traditions are united appear

The *editiones principes* are, for the *D.R.P.*, Valdarfer (?), Venice, *c.*1471; for the bulk of Claudian, B. Celsanus printed by Jac. Dusensis, Vicenza, 1482; for the *carmina minora*, Th. Ugoletus printed by A. Ugoletus, Parma, 1493; the earliest edition of Claudian to begin the process of incorporating the *carmina Graeca* is J. J. Scaliger's Raphelengian, Leiden, 1603. The edition of P. Burman *secundus*, Amsterdam, 1760, is still of great value for its presentation of Heinsius's published notes and unpublished collations, the latter gathered together in a *Sylloge Variantium Lectionum* which remains the fullest collection of information about the readings of manuscripts published to date, though its nomenclature of manuscripts is now obsolete. Among more recent editions the following should be mentioned – editions of the whole of Claudian: L. Jeep, Leipzig, 1876–9; Th. Birt, *MGH, Auct. Ant.* x, Berlin, 1892; J. Koch, Leipzig (Teubner), 1893; editions of *D.R.P.*: L. Jeep, Turin, 1874; J. B. Hall, Cambridge, 1969 (supplemented by 'Notes on Three New Manuscripts of Claudian *De Raptu Proserpinae*', *PACA* 12 (1973), 13 f., and 'Manuscripts of Claudian in the USSR and Poland', ibid. 14 (1978), 15–20, in which Leningrad Lat. O. v. 3, formerly designated Petropolitanus A. O. sect. CIL n. 3, is identified as Heinsius's Mazarinianus); edition of *Gild.*: E. M. Olechowska, Leiden, 1978; edition of *In Eutropium*: P. Fargues, Paris, 1933.

[1] I shall continue my detailed exposition of Claudian's manuscript traditions in a *BICS* Supplement companion volume to my forthcoming Teubner edition.

[2] I take no account here of the pieces included in Birt's *carminum minorum appendix*, most, if not all of which, *pace* D. Romano, *Appendix Claudianea: Questioni d' Autenticità* (Palermo, 1957), are spurious. Nor do I include the Greek epigrams transmitted in the Palatine Anthology, or the Greek *Gigantomachia*, which has its own independent line of descent. This Greek Gigantomachy, incidentally, is preserved not only in Madrid gr. 4691 (*olim* 61), written in 1465 by Constantine Lascaris, but also in Florence, Laur. Conv. Soppr. 164, s. XV, which, interestingly, anticipates a number of modern conjectures.

[3] i.e. what Birt terms 'carmina maiora et publica' = the panegyrics (excluding *Prob.*) and invectives, but not the *D.R.P.*

first in s. XIII, e.g. in Laur. 33. 4. The critic's problems and resources vary considerably from one tradition to another, and contamination, endemic from s. XII especially in *Claudianus maior* and *D.R.P.*, is a constant complication.

(1) The tradition of *Claudianus maior*. Misapplication of stemmatic theory and unjustified *eliminatio* or disregard of manuscripts with a claim to be heard vitiated the editions of Jeep and Birt; and in Olechowska's recent edition of *De Bello Gildonico* stemmatic theorizing (based on much factual error) is inconsistent with, and often indeed contradicted by, the *constitutio textus*. The truth is that only untrammelled eclecticism founded on a recognition of the inapplicability of stemmatics will permit full exploitation of the wealth of the tradition.

Of the numerous manuscripts that offer all or part of *Claudianus maior*, Brussels 5381 and Vat. lat. 2809 commend themselves as *primi inter pares*, the high quality of the latter having been recognized since Heinsius's time and that of the former since it was brought to notice by Breiter in 1852. Each offering as great a concentration of truth as any surviving manuscript (though interpolation is in evidence already in both of them), these two witnesses tend to supplement one another's deficiencies, and their consensus is generally, though by no means invariably, right. The editor's main problem is deciding which manuscripts to use in conjunction with the Brussels and Vatican manuscripts when both are available, and which to use in their stead when one or both are not available. Consideration of the general utility of manuscripts and of their performance in the particular matters of lines only vestigially attested and true readings only tenuously preserved, and also of the need to represent the different orders in which the poems are arranged, suggests a final selection of manuscripts including (in addition to the Brussels and Vatican manuscripts): Cracow 71, Florence, Laur. S. Marco 250 (owned by Niccoli) and Acq. e Doni 672, Florence, Bibl. Naz. Magl. VII. 144, Leiden, Voss. Lat. O. 39, British Library, Burney 167, Milan, Ambros. M. 9 sup., Naples IV. E. 47, Paris lat. 8082 and 18552, and Wolfenbüttel, Gud. lat. 220, all of s. XII or XIII. Other manuscripts also merit being put under contribution, whenever they have something of interest to offer.

The *Excerpta Florentina*, s. XV[2], and *Gyraldina*,[4] written in or after 1523, pose another problem. They offer a good deal of truth otherwise unknown – and therefore their probable immediate source the lost Lucensis was a manuscript with a distinguished pedigree – but intermingled with

---

[4] The *Excerpta Florentina* are to be found in a copy of Celsanus's *editio princeps* now in Florence, Bibl. Naz. Magl. A. 4. 36, and are complemented, in full transcription since Celsanus did not print the *carmina minora*, by Florence, Laur. 33. 9, written in or after 1482 and (probably) before 1493. The *Excerpta Gyraldina* are to be found in a copy of the Aldine edition of 1523 now in Leiden University Library, shelf-mark 757 G 2.

that truth is much specious falsehood, more, I believe, than previous editors have allowed. To isolate the 'grain of truth among the chaff' in these *Excerpta* is a task as important as it is difficult. The testimony of the Isengrin edition (Basle, 1534) is similarly perplexed.

(2) The tradition of the *carmina minora*. Verona CLXIII and Vat. lat. 2809, the two most important witnesses, generally shun one another's company, and even when both are present, their consensus is sometimes wrong. On most occasions their shortcomings are made good by Laur. 33. 9 (whose text of the *carmina minora* complements the *Excerpta* of *Claudianus maior*) and by various manuscripts of s. XII and XIII, which are also of service in *Claudianus maior*.

(3) The tradition of *Prob.* is represented by a mere handful of manuscripts, and the small number of substantial divergences of reading in it suggests a comparatively recent (perhaps s. XI) propagation from a single lost exemplar, very possibly in Italy. In general that exemplar would seem to have been an accurate copy, but four verses it omitted have to be recovered from the Basle edition of 1534 (drawing on some lost manuscript, from Alsace perhaps, or the Palatinate?).

(4) The tradition of the *D.R.P.* is thoroughly contaminated *ab initio* and in consequence largely amorphous. Three lacunae serve to isolate one group, β, but the identity of a second, α, is anything but certain, being inferred from nothing more substantial that the common possession of a borrowed preface;[5] heterogeneous descent is here an evident possibility. Various additional manuscripts form a group, γ, only in the sense that they have all undergone similar processes of supplementation designed to repair the losses of β. The absence, furthermore, of any manuscript of conspicuous worth in this tradition makes the need for editorial eclecticism more manifest here than it perhaps is in other parts of Claudian's œuvre.

J. B. H.

[5] I am not myself persuaded by I. Gualandri's suggestion, *RFIC* 101 (1973), 241 ff., that the third preface was originally designed by Claudian for the *D.R.P.* and subsequently used by him for *VI Cons*. While it is true that there are incidental references to the Giants in *D.R.P.* 3, the equations in the preface of Jove = emperor and gods = courtiers require that Enceladus/Typhoeus should also be understood to represent some contemporary person – and that person can only be Alaric. The preface must therefore, I believe, have been designed by Claudian for *VI Cons.*, and incorporated in the *D.R.P.* by some later editor.

COLUMELLA

From one stock sprang Leningrad Class. Lat. F.v.1 (S, s. IX¾), written at Corbie in Caroline minuscule, and Milan, Ambros. L. 85 sup. (A, s. IX²/₄), less carefully written in an insular script attributable to Fulda.[1] When Poggio acquired A, he could boast that Columella had hitherto been available only 'detruncatus et deformis', and indeed *De re rustica* had scarcely taken root in Italian soil: the defective text, though Petrarch and Boccaccio knew it,[2] quite failed to propagate. Grafted on the text of A, however, it produced a crop of some forty manuscripts – a glut after the medieval famine.

Some readings from the defective text were entered in A after its arrival in Italy, but many more reached the whole of the fifteenth-century tradition through a lost manuscript, R (the manuscript of Niccoli's that Politian collated?). Others appear only in part of the fifteenth-century tradition, not always the same part; they were previously regarded as corruptions because the rest of the manuscripts agreed with SA, but Å. Josephson in a masterly study[3] has shown that the manuscripts most often in agreement with A matter least. His classification has been taken further by S. Hedberg, who also establishes that besides the *Liber de arboribus* the defective text lacked 5.6.17–7.9.4.[4] Progress now čan only come from historical work on the manuscripts. It should be possible, for instance, to identify the scribes of such productive manuscripts as Vienna 81 + 3144 (h, clearly Florentine) and Göteborg lat. 28 (x).[5]

The defective text, whatever its origin,[6] was independent of SA, and

---

[1]   For these precise dates within s. IX see Bischoff ap. P.-P. Corsetti, *RHT* 7 (1977), 109 n. 5, 127 n. 7; for illustrations, Å. Josephson, *Die Columella-Handschriften* (Uppsala, 1955), plates I–II. W. Richter, *WS* 88 (1975), 135–47, attempts to work out from omissions in SA the lineation and date of lost ancestors.

[2]   G. Martellotti, *RCCM* 2 (1960), 391 n. 2, not mentioned by Virginia Brown in her article on Columella in *CTC* iii (Washington, DC, 1976), 173–99.   [3]   Op. cit. n. 1, above.

[4]   *Contamination and Interpolation: a Study of the 15th Century Columella Manuscripts* (Uppsala, 1968). On the sections missing from the defective text see pp. 144–6; Richter, op. cit., 145–7, misinterprets but confirms Hedberg's results when he argues for contamination between an ancestor of the defective text and an ancestor of SA in precisely these sections (and also in Book 10, which he forgets is in hexameters and so would not have been liable to omissions of the lengths that interest him).

[5]   Like h group κ is clearly Florentine, and Dr A. C. de la Mare dates its leading member, B. L. Add. 17295 (j), c.1435–40. Corsetti, *RHT* 8 (1978), 289–93, adds four more manuscripts, and others are Rome, Angel. 1099 and one at Iesi described by C. Annibaldi, *L'Agricola e la Germania di Cornelio Tacito nel ms. latino n. 8 della biblioteca del Conte G-Balleani in Iesi* (Città di Castello, 1907), 4, and discussed by S. Prete in a work that I have not seen, *Il codice di Columella di Stefano Guarnieri* (Fano, 1974).

[6]   R. Sobel, *Studia Columelliana palaeographica et critica* (Göteborg, 1928), 20, surmised that it was the lost Marcianus of Cato and Varro, which once contained Columella.

so of course was the indirect tradition of late Antiquity in Palladius, Pelagonius,[7] and the *Mulomedicina*; but if Columella can thank Palladius for preserving an independent strain of text, he can also blame his narrow circulation in the Middle Ages on Palladius' greater popularity. Apart from an extract in the scrap-book of Walahfrid Strabo († 849) on how to make wine,[8] medieval excerpts and references point to S or at least Corbie, where the beginning of Book 5 went into the making of two geometrical compilations.[9]

All the agricultural writers burst into print together (Venice, 1472). The best edition of Columella was begun in 1897 by V. Lundström, continued in 1955 by Josephson, and completed in 1968 by Hedberg.

M.D.R.

[7] The text of Pelagonius (s. IV[2]), not published until 1826, rests almost entirely on a *recentissimus* (1485) copied from a *vetustissimus* (s. VII/VIII?): Florence, Ricc. 1179, written for Politian. Palimpsest fragments of another *vetustissimus* survive in Naples lat. 2 (Vindob. 16), ff. 37–41 (s. VI[1], uncial, probably Italian, written over at Bobbio in s. VIII; *CLA* III.393). See the Teubner of K.-D. Fischer (Leipzig, 1980), with the important review of H. D. Jocelyn, *LCM* 7 (1982), 54–8.

[8] 'The only pagan works of the classical period which he chose to excerpt were Columella and the *Letters* of Seneca, the first a not surprising choice for the author of a charming poem on his monastery garden' (L. D. Reynolds and N. G. Wilson, *Scribes and Scholars* (2nd ed., Oxford, 1974), 91). On the vexed question of echoes from Book 10 in *De cultura hortorum* see Josephson, 41. The text of the extract in St. Gall 878 (W) shares three errors with S, which was probably written too late to be its source; as Walahfrid had been at Fulda, he may have read the source of SW there, and it may also have been the manuscript that Modius saw there in 1584.

[9] Ullman, *Studi di bibliografia e di storia in onore di T. de Marinis* (Verona, 1964), iv. 279–83 (281 n. 1 is wrong); Corsetti, op. cit. (n. 1, above), 109–32 on Paris lat. 13955 (s. IX³⁄₄) and its descendants, 128 n. 5 on the *Ars geometriae* ascribed to Boethius (see also *AGRIMENSORES*). Virginia Brown, 174, is behind the times both on Corbie and on Walahfrid; on Hugh of Fouilloy (s. XII) see now Corsetti, 110 n. 4.

CONSOLATIO AD LIVIAM

According to the life of Ovid in Calphurnius's edition (Venice, 1474), 'scripsit etiam epistolam consolatoriam ad Liviam Augustam de morte Drusi Neronis filii, qui in Germania perierat; quae nuper inventa est.' It had appeared under his name in an earlier edition (Rome, 1471) and in the first edition of Ausonius (Venice, 1472), which are in fact the main witnesses: most of the fifteen manuscripts and all subsequent editions either certainly or probably derive from them, and the rest, which include one written in 1469,[1] contribute nothing. How old a manuscript turned up, and where, no one knows; for all that the tradition reveals, the poem could perfectly well have been composed shortly before 1469. See M. D. R., 'The Tradition of *Consolatio ad Liviam*', *RHT* 6 (1976), 79–98, which concludes with an apparatus to Lenz's text (Turin, 1956[2]). H. Schoonhoven is working on a commentary.[2]

M. D. R.

[1] Vatican lat. 5160, ff. 119^r–129^v (without title). The text is signed '1469 IO. NY.', in full Iohannes Nydenna de Confluentia, who worked at the time in Padua; see A. C. de la Mare in *The Italian Manuscripts in the Library of Major J. R. Abbey* (London, 1969), 122 nn. 1–2. I have found it since I wrote the article about to be cited; it closely resembles H, on which see pp. 85–6 of the article.   [2] *Gnomon*, 52 (1980), 507.

CURTIUS RUFUS

All manuscripts of Curtius omit Books 1–2, the end of 5 and the start of 6, and parts of 10. It is therefore natural to postulate a single archetype whose mutilation caused these deficiencies.[1] By the ninth century, however, we find a sharp division within our extant manuscripts (all of French origin). On the one hand we have Paris lat. 5716 (P), which for all its inanities represents a truer and uninterpolated stock. On the other, ω, the consensus of Berne 451 (B), Florence, Laur. 64.35 (F), Leiden, B.P.L. 137 (L) and Voss. Lat. Q.20 (c.830, from Tours = V), shows clear signs of scholarly interference[2] (not all of it vain: a marginal note refers us to a parallel[3] in Hegesippus).

There are a large number of later manuscripts,[4] virtually unexamined and therefore classed as *interpolati*. H. Bardon's use of Paris lat. 5717 (s. XII, France) (M) proved unavailing,[5] but Müller reports good readings, confirming later conjecture, from Berne 282, s. XV. A. De Lorenzi[6] has

[1] I rely for my first paragraph on the lucid account of K. Müller, *Q. Curtius Rufus Geschichte Alexanders des Grossen* (Munich, 1954), 783–802, with bibliography. Müller's text is valuable for its exploitation of modern knowledge of rhythm, but E. Hedicke's *editio maior* of 1908 remains indispensable. The earliest critical edition is that of C. T. Zumpt (Brunswick, 1849). The earliest editions, dating to c.1470, appeared in Venice and Rome. Plates of all the early codices in Chatelain, CLXXXVIII–CXC.

[2] An engaging example from Müller: 8.10.25 'murus . . . cuius ima saxo, superiora crudo latere sunt structa': ima *Vogel*: iam P: inferiora ω.

[3] Hegesippus, in fact, drew on Curtius: almost the only trace of our author before the Carolingian period (see Müller, 783).

[4] A list in S. Dosson, *Étude sur Quinte Curce* (Paris, 1887), 315–56. Zumpt gave many readings.

[5] Budé edition (Paris, 1947–8). Müller, *Studi in onore di Luigi Castiglioni* (Firenze, 1960), ii. 629–37, showed M to be a copy of B.   [6] *Curzio Rufo* (Napoli, 1965).

more recently signalled similar results from three Naples manuscripts, IV.C.47–9, s. XV. Only further research will show if he is right to conjecture that these good readings are inherited from at least as early as the ninth century.

M. W.

DE VIRIS ILLUSTRIBUS

Almost everything about this set of brief lives is disputed – author, title, contents, date, sources. It survives in two forms: as an independent work in seventy-seven chapters and, in a longer version of eighty-six chapters, as the central portion of a tripartite corpus.

The shorter version goes under the name of Pliny (the younger if specified); several of the earlier manuscripts call it *Liber illustrium*,[1] which later manuscripts convert into the now traditional *De viris illustribus*. The transmitted title of the corpus reads *Aurelii Victoris historiae abbreviatae ab Augusto Octaviano, id est a fine Titi Livii, usque ad consulatum decimum Constantii Augusti et Iuliani Caesaris tertium* (AD 360), and a subscription in the middle marks off 'prima pars huius operis' from 'secunda'. What immediately follows the title, however, reveals the compiler's title and his conception of the work: he calls it *Origo gentis Romanae*[2] and speaks of three consecutive sources, namely, a Republican assortment, Livy, and 'Victor Afer'. The transmitted title reflects the third source and plainly belongs to 'secunda pars', usually known in consequence as the *Liber de Caesaribus* of Aurelius Victor.[3] Neither this nor the Republican section of 'prima pars', which has come to be known by the compiler's title for the whole corpus, occurs elsewhere. The Livian section of 'prima pars' corresponds broadly to *De viris illustribus*.

Pliny or Livy, then; but enough of Livy survives to acquit him of

---

[1] Cf. W. K. Sherwin, *RhM* 112 (1969), 284–6 (checked where catalogues permit).

[2] Momigliano, *JRS* 48 (1958), 58 = *Secondo contributo alla storia degli studi classici* (Rome, 1960), 148–9.

[3] It may of course be either the original or an adaptation by the compiler. A work that too simply proclaims itself an epitome of the original, *Libellus de vita et moribus imperatorum breviatus ex libris Sexti Aurelii Victoris*, survives in about twenty manuscripts of s. IX–XV (*ed. princ.* Fano, 1504); F. Pichlmayr edited it together with the corpus (Teubner, Leipzig, 1911), and its sources have recently been discussed by J. Schlumberger, *Die Epitome de Caesaribus* (Munich, 1974), and T. D. Barnes, *CPh* 71 (1976), 258–68. Perhaps it was the work *De Caesaribus* 'inauditum' to Guarino when Biondo wrote to him about it from Ferrara or Imola in 1423; cf. Sabbadini, *Scoperte*, i. 101, *Epistolario di Guarino Veronese*, i (Venice, 1915), 374 and Momigliano, *Athenaeum*, 36 (1958), 254–5, neither of whom considers this possibility.

being either the author or the sole source, and though the other attribution continues to enlist adherents,[4] the unadorned style and mechanical
approach suggest instead a scholastic product of later Antiquity.

The corpus is extant only in two fifteenth-century manuscripts,
Oxford, Bodl. Canon. Class. Lat. 131 (o), copied in Italy *c.*1453 and
owned by Cardinal Bessarion, and Brussels 9755-63 (p), copied somewhat later in Flanders or Germany by Johannes de Lumel,[5] and acquired
at Kleve by Theodor Poelman, thanks to whom Andreas Schott was
able to use it for editions of *D.V.I.* (Douai, 1577) and the whole corpus
(Antwerp, 1579, *editio princeps*).[6] Meanwhile a third manuscript of the
corpus, perhaps of s. XII or XIII, was 'in Ubiis Coloniae Agrippinae
apud Io. Metellum Sequanum [Jean Matal, *c.*1520–98] . . . ex bibliotheca
Corn. Gualtheri v.c. [Cornelius Wouters, †1582]',[7] and Schott cites
readings from it at second hand in his notes on *D.V.I.*; there is no
evidence that he owes anything to it in the *Origo* or *Liber de Caesaribus*.[8]
Nothing prohibits the belief that Matal's manuscript was an ancestor of
op.[9]

In op and Matal's manuscript the *Origo* and *D.V.I.* have been
amalgamated by the omission of most of the first chapter of the latter
and the insertion of a bridge passage.[10] It is not known whether this

---

[4] e.g. L. Braccesi, *Introduzione al 'De viris illustribus'* (Bologna, 1973), 97–116, whose contention
that the archetype attributed the work to one or the other Pliny (pp. 100–1) rests on false or
misleading statements of Sherwin about the extant manuscripts of the corpus (n. 1, above) and on
a flagrant misinterpretation of 'quae Plinii titulo circumferuntur' in a description of a lost
manuscript related to them. R. D. Sweeney, *RhM* 111 (1968), 191–2, suggests that the attribution
to Pliny arose not from *Ep.* 6.20.5, the usual view, but from the mention in *Hist. Aug.* 15.4.2 of an
'Aurelii Victoris cui Pinio cognomen erat'.

[5] Dr A. C. de la Mare identifies the scribe with the man of this name who signed Vatican lat.
1815 in 1459 and 434 in 1460; the former is discussed and illustrated by J. Ruysschaert,
Miniaturistes 'romains' sous Pie II (Siena, 1968), 256 n. 61, plate 17. The watermark in p is Briquet 26
(lower Rhine, 1467–95), and its text of Cicero, *Pro Sulla* belongs to the same region; the *ex libris* in
an informal hand on f. 156ᵛ, 'liber Iohannis Loemel capellani ecclesie Sancti Dyonisii Leodiensis
[Liège]', has always been taken to be that of Jan Huybrechts (1489–1532) and may indeed be, but
nothing known about the scribe rules him out (Lumel = Loemel in Flemish pronunciation).

[6] On p see the edition of 1577, f. H 1ᵛ and f. O 3ᵛ, and H. Jordan, *Hermes*, 3 (1869), 390–5; on
both o and p, Momigliano (n. 2, above), 56, and S. D'Elia, *Boll. di studi latini*, 3 (1973), 64–6.

[7] Ed. Antw. 1579, p. 202; cf. Jordan. On Wouters, who lived at Cologne from 1544, see Val.
Andreas, *Bibliotheca Belgica*, 2nd edn. (Louvain, 1643), 151–2, and L. Ennen, *Allgemeine Deutsche
Biographie* iv (Leipzig, 1877), 59–61 s. v. Cassander.

[8] On *D.V.I.* see Momigliano, *Athenaeum*, 36 (1958), 258, and S. Mariotti, *Studi classici e orientali*,
10 (1961), 103 n. 8; on the *Liber de Caesaribus*, R. J. T., *Gnomon*, 50 (1978), 358–9. No one seems to
have pondered how readings from the *Origo* or the *Liber de Caesaribus* might have been conveyed to
Schott before he published the *editio princeps*. Matal himself cites passages from the *Origo* in a letter
published without date or explanation in Schott's *Nepos* (Frankfurt, 1609), 21–3; Mariotti, op. cit.,
goes through the variants. Copies of Schott's editions might be checked for collations by Matal or
anyone else.

[9] D'Elia, *Studi sulla tradizione manoscritta di Aurelio Vittore* (Naples, 1965), 53–95, 112–39.

[10] *Sed horum omnium opinionibus diversis repugnat nostrae memoriae proclamans historia Liviana, quae
testatur quod auspicato Romulus ex suo nomine Romam vocavit muniretque moenibus edixit . . .* Mariotti, 105 n.
13. plausibly emends the last clause by reading with the other version *vocavit ⟨et ut eam prius
legibus⟩ muniret quam moenibus edixit . . .*

operation coincided with the assembling of the corpus or was a later refinement, but the language of the bridge passage has been held to suggest a medieval origin.[11] Certainly of medieval origin are several interpolations in *D.V.I.* peculiar to op and Matal's manuscript; these have been traced to the *Historia miscella* of Landolfus Sagax, written in southern Italy towards AD 1023.[12] As the authorized text of the *Historia miscella*, Vatican Pal. lat. 909, had migrated to Corvey by *c.*1050, the home of the corpus in its present form seems to have been the region of the Lower Rhine, where both p and Matal's manuscript were discovered in the sixteenth century;[13] p and the Italian member of the family, o, could derive from a manuscript discovered there in the previous century by Nicholas of Cues.[14]

When Schott published chapters 78–86 of *D.V.I.*, the short text had already been printed numerous times (*editio princeps* probably Rome *c.*1470: Flodr, *Aurelius Victor* 1), and it appears in over 150 manuscripts of s. XIV–XV, mostly Italian but some of the earlier ones French.[15] The status of chapters 78–86 has been questioned, but nothing in their style or method convicts them of spuriousness,[16] and the simplest explanation for their absence from these manuscripts and editions is a defect in the copy from which they all derive. This hypothesis finds support in chapter 77. Four Florentine manuscripts of s. XV med. (Florence, Laur. 68.29 and Fiesole 181, British Library, Burney 231, Oxford, Corpus Christi College 84) break off at *ad Ptolomaeum Alexandriae*, leaving a sentence unfinished.[17] This is not likely to be a coincidence, especially since the rest of the chapter in all other manuscripts except op is suspiciously different in style from what precedes and is probably an interpolation based on the accounts of Pompey's death given by Lucan and Valerius Maximus.[18]

Where the short text came to light in the fourteenth century, and who

---

[11] D' Elia, *Studi sulla tradizione*, 105–12. Momigliano (n. 2, above), 57–9, assumes that the compiler wrote it and dates the compiler soon after the *Liber de Caesaribus*.

[12] Th. Opitz, *Acta Soc. Phil. Lips.* 2 (1872), 223 n. 31; I. R. Wijga, *Liber de viris illustribus urbis Romae apparatu critico et adnotationibus instructus* (Groningen, 1890), 7; Momigliano (n. 2, above), 59–60; Mariotti, 102 n. 3. On Landolfus Sagax and the manuscript about to be mentioned, see A. Crivellucci, *Landolfi Sagacis Historia Romana*, i (Rome, 1912), xiii–xxi, xxxvii–xlii, and EUTROPIUS. [13] Cf. Momigliano (n. 2, above), 60.

[14] Vatican lat. 1815 (cf. n. 5, above) has the arms of Giovanni Andrea de' Bussi, and Nicholas of Cues is the obvious link between Bussi and the neighbourhood of Liège (cf. again n. 5). On Nicholas's connections with Bessarion see D'Elia (n. 6, above), 64 and n. 42.

[15] Seventy-odd manuscripts have been mentioned in literature on *D.V.I.*, but more can easily be added from catalogues. Two French manuscripts of s. XIV are Vatican, Reg. lat. 1399 and 1494; see Pellegrin, *Manuscrits*, ii. 1 (Paris, 1978), 183, 239. Sherwin (n. 1, above) ignores Pavia 68, an early manuscript discussed by G. Ferrara, *RFIC* 36 (1908), 508–17.

[16] M. M. Sage, *TAPA* 108 (1978), 235–8, against Braccesi, 65–96.

[17] A fifth, Florence, Ricc. 537, ventures its own conclusion; cf. Pichlmayr's edition (Teubner, Leipzig, 1911), xv.

[18] E. Westerburg, *RhM* 37 (1882), 49, saw the debt to Lucan, and Postgate in his edition of Lucan VIII (Cambridge, 1917), xviii–xix, branded the passage as 'late', 'non-classical'.

completed the chapter on Pompey, remains to be determined. Early in
the fourteenth century, however, Giovanni Mansionario of Verona
listed among the works of the younger Pliny 'librum virorum illustrium
a Proca rege Albanorum usque ad Cleopatram in nonaginta octo
capitulis secundum ipsorum virorum numerum'.[19] The corpus lacks
Proca, the short text Caesar–Cleopatra; but Giovanni could well have
seen the copy from which all extant manuscripts of the short text derive
before it lost Caesar–Cleopatra, or for that matter it could have lost
Caesar–Cleopatra already and his knowledge of the original contents
could have come from an index at the front.[20] The latter possibility has
more in its favour than the former, because Vatican lat. 1917 (V), which
seems to have been copied in 1392 from a manuscript written by
Giovanni in 1328,[21] ends with the spurious tailpiece to chapter 77. Did
Giovanni even compose the tailpiece? Be that as it may, no one outside
Como would be sorry if a work supposedly of 'Gaii Plinii Secundi
oratoris Veronensis' should prove to have survived the Middle Ages at
Verona.

Since op are often interpolated and cannot be relied upon, it is
unfortunate that the tradition of the short text has not been properly
investigated.[22] The Florentine group that breaks off before the end of
chapter 77 often agrees with op against the rest, and not in ways that
arouse suspicion of contamination. V and other manuscripts said to be
early have a number of omissions,[23] but manuscripts that share neither
these nor the distinctive readings of the Florentine group are not
necessarily hybrid. The influence of o or a relative has so far been
detected in only one manuscript of the short text.[24]

Fresh information about manuscripts of the short text is unlikely to

[19] *Brevis adnotatio de duobus Pliniis*, ed. E. T. Merrill, *CPh* 5 (1910), 186–8; cf. Sabbadini, *Scoperte*, ii. 89, 193.

[20] A. Barriera, *Athenaeum*, 4 (1916), 434–53, and Sherwin, *Hermes*, 97 (1969), 503–5, connect with Giovanni's description a curious manuscript that may once have had ninety-eight chapters, Naples, Orat. VI.13 (s. XIV according to the catalogue and Sherwin, s. XV[1] according to Barriera, s. XV[2] according to Carlotta Griffiths, who kindly inspected it); no sign of Cleopatra, though. In Ausonius too Giovanni perhaps took information from an index to which the contents no longer corresponded.

[21] Billanovich, in *Tra latino e volgare: per Carlo Dionisotti* (Padua, 1974), i. 83–4.

[22] The most reliable and informative edition is still Wijga's (cf. n. 12, above). The standard edition, F. Pichlmayr's Teubner of the corpus (Leipzig, 1911, reprinted with additions by R. Gruendel, 1961, 1966, 1970), has a very inaccurate apparatus, and Sherwin's recent text (Norman, Okla., 1973) is even more radically deficient, for instance in simply omitting chapters 78–86. Sherwin has continued the work of Titchener (cf. n. 25, below), and it may be that Ohio State University now possesses a large file on manuscripts of *D.V.I.*; but only scrappy accounts appear in the edition and the articles cited here in nn. 1, 20, 24. The *Origo* has recently been edited by G. Puccioni (Florence, 1958), the *Liber de Caesaribus* for Budé by P. Dufraigne (Paris, 1975); on the inadequacy of Dufraigne's edition see R. J. T., *Gnomon*, 50 (1978), 355–62.

[23] See Sherwin's edition, xv n. 4. He does not even mention the Florentine group.

[24] Baltimore W. 388 (De Ricci 471); cf. Sherwin, *CW* 65 (1972), 145–6. Seville, Colombina AA 144 50, singled out by Sherwin (edn.), xii, xv n. 4, as influenced by the text of op, is merely one of many manuscripts that do not share all the corruptions of V and its fellows.

upset the conclusion that both it and the longer text of the corpus descend from one archetype.[25] The corruption of *Fufetius* to *Sufetius* (4.2, 10) even points to an archetype in minuscule script, but more than one such corruption would be needed to outweigh arguments for earlier formation of the corpus.[26]

R. J. T.

M. D. R.

[25] J. B. Titchener, in *Classical Studies in Honor of William Abbott Oldfather* (Urbana, Ill., 1943), 187. In other respects the article might have been written before Wijga's edition (cf. n. 12, above).

[26] Since we wrote this piece, the corpus has been fully discussed by P. L. Schmidt, *P.-W.* Suppl. xv (1978), 1583–1676, but he did not explore the tradition and therefore takes too much on trust. D'Elia has returned to the subject in *La critica testuale greco-latina, oggi: metodi e problemi*, ed. E. Flores (Rome, 1981), 317–29.

AELIUS DONATUS

Commentary on Terence

A commentary by Aelius Donatus on Terence is mentioned by his pupil Jerome, and some forty Italian manuscripts of s. xv ascribe to him a long commentary on five of the six plays. That the latter is at best an adaptation of the former, demonstrated by Parrhasius, has annoyed Terentian scholars more than it would have annoyed Donatus himself, who knew the usefulness of scissors and paste.[1] For an editor it sets two tasks of reconstruction, the second impossible.

The first task, reconstructing the archetype of the extant witnesses, is difficult enough. Besides the fifteenth-century manuscripts, which change their relationship several times in the course of the commentary, the main materials are two older manuscripts, which together contain less than half of the commentary, and two later editions, which drew on important manuscripts without saying much about them.

The older manuscripts are Paris lat. 7920 (A, s. xi), from the Loire valley, and Vatican, Reg. lat. 1595 (B, s. xiii), of uncertain origin. The editions are Stephanus's (Paris, 1529), towards which Ascensius gave him an 'old' manuscript,[2] and Lindenbrog's (Paris, 1602), which used a

[1] The commentary opens with Suetonius' *Vita Terenti* (cf. §8) and a treatise *De fabula* ascribed by Rufinus (s. v ?) to Euanthius (†358). G. Cupaiuolo has collated all the manuscripts of the treatise and edited it (Naples, 1979).

[2] Though there are signs that the manuscript resembled B, Stephanus's printed sources need ascertaining before it can be properly assessed. One was the *ed. Tarvisiana* 1477 of Terence and Donatus.

collation by Pithoeus of a manuscript owned by Cujas (Gronovius later transcribed either Pithoeus's collation or Lindenbrog's transcript of it, but unfortunately into a copy of Lindenbrog's edition, Leiden, Bibliotheek der Rijksuniversiteit 759.C.16).

During the Middle Ages the commentary was also consulted by whoever compiled the *Vita Ambrosiana* of Terence;[3] by three annotators of Terence, one not much later than the scribe in Vatican lat. 3868 (C of Terence, *c*.820–30, Corvey[4]), one of s. x^2/xi^1 in Paris lat. 7899 (P of Terence, s. ix^2, Reims or neighbourhood[5]), and one of s. xii^2 in Florence, Ricc. 528 (E of Terence, s. xi);[6] in s. $xii^3/4$ by Hugh of Orléans;[7] a century later by the annotator of Berne 276, a lexicographer at Orléans or near by who cites it over seventy times;[8] and in s. $xiv^4/4$ by Nicholas of Clamanges.[9] A manuscript at Orléans could easily have been seen by three or more of these people and later acquired by Cujas.

Apart perhaps from a short extract in Milan, Ambros. L.53 sup. (S), owned by Fr. Pizolpasso (†1443), and manuscripts that give only the *argumentum* of *Eunuchus*,[10] the fifteenth-century witnesses derive from manuscripts discovered at Mainz in 1433 by Giovanni Aurispa and at Chartres in the 1440s by Jean Jouffroy.

During the Council of Basle, which gave Aurispa the opportunity of discovering the Maguntinus, Nicholas of Cues also put it at Pizolpasso's disposal,[11] and in 1436 Pier Candido Decembrio transcribed at least *Phormio* from it. As a letter from Decembrio to Pizolpasso precedes *Phormio* in two manuscripts that contain the whole commentary, presumably he went on to make a full transcription and these manuscripts derive from it; the better of the two is Oxford, Bodl. Canon. Class. Lat. 95 (C). The order in which they put the plays, *Andr. Eun. Ad. Hec. Phorm.*, recurs in all but one of the fifteenth-century manuscripts, and it seems to have been the order in B, where *Eunuchus* follows *Andria*.[12]

Aurispa's copy of the Maguntinus seems to have brought only parts of the commentary into circulation and those slowly. It may lie behind a few manuscripts that make a useful contribution to the text of *Eunuchus*,

---

[3] Ritschl edited this from manuscripts of s. xi and later in A. Reifferscheid, *C. Suetoni Tranquilli praeter Caesarum libros reliquiae* (Leipzig, 1860), 534–6, 538. See also K. Dziatzko, *Jahrb. für class. Phil.* 40 (1894), 472, and Sabbadini, *SIFC* 2 (1894) 26–7.

[4] Bischoff, *Mitt. Stud.* i. 60 n. 34. On the various scholiasts see Jachmann's introduction to the facsimile (Leipzig, 1929), 8–11.

[5] Bischoff ap. G. Glauche, *Schullektüre im Mittelalter* (Munich, 1970), 63.

[6] I owe the date of this annotator to Virginia Brown.

[7] Margarethe Billerbeck, *RFIC* 103 (1975), 430–4.

[8] M. D. R. and R. H. R., *Viator*, 9 (1978), 235–49. I have since found another nineteen citations.

[9] Sabbadini, *RFIC* 39 (1911), 541–3 = *Storia e Critica*[2], 153–4.

[10] Claudia Villa kindly tells me that she has found about a dozen, mainly of s. xv but including one of s. xii, Brussels 5329.

[11] As Pizolpasso nowhere mentions Mainz, the manuscript concerned need not have been the Maguntinus, but the supposition is plausible and economical.

[12] Except that *Haut.* is omitted, it agrees with the order in Γ of Terence.

known to Valla by 1441, and of *Hec.* 3.5.8 – *Phorm.* fin., e.g. British Library, Add. 21083, Rome, Cors. 43.E.28, and Oxford, Lincoln College, Lat. 45 (O); in *Phormio* they often agree with Stephanus or the Cuiacianus against the rest of the tradition. Both the *editio princeps* (Venice, *c.*1471) and a partly independent successor (Milan, 1476) have affinities with this group.

In A *Andria* is followed by *Adelphi* (to 1.1.40, where the scribe stopped), and the recurrence of this order in Vatican, Chigi H.VII.240 (K) confirms the close relationship evident in their text.[13] The writing of K was directed and partly carried out by Jacopo Ammannati at Rome in the early 1450s, and much of it must derive from Aurispa's newly acquired copy of the Carnotensis discovered by Jouffroy. When Jouffroy discovered it, however, it lacked part of *Hecyra* and had a 'defectus' in *Phormio*, whereas K has both complete except for a short passage of *Phormio* likewise missing from C (2.1.4–19). Which sections of K after *Ad.* 1.1.40 derive from the Carnotensis is one of the main problems in the tradition.

The remaining witnesses probably derive from a manuscript like C into which readings from the Carnotensis and numerous alterations had been introduced. Among them is the influential edition of Calphurnius (Venice, 1476), in which Donatus was first printed round the text of Terence and a substitute supplied for the missing commentary on *Hautontimorumenos*.

Most of the fifteenth-century witnesses omit or originally omitted all or most of the Greek, for which the best sources besides A, B, and the editions of Stephanus and Lindenbrog are S, K, Vatican, Reg. lat. 1496 (V) and 1673 (G), Cesena S. XXII.5 (M), and B. L. Add. 21083.

The wider stemma is still in doubt. A and B overlap only in about three-fifths of *Andria*, where for bad reasons they have been regarded as close relatives. Nevertheless, the total absence of significant *Bindefehler* between B and C speaks for one or other of these possibilities.

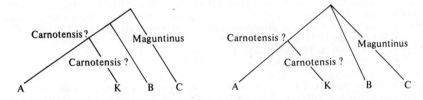

Unless A has a fair amount of emendation or S a fair amount of contamination in its ancestry, the stemma of the short section preserved in S is this:

[13] The order in *Δ* of Terence, or at any rate its main descendants, is *Andr. Ad. Eun. Phorm. Haut. Hec.*, and even though K has *Andr. Ad. Eun. Hec. Phorm.*, its source for *Andr.* and *Ad.* may have agreed throughout with *Δ*.

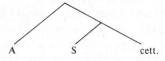

A   S   cett.

In other sections of the commentary no satisfactory stemmata have yet
been extracted from the shifting allegiances of the manuscripts.[14]

Then comes the impossible task, reconstructing the original commentary. Citations from Donatus that do not appear in the extant
version occur in Priscian, in sixth-century scholia on the Bembinus of
Terence (s. IV/V), and in contemporary or not much later scholia on the
Victorianus of Terence (D, s. x^2). The Bembine scholia may have been
taken not from the original commentary but from an abridgement,[15]
and the same could be true of the scholia in the Victorianus.[16] It seems
likely that the extant version was put together from similar scholia,
perhaps two sets in view of the parallel sequences in a scene of *Phormio*
(2.3); and inappropriate lemmata may have led to the incorporation of
extraneous matter. What other extraneous matter the extant version
contains is an open question,[17] and so is the date of its formation. When
Lupus of Ferrières asked Benedict III (855–8) for 'Donati commentum
in Terentio' and Gottschalk of Orbais at about the same time referred in
passing to 'Donatus in Terentium', neither need have meant the extant
version. Insular stages of transmission have been inferred from errors in
manuscripts of the extant version,[18] but the relation of the extant
version to any such stages cannot be determined.

M. D. R.

[14] The first scholar to investigate the tradition at all thoroughly was Sabbadini, who also
collected most of the external evidence known today. Wessner's edition (Leipzig, 1902–5) leaned
heavily on his results but was soon overtaken by the discovery of S and K. For a full study
of K, albeit in isolation from everything except Wessner's apparatus, see O. Zwierlein, *Der
Terenzkommentar des Donat im codex Chigianus H VII 240* (Berlin, 1970), which contains important
discussions of numerous passages. In an article on the whole tradition, *CPh* 74 (1979), 310–26, I
said more about K and pointed out the value of B. L. Add. 21083 and its fellows; I have since found
another manuscript, Salamanca 78, related to C but heavily interpolated. A new edition is called
for, not least because eliminable *Sonderfehler* often swell Wessner's apparatus to half a page.

[15] J. E. G. Zetzel, *HSCP* 79 (1975), 335–54.

[16] W. M. Lindsay, *CQ* 21 (1927), 188–94.

[17] *Commenti Donatiani ad Terenti fabulas scholia genuina et spuria probabiliter separare conatus est H. T.
Karsten*, i–ii (Leiden, 1912–13), but opinions differ on his success.

[18] C. H. Beeson, *CPh* 17 (1922), 283–305. 'No other profane Latin text', says Beeson (p. 287),
'offers such abundant and convincing evidence of the stages through which it has come down to us.
. . . No other text exhibits such bewildering paleographical confusion or betrays such helplessness
on the part of the scribes in dealing with a puzzling script and still more puzzling abbreviations.'

TI. CLAUDIUS DONATUS

Interpretationes Vergilianae

The commentary of Ti. Claudius Donatus on the *Aeneid*, in twelve books,[1] exists in three ninth-century manuscripts and their fifteenth-century descendants, and owes its survival to the efforts of Carolingian monks in the Loire abbeys.

The three Carolingian manuscripts descend from a codex probably once at Luxeuil. The oldest of the three, Vatican lat. 1512 (V) (*CLA* I.10), containing only the second half of the commentary, Books 6–12, was written according to Bischoff at Luxeuil in the late eighth or early ninth century.[2] The second, Florence, Laur. 45.15 (L) (*CLA* III.297a, b), *Tiberi Claudi Donati ad Tiberium Claudium Maximum Donatianum filium suum interpretationum vergilianarum Aeneidos liber I incipit feliciter*, beg. 'Illos qui . . .', containing only Books 1–5, was written at Tours in two parts: I. insular minuscule and II. early Carolingian minuscule, probably during the first years of Alcuin's abbacy (abbot 796–804). It was copied from a Luxeuil exemplar, the influence of which can be traced in its decoration; and this manuscript may have returned to Luxeuil, for it was apparently found there in the fifteenth century. The third manuscript, Vatican, Reg. lat. 1484 (R), *Tiberii Claudii Donati ad Tiberium Claudium Maximum Donatianum filium suum interpretationum vergilianarum Aeneidos incipit liber I*, beg. 'Post illos qui . . .', containing Books 1–5 and Book 10.1–585, was also written at Tours, in the 820s or 30s according to Rand. It belonged to Lupus of Ferrières (d. 862), who revised and corrected the text, and added on f. 168ᵛ an epitaph for the nephew of Aldric, the latter being one of Lupus's predecessors as Abbot of Ferrières and subsequently Archbishop of Sens (d. 836).[3]

Four references exist to what may be additional manuscripts of the commentary. The commentary was known at Bobbio and appears in the tenth-century catalogue of the abbey: '435. Librum Donati super Virgilium unum' (Becker, 32.435, p. 69). The commentary is cited by name by Paul the Deacon in the *Historia Langobardorum*,[4] written at Montecassino in the late eighth century. Given the contact between Bobbio and the two other houses, Montecassino and Luxeuil, perhaps the others were relatives, if not descendants, of the Bobbio codex. The commentary also appears in the anonymous eleventh-century book-list

---

[1] Ed. H. Georgii (Leipzig, 1905–6).
[2] *Mitt. Stud.* ii. 14.   [3] E. Pellegrin, in *BEC* 115 (1957), 13.
[4] Ed. Bethmann and Waitz, *MGH, Script. rer. Lang.* 1 (1878), 85.

in Munich Clm 14436 f. 61ᵛ, 'Commentum Donati super Virgilium'. The list, which Bischoff associated with Hartwic of St. Emmeram, a pupil of Fulbert, has been attributed to both Chartres and Reims.[5] All that can be said, however, is that it perhaps represents the books of a school somewhere in France (Becker, 63.30, p. 147). The anonymous mid-thirteenth-century lexicographer who left profuse annotations in Berne 276 saw a copy of the commentary at St. Columba's in Sens: 'Iste [i.e. Donatus] est qui fecit commentum Virgilii quod est apud sanctum κολῦβαμ σενοῦ: Tiberi Claudi Donati ad Tiberium Claudium Donatianum filium suum. Incipit liber interpretationum librorum Eneidos Virgilii. [incipit] Illos qui Mantuani vatis michi carmina tradiderunt.' Although this does not correspond exactly with the rubric and incipit of either surviving manuscript of the early books, the manuscript referred to may be related to Lupus's codex, given the close relationship between Ferrières and Sens exemplified in Archbishop Aldric. Finally, in the early years of the fifteenth century Poggio reported a discovery while at the Council of Constance (1415–17), which Niccolò Niccoli recorded thus: 'In monasterio Sancti Marci quod est in lacu Constantie sunt commentaria Donati grammatici in litteris vetustissimis in libros octo [sic] Eneidos Virgilii.' Unfortunately this manuscript leaves no trace either in the Reichenau book-lists or in the *recentiores* of the commentary.

The reappearance of Donatus' commentary on Virgil in Italy is the story of the rediscovery not of the Bobbio manuscript but rather of the Carolingian codices. Sabbadini's careful detective work revealed that the first to appear, Laur. 45.15 (Bks. 1–5), was brought to Italy by Jean Jouffroy in 1438 when he attended the Council of Ferrara.[6] Jouffroy, then a young man, was Abbot of Luxeuil and appears to have brought the manuscript from the abbey itself. Once in Italy it soon passed to the library of Pietro de' Medici. The second, Vatican lat. 1512 (Bks. 6–12), came to Italy via an unknown agency by the 1460s.[7] Copies of the whole commentary thereafter spread rapidly. Lupus's manuscript, Reg. lat. 1484, remained in the north, until it passed via Paul and Alexander Petau to the library of Queen Christina of Sweden.

R. H. R.

[5] *Mitt. Stud.* ii. 82–3. Concerning a possible German origin for this list see CICERO, *Speeches*, n. 58.

[6] Cf. Mercati in *Mélanges Felix Grat*, 1 (Paris, 1946), 357–66.

[7] Perhaps the earliest surviving copy is Oxford, Lincoln College Lat. 44, produced by Vespasiano for R. Flemmyng; it appears in the Lincoln inventory of 1474, and was probably given in 1465. I thank A. C. de la Mare for this information.

EUTROPIUS

Such was the need in the late fourth century and later for a summary of the simple facts of Roman history that Eutropius' brief and balanced survey enjoyed an immediate and lasting success. Writing at the request of Valens (364–78) he condensed into ten short books the period from Romulus down to his own time. A Greek version by his contemporary Paeanius is still extant, as are fragments of another translation by Capito (s. v/vi). In the eighth century Paul the Deacon expanded Eutropius' *Breviarium* by inserting extra material from Orosius, Jerome, and others, and added six books of his own composition, bringing the history down to the time of Justinian. In this form it becomes the *Historia Romana*.[1] The *Historia* was itself similarly treated by Landolfo Sagax about the year 1000, who added more books and carried the history down to the ninth century.[2] This is the *Historia miscella*.

Despite powerful competition from the *Historia Romana*, the *Breviarium* did survive in its original form and its relation to its various versions, which are of some use in correcting the text, is clearly set out in the monumental edition of H. Droysen,[3] where Eutropius sits splendidly surrounded by his satellites.

Most of the manuscripts of the *Breviarium* fall into two families, which Droysen called A and B. I shall retain his sigla, since the basic division still obtains even if his families have with time acquired new members.[4] The two early representatives of A are:

G   Gotha Membr. I.101, s. IX, from Murbach.[5] It also contains Festus' *Breviarium* and Frontinus' *Strategemata*.

F   Fuldensis, a lost Fulda manuscript collated by F. Sylburg.[6] Close to G, but better.

Also belonging to the A tradition is a group of manuscripts of dubious

---

[1] Most recently edited by A. Crivellucci, *Pauli Diaconi Historia Romana* (Rome, 1914).

[2] Vatican, Pal. lat. 909 appears to be the copy made for Landolfo himself; see A. Crivellucci, *Landolfi Sagacis Historia Romana*, i (Rome, 1912), xiii–xxi, xxxvii–xlii.

[3] *MGH, Auctores antiquissimi*, ii (Berlin, 1878). Droysen's *editio maior* is still invaluable. There have been two Teubner texts, those of F. Rühl (Leipzig, 1887) and C. Santini (1979). For his view of the tradition Santini is heavily indebted to an important article by N. Scivoletto, 'La tradizione manoscritta di Eutropio', *GIF* 14 (1961), 129–62.

[4] Santini has a new and complex system of group sigla.

[5] R. Ehwald, *Philologus*, 59 (1900), 627–30; R. Schipke, *Die Maugérard-Handschriften der Forschungsbibliothek Gotha* (Gotha, 1972), 59. There is a plate in F. Jacobs and F. A. Ukert, *Beiträge zur ältern Literatur* (Leipzig, 1835–8), i, tab. 3.

[6] In his second edition of Eutropius, *Romanae historiae scriptores Graeci minores* (Frankfurt, 1590). He had been informed of its existence by Franciscus Modius.

value but of some historical interest. Droysen dismissed the two of them known to him as worthless, Rühl made some limited use of them, Santini has constituted them as a group and given them a place in his edition. The earliest of this group is Paris lat. 7240, s. XI (C in Santini). It is of French origin, and Paris lat. 5802, which was written at Chartres[7] in the middle of the twelfth century and presented to Bec by Philip of Bayeux, appears to be a copy of it. Close to C are two manuscripts, also of French origin, British Library, Harley 2729 (s. XII) and Paris lat. 18104 (s. XIII);[8] and, more interestingly, Oxford, Lincoln College Lat. 100, which was written at Malmesbury by William and his collaborators c.1125.[9]

The B family, which has suffered from interpolation, has four main representatives:

V   Vatican lat. 1981, s. XI. Of French origin, it appears to have belonged
    in the eleventh century to the monastery of Saint-Vivant-sous-Vergy,
    in the diocese of Autun.[10] Unknown to Droysen, it was first brought to
    notice by Scivoletto. It is free from some of the errors which join L and
    O.

L   Leiden, B.P.L. 141, ff. 63–151, s. X. Probably of French origin, it
    belonged in the sixteenth century to the Church of St. John and St.
    Bavo in Ghent.[11]

O   Saint-Omer 697, s. XI, which was at Saint-Bertin in the fourteenth
    century. Brussels 6439–51,[12] s. XI[2], is a copy of it.

A   Cambridge, Corpus Christi College 129, s. XIII ex., from Saint
    Augustine's Canterbury. This manuscript was first used by Santini.[13]

This is not the sum of the evidence for B, for Eutropius suffered the diverse tortures of being both extended and excerpted. A florilegium containing extracts from both Eutropius and Justinus was put together in Italy in the ninth century or earlier. From this came the excerpts which were incorporated in the great historical miscellany copied at Verona early in the ninth century and eventually dismembered into four separate units: Leningrad, National Public (Saltykov-Shchedrin) Library, Class. Lat. Q.v.9 (Eutropius) and Lat. Q.v.IV.5 (Justinus);

---

[7] Attributed to Chartres by François Avril: cf. *IMU* 22 (1979), 122 n. 2.

[8] Perhaps also of Chartres origin; on this manuscript see T. Maslowski and R. H. R., 'Twelfth-century Extracts from Cicero's «Pro Archia» and «Pro Cluentio» in Paris B.N. MS lat. 18104', *IMU* 22 (1979), 97–122 (in particular 121 f.).

[9] R. M. T., 'The "scriptorium" of William of Malmesbury', in *Medieval Scribes, Manuscripts and Libraries. Essays presented to N. R. Ker*, edited by M. B. Parkes and A. G. Watson (London, 1978), in particular pp. 118 (plate 28), 129 (plate 33)–130.

[10] It has a contemporary catalogue of St. Viventius.

[11] Whence it was borrowed by Schonhovius, who used it for his 1546 edition.

[12] Attributed to both Lobbes and Saint-Vaast, but there is no real evidence, and its being a copy of O makes Saint-Bertin as likely a home as either: J. Van den Gheyn, *Revue des Bibliothèques et Archives de Belgique*, 2 (1904), 296–301.

[13] Santini has a high regard for A, which is free from some of the errors of VLO. He does not discuss the possibility of contamination.

Berlin (East), Phillipps 1885 and 1896 (Isidore, Jordanes, Anonymus Valesianus, etc.).[14] From the same common exemplar or exemplars is derived the much later collection in Vatican, Pal. lat. 927, written in 1181 at the monastery of the Holy Trinity at Verona. The epitome of Eutropius from which these excerpts were drawn had a basically B text and, though badly mauled, it is earlier than our complete B manuscripts and has some limited use.

Alongside A and B is a third witness of a different order, which Droysen called C. This is the tradition of the *Historia Romana* of Paul the Deacon. The manuscript of Eutropius which Paul had used as the basis for his own history has been lost, so we are left with the problem of deciding whether textual divergences in the *Historia Romana* arise from genuine variants in the text of Eutropius or are arbitrary changes made by Paul himself. It was earlier thought that Vatican lat. 1860, written in Italy in 1313, could be used as a control. More than one of the texts it contains has an affinity with Montecassino traditions and it offers a text of the *Breviarium* of the type used for the *Historia Romana*. But it has been disputed whether it is a genuine descendant of the original manuscript of the *Breviarium* used by Paul (so Droysen), or a text of the *Historia Romana* purged of Paul's additions.[15] In any case it certainly contains a few of Paul's interpolations; there has been contact between it and the *Historia Romana*, and its evidence is suspect.

There are still a lot of loose ends to the text of Eutropius. Even when we have extracted from the *Historia Romana* the C tradition of Eutropius, it is difficult to see where the balance of authority should lie between the various combinations of A, B, and C. Droysen regarded the tradition as tripartite, Mommsen thought that A and C had a common parent,[16] Scivoletto (and Santini) derive A and B from a common (French) hyparchetype. While Scivoletto may well be right in seeing the split in the tradition as medieval rather than antique, our medieval tradition has such early beginnings and so straddled Europe that its initial stages may be more complex than is suggested by a simple stemma with a point at the top. There could have been some interplay with strains of text now lost. Paul the Deacon testifies to the presence of a text of the *Breviarium* at Montecassino in the latter part of the eighth century. This has overshadowed another fact at least as interesting for the history of the transmission, that Eutropius was available much earlier in the century at the opposite corner of Europe; for he was known to the Venerable Bede. The Northumbrian tradition may well pre-date, and

---

[14] R. Cessi, 'Di due miscellanee storiche medioevali', *Archivio Muratoriano*, 13 (1913), 69–96. It seems likely that this was brought with other manuscripts from Verona Cathedral and given to the monastery of St. Vincent at Metz by its founder Bishop Deodericus (†984). Thence to the Jesuit College of Clermont and the parting of the ways.

[15] Scivoletto, 148 ff.   [16] Ap. Droysen, *praef.* xiv.

have no connection with, our extant manuscript groups. It would be a mistake to build on one reading, and a simple banalization at that, but Bede's reading *illic capta* (for *capta illic*) at 7.14 makes it just possible that he was using what was, or was to become, the B tradition of the text.[17] It is the B text which lies behind the Verona epitome of the ninth century and which later re-emerged in France. And there may have been another and superior Italian strain of text which has all but disappeared. The evidence for this is Bamberg Class. 31 (E.III.22), written in Italy in the early tenth century.[18] It contains such excellent texts of Florus and Festus that it must have come from a particularly good home. All it has of Eutropius is his dedicatory letter to Valens, added in a somewhat later hand; but it alone of all the manuscripts preserves the title of our author, *Eutropius v.c. magister memoriae*.

When Eutropius first appeared in print (Rome, 1471) he was still part and parcel of the *Historia Romana* and the *Breviarium* did not appear in its – more or less – original form until edited by Antonius Schonhovius (Basle, 1546).

L. D. R.

[17] *De temporum ratione*, 294.2, ed. Mommsen, *MGH, Auctores antiquissimi*, xiii (Berlin, 1894–8), 284; cf. *Historia ecclesiastica*, 1.3, p. 15. Eutropius was also known to Alcuin: L. Wallach, *Alcuin and Charlemagne* (Ithaca, NY 1959), 18, 28 n. 80.

[18] So Bischoff; cf. P. Jal, *Florus, Oeuvres*, i (Paris, 1967), cxv n. 2.

SEX. POMPEIUS FESTUS

De verborum significatu

Nothing remains (except scattered quotations) from the great Latin dictionary *De verborum significatu* of M. Verrius Flaccus, tutor to the grandsons of the Emperor Augustus.[1] At some point in the second century, this work was digested by Sextus Pompeius Festus. This more manageable text had a long and powerful influence, being used, for example, by Macrobius (*Sat.* 3.5.7) and the compilers of early medieval

The standard Teubner text was edited by W. M. Lindsay, 1913 (reprinted 1965). In *Glossaria Latina*, iv (Paris, 1930, reprinted 1965), 71–506, Lindsay made a bold attempt at re-creating the words of Festus, relying much on the evidence of the later glossaries. A facsimile of F is available: A. Thewrewk de Ponor, *Codex Festi Farnesianus XLII tabulis expressus* (Budapest, 1893).

[1] Suet. *De gramm.* 17. For the remains of Verrius, see H. Funaioli, *Grammaticae Romanae Fragmenta* (Teubner, Leipzig, 1907), 509–23.

glossaries.[2] In the late eighth century, this book of Festus was itself digested by Paul the Deacon in southern Italy, and his prefatory letter shows that this compilation was made for the library of Charlemagne.[3]

The sole surviving witness for Festus is F (Naples IV.A.3), the so-called *codex Farnesianus*, s. XI[2], written in or around Rome.[4] The text (now a mere forty-one leaves, and beginning some way into the letter M) is in two columns, the outer of which has been badly damaged by fire throughout.[5] It can be shown that this book originally consisted of sixteen quaternions, of which the first seven and the larger part of the eleventh had disappeared before F came to light in the fifteenth century.

The rediscovery of F in the Renaissance is due to the Greek Manilius Rhallus, who came upon it[6] in the 1470s, and then produced his edition at Rome in 1475. Rhallus lent F to the scholar Pomponius Laetus, who must have disbound the manuscript, as he was able to keep the eighth, tenth, and sixteenth quaternions, which, as a result, are now lost.

An editor is thus forced to reconstruct part of F from copies made in the fifteenth century. Of these the most useful are:

U   Vatican lat. 3368, in the hand of Politian, lacking its first twelve leaves. It now contains the text of quaternions 11–16 of F.

V   A series of manuscript notes, in a fifteenth-century hand, inserted in the printed text Paris, B. N. Inv. Rés. X. 96, containing the same parts of the text as U.

W   Vatican lat. 3369, containing all the original quaternions 8–16 (except, of course, for the imperfect eleventh) of F as it was in the fifteenth century.

X   Vatican lat. 1549, containing the same 'complete' text as W.

Y   Some scattered readings inserted in Leiden, Voss. Lat. O.9 (itself a copy of X), written in Italy, s. XVI in.

Z   Vatican lat. 2731, an imperfect text. V, Y, and Z appear to have the same source.

It follows that, for long stretches, an editor must rely upon the testimony of W and X (with occasional help from Y). Even more

---

[2] For the glossaries, see the Preface to Lindsay's 1930 edition (pp. 73–90). It is important to observe the southern Italian origin of so much of this work. Festus was still being plundered in this way around the year 1000.

[3] Text in K. Neff, *Die Gedichte des Paulus Diaconus* (Munich, 1908), 124; Lindsay's 1913 edition, 1, 1930 edition, 76.

[4] For the hand and provenance, see Lindsay, 'The Farfa type', *Palaeographia Latina*, 3 (1924), 49–51; also E. Carusi, 'Cenni storici sull' Abbazia di Farfa', ibid. 52–9. Note that Lindsay thinks it not impossible that it was written in Yugoslavia (so 1930 edition). For evidence indicating that Italy had a fuller text of Festus in the tenth century, see B. Bischoff, 'Zu Plautus und Festus', *Philologus*, 87 (1932), 114–17; E. Fraenkel, 'Das Original der Cistellaria des Plautus', ibid. 117–20.

[5] Certainly before the fifteenth-century apographs were made. It would be extremely incautious to suppose that these copies represent a less damaged state of the text.

[6] It was said at the time to have come from 'Illyricum', i.e. Yugoslavia. On Rhallus (or Rhalles) see Cosenza, 3029–30; on Pomponius Laetus, ibid. 2906–14.

lamentable is the fate of the books now lost: for these we have only the brief digest of Paul the Deacon (whose text is well represented by comparatively early manuscripts). A comparison of those books where both Paul and Festus are extant shows the severity of the pruning done by the Carolingian scholar.

P. K. M.

FLORUS

The detailed history of the text of Florus has yet to be written,[1] and only the barest outline of the transmission can be given. In the ninth century Florus was known to Einhard and Freculph of Lisieux. In medieval library catalogues a copy is recorded in the early ninth century at Lorsch; in the eleventh at Chartres; in the twelfth at Bec, Corbie, and Limoges; in the fourteenth at Avignon and Rouen. In twelfth-century England Florus was known to Richard of Devizes, John of Salisbury, and Ralph of Diss.

The author's name is variously given as Iulius Florus (by B), or L. Annaeus Florus (by the majority of manuscripts in the other family). The title is likewise unclear: B has *Epithoma Iuli Flori De Tito Livio Bellorum Omnium Annorum Septingentorum Libri N Duo Feliciter*, whereas N has, more simply, *L. Annaei Flori Epitoma De Tito Livio Incipit Liber Primus Lege Feliciter*. The division of the work also presents problems: B divides it into two books (and is followed in this by most recent editors), while other manuscripts usually offer an arrangement in four books.

Besides relying upon actual manuscripts, the editor of Florus must clearly put great weight upon the massive dependence of Florus on Livy (whose text often allows us to restore the true reading in the later writer), and also upon later authors who use Florus. Important among these is the *Breviarium rerum gestarum populi Romani* of Rufius Festus,[2] but

---

In the confused state of the text, no edition is completely satisfactory. The most useful are: the Teubner texts of O. Jahn (1852), C. Halm (1854), O. Rossbach (1896), together with E. Malcovati (Rome, 1938; second edition, 1972), and the Budé text of P. Jal (2 vols., Paris, 1967). See also H. Nickel, 'Textkritisches zu den Florus-Inkunabeln', *Philologus*, 118 (1974), 166–73.

[1] Much useful evidence has been collected by E. Malcovati, 'Studi su Floro', *Athenaeum*, NS 15 (1937), 69–94. The claim that Florus was known in the ninth century to Servatus Lupus of Ferrières seems to be unfounded.

[2] The latest critical edition is by J. W. Eadie (London, 1967), who also discusses Festus' use of his sources.

of far greater weight is the evidence of Jordanes, who in the middle of the
sixth century excerpted Florus extensively for his *De summa temporum vel
origine actibusque gentis Romanorum*.[3] This text is rightly given the value of
an early manuscript, with the siglum I.

From a source not too dissimilar from I comes B (Bamberg Class. 31
(E.III. 22), of Italian origin, s. x[1] (Chatelain, plate CLXXXIII.1).[4] Since
its discovery in the early nineteenth century, B has been recognized as
being by far the best source for the text: its general superiority is evident
throughout, and one may note in particular B's preservation of the text
(where all others omit) at 2.18.2–6. Its text ends (a quarter of the way
down the page) with the word *profundo* (2.33.60). Its proximity to I
makes it useful to group I and B together as deriving from a common
lost text [A].

The other class [C][5] comes from a text which had lost a leaf containing
2.18.2–6. Of the very large number[6] of manuscripts in this class only the
most important need be mentioned here. They are:

N   Heidelberg, Pal. lat. 894, s. IX, formerly at the monastery of St.
        Nazarius at Lorsch and possibly written there.
Harl. British Library, Harley 2620, s. XI,[7] eastern France or western
        Germany, formerly at Cues.
G   Paris n.a. lat. 1767, s. XI, France.
H   Heidelberg, Pal. lat. 1568, s. X/XI.
L   Leiden, Voss. Lat. O.14, s. X/XI (French?).
U   Berne 249, s. XI, France.
M   Munich Clm 6392, formerly at Freising, s. XI/XII.
P   Paris lat. 7701, s. XII.
Q   Paris lat. 5802, s. XII (written at Chartres, given by Philip of Bayeux
        to Bec, later owned by Petrarch).
J   Paris lat. 18273, s. XIII.
Voss. Leiden Voss. Lat. O.77, s. XI (France, belonged to La-Chaise-Dieu
        in the fifteenth century).
Y   Paris lat. 18104, s. XII[2], formerly at Notre-Dame in Paris, containing
        extracts only; compiled probably at Chartres, see Rouse and
        Maslowski, *IMU* 22 (1979), 97–122.

The interrelationships of the manuscripts of the [C] family have not
yet been satisfactorily established.[8] Their unique ancestor demon-

---

[3] Critical edition by Mommsen, *MGH, Auct. Ant.* v.1 (1882), who clearly presents all passages
where Jordanes borrows from Florus.
[4] The provenance and dating are those given by B. Bischoff (quoted by Jal, i. cxv n. 2); others
have dated it s. IX[1] and viewed it as German.
[5] This class, or something close to it, seems to have been the text of Florus used by Orosius. See
Rossbach, xxiv–xxv.   [6] See Malcovati, op. cit. n. 1, above.
[7] The dating of this manuscript is much disputed, with estimates ranging from the tenth to the
thirteenth century. The date given here is that communicated by Professor B. Munk Olsen.
[8] Jal in his Introduction, cxxxi ff., produces many interesting suggestions, but his final *stemma
codicum* (to face p. clx) is not always convincing. See the review by Malcovati, *Gnomon*, 42 (1970).
275: 'rimango tuttavia scettica sulla legittimità e utilità dello stemma'.

strably suffered from a dislocation of the text at 1.27.3 and 1.40.10, a displacement which some representatives have tried to remedy (of those here cited M and *Voss.*). It is significant that HJY (and other later texts) carry the so-called 'Prologue' (of unknown origin) on the author of the *Epitome.*

Errors common to [A] and [C] demonstrate their derivation from a single copy (presumably in late Antiquity).

P.K.M.

FRONTINUS

De aquis
Strategemata

De aquis

'Impensa monumenti supervacua est: memoria nostri durabit si vita meruimus' (Frontinus ap. Plin. *Ep.* 9.19.6). *Durat memoria.*

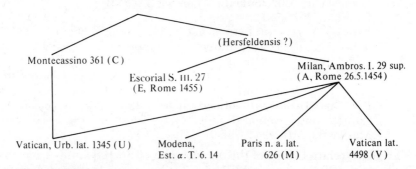

So C. Kunderewicz in the latest edition (Teubner, Leipzig, 1973), viii. The only extant manuscript older than s. xv is C, written at Montecassino *c.*1132–3 mainly by Peter the Deacon.[1] Its antiquity and its loan to Poggio in 1429[2] may have helped to persuade many scholars that all

---

[1] 'Ut ex opusculis adiunctis conicio Petri Diaconi manu scriptus est' Lucas Holstenius (1596–1661), Vatican, Barb. lat. 121 f. 41ʳ; A. Amelli in C. Herschel's edition (Boston, 1899), xviii–xix; H. Bloch, *AJP* 69 (1948), 74; P. Meyvaert, *BRL* 38 (1955–6), 114–38, especially 124 n. 1, 125 n. 1.

[2] Sabbadini, *SIFC* 7 (1899), 132–3. On 9 July 1429 Poggio writes: 'Portavi volumen hoc mecum ut transcribam libellum Frontini, cum sit mendosus et pessimis litteris, adeo ut vix queam legere' (*Ep.* 1, p. 284).

the other manuscripts derive from it; but V and M had supporters even before L. Rubio found manuscripts worthier of support, A and E, and argued their independence of C.[3] An old source for AE lay ready to hand in one of two manuscripts reported from 'monasterio Hispildensi' (Hersfeld) in 1425:[4]

'Iulii Frontini de aquae ductis quae in urbem inducunt liber i. Incipit sic: "Persecutus ea . . ." (ch. 64). Continet hic liber xiii.'

'Item eiusdem Frontini liber. Incipit sic: "Cum omnis res . . ." (ch. 1). Continet xi folia.'

Whether or not these *libri* were two parts of the same volume,[5] a manuscript from Hersfeld or Fulda could easily have entered circulation in s. XV, either by crossing the Alps or, for instance, by being brought to the Council of Basle in the 1430s. It would doubtless have dated back at least to s. XI, when connections between Montecassino and Germany, Fulda in particular, are well documented.[6]

Unfortunately Rubio's elegant demonstration that V and M derive from A must be reckoned the sum of his achievement. Kunderewicz does not add to the six fifteenth-century manuscripts known when Rubio wrote, but here are five more:

B   Berlin (East), Hamilton 254 (ch., s. XV^2/$_4$).
O   Vatican, Ottob. lat. 2089 (ch., s. XV^2/$_3$).
F   Vatican lat. 5122 (ch., 1468).[7]
H   British Library, Harley 5216 (ch., s. XV^2).
S   Siena L.V.26 (ch., s. XV^4/$_4$).

The stemma of all eleven, together with the *editio princeps*, is this:[8]

---

[3] *Emerita*, 31 (1963), 21–41. Poor photographs of AE accompany the article.

[4] Sabbadini, *Storia e critica*², 7, 194–5; R. P. Robinson, *CPh* 16 (1921), 252.

[5] Bloch (n. 1, above), 76–7, assumed that they were and inferred that any descendant ought to have the two books in the wrong order; but the proportion between the two books in the surviving manuscripts is 1:2, not 11:13, and there are ways round the inference in any case. His statement that V shares none of the errors reported from the Hersfeldensis in ch. 1 and ch. 64 rests on Grimal's silence; in fact it shares p. 1.4 *mihi nunc* and p. 25.20 *principium*.

[6] E. A. Lowe, *Casinensia* (Montecassino, 1929), 268–70 = *Pal. Papers*, i.298–9; H Bloch, *CPh* 36 (1941), 185–7; L. D. R., *CQ* 62 (1968), 370 n. 1. Reservations are expressed by G. Cavallo in his useful survey 'La trasmissione dei testi nell' area beneventano-cassinese', *Settimane*, 22 (1975), 389–91; ibid. 397–9, he observes that many manuscripts written at Montecassino in s. XI-XII, among them C, 'sono derivati da modelli in via di deterioramento, di regola mutili', and suggests that these had been decaying at Montecassino itself since s. VIII/IX.

[7] Cf. J. Ruysschaert, *La bibliofilia*, 60 (1958), 353 no. 107. The hand that wrote Frontinus continues to the end of Festus, where it gives the date 20 August 1468 (f. 65ᵛ).

[8] I have established the stemma below A with the aid of microfilms very kindly lent to me by Dr W.-W. Ehlers, who will shortly publish his own results; I had already collated enough of the other manuscripts. R. H. Rodgers, *BICS* 25 (1978), 101–5, rightly challenged Rubio's arguments for the independence of E but wrongly followed Grimal in deriving M from V (M, incidentally, was written not in 1475 but no later; the date 'xvi Iu. 1475' occurs in a marginal note by another hand on p. 40); he missed BOFHS and did not commit himself on U and the Estensis. Both Grimal's apparatus and Kunderewicz's are totally inadequate foundations for an assessment of the tradi-

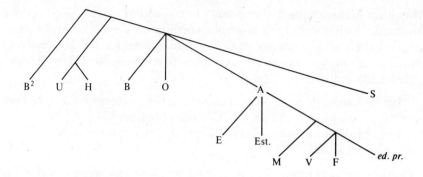

The copy of A that gave rise to MVF and the *editio princeps* would have
won no prizes for accuracy. Of BOAS the most accurate and most
interesting is B, a largely epigraphical miscellany owned by Pietro
Donato († 1447), who corrected Frontinus partly by conjecture and
partly from a manuscript; B^2 is his hand.[9] U, Florentine calligraphy of
the 1470s,[10] outclasses its brother H. Any case against deriving BU and
their fellows from C must rest on readings of their archetype and not, as
it has hitherto done, on readings peculiar to A, which makes emendations, or still worse to VM, which make more.

No passage better illustrates the problem than Frontinus' announcement of what the work will embrace.[11] C presents it as follows (p. 2.7–16
Kund.):

> nomina primum aquarum quae in urbem Romam influant ponam;
> tum . . .; dein . . .; post altitudinem cuiusque modulorumque erogationes
> habiles factae sint quantum extra urbem quantum urbem unicuique
> regioni pro suo modo unaquaeque aquarum serviat

> Romam *del.* B^2
> influant C (?): influunt BU
> modulorumque C: modulorumque rationem BU
> erogationes habiles CB^2: habilis erogationes BU
> factae sint C: *om.* BU
> quantum urbem C: quantum in urbe B^2: quantum intra BU
> unicuique regioni CB^2: quisque modus cuique regioni B: quisque modus
> cuique regioni serviat in urbe unicuique regioni U

tion, and not just because they exclude BOFHS: in Kunderewicz's I have found too many errors
and omissions to list, and his text has others (7.20 *relicto* for *reliquo*, 9.25 *suo* for *sui*, 11.16 the first
passuum for *passus*, 26.20 *ad* om. before *caput*, 32.6 *adquisitionum* for *-em*, and doubtless more). About
one false report of C not peculiar to Kunderewicz, p. 33.16 *sunt* for *si inter*, I have written in *Liverpool
Classical Monthly*, 6.5 (1981), 141–2.

[9] Dr A. C. de la Mare identified it.
[10] Dr de la Mare attributes it to Francesco Contugi.
[11] Oddly Rodgers does not discuss it, even though it contains a word and a phrase that should
have swelled his list of words found in A but not in C (p. 103).

Buecheler, the first editor to found his text solely on C (Leipzig, 1858), made sense of C here by marking a lacuna after *modulorumque* (to be filled by *rationes; denique quae*), reading *ab illis* for *habiles*, and supplying *intra* before the second *urbem*; but Kunderewicz accepts from A *rationem* (BU), *ab illis erogationes* (conjecture), *intra* (BU), and *quisque modus cuique regioni* (B) with *modis* (Rubio) for *modus*. The strongest argument in all this for the independence of BU is *habilis*, closer than *habiles* to *ab illis*; if they are independent, B² will derive from C, with some conjecture thrown in, while the last variant in U suggests collation or conjecture in an ancestor, more likely conjecture, because other signs of contamination are lacking. On the other hand *influunt* in BU could be a misinterpretation of *influant* in C, which is less than clear. How then can the problem be solved?

Compelling enough examples of misinterpretation will surely solve it. Only one has yet been cited (the first in the following list),[12] but several more are available:

(1) At p. 54.15, C has *Pile*, BU *parve*. In C, however, something like + that apparently belongs to the line below makes *P* look like *p*.

(2) At p. 41.24, C has *copiam et grā*, BU *copiam et etiam gratia*. Before the scribe of C wrote his usual compendium for *et*, he had mistakenly written a full stop; instead of erasing this, he wrote the compendium on top of it. The result is at first sight puzzling, and a fifteenth-century scribe might easily have been torn between *et* and *etiam* and written down both in a way open to misinterpretation.[13]

(3) At p. 54.2, C first attached *in recentibus* to what precedes and then superimposed a capital *I* slightly to the left of *i*. The result is again puzzling, and BU have *ideo*.

(4) At p. 53.4, where the true reading is *commoda* (B²), C has *Quom^a* (previously *Quoͫ*) with two lines of deletion through *Quom*. BU have nothing.

(5) At p. 53.19, BU have *id* for *vel*. In C the *u* meets the *t* in a way that invites this misinterpretation.

(6) Listing twenty-five sizes of pipe, Frontinus says of ten *in usu non est*. C abbreviates now *non*, now *est*, now both, now neither, and its spacing is erratic. BU have *unde* for *-u ñ* in the first two places where C writes *ñ*, in both of which the spacing invites this misinterpretation (p. 21.15, 22.9).

(7) At p. 53.27–9, the third *que* of the four has suffered in C from

---

[12] Rodgers, ibid., though he does not present it as compellingly as he might have done. His other two examples cut no ice, because any manuscript could have made *cilvo* look like *alvo* (more so than C does, in fact) and abbreviated *latera* in the same way.

[13] I am grateful to Dr Ehlers for first drawing my attention to this reading of BU, which Kunderewicz neglects to report from A.

damp or wear at the lower corner of the page and looks at first sight
more like *quo*. Only such an accident could have led to *quo* in BU.

(8) At p. 37.11, as elsewhere, C encloses the figure *I* between dots;
the one to the left, clumsily written, is almost as large as the *I*. BU have
II.

(9) The form of the figure *V* in C, not completely constant, invites
just such misinterpretations as *li* (pp. 21.9, 24.13), *ii* (pp. 25.8, 16,
35.14, 38.25), and *vi* (pp. 25.4, 34.18).

The supporters of the fifteenth-century tradition, then, have fought a
losing battle, and it cannot go back to the Hersfeldensis unless the
Hersfeldensis was a copy of C. As there is no external evidence that the
Hersfeldensis ever entered circulation, Poggio should be given the
credit for the diffusion of the text. Exactly how it came about is not clear.
He kept Niccoli abreast of his dealings with C,[14] and Traversari testifies
that it was still at Rome in 1432;[15] but none of the manuscripts can be
connected more than speculatively with either. B[2], which agrees with C
against BU in passages (1), (3), (4), and (6), must derive from C by a
route of its own, conceivably even through the Hersfeldensis.[16]

The first edition, prepared by Pomponio Leto and Giovanni Sulpizio
da Veroli, appeared at Rome together with Vitruvius in the pontificate
of Innocent VIII (1484–92), who spent heavily on buildings;[17] 'quid
aliud novi huic est saeculo reliquum', asks Sulpizio, 'nisi ut aut fontes
inducantur aut theatrum aedificetur?' What amounts to the second
edition (Florence, 1513) brought a great improvement; its editor, the
eminent architect Giovanni Giocondo, plainly used the very distinctive
text of B + B[2], and indeed his hand can be seen emending two or three
passages in B.[18] Another professional, G. Poleni, founded his edition
(Padua, 1722) on CUV. By the time that a hydraulic engineer from
New York, C. Herschel, engagingly made amends for his leaky memory
of Latin by adorning his edition (Boston, 1899) with a complete facsimile of C,[19] technical and scholarly accomplishment in the editing of
Frontinus had drifted apart, and so far the twentieth century cannot
pride itself on either.[20]

M. D. R.

---

[14] *Ep.* I, pp. 154, 155, 159, 167, 170, 284, 295, 304.

[15] Sabbadini, *SIFC* 7 (1899), 133.

[16] A. C. de la Mare, *Trans. Camb. Bibliog. Soc.* 7.2 (1978), 221, shows that the scribe of B worked
for Donato at Basle.

[17] Of the two versions that came from Roman presses at this time – Flodr, *Frontinus* 1 and 2 – 2 is
anonymous and lacks Vitruvius but has the same title as the less rare 1 ('. . . libellus mirabilis').

[18] My surmise ('not impossible' A. C. de la Mare). Did the epigraphical portions of B go into
Giocondo's own *Sylloge*?

[19] M. Inguánez published another (Montecassino, 1930).

[20] Rodgers promises an edition and commentary.

Strategemata

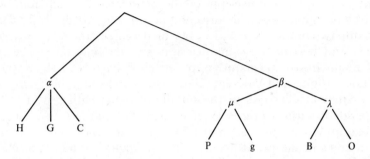

When Paul the Deacon took Eutropius' *Breviarium* as his nucleus and expanded it into his *Historia Romana*, he added five of Frontinus' *stratege-mata*,[1] not enough, unfortunately, to tell us what sort of text he had at his disposal. But the text of Frontinus, unlike that of Eutropius, to which it is at times closely linked, does not appear to have circulated in Italy until reintroduced from the north. In the Carolingian period the arche-type[2] of our extant manuscripts lay north of the Alps, and its descend-ants split into two families. The first seems to be associated with eastern France, the second spreads from northern France to England.

The best manuscript by far and the only complete witness of the better family (α) is British Library, Harley 2666 (H), written in the second quarter of the ninth century in eastern France.[3] The other two α witnesses are both florilegia; for Frontinus' array of exempla is easily culled, and it must be admitted that a little military one-upmanship goes a long way. One is Gotha Membr.1.101, s. IX, formerly at Murbach[4] and known as G. The other is the *Collectaneum* of Sedulius Scottus (C), preserved in a twelfth-century manuscript which may well have come from St. James's Liège (Cues, Nikolaus Hospitalbibliothek 52[5]). Sedulius was himself active at Liège about the middle of the ninth

For our knowledge of the manuscripts of the *Strategemata* we are still dependent on G. Gundermann: on his monograph *De Iuli Frontini Strategematon libro qui fertur quarto* (*Commentationes Philologae Ienenses*, i (Leipzig, 1881), 83–161) and on his edition, *Iuli Frontini Strategematon libri quattuor* (Leipzig, 1888). G. Bendz, *Frontin, Kriegslisten* (Berlin, 1963) offers an up-to-date text, but has nothing to add to the recension except some readings from a manuscript at Uppsala (presum-ably Univ. C. 193), of no particular merit. The *editio princeps* was printed by Eucharius Silber (Rome, 1487).

[1] 2.2.7; 2.11.5; 4.5.4, 5, 6.
[2] In the archetype parts of Book 2 (9.8–10, 10, 11, 12.1–2) were put at the end of 4.
[3] See *Catalogue of Ancient Manuscripts in the British Museum*, Part ii (London, 1884), 72, tab. 56. I am grateful to Professor Bischoff for information about date and provenance.
[4] See EUTROPIUS, n. 5.
[5] J. Klein, *Über eine Handschrift des Nicolaus von Cues* (Berlin, 1866), especially 87–91; S. Hellmann, *Neues Archiv*, 30 (1904), 17–33.

century, though he also had contact with other centres in Germany and eastern France.

The remaining manuscripts of the *Strategemata*, which number a hundred or more, appear to descend from the inferior family β.[6] β itself splits into two branches (μ and λ), of which μ carries the better text. The earliest and best of the μ manuscripts and the only one to be cited individually in Gundermann's apparatus is P, Paris lat. 7240, s. XI. It is of French origin, and Paris lat. 5802, which appears to be a copy of it, was written at Chartres in the middle of the twelfth century.[7] One independent witness of μ is Wolfenbüttel, Gud. lat. 16 (g), a French manuscript written in 1332 'manu Bricii briton(ici) clerici'.

λ emerges in the twelfth century as an Anglo-Norman text. Harley 2729 (B), s. XII, appears to be a French manuscript; Oxford, Lincoln College Lat. 100 (O) is the well-known book containing Frontinus, Vegetius, and Eutropius which was written at Malmesbury c.1125[8] by William and his collaborators. To these may be added a third twelfth-century manuscript, Cambridge, Peterhouse 252,[9] s. XII[1], which could be French or English. A manuscript containing Frontinus is also listed in the catalogue of Christ Church Canterbury compiled for Henry of Eastry (Prior 1284–1331);[10] if this was part of the twelfth-century library, as it may well have been, it was presumably another member of the same group. To the same context belongs the extensive use of Frontinus made by John of Salisbury in his *Policraticus*,[11] and Canterbury may indeed have provided the parent manuscript of this small English tradition.[12] Texts of the *Strategemata* were far-flung in the twelfth century, even if not available in any numbers; for Wibald of Corvey was able to send a copy to Rainald, Prior of Hildesheim, c.1149.[13] It did not become a common text until the fourteenth century, and its later circulation, which is connected with that of other military texts, may repay further investigation.

L. D. R.

[6] So the evidence available suggests, but a large number of later manuscripts have not in fact been inspected.

[7] Attributed to Chartres by François Avril; cf. *IMU* 22 (1979), 121 n. 2.

[8] See EUTROPIUS, n. 9.

[9] Part III of a composite manuscript. It was known to Gundermann (monograph, 109), but dated to the fourteenth century.

[10] No. 267 'Vitruvius, Frontinus de preparatoriis bellicis, Vegetius, Palladius': M. R. James, *The Ancient Libraries of Canterbury and Dover* (Cambridge, 1903), xxxix, 47.

[11] See the preface to Gundermann's edition, xi–xii; C. C. J. Webb, *Ioannis Saresberiensis Episcopi Carnotensis Policratici libri VIII* (Oxford, 1919), xxxiii; J. Martin, 'John of Salisbury's Manuscripts of Frontinus and Gellius', *JWI* 40 (1977), 1–26.

[12] John of Salisbury was using a text closer to O than to any other extant manuscript, and it is possible that William had originally taken his text from a copy at Canterbury: so Janet Martin, op. cit.

[13] P. Jaffé, *Bibliotheca rerum Germanicarum*, i (Berlin, 1864), 328, *epist.* 208.

FRONTO

Fronto was cut to pieces in the Dark Ages. Any author may fall on hard times, when parchment is scarce and other texts are more in demand, but to Fronto belongs the unique distinction of surviving solely as the lower script in no fewer than three palimpsests.

The first preserves a few words from the end of his *Gratiarum actio pro Carthaginiensibus*. It is part of that remarkable manuscript Vatican, Pal. lat. 24, which is a tissue of ancient codices, largely of classical authors and Italian in origin, which were reused in Italy to make up a copy of the Old Testament.[1] The Fronto fragment (ff. 46 and 53, *CLA* I. 72) is written in rustic capitals of s. IV–V; the text was discovered by Angelo Mai in 1820 and published by him in 1823.[2]

The extensive remains of Fronto's *Correspondence* are transmitted as the lower script of Milan, Ambros. E.147 sup. + Vatican lat. 5750,[3] written in an uncial hand of the later fifth century, presumably in Italy; it was rewritten in the seventh century, probably at Bobbio, where it was later housed, with a Latin translation of the Acts of the Council of Chalcedon. Both parts were discovered by Mai, the Ambrosian in 1815, the Vatican in 1819, and published in 1815 and 1823 respectively. The first, in particular, suffered disastrously from his heavy use of chemical reagents.

It seemed, until 1956, that further gains to Fronto's text could come only from strenuous emendation and decipherment;[4] but in that year Bernhard Bischoff pointed out[5] that a third manuscript, published as early as 1750 and conjecturally ascribed to Fronto (then undiscovered) by Dom Tassin in the *Nouveau traité de diplomatique*,[6] contained fragments of *Epist. ad Verum*, 2.1 which actually overlap with the Milan palimpsest. This is one leaf of Paris lat. 12161 (pp. 133–4, *CLA* V. 629), rewritten,

---

[1] For the complicated composition and history of this manuscript, see J. Fohlen, 'Recherches sur le manuscrit palimpseste Vatican, Pal. lat. 24', *Scrittura e civiltà*, 3 (1979), 195–222.

[2] Recently edited by M. van den Hout in his *M. Cornelii Frontonis Epistulae*, i (Leiden, 1954), 241 f.; for further bibliography, ibid. lxxxi f.

[3] 282 leaves, *CLA* III, p. 19, + 106 leaves, *CLA* I. 27. The Milan palimpsest now has a new shelf-mark: S.P. 9/1, 6, 11. There is a complete fascimile of the Vaticanus in [F. Ehrle] *M. Cornelii Frontonis aliorumque reliquiae quae codice Vaticano 5750 rescripto continentur* (Codices e Vaticanis Selecti, vii), Milan, 1906. An interesting feature of this manuscript is the activity of the corrector, who signed himself Caecilius and worked on the manuscript probably about AD 500. The autograph subscription which names him is no longer legible and we are dependent on Mai's drawing of it. For a study of this valuable example of ancient *emendatio*, see van den Hout, xl ff.; J. E. G. Zetzel, 'The Subscriptions in the Manuscripts of Livy and Fronto and the Meaning of *Emendatio*', *CPh* 75 (1980), 38–59.

[4] For the history of the decipherment and editing of Fronto, see van den Hout, lxvii ff.

[5] 'Der Fronto-Palimpsest der Mauriner,' *SBAW* 1958.2. This entails a reordering of the fragments of *Ad Verum*, 2.1.   [6] pp. 144 ff.

probably at Corbie, in the late seventh or early eighth century with Jerome and Gennadius, *De viris illustribus*. The original script, a sixth-century uncial, may perhaps belong to southern France, in which case we have what could be a remnant of the last flowering of rhetorical studies in Gaul.

L. D. R.

GAIUS

The text of Gaius' *Institutiones* rests almost exclusively on a palimpsest, Verona, Chapter Library XV (13) (V: *CLA* IV.488), discovered by B. G. Niebuhr in 1816. The lower script is uncial of the fifth century, and all but about a twelfth has been read.[1] The *editio princeps* was that of I. F. L. Goschen (Berlin, 1820), but a major role was played by W. Studemund (Leipzig, 1874, with supplements in *Collectio librorum iuris anteiustiniani*, i[5] (Berlin, 1905), xvii–xxxix).

More recently, two sets of fragments have been discovered on papyrus: London, Egypt Exploration Society, P.Oxy. 2103 (*CLA* Suppl. 1716),[2] cursive, s. II–III (O), and Florence, Laur. P.S.I. 1182 (*CLA* III.292), uncial, s. V–VI (F).

M. W.

[1] Fascimile published in Anon. [A. Spagnolo], ed., *Gai codex rescriptus in bibliotheca capitulari ecclesiae cathedralis Veronensis cura et studio eiusdem bibliothecae custodis phototypice expressus* (Leipzig, 1909). The standard text is that of E. Seckel-B. Keubler (Leipzig, 1939[8]), but we also have M. David's *editio minor* (Leiden, 1964[2]), based on the fuller edition of David and H. L. W. Nelson, with text and philological commentary (Leiden, 1954–   ).

[2] *CLA* reports 'could not be located in 1965'. But it is safe, in the Ashmolean Library, Oxford.

GALLUS

Fate, so unkind to one of Rome's major poets, has made some small amends.[1] It granted that fragments of the elegiac poetry of Cornelius Gallus should survive in the remains of a papyrus roll which a Roman officer, serving in the very province which the poet had ruled, had brought to solace his hours of duty in the outpost of Qaṣr Ibrîm, some 150 miles south of Aswan. It also arranged that the first of the nine surviving lines should contain an address to the poet's mistress Lycoris; even a schoolboy, with his basic knowledge of who loved whom, could have promptly identified the author. Cast on to the rubbish-dump when the camp was evacuated, perhaps in 20 BC, the book remained buried until a fragment came to light in 1978, in the excavations carried out under the aegis of the Egypt Exploration Society.[2]

The papyrus is at least as remarkable for what it is as for what it contains. Most probably written in the period *c.*50 – 20 BC, it is in any case, with P. Herc. 817,[3] our oldest manuscript of Latin poetry. Elegantly produced, with the pentameters indented, consistent interpunction, and an early orthography (most strikingly EI for long I), it gives us a sample of the books in which a writer of the Augustan period actually saw his works circulating.

L. D. R.

[1] Some took fate into their own hands: the *Elegies* of Maximianus were attributed to Gallus in a group of fifteenth-century manuscripts and appeared under his name in one of the early printed editions (by Pomponius Gauricus, Venice, 1501). For this and other manifestations of pseudo-Gallus in the fifteenth and sixteenth centuries, see W. Schetter, *Studien zur Überlieferung und Kritik des Elegikers Maximian* (Wiesbaden, 1970), 70–4.

[2] First published by R. D. Anderson, P. J. Parsons, and R. G. M. Nisbet, 'Elegiacs by Gallus from Qaṣr Ibrîm', *JRS* 69 (1979), 125–55 (with three plates). P. Qaṣr Ibrîm will eventually be housed in Cairo Museum.

[3] *CLA* III. 385, containing the anonymous *Carmen de Bello Actiaco*. This manuscript, now in the Biblioteca Nazionale at Naples except for a fragment (presented to Napoleon) in the Musée du Louvre, must have been written between the Battle of Actium (31 BC) and the eruption of Vesuvius which entombed it (AD 79). It was excavated in 1752 and unrolled in 1805.

AULUS GELLIUS

Written in the latter half of the second century AD, the *Noctes Atticae* enjoyed great success in Antiquity itself.[1] The list of writers who used this vast compilation includes Apuleius (*De mundo*, 13–14), Lactantius[2] (*Epit. inst. div.* 24.5), Nonius (*passim*), Ammianus Marcellinus (*passim*), the *Historia Augusta* (28.1.1), Macrobius (who, without mentioning his name, quotes Gellius verbatim throughout the *Saturnalia*, and is thus of the highest value for the text), Servius (*Aen.* 5.738; see also on *Georg.* 1.260 and *Aen.* 7.740), and Augustine (*De civ. Dei* 9.4). To late Antiquity presumably belong the verses to be found before Book 10:

C. Aurelii Romuli[3]

Cecropias noctes, doctorum exempla uirorum,
Donat habere mihi nobilis Eustochius.
Viuat et aeternum laetus bona tempora ducat,
Qui sic dilecto tanta docenda dedit.

To the fourth century[4] belongs our oldest manuscript A (Vatican, Pal. lat. 24), a palimpsest, in which Gellius (the original text) is in splendid rustic capitals, apparently written in Italy, and bearing the scribal notice 'COTTA. .SCRIBSIT'. This precious fragment contains large parts of Books 1 and 2, and smaller portions of 3 and 4. As it also has the lemmata to 17 and 18 presented continuously, it is a fair assumption that A originally contained (in how many volumes it is impossible to say) the whole twenty books, with the lemmata correctly preceding the entire work.

With the collapse of Antiquity came the disappearance of Gellius: he is quite unknown, for example, to Isidore and Bede. At this same time must have come the split in the transmission, whereby Books 1–7 circulated separately from 9–20 – a time which also saw the loss of all of

---

The fundamental edition is that of M. Hertz, *editio maior*, Berlin, 1883–5 (2 vols.). This was followed by the Teubner text of C. Hosius (1903), although Hosius did no independent work on the manuscripts. The most recent full critical text is the OCT of P. K. M. (1968, 2 vols.). Still in progress is the Budé text of R. Marache, of which two volumes have so far appeared (Books 1–10). Two English translations have been done: by W. Beloe (London, 1795, 3 vols.) and by J. C. Rolfe (Loeb Classical Library, 1929, 3 vols.).

[1] Still fundamental for Antiquity (as well as the Middle Ages) is M. Hertz, *ed. maior*, ii. v ff. For the Middle Ages, see also Manitius, *Geschichte, passim*.
[2] See R. M. Ogilvie, *The Library of Lactantius* (Oxford, 1978), 46–7.
[3] The identity of Romulus and Eustochius has yet to be discovered.
[4] *CLA* I.74. This manuscript was much damaged in the nineteenth century by the use of chemical reagents. See J. Fohlen, 'Recherches sur le manuscrit palimpseste Vatican, Pal. lat. 24', *Scrittura e civiltà*, 3 (1979), 195–222.

Book 8 (including the lemmata), the lemmata to Book 19 and many of those to 20, and the end of the work (20.10.7 – 11.5).

It is therefore necessary to examine first the circulation of Books 1–7. Evidence has recently[5] come to light suggesting that by the second half of the ninth century a text of Books 1–7 existed in northern France. It may very well be that this manuscript was at or near Laon.[6] However, it is not until the twelfth century[7] that the text of Books 1–7 begins to circulate freely. Our primary witnesses are four in number:

V   Vatican lat. 3452, s. XII[2], written in France. It lacks the Preface, but ff. 1–56 contain the whole of Books 1–7.

C   Cambridge, Clare College 26, s. XIII[2]/4, written in the south of England (possibly at St. Albans).[8] It originally contained the Preface and Books 1–7 complete (with Books 6 and 7 reversed), but has now suffered loss at the end, breaking off at 6.16.4 *hec sunt ferme*. Clearly deriving from the same source as V, this text is remarkable for containing the emendations of an unknown (presumably twelfth-century, French) scholar. It is also invaluable as a check upon V for the final stretches of Book 7, where hitherto V has been the only witness earlier than the fifteenth century.

P   Paris lat. 5765, ff. 61ᵛ–111ᵛ, s. XII[2], written in France. After the Preface and the first nineteen lemmata to Book 1, this manuscript breaks off (leaving half a column blank) to begin again with 1.2.11 *Δείκνυε*: it ends 7.4.3 with the words *ictus solis*.

R   Leiden, Gronov. 21, s. XII, possibly written in northern France. It omits all the lemmata, and ends 6.20.6 *amariores*.

Of textual importance for Books 1–7 and 9–20 are two anthologies, which survive in several witnesses. The first of these, containing substantial excerpts from Valerius Maximus and Gellius, has the following representatives:

S   Cambridge, Trinity College 982 (R.16.34), written at Salisbury Cathedral around 1100. This book was once in the hands of Richard Bentley, who relied upon it for some of his emendations.

T   Paris lat. 4952, s. XII, French ('Liber sancti Arnulfi').

Y   Vatican lat. 3307, s. XII, French.
     A recently discovered text, which has yet to be evaluated: Bremen C.41, s. XII.

---

[5] This evidence is uncertain, and awaits further investigation before it can be published.

[6] The figure of Martin Hiberniensis (819–75) seems to be connected with this text. On this period at Laon see John J. Contreni, *The Cathedral School of Laon from 850–930. Its Manuscripts and Masters*, Munich, 1978 (= Münchener Beiträge zur Mediävistik und Renaissance-Forschung, 29).

[7] For a fuller history of the transmission of Books 1–7, see P. K. M., Janet Martin, R. H. R., 'Clare College Ms 26 and the Circulation of Aulus Gellius 1–7 in England and France', *Mediaeval Studies*, 42 (1980), 353–94.

[8] C has only recently been brought to light (see note 7), and has yet to be used in an edition. It has much to offer.

To these four representatives may be added excerpts in Bonn S 218
(s. XI, but the excerpts are s. XII), and Vatican lat. 4808
(s. XV).

The second anthology (Φ), which for Books 1–7 clearly derives from an
ancestor of P, has to be reconstructed from four witnesses.

K Oxford, Bodleian Library, Rawl. G. 139, ff. 152^v–154^v, s. XII[1],
  associated with William of Malmesbury.

L Oxford, Bodleian Library, Lat. class. d. 39 (formerly London, Sion
  College, Arc. L. 40.2/L.21), s. XII¾, written in England.
  The extracts to be found in the *Polyhistor* of William of Malmesbury
  (d. 1143).
  The extracts in the *Policraticus* of John of Salisbury (finished in 1159).

Of interest also are the extracts to be found in the *Florilegium Gallicum*,
which was compiled s. XII med. in the region of Orléans; the *Abbreuiationes
Chronicorum* of Ralph of Diss (d. 1202), at one time Canon of St. Paul's
Cathedral; the *Manipulus Florum* of Thomas of Ireland, composed at the
Sorbonne *c*.1300; marginal annotations in Berne 276 (s. XIII med.).
 For the text of Books 9–20 the evidence is fuller and earlier.[9]
The manuscripts may be divided into three families:

Family i

F Leeuwarden 55, written in 836 at Fulda,[10] in a large number of hands. It
  was copied (at the instruction of Hrabanus Maurus) from a text lent
  to Servatus Lupus[11] by Einhard (who was then living in retirement in
  Seligenstadt). Despite its impressive origin, F has no known progeny
  or influence in the Middle Ages.

Family ii (γ)

O Vatican, Reg. lat. 597, s. IX[1], once in the hands of Servatus Lupus,
  whose corrections and annotations are to be found throughout.[12] The
  text now begins at 9.14.2 *grammaticam facie dicitur* and ends 20.6.12
  pars uestrorum intellegit, the last folio having been almost entirely lost.

X Leiden, Voss. Lat. F. 112, s. X, written in France, possibly in the

---

[9] For the circulation of Books 9–20 in general, and the manuscripts Π and G in particular, see
A. C. de la Mare, P. K. M., R. H. R., 'Pietro da Montagnana and the Text of Aulus Gellius in Paris
B. N. lat. 13038', *Scriptorium*, 30 (1976), 219–25, with plates of G. To known early witnesses to
Books 9–20 may be added two leaves from a manuscript (s. XI[2]) made for Egmond by Abbot
Stephen (died 1083), Brussels IV.625; and possibly the item in the newly discovered Lobbes
catalogue (for acquisitions between 1074 and 1150), if this does not refer to Books 1–7. See the
references in op. cit. n. 7 above, 378.

[10] G. I. Lieftinck, 'Le Ms d'Aulu-Gelle à Leeuwarden exécuté à Fulda en 836', *Bullettino dell'
'Archivio Paleografico Italiano'*, NS 1 (1955), 11–17 (with eleven plates).

[11] *Epist.* 1 and 5.

[12] Luanne Meagher, *The Gellius Manuscript of Lupus of Ferrières* (Chicago, 1936, with plates),
demonstrates that Lupus often corrects from a source close to X.

region of Chartres, and apparently to be found in the area of Provins[13] in the thirteenth century.

Π Vatican, Reg. lat. 1646, written in 1170 by a Willelmus who can be identified with Willelmus Anglicus, the scribe of a Valerius Maximus (Paris lat. 9688) written in 1167 for Henry Count of Champagne. Π was almost certainly copied from a manuscript from the Benedictine house of St. Columba near Sens. A *gemellus* of Π is G (Paris lat. 13038, possibly the manuscript left to Canterbury by Thomas Becket), which a future editor might well consider using in place of Π.

N   Florence, Bibl. Naz., Conv. Soppr. J.IV.26 (formerly Magl. 329), written by Niccolò Niccoli in, or just before, 1431, and possibly taken from a ninth-century exemplar. The common assertion[14] that the Greek was put in by Ambrogio Traversari would appear to be mistaken, as the Greek hand seems to be that of Niccoli himself.[15]

Family iii (δ)

Q   Paris lat. 8664, s. XIII[1], written in France.
Z   Leiden, Voss. Lat. F. 7, s. XII ex., written in France, possibly at Chartres.
B   s. XII[2], which is incomplete,[16] and is split into two parts: Berne 404 and Leiden, B.P.L. 1925.

The precise interrelationship of the three families, F γ δ, has yet to be worked out, although it seems safe to say that the esteem formerly given to δ is largely unjustified. Like F, δ had no progeny (with the single exception of Göttingen Philol. 162, s. XV, an unfinished text ending at 14.1.22), while γ was clearly the source of the Renaissance copies.

Early in the fifteenth century, the practice was adopted of regularly uniting the two halves of the text in a single volume.[17] To this period also is to be ascribed the rediscovery of the lemmata to Book 8, and the end of Book 20. Where, when, and by whom this important find was made is still completely unknown. It is unfortunate that what must have been an early and good text was not used to improve the texts then current, except for the routine addition of these missing sections.

Mystery surrounds the lost β (*codex Buslidianus*, named after its owner Hieronymus Busleiden, who died 1517), which was once at Louvain. Many of its readings are recoverable from printed texts, above all the

---

[13] So K. A. de Meyier, *Codices Vossiani Latini, Pars I, Codices in Folio* (Leiden, 1973).

[14] So Marshall, text, *Praef.* xv, with the evidence.

[15] Ullman, *Humanistic Script*, 66 and plate 34, where the Greek can clearly be seen.

[16] For a recent view of the date, see L. A. Holford-Strevens, 'A Misdated Manuscript of Gellius', *CQ* 29 (1979), 226–7.

[17] No sure example has been discovered before this date. Thus V, which contains not merely Books 1–7 but also a s. XII text of 9–20, was originally two separate volumes. The story of Gellius in the fifteenth century has yet to be written. See H. Baron, 'Aulus Gellius in the Renaissance, and a Manuscript from the School of Guarino', *Studies in Philology*, 48 (1951), 107–25 (although Baron greatly underestimates the number of extant fifteenth-century manuscripts: there are over ninety known); L. Gamberale, 'Note sulla tradizione di Gellio', *RFIC* 103 (1975), 35–55.

1585 Paris edition of Gellius by H. Etienne, containing the notes of L. Carrio, who describes it as then being 'four hundred years old' (i.e. s. XII). The readings preserved fluctuate between the ridiculous and the highly valuable: for example, β contained the beginning of 1.3, which is otherwise available only in A. Until further evidence shows up, judgement on this witness must be suspended.

P. K. M.

GRANIUS LICINIANUS

What remains of the post-Hadrianic annalist Granius Licinianus was discovered in the British Museum in 1853 by G. H. Pertz, in one of the block of manuscripts which had come to the Museum in 1847 from the monastery of S. Maria Deipara in the Nitrian Desert in Egypt. This manuscript (Add. 17212, ff. 1–8, 10–13) is a palimpsest *ter scriptus*, and the unfortunate Granius is at the bottom. We have fragments of several books of his history (26, 28, 33, 35, 36), written in the fifth century in an uncial hand of African origin. A grammatical text,[1] in African cursive, was superimposed upon this in the seventh century. On top is a Syriac translation of the *Homilies* of John Chrysostom, written in the tenth century in the Near East. The difficult task of decipherment, begun by Georg Pertz, was continued by his son Karl. Despite the continuous rain and cloud which drove him to use artificial light at noon, he gave the *editio princeps* to the world in 1857.[2] Although he was obliged to use one of the milder reagents (the Curators had rightly frowned on stronger compounds), the corrosion was such that subsequent editors have been reduced to using Pertz's transcription, and not the manuscript itself, as the basis for their text.

L. D. R.

[1] Based on Servius, *In Donatum*: cf. B. Bischoff, *SBAW* 1958.2, 29–30.

[2] K. A. F. Pertz, *Gai Grani Liciniani Annalium quae supersunt* (Berlin, 1857). There is a recent edition by N. Criniti (Leipzig, 1981). See also *CLA* ii.167, and E. A. Lowe, 'Codices Rescripti', *Mélanges Eugène Tisserant*, v (*Studi e testi*, 235, Vatican, 1964), no. 63 (= *Pal. Papers*, ii. 499).

GRATTIUS

Vienna 277 contains quires 17–18, written in a pre-Caroline minuscule of s. VIII/IX (*CLA* X.1474, Chatelain, plate CI), from a manuscript produced in France or perhaps western Germany. Jacopo Sannazaro discovered them during the years 1501–3; according to a contemporary, he brought the classical texts that they preserve, *Versus Ovidi de piscibus et feris* and Grattius' *Cynegetica*, 'ex Heduorum usque finibus atque e Turonibus'.[1] In the *Versus de piscibus et feris* lacunae and other corruptions suggest an exemplar of 13–15 lines to the page; Grattius' *Cynegetica* had probably not been transmitted in their company for long. Vollmer surmised 'extitisse aliquando florilegium ut ita dicam ob amorem rei venatoriae compositum, litteris merovingicis descriptum ex variis qui tum extabant codicibus antiquis, fortasse in usum alicuius tum principis velut Pippini regis.'[2]

The same texts, up to *Cyn.* 159, occupy the end of Paris lat. 8071 (Thuaneus, s. IX; Chatelain, plate XIV), perhaps written at Fleury,[3] and H. Schenkl in an important article, 'Zur Kritik und Überlieferungsgeschichte des Grattius und anderer lateinischer Dichter', *Jahrb. für class. Phil.* Suppl. 24 (1898), 383–480, argued that the whole of this manuscript except the text of Juvenal at the beginning was copied from the Vindobonensis before it lost quires 1–16 (pp. 399–400). Attempts at proving it independent continue,[4] but Schenkl's argument still stands.

Sannazaro himself made two copies of the Vindobonensis, and the first edition (Venice, 1534) was apparently printed from a third. The Thuaneus must have been found before Pithoeus used it for his edition (Paris, 1590), because Milan, Ambros. S. 81 sup. (s. XVI) largely derives from it.

The *Versus de piscibus et feris* have been identified since the first edition with the *Halieutica* ascribed to Ovid by Pliny, *N.H.* 32.11, and are invariably printed under that title. J. A. Richmond's edition (London, 1962) is the best;[5] F. Capponi appends to his first volume (Leiden, 1972) plates of the whole text in both the Vindobonensis and the Thuaneus.[6] After being mentioned by Ovid, *Pont.* 4.16.34 (*Gratius*

[1] P. Summontius, preface to J. J. Pontanus, *Actius* (Naples, 1507).

[2] *PLM* II.1 (Leipzig, 1911), 4 n. 2.

[3] U. Knoche, ed. of Juvenal (Munich, 1950), xxvi; cf. *Philologus*, Suppl. 33 (1940), 262–3.

[4] On the latest see E. J. Kenney, *CR* 25 (1975), 218–19.

[5] In *Philologus*, 120 (1976), 92–106, he comes out against Ovidian authorship.

[6] These provide a clear proof, missed by Capponi and everyone else, that Ambros. S. 81 sup. derives from the Thuaneus: it omits 49 *silvas* – 93 *sedes* because of a stain in the Thuaneus.

codd.), and probably quarried by Nemesianus for his own *Cynegetica*,[7] Grattius disappears from view until 1503 except for the manuscripts and an echo in an anonymous poem of s. IX.[8] Enk's edition and commentary (Zutphen, 1918, repr. Hildesheim, 1976) have not been superseded.

M. D. R.

[7] P. J. Enk, *Mnem.* 45 (1917), 61–8.
[8] *PLMA* I.370, v. 174 ~ *Cyn.* 26 (Schenkl, 425).

HORACE

Horace was widely enough read and commented on in late Antiquity to assure his survival; the medieval transmission descends from at least two and possibly three ancient copies of the poems (not counting texts of the scholia). Knowledge of Horace and manuscripts of his work appear rather suddenly in the second half of the ninth century.[1] The court library of Charlemagne may have contained a copy of the *Ars Poetica*, and Alcuin assumed the name 'Flaccus' in the erudite *badinage* of his circle, but neither he nor his contemporaries betray direct familiarity with Horace's poetry.[2] For much of the Middle Ages the lyric poems seem to have been less read than the hexameter *Satires* and *Epistles*, probably because of their greater metrical and linguistic difficulty.

The standard edition is that of F. Klingner (Teubner, 1959³); the most elaborate apparatus is in the edition of O. Keller–A. Holder (Leipzig, 1899²); the most recent survey of the transmission is by C. O. Brink, *Horace on Poetry: the 'Ars Poetica'* (Cambridge, 1971), 1–43. The conventional sigla are retained here. Plates of the following manuscripts are available in Chatelain: A (LXXXII), a (LXXXI), R (LXXXVII), δ (LXXXIII), π (LXXXVI), λ (LXXIX), l (LXXVIII), φ (LXXXIV), ψ (LXXXIII).

[1] P. von Winterfeld, *RhM* 60 (1905), 33–5; cf. also J. D. A. Ogilvy, *Books Known to the English, 597–1066* (Cambridge, Mass., 1967), 162–3.
[2] *Ars Poetica* is mentioned in the book-list added by an Italian hand of the 790s to Berlin (West) Diez B Sant. 66, pp. 218–19, which may disclose part of the contents of the court library at that time, cf. Bischoff, *Karl der Grosse*, 42–62 (plate, p. 54; transcription, pp. 59–60 = *Mitt. Stud.* iii. 149–69, 165–6, plate X), also *CLA* VIII.1044. The entry, however, is unusual, citing the *Ars* by *explicit* alone; the only other use of *explicit* is in the case of Juvenal, where the writer records *incipit* and title of Book 2 of the *Satires*, *explicit* of Book 2, and *incipit* and title of Book 3. B. L. Ullman (*Scriptorium*, 8 (1954), 26–7) suggested that the *Ars* was bound together with the next item in the list, Claudian's *De raptu* and other poems. Perhaps that volume contained only the conclusion of the *Ars*.

The surviving manuscripts, several hundred in number,[3] have not been thoroughly investigated or even catalogued. Study of the transmission has concentrated instead on a small group of relatively early codices, of which the following are regarded as indispensable:[4]

A   Paris lat. 7900A, s. IX/X, Milan, later Corbie.[5] Lacks *Satires*, *Epistles* 2, and *Ars*. (*Epod.* 16.27–17.81 and *Epist.* 1.6.65–1.12.29 are on leaves now in Hamburg.) An important witness for Terence, Lucan, and Juvenal.

a   Milan, Ambros. O.136 sup. (*olim Avennionensis*), s. IX/X, France.

B   Berne 363, s. IX[2] (written in a Continental Irish scriptorium, perhaps in north Italy); a miscellany containing selections from *Carm.* and *Epod.*, also *C.S.*., *Ars*, 1–440, *S.* to 1.3.134.[6]

C/E   Munich Clm 14685, s. XI (St. Emmeram ?). A complete text of Horace (lacking *C.* 4.7.21–*Epod.* 1.23), put together from two sources:

> (1) designated C, provided *C.* 3.27.1–4.7.20, *Epod.* 1.24–end, *C.S.*, *Ars*, 1–440, *S.* 1.4.122–1.6.40, 2.7.118, 2.8, and (probably) *Epist.*
> (2) called E, supplied *Carm.* to 3.26, *Ars* 441–76, and *S.* 1.1.1– 2.5.82, 2.6.34–end (*S.* 2.5.83–2.6.33 were added by a twelfth-century hand on f. 103).[7]

K   Saint-Claude (Jura) 2, s. XI, from Saint-Oyan. Fragments of a palimpsest now bound together with unrelated material, contains *Ars*, *S.* to 2.2.24. Cf. F. Vollmer, *SBAW* 1913.3, 5–7.

R   Vatican, Reg. lat. 1703, s. IX[2]/[4] (Alsace; owned by SS Peter and Paul, Wissembourg). Perhaps the oldest manuscript; corrections in the hand of Walahfrid Strabo. Cf. Pellegrin, *Manuscrits*, ii.1. 370–3.

δ   British Library, Harley 2725, s. IX[4]/[4] (northern France).

π   Paris lat. 10310, s. IX/X (from the Cathedral Library, Autun). Lacking *S.* 1.2.71–end.

λ   Paris lat. 7972, s. IX/X (St. Ambrose, Milan).

l   Leiden, B.P.L. 28, s. IX (from St. Peter, Beauvais).

φ   Paris lat. 7974, s. X (from Saint-Rémy, Reims).

ψ   Paris lat. 7971, s. X (Reims, then Fleury).

V   Blandinius Vetustissimus deperditus, a manuscript of uncertain date from Blankenberg near Ghent, destroyed in 1566. Its readings are primarily known from collations of Jacobus Cruquius as published in his editions beginning in 1565; also from a fifteenth-century copy, Gotha Chart. B. 61 (lacks *C.* 3.10.4–3.15.16 and *Ars*).

[3] H. Buttenwieser, *Speculum*, 17 (1942), 53–5, claimed to have recorded nearly 300, of which 250 were copied before 1300. The number of entries in medieval library catalogues is also striking, cf. Manitius, *Handschriften*, 55–61.

[4] The most important earlier studies are: W. von Christ, *SBAW* 1893, 83–116, F. Vollmer, 'Die Überlieferungsgeschichte des Horaz,' *Philologus*, Suppl. 10 (1905), 259–322, F. Klingner, *Hermes*, 70 (1935), 249–68, 361–403, G. Pasquali, *Storia della tradizione e critica del testo*[2] (Florence, 1952), 373–85.

[5] So Bischoff as reported by H. C. Gotoff, *The Transmission of the Text of Lucan in the Ninth Century* (Cambridge, Mass., 1971), 19.

[6] Complete facsimile edn. by H. Hagen, *Codex Bernensis 363 phototypice editus* (Leiden, 1897).

[7] Brink, 4–6.

These manuscripts (V apart) fall into two groups, each of which almost certainly descends from an ancient codex. One group (Klingner's Ξ) includes ABCK (and a for the portions extant in A, where a is closely related to it), the other (Ψ) R$\delta\pi\lambda$l$\varphi\psi$ (and a where A is not available). These groups are defined by shared errors,[8] by differences in the order of parts of the collection (the *Ars Poetica* appears fourth in Ξ, second in Ψ), and, in the *Odes* and *Epodes*, by differences in the style and form of the titles appended to each poem (e.g. for *C.* 2.16 Ξ gives 'ad Pompeium Grosphum', Ψ 'hypotetice Grospho, ostendens quam iocundum sit otium'). Ξ is on the whole more faithful than Ψ, but both transmit ancient readings – indeed, at times both readings are attested in ancient sources[9] – and in many places the true reading is preserved in Ψ. One such place is the beginning of *Odes* 1.8 (*Lydia, dic per omnes*), where Ψ (= $\varphi\psi\lambda$lπ^2) gives the correct *te deos oro* and Ξ (+R[1]) the ancient interpolation *hoc deos uere*.[10] Since no Ξ source contains a complete text of Horace, this strain is at times poorly represented: in *S.* 1.6.41–2.2.24 by K alone, in *S.* 2.7.118–*Epist.* 2.2.216 by C alone, and in *S.* 2.2.25–2.7.117 by no pure witness.[11]

The division of manuscripts into Ξ and Ψ is perfectly maintained only in a small number of places; much more often the lines of demarcation are blurred or entirely obscured. Each of the Ψ manuscripts agrees on occasion with Ξ, R most often. Since R is the oldest Ψ manuscript, it may have drawn on pairs of variants present in Ψ but progressively lost in later copies.[12] (Klingner cites throughout a third class of manuscripts called Q, which he regards as a ninth-century conflation of Ξ and Ψ. Q includes a, the parts of Munich Clm 14685 called E, and two eleventh-century manuscripts, Paris lat. 7975 and Melk 177. The value of Q seems doubtful: a, at least, is best treated as a Ξ witness where A is extant and a Ψ manuscript where it is not – e.g. in the *Ars Poetica* – and if Q really is a conflation of Ξ and Ψ its only practical value will be in those places where pure Ξ sources are missing or inadequate.)

[8] A tabulation for *Ars Poetica* in Brink, 18–19.

[9] e.g. at *C.* 3.6.22 the scholia transmitted under the name of Porphyrio show knowledge of the readings *artibus* (Ξ) and *artubus* (Ψ); at *C.* 3.17.4 Priscian (2.256.16 *GLK*) explicitly observes, 'apud Horatium duplicem inuenio scripturam et *fastos* et *fastus* in III carminum . . .'.

[10] The interpolated reading seems to have been inadvertently generated by the remarks of Caesius Bassus, who certainly read the line with the correct *te deos oro*, cf. H. W. Garrod, *CR* 35 (1922), 102. At 6.270.14 *GLK* one should therefore read *oro* with B and the *editio princeps*, not *uere* with A.

[11] Here Klingner turned to a group of manuscripts in which he claimed to find 'vestigia recensionis Ξ': St. Gall, Vad. 312 (s. X, St. Gall), Oxford, Bodl. D'Orville 158 (s. XI), Munich Clm 375 (s. XII, Germany), and Oxford, Queen's College 202 (s. XI). He also used Gotha B.61 for this purpose, perhaps unwisely, since that manuscript's non-Ψ readings, if derived from the lost Blandinius Vestustissimus, could reflect a third branch of tradition rather than Ξ.

[12] R also preserves intact some corrupt readings that have been removed by interpolation in later Ψ manuscripts, cf. F. Leo, *GGA* 1904, 851 (= *Ausgewählte Kleine Schriften* (Rome, 1960), ii. 161 n. 1).

As for the mysterious Blandinius Vetustissimus (V), it at least acts the way a descendant of a third ancient branch of tradition might be expected to act: it agrees in good readings with both $\varXi$ and $\varPsi$, sides consistently with neither in error, and contains some remarkable and possibly true readings of its own, of which the most striking is *S*. 1.6.126 *campum lusumque trigonem* for *rabiosi tempora signi* in $\varXi$ (here K), $\varPsi$, and the ancient scholia.[13] Its notable readings must be considered on their merits.

Three manuscripts used by editors (Aλl) contain at the end of the *Epodes* a subscription of the ex-consul Vettius Agorius Basilius Mavortius (cos. AD 527): 'legi et ut potui emendaui conferente mihi magistro Felice oratore urbis Romae.'[14] Vollmer thought Mavortius' copy was the archetype of the entire tradition, but this seems scarcely possible. The subscription was probably copied from a descendant of Mavortius' codex into an unrelated book; since λ and A were both written in Milan at the end of the ninth century, and λ's close relative l originated at the same time north of the Alps, it is simplest to suppose that the subscription passed from λ into A.[15]

The text of Horace has been relatively well preserved: ancient variants are not excessively numerous,[16] interpolated verses are rare[17] – Horace cannot have been easy to imitate – and the indirect tradition offers no certainly correct reading not found in the medieval manuscripts.[18] Some have seen in this relative uniformity the influence of Valerius Probus, the distinguished critic of the first century AD, who is said to have worked on the text of Horace.[19] But there is no evidence that Probus produced an edition of Horace, and it is in fact unlikely that any work he did had the decisive effect claimed for it. In the case of Virgil, Probus' views are often cited by the ancient commentators, but have left few traces in the manuscript tradition; he is not even mentioned in the ancient scholia to Horace.

---

[13] Estimates of V's worth vary from the highly favourable (Pasquali, 381–5, endorsing von Winterfeld's suggestion of an Irish ancestry) to the thoroughly sceptical (R. J. Getty, *Classical Medieval and Renaissance Studies in Honor of Berthold Louis Ullman* (Rome, 1964), 119–31, a vigorous defence of the vulgate at *S*. 1.6.126). E. Fraenkel, *Horace* (Oxford, 1957), 100–1, rejects some of V's alleged good readings as interpolations but does not question the genuineness of *campum lusumque trigonem*.

[14] 'Vettius Agorius Basilius' also appears in Paris lat. 8084, f. 45, a sixth-century copy of Prudentius; his teacher Felix corrected the text of Martianus Capella.

[15] The subscription is also in Gotha B.61, and may therefore have appeared in the Blandinius Vetustissimus.   [16] Vollmer, 291–6.

[17] A notable exception is the passage of eight lines ('Lucili, quam sis mendosus') prefixed to *S*. 1.10, transmitted by several $\varPsi$ manuscripts ($\varphi\psi\lambda$l).

[18] Pasquali, 381, Brink, 34–5. Flavius Caper's *lactea* for *cerea* (*C*.1.13.2) and Servius' *sede* for *fine* (*C*. 2.18.30) are both replacements for difficult or unusual expressions.

[19] 'Probus qui illas [sc. notas] in Vergilio et Horatio et Lucretio apposuit, ut <in> Homero Aristarchus', *GLK* 7.534. On Probus' role in the transmission of Horace cf. Leo, 164–6, Pasquali, 378–9, Brink, 35–8 (showing due reserve).

Appendix: Ancient Scholia

Two sets of ancient scholia survive:[20]

(a) Excerpts from the commentary of Pomponius Porphyrio (third century AD?), edited by A. Holder (Innsbruck, 1894). The main authorities are Vatican lat. 3314 (s. IX in., central Italy[21]), Munich Clm 181 (c. s. IX med., western Germany), and Paris lat. 7988 (s. XV); also a group of fifteenth-century Italian manuscripts descended from a codex brought to Rome in 1455 by Enoch of Ascoli.

(b) A miscellaneous body of ancient material put together perhaps in the fifth century, to which in fifteenth-century manuscripts is attached the name of Helenius Acro (c.AD 200), the author of a lost commentary on Horace; the corpus is usually referred to as 'ps-Acro'. Edited by O. Keller (2 vols., Leipzig, 1902, 1904). The best witness is A (Paris lat. 7900A), to which Vatican lat. 3257 (s. XII = V) is closely related. The testimony of AV can be supplemented from Wolfenbüttel, Aug. 2° 81.31 (c) and Paris lat. 7988 (p), both s. XV, and from Paris lat. 9345 (s. X/XI = γ) and 7975 (s. XI = r).

In addition the marginal scholia in $\varphi\psi\lambda$ (some ancient material with much Carolingian overlay) have been edited by H. J. Botschuyver (Amsterdam, 1935); the same scholar has printed the Carolingian scholia in Paris lat. 17897 and 8223 (Amsterdam, 1942).

R. J. T.

[20] On the character of these collections see R. G. M. Nisbet and M. Hubbard, *A Commentary On Horace: Odes I* (Oxford, 1970), xlvii–li; J. E. G. Zetzel, *Latin Textual Criticism in Antiquity* (New York, 1981), 168–70.   [21] Bischoff, *Lorsch*, 81, 104–5.

HYGINUS

Astronomica
Fabulae

Astronomica

Has any classical text been so ill served by recent scholarship as this?
The Teubner of B. Bunte (Leipzig, 1875), founded on three manuscripts from German libraries, has survived repeated exposure of its
inadequacy and inaccuracy[1] and now reappears in Italian dress (Pisa,
1976). The interval produced only one work of substance, unpublished
at that: Sister L. Fitzgerald, *Hygini Astronomica* (diss. St. Louis, Mo.,
1967), an edition preceded by a list of sixty-one manuscripts, accompanied by a collation of twenty-eight, and followed by a discussion of
these twenty-eight.[2]
Fitzgerald divides her manuscripts into three groups, whose main
members are these:

(1) R Vatican, Reg. lat. 1260 (s. IX, from Fleury?).
     O Paris lat. 8728 (s. IX/X, from St. Remigius, Reims).
(2) Z Paris lat. 11127 (*c*.1000, from Echternach[3]).
(3) D Dresden Dc 183 (s. IX/X); the mainstay of Bunte's edition.
     U British Library, Harley 2506 (*c*.1000, from Fleury[4]).
     M Montpellier 334 (s. IX², Loire valley?[5]).
     N Munich Clm 13084 (s. IX¾, Freising?[6]).

She points out that O has been heavily corrected by two hands and
should be studied on the spot by anyone who wants to dig deeper.
Plainly seven manuscripts selected from sixty-one are better than the
nearest three, but Fitzgerald's conclusions need to be tested and

---

[1] C. Bursian, *SBAW* 1876, 1–56; G. Kauffmann, *Breslauer philol. Abhandl.* 3.4 (1888), 3–15;
Manitius, *Hermes*, 37 (1902), 501–10, 40 (1905), 471–8; Chatelain and Legendre, *Hygini Astronomica*:
texte du manuscrit tironien de Milan (Bibl. de l'École des Hautes Études, 180, Paris, 1909), viii–ix.
J. Tolkiehn, *P.-W.* x.1 (1917), 640–50, gives a useful survey of these and other contributions; see
especially §§ 1 (*Titel*), 6 (*Fortleben*), 7 (*Überlieferung*), 9 (*Das sog. Anecdoton Hygini*), 10 (*De duodecim
signis*).

[2] *DA* 28 (1968), 3656A; the Bodleian has an authorized copy (2954 e. 1). Several of the sixty-one
manuscripts contain only excerpts or adaptations. Sister Fitzgerald discusses another manuscript,
Baltimore W. 734 (s. XII², from northern Italy according to Professor B. Munk Olsen), in *Essays in
Honour of Anton Charles Pegis* (Toronto, 1974), 197–200. It appears from *Gnomon*, 52 (1980), 83 that
someone proposes to edit the text with the aid of a computer.

[3] J. Schroeder, *Bibliothek und Schule der Abtei Echternach um die Jahrtausendwende* (diss. Freiburg,
1975, publ. Luxembourg, 1977), 57–9.   [4] See *ARATEA*, n. 29.

[5] Information kindly supplied by Professor Bischoff.

[6] B. Bischoff, *Die südostdeutschen Schreibschulen und Bibliotheken in der Karolingerzeit*, 1: *Die bayerischen
Diözesen* (Wiesbaden, 1974³), 120.

amplified. In the first place, much remains to be done on dates and provenances. Secondly, though she asserts that DUMN have numerous errors (p. 345), she cites none.[7] Thirdly, she misses manuscripts that may be important, for instance Valenciennes 337 (s. IX, from Saint-Amand)[8] and two of the earliest illustrated manuscripts, Leiden, Voss. Lat. O.15 (s. XI[1], written by Adémar of Chabannes) and St. Paul in Carinthia XXV/4.20 (s. XI[1], from Weingarten).

Frustrating hours of poring over catalogues suggest that even a reliable list of manuscripts would be no mean service. Both in the Middle Ages and in modern catalogues other texts besides the complete *Astronomica* go under the name of Hyginus, and historians of art have a habit of disagreeing with cataloguers over what a manuscript contains;[9] furthermore, a deviation from the usual order of books may give a misleading appearance to a mere *incipit* and *explicit*. A list that specified the books present together with the *incipit* and *explicit* would not only clear away uncertainties but also expedite the process of classification. Three examples:

(1) The work breaks off unfinished, in DM[1]N actually with an unfinished sentence, *annum voluerunt esse cum sol ab aestivo circulo.*[10] Other manuscripts supplement the sentence in various ways and thereby change the *explicit*.

(2) P. McGurk has drawn attention to a form of the text that appears first in Vatican lat. 3110 (s. XIV, owned by Salutati[11]) and then in four Florentine manuscripts of s. XV[2] (derived from it?); it begins with Books 3–4 (*Igitur incipiemus* . . .), condenses Book 2, and intersperses material from Martianus Capella and elsewhere. Other Italian manuscripts of s. XV have only Books 2 and 3, usually reversed.[12]

(3) At least nine manuscripts end at 106.26 (Bunte) *montium magnitudine*: Berlin (West) lat. 4° 576, Florence, Laur. 29.30, Ricc. 3011, Holkham Hall 331, Leiden, Voss. Lat. O.3, O.18, B. L. Egerton 1050, Vatican lat. 11460, Ottob. lat. 2056. All but the Laurentianus (s. XII/XIII, Italian[13]) are Italian manuscripts of s. XV (derived from it?).

---

[7] MN certainly seem related if her stemma is sound: they must have interpolated the words that on p. 346 she charges ROZDU with omitting.

[8] A. Boutemy, *Hommages à M. Renard* (Brussels, 1969), i. 108–18. It is related to Milan, Ambros. M.12 sup. (s. IX, not s. XV as Fitzgerald says), another part of which comes from Corvey; cf. F. Steffens, *Lateinische Paläographie*[2] (Trier, 1909), 56. Both are fragments: the Ambrosianus has about half the text, Val. 337 about two-fifths. Incidentally, Fitzgerald calls fragmentary a manuscript that the catalogue explicitly describes as complete, St. Gall 250 (s. IX[4]/[4], St. Gall, according to Bischoff).

[9] Two manuscripts in point are Munich Clm 10270 and St. Gall 902.

[10] Bunte and Fitzgerald print ⟨*redit*⟩ (RO). Fitzgerald implies that M has it, but see Bursian, 4.

[11] Ullman, *Salutati*, 189.

[12] *Catalogue of Astrological and Mythological Illuminated Manuscripts of the Latin Middle Ages*, iv (London, 1966), xix. Add Milan, Ambros. H. 139 inf., Vatican, Chigi H. IV. 120.

[13] Date and origin kindly supplied by Professor B. Munk Olsen.

How many manuscripts came through the Dark Ages will not be known until more work has been done on their descendants. Isidore, *De natura rerum*, 17.1 mentions 'Aratus et Hyginus' and certainly uses the latter. Scholia on Cicero's version of Aratus derive from a text of Hyginus less corrupt in places than the extant manuscripts.[14]

Illustrations in the *Astronomica* have been discussed by Byvanck and McGurk, who agree that they were borrowed in s. XI[1] from other texts.[15] The earlier illustrations mostly accompany Book 2; the later, for instance in the second edition (Venice, 1482), Book 3.[16]

M. D. R.

[14] G. Kauffmann, 2. This expanded dissertation of Kauffmann's is thorough and informative; see *ARATEA*, n. 23 for one of its merits, and another is the collection of material on Carolingian astronomy and Hyginus' place in it (pp. 70–9).

[15] *Meded. der Kon. Ned. Akad. van Wet.*, N.R. 12 (1949), 189–90, 229–33; *Catalogue*, xxii–xxv. Chatelain, *Hygini Astronomica*, x–xi, argues from F⟨IGVRA⟩ SERPENTIS and the like that Milan, Ambros. M. 12 sup. (s. IX, partly in *notae Tironianae*) was copied from an illustrated exemplar; but the *F* can equally well be expanded to *FABVLA* or *FORMATIO*, as it is in other manuscripts.

[16] The *editio princeps* (Ferrara, 1475) leaves spaces in Book 3.

Fabulae

Jacobus Micyllus published the *editio princeps* of Hyginus' *Fabulae* (Basle, 1535) from a manuscript in the cathedral library at Freising that he found hard to read and make sense of. Fragments of it discovered in bindings at Regensburg in 1864[1] and at Munich in 1942[2] reveal why: it was written *c*.900 in Beneventan.[3] It may have been the Hyginus catalogued at Freising in s. XI, though manuscripts of the *Astronomica* were common by that date.[4] An inscription on one of the leaves discovered in 1942 shows that it had been dismembered by 1558. The blame need not attach to Micyllus, except that his edition might be thought to have made it redundant; but he has incurred another charge, negligence in transcribing it.[5]

[1] K. Halm, *SBAW* 1870, 317–26. Halm acquired these fragments for the library at Munich, where they are Clm 6437 (Freising 237). For a description and illustration see Lowe, *Scriptura Beneventana* (2 vols., Oxford, 1929), xxvii.

[2] P. Lehmann, *ABAW* 23 (1944), 37–41, plates IV–VIII. Bischoff made the discovery in Munich, Erzbischöfl. Ordinariatsarchiv 934. Lehmann identifies the fragments with ff. 7–8 and the lower halves of ff. 1–2, but he gives no reasons, and to judge from the text 'f. 1' is more likely to have been f. 2, 'f. 2' f. 7, and 'ff. 7–8' two leaves that came much further on in the manuscript, next but one to each other. [3] Lowe assigns it to Capua.

[4] Manitius, *Handschriften*, 80.

[5] Halm, 325–6; K. Meuli, *ANTIΔΩPON: Festschrift Jacob Wackernagel* (Göttingen, 1923), 232. Lehmann, 40–1, offers extenuations. Micyllus says, 'nonnihil adiuvit is qui prior illum latine describendum ceperat, cuius nos exemplum principio ceu filum quoddam secuti sumus.' Lehmann's plate VI convicts Micyllus of omitting an *ubi* and Lehmann himself an *in*.

Not surprisingly for so useful an aid to understanding the poets, the work has come down not in its original form, which probably bore the title *Genealogiae*, but chopped about.[6] Other evidence available to the editor is: the *Hermeneumata Leidensia*, a series of parallel Greek and Latin texts of which one, introduced by a preface dated AD 207, uses Hyginus;[7] quotations in commentaries of late Antiquity; and a deviant version of chapters 67–71 preserved in a palimpsest leaf of s. V, Vatican, Pal. lat. 24, ff. 38 + 45 (uncial; overwritten c.s. VII/VIII; probably at Lorsch in s. VIII).[8]

M. Schmidt edited the text after the first set of fragments came to light (Jena, 1872). H. J. Rose's edition (Leiden, 1933) was reprinted in 1963 and 1967 without so much as a mention of the other set.[9]

M. D. R.

[6] C. Bursian, *Jahrb. für class. Phil.* 12 (1866), 771–3; Rose (edn.), xii–xv.

[7] G. Goetz, *Corp. Gloss. Lat.* III (Leipzig, 1892), 56.30– 60.20. The relationship beween the Greek and Latin versions has been debated by L. C. Valckenaer, 'De Hygini fragmento Dositheano schediasma', *Misc. obss. crit.* 10 (Amsterdam, 1739), 108–23; Lachmann, *Versuch über Dositheus* (Berlin, 1837); Bursian, op. cit.; Rose, *CQ* 23 (1929), 96–9. It would be easier to determine if both versions were less corrupt, but Bursian, 769–70, seems right to hold that the date pertained to an original preface in Latin. Rose, 172–6, prints only the Greek version, but even if Bursian was wrong both are indispensable; at 57.4, for instance, the Greek alone has preserved ἑνὸς ἑκάστον ἐξήγησιν, the Latin alone *ex subiectis recognosces*, and a few words in between must be missing from both. D. A. van Krevelen, *Philologus*, 110 (1966), 315–18, makes the same mistake in quoting only the Greek version of the *Hermeneumata Montepessulana* (*Corp. Gloss. Lat.* III.291.53–292.45) to expose corruption in the *Leidensia*. Rose's attribution to Hyginus of 60.21–69.38, a headless and tailless summary of the *Iliad*, needs reappraisal.

[8] *CLA* I.71, first published by B. G. Niebuhr, *M. Tulli Ciceronis orationum pro M. Fonteio et C. Rabirio fragmenta* (Rome, 1820).

[9] Micyllus's edition (Basle, 1535) has also been reprinted (Garland Publishing, New York and London, 1976).

ILIAS LATINA

Written probably during the reign of the Emperor Nero,[1] this unattractive compendium (whereby the *Iliad* is reduced to 1,070 hexameter lines, much indebted to Virgil and Ovid) is first noticed in late Antiquity, when Lactantius Placidus[2] quotes lines 1048–50. In the sixth century Columban appears to have come under its influence.[3] Then there is silence until the middle of the ninth century, when Ermenric (*MGH, Epist.* 5.545) quotes line 7. Thereafter the work enjoyed great popularity in the schools. In the early tenth century its influence is evident in the so-called *Gesta Berengarii* (*MGH, Script.* 4.189–210), written in northern Italy.[4] At the end of the tenth century 'Homer' is mentioned by Walter of Speyer as one of the common school poets, a fate likewise given the work a century later by the Frenchman Haimeric in his *Ars Lectoria*.[5] In

The only serviceable text is the 1913 Teubner edition of Fr. Vollmer (= *Poetae Latini Minores*[2], ii.3). In the same year Vollmer also published the important *Zum Homerus Latinus. Kritischer Apparat mit Commentar und Überlieferungsgeschichte* (= *SBAW* 1913.3). A new edition by M. Scaffai is in preparation. The first extensive study of the manuscripts was produced by a pupil of Vollmer's, H. Remme, *De Homeri Latini codicum fatis atque statu disputatio critica* (diss. Munich, 1906). This has now been superseded by M. Scaffai, 'Tradizione manoscritta dell' *Ilias Latina*', in *In verbis verum amare. Miscellanea dell' Istituto di Filologia Latina e Medioevale, Università di Bologna* (a cura di Paolo Serra Zanetti, 1980), 205–77, a thorough and illuminating study, to which the present article is much indebted.

[1] See, most recently, G. Scheda, 'Zur Datierung der *Ilias Latina*', *Gymnasium*, 72 (1965), 303–7. The question of authorship has been much discussed. As the first eight and the last eight lines (after emendation) can present the acrostic *Italicus scripsit*, one obvious candidate has been Silius Italicus, a view championed by L. Herrmann, 'Recherches sur l'*Ilias Latina*', *AC* 16 (1947), 241–51. H. Schenkl in *WS* 12 (1890), 317, observed that a fifteenth-century manuscript in Vienna (3509) attributes the poem to one Baebius Italicus, and many have been ready to believe the evidence of a manuscript otherwise totally worthless. From the eleventh century on, one finds Pindar frequently given the credit. For an ingenious attempt to explain this bizarre attribution, see M. Scaffai, 'Pindarus seu Homerus. Un' ipotesi sul titolo dell' *Ilias Latina*', *Latomus*, 38 (1979), 932–9. All the better manuscripts call the author 'Homer'.

[2] *Comm. in Statii Thebaida*, 6.114 (ed. R. Jahnke (Leipzig, 1898), 305). The clear superiority of the text given by Lactantius makes evident the poor quality of the surviving manuscripts of the *Ilias Latina*.

[3] So Manitius, *Geschichte*, i. 186. Manitius (p. 634) claims that it is possible that early in the ninth century Hrabanus Maurus at *De universo*, 12.4 (*PL* 111.344) drew on the *Ilias Latina* for his remark: 'de quo [sc. Dardano] Homerus ait: Quem primum genuit coelesti Iupiter arce', a line which does not appear in our extant manuscripts of the *Ilias Latina*. However, Manitius fails to see that this comes directly from Isidore, *Etym.* 14.3.41. Isidore's source is unknown.

[4] Manitius, i.632, suggested Verona, an interesting idea in view of its later use by Laurence of Verona.

[5] For Walter, see Manitius, ii. 505; Haimeric, iii.181; Konrad, iii.317; Osbern, iii.189; Lambert, iii.501. Desiderius had a copy of the *Ilias Latina* made, as recounted by Petrus Diaconus in his *Chronica* (*MGH, SS* 7, 746.34). A great debt is owed to the *Ilias* by Laurence in his epic poem *De Bello Balearico* (*PL* 163.513–76). For Primas, see W. Meyer, 'Eine gereimte Umarbeitung der *Ilias Latina*', *Nachrichten von der königlichen Gesellschaft der Wissenschaften zu Göttingen, Phil.- hist. Kl.* 1907, 235–45.

the eleventh century the work was known to Desiderius Abbot of
Montecassino and to Konrad of Hirschau; in the twelfth to Laurence of
Verona, Hugh Primas of Orléans, Osbern of Gloucester, and Lambert
of Ardres.

Library catalogues show a 'Homer' in the ninth century at Saint-
Riquier and at Freising; in the eleventh at Blaubeuern and Hamersleven
(three copies); in the twelfth at Durham, Engelberg (two copies), Muri,
Pfäffers, Prüfening, Rouen, Salzburg, Wessobrunn (two copies), and
Whitby.

It is demonstrable that all extant manuscripts descend from a single
copy,[6] which survived into the Carolingian period. These manuscripts
can be divided into two families, of which the first (and by far the better)
has two representatives:

P   Antwerp 89[7], s. XI, ff. 17^v–35^v, with the *ex libris* of Koningsdaal (near
        Ghent).
W   Valenciennes 448, s. XI, ff. 100^v–116^v, from Saint-Amand.

In both P and W the *Ilias Latina* follows the text of Dares Phrygius.[8] A
single leaf preserved in Brussels 4344, s. XI (known as A, and containing
now only verses 1048–57 and 1065–70) was once considered to be part
of the copy from which both P and W were derived.[9]

The second family splits into four main divisions,[10] of which (in
descending order of fidelity to the archetype) the main representatives
are:

Division i

O   Oxford, Bodl. Rawlinson G.57, s. XI[2], ff. 6^r–27^r, written in
        England (N. R. Ker, *Catalogue of Manuscripts containing Anglo-Saxon*
        (Oxford, 1957), 427).
X   Oxford, Bodl. Auct. F.2.14, s. XI[2], ff. 90^r–104^v, written in England,
        possibly at Sherborne (Ker[2], 179).

[6] Vollmer suggested that this single copy came from Spain, but Scaffai, 'Tradizione manoscritta', 251, convincingly refutes this theory. As the inventory for 831 shows that Abbot Angilbert
had a copy made for Saint-Riquier in north-east France (see Manitius, *Handschriften*, 123), Scaffai
offers the attractive theory that this manuscript of Angilbert (s. VIII/IX) is the exemplar from
which all extant manuscripts ultimately derive. Significant is the connection of Angilbert with the
Carolingian court; see N. Scivoletto, 'Angilberto di S. Riquier e l'humanitas carolingia', *GIF*, 5
(1952), 289–313.

[7] For a full description of P, see Fr. Vollmer, 'De recensendo Homero Latino', in *Festschrift
Johannes Vahlen* (Berlin, 1900), 466–89, esp. 468–9.

[8] It is noteworthy that Dares Phrygius is also in manuscripts C and F. It seems that from the
tenth (possibly the ninth) century on, the *Ilias Latina* was transmitted with other works dealing
with Troy, especially Dares and Dictys Cretensis. In later centuries the *Ilias* circulated in different
company.

[9] So Vollmer (n. 7, above), 477. This leaf is part of the binding of a manuscript which was in
Aarschot (in Belgium, ten miles north-east of Louvain) as early as the thirteenth century. Scaffai,
'Tradizione manoscritta', 240, gives powerful reasons for rejecting the primacy of A.

[10] A stemma is given by Scaffai, 'Tradizione manoscritta', 259. Until Scaffai's edition appears,
these groupings must be considered tentative.

B   British Library, Add. 15601, s. XII/XIII, ff. 102^v–108^r, containing only verses 1–882, northern France; formerly at Avignon, since at least the fifteenth century.

d   Dijon 497, s. XIII ex., ff. 248^v–251^v, northern France, formerly at Cîteaux.

Division ii

C   Saint-Claude 2, s. XI^1, ff. 75^v–95^v, possibly written at Saint-Claude (Saint-Oyan).

F   Florence, Laur. 68.24, s. XI^1, ff. 55^v–74^v, central France.[11]

V   Venice, Marc. Lat. Z.497 (1811), s. XI ex., ff. 59^r–65^r, southern Italy (Farfa?).

t   Turin E.V.20, s. XI, on six leaves used to bind a twelfth-century copy of the *Liber Regulae Pastoralis* of Gregory, containing verses 62–174 and 231–454, central France.

Division iii

This class betrays evident contamination from a source close to P and W:

D   Prague 1625 (VIII H 7), s. XII, ff. 12^v–14^v, Germany (probably St. Lambrecht in Stiria), containing verses 1–337.

E   Erfurt, Amplon. 12°.20, s. XI/XII, ff. 105^r–131^v, Germany.

L   Leiden, Voss. Lat. O.89, s. XI^2, ff. 29^r–56^r, France, possibly from Fleury (owned by Pierre Daniel at the end of the sixteenth century).

R   Regensburg, Bischöfliche Zentralbibliothek, S.N., s. X/XI, pp. 1–24, containing only verses 497–586 and 648–906, southern Germany (previously at the convent at Obermünster).

h   Wolfenbüttel, Helmst. 349, s. XIII, ff. 1^r–7^v, containing only verses 267–1070, Germany.

Division iv

These witnesses form, in effect, an inferior branch of Division iii:

M   Munich Clm 19463, s. XII^1, ff. 13^r–35^v, Germany (from Tegernsee).

N   Munich Clm 19462, s. XII^1, ff. 1^r–18^r, Germany (from Tegernsee), a *gemellus* of M.[12]

m   Munich Clm 29200 (*olim* 29038), s. XII, comprising four bifolia containing verses 32–401, 465–525, and 970–1032, Germany (probably Tegernsee).

p   Pommersfelden 12 [2671], s. XIII/XIV, ff.228^v–238^v, Germany.

Of some interest, but hard to place in any of the above divisions is:

---

[11] In the fifteenth century F was owned by Francesco Sassetti, who probably acquired it in France. See Sabbadini, *Scoperte*, 165. Like P, F also contains Persius.

[12] It is noteworthy that P and N also contain Theodulus, as do D, L, and p.

G   Wolfenbüttel, Extrav. 301, s. XII/XIII, ff. 17^v–29^r, containing only
     verses 1–181 and 626–1070, southern Germany.

After the reconstruction of the common archetype from all the above
witnesses, the editor must still exercise considerable ingenuity in
emendation. The poor quality of this archetype is all too evident.

P. K. M.

ISIDORE

Etymologiae

The *Etymologiae* (or *Origines*) of Isidore of Seville (d. 4 April AD 636)
would seem first to have been dedicated to King Sisebut (d. 621). Yet
the author, clearly reluctant to let go of his vast work, had still not
finished it at the end of his life. His friend, Bishop Braulio of Saragossa,
writes that even before Isidore's death the work was (apparently without authorization) in the hands of many people in a state described as
'*libri . . . detruncati conrosique*'. Finally (in or after 633) Isidore sent the
Etym. to Braulio in its unfinished state, and it is to Braulio that we owe
the final editing and the division into twenty books (whereas Isidore
had left it simply divided into chapters). It is tempting to see the origin
of the three main families of manuscripts as coming from these three
states of the text: (1) the 'pirated' version; (2) the uncorrected and
unedited text of Isidore himself; (3) the version prepared for publication
by Braulio. There may be some kernel of truth in this theory, although
all manuscripts show marks of the editing by Braulio (e.g. in the
division into twenty books).

The spread of the *Etym.* was swift and extensive. The earliest trace
outside Spain is in a fragment of Book XI in an Irish hand, possibly

The only critical edition is that of W. M. Lindsay (OCT, 2 vols., 1911). This text is serviceable,
but makes no claim to being definitive. Its greatest weakness is that Isidore's sources are not
cited in the apparatus criticus. The following studies are of fundamental importance: W. M.
Lindsay, 'The Editing of Isidore's *Etymologiae*', *CQ* 5(1911), 42–53; C. Beeson, *Isidor-Studien*
(Munich, 1913); W. Porzig, 'Die Rezensionen der *Etymologiae* des Isidorus von Sevilla', *Hermes*,
72 (1937), 129–70; M. C. Díaz y Díaz, *Index Scriptorum Latinorum Medii Aevi Hispanorum*
(Salamanca, 1958), no. 122; B. Bischoff, 'Die Europaeische Verbreitung der Werke Isidors von
Sevilla', in *Isidoriana*, ed. M. C. Díaz y Díaz (León, 1961), 317–44 (= *Mitt. Stud.* i. 171–94);
J. M. F. Catón (ed.), *Las Etimologías en la Tradición Manuscrita Medieval estudiado por el Prof. Dr.
Anspach* (León, 1966); M. Reydellet, 'La Diffusion des *Origines* d'Isidore de Séville au Haut
Moyen Âge', *MEFR* 78 (1966), 383–437.

coming from Ireland itself[1] (*CLA* VII.995). In England the work was known to Aldhelm (d. 709).

The extant manuscripts are early and numerous.[2] They may conveniently (and broadly) be divided into three national groups, in the sense that Spain, France, and Italy are each the home of a version of the text. Unless otherwise specified, all manuscripts contain all of Books I–XX.

(a) 'Spanish' Manuscripts

This family generally shows a fuller, and more polished, form of the text. It is thus tempting to see the editorial hand of Braulio here.

T   Madrid Vitr. 14–3, s. VIII, written in a Visigothic minuscule in a Mozarabic location (*CLA* XI. 1638). A full facsimile was published in 1909 by R. Beer (A. W. Sijthoff, Leiden).

U   Escorial T.II.24, Spain. This witness bears the date 743, apparently copied from its exemplar. Bischoff assigns U to s. X.[3]

V   Escorial & I.14, s. IX, Mozarabic. Contains only Books III. 20.12–XX.

W   Escorial P.I.7, s. IX, formerly in the library of King Alfonso the Great (848–913).[4]

X   St. Gall 237, s. IX[1], possibly written at St. Gall.

C   Leiden, Voss. Lat. F.74, s. IX[1]. This text is formed by joining two separate books: thus XI–XX were written at Fulda, whereas I–X may have been written at Autun or Ferrières. In Books I–X the correcting hand of Servatus Lupus of Ferrières is much in evidence.

(b) 'French' Manuscripts

This family has by far the greatest number of representatives, and offers what was long the 'standard' text.

I   Brussels II.4856, s. VIII[2], copied at Corbie (*CLA* X. 1554) from a Spanish exemplar. Contains only Books I–X.

D   Basle F III 15, s. IX, France. Contains only Books II–XIX.

B   Berne 101, s. IX, France.

q   Laon 447, s. IX, Mainz.

---

[1] B. C. B.-B. observes, however, that the parchment is of the Continental, not the Irish type. For evidence that the *Etymologiae* may have been known in Ireland as early as the middle of the seventh century, see M. Herren, 'On the Earliest Irish Acquaintance with Isidore of Seville', in *Visigothic Spain: New Approaches*, ed. E. James (Oxford, 1980), 243–50.

[2] Those given here form the basis for the new collaborative edition of the *Etymologiae* in progress under the direction of Professor J. Fontaine, of which so far only Book XVII (ed. J. André, Budé, Paris, 1981) has appeared. This list deliberately excludes many ninth-century witnesses, and takes no account of the extensive indirect tradition from writers throughout the Middle Ages. After all twenty books have been edited, a further volume will be devoted to a minute examination and evaluation of all the manuscripts.

[3] *Mitt. Stud.* i. 174.

[4] The hand may be seen in P. Ewald and G. Loewe, *Exempla scripturae Visigothicae* (Heidelberg, 1883), pl. 14.

f   Reims 425, s. IX, Reims. Once owned by Hincmar, Archbishop of Reims (d. 882).

H   British Library, Harley 2686, s. IX, western France.

Y   Valenciennes 399, s. IX, northern France.

A   Milan, Ambros.L99.sup., s. VIII, Bobbio (*CLA* III.353). Contains only Books I–III and V–X.

(c) *'Italian' Manuscripts*

This family presents a somewhat shorter text, and constantly varies from the other two families.

K   Wolfenbüttel, Weissenb. 64, s. VIII, northern Italy (*CLA* IX. 1386).

M   Cava, Archivio della Badia 2 (XXIII), s. VIII², written in Beneventan minuscule at Montecassino, between the years 779 and 797 (*CLA* III.284). For the early books, this manuscript derives from a source which has been 'corrected' from a copy of Cassiodorus' *Institutiones*.

The editor of the *Etym.* faces many acute difficulties: above all he must decide if he can (or should) reproduce the text as left by Isidore, or whether he must rather content himself with coming as close as possible to the corrected edition of Braulio.

P. K. M.

JULIUS OBSEQUENS

The *Liber Prodigiorum* in which Julius Obsequens (perhaps in the fourth century AD) listed prodigies for purposes of pagan edification appears first, in a mutilated state,[1] in an Aldine edition of 1508, where it is appended to the letters of Pliny and to Suetonius, *De grammaticis et rhetoribus*. Aldus says he had it from Iucundus, but no manuscript survives, and all subsequent editions (most recently in O. Rossbach's edition of the *Periochae* of Livy in the fourth part of the Teubner Livy, 1910; see his Praefatio, xxviii ff.) depend on the Aldine.

M. W.

[1] The title appears to have been *Ab anno urbis conditae quingentesimoquinto prodigiorum liber*; as the list now starts at AUC 564, the beginning must be lacking (Rossbach, xxxvi).

JUSTINUS

It is a pity that the *Historiae Philippicae* of the Augustan historian Pompeius Trogus, with their concentration on the history of peoples outside Italy, have been lost to us. But we do have the epitome made around the third century by M. Iunian(i)us Iustinus, which reduced Trogus' forty-four books to something like a tenth of their original compass. Full of fact, concise, and written in a simple style, the epitome became so popular in late Antiquity and throughout the Middle Ages that it made Justinus a household name.

Justinus was widely known and read, both north and south of the Alps; more than two hundred manuscripts survive. Four families of manuscripts have been distinguished ($\tau\pi\iota\gamma$).[1] The first is traditionally known as the transalpine family, the third as the Italian, but the latter term is somewhat misleading; an early witness of the Italian family is probably French, and $\pi\gamma$ are no less Italian than ι.

The transalpine family offers the best text. Its oldest member, which has persisted in escaping the notice of editors, is a single leaf formerly at Weinheim, E. Fischer Sammlung S.N., written in Northumbria in the middle of the eighth century.[2] This fragment has a significance quite out of keeping with its size. It can hardly be unconnected with a reference in Alcuin's famous poem in praise of York; when offering us a glimpse of the resources of the cathedral library, he lists Pompeius alongside the 'historici veteres'.[3] A copy of Justinus was also among the books which came to Lorsch from the library of its former monk Gerward.[4] Gerward had been at the Carolingian court as early as 814, and was palace librarian under Louis the Pious. He had come by some remarkable books, which may even have included the Palatine Virgil; and it has been attractively conjectured[5] that the Weinheim leaf may be

---

[1] The fundamental work on the tradition was done by F. Rühl, 'Die Textesquellen des Justinus', *Jahrb. f. class. Phil.* Suppl. 6 (1872), 1–160, remarkable for its time in the large number of manuscripts it lists and describes; see also *Die Verbreitung des Iustinus im Mittelalter* (Leipzig, 1871) and his Teubner edition (1886). Rühl's work on the text was carried on in this century by O. Seel, in his two Teubner editions (1935, 1972); also 'Die justinischen Handschriftenklassen und ihr Verhältnis zu Orosius', *SIFC* 11 (1934), 255–88, 12 (1935), 5–40, and *Eine römische Weltgeschichte. Studien zum Text der Epitome des Iustinus und zur Historik des Pompeius Trogus* (Erlanger Beiträge zur Sprach- und Kunstwissenschaft, 39), Nuremberg, 1972. The *editio princeps* was printed in Venice by Nicolaus Jenson in 1470; the first really critical edition was that of Jacques Bongars (Paris, 1581), which earned him the name of the Sospitator Justini.

[2] *CLA* IX.1370; first published by S. Brandt, *Neue Heidelberger Jahrbücher*, 16 (1909), 109–14, still valuable, since the present location of the manuscript is unknown.

[3] Line 1548 (*MGH, Poetae latini aevi Carolini*, ed. E. Dümmler, i (Berlin, 1880–1), 204).

[4] Becker, 37.579. The book-list has been re-edited by P. Lehmann, in *Het Boek* (1923), 207 f., reprinted in *Erforschung des Mittelalters*, i (Stuttgart, 1959), 207 f.

[5] By B. Bischoff, most fully developed in *Lorsch*, 55–7; see also Lehmann, *Erforschung*, iii, 161.

a remnant of Gerward's Justinus, which would in that case have been brought to the court from England, probably in the time of Charlemagne. If that is true, our leaf is part of a very rare thing, the only extant English classical manuscript to have generated a Carolingian tradition. For it is difficult to believe that the transalpine tradition of Justinus did not spring from the court library of Charlemagne. Its earliest Carolingian witness, Paris lat. 4950, was written in north-east France about the year 800 and was later at Corbie.[6] There was a text of Justinus at Saint-Riquier by 831,[7] and there was probably an early copy at Fulda, for the epitome was used by Einhard, Hrabanus Maurus, and Walahfrid Strabo. The medieval catalogues tell us that there were also copies at Reichenau, Murbach, and St. Gall, and extant manuscripts demonstrate that the transalpine text was well established in the area of Lake Constance. Giessen 79 (s. IX¾) is a product of this area,[8] and an extant copy of it, St. Gall 623, is to be identified with an item in the ninth-century St. Gall catalogue. This text of Justinus quickly spread to France: Leiden, Voss. Lat. Q. 32 (s. IX[1]) and Paris n.a. lat. 1601[9] (s. IX[2]/4 or IX med.) are both of Fleury origin.

The π family of manuscripts originated in Italy, possibly at Verona. The earliest two witnesses, which contain only parts of the text, are derived independently from a selection of Justinus and Eutropius put together in Italy in the ninth century or earlier. The first, Leningrad, National Public (Saltykov-Shchedrin) Library, Lat.Q.v.IV.5, is part of the great historical miscellany copied at Verona early in the ninth century and now divided into four separate books.[10] The other, Vatican, Pal.lat.927, was written in 1181 at the monastery of the Holy Trinity in Verona. British Library, Add.19906 has its roots in the same corner of Italy; this is the now well-known manuscript copied by Lovato Lovati about 1290 from an original written, as its subscription (duly reproduced) tells us, by a monk at Pomposa just before 1100.[11] Naples IV.C.43, which has a long humanist history, was written in 1279 by Petrus de Dolcanis de Verona.[12] Other π manuscripts which have come to light are Florence, Laur. 66.19 and B. L. Harley 4822, both of the fourteenth century; the latter, though not a humanist book, has humanist notes and belonged to Sozomeno da Pistoia.

[6] *Karl der Grosse*, 48 n. 43, 238 f. (= Bischoff, *Mitt. Stud.* iii. 14, 158 n. 45); *Mitt. Stud.* i. 60.

[7] Becker, 11.190.

[8] The manuscript was at one time at Constance (Dombibliothek) and later at Weingarten. Information about date and origin kindly supplied by Professor Bischoff.

[9] This manuscript still appears in editions with the shelf-mark Laur. Ashburnham L.29. It was stolen by Libri from Montpellier: cf. L. Delisle, *Notices et extraits des manuscrits de la Bibliothèque Nationale*, 32 (Paris, 1886), 105; *Catalogue des manuscrits des fonds Libri et Barrois* (Paris, 1888), 43 f. I am grateful to Professor Bischoff for advice about date and origin.

[10] See EUTROPIUS, n. 14.

[11] Gius. Billanovich, *I primi umanisti e le tradizioni dei classici latini* (Fribourg, 1953), 17 f.

[12] M. Galdi, *Rivista Indo-Greco-Italica*, iv. 1–2 (1920), 59–64.

The ι manuscripts all lack the prologue and have a number of lacunae. Their common parent is reconstructed from four early witnesses: Vercelli, Eusebianus CLXXVII, s. X, written at Vercelli; Laur. 66.20 (s. XI), of unknown provenance; Rome, Bibl. Naz. Sessoriano 17, s. XI (Nonantola?); Leiden, Voss. Lat. Q.101, s. X or even late IX. The last is interesting: it does not appear to fit the geographical pattern, since it is probably of French origin; and it was used and annotated by Landolfo Colonna, so that it is likely to be the very book which be borrowed from Chartres Cathedral on 12 November 1309.[13]

γ poses the main problem of the text. Its home is Montecassino. Two copies of γ survive, Laur. 66.21, written at Montecassino in Beneventan script in the late eleventh century, and Vatican lat. 1860 (s. XIV). It is now accepted that the Vaticanus is derived from the Laurentianus for those parts of the text which the latter contained;[14] where the Laurentianus was defective, it took its text from another γ manuscript, perhaps from γ itself.[15] The γ text is idiosyncratic and by general agreement heavily interpolated. It is problematic because it shows a clear affinity in places with the text used by Orosius, and this led Rühl to give it considerable authority. But Orosius was widely read, and indeed available at Montecassino, so that Seel's view, that γ had derived readings from Orosius, may well be right.[16] It is γ which has preserved the name of our epitomist.

Justinus has a rich tradition, with an unusually large number of medieval Italian witnesses, and further exploration is overdue.

L. D. R.

[13] É. Pellegrin, 'Un manuscrit de Justin annoté par Landolfo Colonna (Leyde, Voss. lat. Q.101)', *IMU* 3 (1960), 241–9, tav. 9.

[14] 16–26.1.8, 30.2.8–44.4.3.   [15] Seel, *SIFC* 11 (1934), 272 ff.

[16] *Contra* H. Hagendahl, who maintains that the γ text pre-dated Orosius: *Orosius und Iustinus. Ein Beitrag zur iustinischen Textgeschichte* (Göteborgs Högskolas Årsskrift, 47.12), Göteborg, 1941. Seel replies in his second edition, xv f., and in *Eine römische Weltgeschichte*, 11 ff.

JUVENAL

In the last quarter of the fourth century Juvenal's satires emerged from a long period of neglect into sudden popularity. Not cited by Donatus or Jerome, Juvenal appears more than seventy times in the Virgilian commentaries of Servius, who may himself have contributed to the new interest in the satires.[1] By the last decade of the century the vogue of Juvenal was at its height,[2] and the poems had been equipped with an ample commentary, large parts of which survive.[3] Juvenal retained this central position when interest in the classics revived in the ninth century. His works formed part of Charlemagne's court library[4] and rapidly engaged the attention of Carolingian scholars. From this time onwards Juvenal circulated widely (often together with his fellow satirist Persius); the number of surviving manuscripts of his work far exceeds five hundred.[5]

The texts available in fourth-century Rome already contained a significant number of spurious lines, which therefore passed into the entire later tradition.[6] The revived attention of readers and expositors made its own mark on the text, difficult or obscure language often being replaced by more straightforward equivalents. The vast majority of the medieval manuscripts derive from ancient copies much affected by this process of interpolation; fortunately, however, a few manuscripts and fragments bear witness to another ancient form of the tradition, often

The best edition is that of W. V. Clausen (OCT, 1959); the most elaborate critical apparatus is in the edition of U. Knoche (Munich, 1950). Knoche's *Handschriftliche Grundlagen des Juvenaltextes* (Leipzig, 1940, *Philologus*, Suppl. 33.1) is the most detailed study of the transmission.

[1] Two manuscripts (KL in the second list below) contain the subscription 'Legi ego Niceus apud M. Serbium Romae [so K; L has 'Rome apud Servium magistrum'] et emendavi.' Some connection between Nicaeus and Servius the famous *grammaticus* is plausible, but the exact nature of Nicaeus' activity and its influence on the later tradition is impossible to determine. On *emendare* in such subscriptions see now J. E. G. Zetzel, *CPh* 75 (1980), 38–59. A second ancient subscription is preserved in Paris lat. 9345 (Clausen's H), f. 129ᵛ: 'Legente Aepicarpio scrinbentis Exuperantio servo' (Chatelain, pl. CXXXV).

[2] Amm. Marc. 28.4.14: 'quidam detestantes ut venena doctrinas Iuvenalem et Marium Maximum curatiore studio legunt, nulla volumina praeter haec in profundo otio contrectantes.' For Juvenal in the *Historia Augusta* (itself a product of the 390s), cf. A. D. E. Cameron, *Hermes*, 52 (1964), 363 ff.

[3] Edited by P. Wessner (Teubner, 1931). On the date, Th. Mommsen, *Gesammelte Schriften*, vii (Berlin, 1909), 509–11; a *terminus post quem* of 352/3 is provided by the reference to a *praefectus urbis* named Cerealis in the note on 10.24, but much of the material is of earlier date, cf. G. B. Townend, *CQ* 22 (1972), 376–87.   [4] *Karl der Grosse*, 42–62 (= Bischoff, *Mitt. Stud.* iii. 149–69).

[5] Handlist (far from complete) in Knoche, *Grundlagen*, 1 ff.; edn., xii ff.

[6] The precise number of such lines is disputed: Clausen brackets approximately fifty, Knoche about twice as many; cf. G. Jachmann, *NGG* 1943, 187–266, R. G. M. Nisbet, *JRS* 52 (1962), 233–8, E. Courtney, *BICS* 22 (1975), 147–62. I have not seen H. Högg, *Interpolationen bei Juvenal* (diss. Freiburg, 1971).

more corrupt but less subject to interpolation than the common class. The representatives of this relatively pure strain are as follows:[7]

P   Montpellier 125 (s. IX[1], Lorsch),[8] owned by P. Pithou and used for his edition of 1585. (Also contains Persius.)

Arou.   Fragmenta Arouiensia, parts of five leaves of a complete manuscript (s. X, Germany) broken up for binding, now in the Kantonsbibliothek in Aarau (contains 2.148–55, 3.6–13, 35–92, 6.136–93, 252–310, 311–39 (beginnings), 340–68 (ends), 427–55 (beginnings), 456–84 (ends), 7.57–85 (ends missing), 86–114 (beginnings missing), 115–72, with scholia.[9]

Sang.   St. Gall 870 (s. IX[2]), a florilegium (pp. 6–31) including 280 lines of Juvenal; pp. 40–326 contain the ancient scholia.[10]

S   Lemmata of the ancient scholia as preserved in P Arou. Sang. (the text of the scholia themselves often departs from that of the lemmata).

R   Paris lat.8072 (s. X ex., France?), ff. 94[v]–97[v] containing 1.1–2.66, ff. 98[r]–105[v] 5.98–6.437, ff. 106[r]–113[v] 3.32–5.97.

V   Vienna 107 (s. IX ex.), 1.1–2.59, 3.107–5.96.

The relationship of P Arou. Sang. is very close, the first two being nearly identical twins with the same mise-en-page.[11] R and V are less faithful witnesses to this strain; V in particular has been much influenced by readings of the other class.

The relationships of the manuscripts in the vulgate class are too thoroughly blurred by contamination to be depicted stemmatically, and even groupings based on geographical origin and shared lacunae are too unstable to be of much use.[12] The representatives of this vast group used by Clausen (the consensus of which he calls Φ) are these:[13]

A   Munich Clm 408 (s. XI, Germany).

F   Paris lat. 8071 (s. IX, France).

G   Paris lat. 7900A (s. IX/X, Milan?).[14]

---

[7] Sigla as in Clausen. Plates of the following manuscripts in Chatelain: P (CXXIII, CXXVII), Sang. (CXXIXb), R (CXXVIII), F(XIV), G (LXXXII), H (CXXXV), K (CXXXIVb), L (CXXXIVa), Z (CXXIXa).   [8] Bischoff, Lorsch, 38, 98 f.

[9] H. Wirz, Hermes, 15 (1880), 437–48; Wessner (n. 3, above), x–xi.

[10] C. Stephan, RhM 40 (1885), 263–82; Wessner, xi–xii.

[11] Wirz (n. 9, above), 442, E. Courtney, 'The Transmission of Juvenal's Text', BICS 14 (1967), 38–50 (an admirably lucid account of the entire tradition), esp. 46 f. The excerpts from Juvenal (thirty-two verses) in the metrical florilegium of Mico of Saint-Riquier (c.825) also belong to this group; cf. L. Traube, PLAC III.1.279 ff.

[12] For the attempt cf. Knoche, Grundlagen. A 'taxonomic' study was undertaken by J. G. Griffith, MH 25 (1968), 101–38, on which cf. M. L. West, Textual Criticism and Editorial Technique (Teubner, Stuttgart, 1973), 46–7. Clausen dispenses with all grouping of his Φ witnesses.

[13] Of the many other manuscripts reported by Knoche perhaps the most noteworthy are Leiden, Voss. Lat. F.64 (s. X[2], France = B) and Voss. Lat. Q.18 (s. X[2], France, perhaps Auxerre, = V). B is used by Clausen along with KHU for the vta of Juvenal.

[14] B. Bischoff cited in H. C. Gotoff, The Transmission of the Text of Lucan in the Ninth Century (Cambridge, Mass., 1971), 19. G's affiliations are remarkably various: from 1.1 to 6.476 it displays no consistent affinities; it then agrees often with P in the remainder of the sixth satire, combines with U in 7–13, and thereafter reverts to its unaligned state. (Cf. Knoche, Grundlagen, 143–7; Griffith (n. 12, above), 136–8).

H   Paris lat. 9345 (s. XI, from Cluny).
K   Florence, Laur. 34.42 (s. XI).
L   Leiden B.P.L. 82 (s. X/XI).
O   Oxford, Bodl. Canon. Class. Lat. 41 (s. XI/XII, south Italy, perhaps Montecassino).
T   Cambridge, Trinity College 1241 (O.4.10) (s. X², England; from St. Augustine's Canterbury).
U   Vatican, Urb.lat. 661 (s. XI in., Germany?).
Z   B.L. Add.15600 (s. IX ³⁻⁴/₄, France).

Although P with its relatives and Φ comprise the two main channels of tradition, ancient readings have also been preserved in several other sources:

(a) the extensive ancient commentary of which large extracts are preserved in P Arou. Sang., and of which some additional fragments are embedded in the Carolingian scholia found in several Φ manuscripts and, probably, in the comments attributed to 'Probus' by Giorgio Valla in his Venice edition of 1486.[15]

(b) fragments of ancient books:

(1) Bob. = Vatican lat. 5750, pp. 77–8 (s. VI¹, probably Italy = *CLA* I.30), containing 14.324–15.43 with scholia (also Persius, 1.53–104).[16]

(2) Ambr. = Milan, Ambr. Cimelio 3 (s. VI, probably Italy = *CLA* III.305), containing 14.250–6, 268–91, 303–19.[17]

---

[15] On the Carolingian scholia (perhaps compiled by Heiric and Remigius of Auxerre) cf. Wessner (n. 3, above), xxiii–xxxii. On medieval and Renaissance commentaries generally see E. M. Sanford, *CTC* i (1960), 175–238, F. E. Cranz and P. O. Kristeller, *CTC* iii (1976), 432–45. On Valla's 'Probus' cf. W. S. Anderson, *Traditio*, 21 (1965), 383–424, A. Bartalucci, *SIFC* 45 (1973), 233–57. Valla apparently used a second commentary throughout to supplement the 'Probi interpretamenta . . . plane perexigua' that gave out at 8.198; most of the comments not attributed to 'Probus' overlap with either the P-group material or the Carolingian scholia. Valla also cited a *codex antiquissimus* (or *uetustissimus*) whose readings show significant agreements with the strain of text represented by U (at times with the support of G and other manuscripts). After 6.614, U, 'Probus', and the *codex antiquissimus* offer three lines not found in the majority of manuscripts; the lines are certainly ancient, though not necessarily genuine (as argued by G. Luck, *HSCP* 76 (1972), 229–30). U itself contains a commentary under Probus' name on ff. 62ʳ–134ʳ. (O. Jahn suggested that the name 'Probus' migrated to a set of scholia on Juvenal from the *vita* of Persius, 'de commentario Probi Valeri sublata'.) Lombardy is the most likely place for Valla to have discovered his old manuscript of Juvenal: G was probably written at Milan and U might have been produced by a German scribe in a Lombard centre, like Munich Clm 14420, the *Commentum Monacense* on Terence (Brescia, *c*.1000, cf. B. Bischoff, *IMU* 15 (1972), 53–61). The writer of a verse letter in the Munich manuscript (f. 144ʳ) recalls reading Juvenal with his correspondent at Brescia and being hampered by the lack of a commentary on the last two books; G. Billanovich, *IMU* 17 (1974), 56–8, suggests that the writer (whom he identifies as Hildemar of Corbie) had used the manuscript in which Valla found his 'Probus', whose comments extended nearly to the end of the third 'book' of Juvenal. On Juvenal scholia see also J. E. G. Zetzel, *Latin Textual Criticism in Antiquity* (New York, 1981), 179–91.

[16] Plate in F. Ehrle-P. Liebaert, *Specimina codicum latinorum Vaticanorum*² (Berlin, 1932), 6d.

[17] A. Ratti, *Rend. Istituto Lombardo*, 42 (1909), 961–9.

(3) Ant. = Fragmentum Antinoense, a parchment leaf from Antinoë (*c*.500), containing 7.149–98 (*CLA* Suppl. 1710).[18]

None of these fragments agrees consistently with either branch of the medieval tradition.[19]

(c) occasional ancient readings preserved by indirect transmission[20] or in individual manuscripts. The most spectacular of these isolated survivals came to light in 1899 when an Oxford undergraduate, E. O. Winstedt, discovered in O thirty-six otherwise unknown verses in the sixth satire (O1–34 after 6.365, 6.373A–B).[21] The lines are still variously regarded as genuine (now the majority view), as interpolated, and as a remnant of a lost first edition of the satires.[22] They are clearly ancient (having left traces in the scholia) and the work of a writer of some ability. If genuine, this section was not only omitted in both main branches of the tradition, but three lines based on part of it (i.e. 346–8, cf. O29–34) were invented as a substitute. Like the other serious disturbances in Juvenal's text, the excision or intrusion of the 'Oxford fragment' took place during the earliest stages of the transmission, before the relative stability imposed by the fourth-century revival.

R. J. T.

[18] C. H. Roberts, *JEA* 21 (1935), 199–209 (with facsimile).

[19] The same appears true of the two leaves (s. IX²/₄, Fleury) removed from the binding of Orléans 295, containing 2.32 –89 and 3.35–93 ('Aurel.' in Clausen), cf. A. P. McKinlay and E. K. Rand, *HSCP* 49 (1938), 229–63. The text of Aurel. is better than that of P or Φ taken singly and has no significant error in common with P, even though its format is identical with P's (and in 3.35–93 with that of P Arou.); Courtney (n. 11, above), 47 f., regards it as a contaminated text.

[20] e.g. *Cocytum* at 2.150 restored from Liutprand of Cremona, *Antapodosis*, 5.8 (*et contum* VΦ, *et pontum* PSTU Arou. Σ); cf. J. Willis, *Latin Textual Criticism* (Urbana, Ill., 1972), 187 ff.

[21] *CR* 13 (1899), 201 ff.

[22] A selection only. Genuine: E. Courtney, *Mnem.* ser. 4.15 (1962), 262–6, M. Coffey, *Lustrum*, 8 (1963), 179–84; interpolated: Knoche, B. Axelson, *ΔΡΑΓΜΑ Martino P. Nilsson . . . dedicatum* (Lund, 1939), 41–55; remnant of first edition: F. Leo, *Hermes*, 44 (1909), 600–17, G. Luck, *HSCP* 76 (1972), 217–32. The case against authenticity has not yet been stated in the most forceful possible form, but the alternative to Juvenal's authorship is not necessarily conscious interpolation (which is indeed unlikely at such length and with such quality). Perhaps O1–29 *pergula* are from another satirist's work (for the domestic *cinaedus* as a figure of jest Courtney aptly compares Lucian, *De merc. cond.* 33) and only the bridge passage *noui*–O34, generally admitted to be less successful than 346–8, is the work of an interpolator. Luck may be right in giving the scholiastic tradition credit for the early transmission of the lines, but Servius' handling of the 'Helen episode' (*Aen.* 2.567–88), which Luck regards as another instance of genuine material preserved by a commentator, shows instead that even good fourth-century scholars could be taken in by allegedly 'lost' fragments of classical authors.

These lines (whatever their status) are probably one of several important classical texts whose survival is due to the active scriptorium of Montecassino under Abbot Desiderius, cf. H. Bloch, 'Montecassino's Teachers and Library in the High Middle Ages', *La scuola nell'occidente latino dell'alto medioevo* (*Settimane*, 19 (1972), 563–605, esp. 582–6).

In a discussion not yet published, F. Newton argues that O and Vatican, Urb. lat. 341 (manuscript of Ovid's *Metamorphoses*) were at Montecassino in s. XIII, since both contain corrections by the scribe who also corrected Montecassino 374 (Prudentius, at the abbey since s. XI). O, or a manuscript related to it, may have been in Rome at the end of s. XVII; Latin satires written in the early 1690s by Ludovico Sergardi, an associate of Cardinal Pietro Ottoboni, contain verbal echoes of the O verses (cf. S. Citroni Marchetti, *Maia*, 29/30 (1977/8), 61–8).

LAUS PISONIS

The text of the anonymous panegyric of Calpurnius Piso rests on two sources: (1) the 1527 Basle edition of Johann Sichard, taken from a manuscript then at Lorsch which has since disappeared; and (2) the *Florilegium Gallicum*, compiled at Orléans in the middle of the twelfth century, which contains 196 of the 261 verses. B. L. Ullman sorted out the transmission of the panegyric in his series of studies on the texts in medieval florilegia, published in *Classical Philology*, 1928–32.[1]

In both traditions, that of the Lorsch manuscript and that of the *Florilegium Gallicum*, the *Laus Pisonis* is associated with the transmission of the minor poems of Virgil. According to Sichard, the panegyric was attributed to Virgil in the Lorsch codex, which also contained twenty lines of epigrams about Virgil, attributed to Ovid. Ullman points out that the epigrams circulate in at least one group of manuscripts with the *Appendix Vergiliana*, and suggests that the latter was also in the Lorsch manuscript, preceding the *Laus Pisonis*. As evidence for this, he notes that the minor Virgil appears in the ninth-century catalogue of the library of Murbach: '281. Liber Eneydos. 282. Eiusdem Dire, Culicis, Ethne, Copa, Mecenas, Ciris, Catalepion, Priapeya, Moretum.' This, Ullman suggested, is a relative of the Lorsch manuscript, given the proximity of the two houses and the known overlap in contents of the Murbach and Lorsch catalogues.

The *Florilegium Gallicum* contains lengthy extracts from the *Laus Pisonis* (amounting to 75 per cent of the whole) and extracts from the minor works of Virgil in the following sequence: *Culex, Aetna, Laus Pisonis*. Although this last has the rubric *De laude Pisonis*, the headline reads *Lucanus in Catalecton*; and the first line is from the *Ciris*, followed by the 196 lines of the panegyric. In the process of the florilegium's compilation, the *Laus Pisonis* was mixed up with the *Ciris* and the *Catalepton*. The sequence of the florilegium's exemplar was clearly similar to that reflected in the Murbach book.

The *Florilegium Gallicum* is a large collection of extracts from ancient Latin authors, of both prose and verse, containing texts from a number of rather rare authors – Tibullus, Petronius, Calpurnius, and Nemesianus, among others. It must have been compiled by the middle of the twelfth century, since it was used in the *Moralium Dogma Philosophorum*, which is thought to have been written for Henry II of England before his accession in 1159. The florilegium can be associated

---

[1] See esp. 'The Text Tradition and Authorship of the *Laus Pisonis*', *CPh* 24 (1929), 109–32; see also R. Verdière, in *Collection Latomus*, 19 (1954); A. Seel, diss., Erlangen-Nürnberg, 1969.

with the Loire region on the basis of the texts that it contains; moreover, it has been shown, for its text of the *Querolus*, to have drawn on Vatican lat. 4929, which evidently then belonged to the cathedral of Orléans.[2]

The one appearance of the panegyric in a medieval catalogue is in an anonymous book-list of the eleventh century: 'Liber catalepton Pisoni' (Delisle, ii. 446–7). Clearly, the *Laus Pisonis* was already embedded in the Virgilian appendix at this date. Unfortunately, the home of this list is not known. It appears on a blank leaf immediately following the tenth-century pontifical of Sherborne Abbey (now Paris lat. 943), and is headed, 'Hic continetur numerus divinorum librorum Sanctae Mariae quos custodit Dodo'. While the manuscript was at Sherborne in the early eleventh century, it eventually belonged to Notre-Dame in Paris, where it was seen in the sixteenth century by François Pithou. D. de Bruyne thought it to be an inventory of the library of Notre-Dame[3]; but it might more probably be the inventory of some other church dedicated to the Virgin, one with a school which drew scholars from England in the eleventh century – such as Chartres.

Once in the *Florilegium Gallicum* the *Laus Pisonis* was assured of an audience, since the florilegium is known in ten copies and a large number of manuscripts which contain parts of it. This florilegium was the source of the *Laus Pisonis* known to the Verona florilegist and to Guglielmo da Pastrengo in Italy in the fourteenth century, and of the texts known to Junius, Scaliger, and Martyni-Laguna.

R. H. R.

---

[2] A. Gagnér, *Florilegium Gallicum*, Skrifter utgivna av Vetenskaps-societeten, 18 (Lund, 1936); J. Hamacher, *Florilegium Gallicum*, Lateinische Sprache und Literatur des Mittelalters, 5 (Frankfurt a.M., 1975); R. H. R., '*Florilegia* and Latin Classical Authors in Twelfth- and Thirteenth-Century Orléans', *Viator*, 10 (1979), 131–60.   [3] *Rev. bén.* 29 (1912), 481–5.

LIVY

Livy's *Ab urbe condita* was so monumentally large that it could only survive piecemeal. Also, Livy's method of composition was such that the work naturally fell into smaller units, into decades and pentads, and these found their separate ways to the Middle Ages. Of the original 142 books we have only the First Decade (Books 1–10), the Third Decade (21–30), the Fourth Decade (31–40), and the first pentad of the Fifth

Decade (41–5); the rest is lost, apart from an isolated fragment of Book 91.[1] The transmission is complex, being fundamentally different for each decade; but since it was only a matter of time before chance and human initiative succeeded in uniting the surviving portions of Livy, eventually the distinct streams of transmission converge and combine. The traditions of Books 26–30 and 31–40 merged at an early stage; and Petrarch, who devoted more critical attention to more of Livy than anyone had since Antiquity, features in the transmission of all but the last surviving pentad. The following account is essentially a simplification of this large and complex phenomenon.

First Decade

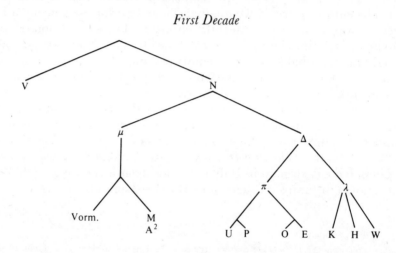

The text of the First Decade rests on two foundations of great antiquity.[2] The first is an uncial codex of the early fifth century, Verona XL (38) (*CLA* IV. 499), known as V. It was written in Italy, was palimpsested at Luxeuil at the beginning of the eighth century, and had

The above account can be readily supplemented from the excellent material on Livy's text already available in print. Of particular importance are two articles by Professor G. Billanovich, 'Petrarch and the Textual Tradition of Livy', *JWI* 14 (1951), 137–208, and 'Dal Livio di Raterio (Laur. 63, 19) al Livio del Petrarca (B. M. Harl. 2493)', *IMU* 2 (1959), 103–78; the prefaces to the OCT editions of R. M. Ogilvie (vol. i, Books 1–5, 1974) and A. H. McDonald (vol. v, Books 31–5, 1965); and, on Books 21–5, T. A. Dorey, 'The Agennensis (Livy 21–25)', *CQ* 7 (1957), 146–50, 'The Textual Tradition of Livy 21–25', 8 (1958), 161–4, 'Livy XXI–XXV: Petrarch and the Codices Deteriores', *Euphrosyne*, 3 (1969), 59–72, together with his prefaces to the Teubner editions of Books 21–2 (1971) and 23–5 (1976). Billanovich's comprehensive study of the transmission, *La tradizione del testo di Livio e le origini dell' umanesimo*, reached us too late to influence this account; vols. i.1 and ii have now appeared (Padua, 1981).

[1] Vatican, Pal. lat. 24 (*CLA* 1.75), ff. 73, 75, 76, 78. On the composition and history of this manuscript, see J. Fohlen, 'Recherches sur le manuscrit palimpseste Vatican, Pal. lat. 24', *Scrittura e civiltà*, 3 (1979), 195–222. The Livy manuscript is written in rustic capitals of the fourth century.
[2] There is also a fourth-century papyrus fragment, too small to be of any significance: Oxford, Bodl. Lat. class. f. 5 (P), P. Oxy. xi. 1379, *CLA* II.247.

found its way by the ninth century to Verona, bearing Gregory's *Moralia* as its upper text. It contains fragments of Books 3–6.

All our medieval manuscripts belong to a different tradition (N); this is in general superior to V, ancient, and of illustrious ancestry. By a lucky chance we know, from a letter written by him in AD 401, that Q. Aurelius Symmachus, the vigorous opponent of Ambrose, was engaged on the massive enterprise of correcting the whole of Livy.[3] A famous series of subscriptions appended in our manuscripts to the books of the First Decade reveal that this was a co-operative venture undertaken by the related and equally distinguished families of the Nicomachi and Symmachi and that our medieval text is a descendant of what is traditionally called the Nicomachean 'recension'.[4] It emerged from the romantic background of the pagan revival of the late fourth century,[5] the positive product of a lost cause. The descendants of N divide into two families, those which belong to the thin line of descent through the cathedrals (μ), and those which derive from the much broader stream of the tradition (Δ) which ramifies through the activity of the Carolingian monasteries.

μ is represented by two manuscripts, probably *gemelli*, the extant Florence, Laur. 63.19 (M) and the lost codex Vormatiensis. M is a marvellous book, written by five different scribes at the Cathedral of Verona sometime before 968; its execution was the inspiration of Ratherius, then for the third time Bishop of Verona; his particular interests and splenetic temper are amply mirrored in M's marginalia.[6] Its twin was discovered in the sixteenth century at the Cathedral of Worms (Vorm.); it was used by Beatus Rhenanus and Gelenius for the second Froben edition of Livy (Basle, 1535), and then it disappeared. It has been plausibly conjectured that Vorm. was copied at Verona at the same time as M and presented to Otto I on his visit to Verona in 967.[7] The only other evidence for μ are the variants which Petrarch (A[2]), who had access to a manuscript of this group,[8] copied into his text of the First Decade (A = British Library, Harley 2493).

On the monastic side of the tradition we have a large number of manuscripts dating from the mid-ninth century onwards. These fall into two classes, λ and π. So much is clear, but there is an editorial problem in choosing from the manuscripts available those which best

---

[3] *Epist.* 9.13: 'Munus totius Liviani operis quod spopondi etiam nunc diligentia emendationis moratur.'

[4] The subscriptions in Livy and the work of the subscribers have been studied by J. E. G. Zetzel, 'The Subscriptions in the Manuscripts of Livy and Fronto and the Meaning of *Emendatio*', *CPh* 75 (1980), 38–59. A Nicomachean subscription is reproduced from O in *Survival*, no. 88 and pl. X(a).

[5] H. Bloch, in *The Conflict between Paganism and Christianity in the Fourth Century*, ed. A. Momigliano (Oxford, 1963), 215 f.

[6] Billanovich, 'Dal Livio di Raterio', 112 ff.   [7] ibid. 174 ff.

[8] ibid. 147 f. Billanovich conjectures that Petrarch had access to a copy of M made by Simon of Arezzo about 1328, when he was canon of Verona.

represent their respective families;[9] the stemma depicted above is that used by Ogilvie in his OCT edition. The manuscripts which he brings on to the stage to represent λ are K = Copenhagen, Fragm. 19 IX, the remains of a manuscript written at Corbie in the time of Hadoard;[10] H = Harley 2672, s. X ex., written in Germany and later in the possession of Nicolaus of Cues; W = a bifolium recently found at Marburg, German, perhaps from Fulda.[11] Among the understudies relegated to the wings are Petrarch's Livy (as above, c.1325) and a ninth-century Lupus manuscript, Paris lat. 5726. On the π side we have U = Uppsala C.908, s. X ex.; P = Paris lat. 5725, s. IX med., France; O = Bodl. Auct. T.1.24, s. XI in., eastern France; E = Einsiedeln 348, s. X in., France. Two other closely connected manuscripts of this group indicate that the π text had reached Italy at an early date; these are Bamberg Class. 34 (M.IV.8), s. IX², written in Italy, and a bifolium at Prague (Univ. 1224 (VII A 16), s. X) written in a Beneventan hand, possibly for Duke Giovanni of Naples.[12]

Third Decade

For the purposes of recension the Third Decade is best divided into its constituent pentads.

Books 21–5

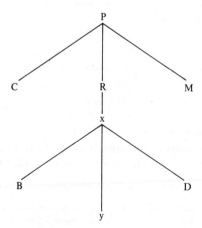

  [9] In his review of Ogilvie's edition (*JRS* 67 (1977), 239–41), J. Briscoe criticizes the editor for simplifying his earlier stemma (*CQ* 7 (1957), 68–81) and ousting manuscripts which still have a part to play; for other doubts see Zetzel, 41 f.   [10] Bischoff, *Mitt. Stud.* i.58.
  [11] R. M. Ogilvie, 'Fragments of a new MS. of Livy', *RhM* 114 (1971), 209–17.
  [12] *Beneventan Script*², i.18, ii.119; E. A. Lowe, *Scriptura Beneventana* (Oxford, 1929), pl. XLVII.

For these books of Livy we still have the archetype. This is a handsome but corrupt uncial manuscript of the first half of the fifth century, the Puteanus (P = Paris lat. 5730, *CLA* v. 562). A subscription indicates that it was read at Avellino near Naples shortly after it was written. The pattern of its copies strongly suggests that by the end of the eighth century it had found a home in the Court Library of Charlemagne.[13] Its earliest extant copy is Vatican, Reg. lat. 762 (*CLA* I. 109) = R, a beautiful book transcribed directly from it by eight scribes at Tours about 800.[14] By the third quarter of the ninth century P had moved, with some other manuscripts from the Court Library, to Corbie, for another copy (M = Florence, Laur. 63.20) is one of the manuscripts executed at Corbie while Hadoard was *custos librorum*.[15] The third copy (C = Paris lat. 5731, s. XI[1]) is also French. Apart from some fragments at Munich (FM = Clm 29224 (1.2 (*olim* 29000) s. XI, probably derived from C), the rest of the tradition descends from the Tours manuscript, via a hypothetical copy (x). The two extant representatives of the next stratum of descent are B (Bamberg Class. 35 (M. IV. 9), s. XI (*inc.* 24.7.8)) and D (Cambridge, Trinity College 637 (R.4.4), s. XII[2]). D was earlier at Christ Church Canterbury and belonged to Thomas Becket; it is probably one of the books which he had copied during his exile (1164–70) in France, at Pontigny and Sens, and which he brought back to Canterbury in 1170.[16] A third copy of x is the putative progenitor of the whole Italian tradition of these books of Livy (y). The best known of the Italian manuscripts, about fifty in number, are the Laurentianus Notatus (Laur. 63.21, s. XIII = N) and Petrarch's manuscript (A). The latter, and the corrections which Petrarch made to it, play a dominant role in the evolution of the Italian tradition.[17]

Books 26–30

In these books the traditions of the Third and Fourth Decades overlap. The Puteanus and its descendants, which have provided us with our text of Books 21–5, are still in business and there is no new problem here. But for Books 26–40 (and thus overlapping with P for 26–30) we also have what has been called the Spirensian tradition. This owes its name to a

---

[13] *Karl der Grosse*, 62 (= Bischoff, *Mitt. Stud.* iii.168 f.). A complete reduced facsimile of P was published by H. Omont (Paris, 1907).

[14] E. K. Rand, *Studies in the Script of Tours, I: A Survey of the Manuscripts of Tours* (Cambridge, Mass., 1929), vol. i, especially p. 96.; vol. ii, plates XXVI–XXVII.

[15] Bischoff, loc. cit. n. 10, above.

[16] M. R. James, *The Ancient Libraries of Canterbury and Dover* (Cambridge, 1903), 83; F. Whitehead, 'Codex Cantabrigiensis (D) in Trinity College Library, Cambridge', *CQ* 11 (1917), 69–80.

[17] Billanovich, 'Petrarch and the Textual Tradition', 172 ff.; T. A. Dorey in the articles listed above.

lost manuscript, the *codex Spirensis*, which contained Books 26–40 and belonged to the Chapter Library of Speyer. But in 1951 Billanovich[18] demonstrated that a similar and in many ways more dramatic part had been played in the tradition of these books by another lost manuscript from another great cathedral, the *vetus Carnotensis* of Chartres. The precise implications of this discovery for the text of Livy were worked out by McDonald in the revised OCT edition of Books 31–5, in which the complementary researches of these two scholars bore fruit. But the same has not yet been done for Books 26–30,[19] which consequently remain a rather grey area of Livy's text. Billanovich's original view that the Spirensis was copied from the Carnotensis did not hold up for the Fourth Decade[20] and appears to be equally mistaken in the case of Books 26–30.[21] Consequently, though the details will only become clear with a new edition, the basic pattern for the transmission of Books 26–30 is as follows:

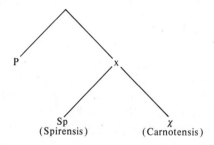

P is, as before, the Puteanus. The evidence for x, the so-called Spirensian tradition, is as follows:

1. Part of a palimpsest which, until its destruction by fire in 1904, was in the Biblioteca Nazionale at Turin (A.II.2*, ff. 47–53; cf. *CLA* IV, p. 12).[22] This manuscript, apparently written in uncials in Italy in the fifth century, was rewritten at Bobbio in the seventh. Known to editors as Ta, it contained parts of Books 27 and 29.

2. The *folium Monacense*, Munich Clm 23491, s. XI, Italian = S: a single leaf containing a fragment of Book 28.

3. Sp = those readings which are explicitly cited from the Speyer manuscript by Beatus Rhenanus in the edition which he and Gelenius published at Basle in 1535. (Sp ut vid. or Sp? are used when the provenance of the readings is less certain.)

[18] 'Petrarch and the Textual Tradition'.

[19] A Teubner text of 26–30 is being prepared by P. G. Walsh.

[20] McDonald, praef. xxxvi f.; Dorey, *JRS* 57 (1967), 279.

[21] Dorey, *Euphrosyne*, 2 (1968), 180; H. Testroet, ibid. 7 (1975–6), 64 ff.

[22] The Livy is the one text in the palimpsest collection for which *CLA* was unable to reproduce or record any photograph.

4. χ = the lost Carnotensis, which has to be reconstructed from its descendants. This process is best seen in the Fourth Decade, where we are on firmer ground; *mutatis mutandis* the same will have to be done for Books 26–30.

5. Any of the *recentiores* which can be of help in reconstructing x.[23]

When so much of the evidence is fragmentary or lost, it is difficult to build up a coherent picture. It seems almost certain, as had been earlier conjectured, that S is in fact a surviving leaf of the Spirensis itself,[24] which would in that case be an eleventh-century book of Italian origin. The transmission of the Fourth Decade suggests that the Chartres manuscript was likewise of Italian origin,[25] and so is the Turin palimpsest. It would make a tidier picture if further investigation confirmed that our two cathedral codices ultimately descend from the Turin palimpsest (Ta) for Books 26–30, just as they descend from the Piacenza fragments (F) for Books 31–40. The pentad and the decade would then have been joined together at an early date in northern Italy.[26]

Fourth Decade

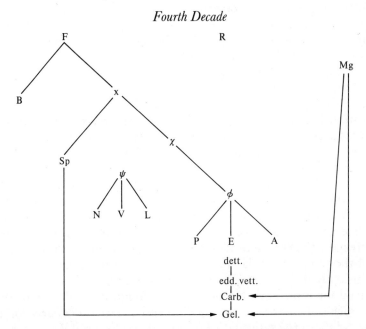

[23] These require further investigation. For instance, Harley 2684 (s. xv = H) has been influenced by the Spirensian tradition for one small area of its text; see S. K. Johnson, OCT vol. iv, praef. vii, xxix f.; Dorey, *Euphrosyne*, 2 (1968), 177–81.

[24] H. Testroet, '*Folium Monacense* and the Spirensian Tradition of the Third Decade of Livy', *Euphrosyne*, 7 (1975–6), 63–71.

[25] Billanovich, 'Petrarch and the Textual Tradition', 187–8; McDonald, praef. xxxvii.

[26] Possibly pooling the resources of Bobbio and Nonantola, as Billanovich suggested, 188 n. 1.

Before dealing with the main stream of the tradition of the Fourth Decade, which derives from F, mention must be made of two manuscripts of different origin. The first is Vatican lat. 10696 (*CLA* I.57 = R), fragments of an ancient codex (s. IV/V). This had a more distinguished fate than most wrappers: it was used to preserve relics from the Holy Land and was found in 1906 in the Sancta Sanctorum of St. John Lateran, in a cypress box made for Pope Leo III (795–816). It contains fragments of Book 34. The other is a lost manuscript (Mg) at one time in Mainz Cathedral, conjecturally written in a ninth-century insular hand.[27] It was used by Nicholaus Carbach for the edition of Livy which he and Wolfgang Angst published at Mainz in 1519 (Carb.) and again collated by Gelenius for the Basle edition of 1535 (Gel.). It is our only source for part of Book 40 (37.3 *ad fin.*).

Both these fine books came to grief. F too exists only as fragments of binding, Bamberg Class. 35ª (*CLA* VIII. 1028, s. V). This uncial manuscript was at one time at Piacenza. It was given to Bamberg Cathedral by Henry II in 1007 from the inheritance of Otto III. Otto had acquired the book at Piacenza during the years 996–1001 through the agency of his former tutor John Philagathos, Bishop of Piacenza and Abbot of Nonantola, though the precise nature of the transaction is unclear.[28] Fortunately a copy of F, made at Bamberg in the eleventh century, still survives, Bamberg Class. 35 (M.IV.9) (= B). From an earlier copy of F, written in northern Italy, descend our two cathedral codices of Speyer and Chartres, though, as we have seen, x had succeeded in adding Books 26–30 to those of the Fourth Decade.[29]

Mention has already been made of the Spirensis, here reduced to such readings as we can assume, from a study of the Basle edition, to have been in it. The vast majority of the extant manuscripts, more than ninety in number, descend from the lost Chartres codex (χ) and it is this story which was so excitingly unravelled by Professor Billanovich in 1951. Landolfo Colonna, canon of Chartres and uncle of Petrarch's patron Giovanni Colonna, is known to have twice borrowed a copy of Livy from Chartres Cathedral Library, in 1303 and 1309. He left Chartres after a dispute in 1328 and settled at Avignon, at this time the seat of the papal curia. He had made a copy of the Chartres Livy and from his copy (φ) was transcribed the sumptuous book which was later produced for him, Paris lat. 5690 = P (though it is called L in Books 26–30 to avoid confusion with the Puteanus). Two other early copies of φ exist, of about the same date (*c.*1330). One is Escorial R.I.4 (= E), the other part of Petrarch's famous Livy (A). Petrarch too was at Avignon at this time and putting together his own text of Livy. This was a

[27] L. Traube, *ABAW* III Kl. 24.1 (1904), 24 f.

[28] McDonald, praef. xi f.; Billanovich, 'Petrarch and the Textual Tradition', 188 n. 1.

[29] It also succeeded in losing Book 33 and the end of 40.

composite book. The nucleus was a manuscript of the Third Decade (s. XII/XIII), an Italian descendant of the common Puteanus tradition. Now that Petrarch had access to φ, he was able to improve his text of Books 26–30 by adding variants and supplements (P had omissions) from the Chartres tradition. To the Third Decade he appended copies of both the First and the Fourth Decade, having the latter transcribed from φ. Thus he became the proud possessor of all three Decades available at the time and had a better text, one would imagine, than anyone since Antiquity. His Livy was later used to great effect by Lorenzo Valla.[30]

Most of the later manuscripts are corrupt and contaminated descendants of φ. But McDonald was able to isolate from this ruck a group of five manuscripts which were derived from another examplar (ψ). These are all Florentine[31] and were written between the years 1413 and 1453. From these he chose three as the best representatives of ψ: Oxford, New College 279 ($c.$1430–40, = N); Vatican lat. 3331 (1453, = V); Laur. 89 inf. 3.3 (mid 1440s, = L). As ψ was closely related to φ, McDonald made the natural assumption that they were twin offspring of χ, and this was the position adopted in his edition of Books 31–5.

ψ and to some extent φ are now back in the melting-pot. It seems probable that ψ is an older manuscript,[32] venerable enough to join the company of χ itself, and both its origin and its position in the stemma have to be reconsidered. Moreover, it had long been clear that the Fourth Decade had begun to circulate again in Italy before its rediscovery at Chartres: it was known to Lovato Lovati and his friends at Padua in the latter part of the thirteenth century,[33] and to Gervasio Riccobaldo in the early years of the fourteenth.[34] Billanovich has recently reported that he has evidence that Petrarch had at his disposal not only a copy of the Chartres manuscript but also a copy of the text known forty years earlier to Lovato, and that he combined readings from them.[35] Until the mystery of the Paduan connection is elucidated and its implications for the text explored,[36] ψ must remain in limbo and the reconstruction of φ, in so far as it depends on Petrarch, be in some doubt.

[30] Billanovich, 'Petrarch and the Textual Tradition', *passim*. The presence of a third hand, belonging to neither Petrarch nor Valla, has been recognized by some and strenuously denied by others.

[31] A. C. de la Mare, 'Florentine Manuscripts of Livy in the Fifteenth Century', in *Livy* (ed. T. A. Dorey, London, 1971), 177–99.

[32] Suggested by A. C. de la Mare, ibid. 177. For evidence that this may indeed be the case, see J. Briscoe, 'Notes on the Manuscripts of Livy's Fourth Decade', *BRL* 62 (1980), 311–27.

[33] Billanovich, 'Petrarch and the Textual Tradition', 208; A. Perosa, *Atene e Roma*, 13 (1954), 26.   [34] T. Hankey, *JWI*, 21 (1958), 220.

[35] 'Petrarca e Padova', *Convegno Internazionale Francesco Petrarca 1974, Acc. Naz. dei Lincei, Atti dei Convegni Lincei*, 10 (Rome, 1976), 197.

[36] The task of editing the new OCT volume of Books 36–40 has passed, on the death of McDonald, to P. G. Walsh. In the meantime, there are pertinent observations in Briscoe, 'Notes on the Manuscripts'.

Fifth Decade

After the complication of the earlier books, it is a relief to pass to the monolithic simplicity of the Fifth Decade. Our only source for these books is Vienna 15 (V), written in uncials in Italy in the early fifth century.[37] By about the late eighth century it had crossed the Alps and was in the possession of 'Theatbertus episcopus de Dorostat' (Durstede, near Utrecht), possibly[38] Thiatert, Bishop of Utrecht c.784. By the ninth century it had moved to Lorsch and there it sat on the shelf, unread and unsung, until discovered by Simon Grynaeus in 1527. It seems to have originally contained the whole Decade,[39] but the second pentad was already lost when the book came into the hands of Theatbertus and there were further losses of leaves; the editio princeps, edited by Grynaeus and printed by Froben (Basle, 1531), is our only source for the first chapters (1.1–9.10) of Book 41.

L. D. R.

[37] CLA x.1472. There is a complete facsimile in S. de Vries, Codices Graeci et Latini photographice depicti, xi (Leiden, 1907), with a detailed description by C. Wessely. The manuscript is noted for the peculiar nature of the corruptions which it contains, and the theory has been recently advanced that these are due to transcription from an exemplar in early cursive script: see M. Zelzer, 'Palaeographische Bemerkungen zur Vorlage der Wiener Liviushandschrift', Antidosis, Festschrift für Walther Kraus zum 70 Geburtstag (WS Beiheft 5, 1972), 487–501. These Books have been edited by C. Giarratano (Rome, 1933) and P. Jal (Budé, 3 vols., Paris, 1971–9); J. Briscoe is working on a new edition for Teubner.

[38] Bischoff would not rule out an early ninth-century date for the Theatbertus entry: Lorsch, 88 n. 8. On ff. 20ʳ and 24ᵛ there are marginalia in Anglo-Saxon minuscule; Bischoff (p. 64) points out that Durstede had commercial links with England and suggests that an Anglo-Saxon missionary might have brought the book from England or from a journey to Rome.

[39] On the last page is the incipit of Book 46.

LUCAN

The great popularity of Lucan's *Bellum ciuile*[1] in Antiquity and the Middle Ages is reflected in the richness of the tradition: more than 400 complete and partial copies,[2] including fragments of three ancient books,[3] five complete ninth-century manuscripts and a fragment of a sixth, and two sets of ancient commentary.[4]

The tradition is also untidy, probably from the first edition onwards. Lucan died with his epic unfinished and except for the first three books unrevised. His executors may in some places have incorporated rejected or alternative drafts in the published text, perhaps marking them with critical signs that were not transcribed in later copies.[5] Several ancient codices survived into the Carolingian period, each offering a somewhat different combination of the readings current in late Antiquity.

So far only the ninth-century manuscripts have received thorough

The edition most widely used is that of A. E. Housman (Oxford, 1926). Its reporting of manuscript readings (derived from the 1913 Teubner of C. Hosius) is inadequate and many of the conjectures printed in it have not won general acceptance. A new Teubner text is being prepared by G. Luck.

[1] So the poem is entitled in the manuscripts. The title *Pharsalia* rests on a misunderstanding of 9.985 f.: *Pharsalia nostra/viuet* ('*Pharsalia nostra*, proelium a te [sc. Caesare] gestum, a me scriptum', Housman *ad loc.*); Stat. *S.* 2.7.66, *Pharsalica bella detonabis*, is no help. Lucan may not have fixed on a title for the epic before his death.

[2] R. Badalì, 'I codici romani di Lucano', *Bollettino*, 21 (1973), 3–47, inaugurating a series of articles intended ultimately to describe all surviving codices; cf. *Bollettino*, 22 (1974), 3–48; 23 (1975), 15–89; *RCCM* 16 (1974), 191–213.

[3] (1) Parts of fifteen folios of a fourth-century codex in rustic capitals written probably in Italy, reused at Bobbio in the eighth century: Naples Lat. 2 (formerly Vindob. 16) + IV. A. 8 = *CLA* III.392 (N in editions), containing 5.31–91, 152–211, 272–301, 331–45 (beginnings), 346–60 (ends), 361–90, 631–60, 6.153–63, 168–78, 215–74, 305–34, 395–424, 545–76, 667–98. (2) Vatican, Pal. lat. 24, ff. 11–14, two bifolia from a codex of unknown origin in rustic capitals (s. IV/V), at Lorsch in the eighth century = *CLA* I.70 (*Π* in editions, S in H. C. Gotoff, *The Transmission of the Text of Lucan in the Ninth Century* (Cambridge, Mass., 1971)), containing 6.21–61, 228–67, 7.458–537. (3) B.L. Add. 34473 (6), fragments of four lines (2.265 f., 247 f.) in a good uncial (s. V ex.) found in the Fayûm on a strip of parchment used in a binding = *CLA* II. 175. Note also Vatican lat. 5755, containing, on pp. 292–307, 8.60–254 in seventh-century uncials, now illegible = *CLA* I.33.

[4] (A) The *Commenta Bernensia* preserved in Berne 370 (s. IX ex., north-eastern France, conjecturally Reims; cf. O. Homberger, *Die illustrierten Handschriften der Burgerbibliothek Bern* (Berlin, 1962), 16 n. 2) and printed by H. Usener (Leipzig, 1869); (B) the *Adnotationes super Lucanum* found in an abbreviated version in Berne 370 and in a fuller form in Bodmer lat. 182 (*olim* Harburg I.2.2°7, s. XI, Tegernsee?), printed by J. Endt (Leipzig, 1909).

[5] E. Fraenkel, *Gnomon*, 2 (1926), 517–27 (= *Kleine Beiträge zur Klassischen Philologie* (Rome, 1964), ii. 290–303), G. Pasquali, *Storia della tradizione e critica del testo*[2] (Florence, 1952), 433 f. As Fraenkel knew, the distinction between interpolations and material rejected by the author is often hard to draw. G. Luck has tried, in *RhM* 112 (1969), 254–84, to relate Fraenkel's hypothesis of an ancient edition containing marginal verses to the lines omitted by one or more of the primary medieval witnesses.

study,[6] but it is clear that contamination and interpolation are abundantly present in the entire tradition, and that attempts at stemmatic recension can hope for only limited success. On the other hand, the intermingling of readings has preserved many ancient variants, so that the editor's task is often that of selection rather than of emendation.[7] (The evidence of the two substantial surviving fragments of ancient codices tends to bear out this conclusion: neither agrees consistently with any later manuscript or group of manuscripts, and neither contains a certainly true reading not found in at least one ninth-or tenth-century manuscript.[8])

The earliest medieval witnesses are:[9]

Z Paris lat. 10314 (s. IX²/₄, eastern France, perhaps Luxembourg; Echternach?).

M Montpellier 113 (s. IX²/₄, partly in Orléans script).

A Ashburnhamensis, Paris n. a. lat. 1626, ff. 63, 64ʳ (s. IX²/₄); ff. 76–7 (s. IX³⁻⁴/₄, western France).

B Berne 45 (s. IX med. – ¾, probably Fleury).

R Montpellier 362 (s. IX⁴/₄, France).

F Paris lat. 10403, ff. 49–50 (s. IX²/₄, France), containing 8.575–9.124 (Q in Housman and Hosius).

Q Paris lat. 7900A (s. IX/X, perhaps written in Milan, later at Corbie).

G Brussels 5330–2 (s. X, Gembloux).

U Leiden, Voss. Lat. F. 63 (s. X, origin not determined).

V Leiden, Voss. Lat. Q. 51 (s. X⁴/₄, western Germany?).

P Paris lat. 7502 (s. IX/X?, Tours[10]).

Y Leiden, Voss. Lat. Q. 16 (s. X and XI, France).

From 1.483 to 9.85 ZM derive from a common source (ζ), as shown by some 1,200 errors shared against the tenth-century manuscripts. This source lost one quaternion at the beginning and several at the end between the copying of ζ and that of M (or, more probably, its exemplar).[11] The missing parts were apparently made up from two other manuscripts, of which the one used for 9.86–end was closely related to,

---

[6] By Gotoff (n. 3, above). The account given here adopts Gotoff's main conclusions but omits his more subtle arguments.

[7] Housman, preface, xxvi; Gotoff, 1. Scrutiny and, where necessary, correction of the paradosis are of course still required: cf. L. Håkanson. *PCPS* NS 25 (1979), 26 ff.

[8] Excluding the orthographical improvement *echenais* in N at 6.675 (*ethenaeis* Z); N's *obstrinxit* for *obstruxit* at 4.197, praised by A. Souter (*CR* 44 (1930), 174) and R. J. Getty (*M. Annaei Lucani De bello civili liber I* (Cambridge, 1940), ix), is not certainly correct; at 7.462 Housman preferred the reading of the Palatine palimpsest (*vultus quo no* [*scere possent*) to the variants found in the medieval witnesses (*tempus q.n.p., vultusque agnoscere quaerunt*), but cf. E. Fraenkel, 515 (288 f.), Gotoff, 25, Håkanson, 43–5.

[9] Dates and locations after Gotoff, 11–26, who acknowledges the assistance of B. Bischoff for the ninth-century codices. Plates in Chatelain of Z(CLIV), M(CLVIII), A(CLIV), R(CLV), G(CLVII), U(CLX), V(CLVII), P(CLIX).

[10] E. K. Rand, *Studies in the Script of Tours, I: A Survey of the Manuscripts of Tours* (Cambridge, Mass., 1929), i. 176 f., no. 154.   [11] Gotoff, 52–5.

and probably the source of, P.[12] In the section of the poem in which both derive from ζ, ZM differ in about 175 places; some of these disagreements are most plausibly explained by supposing that ζ carried marginal or interlinear variants. The fragment F is clearly related to ZM but is free of about forty of their shared errors; where Z and M divide F agrees nearly as often with one as with the other.

The remaining ninth-century manuscripts (ABR) derive ultimately from Z, since they contain a displacement (3.211 following 193) which has its origin in the physical conditions of Z.[13] A similar displacement (9.944 after 938) in B, the result of misreading a correction in A, shows that A is the source of B; B and R are very closely related, so R too is ultimately derived from A.[14] Editors have neglected ABR as *descripti*, but Gotoff has demonstrated their usefulness. The presence of Z^2 corrections in A or of A^2 corrections and A^v variants in B permits a secure ninth-century *terminus ante quem* to be assigned to hundreds of Z^2, A^2, and A^v readings, some of which are true or at least ancient and which are otherwise known only from tenth-century sources. In addition, R shows the results of contamination from a manuscript unrelated to ZM, and is thus the earliest extant source of more than a hundred correct readings.[15]

The tenth-century manuscripts QGUPV are independent of ZM; the new readings they offer are more often specious than true, but some are certainly correct[16] and even more are undoubtedly ancient.[17] No stemmatic analysis has yet been undertaken, and Housman's words about the entire tradition still seem applicable to them: 'the manuscripts group themselves not in families but in factions; their dissidences and agreements are temporary and transient . . . and the true line of division is between the variants themselves, not between the manuscripts which offer them.'[18]

The manuscripts later than the tenth century are still for the most part unexplored.[19] They may therefore contain traditional readings not

---

[12] The source of P and of M after 9.85 was ultimately derived from a manuscript corrected free-hand by a Constantinopolitan of uncertain date named Paulus: the subscription 'Paulus Constantinopolitanus emendavi manu mea solus' appears consistently in P, in M at the end of Books 8, 9, and 10. (It is also found in U at the end of Books 2, 7, and 10, raising the possibility that an ancestor of U had access to a manuscript resembling P or its source.) See Housman, preface, xiii–xviii.

[13] Gotoff, 30, 34 f. (first pointed out by P. Lejay in his edition of Book 1, Paris, 1894).

[14] Gotoff, 70 f., 84–9.

[15] Gotoff, esp. 111–78 (appendices listing the readings originating in Z^2, A^2, and A^v).

[16] e.g. 1.229 *it* for *et* (PV), 254 *ruentem* for *furentem* (G), 583 *fracto Marium* for *M.f.* (PGU), 614 *laxo* for *largo* (QGPUV *Comm. Bern.*).

[17] Housman (preface, ix) pointed out that the two ancient palimpsests often agree with G against the other early manuscripts.   [18] Ibid. vii.

[19] Gotoff (pp. 21–4) gives some information about three later manuscripts; Getty (n. 8, above) supplied reports for Book 1 of the manuscripts in the Bibliothèque Nationale in Paris; Fraenkel (p. 515 = pp. 288 f.) invoked four Laurentiani (s. XII and XIII) in his discussion of 7.462 f.

preserved in earlier codices, but this has not yet been decisively proved to be the case. For the present an editor must regard any reading or variant not an obvious blunder that is found in one or more of the ninth- and tenth-century manuscripts as potentially ancient.

R. J. T.

LUCRETIUS

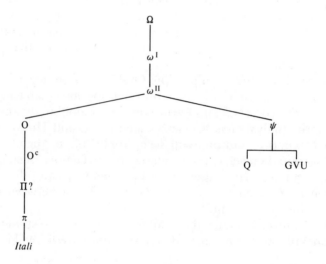

The stemma of Lucretius has long been one of the great show-pieces of classical scholarship. It was first given its basic shape by Jacob Bernays in 1847,[1] three years before Karl Lachmann stole his thunder with his magisterial edition of 1850. There have been four modifications of the basic pattern, determined by the degree of independence one granted to the Italian manuscripts of the fifteenth century. Recent scholars[2] have

---

[1] *RhM* 5 (1847), 533–85.

[2] K. Müller, *MH* 30 (1973), 166–78; also in his edition (Zürich, 1975), 297–319. G. F. Cini, after a more exhaustive treatment, confirms Müller's view in its essentials: *Atti e Memorie dell' Accademia Toscana la Colombaria*, 41 (1976), 115–69. For a reaction against this view see E. Flores, *Le scoperte di Poggio e il testo di Lucrezio* (Naples, 1980), not in my opinion a very helpful contribution to the problem.

in the main returned to the position taken by Diels in 1923, and it may now be regarded as established that π, the parent of the Renaissance tradition, was a copy, direct or at one remove,[3] of O in its corrected form. The stemma here given differs in some details[4] from that published by Konrad Müller in 1973.

The lost archetype of Lucretius (ω^{II}) is as familiar to generations of classical students as any extant manuscript. Its fabric suffered a singularly convenient series of mishaps, both before and during its being copied, and calculations based on these have made it possible to reconstruct its actual pagination.[5] It was this conjuring up of a lost manuscript in its physical detail, combined with the application of stemmatic theory to a closed tradition – equally striking at the time – which gave Lachmann's edition its dramatic impact on textual studies.[6] Strata of corruption embedded in the text point to a pre-archetype in pre-Caroline minuscule (ω^{I}) and an antique codex in rustic capitals (Ω, s. IV or V).[7] The once fashionable notion of an insular stage in the transmission has been demolished.[8]

In practice the text of Lucretius rests upon two Leiden manuscripts, traditionally known from their format as the Oblongus (O) and Quadratus (Q). The older and better is O (Voss. Lat. F. 30). It was written not long after 800 in the Palace School of Charlemagne. A contemporary corrector, using a distinctive insular hand, emended the text and in places filled up lacunae left by the original scribe. This hand has been recognized as that of Dungal, who became, after the death of Alcuin, the foremost Carolingian authority on astronomy and computus.[9] It is agreeable to wonder, in the duller moments of life, if this formidable Irishman would have much rejoiced in his posthumous title of the 'corrector Saxonicus' (O^s). The history of O during the later Middle Ages is obscure, but by 1479 it had reached St. Martin's at Mainz. Q (Voss. Lat. Q. 94) was written in the ninth century in

---

[3] Cini (163 ff.) does not accept Müller's postulation of an intermediary (Π) between O and π and argues that Poggio's transcript was made directly from O. A certain decision is difficult on present evidence.

[4] In particular, I have discarded his stemma of the Italian tradition (descended from π), which is unsatisfactory. See below.

[5] Lachmann's reconstruction of the archetype has been confirmed and elaborated in an interesting article by G. P. Goold: *Acta Classica*, 1 (1958), 21–130. Lachmann wrongly believed that the manuscript he was reconstructing was Ω.

[6] S. Timpanaro, *La genesi del metodo del Lachmann* (new edn., Padua, 1981) puts Lachmann's contribution into proper perspective.

[7] L. Duveau, *RPh* 12 (1888), 30–7; Timpanaro, 113 ff.

[8] F. Brunhölzl, *Hermes*, 90 (1962), 97–104; V. Brown, *HSCPh* 72 (1967), 301–10.

[9] For the Oblongus and Dungal, see B. Bischoff in the catalogue to the 1965 Charlemagne Exhibition at Aachen, *Karl der Grosse, Werk und Wirkung* (Aachen, 1965), 202–3. There is an excellent article on Dungal by Mirella Ferrari: 'In Papia conveniant ad Dungalium', *IMU* 15 (1972), 1–52, in which (38 n. 3) Bischoff's more precise attribution of O to the Palace School is reported.

north-east France; it appears to have spent most of the Middle Ages at Saint-Bertin.[10]

In addition to OQ we have the fragmentary Schedae, the Gottor-pienses (G), eight leaves formerly at Gottorp and now in Copenhagen (Gl. Kgl. S. 211 2°), and the Vindobonenses, ten leaves now in Vienna (MS 107, ff. 1–6 = V, and ff. 7–10 = U). G and V are clearly parts of the same book; U has been thought to have an alien origin, but the distinction is probably artificial.[11] The Schedae were written in the middle of the ninth century in south-west Germany.[12]

It would seem that Lucretius emerged towards the end of the eighth century, that the archetype of our manuscripts found its home in the Carolingian court, and that the text was disseminated from there, radiating westwards into the Low Countries and northern France and southwards along the Rhine. Excerpts[13] show that the text was read and used, and it seems to have been well established in the area of Lake Constance. Lines from the *De rerum natura* occur in two metrical florilegia, that of Mico of Saint-Riquier, put together at Reichenau about 825, and the *Florilegium Sangallense* (St. Gall 870, c.900). Lucretius is also quoted in a letter written from St. Gall by Ermenrich of Ell-wangen c.850,[14] and there was a copy of his poem in the ninth century at Murbach.[15] Then, despite this promising start, Lucretius went under-ground for the rest of the Middle Ages, an eclipse which may be partly explained by the passionately anti-religious nature of his message. All we have until the fifteenth century are a few fleeting glimpses. The abbey of Lobbes acquired a Lucretius, probably in the early twelfth century,[16] and he is listed in the twelfth-century catalogue of Corbie.[17] The presence of Q at Saint-Bertin may well explain the echoes of Lucretius in the *Encomium Emmae*[18] and the Lucretian gloss in Sigebert of Gembloux (c.1030–1112)[19] fits with the availability of his poem in the

[10] Q was at Saint-Bertin in the sixteenth century (preface to Lambinus's edition, Paris, 1563) and possible echoes in the *Encomium Emmae* (*MGH SS* 19, 509–25), written by the Chaplain of Queen Emma, who was associated with Saint-Bertin, suggest that it was there in the eleventh century, despite its non-appearance in the twelfth-century catalogue: cf. R. W. Hunt, in *Classical Influences on European Culture A.D. 500–1500* (ed. R. R. Bolgar, Cambridge, 1971), 51.

[11] The alien origin of U was advocated on grounds of script and format by E. Göbel, *RhM* 12 (1857), 449–56. But Professor Bischoff is not convinced that this degree of irregularity is incom-patible with a single origin; and one has the strong impression with GVU that one is dealing with a single entity.   [12] Bischoff, *Lorsch*, 74.

[13] For two sets of excerpts in manuscripts of s. IX–X additional to those mentioned below, see U. Pizzani, 'Versi Lucreziani nel codice Vaticano Reginense Lat. 598', *RCCM* 1 (1959), 399–402 (cf. Müller (edn.), 356); C. E. Finch, 'Lucretius in Codex Vat. Reg. Lat. 1587', *CPh* 62 (1967), 261–2.   [14] *MGH, Epist.* 5, 554.6 ff.

[15] W. Milde, *Der Bibliothekskatalog des Klosters Murbach aus dem 9 Jahrhundert* (Beihefte zum Euphorion, 4), Heidelberg, 1968, 48 no. 318.

[16] See F. Dolbeau, 'Un nouveau catalogue des manuscrits de Lobbes aux XIe et XIIe siècles', *Recherches Augustiniennes*, 13 (1978), 3–36; 14 (1979), 191–248; in particular, pp. 36, 233.

[17] Becker, 79. 289.   [18] See above, n. 10.

[19] Manitius, *Geschichte*, iii. 340; Dolbeau, 233.

closely connected abbey of Lobbes. The degree to which the *De rerum natura* was known in Italy before the fifteenth century is more problematical. There was a manuscript at Bobbio in the ninth century,[20] faint echoes have been detected in medieval Italian works,[21] and one line, probably quoted at second hand and imported from northern Europe, occurs in a florilegium of south Italian origin preserved in Venice, Marc. Lat. Z. 497 (1811).[22]

Lucretius was rediscovered by Poggio in 1417, during the Council of Constance. He found the manuscript, not in one of the local monasteries, but in a 'locus satis longinquus'[23] which he does not bother to name. Poggio sent his only copy to Niccolò Niccoli for him to transcribe and, despite increasingly querulous requests for its return,[24] Niccoli was still sitting on the manuscript in 1429. Niccoli's autograph survives and is now Florence, Laur. 35.30 (L). There are more than fifty extant descendants of Poggio's manuscript and the effort devoted to sorting them out, at times half-baked, has been slow to produce results. It seems to be established at long last that π is derived from O, so that the *Itali* have no textual value except as a repository of conjectures. But Lucretius passed through such distinguished hands in the course of the Renaissance that the later history of his text can throw a great deal of light on the capacity and cross-currents of humanist scholarship, as a recent and significant contribution to the subject amply demonstrates.[25] The manuscripts which have commonly been used to reconstruct π are (in addition to L) Florence, Laur. 35.31 (F), Cambridge, University Library Nn.2.40 (C), Vatican lat. 3276 (A), and Vatican, Barb. lat. 154 (B), but the list of interesting manuscripts does not end here.[26] The precise interrelationship of the main manuscripts and manuscript groups is not easily determined, complicated as it is by contamination and readings possibly derived from the recollation of older witnesses. In particular, one is reluctant to accept any stemma

[20] Becker, 32. 375.

[21] Guido Billanovich, *IMU* 1 (1958), 164–8, 182–90.

[22] F. L. Newton, *TAPA* 93 (1962), 264, 266 and n. 25. The line (1.155) was also known to Ermenrich of Ellwangen.

[23] As he tells us in a letter written from Constance to Francesco Barbaro, late in 1417 or early in 1418: cf. *CR* 13 (1899), 125. The identity of the 'locus' has still to be revealed.

[24] *Epist.* I (ed. de Tonellis), pp. 148, 150, 154, 189, 295, 303.

[25] M. D. R., 'The Italian Tradition of Lucretius', *IMU* 23 (1980), 27–48.

[26] See Reeve *passim*. In particular, he draws attention to two manuscripts which indicate that some humanist other than the scribe of π had had access to O or a manuscript very like it; these are Laur. 35.29 (with notes in Politian's hand) and Rome, Bibl. Naz. Fondi Minori 437 (S. Onofrio 85). We learn from Poggio's correspondence that in 1427 Bartolomeo da Montepulciano was trying to procure a Lucretius for him from northern Europe (*Epist.* I, p. 208): 'Bartholomaeus de Monte Politiano dat operam ut habeamus Lucretium; id si assequetur, tunc alia aggrediemur. Non enim est nunc de aliis libris tractandum, ne multa petendo daremus occasionem istius denegandi. Paulatim incedendum est; barbari enim sunt et suspiciosi.'

which does not allow L to be a direct copy of π,[27] but any that does must postulate the infusion into the Italian tradition of further material from O or some non-π manuscript.

L. D. R.

[27] In Müller's stemma L is at two removes from π, which is very difficult to square with the story which emerges from Poggio's letters. Reeve offers a tentative new stemma.

MACROBIUS

Introduction

Commentary on Cicero's Somnium Scipionis
Saturnalia

Introduction

The medieval traditions of *Saturnalia* and *Commentary* are separate. The two texts have almost always been printed together, from the *editio princeps* onwards (N. Jenson, Venice, 1472); yet before the fifteenth century they are combined in only five manuscripts,[1] a negligible total in comparison with the numbers of copies in which they appear separately. Although one of the five is an important early manuscript, Paris lat. 6370 (French, probably written at Tours, s. IX[1]/[3]), there is an indication that the union of the two texts had occurred only recently in its ancestry: the *Saturnalia* (of which only the first leaf now survives, f. 112[r-v]) follows the *Commentary*, but lacunae at the end of the *Commentary* suggest a descent from a volume which contained only the *Commentary* and which was damaged at the end. The next two of the five manuscripts are twins, Paris lat. 6371 (French?, s. XI) and Troyes 514 (French, s. XII ex.); their tradition (which thus reflects only one amalgamation, not two) is possibly connected with Paris lat. 6370. The final two, Cambridge, Corpus Christi College 71 (written at St. Albans, s. XII) and Paris lat. 6367 (probably written for Richard de Fournival,[2] s. XIII

[1] Willis's edition (Teubner, Leipzig, 1963) is deceptive here: he uses the same siglum, 'B' (following Eyssenhardt), to denote two separate Bamberg manuscripts, Class. 37 (M.V.5) of the *Saturnalia* (s. IX), Class. 38 (M.IV.15) of the *Commentary* (German?, s. XI); and he appears to be unaware that his D (Oxford, Bodl. Auct. T. 2. 27) consists of two independent manuscripts (ff. 1–50, *Commentary*, south German, s. X ex./XI in.; ff. 51–98, *Saturnalia*, east French?, s. XI in.), which need not have come together until the eighteenth century.

[2] R. H. R., 'Manuscripts belonging to Richard de Fournival', *RHT* 3 (1973), 266.

med.), were both made for expanding libraries where the assembling of 'collected editions' might well have been encouraged.

The process also found favour with Renaissance collectors: a further twelve omnibus manuscripts,[3] mostly Italian, survive from the second half of the fifteenth century. Close textual links can sometimes be detected between these and various manuscripts containing just one of the two texts.[4] When Bartolomeo Fonzio wrote out an omnibus volume (now Munich Clm 15738) for the Hungarian Petrus Garazda at Florence in the late 1460s, he took his text of the *Commentary* from an eleventh-century exemplar containing that text only (Florence, Laur. S. Croce 22 sin. 9). In the *editio princeps*, the *Commentary* and *Somnium Scipionis* texts descend from the same parent[5] as British Library, Harley 4794 (north-east Italy, s. xv¾), a manuscript which does not contain the *Saturnalia*. The conclusion is that the union of the two Macrobian texts in the *editio princeps*, a union tacitly accepted by most subsequent editors, is merely one of several independent and recent amalgamations, following a natural tendency of a period of renaissance. The vandal who redivided the beautiful omnibus copy written by Antonio Tophio in 1466 (Cambridge, University Library, Add. 4095 + Vatican, Ottob. lat. 1137) was thus acting on sound editorial principles.

Excerpts from the *Commentary* and from Macrobius' third work, the *De differentiis et societatibus graeci latinique verbi*, were written side by side at Bobbio in the eighth century (Naples lat. 2 (Vindob. 16), ff. 111ᵛ, 157–8, *CLA* iii.397b), but this is our one glimpse into the prehistory of Macrobian texts, and the *De differentiis* did not survive much later.

A count of extant manuscripts is a clumsy criterion in textual matters, given the freaks of survival and the inherent subjectivity of such totals.[6] But in the case of Macrobius the danger of approximation is outweighed by the dramatic differences in the totals for the two main

---

[3] Vatican, Ottob. lat. 1197 (northern European, 1449, with only Book 7 of *Sat.*); Paris lat. 8677 (Paduan?, s. xv med.); Cambridge, University Library, Add. 4095 + Vatican, Ottob. lat. 1137 (written at Rome by A. Tophio, 1466); Munich, Clm 15738 (written at Florence by B. Fonzio, late 1460s); Warsaw, MS.F.v.Cl. lat. 13 (Roman?, s. xv¾); Valencia 848 (Italian, 1472, two companion volumes); Leiden, B.P.L. 46 (northern European, 1476); Vatican, Pal. lat. 1575 (Florentine?, s. xv²); Milan, Ambros. A.128 inf. (Italian, s. xv, prob. second half); Modena α.R.4.1 = Lat. 1085 (s. xv); Siena K.v.18 (s. xv); Vat. lat. 6763 (Italian, s. xv). Now destroyed: Tournai 96 (AD 1500–1).

[4] Paris lat. 8677 is probably a direct descendant of Vat. lat. 1546 (Italian?, s. xi ex.), *Comm.* and *Somnium Scipionis* only; Vat. lat. 6763 is closely related to Florence, Laur. Edili 168 (Ferrara, 1438), *Comm.* only.

[5] The parent constantly wrote *autem* for *enim* and vice versa, a classic symptom of insular ancestry. The confusion is especially noticeable in the *Somnium Scipionis*.

[6] Some of the datings are derived from catalogues rather than from personal inspection and it is often difficult to decide whether to include certain classes and marginal individual manuscripts. The above totals include fragments (presumably of manuscripts once complete) but not minor excerpts. Fragments containing parts of the *Somnium* only have nevertheless been classed under 'Comm.' not 'Somnium alone'. Manuscripts recently destroyed are excluded. Those dating from the turn of a century are counted under the later century.

works over the centuries. Medieval enthusiasm for the *Commentary* reached its peak in the twelfth century, while the *Saturnalia* did not come fully into favour until the Renaissance.

Saec.	IX	X	XI	XII	XIII	XIV	XV	Total
Sat.	6	1	5	13	14	13	61	113
Comm.	6	8	31	106	28	11	40	230
Somnium alone	–	1	5	2	1	*c.*17	*c.*250	*c.*276

B. C. B.-B.

Commentary on Cicero's Somnium Scipionis

Of the 230 medieval manuscripts of Macrobius' *Commentary*, ten contain a subscription at the end of Book 1: 'Aur(elius) Memm(ius) Symmachus ū. c̄. emendebam uel distinguebam meum Rauennae cum Macrobio Plotino Eudoxio ū. c̄.' The Symmachus who wrote this into his own copy at Ravenna can be identified with reasonable certainty as the consul of 485, the father-in-law and a dedicatee of Boethius; the latter, in turn, knew the text well. Alan Cameron[1] proposes that the Macrobius Plotinus Eudoxius who helped Symmachus might have been the author's own grandson – a theory which depends on his later dating of the author as the praetorian prefect of Italy ('Theodosius') in 430.

The transmission of the subscription in the ten manuscripts argues that Symmachus' copy lies somewhere in their ancestry; but the arguments are complicated, for in three it can be proved that the subscription was added in a recent ancestor,[2] and in another three it has been added by a later hand.[3] Its addition in Paris lat. 6370 (s. IX⅓) is by a ninth-century hand associated with Lupus and Heiric,[4] possibly by

The most useful edition for manuscript readings: L. von Jan (Ludovicus Ianus), vol. i (Quedlinburg and Leipzig, 1848). The only edition in print, resting on a narrow, ill-chosen and ill-collated manuscript base: J. Willis (Teubner, Leipzig, 1963), vol ii (reprinted in 1970 from corrected sheets). English translation: W. H. Stahl, *Records of Civilization, Sources and Studies*, 48 (Columbia Univ. Press, 1952, reprinted 1966). Survey of the earlier manuscripts: B. C. B.-B., 'The Manuscripts of Macrobius' Commentary on the *Somnium Scipionis*' (2 vols., Oxford D. Phil. thesis, 1975).

[1] 'The Date and Identity of Macrobius', *JRS* 56 (1966), 25–38.
[2] Paris lat. 6371 (French?, s. XI); Florence, Laur. S. Croce 22 sin. 9 (s. XI, origin unknown, later in Italy); B. L. Egerton 2976 (Italian?, s. XII¹).
[3] Besides Paris lat. 6370, the other two are Paris lat. 16677 (addition by a hand of the angular Fleury type, s. X ex./XI in.) and Vat. lat. 4200 (addition, by an Italian hand of s. XIV ex., directly derived from B. L. Egerton 2976).
[4] The presence of Heiric's hand was first suggested by É. Pellegrin, 'Les Manuscrits de Loup de Ferrières', *BEC* 115 (1957), 6, 11; I believe that one of the major additional hands is definitely Heiric's, but it is difficult to be certain that the subscription was added by this hand.

Heiric himself. Certain letter-forms in the addition suggest that it was transcribed directly from an ancient copy of the subscription written in rustic capitals, presumably of the late fifth or sixth century. The theory is supported by the parallel with another ancient manuscript which travelled from sixth-century Ravenna to the ninth-century French circle of Lupus and Heiric, the geographical miscellany formed by Flavius Rusticius Helpidius Domnulus (Heiric's copy, preserving ancient letter-forms, survives in Vat. lat. 4929, ff. 79ᵛ–195ʳ, see JULIUS PARIS).

The ancient copy of Macrobius' *Commentary* had probably engendered at least one earlier child in a scriptorium trained in insular script: the ancestor of either or both of the two groups of manuscripts in which the subscription cannot be proved to be a recent addition. The first group consists of only one manuscript, Wrocław R.69 (German?, s. XII). P. Lehmann detected its insular ancestry,[5] which raises it from the surrounding twelfth-century contamination and makes it at least the equal of the surviving ninth-century manuscripts; it seems to have no close relatives. The second group consists of British Library, Harley 2772, ff. 44–74 + Munich Clm 23486, ff. 1–2 (German?, s. XI) and Florence, Laur. Conv. Soppr. 444 (Italian, south?, s. XII); since both of these belong to the π family, and the related φ family (of insular descent) contains a probable echo of the subscription ('emendatum est' at the end of Book 1), the common ancestor of φ and π presumably contained the subscription.[6] The insular background of the text, otherwise hypothetical, emerges concretely in one frail witness: the eighth-century Bobbio excerpts (see above) are written in insular script. Irish scholars on the Continent, or their pupils, must have played an important if now largely irrecoverable part in the transmission of Macrobius' *Commentary* in the eighth and early ninth centuries. It is still unclear whether Symmachus' copy was the only text-carrier of Macrobius' *Commentary* to survive the Dark Ages; probably it was not.

In the ninth century, Macrobius' *Commentary* was studied and copied in the great centres of Carolingian France. Towards the beginning of the century, Paris lat. 6370 was copied out probably at Tours, its text still reflecting the peculiarities of eighth-century spelling.[7] At around the same time, Adalbaldus, an important scribe of St. Martin's of Tours, perhaps made another copy which was lost in the nineteenth

---

[5] 'Enim und autem in mittelalterlichen lateinischen Handschriften', *Erforschung des Mittelalters*, iv (1961), 22–5 (first printed in *Philologus*, 73 (1916), 543–8).

[6] The tenth subscription-bearing manuscript (Aachen, Ludwig Collection XII 4, formerly Phillipps 1287 and H. D. Horblit Collection, German, s. X²/XI¹) is so heavily corrected that it is difficult to define its original textual affiliations; but its main contemporary corrector seems identical with a hand which also makes additions in Harley 2772.

[7] The importance of this manuscript was first fully realized by A. La Penna, 'Le Parisinus Latinus 6370 et le texte des Commentarii de Macrobe', *RPh* 24 (1950), 177–87. It is 'S' in Willis's edition.

century: formerly Tours, Bibl. Municipale, St. Martin's 33.[8] If this is
not a ghost, it was one of four ninth-century manuscripts known to
contain Cicero's *De senectute* preceding Macrobius' *Commentary*; the two
texts were presumably amalgamated because the *Somnium Scipionis*
seemed the natural companion piece to the *De senectute*, both in subject-
matter and in interlocutors. Of the others, two (Vat. Reg. lat. 1587, ff.
65–80 + Paris lat. 16677[9] and Leiden, Voss. Lat. F.12β + F.122 + B. L.
Royal 15.B.XII, ff. 1–2) were probably written at Fleury, the third
(Paris n. a. lat. 454) at Corbie in the time of Hadoardus.[10] Hadoardus's
excerpts from the *De senectute* and from Macrobius' *Commentary*, derived
from a child of Paris n. a. lat. 454, survive in his Ciceronian *collectanea*,
Vatican, Reg. lat. 1762.

The three survivors of the *De senectute* + *Commentary* group share a
large number of characteristic readings, of which only a faint impression can be gleaned from the sparse selection from Paris lat. 16677
printed by Willis under the siglum E. They descend independently
from a common ancestor, φ, which must have been written in insular
script. Both Paris lat. 16677 and n. a. lat. 454 show some contamination
from 'non-φ' sources. The Leiden + British Library fragment is full of
superficial mistakes arising from the misunderstanding of insular abbreviations (especially the substitution of *quam* for *quod*), but appears to
transmit φ in an uncontaminated form; although for the Macrobius text
all but nine sides of this faithful incompetent are now lost, a partial
descendant survives in Paris lat. 16678, ff. 1–8 + 6620 (s. X ex./XI in.).
The end of the *Commentary* in Paris lat. 16677 and n. a. lat. 454 (it is lost
in Leiden + British Library) is followed by a four-line verse colophon
entitled *De errore emendationis*,[11] an apology to modern editors from the
ghost of φ.

It seems likely from its contents that the hypothetical Tours manuscript written by Adalbaldus was also a descendant of φ. This is not the
case with Paris. lat. 6370, the surviving Tours manuscript, which
shortly passed into the hands of Lupus of Ferrières. Lupus made
extensive corrections, often in erasure, and supervised the addition of

---

[8] L. Delisle, in *Notices et extraits des manuscrits*, 31.1 (1884), 264–6 no. LXXXII, identifies the lost
Tours manuscript with Paris n. a. lat. 454 – wrongly, in my view. Bréquigny tells us that the lost
Macrobius was marked by Adalbaldus in the same way as his copies of the letters of St. Augustine
and St. Jerome etc. (now Tours 281 + Paris n. a. lat. 445 + n. a. lat. 405), and of Orosius (now
entirely lost, *pace* Delisle). Our Adalbaldus is possibly also identifiable as the *indignus Adalbaldus*
who wrote Quedlinburg 79 (*Martinellus*).

[9] See A. La Penna, 'Note sul testo dei «Commentarii» di Macrobio', *Annali della Scuola normale
superiore di Pisa*, 20 (1951), 239–54. 'E' in Willis's edition. The join with Reg. lat. 1587 was first
noticed by B. C. B.-B., 'A Ninth-Century Manuscript from Fleury: *Cato de senectute cum Macrobio*',
Medieval Learning, 145–65.

[10] B. Bischoff, 'Hadoard und die Klassikerhandschriften aus Corbie', *Mitt. Stud.* i (1966), 53–4,
59 (first published in 1961).

[11] Published most recently by K. Strecker in *MGH: Poetae*, vi.1 (Weimar, 1951), p. 169, from
n. a. lat. 454; the colophon also occurs in Clm 6369.

the five standard diagrams; his pupil Heiric of Auxerre added further corrections and variants. The letter-forms of the added subscription suggest that Lupus and Heiric may have had access to an ancient manuscript. Further evidence emerges from Lupus's correspondence: he was in touch with a friend who had a manuscript 'revera venerabilis et exactissimae diligentiae'.[12] The friend had sent him a sample leaf from it, probably connected in some way with the bifolium written entirely in Lupus's hand in Paris lat. 6370, ff. 108^r–109^v (*Comm.* 2.16. 10–17. 3 Willis, pp. 147.29–151.15, *non nocebit–abstrahet*). The name of the correspondent, otherwise unidentified, is given as 'Adℓgdo' or 'Adalg.', and were it not for the fact that names beginning 'Adal-' were very common at this period, the temptation to emend 'Adℓgd.' to 'Adℓbd.' would be very strong. So far no relationship has been defined between Paris lat. 6370 and any other extant manuscript, a difficulty possibly due to the decisive nature of Lupus's interventions. Willis's error rate of 20 per cent in recording the readings of this manuscript in his apparatus criticus is mainly the result of his failure to distinguish Lupus's corrections in erasure from original readings.

Auxerre, where Heiric spent the last years of his life, appears to have been the original home of the giant miscellany, Berne 347 + 357 + 330 + Leiden, Voss. Lat. Q.30, ff. 58–7 + Paris lat. 7665 (s. IX^2). This is the earliest extant manuscript not only of the *excerpta uulgaria* of Petronius but also of an abbreviated version of Macrobius' *Commentary*. In spite of the Auxerre link there seems no obvious textual connection between Heiric's corrections in Paris lat. 6370 and the abbreviated version of Berne 347, ff. 1^r–22^r. The version includes the central section, with most of the astronomical and geographical material and all five standard diagrams, but omits the more philosophical discussions at beginning and end. The main characteristics of the form are described by Jan in his edition (i.lxiv–lxvi, lxxix). The opening title is usually given as *Ex libris Macrobii Ambrosii de differentia stellarum et siderum*, and there are further characteristic titles within the text (e.g. *De musico stellarum modulamine* at the beginning of Book 2). The text starts at 1.14.21 (Willis 59.13) *Nunc videamus quae sint haec duo nomina* and ends at *quam in tam parvo magna esse non poterit*. 2.9.10 (Willis 124.19), followed without a break by the additional clause *ut contentus potius conscientiae praemio, gloriam non requirat*. This is followed by an unrelated passage on the gates of horn and ivory, from the end of Macrobius' discussion of dreams: 1.3.17 (Willis 12.9) *Siquis forte quaerere vult cur porta ex ebore . . . nullo visu ad*

---

[12] E. Dümmler (ed.), *Lupi abbatis Ferrariensis epistolae* (*MGH: Epistolae*, vi = *karolini aeui*, iv), Berlin, 1925, 19–20, no. 8; L. Levillain (ed.), *Loup de Ferrières. Correspondance* (*Les Classiques de l'histoire de France au moyen âge*, 10 and 16), i (Paris, 1927), 106–111, no. 21. The date of the letter (between 837 and 841?) and the identity of the correspondent (probably the person associated with Lupus in Dümmler no. 6) are still matters of guesswork.

ulteriora tendente penetretur. 1.3.20 (Willis 12.28). There are several major
and minor omissions in the body of the text (e.g. 1.19.18–19 and 23–7;
1.20.5–8; 1.22.13–2.1.1) and an interpolation at 1.15.7 (after *temperaret*,
Willis 62.2). The Macrobian text is usually followed by four astronomical excerpts from the second book of Pliny's *Natural History*, with
diagrams (see ELDER PLINY, p. 310). The omissions and variants
have such an editorial look about them that the abbreviated version
must have been adapted from a full copy of Macrobius' text by a single
scholar. The physical make-up of the leaves in Berne 347 suggests that
the editorial process reached its completion in this very manuscript; it
may well, therefore, be the archetype of the later manuscripts of the
abbreviated version, though the conclusion has still to be tested by
detailed comparisons.

    France appears to have been the centre for the study of Macrobius'
Commentary during the ninth century, to judge by the surviving ninth-
century manuscripts so far discussed. We do not know the original
home of the remaining ninth-century copy, Cologne 186, ff. 73–120.
Although this shares many readings with φ, there is some evidence to
suggest that it is descended not from φ itself but from a *gemellus* of φ,
which may be christened π. Superficially, the text of Cologne 186 is
extremely corrupt, but the naïvety of the scribe(s) is in some ways
preferable to the sophistication of a Lupus or Heiric. Three later manuscripts may be loosely associated with Cologne 186: B. L. Harley 2772,
ff. 44–74 + Munich Clm 23486, ff. 1–2 (German?, s. XI); Florence,
Laur. Conv. Soppr. 444 (Italian, south?, s. XII); Vatican, Reg. lat. 1367
(Italian?, s. XII). These three share a sprinkling of φ readings with
Cologne 186, but for the great majority they show the vulgate readings
against the φ readings of that manuscript. However, the characteristic
shared by all four manuscripts is that a number of Greek words which
are written in Latin letters in all other manuscripts are here written in
Greek letters. Since it is very likely that the bilingual Macrobius himself
wrote these words in Greek letters, it may be that π is tapping a
particularly pure textual stream. The three later manuscripts perhaps
descend from a heavily contaminated descendant or twin of Cologne
186. Harley 2772 and Conv. Soppr. 444 are two of only four manuscripts
where the subscription cannot be proved to have been recently added in
the textual tradition.

    The table of manuscript totals (see *Introduction*) shows how the
number of extant manuscripts gradually swells for the tenth and
eleventh centuries, to reach a climax in the twelfth. By the twelfth
century, the tradition has become so thoroughly contaminated that
although small groups of related manuscripts or exemplar/copy pairs
may be detected, it is impossible to define larger families which may be
linked in a stemmatic relationship with earlier manuscripts – perhaps

the inevitable consequence of so rich a tradition. However, some of the tenth- and eleventh-century copies can be classified.

The φ family produced both French and German descendants. The *Commentary* was copied out and studied extensively at Fleury in the late tenth and early eleventh centuries under the great scholar-abbot Abbo (*d.* 1004). One of the ninth-century φ manuscripts, Vatican, Reg. lat. 1587, ff. 65–80 + Paris lat. 16677, was collated both with a manuscript bearing the subscription and with a manuscript of the abbreviated form; the major correcting hand is possibly that of Abbo himself. Three φ manuscripts are written in the angular type of script characteristic of Fleury around Abbo's time.[13] Paris lat. 7299 is a φ copy independent of the ninth-century manuscripts, though an intelligent medieval emendator had altered some φ readings in its immediate ancestry. Paris lat. 6365, ff. 2–23, is a direct descendant of Paris lat. 16677 (as corrected by its Fleury annotators), but its diagrams are derived from Paris lat. 7299 and its *Somnium Scipionis* from another source. Paris lat. 6365 transmits to us the readings of the lost first leaf of 16677, and these may be confirmed from Paris lat. 16678, ff. 1–8 + 6620. The latter, which shows evidence of quire-for-quire copying at speed, is a direct descendant in some parts from 16677 (after correction), in others from the Leiden + British Library fragment; the two sources may be distinguished by reference to 16677 and to the *quam*-for-*quod* mistakes characteristic of the Leiden + British Library fragment.

Two south German manuscripts are direct descendants of the ninth-century Corbie copy, Paris n. a. lat. 454: Oxford, Bodl. D'Orville 77 + 95 (s. x ex./xi in.) and Munich Clm 6369, ff. 35ᵛ line 16–62ᵛ (s. xi, late evidence of Freising ownership, *Comm.* 1.20.16, Willis 81.24 *longitudo* – end; the earlier part of the manuscript is copied from an exemplar containing an expanded version of the abbreviated form). A third German manuscript also belongs to the φ group: Paris lat. 10195 (probably written at Echternach, s. xi).

The abbreviated version in its pure form survives in six manuscripts from the Germanic area: Munich Clm 6364 (written at Freising, s. x^2); Clm 14436, ff. 34–61 (s. x, German?, at St. Emmeram's, Regensburg, by s. xv) and its direct descendant Zürich Car. C 122 (s. x^2 or xi^1, at Zürich by s. xv); Clm 14353, ff. 94–117 + Clm 29020, ff. (3–4) (s. x ex./xi in., ?corrected by or for Hartwic of St. Emmeram); Cologny (Geneva), Fondation Bodmer, lat. 111 (s. x^2 or xi^1, at Admont by s. xii) and its twin Vatican, Pal. lat. 1577 (s. xi^1, possibly belonged to Lorsch). Two further 'pure' copies are French, in addition to the possible ninth-century archetype in Berne 347: Leiden, Voss. Lat. F.96, ff. 71–8 (s. xi, Fleury??) and Berne 265 (s. xi, at Metz by s. xii or xiii). The solitary

[13] See É. Pellegrin, 'Membra disiecta Floriacensia', *BEC* 117 (1959), 14–16.

twelfth-century copy is English: B. L. Royal 12.C.IV, ff. 1–43 (s. XII¹, probably written at Rochester). Three further manuscripts are descended from exemplars where the abbreviated form was filled out by additions from the full text: Oxford, Bodl. Auct. T. 2. 27, ff. 1–50 (s. X ex./XI in., south German), the most heavily contaminated of all Macrobian manuscripts, used by Willis under the siglum 'D'; Clm 6362, ff. 35–85 (s. XI, south German, at Freising by s. XII); and Clm 6369, ff. 1ʳ–35ᵛ line 15 (s. XI, see above). Two manuscripts contain those parts of the text *not* contained in the abbreviated form, and so must have been written to accompany manuscripts of that form: Clm 14436, ff. 10–33 (s. XI⅓, written by or for Hartwic of St. Emmeram, probably to accompany not the present ff. 34–61 but Clm 14353, ff. 94–117); and Leiden, Voss. Lat. Q.2, ff. 3–30 (s. XI, origin unknown).

The most important remaining task is to classify those pre-twelfth-century manuscripts which belong neither to φ nor to π nor to the abbreviated group. Paris lat. 6370, the ninth-century manuscript, belongs to this category. A further fourteen are more or less complete, and there are small fragments of four more. *Complete*: Brussels 10146 (French?, s. X in., possibly IX ex.); Vatican, Pal. lat. 1341, ff. 62–109 (written at Lorsch, s. X²); St. Gall 65, pp. 1–(153 ter) + Leiden, Voss. Lat. Q.33, f. 58 (written at St. Gall, s. X); Aachen, Ludwig Collection XII 4 (German, s. X²/XI¹); Paris lat. 8663 (written at Fleury, s. X ex./XI in.); Oxford, Bodl. Auct. F. 2. 20 (English, possibly belonged to Exeter Cathedral, s. XI²); Paris lat. 6371 (French?, s. XI, perhaps XI²); Vatican, Ottob. lat. 1939 (written in Beneventan script at Montecassino, s. XI ex.), and its twin Florence, Laur. 51.14 (probably Italian, s. XI); Vat. lat. 1546 (probably Italian, s. XI ex.); Bamberg Class. 38 (M. IV.15) (German?, s. XI); Florence, Laur. 76.33 (German?, s. XI); Florence, Laur. S. Marco 287 (possibly Spanish, s. XI); Troyes 804, ff. 181–248 (possibly German, s. XI). *Fragments*: Wolfenbüttel 404.1 (1, 5) Novi (German, s. X); Leiden, Gronov. 20 (Italian?, s. X, possibly XI); Berlin (West) lat. 2° 389 (German, s. XI¹, a fragment of the *Somnium Scipionis*); and Berlin (West), Nachlass Grimm, Nr. 132, 3 (German, s. XI, ?XI¹). The range of origins, from England to southern Italy, shows the widespread distribution of the text by the end of the eleventh century. The list has been established solely by the process of eliminating manuscripts of recognizable families – not a good way of establishing a new textual family. These manuscripts present 'clean' texts, relatively close to the 'vulgate' tradition which has held sway from the twelfth century to Willis, with few gross characteristics to betray their affiliations; it may be their very excellence which makes them so elusive. They may well represent several textual streams independent of the families so far defined.

This textual story concerns not one text but two: Macrobius' *Com-*

mentary and the text of the *Somnium Scipionis* itself. The assumption is that the fragment from the end of Cicero's *De re publica* survived only through its attachment to Macrobius' popular *Commentary*; and the figures for manuscripts of the *Somnium* without the *Commentary* (see *Introduction*, table) illustrate how it achieved widespread independence from Macrobius only in the fourteenth and fifteenth centuries (the flashpoint was possibly provided by Petrarch's search for new Ciceronian works).[14] Of the eight pre-thirteenth-century manuscripts of unaccompanied *Somnium*, Aberystwyth 735 C (French, s. XI) is accompanied by excerpts from the beginnings and ends of the two books of the *Commentary*. No particular textual affiliations leap out either for B. L. Add. 11035 (written at St. Eucharius, Trier, s. XI[1]) or for Hildesheim, Dombibl. J. 70 (German?, s. XI[1]).[15] The remaining manuscripts fall into two groups: a French group, consisting of Berlin (East), Phill. 1786–7 (s. X[2]) and its two descendants Orléans 267 (223) + Paris n. a. lat. 1611 (written at Fleury, s. X[2]) and Vatican, Reg. lat. 1207 + 1405 (s. XI[1]); and a pair of Beneventan manuscripts, Vat. lat. 3227 (probably written at Montecassino, s. XII in.) and Florence, Laur. Strozzi 49 (Bari type, s. XII[1]), not particularly closely related either to each other or to Ottob. lat. 1939, the Beneventan manuscript of *Somnium Scipionis* with *Commentary* (written at Montecassino, s. XI ex.).[16] All the remaining early copies of the *Somnium* accompany copies of the *Commentary*, though there is a fair amount of independent mobility. Only one extant ninth-century manuscript of the *Commentary* includes the *Somnium* as part of the original writing plan, Paris n. a. lat. 454; the *Somnium* was never present in Paris lat. 6370 or Berne 347, and is not now to be found in Leiden, Voss. Lat. F.12β etc., while it is a later addition in the remaining φ manuscript of the ninth century, Paris lat. 16677, and in the oldest π manuscript, Cologne 186. One of the later φ manuscripts from Fleury, Paris lat. 6365, inherited its text from Berlin Phill. 1786–7. Nearly all[17] the unclassified tenth- and eleventh-century copies of the *Commentary* listed above are accompanied by original copies of the *Somnium*. The conclusion is that the *Somnium* occurred with the *Commentary* in some but not in all of the older textual families.

---

[14] A list of manuscripts up to the end of the twelfth century (i.e. mainly of the *Somnium* with Macrobius' *Commentary*) is printed by B. Munk Olsen, 'Quelques aspects de la diffusion du "Somnium Scipionis" de Cicéron au moyen âge (du ix[c] au xii[c] siècle)', *Studia Romana in honorem Petri Krarup Septuagenarii* (Copenhagen, 1976), 146–53. The list omits about twenty-five manuscripts, and there are some errors of detail.

[15] I am grateful to M. D. R. for drawing my attention to the Hildesheim manuscript.

[16] A manuscript of the *Somnium* without Macrobius, closely related to Strozzi 49, is Baltimore, Walters Art Gallery W.361 (De Ricci 463) (Italian, *c*.1310).

[17] The exception is Florence, Laur. 76.33 (*Somnium* added in s. XIV[2]). We do not know whether three of the manuscripts now represented by fragments of the *Commentary* once contained the *Somnium*; the fourth fragment, Berlin (West) lat. 2° 389, is the first leaf of a copy of the *Somnium*, and it seems more likely than not that it would have been followed by a copy of the *Commentary*.

Appendix: Diagrams

Macrobius' text specifically mentions five circular diagrams, which are more or less faithfully reproduced in most manuscripts, at standard places in the text.

1. The seven 'planets' moving within the zodiacal signs. *Comm.* 1.21.4/5 (Willis 85.30/1), *dicetur./Atque.*
2. 'Rain falling off the earth', an impossibility illustrating what we would call the force of gravity. End of Book 1.
3. The five zones of the earth. *Comm.* 2.5.15/16 (Willis 112.22), *addetur./Licet.*
4. The five zones of heaven over those of the earth, with the ecliptic. *Comm.* 2.7.6/7 (Willis 118.24), *perustam./Et.*
5. World map, showing the tides of Ocean. *Comm.* 2.9.7/8 (Willis 124.1), *perseverat./Quod.*

Willis prints representations of diagrams (1), (3), (4), and (2), in that order, on pp. 164–7 (but the earlier manuscripts contain no wording in diagrams (2) and (3), and often illustrate the falling rain in (2) by numerous parallel lines). He completely omits (5), the *mappa mundi* which is of fundamental importance to the medieval view of world geography.[18] Jan's plates provide versions of all five diagrams, but also some additional diagrams not specified by Macrobius (most of Jan's diagrams are from Munich Clm 6362). Many manuscripts contain such additions, some spontaneously invented by medieval readers to elucidate the text, others copied from works such as Calcidius' commentary on the *Timaeus*, Boethius's *De institutione musica*, and Isidore's *De natura rerum*.

B. C. B.-B.

---

[18] A list of Macrobian manuscripts containing the map – a good proportion of the total – is printed by M. Destombes, *Mappemondes A.D. 1200–1500* (*Imago Mundi*, Suppl. iv, *Monumenta Cartographica Vetustioris Aevi*, i), Amsterdam, 1964, 43–5, 85–95, which also provides convenient references to the many reproductions in Youssouf Kamal, *Monumenta Cartographica Africae et Aegypti* (5 vols. in 16 fascicules, Cairo, 1926–51). Kamal (vol. iii, fasc. i (1930) fol. 554^r) reproduces the one surviving photograph of Metz 271 (s. x^2 or xi^1, destroyed in 1944).

Saturnalia

Written in the first half of the fifth century,[1] the *Saturnalia* is a hùgely complex work, which draws extensively upon a great variety of predecessors, both Greek and Latin. One of the most obvious of these is Aulus Gellius,[2] whom Macrobius follows so closely so frequently that the *Sat.* comes to have almost the authority of an early manuscript for the text of Gellius (and vice versa).

Although it is often assumed that Isidore knew the work, it is highly doubtful that he had read it at first hand.[3] There is no sign that Bede knew anything other than a brief set of excerpts.[4] In the ninth century,[5] the *Sat.* was known to Servatus Lupus,[6] and also apparently to Erchanbert of Freising, Milo of Saint-Amand, and the compilers of the Carolingian

The only modern critical edition is the Teubner text of J. Willis (1963; 2nd edn., 1970). This is in general a reliable text, although it does not use the full range of manuscripts given below. There is an English translation by P. V. Davies, *Macrobius: the Saturnalia* (Columbia University Press, 1969). Unfortunately this is based not on Willis, but on Eyssenhardt's 1893 Teubner text.

[1] For the date see Alan Cameron, 'The Date and Identity of Macrobius', *JRS* 56 (1966), 25–38; also S. Döpp, 'Zur Datierung von Macrobius' Saturnalia', *Hermes*, 106 (1978), 619–32.

[2] For a spirited attempt to find greater 'independence' in Macrobius, see E. Tuerk, 'Macrobe et les Nuits Attiques', *Latomus*, 24 (1965), 381–406.

[3] The question of the influence of the *Sat.* in the Middle Ages is virtually unexplored, much more attention being paid to the *Commentarii in Somnium Scipionis*. The standard works are uncritical and highly unreliable: Manitius, *Geschichte*; M. Schedler, *Die Philosophie des Macrobius und ihr Einfluss auf die Wissenschaft des christlichen Mittelalters* (= *Beiträge zur Geschichte der Philosophie des Mittelalters*, 13), Münster i.W., 1916. A much more sceptical approach is found in R. Bernabei, *The Treatment of the Sources in Macrobius' Saturnalia, and the Influence of the Saturnalia during the Middle Ages* (diss., Cornell University, 1970).

[4] The so-called *Disputatio Hori et Praetextati*, a series of excerpts from Book 1; see C. W. Jones, *Bedae Opera De Temporibus*, Mediaeval Academy of America (Cambridge, Mass., 1943), 105–8 and 206–10. Jones knows of only three manuscripts of these excerpts. To these must now be added Padua, Bibl. Antoniana 27, ff. 66ʳ–71ᵛ. See the transcript given by Sister Mary Josepha Carton, *Three Unstudied Manuscripts of Macrobius's Saturnalia* (diss., Saint Louis University, 1966), 160–201. Carton dates this manuscript *c*.820, but is unaware that it represents another witness to the *Disputatio*. P. McGurk, *Catalogue of Astrological and Mythological Illuminated Manuscripts of the Latin Middle Ages*, iv (Leiden, 1966), dates the Padua manuscript to s. X in. Yet another manuscript of the *Disputatio* to come to light is Vienna 15269 + ser. nov. 37 (written at Salzburg, s. VIII ex. = *CLA* X. 1510). See B. C. B.-B. in *Survival*, no. 93.

[5] The possibility must always remain open that in some cases this knowledge was derived not from a full text, but from excerpts.

[6] Paris lat. 6370 (s. IX¹, from Tours) contains a text of the *Comm.*, while the last leaf (f. 112ʳ⁻ᵛ) has the beginning of the *Sat.* (ending at *Praef.* § 6 *committemus*). This book is heavily annotated in the hand of Lupus. Unfortunately it is not possible to say what the original state of the *Sat.* text must have been: its brevity frustrates all efforts at relating it to the other manuscripts. See É. Pellegrin, 'Les Manuscrits de Loup de Ferrières', *BEC* 115 (1957), 5–31, esp. 11; E. K. Rand and L. W. Jones, *The Earliest Book of Tours*, Mediaeval Academy of America (Cambridge, Mass., 1934), 100–1; A. La Penna, 'Le Parisinus Latinus 6370 et le texte des *Commentarii* de Macrobe', *RPh* 24 (1950), 177–87. Further clues to associate the *Sat.* with the circle of Lupus are (a) a fragment of the *Sat.* in Leiden, Voss. Lat. Q. 2, ff. 31–3, dated by Bischoff to before 850, with the provenance 'ager Ligerae fluminis ab latere monasterii Ferrierensis'; (b) the association noted for M below.

commentaries on Martianus Capella. Although the *Sat.* never attained the popularity given to the *Comm.*, nevertheless in the twelfth century the *Sat.* comes into its own with such writers as William of Conches, Giraldus Cambrensis, and John of Salisbury.[7]

Our knowledge of the text[8] is derived ultimately from a single (now lost) copy, which was available in the late eighth/early ninth centuries. From this single copy were derived two families:

Family I

The most important representatives of the first family are:

N   Naples V. B. 10, s. IX med.–IX¾ (France), ending[9] at Book 7.5.2.
G   Strasbourg 14, s. XI, Germany, containing all seven books.[10]
D   Oxford, Bodl. Auct. T. 2. 27, s. XI in., east French? (from Metz), ending[11] at 3.4.9.
P   Paris lat. 6371, s. XI, containing all seven books.
T   Escorial Q.I.1, s. XV, all seven books.[12]

The second family splits into two groups, the first of which (a) is characterized by its preserving only the first three books, while the second (b) has all seven.

Family II(a)

M   Montpellier 225, s. IX med. (France), containing 1.12.21–the end of Book 3. B. C. B.-B. reports that M 'is written in a hand reminiscent of Heiric of Auxerre's (though not his)'.
B   Bamberg Class. 37 (M.V.5), s. IX¾ (northern or eastern France); first three books.
L   Vatican lat. 5207, s. X[1] (Italy); first three books.[13]
V   Vatican, Reg. lat. 1650, s. IX⁴/₄ (France, area of Soissons); first three books.
Z   Escorial E.III.18, mainly a worthless fifteenth-century text of

[7] C. C. J. Webb, 'On Some Fragments of Macrobius' *Saturnalia*', *CR* 11 (1897), 41, even maintained that John had access to a fuller text of the *Sat.*, in which the end of Book 7 (now lost) was still available.
[8] This account accepts the stemma of J. Willis, 'De codicibus aliquot manuscriptis Macrobii *Saturnalia* continentibus', *RhM* 100 (1957), 152–64, against A. La Penna, 'Studi sulla tradizione dei *Saturnalia* di Macrobio', *Annali della Scuola normale superiore di Pisa*, 22 (1953), 225–52. La Penna is still useful for his descriptions of most of the manuscripts.
[9] See U. Lepore, 'I codici Napoletani dei Saturnalia di Macrobio', *Biblion*, 1 (1946–7), 75–91.
[10] This manuscript was not used by Willis for his Teubner text. For its importance see Carton (n. 4, above), who gives a complete collation of G (pp. 11–97) and concludes that it is a *gemellus* of N and hence of the greatest value for the end of Book 7.
[11] W. M. Lindsay, 'A Bodleian Ms. of Macrobius', *CR* 14 (1900), 260–1.
[12] Willis has been censured for bothering to use T in a critical edition (e.g. J. Préaux, *Latomus*, 24 (1965), 957). It might indeed be excluded with little or no loss.
[13] Willis did not use L. A full collation is given by Carton, 98–139; she judges that it is a *gemellus* of B.

Books 1–7, although the text up to 1.17.6 is of some value, being s. XII/XIII.

To these must be added British Library, Cotton Vit. C.III, s. IX med.–IX¾ (northern France); first three books.[14]

Family II(b)

R   Vatican, Reg. lat. 2043, s. X/XI (France, Mont-Saint-Michel), ending at 7.14.11.

J   Vatican lat. 3417, s. XII, containing[15] Books 1–4 and Book 7.

F   Florence, Laur. 90 sup. 25, s. XII.

A   Cambridge, University Library Ff. 3.5, s. XII (Bury St. Edmunds).

With the use of all these witnesses, it is usually possible to reconstruct the archetype with reasonable certainty and thus to come possibly as close as 350 years from the publication of the *Saturnalia*.

P. K. M.

[14] Another witness not used by Willis.
[15] J is ignored by both La Penna and Willis – see Carton, 'Vat. Lat. 3417 and its Relationship to the Text of Macrobius' *Saturnalia 7*', *TAPA* 96 (1965), 25–30.

MANILIUS

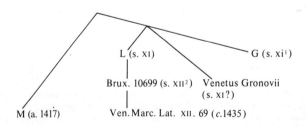

The text of Manilius rests primarily on three manuscripts, Leipzig 1465 (L), Brussels 10012 (G), and Madrid 3678 (M). M, the most honest but most corrupt of the three, was written for Poggio during the Council of Constance by a local scribe. During the next Council Nicholas of Cues brought to Basle a copy of L, Brussels 10699 (Cusanus), from which Venice Marc. Lat. XII. 69 (3949) was copied on the spot by an Italian hand. M and the Marcianus were subsequently collated with each other, and from the Marcianus thus transformed derive sixteen manuscripts,[1] the *editio princeps* (Nuremberg, *c*.1473, prepared by the eminent astronomer Regiomontanus), and the first Italian edition (Bologna, 1474).

The first editor to reach beyond these hybrid *recentiores* was Scaliger, who for his second edition (Leiden, 1600) secured a collation of G.[2] Bentley (London, 1739) went further by using collations not only of a manuscript largely derived from M, Leiden, Voss. Lat. O.3, but also of L and a lost *membranaceus Venetus coenobii D. Antonii* collated by Gronovius, who assigned it to s. XI; Gronovius's collation has been used only in Bentley's copy, but the original survives in Leiden 755 H 15. M was not brought back into service until Housman used Ellis's 'voluminous excerpts' for his edition of Book 1.[3]

LG and Gronovius's Venetus often agree in error against M, and so it is satisfying that LG can both be assigned to the region of Liège. G, in which Priscian's *Periegesis* follows the inadequately or incorrectly labelled Manilius,[4] is one of many classical manuscripts written at Gembloux in the abbacy of Olbert (1012–48),[5] and a newly published catalogue of *c*.1049–1160 from Lobbes, near Gembloux and closely connected with it, includes 'Astronomicon lib. VI. T. Claudii Caesaris Arati Phenomena. Periegesis Prisciani. Vol. I'.[6] Traube assigned L to the same region as G,[7] and its title, 'Arati philosophi astronomicon liber primus incipit', may be due to the conjunction of texts seen in the manuscript at Lobbes. Another member of the family was at Toul by 1084: 'cuiusdam de astronomia cum peryesi Prisciani et Girberto de astrolapsu. Vol. I'.[8]

M has lost its first leaf, but three descendants step in, and these cast

---

[1] See M. D. R., *CQ* 71 (1977), 223–4, and add Vatican Chigi H.IV.133 and Vienna 3128. A Ferrarese family attested by 1457 incorporates numerous emendations. Savignano sul Rubicone 68 derives from the Cusanus by another route.

[2] On this and other materials of Scaliger's see M. D. R., *Mnem.* 33(1980), 177–9. The relationship of the editions before Scaliger's was discussed by A. Cramer, *Über die ältesten Ausgaben von Manilius' Astronomica* (Ratibor, 1893), who for want of information about the manuscripts could not say how many editions other than the first two and Bonincontrius's (Rome, 1484) used something besides their predecessors. Bonincontrius's recovery of 2.716–7 reveals a debt to some manuscript independent of the Marcianus, presumably M or a descendant (four survive); but no evidence has been offered that he made more than the most desultory use of it.

[3] Housman later acquired photographs of MLG and other manuscripts, which are now in Cambridge University Library.

[4] 'Manilius poeta' is not earlier than s. XV, and the erased title has not been deciphered.

[5] A. Boutemy, *Annales de la Société archéologique de Namur*, 41 (1934), 43–85, and *Mélanges Félix Rousseau* (Brussels, 1958), 111–20.

[6] F. Dolbeau, *Recherches Augustiniennes*, 13 (1978), 33 no. 302; 14 (1979), 227 no. 302.

[7] *Philologus*, 66 (1907), 122–3. Its copy the Cusanus probably comes not from Liège but from St. Eucharius Trier: see *APPENDIX VERGILIANA*, n. 6.

[8] Becker, 68.210. The annotator of Berne 276, who worked in central France about 1250–60, says on *Ofiucus* '. . . P's de situ orbis *serpentem magnis Ophiucus nomine signis dividit* [Manil. 1.331–2]'. 'P's' is presumably 'Priscianus', whose *Periegesis* bears the title *De situ orbis* in a few manuscripts (though not in G); but no other trace of Manilius even in this guise has been found in central France.

doubt on whether M had any title at the beginning. Nevertheless, it does elsewhere call the poet something like Manilius. In the subscription to Book 2, it adds 'Boeiii' to 'M. Manlii', and this has suggested confusion with Boethius, whose full name included Manlius. A victim can even be found for the confusion: Gerbert, having come across 'viii volumina Boetii de astrologia' at Bobbio in 983, sent five years later for 'M. Manlius de astrologia'.[9] The cause of confusion, however, is less likely to have been one of Boethius's minor names than his conjunction with Manilius in a manuscript; and the ninth-century catalogue from Bobbio includes just such a manuscript, nos. 384–7: 'libros Boetii iii de aritmetica et alterum de astronomia', if the work 'de astronomia' is identified with the five books of Manilius.[10]

The question now arises whether Gerbert's request succeeded and if so whether M, the family of LG, or both, owe their existence to him. The presence of his 'De astrolapsu' in the manuscript at Toul does not suffice to answer it. It might be easier to answer if Poggio had disclosed where he found the exemplar of M, especially since it has sometimes been regarded as the archetype.

Fresh light on the medieval circulation and the stemma comes from an unexpected quarter. Parma 283, a miscellany of which the relevant part dates from 1452 or after, offers on f. 37ᵛ the first fifteen lines of Book 1 preceded by 'M. Manilii Stronomicon liber primus sic incipit et est in bibliotheca Spirensi'.[11] The title rules out any association with the family of LG, and in line 11 the Spirensis had *iam propius mundusque favet* like M and not *iam propiusque favet mundus* like LG. Either, therefore, LG have not inherited the truth in line 11, or M and the Spirensis share an error. Further evidence is provided by British Library, Add. 22808, ff. 2–11, a text of 1.1–727 written in s. xv²/₃ at or near Amorbach and probably copied from the Spirensis.[12] Though this manuscript shares interpolations with LG, it appears to derive independently from the archetype, which presumably carried corrections. Corrections in the archetype will also account for the sporadic preservation of truth by L^2 or G against MLG or ML; the source of LG need only have taken most of them over while M ignored them.[13] Whether the Spirensis was the archetype or a copy of it does not emerge from its descendants.[14] The six books attributed to it by the Parmensis ('sunt libri sex, ultimus est

[9] F. Weigle, *Die Briefsammlung Gerberts von Reims* (Weimar, 1966), *Epp.* 8, 130.

[10] G. P. Goold (Loeb edn., 1977), cvii–cix, offers this attractive explanation of Gerbert's 'viii volumina Boetii'.

[11] P. O. Kristeller, *Iter Italicum*, ii (Leiden, 1967), 46, with further details from my own inspection.   [12] See M. D. R., *CQ* 74 (1980), 519–22.

[13] Goold, *Phoenix*, 13 (1959), 97–8.

[14] Goold, *RhM* 97 (1954), 359–72, follows Jacob and Garrod in hazarding a reconstruction of the archetype on the evidence of displacements. See also D. B. Gain, *RhM* 114 (1971), 261–4.

completus') recur in the manuscript at Lobbes but can be variously explained away.

More could be said about the manuscript that Politian borrowed from Pietro Leoni at Padua in 1491, 'libro che io per me non ne viddi mai più antiqui',[15] if the printed edition in which he collated it were to reappear; at 5.126 it read *ut fidum nerea dii genuere syboeten*,[16] and it included astronomical and meteorological poems from the *Anthologia Latina*.[17] If Bonincontrius really received an old Casinese fragment from Panormita, it should have made more of a difference to his edition (Rome, 1484).

For knowledge of Manilius in Antiquity see van Wageningen's edition (Leipzig, 1915), xvii–xix. Who knew him in the Middle Ages depends partly on the name he went by, but everything certain has been mentioned above.

Even after the labours of Scaliger and Bentley, Housman's five volumes (London, 1903–30) are a monument of criticism; the conclusions to which his gradual acquaintance with the tradition eventually brought him are set out in the fifth (pp. v–xxiii). See also, especially on the history of Manilian recension, H. W. Garrod, *Manili Astronomicon liber II* (Oxford, 1911), xv–lxi. Ordinary mortals who wish to read and understand the poet will be grateful for the excellent Loeb edition of G. P. Goold (1977).

M. D. R.

---

[15] People repeat Sabbadini's inference that it was 'in maiuscolo o comunque anteriore al sec. IX' (*Scoperte*, i. 170), but may Politian not have meant that he had seen no older manuscripts of Manilius? Perhaps it became Gronovius's Venetus; cf. the next note.

[16] *Angelo Poliziano, Miscellaneorum centuria secunda*, ed. V. Branca and M. Pastore Stocchi (Florence, 1972), iv.34. As Politian reports *fidum* (Scaliger) from both M and the *ed. Bonon.*, which have *fidunt*, the Leoninus may not have had *fidum* either; and as he gives his conjecture once with *et* and once with *ut*, perhaps *ut* too cannot be trusted. Is it a coincidence, however, that according to Gronovius the Venetus read *ut fidum nereadii genuere syboten*?

[17] Collations of these appear in Munich Clm 807, ff. 53^v–57^r; cf. C. di Pierro, *Giornale storico della letteratura italiana*, 55 (1910), 9. If the manuscript of Priscian's *Periegesis* collated on ff. 60^r–61^v was the same, the case for identifying it with Gronovius's Venetus is strengthened; cf. the third paragraph above. Nothing looks like Manilius in the inventory of Leoni's manuscripts published by L. Dorez, *Rev. des. Bibl.* 7(1897), 84–92.

MARTIAL

Despite unsolved problems at all stages, the transmission of Martial's epigrams presents both in the stemma and on the map a sharp and striking outline. Much of the credit for sketching it goes to Schneidewin, who in his monumental edition (Grimma, 1842) first distinguished the three families of manuscripts whose character and history are now familiar.[1]

Northern Europe in the Middle Ages owed its acquaintance with Books 1–14 to Schneidewin's C, best represented by:

E   Edinburgh, Adv. 18.3.1 (s. IX[2], northern France[2]).
X   Paris lat. 8067 (s. IX³⁄₄, Corbie[3]; Chatelain, plate CLI).
V   Vatican lat. 3294 (s. IX²⁄₃, Auxerre?;[4] Chatelain, plate CLII).

The archetype of this family seems to have been a manuscript in minuscule.[5] It lacked 10.56.7–72 and 87.20–91.2, and many of its later descendants transpose 3.22.1–63.4 after 5.67.5.

Meanwhile the archetype of Schneidewin's B was lying scarcely noticed in an Italian library. Until the 1820s no descendants earlier than s. XV had come to light, and few even of s. XV:

P   Vatican, Pal. lat. 1696 (from Padua?[6]).
Q   British Library, Arundel 136 (s. XV²⁄₃, acquired presumably at Padua by Joh. Pirckheimer c.1460; Chatelain, plate CLI).
f   Florence, Laur. 35.39 (s. XV³⁄₄, written by the Florentine humanist G. A. Vespuccci[7]).

---

[1] On the merits of Schneidewin's edition, unusual merits for its date, see S. Timpanaro, *La genesi del metodo del Lachmann* (new edn., Padua, 1981), 61–2. The latest account of the tradition, M. Citroni's in his excellent edition of Book 1 (Florence, 1975), xlv–lxx, supersedes all others in some respects, but reference will be made below to W. M. Lindsay, *Ancient Editions of Martial* (Oxford, 1903), 1–12; W. Heraeus, *RhM* 74 (1925), 314–36; G. Pasquali, *Storia della tradizione e critica del testo* (Florence, 1934), 415–27. Outside Book 1 the best achievement of *recensio* is Lindsay's OCT (1903), which Housman, *CR* 39 (1925), 199, called 'one of those works which are such boons to mankind that their shortcomings must be forgiven them'; for *emendatio* he preferred the editions of J. D. Duff (*Corpus poetarum latinorum*, ed. J. P. Postgate, ii (London, 1905), 431–531) and Heraeus (Leipzig, 1925¹, rev. J. Borovskij, 1976²).

[2] 'Written by several hands in a French scriptorium north of the Loire' according to I. C. Cunningham, *Scriptorium*, 27 (1973), 70.

[3] Bischoff, *Mitt. Stud.* i. 55, 59 (where 8061 is a misprint).

[4] Bischoff ap. A. C. de la Mare, in *Cultural Aspects of the Italian Renaissance: Essays in Honour of P. O. Kristeller*, ed. C. H. Clough (Manchester, 1976), 187, no. 72.

[5] Lindsay in Friedlaender's edition (Leipzig, 1886), i. 85 with n. 1. 11.70.3 *quepelle* for *querellae* suggests a pre-archetype in pre-Caroline minuscule. F. Brunhölzl, *Festschrift Bernhard Bischoff* (Stuttgart, 1971), 27–8, offers tenuous evidence of corruptions caused by cursive in the earliest centuries of transmission.

[6] Th. Simar, *Mus. Belge*, 14 (1910), 196.   [7] De la Mare, *Handwriting*, 125.

In the 1820s K. Witte discovered in a binding at Perugia a thirteenth-century fragment of Book 10.[8] Then in 1900 a manuscript of s. XII once at S. Maria Corteorlandini Lucca found its way to Berlin and fame:[9]

L   Berlin (West) lat. 2° 612.

Errors in L and PQf betray a Beneventan archetype.[10] Four similar manuscripts, which may have included the archetype, were consulted at Florence, Verona, and Rome by Politian, whom they misled into defending *mulo* at 6.77.7.[11] The family disarranges Books 1–4 as follows: 1 praef.–14 (1–2 *om.*), 48–103.2, 15–41.3 (41.4–47 *om.*), 4.24.2–69.1, 1.103.3–4.24.1, 4.69.2–end of Book. Subscriptions, most fully preserved in L and Q, take the family back to a copy 'emended' in AD 401; the most informative reads 'emendavi ego Torquatus Gennadius in foro divi Augusti Martis consulatu Vincentii et Fraguitii virorum clarissimorum feliciter.'[12]

Schneidewin's A, a family of anthologies, offers excerpts from a *Liber spectaculorum* unknown to C and B, excerpts again (amounting to about half the total) from Books 1–12, and then Books 13–14 in full. The oldest member of A, indeed the oldest manuscript of Martial, is:

H   Vienna 277, ff. 71–3 (s. VIII or IX, probably French; *CLA* X.1474).

Unfortunately H has lost *Spect.* 1.1–18.4 and everything after 1.4.2, so that little chance remains of determining its relationship to:

T   Paris lat. 8071 (s. IX, central or southern France; Chatelain, plate XIV).
R   Leiden, Voss. Lat. Q.86 (*c.*850,[13] Tours?;[14] Chatelain, plate CLII, wrongly cited as Q. 36).

---

[8] Schneidewin i. lxx–lxxi. It contained 36.7–41.5, even that not all legible. Where is it now?
[9] Lindsay, *CR* 15 (1901), 413–20; *Ancient Editions*, 5, 61–120.
[10] Lindsay, *CR* 15 (1901), 416–17.
[11] *Misc.* 1.23. The 'codex vetustissimus . . . langobardis litteris' at S. Marco is no. 947 in the catalogue published by Ullman and P. A. Stadter, *The Public Library of Renaissance Florence* (Padua, 1972), 236; Politian saw at Verona 'pagellas quaspiam antiquissimi item voluminis'; at Rome in the possession of Bernardinus Valla 'volumen item Martialis langobardis characteribus' (cf. *Misc.* II.35.5); and at Florence 'alium . . . codicem semiveterem'. On 6.77.7 see S. Timpanaro, *Rinascimento*, 2 (1951), 311–18 = *Contributi di filologia e di storia della lingua latina* (Rome, 1978), 333–43.
[12] For details of the subscriptions see Lindsay, *Ancient Editions*, 3–4, 119–20 (where read Add. 12004 for Harley, 12004).
[13] Bischoff ap. K. A. de Meyier, *Codices Vossiani latini II: codices in quarto* (Leiden, 1975), 197.
[14] A. Wilmart, *Codices Reginenses Latini*, ii (Vatican, 1945), 245. Another argument can be added with the aid of Manitius, *Geschichte*, iii. 291, 300. Hrabanus Maurus pillaged three poems from the *Anthologia latina* that have come down only in R, and he also cites Mart. 9.5.1 as from 'Calpurnius in X' (*PL* 111, 623A), of which at least 'in X' fits Schneidewin's A: *Spect.* = 'Book 1', Book 1 = 'Book 2', and so on. One manuscript like R would account for both debts, and he spent at Tours such time as he did not spend at Fulda or Mainz.

Between *Spect*. 18.5 and 1.4.2 neither contains anything absent from H; both there and thereafter T is much fuller than R, which prefers single couplets.[15] In other texts common to H and T, such as Grattius' *Cynegetica*, T is widely regarded as a copy of H, but no one has found conclusive proof.

Early manuscripts that cannot be assigned to any family are two known only from laconic catalogues, an unaccompanied Martial at Lorsch in s. IX and a combined Juvenal, Martial, and Persius at Bobbio in s. IX[2];[16] a third in the library of Charlemagne less laconically described as 'Valeri Martialis epigrammata in (?) libri VIIII ad Lucanum et Tullum';[17] the *Florilegium Sangallense*, St. Gall 870 (s. IX), which cites five lines for points of prosody;[18] and two sets of excerpts: Leipzig Rep. I.4°.74 (s. IX[2]/4, Orléans?[19]), ff. 25[r]–26[v], which contains an epigram each from the *Xenia* and *Apophoreta* (Books 13–14) and Books 1, 2, 3, 11, and 12 followed by nine more in no recognizable order; and Munich Clm 6292 (s. XI, Freising), ff. 118[r]–119[v], which contains excerpts from Books 1–6 under the title 'Martialis e xeniorum'.[20] The last phrase in the description of Charlemagne's manuscript is the title in C and B (*Tullium* B) of an epigram absent from T and R, 1.36; the Sangallensis, the Lipsiensis, and the Monacensis likewise include things absent from T and R, and they do not belong to C either.

Contamination amongst ABC not surprisingly began in France, the home of both C and A. The compiler of the *Florilegium Gallicum* (s. XII[2]/3, Orléans or thereabouts) used for the staple of his text a member of C in which 3.22.1–63.4 stood after 5.67.5;[21] but after Book 14 he put *Spect*. 13–14, known only from A, and 31–2, not known from elsewhere, and furthermore he drew on a source like A for additions and alterations to

---

[15] U. Carratello, *GIF* 26 (1974), 145, draws attention to the curious fact that in *Spectacula* T and R each omit what the other includes. Cf. M. D. R., *Prometheus*, 6 (1980), 198, which should be consulted on anything that pertains to *Spectacula* in what follows; it appeared too late to affect Carratello's edition, *M. Valerii Martialis Epigrammaton liber* (Rome, 1981, 'ristampa dell' edizione fuori commercio del 1980').

[16] Manitius, *Handschriften*, 130, 131; on the date of the catalogue from Bobbio see G. Mercati, *M. Tulli Ciceronis De re publica libri e codice rescripto Vaticano Latino 5757 phototypice expressi*, i (Vatican, 1934), 26–7.

[17] *Karl der Grosse*, 60 (= Bischoff, *Mitt. Stud.* iii. 166), and Bischoff, *Sammelhandschrift Diez. B Sant. 66* (Graz, 1973), 39, 218.

[18] Chr. Stephan, *RhM* 40 (1885), 263–82.

[19] Haupt, *Opusc.* i (Leipzig, 1875), 290–1. For the date and origin of this manuscript see OVID, *Metamorphoses*; I have used a microfilm at the Institut de Recherche et d'Histoire des Textes, in Orléans, and s. IX is certain.

[20] On the importance of this manuscript see TIBULLUS. A transcript would be easier to use than the bits and pieces plucked out by Friedlaender, i. 89–90, Hosius, *RhM* 46 (1891), 297–8, Citroni, lxx.

[21] M. D. R., *Prometheus*, 6 (1980), 199–200. One such manuscript older than the Renaissance is Wolfenbüttel, Gud. lat. 157 (G, s. XIII), whose agreements with the *Florilegium Gallicum* are mentioned by Citroni, lxix; others are Leiden, Voss. Lat. O.56 (s. XII[1]), B. L. Harley 2700 (s. XII), and Milan, Ambros. H. 39 sup. (s. XII).

Books 1–14. It appears, therefore, that a manuscript like A but fuller survived into s. XII.[22]

More contamination between C and A had taken place in either France or England by s. XIII[1], the date of:

W   Westminster Abbey 15 (apparently at Wilton in s. XVI[23]).

This manuscript, a member of C in Books 1–14, adds without titles the *Liber proverbiorum* composed *c*.1100 by Godfrey of Winchester, who imitates Martial, and *Spectacula*. A hand not much later than the scribe's labelled them Books 15 and 16.

How early C and A reached Italy is not known, but already in s. XIV *Spectacula* had been prefixed to a member of C: Bologna, Univ. 2221.[24] Of the two leaves that contained *Spectacula* only the second survives, not written by the same hand as Books 1–14, but both were copied in s. XV¾ by the scribe of Vienna 316. By 1451 another manuscript that began with *Spectacula* had entered the library of S. Spirito Florence, no doubt at one remove from Boccaccio; the reported *explicit* of the penultimate leaf does not correspond exactly to anything in the usual text, and no other readings are preserved.[25]

In s. XV²/₄ manuscripts of Martial started to proliferate among Italian humanists.[26] Attempts at squaring the dislocated and lacunose texts of C and B led to numerous varieties of order, and *Spectacula* occur at the beginning, at the end, after Book 12, or nowhere. Two of the first three editions, Flodr, 3 (Rome, *c*.1470–1) and 1 (Venice, *c*.1469–73), begin with *Spectacula* and exhibit in Books 1 and 5 the dislocations of both B and C. One thing is clear, that apart from Vienna 316 and a few manuscripts similar to and perhaps derived from W, all fifteenth-century copies of *Spectacula* have a common source, which seems to have put them at the beginning.[27]

---

[22] Strictly, *Spect.* 31–2 could have appeared in H between 14 and 18; but 31 is ill suited to the middle of a book, and O. Weinreich, *Studien zu Martial* (Tübinger Beiträge zur Altertumswiss. 4, Stuttgart, 1928), 24–8, gives reasons for supposing it to be the last couplet of the last poem.

[23] M. D. R., *Prometheus*, 6 (1980), 193–4.

[24] G. Götz and G. Löwe, *Leipziger Stud.* 1 (1878), 365–7; Sabbadini, *RFIC* 39 (1911), 248–9.

[25] Sabbadini, *Scoperte*, i. 29; most recently Antonia Mazza, *IMU* 9 (1966), 6, 14, 49. As Boccaccio cites 7.74.1–2, *tossica seva gerit* is taken for a corruption of 10.36.4 *toxica saeva vias* rather than 1.18.6 *toxica saeva mero*; but no one has mentioned that in both passages C reads *vina* for *saeva*. 10.36.4 is not in A. As for Petrarch, G. Martellotti, *RCCM* 2 (1960), 388–93, finds four quotations in earlier works and two allusions to 1.61.9–12 in revisions of 1365 and 1371; all four quotations, 1 *praef.* 8, 1.15.11–12, 1.61.7–8, and 5.81.2, occur in an anthology, Oxford, Bodl. Add. A.208 (s. XIII, French), which also has eight of the ten quotations reported from Geremia da Montagnone by F.-R. Hausmann, 'Martial in Italien', *Studi medievali*³, 17 (1976), 177 n. 18, and quotes other parts of the epigrams that furnished the remaining two.

[26] Besides the manuscripts already mentioned, most of which are medieval, I know of at least another 135, of which only five appear to be medieval: Aberdeen 152 (s. XII/XIII), Cambridge, Corpus Christi College 236 (s. XIII), Ivrea 37 (s. XI, 13.1–110 only), and Leiden, Voss. Lat. Q.89 (s. XIII) and 121 (s. XI/XII). Excerpts abound in the Middle Ages and the Renaissance alike.

[27] Besides *Spectacula*, Italian manuscripts often include as the penultimate poem of Book 4 *Anth. Lat.* 26, *Rure morans*, transmitted at the beginning of Book 5 in A; see AVIANUS, n. 19. Its circulation in Italy might repay investigation.

The sixteenth century recovered the older members of A and with them superior readings in Books 1–14. Sannazaro *c.*1501–3 brought H to Italy 'ex Heduorum usque finibus atque e Turonibus';[28] the margin of a Gryphian edition (Lyon, 1539) gives readings from T or something very like it; and Scaliger, *Publii Virgilii Maronis appendix* (Lyon, 1572), 215–16, published *Spect.* 29–30 from R. When the libraries of central France yielded copies of the *Florilegium Gallicum*, Adr. Junius printed *Spect.* 31–2 for the first time (Antwerp, 1568).

A thorough study of the tradition, however rewarding, would hardly benefit editors. They have enough on their hands anyway, because the three families diverge considerably and not always for obvious reasons. A has certainly expurgated the text,[29] though not at the cost of metre or Latinity; but no purpose has been discerned in the behaviour of B and C. Many variants occur in names, a phenomenon not confined to Martial.[30] Most editors since Schneidewin have attributed some variants, whether in names or not, to Martial himself.[31] Before the three families can be taken back separately to Martial, however, three conditions must be met: it must be shown that Martial either did publish or could have published in such a way that different versions circulated; neither all three families nor any two must share significant errors; and no other explanation must fit the variants so well. Statements of Martial's own meet the first condition, and even without them it would be unlikely that he had run together unaltered fifteen books of epigrams composed over twenty years.[32] The second condition is flouted by BC at, for example, 2.84.4,[33] 4.23.3, 6.12.2, 7.47.6, 79.3,[34] 11.24.15, 56.11, 80.7, 12.2.4, 94.5;[35] by AC at 3.3,[36] 7.18.9–10, 9.71.6, 12.40.3–6;[37] by ABC at 2.46.8, 53.7, 5.19.12, 6.75.4,[38] 9.48.8, 11.8.1.[39] As for the third condition, no one has produced positive reasons for regarding the variants of wording as author's variants anywhere except at 10.48.23,

---

[28] P. Summontius, preface to J. J. Pontanus, *Actius* (Naples, 1507).

[29] 'What is termed modesty in a [= A] by Mr Heraeus and elegance by Mr Lindsay,' says Housman, *CR* 39 (1925), 202, 'is mere monkish horror of woman: a will copy down the grossest and filthiest words, such lines as III.71.1 and VII.10.1, if only they do not call up thoughts of the abhorred sex.'   [30] Pasquali, 421–7.

[31] Lindsay, *Ancient Editions*, 13–34, went further in this than others. Cf. Friedlaender, i. 92–6, Heraeus, 318–23.

[32] Pasquali, 415–16, with Italian analogies. A modern English one may be added, the poems of Robert Graves; see, e.g., the foreword of *Collected Poems (1914–1947)*.

[33] ⟨Alter⟩ ab hoc caesus J. Delz, *MH* 28 (1971), 59.

[34] Housman, *J. Phil.* 30 (1907), 242–4.

[35] Cf. also Lindsay, *Ancient Editions*, 55–9, who wonders whether Torquatus Gennadius 'emended' a text like that of C.

[36] Ibid. 60–1.   [37] Ibid. 45.

[38] *Has ego non metuam* Th. Birt, *RhM* 79 (1930), 309.

[39] Housman, *CR* 44 (1930), 114–15. For a list of insignificant errors see Heraeus, 323–4. E. Lehmann, *Antike Martialausgaben* (Jena diss., Berlin, 1931), 53, sees evidence of a common source in the position of Books 13–14, composed before 1–12, and Pasquali, 418, assumes that Martial himself could not have been responsible for it; but as Books 13–14 differ in character from 1–12, surely he could. Lehmann argues for other reasons that he could not; cf. n. 43, below.

and even there the reasons are unconvincing.[40] The other variants of wording, though puzzling to anyone who believes that corruptions always arise through visual confusion and result in nonsense,[41] amount at best to evidence of a revision so desultory and superficial as to be quite pointless. Most analogies suggest, however, that revision of collections like Martial's epigrams consists largely in pruning, the process most liable to be reversed in transmission.[42] Martial may have revised thoroughly, therefore, and the tradition have covered his traces either wholly or in part. It did so only in part if the omission by B or C of prefaces and the occasional epigram is not due to accident or whim.[43] Another omission to be accounted for is that of the couplet ascribed to Martial by the scholiast on Juv. 4.37; editors accept it (and absurdly print it as *Spect.* 33), but ABC all omit it.

Martial has never lacked readers or imitators,[44] but he has not always been understood. The archetypes of ABC furnished some of the epigrams with ludicrous titles,[45] and someone in the Middle Ages put about the notion that their author was Martial the Cook.[46]

M. D. R.

---

[40] Heraeus, 319, against Lindsay, *Ancient Editions*, 14; Pasquali, 420, nevertheless follows Lindsay.

[41] e.g. 13.65.2 *piscina ludere* A, *lautorum condere* B, *lautorum mandere* C, on which see W. Schmid, *Hommages à Jean Bayet* (Brussels, 1964), 668–71.

[42] Wilamowitz and other scholars in this century not averse to diagnosing interpolation have rightly stressed the desire of Alexandrian editors *nichts umkommen zu lassen*, and long before them Joh. Rhodius in his edition of Scribonius Largus (Padua, 1655), f. b3ʳ, spoke of extraneous matter incorporated by scribes 'modo nihil praeteriissent'. This principle of transmission is still insufficiently recognized. It weakens the common argument that manuscripts of a headless or tailless text must all derive from one headless or tailless copy; why not from several headless or tailless copies of which the fullest supplied the parts missing from the others?

[43] See especially Lehmann, *Antike Martialausgaben*, 48–52, on the epigrams omitted by C in Book 12. At 53–61, Lehmann postulates a critical edition in which someone augmented a copy of Martial's final version with material from earlier versions; but nothing so formal as a critical edition was needed to bring about such contamination. Cf. Citroni, lxxii, and n. 42, above.

[44] For recent bibliography see Hausmann, op. cit. (n. 25, above) and *CTC* iv (Washington, 1980), 249–96.

[45] Lindsay, *Ancient Editions*, 34–55, e.g. 38 (4.76 *AD BISSENAM* from v. 1 *milia . . . bis sena*).

[46] Schneidewin, i. 21–2, who suspected misconstruction of 6.60.8; Manitius, *Philologus*, 49 (1890), 562 n. 1; P. Lehmann, *Pseudo-antike Literatur des Mittelalters* (Leipzig, 1927), 97 n. 86. 'Marcialis Cocus ideo sic est dictus', according to B. L. Cotton Tit. D. xx (s. xv¹, English), f. 134ᵛ, 'quia quemadmodum cocus per ignis decoctionem a carnibus humorem noxium extrahit et eas homini ad gustandum aptas facit, sic iste per invectivum calamum viciorum saniem ab humano corde eicit quodque prius erat cloacha sordium posterius per huius eiectionem sorditatis vas sincerum in susceptionem virtutis efficit atque mundum.'

MARTIANUS CAPELLA

Martianus Minneius Felix Capella keeps his secrets: notably that of his date.[1] Much remains to be learned, too, about the transmission of the *De nuptiis Philologiae et Mercurii*. J. Willis's new Teubner is in the press; his preliminary papers[2] show the acuteness he will bring to the constitution of this most difficult of texts, but suggest a narrow manuscript basis. The recent death of J. Préaux has blighted hopes of a Budé of Books 1–2, and his published work on the manuscripts does not seem definitive.

A *subscriptio*[3] appearing, in most of the manuscripts that contain it, at the end of Book 1 witnesses to the activity in 534 of 'Securus Melior Felix[4] . . . rhetor Urbis R.' 'emending' the text 'ex mendosissimis exemplaribus'. What he produced may be the basis of the flourishing ninth-century tradition, represented for us by an impressive number of extant books,[5] localizable mainly in France and Germany. A corrupted and contaminated vulgate soon established itself to meet the needs of students and teachers of the liberal arts, and a number of commentaries survive from this time.[6] Later, the complete text is relatively less frequent, and the separate copying of Books 1–2 becomes popular. C. Leonardi's monumental article listed 241 manuscripts of Martianus,[7] and despite various detailed studies of single codices much remains to be elucidated in a tradition that can only be highly contaminated.

Such is the wealth of ninth-century material that even the outdated, though still standard, edition of A. Dick (Teubner, 1925)[8] could employ nine books that have since been dated to that early period, including

---

[1] He precedes Fulgentius (for this testimonium and others see Dick, xxix–xxxi; full discussion in C. Leonardi, *Aevum*, 33 (1959), 459 ff.; J. Préaux, 'Les Manuscrits principaux du De nuptiis Philologiae et Mercurii de Martianus Capella', in G. Cambier, C. Deroux, J. Préaux, *Lettres latines du moyen âge et de la Renaissance* (Collection Latomus, 158, Brussels, 1978), 82 ff., adds nothing. But when was Fulgentius? See, still, R. Helm, *RhM* 54 (1899), 111–34.

[2] Most notably, *De Martiano Capella emendando* (Leiden, 1971), and most recently *Mnem.* 33 (1980), 163–74.

[3] Discussed by Préaux, *Corona Gratiarum . . . Eligio Dekkers . . . oblata*, ii (1975), 101–21 (see also 'Les Manuscrits principaux' 77–8).   [4] See HORACE, n. 14.

[5] See Préaux, 'Les Manuscrits principaux', 79–80.

[6] For details see C. E. Lutz in *CTC* ii (Washington, 1971), 370 f. The version of the commentary by Johannes Scottus Erigena in Oxford, Bodl. Auct. T.2.19 (see *Survival*, 52 no. 101) has now been published by E. Jeauneau, *Quatre thèmes érigéniens* (Montreal and Paris, 1978), 91–166.

[7] *Aevum*, 33 (1959), 443–89; 34 (1960), 1–99, 411–524. There is also a book.

[8] The latest reprints (most recently 1978) contain excellent bibliographies on all aspects of Martianus, together (xxxvii–xxxviii) with Préaux's redating of Dick's manuscripts. I follow for the most part Préaux's latest datings (from 'Les Manuscrits principaux').

Karlsruhe Aug. LXXIII (Dick's R: s. IX⅓, probably written in the palace scriptorium of Louis the Pious)[9] and Bamberg Class. 39 (M.v.16) (B: s. IX$^{2-3}$/₄, French), whose merits had been recognized by F. Eyssenhardt (ed. 1866).[10] Préaux's papers[11] suggest a tendency to dismiss the rest of Dick's manuscripts in favour of a 'Corbie' group containing Vatican, Reg. lat. 1535 (s. IX¾, Auxerre) and 1987 (s. IX¾, north (-west) France), British Library, Harley 2685 (s. IX$^{3-4}$/₄, also containing Boethius and Fulgentius), and Paris lat. 8670 (s. IX$^{2-3}$/₄, Corbie). But the evidence for this preference has not been fully stated.

Dick (iii ff.) sketches the editorial work since the *editio princeps* of 1499 (Franciscus Vitalis Bodianus, Vicenza), and Willis goes, polemically, over the more recent ground.[12]

M. W.

[9] B. Bischoff, in *Medieval Learning*, 21.
[10] The two are argued to be uniquely primary by Willis, *De Martiano*, 83–8.
[11] See especially *Corona*, 118 n. 2; *Sacris Erudiri*, 17 (1966), 142–3, and 'Les Manuscrits principaux', esp. 121–5.   [12] *De Martiano*, 4–12.

NEMESIANUS

Cynegetica

Hincmar of Reims read the *Cynegetica* as a 'puer scholarius'.[1] Born about 806, he was educated under Alcuin's pupil Hilduin at Saint-Denis, where the earliest manuscript, Paris lat. 7561, pp. 13–18 (A), was written c.825.[2]

In s. XI the *Cynegetica* followed Claudian, *In Rufinum* in a manuscript at Saint-Oyan that may have been A but cannot have been the other medieval manuscript that survives, Paris lat. 4839 (B, s. X), which has different contents and apparently comes from England.[3] B was once suspected of being a poor copy of A,[4] but more recently its independence has been upheld.[5]

[1] *PL* 126 (Paris, 1852), 383c. Pithoeus pointed this out in *Epigrammata et poematia vetera* (Paris, 1590), 470.
[2] Bischoff, *Mitt. Stud.* iii 150 n. 8. An erasure at the foot of pp. 14–15 may conceal something helpful.
[3] Manitius, *Geschichte*, i.347: Bischoff ap. A. Beccaria, *I codici di medicina del periodo presalernitano* (Rome, 1956), 140.
[4] H. Schenkl, *Jahrb. für class. Phil.* Suppl. 24 (1898), 401.
[5] P. van de Woestijne in his edition (Antwerp, 1937), 20–1.

The only other manuscript, Vienna 3261, was copied by Jacopo Sannazaro from one that he found during 1501–4 in France. It was probably A,[6] though some scholars have wondered whether Nemesianus' *Cynegetica* occurred somewhere in quires 1–16 of the manuscript that supplied Sannazaro with Grattius' in quires 17–18 (Vienna 277, s. VIII/IX); a third possibility, unexciting and not yet aired, is a lost manuscript.

The first edition (Venice, 1534) was printed from something like Vienna 3261.[7] The only editors who report all three manuscripts are Baehrens, *PLM* III (Leipzig, 1881), 190–202, and P. Volpilhac (Budé, Paris, 1975).

The poem was incomplete in the archetype.

M. D. R.

[6] Schenkl, 401–2.   [7] Ibid. 401; van de Woestijne, 28 n. 2.

CORNELIUS NEPOS

The collection of twenty-three *Lives*, preceded by a *Prologus*, is attributed in the manuscripts to one Aemilius Probus, with the title *De excellentibus ducibus exterarum gentium*. To these are appended the *Lives* of Cato and Atticus, together with two fragments from the letters of Cornelia, mother of the Gracchi, all of which are correctly attributed to Cornelius Nepos, and cited from his work *De Latinis historicis*.

The work of Nepos was unknown after late Antiquity, until the appearance, probably in the twelfth century, of the unique source of all extant manuscripts. This is a manuscript, now lost, which belonged in the sixteenth century to Pierre Daniel or (more probably) Gifanius. It is known, therefore, as *Dan.* or *Gif.*, and some of its readings can be recovered from several printed sources in the sixteenth and seventeenth centuries, together with some manuscript notes of Paul Petau.

Two direct copies of *Dan.* are known:

L   Leiden B. P. L. 2011, written in the third quarter of the fifteenth century in the Netherlands/Rhine region. This copy does not contain the *Life* of Cato or the Cornelia fragments.

P   The codex Parcensis (from the library of le Parc in Belgium), which was transferred to Louvain, where it was destroyed in the bombardment of August 1914. Various detailed collations survive, notably that of

K. L. Roth preserved in the University Library at Basle. A photograph of one page is preserved in Chatelain, plate CLXXXII, showing a Flemish hand of the second half of the fifteenth century. This copy does not contain the *Life* of Atticus or the Cornelia fragments.

Also descended from *Dan.*, but further removed, is A, Wolfenbüttel, Gud. lat. 166, written at the very end of the twelfth century, possibly in northern France. The text of A is markedly inferior to that produced by the combined witness of L and P, although its value for the *Lives* of Cato and Atticus, and for the Cornelia fragments, remains considerable.

A large number of fifteenth-century Italian manuscripts survive, but these are all demonstrably derived from A.

P. K. M.

For further information see P. K. Marshall, *The Manuscript Tradition of Cornelius Nepos* (*BICS* Suppl. 37), London, 1977; *Cornelii Nepotis Vitae cum Fragmentis*, Leipzig, 1977. Photographs of P and A are given by Chatelain, plate CLXXXII, of L and A by Marshall, *The Manuscript Tradition*.

NONIUS MARCELLUS

Nonius Marcellus' *De compendiosa doctrina* is important not only as a dictionary of early Latin usage but as the main source for a number of works which have no transmission of their own. It is Nonius who has preserved many, and in some cases most, of the fragments of lost works of writers of the Republic, among them Accius, Lucilius, Varro's *Menippean Satires*, the *Tragedies* of Ennius, Sisenna, and the *Historiae* of Sallust.

The *De compendiosa doctrina* is one of those works which might have been designed to be edited by W. M. Lindsay, and it is his edition of the text[1] which we still use. The manuscript tradition is rather complex,

[1] Leipzig, 1903. Lindsay had seen through the press the posthumous edition of J. H. Onions (Books 1–3, Oxford, 1895), who had done important work on the manuscripts. Lindsay's other book, *Nonius Marcellus' Dictionary of Republican Latin* (Oxford, 1901), is a fundamental study of Nonius' method of compilation. More information may be found in Lindsay's articles, in particular: 'Die Handschriften von Nonius Marcellus I–III', *Philologus*, 55 (1896), 160–9; 'Die Handschriften von Nonius IV', *Philologus*, 60 (1901), 217–28; 'Die Handschriften von Nonius V–XX', ibid. 628–34; 'The Lost "codex optimus" of Nonius Marcellus', *CR* 10 (1896), 16–18; 'A Study of the Leyden MS of Nonius Marcellus', *AJP* 22 (1901), 29–38; 'Sur la provenance de quelques manuscrits de Nonius Marcellus', *RPh* 26 (1902), 211–12. Recent work on Nonius is best followed in *Studi Noniani*, of which five volumes have so far appeared (Genoa, 1967–78); see especially F. Bertini, 'Errori nella tradizione manoscritta della *Compendiosa Doctrina*', *Studi Noniani*, i. 9–66, who points to certain inadequacies of Lindsay's edition, and R. Mazzacane, 'Il codice *Gudianus di*

tripartite in more ways than one. Nonius' compilation ran to the twenty books traditional for works of grammar and, in Carolingian times it would appear, this lengthy text was split for convenience into three parts; some of the manuscripts contain only one of the three, others, though complete, have clearly derived the different sections from different sources. Nonius' division of his material into books was so unbalanced that Book 4 is longer than the sixteen books which follow; consequently the volumes into which the book was split contain respectively Books 1–3, Book 4, Books 5–20. The manuscripts also fall into three families, depending not on the books they contain, but on the type of text they offer. The first family carries the 'pure' text. The second offers what has been called the 'doctored' text. This is in places more faithfully transcribed from the archetype, but in general has been worked over by some Carolingian scholar to provide a more readable version; a text once described as 'ulcerated from top to toe'[2] was not easy fodder for those having a struggle to learn the Latin tongue. The third family carries the 'extract' version, in which the words and their explanations are given but the examples are mostly omitted; the book has been adapted to the form of a glossary, doubtless to provide a Latin dictionary for monastic use. All manuscripts of all three families descend from a common archetype, in which a leaf from Book 4 had been placed for safe keeping after the first leaf of Book 1.[3]

Thus the basic stemmatic pattern is tripartite; the head of each family derives independently from the archetype, but the membership and structure of each family group varies over the three sections of text. To provide a critical basis for his edition Lindsay had to construct three full stemmata,[4] but the geographical and historical context of the transmission may perhaps be more easily explored if we concentrate on the descent of the 'pure' text (Family I).

The manuscripts used in the reconstruction of the hyparchetype of the first family are these:

L   Leiden, Voss.Lat.F.73, s. IX in., Tours.[5]

F   Florence, Laur.48.1, s. IX[1], corrected by Lupus of Ferrières.[6]

H   British Library, Harley 2719, s. IX/X, written in or near Brittany.

Nonio Marcello', ibid. v. 117–201, who challenges the supremacy given by Lindsay to L. Of great importance for the transmission is what Bischoff has to say in *Settimane*, 22.1, 78–9 (= *Mitt. Stud.* iii. 67).

[2] 'A vertice, ut aiunt, usque ad extremum unguem ulcus est': Angelo Mai, in the *editio princeps* of Cicero's *De re publica* (Rome, 1822), xlii.

[3] Thus 406.13 M. *interiere tamen* – 409.15 M. *auster nascitur* appears in the manuscripts at 3.13 M. after the word *Pausimacho*. The omission of Book 16 may be pre-archetypal.

[4] xxx–xxxii.

[5] E. K. Rand, *Studies in the Script of Tours*, i (Cambridge, Mass., 1929), 105 no. 26, plates XXXVIII–XXXIX; W. Köhler, *Die karolingischen Miniaturen, i, Die Schule von Tours* (Berlin, 1930), Text I, 68 f., 368, Taf. 7 e-i.   [6] Bischoff, loc. cit.

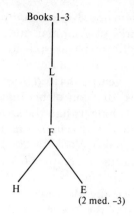

Books 1-3

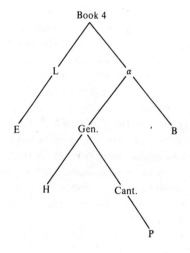

Book 4

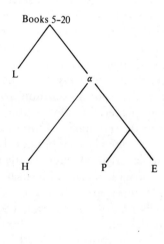

Books 5-20

E   Escorial M.III.14, s. IX²/₃, Auxerre?; in the eleventh century at
       St. Peter's Ghent.[7]
Gen.   Geneva lat.84, s. IX, Fulda.[8]
B   Berne 83, s. IX, written at Reims in the time of Hincmar.[9]
Cant. Cambridge, University Library Mm.5.22, s. IX ex., from Bourges.[10]
P   Paris lat. 7667, s. X, Fleury.[11]

The manuscript L, which contains all three sections of the text and
which Lindsay regarded as the most faithful representative of the
archetype, is a fine and carefully executed book written at Tours in the
early years of the ninth century, probably while Alcuin was still Abbot

---

[7] I am grateful to Professor Bischoff for information on date and provenance.
[8] Bischoff, loc. cit.   [9] Ibid.
[10] Lindsay, *RPh* 26 (1902), 211–12.   [11] Ibid.

of St. Martin's. In Books 1–3 it is the progenitor of all the surviving manuscripts. Tours clearly played a leading part in the diffusion of Nonius' text, and it may be significant that two of the correctors in L had access to texts of the second and third families; L^2 incorporated readings from the third or 'extract' family, L^3 from the second or 'doctored' tradition.

F, which is derived from L, does not take us far from Tours, for it has been recognized as another of the manuscripts corrected and annotated by Lupus of Ferrières, at an early stage in his career. The corrections in F will need further investigation, for one of the correctors occupies a place of special significance in the transmission of the *Compendiosa doctrina*. F^3 had access to a manuscript containing variants and supplements not known from any other source and clearly right; he had been able to consult a good manuscript now lost, perhaps the archetype itself at an earlier stage in its history or a copy taken from it before its text had begun to suffer.[12] The valley of the Loire must be the centre of Nonius' transmission, and the evidence provided by the two copies of F (H and E) strengthens this supposition. H has been glossed in Breton, which serves to place it in or near Brittany, an easy step from the Loire valley. E is closer to home, for the annotations belong to the school usually associated with Auxerre. In Books 2 med.–3 it is a descendant of F (Lupus's manuscript), in 4 of L itself (no intermediary like F has survived), in 5–20 (and also in 1–2 med., where it joins the second family) its closest relative is another Loire manuscript, P, from Fleury.

When we move to Book 4 a new element enters the tradition. The best manuscript of this family after L is the Geneva manuscript (Gen.), undoubtedly written at Fulda. Tours – Fulda is a common axis, as other texts, Apicius and Suetonius for example, demonstrate, and it is difficult in this context not to think of Lupus, whose strong connection with Fulda would explain this German intrusion into an otherwise exclusively French tradition. If Lupus's long arm had plucked Gen. from Fulda, this would explain part of the puzzle, and indeed some of the corrections in Gen. could be in Lupus's hand.[13] But this would imply that Gen.'s exemplar (a or a copy of it) was also of German origin, and the other evidence does not support the theory that in a we have a German branch of the tradition. Until new facts come to light, Gen. must remain something of a mystery, but we can be reasonably certain that it was brought from Fulda to the area of the Loire. A text similar to Gen. but vastly inferior is found in B, written in Reims in the time of Hincmar, and Gen. itself can count at least three surviving French descendants, H (Brittany), Cant. (from Bourges), and P (Fleury).

---

[12] Lindsay, *CR* 10 (1896), 16–18. F^3 does not correct the passage transposed from Book 4 and marks it with asterisks.   [13] Bischoff, loc. cit.

Books 5–20 throw little new light on the tradition but illustrate the shifting relationship of HPE from one part of the text to another.

The second and third families of manuscripts do not provide much new information about the transmission of Nonius' text but confirm that during his period of popularity in the early Middle Ages the circulation of his text was largely concentrated in one area. The only complete representative of Family II, the 'doctored' text, is Wolfenbüttel, Gud.lat. 96 (G). This manuscript takes us straight back to Tours, where it was written in the first to second quarter of the ninth century.[14] For Books 1–2 med. it is joined by two of the manuscripts of the pure text, P and E. The version of the text which it carries was extremely influential: it succeeeded in imposing itself, in the form of variants and corrections, on to the text of the purer family and its influence can be detected in the work of L³, H², Gen.², Cant.², P², E². The 'extract' version, Family III, existed in two forms, which Lindsay called C^A and D^A respectively. The provenances of the third family, where known, fit the pattern of distribution already indicated by the representatives of the other two families:

C^A   Paris lat. 7666, s. X, Fleury.[15]
      Leiden, Voss. Lat. Q.116, s. IX, written at Reims in the time of Hincmar.
      Bamberg, Class. 30 (M.v.18), s. IX³⁻⁴/₄, Reims.[16]
      Zürich C 79b, s. X/XI, St. Gall.

D^A   Berne 347 + 357 + Paris lat. 7665, s. IX, probably written at Auxerre.
      Oxford, Bodl. Canon.Class.Lat. 279, c.900, Auxerre.
      Montpellier 212, s. X¹, France.

Nonius is hard tack, a diet for pioneers and enthusiasts. As Carolingian scholarship waned he went out of favour and did not circulate widely again until the fifteenth century.[17]

L. D. R.

---

[14] Information given to me by Professor Bischoff. For the disputed identification of G with the Victorinus of Mercier, see Mazzacane, 196 ff.

[15] See note 10, above.

[16] Date and provenance supplied by Professor Bischoff.

[17] Nonius is listed in only two medieval catalogues: St. Vincent, Metz (s. XI), Saint-Amand (s. XII). He is quoted extensively by the lexicographical annotator of Berne 276 in the mid-thirteenth century, and there are excerpts from Nonius in Cambridge, Corpus Christi College 229 (s. XII/XIII) and Paris lat. 7596A (s. XIII). The only study of the fifteenth-century manuscripts which has come to my notice is in Onions, xxiv–xxvi. In 1947 R. P. Oliver published 'new fragments' of Republican writers, in particular Ennius, Plautus, and Sallust, extracted from the *Cornucopia* of Niccolò Perotti and derived, he suggested, from a Nonius Auctus: ' "New Fragments" of Latin Authors in Perotti's Cornucopiae', *TAPA* 78 (1947), 376–424. Since the Nonius Auctus was not too big for Bertini to swallow (pp. 58–61), it should perhaps be looked at again, if only as an example of Renaissance forgery; in the meantime, see S. Timpanaro, *Anzeiger für die Altertumswissenschaft*, 5 (1952), cols. 208 ff.

NOTITIA DIGNITATUM

Virgil alone of Latin authors has come down to us in manuscripts illustrated before the fall of the western Empire in 476. From the sixth century, however, we have the Arcerianus of the *Agrimensores* and Leiden, Voss. Lat. Q. 9 (*CLA* x.1582) of the pseudo-Apuleian *Herbarium*; Carolingian artists copied ancient illustrations of Terence and the *Aratea*; and a line of transmission barely glimpsed before the Renaissance has given us a collection of six works illustrated in Antiquity. The best known and most richly illustrated of the six is the last, a register of imperial officials entitled *Notitia dignitatum omnium tam civilium quam militarium*; originally drawn up when the Empire split in 395, it treats first *partes orientis* and then *partes occidentis*. The other five works are:

1. *De rebus bellicis*
2. *Altercatio Hadriani Augusti et Epicteti philosophi*
3. *Notitia urbis Romae*
4. *Notitia urbis Constantinopolitanae*
5. *De gradibus cognationum.*

The manuscript that preserved the illustrations through the Middle Ages belonged in the fifteenth century to the cathedral library at Speyer. Resemblances between those in *De rebus bellicis* and those in Conrad Kyeser's *Bellifortis*, written during 1402–5, may be the first sign that the Spirensis had come to notice.[1] If not, certainly Cardinal Orsini, papal legate in Germany from 1425, acquired a copy, and either that copy or more probably a copy of it, written at all events in 1427, very appropriately went on a long tour of *partes occidentis* before being pulled to pieces and finishing up framed on the walls of cottages in Norfolk. Of this manuscript, L, all that survives is five leaves, now Cambridge, Fitzw. Mus. 86–1972, and copies of three pages made in Norfolk by Frederick Sandys (1829–1904) and now to be seen in the Castle Museum at Norwich. Not many nineteenth-century artists can be independent witnesses to a classical text.[2]

[1] M. Berthelot, *Journal des savants*, 1900, 10, 86, 88, *Annales de chimie et de physique*, ser. VII, 19 (1900), 307–8, 342, 343–4; R. Neher, *Der Anonymus de rebus bellicis* (Tübingen, 1911), 1, 6, 33–5, 43. On the date of composition see G. Quarg in the introduction to the facsimile of the final version (Düsseldorf, 1967), xxv; no mention, alas, of *De rebus bellicis*.

[2] Sandys's drawings were identified as copies of L by B. C. B.-B. ap. J. J. G. Alexander, 'The Illustrated Manuscripts of the *Notitia dignitatum*', in *Aspects of the* Notitia dignitatum, ed. R. Goodburn and P. Bartholomew (*BAR* Supplementary Series, 15, Oxford, 1976), 21 n. 18; see also 12–13, frontispiece, plates IV, VI–VIII. The five leaves in Cambridge, then Phillipps 16397, were discussed and transcribed by H. Omont, *Mem. de la Soc. nat. des antiq. de France*, ser. VI.1

During the Council of Basle Orsini's example was followed by Pietro Donato, Bishop of Padua, and Francesco Pizolpasso, Archbishop of Milan, who both had the Spirensis copied. Donato's copy, made in 1436, is Oxford, Bodl. Canon. Misc. 378 (C or O), Pizolpasso's Paris lat. 9661 (P). The texts of O and P were taken independently from the Spirensis by Italian scribes,[3] but the illustrations in both are the work of the French miniaturist Peronet Lamy.[4] All other Italian manuscripts derive from O or P, mainly from O.[5]

In 1484 or earlier someone made a fourth and very careless copy of the Spirensis known from one illustrated leaf, Frankfurt lat. Q.76, and two unillustrated descendants, Trento, Bibl. Com. già Vienn. 3103 and Trento, Mus. Naz. già Vienn. 3102.[6]

More faithful to the Spirensis than the illustrations in L and OP are the second set in Munich Clm 10291 (M), which were copied from tracings in 1550/1 for the Pfalzgraf Ottheinrich after he had expressed his dismay at the modern style of the first set.[7] The first set and the accompanying text apparently reproduce not the Spirensis itself but a copy made in 1542 or earlier, from which Vatican, Barb. lat. 157 (B) also derives.[8]

For whatever reason, whether that printers were daunted by the illustrations or that manuscripts never reached antiquarian circles such as the Roman academy under Pomponio Leto, the *editio princeps* waited until well into the sixteenth century, and even then the earliest editions were partial and unillustrated. Alciatus's *editio princeps* of the *Notitia orientis* (Lyon, 1529) was printed from a remote descendant of O,[9] and two editions and a manuscript that present an abbreviated text of the *Notitia occidentis* also derive from O.[10] When Alciatus printed the whole *Notitia* (Basle, 1546), he added to his previous text of the *Notitia orientis* a

(1890), 225–44; see now F. Wormald and P. M. Giles, *A Descriptive Catalogue of the Additional Illuminated Manuscripts in the Fitzwilliam Museum acquired between 1895 and 1979* (Cambridge, 1982), ii.563–6 and plates 74–6.

[3] On the scribe of O see A. C. de la Mare in *Survival*, 85–6; on the scribe of P, ibid. Addenda (1976), 108, and *Trans. Camb. Bibliog. Soc.* 7.2 (1978), 221.
[4] S. Edmunds, *The Art Bulletin*, 46 (1964), 139. Those in P were published by H. Omont (Paris, n.d.).
[5] This has never been proved, but it seems plausible and no refractory evidence has come to light.
[6] Confident assertions have not settled whether 3102, written in 1529, was copied from 3103, which bears the date 1484. Before I. G. Maier first mentioned the Francofurtanus in *Latomus*, 27 (1968), 100 with nn. 1–2, and derived 3103 and 3102 from it, L. Bieler, *Proc. of the Royal Irish Acad.* 64 C 1 (1965), 7–8, had already wondered whether the date 1484 came from their exemplar.
[7] Minutes of his negotiations with the Chapter were published by K. Preisendanz, *Zeitschr. für Buchkunde*, 1 (1924), 15–16; cf. Maier, *Latomus*, 28 (1969), 995–7.
[8] Maier, *Latomus*, 28 (1969), 960–1035. The date 1542 occurs twice in M, but the same thing may have happened as in Trento 3103 (cf. n. 6).
[9] P. F. Girard in *Studi in onore di Silvio Perozzi* (Palermo, 1925), 65–74.
[10] Maier, *Latomus*, 27 (1968), 96–141, after spending twenty-odd pages proving that one of the Italian manuscripts derives from another and the other from O with corrections from Giessen

text of the *Notitia occidentis* derived from a copy of the Spirensis that had been in the hands of Frobenius and Rhenanus since the 1520s.[11] Gelenius's *editio princeps* of the illustrated collection (Basle, 1552) announces its recovery 'ex ultimis Britannis',[12] but in fact the manuscript of Frobenius and Rhenanus supplied his text of the *Notitia*[13] and presumably of the rest too.[14]

By 1566 Ottheinrich's perseverance had brought him a greater prize than M: the Spirensis itself.[15] He would have been appalled by the negligence of his heirs or whoever *c.*1602–3 allowed it to be dismembered and used for binding legal documents. The mute evidence of this calamity, one of all too many that befell old manuscripts from Speyer in the sixteenth century, lies in the Fürstlich-Oettingen-Wallerstein'sche Bibliothek, now at Augsburg: a fragmentary bifolium in a Caroline minuscule of s. x¹ (1.2.2°37) found in 1906 and since 1927 generally acknowledged to be a relic of the Spirensis.[16] The work of which it preserves a fragment, however, is not one of the six listed above but the *Itinerarium Antonini*, the second of six unillustrated works that preceded them. Some of these circulated quite widely in the Middle Ages, and in the stemma of the *Itinerarium* the Spirensis occupies so lowly a place that the latest editor does not report it.[17] It therefore seems

Univ. 946, refers to his 'collation' (in reality a list of attractive readings) for evidence that the Gissensis and the editions of G. Fabricius (Basle, 1550) and A. Schonhovius (Basle, 1552) derive from a collateral of the Spirensis. If instead he had checked whether their source had errors that recur in any descendant of the Spirensis, he would have found four omissions shared with O: *Occid.* 1.70 *primae*, 6.57 *equites Dalmatae*, 9.7 *scola gentilium seniorum*, 21 *Lauriacensis scutaria* (I have consulted only Schonhovius, but that is enough). So much for the alleged irresponsibility of O. Seeck, *Hermes*, 9 (1875), 224, in deriving the Gissensis from O. Though Maier's two articles offer new information in their 122 pages, they labour simple or trivial points and yet have holes like this.

[11] E. Böcking, *Ueber die Notitia dignitatum* (Bonn, 1834), 45–6, 50–3; Girard, 74–83.
[12] C. E. Stevens in *Aspects* (n. 2, above), 211–24, argues that Giraldus Cambrensis consulted the *Notitia* in a copy sent over the Channel by Alcuin, which Gelenius somehow obtained.
[13] Böcking and Girard, *locc. cit.* (n. 11, above); Maier, *Latomus*, 27 (1968), 127 n. 5, and ibid. 28 (1969), 962–3, 964 n. 2. Maier regards the manuscript as independent of the Spirensis, but see R. I. Ireland in part 2 of *De rebus bellicis* (*BAR International Series*, 63, Oxford, 1979), 43–66. Ireland's edition of *De rebus bellicis* is the latest of any work in the collection; Maier, *Latomus*, 27 (1968), 96 n. 1, promises to replace O. Seeck's edition of the *Notitia* (Berlin, 1876).
[14] Ireland, loc. cit., concludes that in *De rebus bellicis* he worked from the Spirensis and emended it rather impatiently, sometimes even for typographical convenience, which may also explain his omission of *De gradibus cognationum*; but one of his errors, 5.4 *Arabum* (*arabunt* OPM), recurs in Oxford, Bodl. Dep. Bridges 71, ff. 62–3, two leaves in an elegant italic hand of s. xvi¹ (watermark of a type common at the time in northern Italy and Germany, similar to Briquet 3067) that contain chs. 4–6 of *De rebus bellicis* neither taken from his edition (5.5 *minori ut maiori: minori ut minori* OPM, *minori* Gelenius) nor used for it (5.5 *his itaque: his ïta* OPM, Gelenius). The leaves doubtless derive from the manuscript of Frobenius and Rhenanus. I should like to thank Bruce Barker-Benfield for drawing my attention to them and Lord Bridges for permission to inspect them.
[15] K. Schottenloher, *Pfalzgraf Ottheinrich und das Buch* (Münster, 1927), 192; Maier, *Latomus*, 28 (1969), 1029 n. 2.
[16] Schottenloher, 9–11. The date is Bischoff's ap. Alexander in *Aspects* (n. 2, above), 12; plate I (ibid.) shows the hand.
[17] O. Kuntz (Leipzig, 1929); see the stemma of J. W. Kubitschek, *WS* 13 (1891), 209. The other works are the *Cosmographia* of pseudo-Aethicus, ed. A. Riese, *Geographi latini minores* (Heilbronn,

likely that the Spirensis had at least two parts, so that the date and script of the surviving bifolium need convey nothing about the illustrated part.[18] On the contrary, corruptions in the illustrated part suggest that both it and its exemplar were written in insular script.[19] That would account for Gelenius's reference to 'ultimi Britanni'. Furthermore, the one other manuscript of the *Notitia urbis Romae* and *Constantinopolitanae*, Vienna 162 (s. IX²/4), was copied at Fulda from an insular exemplar[20] and corrected by an insular hand.[21] The abbot at the time was Alcuin's pupil Hrabanus Maurus, and Alcuin had drawn on the *Altercatio* for a work of his own.[22] The illustrations in the three *Notitiae* may even have impressed Alcuin's master Charlemagne: his will mentions 'tres mensas argenteas', of which one 'forma quadrangula descriptionem urbis Constantinopolitanae continet,' another 'forma rotunda Romanae urbis effigie figurata est,' and the third 'ex tribus orbibus conexa totius mundi descriptionem subtili ac minuta figuratione complectitur'.[23] If the ruler of the west knew that the *Notitia dignitatum* had come to him from a pigeon-hole in Ravenna after serving the needs

1878), xxvii–xxix, xl–xliii, 71–103; *Nomina montium et aquarum*, ed. R. Valentini and G. Zucchetti, *Codice topografico della città di Roma*, i (Fonti per la storia d'Italia, 81, Rome, 1940), 294–6; the *Liber de mensura orbis terrae* of Dicuil (a. 825), ed. L. Bieler in *Scriptores Latini Hiberniae*, vi (Dublin, 1967); the *Notitia Galliarum* and *Laterculus Polemii Silvii*, ed. Th. Mommsen, *Chronica minora saec. iv.v.vi.vii, 1* (*MGH Auct. Ant.* ix Berlin, 1892), 511–612; and *De montibus portis et viis urbis Romae*, ed. Valentini and Zucchetti, 296–301. As far as Dicuil the Spirensis had until 1945 a close relative in Dresden Dc 182, at Reims *c*.1000 and later at the Michelsberg, Bamberg; Bischoff ap. P. Lehmann, *SBAW* 1934, 16, assigned the script to the end of s. IX.

[18]   P. Schnabel, *Sitzungsber. der preuss. Akad.*, 1926, 247–57, first abandoned the assumption that the Spirensis was all of a piece. His initial division into an unillustrated and an illustrated part also commended itself to Ireland (edn., 53), but Schnabel went on to divide the former into two and the latter into three, partly because he did not realize that *De gradibus cognationum* was illustrated.

[19]   Seeck (edn.), xxvi, followed by Schnabel, 253–5; Lehmann, *SBAW* 1934, 19–20, disagreed, but see now Ireland (edn.), 42, 43, 54–5, who unlike Schnabel finds insular symptoms in *De rebus bellicis* as much as in the other illustrated works.

[20]   Schnabel, loc. cit. (n. 19, above); Ireland (edn.), 51.

[21]   *Umbrae codicum occidentalium*, ii (Amsterdam, 1960), with an introduction by F. Unterkircher. A different version of the *Notitia urbis Romae* usually known as the *Curiosum* appears in Vatican lat. 3321 (s. VIII, central or southern Italy; *CLA* I.15) and several descendants, and the two versions are conflated in Florence, Laur. 89 sup. 67 (s. X) and several relatives; see A. Nordh, *Libellus de regionibus urbis Romae* (Lund, 1949).

[22]   *Disputatio Pippini cum Albino*, edited with the *Altercatio*, an abridgement, and related material by W. Suchier, *Illinois Studies in Language and Literature*, 24 (1939), 95–166; cf. L. W. Daly, ibid. 79–82. Suchier infers from one reading (p. 112), but reasonably, that the abridgement does not derive from the Spirensis.

[23]   Einhard, *Vita Caroli*, end, pointed out by Schnabel, 255. Though illustrations of Constantinople appear in OP and Gelenius's edition, the absence of any from MB, together with the headless state of the corresponding text in all descendants of the Spirensis (they begin with the last word of Vienna 162, f. 5ᵛ), shows that the Spirensis had none in the fifteenth century. Was it torn out by someone who had a special interest in Constantinople, for instance during the reign of Otto II (972–83), who married the Byzantine princess Theophano, or of their son Otto III (983–1002)? In October 984 the court met at Speyer; see K. and M. Uhlirz, *Jahrbücher des deutschen Reiches unter Otto II. und Otto III.*, ii (Berlin, 1954), 37–9. For the possibility that artists of s. IX–XI flattered their emperors with the aid of illustrations from the *Notitia dignitatum* see Alexander in *Aspects* (n. 2, above), 19 with n. 56.

of the *magister utriusque militiae,* 'the virtual ruler of the west from the mid-450s down to the end of the western empire in A.D. 480', then he knew what modern scholars have only been able to guess;[24] but it would be nice if they were right.

M. D. R.

[24] J. C. Mann in *Aspects*, 8. He does not ask, and no one can say, when the *Notitia* and the other five works came together.

OVID

Introduction

Amores, Ars amatoria, Remedia amoris
Epistulae ex Ponto
Fasti
Heroides
Ibis
Medicamina faciei feminaae
Metamorphoses
Tristia

Introduction

The emperor Augustus may have banished Ovid from Rome and ordered his works removed from its libraries, but he was unable to prevent Ovid's poetry from finding a large and receptive audience. From his own time until the end of Antiquity Ovid was among the most widely read and imitated of Latin poets; his greatest work, the *Metamorphoses*, also seems to have enjoyed the largest popularity. What place Ovid may have had in the curriculum of ancient schools is hard to determine: no body of antique scholia survives for any of his works,[1] but it seems likely that the elegance of his style and his command of rhetorical technique would have commended him as a school author, perhaps at the elementary level.

[1] The prose summaries and *tituli* preserved in some manuscripts of the *Metamorphoses* are probably the work of a late-antique *grammaticus*, but it is not clear that they were composed with a scholastic purpose or were part of a larger commentary.

Well-read writers of the Carolingian period were familiar with some or most of Ovid's works (the *Metamorphoses* retaining its pride of place), but Ovid was overshadowed both in general popularity and in scholarly attention by Horace, Lucan, and Juvenal as well as by the omnipresent Virgil and Terence. The situation can be seen changing in the latter part of the eleventh century, and in the twelfth century – the 'aetas Ovidiana', as Ludwig Traube called it – the circulation and influence of Ovid's poetry increased dramatically. Minor works such as the *Ibis*, *Nux*, and *Medicamina faciei femineae* emerge from obscurity and take their place beside the longer-established compositions. By the end of the century omnibus editions containing all of Ovid's elegiac poetry (sometimes including *Metamorphoses* as well, and often with an admixture of medieval pseudo-Ovidiana) had become a popular alternative to the independent circulation of individual works.[2]

Ovid's entry into the ranks of standard authors (a position he retained through the Renaissance and beyond) can be clearly traced in the treatment accorded his poetry in the most active centre of twelfth-century classical studies, the valley of the Loire. The compiler of the influential *Florilegium Gallicum* included generous extracts from all the works of Ovid available in the area,[3] and the leading literary scholar of the day, Arnulf of Orléans, lectured and commented on *Metamorphoses*, *Fasti*, and other works.[4] Ovid also travelled in less exalted scholastic circles: the *Remedia amoris* was often added to the so-called *Liber Catonianus*, a set of poetic texts widely used in teach-

---

[2] In general Ovid's works have distinct manuscript traditions; *Amores, Ars amatoria*, and *Remedia amoris*, however, were probably combined (perhaps along with *Heroides*) in at least one ancient codex, and there is also a close association between *Medicamina faciei femineae* and *Nux*.

[3] The role of medieval florilegia, and of the *Florilegium Gallicum* in particular, in the transmission of several Latin authors was discussed by B. L. Ullman in an important article, 'Classical Authors in Medieval Florilegia', *CPh* 27 (1932), 1–42; most recently see R. H. R., 'Florilegia and Latin Classical Authors in Twelfth- and Thirteenth-Century France', *Viator*, 10 (1979), 131–60. Partial editions of the *Florilegium Gallicum*: S. Rackley, *The Amatory Poems of Ovid in Four Manuscripts of the Florilegium Gallicum*, diss. Duke University, 1973; J. Hamacher, *Florilegium Gallicum: Prolegomena und Edition der Exzerpte von Petron bis Cicero, De Oratore* (Lateinische Sprache und Literatur des Mittelalters, 5), Frankfurt, 1975; R. J. Burton, *Classical Authors in the Florilegium Gallicum and Related Manuscripts*, diss. Toronto, 1981 (selected portions of all the poetic texts).

[4] Extracts from Arnulf's glosses on the *Metamorphoses* were published by F. Ghisalberti, *Memorie dell'Istituto lombardo*, 24 (1932), 157–234, but no complete edition of a commentary by Arnulf on Ovid has yet appeared. (A partial edition of an influential thirteenth-century *Metamorphoses* commentary, which includes material from Arnulf and other twelfth-century sources, is being prepared by Dr Frank Coulson of Ohio State University.) Selections from many twelfth- and thirteenth-century Ovidian commentaries, together with sympathetic discussion of the literary attitudes displayed in them, may be found in two books by J. B. Allen: *The Friar as Critic* (Nashville, 1971) and *The Ethical Poetic of the Later Middle Ages* (Toronto, 1982). Other important discussions or collections of material: G. Przychocki, *Accessus Ovidiani* (Cracow, 1911); E. H. Alton, 'The Mediaeval Commentators on Ovid's *Fasti*', *Hermathena*, 60 (1926), 119–51, also ibid. 94 (1960), 21–38, and 95 (1961), 67–82; E. Martini, *Einleitung zu Ovid* (Vienna, 1933), with earlier bibliography.

ing elementary grammar,[5] and even the less edifying erotic poetry occasionally found its way into the schoolroom.[6]

With acceptance and respectability came assimilation to medieval habits of understanding. Even when they were not interpreted allegorically (as the *Metamorphoses* often was), Ovid's poems were read as a form of ethical discourse, and Ovid himself often seen as a serious *praeceptor morum*: a transformation that the author of the *Ars amatoria* would have relished for its incongruity, and in which the poet of the *Metamorphoses* might have recognized a measure of justice.

R. J. T.

[5] É. Pellegrin, *BEC* 115 (1957), 172–9.

[6] This seems a fair inference from the outraged protest of Conrad of Hirsau: 'etsi auctor Ovidius idem in quibusdam opusculis suis, id est Fastorum, de Ponto, de Nuce et in aliis utcumque tolerandus esset, quis eum de amore croccitantem, in diversis epistolis turpiter evagantem, si sanum sapiat, toleret?' (*Dialogus super auctores*, ed. R. B. C. Huyghens (Brussels, 1955), 51). The existence of glossed texts of the *Ars amatoria* points in the same direction.

Amores, Ars amatoria, Remedia amoris

These poems are transmitted in a small group of older manuscripts (s. IX–XI) and in a much larger mass of *recentiores*.[1] The older codices give evidence of derivation from a common source, a manuscript (α) written on the Continent around the year 800, which contained the *Heroides* as well as the *Ars, Remedia*, and *Amores* (probably in that order).[2] The *recentiores* do not derive from α, as shown most clearly by their preservation of genuine lines missing in the α group;[3] they need not have a single source.[4] Some later manuscripts possess individual

The standard edition is by E. J. Kenney (OCT, 1961); the edition of *Amores* by F. Munari (Florence, 1964) is also valuable. This account is primarily based on Kenney's discussion, 'The Manuscript Tradition of Ovid's *Amores, Ars Amatoria*, and *Remedia Amoris*', *CQ* 12 (1962), 1–31, which incorporates the results of earlier treatments, e.g. S. Tafel, *Die Überlieferungsgeschichte von Ovids Carmina Amatoria* (diss. Tübingen, 1910). The important Hamiltonensis, brought to light after Kenney's edition had appeared, is discussed in the exemplary monograph of F. Munari, *Il Codice Hamilton 471 di Ovidio* (Rome, 1965); its readings are included in the edition, with commentary, of *Ars* 1 by A. S. Hollis (Oxford, 1977). (F. W. Lenz's 1969 Paravia edition of *Ars* gives an account of the Hamiltonensis, but the collation is less reliable than Munari's and the text much inferior to Kenney's.) Many passages in all three works receive acute discussion from G. P. Goold in '*Amatoria Critica*', *HSCP* 69 (1965), 1–107.

[1] Kenney, 3–5 (all references are to his article cited above), lists thirty-two later manuscripts, almost all of s. XII ex. or s. XIII.

[2] The existence of such a manuscript had been postulated by Lucian Müller, *De Re Metrica*[2] (St. Petersburg, 1894), 24 ff. The order *Ars, Rem., Am.* is common to R and Y, the only close descendants of α to contain more than one of the three works.

[3] *Am.* 1.13.11–14 and 2.2.18–22, 25–7, *Ars* 1.466–71; Kenney, 9 and 17.

[4] Following Munari (ed., xix), Kenney (p. 9) assumed for the sake of convenience that they did descend from a common source (called β); note, however, the later disavowal in *The Classical Text* (Berkeley, 1974), 134.

interest, but in general the *recentiores* are valuable as a group for their non-α readings. Their contributions to the text are neither as numerous nor as substantial as those of α, but their testimony can never be simply disregarded. Contamination is endemic among them and is not absent in the α family; α itself almost certainly carried variant readings.[5] The scope of stemmatic criticism is therefore limited, and most editorial decisions will be based on the intrinsic merit of the transmitted readings.[6]

These remarks apply equally to all three works, but the shifting identity of the α witnesses makes it desirable to set out the manuscript evidence separately for each.

Amores

The representatives of α are:[7]

R   Paris lat. 7311, ff. 50ᵛ–103ᵛ (s. IX, France), containing *Am.* only to 1.2.50 (following *Ars* and *Remedia*).

P   Paris lat. 8242 (s. IX¾, Corbie), containing *Am.* 1.2.51–3.15.8 (om. 3.12.37–3.14.2), also *Heroides*.

S   St. Gall 864 (s. XI, Germany), containing *Am.* to 3.9.10 (om. 1.6.46– 1.8.74).

Y   Berlin (East), Hamilton 471 (s. XI, Italy), containing *Am.* complete (following *Ars* and *Remedia*).[8]

P was almost certainly copied from the lost part of R (= R′, which may have been its source for the *Heroides* as well).[9] Y and S seem to be independent descendants of α; Y is equal or even superior to P in worth, but S agrees often with the *recentiores* in non-α inferior readings. (In P and Y readings of this kind have been added by later hands, called p and y.[10])

Among the *recentiores* special mention should be given to Dijon 497 (D, northern France), a vast thirteenth-century corpus of Latin poetry known to Heinsius as the 'Jureti liber' or 'excerpta'; it has more agreements with α than any other late manuscript (including the significant error *honores* for *inanes* at 2.2.31, also found in PY) and may even be a debased α manuscript.

The pseudo-Ovidian poem printed in modern editions as *Amores*

---

[5] Kenney, 24.   [6] Ibid. 10–11, 19–20, 22–3, 27–9.

[7] Chatelain has plates of R (XCIII), P (XCI), and S(XCI).

[8] The manuscript escaped the notice of editors through having been catalogued as s. XIV rather than s. XI; description, full collation, and plates in Munari's monograph. Y contains numerous additions and corrections by Pontano, discussed by B. L. Ullman, ibid. 73–8 (and cf. plates ii, iii, iv 3, vi).   [9] Kenney, 6–7, after Tafel, 31.

[10] Kenney, 10 (p); Munari (monograph), 62 (y). Goold (p. 6) argues that S could be a contaminated descendant of R′; whatever S's status, its value has sunk nearly to the vanishing point with the accession of Y.

3.5 (the so-called *Somnium*) owes that position to α alone (= PSY). Only a.handful of *recentiores* place it there, presumably by conflation with a manuscript of the α group; the great majority of those that transmit it separate it from the body of the *Amores*.[11] With 3.5 removed and 2.9 and 3.11 divided into two poems (as proposed by L. Müller, *Philologus*, 11 (1856), 89–91), the second edition of the *Amores* may be seen to comprise three books of fifteen, twenty and fifteen poems respectively.

Ars amatoria

The representatives of α are, besides R and Y (which omits 2.113–258):

O   Oxford, Bodl. Auct. F.4.32. ff. 37–47 (s. IX, probably Wales), containing *Ars*, 1.[12]

Sa   St. Gall 821 (s. XI, Germany?), containing *Ars*, 1.1–230.

b   Bamberg Class. 30 (M. V. 18) (s. IX$^{3-4}$/4, Reims), containing excerpts[13] from *Ars* on margins of ff. 110–12.

These may be treated as independent witnesses,[14] of which RY are the most important (and the only ones extant in books 2 and 3). A fifteenth-century manuscript, Oxford, Bodl. Canon. Class. Lat. 18 (Og), is of some interest for its affinity with α.[15]

Among other manuscripts a special place is occupied by British Library, Add. 14086 = A (*c.*1100). It shares several errors with the α manuscripts (though not enough to justify treating it as a member of the group) and is the only or the earliest source for a number of true non-α readings.[16]

---

[11] Kenney, 11–13, with elaboration of arguments against Ovid's authorship in *Agon*, 3 (1969), 1–14. The earliest text of the *Somnium* is in the miscellany Leipzig Rep. I. 4°. 74, ff. 27^v–28^v (s. IX²/4, France), wrongly described by Kenney (p. 5) as 'saec. xii'.

[12] Plate in Chatelain (XCIII.2), complete facsimile in R. W. Hunt, *Saint Dunstan's Classbook from Glastonbury* (Leiden, 1961; *Umbrae Codicum Occidentalium*, 4); palaeographical and codicological discussion in M. C. Bodden, 'Detailed Description of Oxford Bodleian Manuscript Auct. F.4.32' (diss. Toronto, 1979), 8–42, 198–246. The last leaf of the Ovid (f. 47) may have been written by St. Dunstan himself, although there are differences between the script of f. 47 and the insertion on f. 1^r more confidently attributed to Dunstan. O was probably copied from a Continental exemplar (cf. Kenney, 15 n. 1) and does not therefore represent a distinctive insular strain of tradition.

[13] List in Kenney, 6 n. 1.

[14] So Goold, 7; Kenney (p. 14) had followed Tafel (p. 21) in deriving RSab from one common ancestor (ϕ) and O from a second (η).

[15] Og is much less useful as a means of reconstructing α than ROY, but it is not entirely without value. At 1.119, for example, Og agrees with O in reading *furentes* against *ruentes* RYSa and thereby increases the likelihood that α contained both readings. (Kenney, 18, adduces the imitation of Theodulf, *Carm.* 28.426 *ne* ruat *interius plebs sine lege* furens, which may also point to a source with both *furentes* and *ruentes*.)

[16] e.g. 1.268 *adeste* (*adesse* ROY), 619 *nunc sit* (*non sit* ROY) 686 *graiaque* (*grataque* ROY); Kenney, 16.

Remedia amoris

The representatives of α are, besides RY:

E   Eton College 150 (s. XI, southern Italy; in Beneventan script of the
     Bari type); an early *Liber Catonianus*.[17]
K   Paris lat. 8460 (s. XII or XIII).[18]
Pc   Excerpts in Paris lat. 8069 (s. X/XI), ff. 1ᵛ–3ʳ.[19]

EK have undergone extensive contamination with non-α sources.[20]
K is the more interesting; it is equipped with numerous variants, most
of them probably derived from its exemplar, of which some may
represent a good non-α source.[21]

Finally, additional information on the α text of the amatory poems
seems to be available in two closely related, but independent, sets of
excerpts cited by Nicolaus Heinsius as the 'excerpta Puteani' and the
'excerpta Scaligeri';[22] in *Ars* and *Remedia* the excerpts clearly have
drawn upon an α-type manuscript.[23]

                                                                    R. J. T.

[17] *Beneventan Script*,[2] i.152, ii.40. On the scholastic anthologies called *libri Catoniani*, cf. P. M.
Clogan, *The Medieval Achilleid of Statius* (Leiden, 1967), 2–3.
[18] Kenney, 2, dates it to the twelfth century, F. W. Lenz, *SIFC* 29 (1957), 1–3, to the thirteenth.
[19] The manuscript also contains the non-Ovidian couplet found as a Pompeian graffito and
transmitted as *Am.* 3.11.35–6, and *Ars* 3.65–6 and 73–4 via the *Anthologia Latina* (269 Riese); cf.
Riese's preface to *Anth. Lat.* (Teubner, 1894), xli–xlii.
[20] The attempt by Goold (*HSCP* 69 (1965), 8–9) to remove EK from α is unpersuasive: the
non-α readings cited are evidence rather of extensive contamination.
[21] e.g. 13 *ardens* (*ardet* REK¹Y p₆ω).
[22] Kenney, 30–1; in greater detail, M. D. R., *RhM* 117 (1974), 162–4; 119 (1976), 73–4. The *exc.*
Puteani cover the *Amores* and *Ars* to 2.239, the *exc. Scaligeri* all three works.
[23] In *Ars* the source of the excerpts 'bears a strong resemblance to Parisinus 7311 [= R] (e.g.
3.527 *vite*, 709 *passis*) and in spite of discrepancies (1.244 *venis*, 581 *sorte*, 2.164 *valet*) is unlikely to
have been anything else; the resemblance is equally marked in *Remedia* (e.g. 446 *haesaque*)'
(M.D.R., *RhM* 117 (1974), 163; cf. also 119 (1976), 73 n. 11). It might be added that Y shares some
of the readings linking the excerpts to R (e.g. *Ars* 3.527 and 709, *Rem.* 446), and that some of the
readings not traceable to R are present in Y, e.g. *Ars* 1.581, *Rem.* 486, 753.

Epistulae ex Ponto

Perhaps because of their relative lack of popularity, the *Epistulae ex
Ponto* have a less intricate tradition than most of Ovid's major works.

   There is as yet no comprehensive modern treatment of the transmission and no fully
satisfactory edition. The most extensive discussion is in the introduction to F. W. Lenz's
Paravia text (1938), vii–lix; other editions by O. Korn (Leipzig, 1868), S. G. Owen (OCT,
1915, quite inadequate), R. Ehwald–F. W. Levy (= Lenz) (Teubner, 1922), and J. André
(Budé, 1977). On the transmission cf. R. Ehwald, *Kritische Beiträge zu Ovids Epistulae ex Ponto*
(Gotha, 1896).

They also boast the only surviving ancient witness to any Ovidian text, twenty-five lines of Book 4 from a codex in fine uncial script (s. V^2, probably Italy) reused in the eighth century at Luxeuil: Wolfenbüttel Aug. 4° 13. 11 (= G).[1] The text of this fragment excels that of the medieval manuscripts in one place (4.9.103 *sit* for *est*) but shares a corruption with them in another (4.9.128 *ut* for *et*), and so is descended from the same ancient archetype as the rest of the tradition; it is not part of the archetype itself, since it contains errors not found elsewhere (e.g. 4.12.19 *naia* for *nota*). This archetype can be further described: it contained several lacunae (e.g. a pentameter missing after 1.2.9 and 1.8.19, only the first word of 3.1.143 preserved), and errors caused by miscopying of capital script (e.g. 2.1.39 *proelia* read as *proflua* under the influence of *flumina* earlier in the line). It also carried the titles that an ancient editor had affixed to each of the letters, which still appear in some modern editions.[2]

As with several other works of Ovid, aspects of the text's circulation not documented by surviving manuscripts can be recovered from other sources. For example, imitations in Carolingian writers show that copies were available in several French and German centres during the ninth and tenth centuries; the collection is referred to by Rather of Verona (*PL* 136.374), but it is not clear from his citation whether he knew it at first hand or, if so, where he had encountered it; extracts appear in florilegia compiled in northern Europe between the ninth and twelfth centuries (e.g. St. Gall 870, s. $IX^4/4$ or IX/X, St. Gall, and Paris lat. 8069, s. XI, France); the *Epistulae* are named in the book-lists of several northern libraries in the eleventh and early twelfth centuries (Blaubeuern, Tegernsee, Bamberg, Egmond, Cracow); and the presence of the poems in north-central France can be traced from the late eleventh century onwards, first from echoes in Hildebert of Lavardin and Baudri de Bourgeuil, later from the extracts in the *Florilegium Gallicum*, and finally from the complete texts (often parts of compendious collections of Ovidiana) that emanate from this region toward the end of the twelfth century.

The direct medieval tradition comprises a single Carolingian codex and a large number of *recentiores* (s. XII^2 onwards); in this case chronological and textual divisions coincide. The early manuscript is Hamburg, Staats- und Universitätsbibl. 52 in scrinio (= A), written in

---

[1] G contains 4.9.101–8, 4.9.127–33, 4.12.15–19, and 41–4; cf. *CLA* IX.1377 (plate of 4.9.105–8), Chatelain, plate XCIX.2.

[2] More can be said about the archetype of these poems than about any other Ovidian archetype, so it is odd that less space is given to it than to the others in G. Luck's *Untersuchungen zur Textgeschichte Ovids* (Heidelberg, 1969). Luck's attempt to reconstruct the mise-en-page of an ancient edition of Ovid is an exercise of the imagination with little bearing on the actual history of these texts; cf. M. W., *CR* 21 (1971), 208–9, H. Dörrie, *Gnomon*, 46 (1974), 664–9.

northern France (perhaps Paris or environs) in the mid-ninth century.[3]
It preserves many good readings not found in the later manuscripts,
but exhibits even more unique errors; it is therefore likely that A
derives from one ancient copy of the archetype and the later tradition
from another.[4] The text in A breaks off at 3.2.67, and poem 1.3 is
omitted. No other extant manuscript is closely related to A, but some
readings entered by Scaliger in his copy of the *editio Gryphiana* (1546)
show knowledge of A or a related manuscript.[5]

The primary extant representatives of the later tradition are:

B   Munich Clm 384, s. XII, Germany.
C   Munich Clm 19476, s. XII, Tegernsee, also contains Theodulus'
        Ecloga.
D   Gotha Membr. II. 121, s. XIII.[6]
T   Tours 879, s. XII/XIII, France, an *Opera omnia Ovidi* (plate of *Tr.*
        4.10.83–5.1.68 in S. G. Owen's *editio maior* (Oxford, 1889), facing
        p. 1).

A Strasbourg manuscript of s. XI or XII[7] destroyed in 1870 and now
known only from Korn's apparatus also seems to merit attention
(= S); its text ended at 3.5.34. The common source of these manuscripts presents a text often more correct than that of A, but also more
heavily interpolated: for example, the lacunae of the archetype have all
been filled, sometimes in two or even more ways.[8] (For an approximate
analogy one might cite the respective characters of the Pithoeanus and
its kin on the one hand and the vulgate manuscripts on the other in the
tradition of Juvenal.)

The clearest division is between BC and DT, with the latter showing

---

[3] T. Brandis, *Die Codices in scrinio der Staats- und Universitätsbibliothek Hamburg 1–110* (Hamburg,
1972), 108–10 (who cites B. Bischoff for the date and place of origin). The *Epistulae* follow a text of
Virgil with Servius' commentary; the text of Servius belongs to Murgia's 'Tours family' (cf. C. E.
Murgia, *Prolegomena to Servius 5 – The Manuscripts* (Berkeley, 1975), p. 89). J. J. H. Savage, *HSCP* 45
(1934), 179, thought the hand of the Ovid noticeably later than that of the Virgil.

[4] Good readings in A: e.g. 1.1.67 *si* (*est si*), 1.8.4 *si* (*sit*), 2.1.33 *caste* (*castos/claros*), 46 *Bato*
(*fuit/tenet*), 2.5.67 *gustata* (*gest-*), 2.7.55 *horruerit* (*obruerit/-et*), 3.1.89 *suscense* (*succ-*). Unique errors of
A: e.g. 1.1.19 *haec* (*nec*, also 1.2.75), 68 *de niue* (*denique*), 1.2.17 *per terram et* (*perterrita*), 41 *medici cum*
(*medicinaque*), 50 *uita* (*multa*), 99 *publica saro* (*sub caesare*), etc. If a single ancient codex lies behind A
and the *recentiores*, A was copied with remarkable negligence.

[5] Note in particular *Bato* in 2.1.46. At 1.4.37 the *excerpta Scaligeri* give the correct *densa*, where A
preserves the nonsensical *sa* of the archetype (*den* having fallen out by haplography after *aesoniden*)
and the later manuscripts repair the damage by interpolation (*sacra, firma*). Here Scaliger may
have emended the text himself on the basis of A's reading. On these *excerpta* see M. D. R., *RhM* 117
(1974), 163–4, 119 (1976), 73–4.

[6] So editors; s. XII according to R. Schipke, *Die Maugérard-Handschriften der Forschungsbibliothek
Gotha* (Gotha, 1972), 75.

[7] Heinsius dated it to s. XI, Korn to s. XII (and Lenz to s. XIII, *praef.* xxxi).

[8] At 3.1.143–4, for example, where A gives only *omnia* at the start of the hexameter, differing
versions of the couplet appear in B¹C, B² *mg.* S, and DT. The language of these supplements
suggests ancient rather than medieval origin.

a greater propensity to interpolation.[9] For much of the time the manuscripts conform to the patterns observed in closed transmissions,
agreement of A with BC or DT yielding the reading of the archetype.
Other evidence shows, however, that this simple picture will not do.
ABC and ADT at times concur in errors not likely to have arisen twice
by coincidence and not easily removed by conjecture; B, C, D, T, and S
each agree individually on occasion with A in good readings; B exhibits
hundreds of corrections and double readings ($= B^2$), most often coin-
ciding with DT but sometimes with A or with no known source;[10] and
S agrees consistently with neither BC nor DT.[11] These complications
all point toward pairs of readings in an ancestor of BCDTS, as do such
places as 2.9.52 *negem* AB^1CT: *putes* B^2: *negem putem* D.[12] On this
assumption the basic relationship of ABCDGST may be depicted thus:

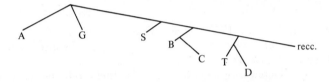

Where A and BCDTS are extant the contribution of other *recentiores*
is slight, perhaps restricted to astute correction of archetypal errors.
For nearly half the collection, however, A is not available, and here
closer attention to the later witnesses is justified. Among the leading
secondary manuscripts some play a similar role in other Ovidian
transmissions, e.g. Antwerp, Plantin 68, Dijon 497, Oxford, Bodl.
Canon. Class. Lat. 1, and Paris lat. 7993, all products of the intense
scholastic interest taken in Ovid shortly before and after 1200.[13]

R. J. T.

[9] One need go no further than 1.1.24 *scrinia* BC *recte* (*carmina* ADT); for ABC in error cf. e.g.,
1.8.51 *rure* (*rupe* B^2DT), 2.2.5 *quid/quod* (*si* B^2DT), 2.7.5 *sic* (*sed*), 2.9.76 *pateat* (*lateat*), 3.1.154
premente (*tre-*).

[10] At 1.2.99 B^2 gives *publica sarcina*, obviously connected with A's *publica saro*, for *sub caesare*; B^2's
venae for *vires* in 1.4.3 and its *terra remota tenet* at 3.2.44 (*pontus et hister* B^1C, om. A, *alii alia*) are unique;
it alone gives the correct *indelebile* for *indeflebile* in AB^1C at 2.8.25, but this might be the result of
conjecture, cf. *Met.* 15.876. Editors seem not to have examined Vat. lat. 3254, ff. 87–94 (*Pont.*
1.1.1–2.7.51), which is perhaps as early as BC (s. XII, perhaps Germany) and which offers a text
related to theirs but with interesting features of its own (e.g. reading *publica sarcina* at 1.2.99 with
B^2, omitting 1.3 with A).

[11] Note, for example, its behaviour in dealing with the archetypal lacunae, conveniently
summarized by André, xliii. Ehwald (*Krit. Beiträge*, 24) placed S at the head of the 'vulgate' group.

[12] The existence of pairs of variants in a forerunner of B is also revealed by cases where the
normal pattern B^1C–B^2DT is reversed, e.g. 2.2.67 *ille* B^1DT: *illa* AB^2C, 2.7.29 *laborum* AB^2CD:
malorum B^1T, 2.8.29 *reperta* AB^2CD^2T: *recepta* B^1D^1, 3.1.113 *icariotide tela* (*vel sim.*) AB^1DT: *instru-
menta parare* B^2C.

[13] To these manuscripts should be added Boccaccio's copy, Florence, Laur. 36.32, the 'primus
Mediceus' of Heinsius (s. XIII, not XI as Heinsius thought), on which cf. F. W. Lenz, *Rend. Ist.
Lomb.* ser. III. 1–2 (1937–8), 133–44.

Fasti

When Ovid was relegated to Tomi he had planned, and perhaps to an extent drafted, all twelve books of his poem on the Roman calendar,[1] but only the first six books seem to have reached a publishable state; these alone survive, in a draft incompletely revised by Ovid in exile.[2]

Though not one of Ovid's most popular works in the Middle Ages, the *Fasti* enjoyed a fairly widespread circulation from the ninth century onwards. Unfortunately, the early Carolingian phase of the direct tradition has entirely disappeared, and the text must be established from, so to speak, second-generation or later medieval witnesses.

Of the approximately 170 surviving manuscripts[3] five far excel the rest in importance:[4]

A   Vatican, Reg. lat. 1709 (s. X ex., France[5]); ends at 5.24.
U   Vatican lat. 3262 (Ursinianus) (s. XI, Montecassino: old shelfmark IV° 743).[6]
I   Cologny-Geneva, Bodmer lat. 123 (*olim* Ilfeld, Bibl. der Klosterschule 3) (s. XI/XII, Germany); contains only 2.568–3. 204 and 4.317–814 (and scraps from the end of 1 and the beginning of 2).
G   Brussels 5369–73 (s. XI, Gembloux?); begins at 1.505.
M   Oxford, Bodl. ·Auct. F. 4.25, *olim* Mazarinianus (s. XV, perhaps Ferrara).

IGM form a clearly distinct family, called Z (ζ where I is missing);

The standard edition is now (and is likely to remain for some time) the Teubner (1978) of D. E. W. Wormell and E. Courtney, which builds on the preliminary work of E. H. Alton; the preface to that edition (cited as 'Praef.') is the basis of this account. The older editions by Sir James Frazer (London, 1929) and F. Bömer (Heidelberg, 1957–8) remain valuable for their commentaries. F. Peeters's *Les Fastes d'Ovide: Histoire du texte* (Brussels, 1939) assembles much useful information, but the exaltation of G and the attempt to incorporate all extant manuscripts into a stemma are generally thought to be misguided.

[1] This seems the correct interpretation of *Tr.* 2.541 *sex ego Fastorum scripsi totidemque libellos*; cf. F. Leo, *Plautinische Forschungen*[2] (Berlin, 1912), 44; Praef. v–vi.

[2] A new prologue (addressed to Germanicus) was written for Book 1, and the original invocation to Augustus was incorporated in the prologue to Book 2. These changes, and the pathetic aside at 4.81–4 prompted by the mention of Sulmo, are the only certain evidence of revision; the transmission contains no true author's variants. (Praef. vi–vii.)

[3] D. E. W. Wormell and E. Courtney, *BICS* 24 (1977), 37–63.

[4] The sigla of the Teubner text are retained, although (among other reservations) one might have wished Z, which is not an extant manuscript, to be distinguished more obviously from A and U, which do exist. Plates of AUG in Frazer (vol. 5, pls. 1, 2, 4), of A in Chatelain (XCIX), of IM in Wormell–Courtney (after p. 185).

[5] Pellegrin, *Manuscrits*, ii.1., 383–6. The *Fasti* bear the title 'Ovidius maiolii', which might refer to S. Maieul, Abbot of Cluny (d. 984). Chatelain suggested that A was no. 71 in the 1552 Fleury catalogue.

[6] A twelfth-century Italian copy of U, Berlin (West) lat. 8° 134 (Y), permits the three early correctors of U to be distinguished from the last two; cf. E. H. Alton, *Hermathena*, 45 (1929), 371.

both Z and A descend from ancient exemplars and carry equal weight
in establishing the text, although A is on the whole superior in quality.
The position of U is harder to make out. It cannot be assigned simply to
the A or Z branch of tradition, since it agrees with each in both true
and false readings and on occasion gives the right reading against AZ.[7]
One must therefore postulate the existence of three streams of ancient
tradition and reckon with the likelihood of contamination. U agrees
with Z more often than with A, it is right against AZ much less often
than A is against UZ or Z against AU,[8] and it shows evidence of being
the product of conscious thought and effort.[9] The facts might best be
accounted for on the following hypothesis:

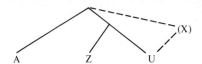

(X) would thus be the source both of U's good readings against ZA
and also of the readings that it shares with A against Z (almost all of
which are of a kind suitable to horizontal transmission).[10]

Where AZU are extant they contain virtually all the readings that
must be considered traditional; the isolated good readings offered by
the *recentiores* are hardly ever beyond the powers of a twelfth- or
thirteenth-century master.[11] In 1.1–505, however, Z is represented
only by M and A is missing after 5.24. These losses can be mitigated to
a degree with the help of secondary manuscripts:

(1) related to A: Cambridge, Pembroke College 280 (s. XII,
Canterbury?) = F; Florence, Laur. 36.24 (s. XII/XIII, Italy) = L; Paris
lat. 7993 (s. XIII, northern France) = Δ.

[7] Praef. xi–xii.
[8] In 2.568–3.204 A alone gives the correct reading about twice as often as Z and nearly eight
times as often as U (roughly 30: 15: 4, based on Wormell–Courtney's text and apparatus); in
4.317–814 A and Z are nearly equal in right readings (about fifteen each) and U is not as far
behind (six).
[9] Praef. xii. Several good readings unique to U could be the result of 'editorial' acuteness, e.g.
3.133 *in anno* (*-os* AZ), 4.422 *henna* (*hensa* A, *(a)ethna* Z), 692 *cum duro* (*duro* A, *cum uestro* Z), 756 *fano*
(*fauno* AZ), 795 *feribant* (*ferebant* A, *ferirent* Z).
[10] The behaviour here suggested for U is very similar to that of one of the two Beneventan
manuscripts of the *Metamorphoses*, Vatican, Urb. lat. 341 (also called U); see below. In the case of
the *Metamorphoses* we are fortunate in having manuscripts N and E(P) to reveal U's primary
affiliation and the nature of the contamination it has undergone; without them, U's readings
would raise precisely the same problems as those of the Ursinianus do in the *Fasti*.
[11] Typical examples are 2.587 *latebat* (*iacebat*), 645 *huc* (*hic/hinc*), 3.37 *pugnant* (*-at*), 96 *utrique*
(*uterque*), 131 *titiensibus* (*tot-* A), 145 *isse* (*esse*), 167 *si licet* (*scil-*). 3.176 *solam* (*-um*) and 4.745
mul(c)tramque (*in utramque* U, *in utrumque* AZ) show rather more skill.

(2) related to Z: Milan, Ambros. N.265 sup. (s. XII), contains 1.95–394, 2.467–660, 3.1–6.640 = θ; Berlin (East), Diez. B Sant. 29 (s. XV) = σ; Oxford, Bodl. D'Orville 172 (s. XV) = d.[12]

None of these manuscripts, however, is an entirely faithful representative of its type. The consequences for the quality of the text are especially serious in the last two books, where A's often uniquely valuable testimony is not available.[13]

R. J. T.

[12] Among other manuscripts Wormell–Courtney give preference to Leiden, Voss. Lat. O. 27 (s. XII ex., France? = B), Oxford, Bodl. Auct. F. 4. 29 (s. XII/XIII = C, with interesting marginal commentary), and Munich Clm 8122 (s. XII), a conflation of A and Z once thought to possess an independent status comparable to AZU (cf., e.g., Bömer, 52).

[13] The situation is analogous to *Metamorphoses* 15, where the best specimens of the so-called 'Lactantian' group (MN) are missing and are not adequately replaced by later members of the class.

Heroides

The *Heroides*[1] are the least well-preserved of Ovid's works, in large part because of the circumstances of their transmission: the text of *Heroides* 1–14 and 16–21 (with possible exceptions to be noted below) is based on a single early Carolingian codex (Ω) written in France around 800. (The *Epistula Sapphus*, usually printed as *Heroides* 15, has a distinct transmission, discussed below.) It is very likely that Ω also contained the *Remedia amoris*, *Ars amatoria*, and *Amores*, and that it was the source of the better class of manuscripts of those works (called α).[2] In the amatory poems, the shortcomings of Ω can often be detected with the help of a second independent stream of ancient tradition, but this resource is not available for the *Heroides*. The approximately 200 surviving manuscripts represent successive stages in the degradation (and attempted correction) of the already debased text of Ω.

The oldest surviving manuscript is Paris lat. 8242 (s. IX¾, Corbie =

The fundamental study of the manuscript tradition is by H. Dörrie: 'Untersuchungen zur Überlieferungsgeschichte von Ovids *Epistulae Heroidum*', *NGG* Phil.-Hist. Kl. 1960 (I.113–230; II.359–423); some of his conclusions are modified by E. J. Kenney in *Gnomon*, 33 (1961), 478–87. The principal editions are by H. Sedlmayer (Vienna, 1886), A. Palmer (Oxford, 1898), and Dörrie (Berlin, 1971); this last, although valuable for its detailed reports of the manuscripts, is seriously deficient in almost every respect: cf. G. P. Goold, *Gnomon*, 46 (1974), 475–84, M. D. R., *CR* 24 (1974), 57–64, J. M. Hunt, *CPh* 70 (1975), 215–24. An OCT edition is being prepared by E. J. Kenney.

[1] The title *Heroides* is ancient (Priscian *GLK* 2.544.4), but not necessarily original. Ovid refers to the work simply as *Epistula* at *Ars* 3.345, and this suggests that that word figured in the title (perhaps, therefore, *Epistulae Heroidum*). The manuscripts vary between *Liber epistularum* and *Liber heroidum*.   [2] E. J. Kenney, *CQ* 12 (1962), 24 and n. 1.

P),[3] now incomplete (contains 2.14–4.47, 4.104–5.96, 6.50–20.175[4]). It was almost certainly copied from the now lost part of Paris lat. 7311 (R of *Ars*, *Remedia*, and *Amores*).[5] Since P is more than two centuries older than any other extant witness, it is, not surprisingly, less subject to interpolation and occasionally preserves a slight corruption that later manuscripts have emended away (e.g. 20.129 *in caput* P whence *in caput ut* Ehwald: *in caput et/inque caput* rell.). P's readings thus deserve close attention, although they possess no unique authority.

P is the only surviving Carolingian manuscript of the *Heroides*, and these poems appear to have been much less read in the ninth and tenth centuries than the *Metamorphoses* and the amatory works, and rather less well known than the *Fasti* and the letters from Tomi. Some evidence for the circulation of the *Heroides* in this period is found, though, in library catalogues (s. IX, Murbach) and in imitations by Carolingian writers (e.g. Angilbert and Mico at Saint-Riquier, not far from Corbie, the home of P, and Walahfrid Strabo at Reichenau, the mother house of Murbach). From the late eleventh century onwards the presence of the *Heroides* can be registered in several parts of Europe: in France from echoes in the poetry of Hildebert of Lavardin and Baudri de Bourgeuil, and shortly afterwards from the extensive excerpts included in the *Florilegium Gallicum*, in the Beneventan zone of Italy (see manuscript E in the list below), in southern Germany and Austria (in the eleventh-century book-list of Blaubeuren and the fragments from Mondsee, W in the list below). By about the mid-twelfth century the text was in general circulation north of the Alps.

A codicological study of the surviving manuscripts would make it possible to trace the history of the text in greater detail. Investigation of the manuscripts has concentrated up to now on their textual evidence, and conclusions have been modest and guarded.

Extensive contamination makes it impossible to isolate clear-cut families, but several manuscripts are related in some degree to P: Frankfurt, Univ. Barth. 110 (s. XIII[1], France = F),[6] Louvain 411 (s. XII, destroyed in 1940; text ends at 9.133 = L), and Wolfenbüttel, Gud.

---

[3] Plates in Chatelain (XCI) and in Palmer's edition (frontispiece).

[4] The traditional numbering is used; Dörrie departs from it in several poems because he reckons an additional introductory distich as lines 1–2 (7, 8, 11, 12, 17, 20, 21). The *Concordance of Ovid* by Deferrari–Barry–McGuire (Washington, DC, 1939) reports the *Epistula Sapphus* as a separate work and therefore refers to *Heroides* 16–21 as 15–20.

[5] S. Tafel, *Die Überlieferungsgeschichte von Ovids Carmina Amatoria* (diss. Tübingen, 1910), 31; Kenney (n. 2), 6–7.

[6] An *Opera omnia Ovidi*: brief description in F. Munari, *Catalogue of the MSS of Ovid's Metamorphoses*, London, 1957 (*BICS* Suppl. 4), no. 95; fuller account in G. Powitz and H. Buck, *Die Handschriften des Bartholomaeusstifts und des Karmeliterklosters in Frankfurt-am-Main* (Frankfurt, 1974), 253–7. Dörrie dates the manuscript 'saec. XII ex.' in the list of sigla and in the introduction to his edition (p. 14), 'saec. XIII' in the introduction to the *Epistula Sapphus* (p. 297).

lat. 297 (= Gu), a fifteenth-century copy of a manuscript similar to but independent of P.[7] The most remarkable feature of Gu is that its text, and almost certainly that of its Carolingian exemplar, extended to 21.144 whereas that of almost all other extant manuscripts breaks off at 21.12.[8]

The remaining manuscripts are more heavily interpolated than PFL Gu, but their testimony cannot be disregarded. Dörrie reports the readings of about forty witnesses (plus a number of fragments and florilegia), of which the following are accorded preferred status, mainly because of their date:

E   Eton College 150, s. XI ex., written in Beneventan script of the Bari type;[9] ends at 7.159.

G   Wolfenbüttel, Extrav. 260, s. XII, Italy (?).

V   Vatican lat. 3254, s. XII[2], Italy (?), ends at 17.236. *Heroides* bound between unrelated texts of *Eclogues* and *Georgics* and *Epistulae ex Ponto*.

W   Vienna ser. nov. 107, s. XII or perhaps XI ex., Mondsee, contains 10.14–11.66, 12.19–98, 12.180–16.319, 16.368–17.66, 17.112–18.4, 18.169–20.224.

In this transmission there is no room for *eliminatio codicum* and very little for *recensio* as a whole. All inherently plausible readings, whatever their source, must be taken seriously, and sense and usage are the only sure criteria for deciding among them.

In several places single couplets or extended passages are found in a minority of witnesses. None of this material is certainly genuine, but at least some of it is indubitably ancient. It may therefore owe its survival to a text of the corpus independent of Ω.[10] The passages in question are of three kinds.

(a) Introductory distichs, found in all the poems except 1–4, 13–14, 16, and 19. The witnesses supporting these additional couplets differ from poem to poem: those preceding 9, 10, and 12 appear only in the

---

[7] Dörrie, i.179–84, with a plate of f. 24ᵛ facing p. 184. The manuscript was in the Veneto in the 1660s, and may have been written there.

[8] *Her.* 21.13–144 are also present in the printed editions of Sweynheim and Pannartz (Rome, 1471) and Jacobus Rubeus (Venice, 1474), and in several late fifteenth-century manuscripts. Dörrie (ii.371 ff.) eliminates all but two of these as derived from the printed texts, but regards Florence, Laur. 36.2 and Paris lat. 7997 as independent, though closely related to the Rome and Venice editions respectively (pp. 379–84). Paris lat. 7997 is the work of Bartolomeo Sanvito and Laur. 36.2 was executed by Bartolomeo Fonzio for Francesco Sassetti, cf. M. D. R., *RHT* 6 (1976), 85 n. 1 and 89.

[9] *Beneventan Script*[2], i. 152, ii. 40.

[10] Kenney (*Gnomon*, 33 (1961), 484) constructs a stemma that would explain the survival of 16.39–144 and 21.13–144 by physical losses in Ω. The material in (a) and (b) above, however, still requires a non-Ω source; as Kenney observes (p. 480), such a source might be responsible for verbal variants found in isolated manuscripts.

early printed editions,[11] whereas those preceding 5, 6, and 7 are present in E, the second oldest manuscript (which breaks off at 7.159). Some of the lines are obviously spurious, and all can be accounted for as interpolations designed to identify the sender and recipient of each 'letter' in its opening words; the poems for which no additional verses survive are those in which this function is performed by the first lines as generally transmitted.[12]

(b) Distichs found in the body of poems. Again, the manuscript support varies from passage to passage, but includes in all cases at least one medieval witness. Several of these insertions are manifestly spurious, and perhaps medieval in origin: these are found after 4.132, 9.114, 12.158, 16.166, and 16.266.[13] Other additional lines, however, are not clearly inauthentic and appear in places where the paradosis is certainly or arguably lacunose: of this kind are 2.18–19, 7.24–5, 7.97–8, 8.19–20, and 13.74–5. These are therefore either genuine Ovidian couplets omitted in Ω or ancient interpolations composed to replace Ovidian verses now irretrievably lost.[14]

(c) Two passages (16.39–144, 21.145–248) for which the only witness is the 1477 Parma edition. The cases are not exactly comparable: 16.39–144 can be bracketed as an interpolation with no ill effect on 16 as a whole,[15] whereas 21.145–248, like the disputed couplets in (b) above, are either part of the original text lost in Ω or an attempt to complete a permanently mutilated poem.

Ovid took pride in the novelty of the *Heroides* (*Ars* 3.346), and the

---

[11] They have been added by a second hand in Paris lat. 7997, almost certainly from one of the printed texts. In his edition Dörrie retracted the earlier statement (1.210 f.) that the introductory verses to 17 are found in Eton College 91 and Oxford, Bodl. Canon. Class. Lat. 1 (Heinsius mistakenly reported them as a marginal addition in P); Heinsius's source turns out to have been Brussels 21368 (Dörrie's Bx), cf. O. Zwierlein, *RhM* 116 (1973), 275–9, M. D. R., *RhM* 117 (1974), 137 n. 15.

[12] The most detailed treatment of these distichs, by E.-A. Kirfel, *Untersuchungen zur Briefform der Heroides Ovids* (Bern, 1967), comes to different conclusions, regarding as genuine the additional introductory couplets to 7, 8, and 17, and as spurious the unanimously transmitted opening couplets of 2, 10, 13, 18, and 19. Dörrie (edn. 7 f.) treats them all as spurious and suggests that they were composed for an ancient edition. There is an earlier discussion (sceptical) by W. Schmitz-Cronenbroeck, *Die Anfänge der Heroiden des Ovid* (diss. Cologne, 1937). The view advanced above presupposes the authenticity of the headings (e.g. *Penelope Vlixi*) affixed to each letter in many of the manuscripts (though not P[1]); cf. Kenney, *Gnomon*, 33 (1961), 485; H. Jacobson, *Ovid's Heroides* (Princeton, 1974), 404–6.

[13] *Her.* 5.25–6 is in a different class: ELV and Gu offer it (after line 21 or 22), and it was thus probably present (as a marginal addition?) in Ω.

[14] Housman, *CR* 11 (1897), 200–2 (= J. Diggle and F. R. D. Goodyear (edd.), *The Classical Papers of A. E. Housman* (3 vols., Cambridge, 1972), 388–92) defended the authenticity of three of the passages, doubting 8.19–20 and regarding 13.74–5 (the latter transmitted by the main manuscripts) as spurious; M. Sicherl, *Hermes*, 91 (1963), 190–212, accepts all except 13.74–5 as genuine. The case against these lines has not been argued in detail; Goold, *Gnomon*, 46 (1974), 483, thinks they are more likely to be ancient interpolations. Dörrie (edn. 8) most implausibly suggests that Ovid himself rejected the lines in preparing a second edition of *Heroides*.

[15] Cf. U. Fischer, *Ignotum hoc aliis ille novavit opus* (diss. Berlin, 1968), 132–51.

collection provoked immediate attempts at imitation (*Am.* 2.18.27 ff.). Perhaps as a result of their popularity, the text of these poems as preserved in Ω contains proportionally more spurious couplets of ancient origin than Ovid's other elegiac works. The problem of authenticity also arises in regard to entire poems: setting aside the *Epistula Sapphus* (discussed below), the Ovidian authorship of the double letters 16–21 has often been questioned,[16] and doubts have also been entertained about several of the single letters (8, 9, 12–14).[17] Only nine poems (1–7, 10–11), have remained immune to scepticism, all but one of those (3) being mentioned in *Amores* 2.18. Most writers still accept Ovid's authorship of at least 1–14, but a careful stylistic analysis of the collection has not yet been undertaken and the question therefore remains open.

Epistula Sapphus

The transmission of the *ES* is independent of that of the *Heroides*, and the poem owes its traditional position as fifteenth in the corpus to Daniel Heinsius, who placed it there in his edition of 1629.[18] (Excerpts from the *ES* appear in the twelfth-century *Florilegium Gallicum* between *Heroides* 14 and 16, but this does not prove that the compiler used a manuscript that included the *ES* with the *Heroides*. The *FG* was put together by a well-read scholar using the resources of a library (at Orléans?) rich in extremely rare texts: the compiler could have anticipated Heinsius by incorporating excerpts from the separately transmitted *ES* into the *Heroides*.[19])

Apart from the lines cited in the *Florilegium Gallicum*, the *ES* survives in only one medieval witness, F. (It is surely significant that F, like the florilegium, probably had its origin in the Loire valley.) In F the *ES* precedes the *Heroides* and there are signs (such as the absence of annotation, abundant elsewhere, in the *ES*) that it was copied from a different exemplar.

The poem is also found in about 200 manuscripts written from 1420 onwards and descended from a common source;[20] the source of the *recentiores*, though inferior to F, is independent of it, and so the consensus of the *recentiores* can often be used to correct errors of F.

---

[16] e.g. by Palmer in his edition (pp. 436 ff.).

[17] Most notably by Karl Lachmann, *Kleinere Schriften* (Berlin, 1876), ii.56–61; doubts about 9 are expressed by E. Courtney, *BICS* 12 (1965), 63–6 and D. W. T. C. Vessey, *CQ* 19 (1969), 349–61.

[18] Heinsius was guided by *Amores* 2.18.26, where a letter of Sappho is mentioned at the end of a series of nine *epistulae*.

[19] Dörrie (edn.), 289; more tentatively in *P. Ovidius Naso: Der Brief der Sappho an Phaon* (Munich, 1975), 52–3.

[20] The *recentiores* display their common origin by many shared wrong readings of which F is free: e.g. 15 *pierides* (*pyrrhiades*), 45 *omnique a* (*omni tibi*), 84 *dedit* (*facit*), 101 *summa* (*nostra*).

(Readings of interest found in a small minority of the *recentiores* are probably to be treated as conjectures.)

Ovid's authorship of *ES* has been vigorously impugned and defended; the evidence of style strongly suggests that the work is a product of the Neronian or Flavian period.[21]

R. J. T.

[21] In favour of authenticity, S. de Vries, *Epistula Sapphus ad Phaonem apparatu critico instructa commentario illustrata et Ovidio vindicata* (Berlin, 1888), Dörrie (n. 19, above); against, R. J. T., *HSCP* 85 (1981), 133–53, arguing as well that the references to a letter of Sappho in *Am.* 2.18.26 and 34 are interpolations.

Ibis

The earliest evidence for the circulation of the *Ibis* comes from the indirect tradition. No extant copy of the poem is certainly earlier than 1200,[1] but manuscripts were available in twelfth-century England, Belgium, and Germany,[2] the compiler of the *Florilegium Gallicum* had access to a text, and the *Ibis* formed part of the impressive body of classical poetry put to use by Walter of Châtillon in his *Alexandreis*.[3]

The surviving manuscripts descend from an archetype (probably s. IX or X) in which a spurious couplet of medieval origin had been added in the margin at line 130. The several ways in which the older manuscripts treat this interpolation, combined with other significant errors and displacements in the order of verses, suggest a tripartite division:

group 1

G   Cambridge, Trinity College 1335 (O.7.7) (s. XIII in., England?), a miscellany of ancient and medieval material, including the *Megacosmus* and *Microcosmus* of Bernard Silvester, the cento of Proba, and Senecan and pseudo-Senecan moral treatises.

P   Berlin (East), Phill. 1796 (Rose 210) (s. XIV?),[4] Ovidiana and pseudo-Ovidiana.

Edition with commentary by A. La Penna (Florence, 1957), including a full textual analysis of the tradition.

[1] According to the dates assigned in La Penna's list of manuscripts. (The following manuscripts may be added to La Penna's list, from information provided by M. D. R.: Genoa, Univ. E.II.31, Padua, Bibl. Univ. 1010, Rome, Bibl. Cors. 43.E.43, Bibl. Naz., Vitt. Eman. 1417, and a manuscript in the possession of Mr John Sparrow (all s. XV or later).)

[2] Manitius, *Handschriften*, 63, 69, records appearances of the *Ibis* in twelfth-century book lists from Durham (shortly after 1150), Christ Church Canterbury (1170), Egmond (1129), Brogne, and Lambach.

[3] M. L. Colker's edition (Padua, 1978) gives three verbal echoes of the *Ibis*: 170 (*Alex.* 6.262), 191 (7.235), and 432 (6.262).

[4] La Penna (p. lxxxix) dates P to s. XIII/XIV, V. Rose to s. XIV/XV, *Verzeichniss der lateinischen Handschriften der kön. Bibliothek zu Berlin*, i (Berlin, 1893), 447–9.

P₁   Paris lat. 7994 (s. XIII, France), Ovidian material and Bernard
      Silvester.
E   Berlin (West), lat. 8° 167 (formerly Phillipps 124) (s. XIII).

PP₁E derive from a common source within this group.

group 2

T   Tours 879 (c.1200, France); contains all of Ovid except *Med. fac.*

group 3

F   Frankfurt, Univ. Barth. 110 (s. XIII¹, France), Ovidian and pseudo-
      Ovidian material forming an *Opera omnia.*
V   Vienna 885 (s. XIII or s. XII ex.), also containing Theodulus and the
      Disticha Catonis.
H   British Library, Add. 49368 (formerly Holkham Hall 322) (s. XIII¹,
      France, with links to Orléans), Ovid and pseudo-Ovid.
A   Antwerp 68 (s. XII/XIII), Ovidiana.
Z   Paris, S. Geneviève 1210 (s. XIII), a miscellany of mainly theological
      texts; also contains *De utensilibus* of Alexander Nequam.

The first group is the most influential: its later descendants comprise
nearly all the fourteenth- and fifteenth-century manuscripts, with a few
exceptions related to FHVAZ.[5]
Even at the earliest visible stage of the tradition contamination is far
advanced; each of the three groups listed has influenced the other two to
a degree and AZ seem to have drawn on sources no longer extant.[6]
Little if anything of value is contributed by the later thirteenth- and
fourteenth-century manuscripts,[7] but some of the humanist copies
stand out for rare good readings: for example, Paris lat. 7997 (a Sanvito
book) and in particular Oxford, Bodl. Canon. Class. Lat. 20 (s. XV/
XVI), the only extant manuscript to have removed the spurious couplet
inserted after 130 in the archetype.[8]
A set of late-antique scholia survives, best reflected in P (Berlin
(East), Phill. 1796). Other extant copies offer an expanded but also
debased form of the notes; the oldest representative of this class is
Berne 711 (s. XII, France = B), which also contains the fullest set of
lemmata; the portions of the text in B are markedly inferior to the

----

[5] La Penna, xci–c, cxiv–cxliv. The excerpts in the *Florilegium Gallicum* seem related to HZ
(pp. cxi–cxii).
[6] See the stemma in La Penna, cvii.
[7] Dijon 497, however, excels the others in the ambitiousness and occasional acuteness of its
interpolations; La Penna, xcvii–xcviii; E. J. Kenney, *CQ* 12 (1962), 3 n. 4, 9–10.
[8] La Penna, cxxx–cxxxvi. He reports as well the readings of Vatican lat. 1595 (c.1450? with
notes by Pietro Odi da Montopoli), the best representative of a group of manuscripts that includes
the source of the *editio princeps* (Rome, 1471).

consensus of thirteenth-century manuscripts. This recension of the scholia is also represented by less extensive notes of GEFHZ.[9]

R. J. T.

[9] Edition by La Penna (Florence, 1959); his text of *Ibis* cites only the lemmata of B, which show some affinity with the FHVAZ group (cf. 275, 319, 455, 472, 507, 543, 615) as well as a number of rare or unique interpolated readings (321, 351, 413, 479 (E), 517, 549 (D), 568, 587, 651 (E)).

Medicamina faciei femineae

Only 100 lines of this didactic poem[1] survive, perhaps the contents of a bifolium in a late-antique or Carolingian codex.[2] The earliest extant text occupies part of the last verso (originally blank) of a manuscript of the *Metamorphoses*, Florence, Laur. S. Marco 223 (s. XI ex., France = M).[3] The rest of the verso is occupied by the *Nux*; this conjunction may derive from the archetype, since the two poems are found together in virtually all extant copies, as well as in medieval catalogue-entries.[4] After M follows a hiatus of about a century in the visible transmission: the *Med. fac.* (like the *Nux*) remained unknown to the eager French Ovidians of the early and mid-twelfth century – it is, for example, absent from the *Florilegium Gallicum* – and the earliest of the *recentiores* that comprise the rest of the tradition date from around 1200.[5]

The most recent edition uses the following witnesses to represent the later tradition:

B   Berlin (East), Diez. B Sant. 1 (s. XIV[1], Italy); *Med. fac.* at end of a corpus of Ovid's elegiac poetry.[6]

Edition, E. J. Kenney (OCT, 1961); text and commentary, A. Kunz (Vienna, 1881).

[1] The poem is headed *De medicamine faciei* (*femineae*) in the manuscripts, but the verbal sense of *medicamen* is not attested in classical Latin. Seventeenth-century editors introduced the form *medicamina* from *Ars* 3.205. The oldest manuscript (M) gives the title in a mixture of Greek and Roman capitals (DH MHDICAMINH FACIHY ΦHMYNHH), perhaps preserving a piece of Carolingian whimsy.

[2] Ovid's words at *Ars* 3.205 f. show that the poem was not left unfinished: 'est mihi, quo dixi uestrae medicamina formae,/ paruus, sed cura grande, libellus, opus'.

[3] The San Marco manuscript comprises two originally distinct books. *Med. fac.* and *Nux* are on f. 56ᵛ, in a hand contemporaneous with, but different from, that of *Met.* (ends f. 56ʳ) or *Tristia* (starts f. 57ʳ), although closely resembling the latter. The manuscript was left to San Marco in 1499 by Giorgio Antonio Vespucci (f. 1ʳ).

[4] In Richard de Fournival's *Biblionomia*, for example, *Med. fac.* and *Nux* are bracketed with a group of pseudo-Ovidian works (*De cuculo, De pulice, De sompno* (= *Am.* 3.5), *De medicamine surdi*); the two poems appear in similar company in a fourteenth-century catalogue from Peterborough (Manitius, *Handschriften*, 67, 70) and in several manuscripts, e.g. Milan, Ambros. H. 225 inf. (see under *Nux*).

[5] Walter of Châtillon may have known the *Med. fac.*, but the single parallel cited in M. L. Colker's edition (Padua, 1978) is not certain proof of direct imitation: *Alex.* 3.14 (*fames*) *forme populatur honorem* (*M. f.* 45 *formam populabitur aetas*).

[6] The text of the *Metamorphoses* in ff. 1–122 is an originally distinct manuscript.

Be   Berlin (East), Phill. 1796 (Rose 210) (s. XIV, Italy), contains *Fasti, Ibis, Amores, Ex Ponto, Ars*, and pseudo-Ovidiana including *Nux*.

Ce   Collection of the late major J. R. Abbey, JA. 6654 (formerly Phillipps 6912) (s. XIII).

G   Gotha Memb. II.120 (s. XII/XIII, Hildesheim, St. Gottardskloster?[7]).

La   Leiden, Periz. Q. 7 (s. XV, Italy); *Med. fac.* and *Nux* now bound with Pomponius Mela.

N   Naples IV. F. 13 (s. XII/XIII), also contains *Amores* and *Ars*.

N_b Naples IV. F.12 (1385–6, Italy).

P_b Paris lat. 7994 (s. XIII, France), containing *Heroides, Ibis*, and the amatory poems.

Q   Antwerp 68 (s. XII/XIII), another corpus of Ovidian elegy.

U   Florence, Ricc. 489 (s. XIII), also contains *Heroides, Am.* 3.5, *Fasti, Tristia*, and *Ars* (owned by Boccaccio).

None of the *recentiores* individually offers a text as good as M's, but the later manuscripts are independent of M (at 65 they have *gummi* (i.e. *cummi*, cf. 87) while M has *bulli*, a repetition of its garbled *bullos* for *bulbos* in 63) and in groups of shifting configuration they often give the correct reading where M is corrupt; at least some of these good readings are likely to be traditional (e.g. 21 *oriente* (*stridente*), 44 *facies* (*facile*)).[8]

R. J. T.

[7] So R. Schipke, *Die Maugérard-Handschriften der Forschungsbibliothek Gotha* (Gotha, 1972), 73–4.

[8] Others, such as 19 *positu* (*-tos*), 30 *altus* (*saltus*), 76 *tritis* (*tristis*), 88 *cubum* (*cibum*), 97 *molli* (*mollis*), could be acute corrections; of this kind are perhaps N's *quos* in 64 (*quas* M *recc.*) and *sint* in 97 (*sit* M *recc.*). On the other hand, it probably took more than scribal enterprise for N_b to avoid the two distinctive errors of the *recentiores* as a class: 69 *pallore* (from *pallentes* earlier in the line) for *torrere* and 86 *trahens* for *triens*. In the former passage N_bBe have *torquere* and U *terrere* (?), in the latter N_b is joined by G (which also has the true readings *sint* and *molli* in 97).

Metamorphoses

The tradition of the *Metamorphoses* is remarkable for the total absence of extant complete manuscripts before the second half of the eleventh century. Only small fragments remain from the early Carolingian period, when the text was first rediscovered and subjected to critical scrutiny. Fortunately, the fragments and the surviving manuscripts written before 1150 are sufficient to permit certain conclusions to be drawn. The picture that emerges resembles in its main outlines the transmission of the amatory poems: on the one hand a small group of closely related manuscripts ultimately descended from a single ancient exemplar, on the other a great mass of manuscripts whose relationships cannot be securely plotted and which seem to present in an intermingled form more than one stream of ancient tradition. As in the amatory poems there is clear evidence of readings being horizontally as well as vertically transmitted; it is also likely that lost hyparchetypes carried alternative readings, which have been variously adopted in their descendants. It is therefore seldom possible to eliminate the individual readings even of secondary manuscripts on stemmatic grounds; enlightened eclecticism based on sense and usage must guide future editors just as it did the greatest of their predecessors, Nicolaus Heinsius.

The oldest surviving witnesses are three fragments from the ninth century:[1]

α   (Bern) Berne 363 (s. IX ex., in insular minuscule; Munari, 37²), a miscellany containing 1.1–199, 304–9, 773–9, 2.1–22, 3.1–56.

λ   (Lips) Leipzig Rep. I.4°.74 (s. IX²/₄, France (Orléans?); Munari, 151), a miscellany including the episode of Actaeon (3.131–252).

π   (Par) Paris lat. 12246 (s. IX², France; Munari, 270), contains 1.81–192, 2.67–254 (161–254 mostly illegible).

None of these early fragments can be definitely assigned through shared errors to either main class of the medieval tradition; each preserves at least one good reading not otherwise attested.[3] For α and λ direct descent from ancient miscellanies is likely. With π matters are less clear; it too may have an independent ancient source, or it may represent at an early stage the strain of tradition of which the first complete examples are EFP (see below), written in France/Germany around 1100. (π offers sets of double readings in places where an ancestor of EFP must have done so, e.g. 2.179 *iacentes/patentes*.)

All three fragments present headings for some of the individual episodes (e.g. 'Acteon in ceruum' in λ), and π also contains prose

The most recent edition, by W. S. Anderson (Teubner, 1977), is the first to report the readings of the essential manuscripts and fragments; the reports, however, cannot always be relied upon and the apparatus does not make full use of information amassed by previous editors. Much can still be gleaned from the compilations of H. Magnus (in his Weidmann edition of 1914) and D. A. Slater (*Towards a Text of the Metamorphosis of Ovid* (Oxford, 1927) – apparatus only, based on A. Riese's 1889 Tauchnitz text). The Loeb text of Books 1–8 by F. J. Miller, revised by G. P. Goold (London, 1977), offers a well-constructed text without apparatus. A critical edition is being prepared by R. J. T. There is no comprehensive study of the transmission. R. T. Bruère attempted a stemmatic analysis in *HSCP* 50 (1939), 95–122; F. W. Lenz produced a somewhat chaotic summary of progress to 1967 (*Ovid's Metamorphoses. Prolegomena to a Revision of Hugo Magnus' Edition*, Zurich, 1967); there is a brief statement in the preface to Anderson's edition (pp. v–xxiii). See also R. J. T., *CPh* 77 (1982), 342–60.

[1] The sigla given are those in common use, with proposed additions and replacements added in parentheses where appropriate. Plates of π (XCIV), M (XCVI), β (XCV), ε (XCVII.1), F (XCVIII), L (XCVII.2) in Chatelain; complete facsimile of α ed. H. Hagen (Leiden, 1897); plate of λ f. 28ᵛ in Slater, facing p. 18; of MNF in Magnus (at back); of US in Slater (frontispiece, facing 'Lactantius' Book 10).

[2] F. Munari, *Catalogue of the MSS of Ovid's Metamorphoses* (London, 1957, *BICS* Suppl. 4), no. 37. This indispensable work contains a brief description with bibliography for each manuscript. Occasional corrections of Munari's accounts have not been signalled.

[3] e.g. α has 1.56 *fulgora* (*frigora*), 173 *hac parte* (*hac fronte/a fronte*), 3.49 *funesti* (*funesta*); λ has 3.233 *Therodamas* (*theri-*) and, probably correctly, 206 *primique* (*-usque*) and 213 *fero* (*ferox*); π alone preserves *et* before *Eous* in 2.153.

summaries. This material, which is commonly referred to as the work of 'Lactantius', was probably composed for an ancient edition of the poem. It survives complete in only one group of medieval manuscripts, which has as a result often been called the 'Lactantian' family, but the evidence of α λ π suggests that 'Lactantian' material was present in some form in all of the ancient codices that survived into the Carolingian period.[4]

The most clearly defined group includes several complete and fragmentary manuscripts associated both by the presence of the 'Lactantian' *tituli* and *narrationes*, and by shared errors, among them many omissions of genuine lines. The members of this group so far identified are as follows:

(a) *complete manuscripts*

M   Florence, San Marco 225 (s. XI[2], central/north Italy; Munari, 178), ends at 14.830.

N   Naples IV.F.3 (s. XII in., south Italy – Bari-type Beneventan script; Munari, 206), first hand ends at 14.838.[5]

U   Vatican, Urb. lat. 341 (s. XI/XII, south Italy – Bari-type Beneventan script; Munari, 370); 15.494–879 (along with portions of earlier books) added in Gothic script (s. XIII ex.). See p. 203 n. 22, above.

(R)   Naples IV.F.2 (s. XII[2], Italy?; Munari, 205); contains the *tituli* of 'Lactantius' for all fifteen books.

W   Vat. lat. 5859 (Italy, 1275; Munari, 345); *tituli* and *narrationes* for all fifteen books.[6]

(Z)   Vienna ser. nov. 12746 (Milan?, c.1470;[7] Munari, 385); *tituli* and *narrationes* for all fifteen books.

(b) *incomplete, fragmentary, or lost manuscripts*

β(E)   British Library, Add. 11967 (s. X, Italy; Munari, 154), contains 2.833–3.510, 4.292–5.389, 5.588–6.411.

---

[4] For this reason the designations 'Lactantian' and 'non-Lactantian' appear in inverted commas. On the origin and character of 'Lactantius', cf. B. Otis, *HSCP* 47 (1936), 131–63. The name is not attached to the *tituli* and *narrationes* before the fifteenth century, and was probably inspired by the well-known commentator on Statius. The material has been printed by Magnus and Slater, but still awaits a thorough study, which would now include the evidence of RWZ (see below).

[5] For the date cf. *Beneventan Script*[2] i.151, ii.99; a slightly earlier date (s. XI ex.) is proposed without argument by G. Cavallo, *Settimane*, 22 (1974), 402. The remainder of f. 189[v] contains 14.839–51 in a Beneventan hand (not identical with N[1]), 15.1–16 in a later Gothic hand (s. XIV); the rest of Book 15 is written in Gothic script of s. XIV, the text being derived from a different source.

[6] Berlin (East), Diez. B. Sant. 1 is similar to W in contents and elegant format, but was written approximately 25–50 years later.

[7] Information kindly provided by Dr A. C. de la Mare.

ε(H) British Library, Harley 2610 (s. x², Germany; Munari, 166), contains
       1.1–3.622 with 'Lactantian' *narrationes* in margin in Books 1–2.[8]

v(Urb) Vatican, Urb. lat. 342, ff. 77–8 (s. x ex., France?; Munari, 371),
       contains 5.483–6.45, 7.731–8.104 on the first and eighth leaves of a
       gathering, sewn into the back of a text of Juvenal (s. IX/X, Fleury?); no
       'Lactantius'.

J   Padua, S. Johannes in Viridario (s. XII; Munari, 281). Now lost;
       briefly inspected by Heinsius, who noted the presence of 'argumenta
       Luctatii (i.e. Lactantii) omnia'. It may have been an earlier specimen
       of the type represented by RWZ.

S   Speyer (Munari, 313), now lost except for the quaternion containing
       9.324–10.707 in Copenhagen Ny Kgl. S. 56 2° (s. XI/XII, Germany?;
       Munari, 111). Readings from the Spirensis were communicated to
       Heinsius by C. Langermann and noted by Heinsius with the siglum g
       in Bodl. Auct. 2. R. VI.23.[9]

This class is predominantly Italian (with ε(H) and v (Urb) perhaps
imported from south of the Alps[10]); within it smaller sub-groups can be
made out. M and β(E) are so similar as to seem like twins, a fact that
speaks well for the purity of M despite its relatively late date. The two
Beneventan manuscripts NU share scores of distinctive errors that give
them a place apart. RSWZ, although independent of the early manuscripts, have lost many characteristic errors (particularly lacunae)
through consultation of other sources. They are in general, therefore,
less valuable for reconstructing the 'Lactantian' text, although in Book
15 the absence of MN gives RWZ greater importance. At times nearly
all the members of this group agree individually with other sources in
significant readings (many of them potential ancient variants), and at
least some of these agreements may stem from alternative readings
present in the ancient copy from which the group derives. In U,
however, the loss of characteristic 'Lactantian' readings has gone so far
that it almost obscures the manuscript's basic affiliation, and
systematic contamination from a text of a different family seems likely
(see below).

The 'Lactantian' group is less subject to interpolation than the

---

[8] The fragments of *Met.* 1 from a Tegernsee manuscript (s. XI; Munari, 321) now in Munich
Clm 29208 (1–12 and Cgm 4286 (back flyleaf) derive, perhaps directly, from Harley 2610; cf.
W. S. Anderson, *CSCA* 11 (1978), 1–19. The fragments from Books 4–15, however, are of a different
textual character, similar to that of the oldest 'non-Lactantian' manuscripts FP(B). The Harley
manuscript could be the text of *Met.* named in a s. X/XI Tegernsee book-list (in Clm 18541, f. 1ʳ) as
donated by 'quidam frater Reginfridus'.

[9] The manuscript was said to contain 3.506–4.786 and 6.439–12.278. The source of the
readings in Book 1 cited by Heinsius as from the Spirensis is therefore obscure.

[10] It is theoretically possible that more than one ancient copy of the 'Lactantian' text survived
in various parts of Europe, but difficult to believe that the numerous lacunae shared by ε(H) and
M were independently produced.

majority of manuscripts,[11] but its readings do not possess any superior authority.

From the throng of 'non-Lactantian'[12] manuscripts the following stand out on grounds of age:

E(P) Vatican, Pal. lat. 1669 (s. XI/XII, France?;[13] Munari, 365), portions of text missing on ff. 14–24, cf. Anderson, praef., xiv.

F   Florence, S. Marco 223 (s. XI/XII, France?; Munari, 177), several folios replaced in s. XV Italian hand.

L   Florence, Laur. 36.12 (s. XII¹; Munari, 131), text ends at 12.298; some marginal notes in hand of Poliziano.

P(B) Paris lat. 8001 (s. XII in. ff. 1–24ʳ, 1.1–6.590; s. XII ex. 6.591–end, France?; Munari, 240).[14]

τ(T) Munich Clm 29208 (1–12 *olim* 29007a) (s. XI, Tegernsee; Munari, 321); fragments from Books 4, 6, 8–15 comprising about 2,200 lines.

The derivation of EFLPτ from a single source cannot be conclusively demonstrated as for the 'Lactantian' group. On the other hand, these manuscripts do agree in many wrong readings not found in the 'Lactantians'; some of these are probably ancient variants, but the agreements seem too numerous to be the product of random coincidence.[15] Whether or not EFLPτ are thought, for the sake of convenience, to have a common source, a special position is occupied by E, which avoids many errors of FLPτ and which contains hundreds of readings found neither in FLPτ nor in the major 'Lactantian' manuscripts MN. Most of E's distinctive readings are trivializations, but enough are true to require postulating an ancient source for them.[16] Many of E's readings are also found in U, but neither is likely to have derived them from the other; the most probable explanation for the close agreement of EU is that each has contaminated its basic text with that of another form of ancient tradition. Each was well placed for such activity, since around 1100 the

---

[11] MN, for example, are free of the interpolated lines 8.652–6 and 693a–b; these and several other passages have often been mistakenly regarded as alternative versions composed by Ovid, cf. R. J. T., *CPh* 77 (1982), 354. Other interpolations avoided by the 'Lactantians' include 8.87 and, probably, 1.477.

[12] The term is not strictly accurate, since, e.g., L has the *tituli* in the margins (added by the rubricator) and a (B. L. King's 26) has them for Book 1.

[13] The manuscript was in Bourges by 1200. A twelfth-century hand has written part of an episcopal letter on the last folio: 'P. dei gratia bituricensis ecclesie archiepiscopus' refers either to Petrus de la Chastre (bishop *c.*1141–71) or Petrus II (1180–4).

[14] Anderson (praef. xv) suggests that not only the hand but also the exemplar changes at 6.591. This is possible (and the shift from *Metamorphoseon* to *Metamorphoseos* in the colophons of 6–15 might support the idea), but the character of the text remains the same.

[15] e.g. 1.317 *superatque cacumine* (*-antque -ina*), 3.76 *herbas* (*auras*), 5.18 *cur quis* (*quisquam*), 6.142 *om. est*, 9.624 *urit et ussit* (*urget et urit*), 10.291 *agat* (*agit*), 590 *mirator* (*miratur*), 12.333 *minorem . . . dederunt* (*inu. ord.*), 545 *quoque* (*di*), 13.77 *ad* (*in*), 184 *sunt* (*erant*), 544 *ira* (*iram*), 929 *nec* (*neque*), 14.356 *aethera* (*aera*).

[16] e.g. 7.118 *suppositosque* (*-toque*), 225 *othrysque pindusque*, 413 *abstraxit* (*attraxit*), 417 *fecundique* (*-asque*), 520 *morer uos* (*moreris*); 8.206 *nec* (*neu*), 641 *inde* (*inque*), 749 f. *tantum . . . quantum* (*-o . . . -o*).

Loire valley and the area of Beneventan dominance were the most promising regions in Europe for the survival of rare texts or rare branches of tradition.[17]

The strain of text represented by E was the single most influential component of the vulgate text of the *Metamorphoses* as it took shape in the late twelfth and thirteenth centuries.[18] From this period come several manuscripts clearly related to, although independent of, E; as a group they add virtually nothing of value to the information available in E, but individually each offers good readings not previously preserved:

a (k)   British Library, King's 26 (s. XII[1], Italy; Munari, 172).
e   Erfurt, Amplon. F. 1 (s. XII ex., Germany; Munari, 81), lacking 1.608–2.227.
g   Graz 1415 (s. XII/XIII; Munari, 102); related to FL.
h   Copenhagen Gl. Kgl. S. 2008 (s. XII ex. or XIII in., Italy?; Munari, 112).
(l)   Lucca, Bibl. Gov. 1417 (s. XII med., Italy?; Munari, 176), lacking 4.113–6.298 and 8.684–9.6.
(o)   Leiden, Voss. Lat. O. 51 (s. XII[2], France; Munari, 148).
p   Heidelberg, Pal. lat. 1661 (s. XII/XIII, Germany?; Munari, 115).
r   Vatican lat. 11457 (s. XII[2], Germany; not in Munari.)[19]
v   Vatican lat. 1593 (s. XII/XIII; Munari, 334).

Beyond this point distinct text-types can no longer be defined. True readings too subtle to be medieval conjectures turn up in individual manuscripts as late as the fourteenth century (the humanist manuscripts add little of interest), and further discoveries are still to be made.[20] Failing complete collations of all the manuscripts (nearly a lifetime's labour), an editor must exploit the information already available; the collations made by Nicolaus Heinsius in preparation for his edition of Ovid are an especially valuable resource.[21]

The foregoing summary can be depicted in a stemma, but it must be borne in mind that no stemmatic elimination of individual readings is possible. (Δ is used for the ancestor of the so-called 'Lactantian' group,

[17] Compare the remarks made above on the Montecassino manuscript of *Fasti* (U).
[18] It has also left its mark on the later 'Lactantians' RWZ, most deeply on W. A manuscript related to E (or perhaps more probably to the group aeghloprv) seems to have been used in the *Derivationes* of Osbern of Gloucester, completed between 1148 and 1179. (I am indebted to Mr David Carlson for information on this point.)
[19] Described by J. Ruysschaert, *Codices vaticani latini 11414–11709* (Vatican City, 1959), 92–3.
[20] For some examples from Paris lat. 8008 and Gotha Membr. II.58 see R. J. T., *CPh* 77 (1982), 352. The Greek translation of the *Metamorphoses* by the thirteenth-century Byzantine monk Maximus Planudes has been regarded (by Slater, for example) as a witness of unusual interest, but its value has shrunk with better knowledge of the twelfth-century tradition. (Edition by J. Boissonade, Paris, 1822.)
[21] On the identification of Heinsius's manuscripts of *Met.*, cf. F. Munari, *SIFC* NS 29 (1957), 98–114, 265; *Ovidiana*, ed. N. Herescu (Paris, 1958), 347–9; F. W. Lenz, *Eranos*, 51 (1953), 66–88, 61 (1963), 98–120; M. D. R., *RhM* 117 (1974), 149–56, 119 (1976), 67–8.

Σ for the source or sources of EFLPτ, φ for aeghloprv collectively, and (X) for the source of those ancient readings in EUφ not present in $\varDelta\Sigma$.)

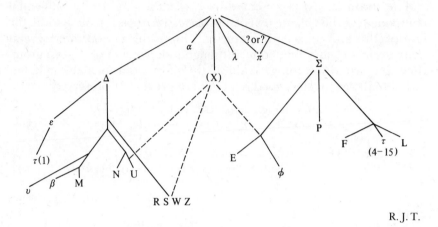

R. J. T.

Tristia

The textual history of the *Tristia* has not yet been seriously investigated. France and Germany will figure prominently in this story, since they provide nearly all the definite evidence of the text's medieval circulation down to the end of the eleventh century.[1] The *Tristia* were known to the scholars of twelfth-century Orléans, and this area may have played a part in the proliferation of copies from the second part of the century onwards.[2]

The *Tristia*, like the *Heroides, Metamorphoses*, and amatory poems, have

The basic discussions of the manuscript tradition are F. Tank's dissertation *De Tristibus Ovidi recensendis* (Greifswald, 1879) and the preface (xii–xciv) of S. G. Owen's *editio maior* (Oxford, 1889). Owen's edition also offers the fullest and most reliable critical apparatus now available. Other editions by Owen (OCT, 1915), R. Ehwald–F. W. Levy (= Lenz) (Teubner, 1922), J. André (Budé, 1968), G. Luck (Heidelberg, 1967–77, with commentary). No edition, however, reports all significant readings of the major manuscripts (MTr, AGHPV, DKT).

[1] This evidence includes imitations in writers of the ninth century (e.g. Theodulf, Mico of Saint-Riquier, Hrabanus Maurus, Walahfrid Strabo) and in French poets of the late eleventh century (Hildebert, Baudri), collections of excerpts (Paris, lat. 8069, s. XI, France; later note Douai 749, s. XII[2], perhaps Cambrai, and Heiligenkreuz 227, s. XII[2], south Germany/Austria), appearances in library catalogues (Bernardus, s. XI), and extant manuscripts (Tr and perhaps M, see below). Some part may have to be allotted to Italy as well, if the relatively early copy in Vat. Ottob. lat. 1469 is really of Italian origin (see n. 8, below).

[2] The excerpts from *Tristia* in the *Florilegium Gallicum* antedate all but a handful of surviving complete manuscripts, but have not been used by any editor. Collation of the excerpts from Books 1 and 2 in Paris lat. 17903 suggests that the text used by the compiler generally resembled that found in manuscripts such as DKT, with a somewhat closer affinity to D than to any other manuscript so far reported.

a complex and highly contaminated tradition, made even more difficult to sort out by the absence of early manuscripts. Only two extant witnesses clearly antedate the twelfth century, and neither of these is complete. One is a fragment in the Stadtbibliothek in Trier (Tr), two leaves of a manuscript (s. x) used in a binding, containing *Tristia* 1.11.1–31, 1.11.33–2.21; 4.4.35–65, 4.4.67–4.5.9.[3] The other is Florence, Laur. S. Marco 223 (M, s. xi ex.), containing 1.5.11–3.7.1 and 4.1.12–4.7.5 in two hands of uncertain geographical origin (the rest of the text has been supplied in a later hand (m), and is of no interest).[4] TrM are related, agreeing in both good and bad readings against other manuscripts. Each displays variants contemporary with the first hand, many of which reappear in later parts of the tradition.[5] At least some of these pairs of readings must have been present in a common source of MTr, and it is highly probable that some were already in the archetype of all manuscripts.

MTr perpetrate serious blunders,[6] but they preserve a distinctly purer text than any other manuscript or group of manuscripts, and it is unfortunate that neither is available for the whole collection. The remaining manuscripts illustrate the gradual formation of a vulgate text, and Nicolaus Heinsius (who did not know MTr) can be pardoned for declining to pass more time 'inter sordes exemplarium mendosissimorum'.[7] In this unruly mass two distinct groups have been isolated.[8] The first comprises five manuscripts:

[3] Published by R. Ehwald, *Ad historiam carminum Ovidianorum recensionemque symbolae*, ii (Gotha, 1892).

[4] Plate of f. 59ʳ (*Tr.* 1.5.11–1.6.35) in Owen, frontispiece. The manuscript is F in the tradition of *Metamorphoses* (= Munari, 177) and *Nux*, M in the *Medicamina*. *Nux* and *Med. fac.* appear together on f. 56ᵛ in a hand similar, but not identical, to one of those in the *Tristia*.

[5] e.g. 4.4.52 *locus* TrM (*recte*), *locum* M²GK; 58 *adit* TrM² (*recte*), *adis* M; 64 *spargitur* M (*recte*), *pascitur* M²TrAV; 1.11.31 *ad aethera* M, *substrata* M²Tr²G (*de* Tr¹ *non liquet*).

[6] M is more deeply corrupt than Tr, and indeed seems to have been copied from an exemplar in which the ends of many lines were damaged or illegible, giving rise to numerous grotesqueries (examples in Owen, xxxix).

[7] On 5.14.51, cited by Luck, 11.

[8] Descriptions in Owen, xii–xxviii. André groups the manuscripts differently, putting AGHKT in one class and D alone in another. He does not use H, P, V, and instead includes with AGKT in his second class Copenhagen Gl. Kgl. S. 2014 (F, s. xii) and Vatican, Ottob. lat. 1469, discussed by C. Questa, *Atti del Convegno Internazionale Ovidiano*, i (Rome, 1959), 81–90, and *Scriptorium*, 13 (1959), 217–32. The latter (which contains the text to 4.8.17 on ff. 23–40) is clearly of some interest; it is early (Questa dates it as s. xi/xii, but s. xii¹ is perhaps also possible) and may show a stage of the vulgate text prior to that found in the other manuscripts listed here. (At 2.8, for example, it gives *pridem iussa*, the first word agreeing with DKT and the second with MTr.) Unfortunately, Questa's collation in *Scriptorium* is highly selective and neither André nor Luck has gone beyond it. Questa shows that the Vatican manuscript is related to Oxford, Bodl. Rawlinson G. 101 (s. xv = Q), which Luck includes in his stemma as a late member of the AGHPV group. Collation of Ottob. lat. 1469 for Book 1 makes it clear that the manuscript ought to be reported more fully by a future editor. Besides showing noteworthy agreements in error with M, Tr, and A (1.2.92 *iuuant*, 1.5.62 *sarmaticosque*, 1.6.2 *clario*, 1.7.1 *nostros*, 1.8.33 *om. ante corr.*), it offers the earliest known attestation of several good readings (e.g. 1.1.2 *fuco*, 1.2.104 *tu rapius* (i.e. *tura pius*), 1.5.57 f. *neritio*, 1.10.35 *thiniacosque*).

A   Florence, S. Marco (s. XII–XIII?); now lost, and known from Poliziano's collation in a copy of the Parma 1477 edition now in the Bodleian (printed book Auct. P 2.2; Owen, xii–xvi).[9]

G   Wolfenbüttel, Gud. lat. 192 (s. XIII?).

H   British Library, Add. 49368, formerly Holkham Hall 322 (s. XIII[1], France, with links to Orléans).

P   Vatican, Pal. lat. 910 (c.1467, Italy, perhaps Rimini).

V   Vatican lat. 1606 (s. XII/XIII, Italy).

The second consists of four codices:

D   Gotha Membr. II.122 (s. XIII); lacking 3.2.6–3.12.50.

G[2]   Readings of the second hand in G.

K   Leiden, B. P. L. 177 (s. XIII ex.).

T   Tours Bibl. Mun. 879 (s. XIII[1] France,), an *Opera omnia Ovidi* (plate of 4.10.83–5.1.68 in Owen, facing p. 1).

AGHPV and DG²KT represent two phases in the development of the vulgate. The AGHPV group is capable of blatant interpolation (e.g. 1.8.41 *nati* for *venae*, corrupted to *neve* in M), but remains in general closer to the genuine text; it shows nothing remotely comparable to DK²T's rewriting of 5.1.18 *aptior, ingenium come, Tibullus erit* as *et plures quorum nomina magna vigent*.[10]

A stemmatic depiction of the relationships of MTr, AGHPV, and DG²KT is complicated by extensive horizontal movement of variants, especially in the latter two groups; a stemma that makes allowances for all the facts will be so open as to be of little practical value.[11] True readings can be found in any of the three groups (least often in AGHPV except where M is lacking) and also in any one of the major manuscripts (usually in agreement with other *recentiores*).

Manuscripts other than MTr AGHPV DG²KT cannot be disregarded, and their contribution goes beyond correction of archetypal errors. Places like 1.11.9, where three later manuscripts agree with Tr's *ipse etenim* for *ipse ego nunc* (present in Tr as a variant reading), or 2.11, where the true reading *curae* was known only from Heinsian manuscripts until it was found in Tr, show clearly that traditional variants can bypass the major manuscripts and surface only in *recentiores*. Especially where Tr and M are not available, the editor must cast the net widely[12] and recognize readings of merit whatever their provenance.

R. J. T.

[9] André (xxxvi) cites I. Maier for the view that the collations are in the hand of a pupil rather than that of Poliziano himself.

[10] On the character of the two groups cf. Luck, 15–17; Owen, lxvii–xciv, offers a valuable summary of the faults of the transmission in general.

[11] Luck's stemma (p. 18) illustrates the difficulty: for example, the common source of AGHPV (N) is shown as a blend of two copies of the archetype, of which the second had been contaminated from the first before N was written.

[12] In Owen's more exalted metaphor, 'Acheronta, ut ita dicam, saepe mouendum esse confirmo' (p. xlviii, a precept followed perhaps too faithfully in his apparatus).

PSEUDO-OVID

Nux

This curious elegy, the most accomplished of pseudo-Ovidian poems,[1] has a suitably intriguing textual history. Quite unknown in the Carolingian period, the *Nux* suddenly comes to light in several parts of Europe in the decades before and after 1100. The earliest extant copy was written in England, perhaps at Sherborne (Oxford, Bodl. Auct. F. 2.14, s. XI^2 = O_1); in it the *Nux* appears amid texts used in teaching grammar and composition.[2] The work's pedagogic value was also acknowledged early in the twelfth century by Conrad of Hirsau, who listed it among Ovid's morally unobjectionable poems in his *Dialogus super auctores*.[3] In the next oldest copy, Florence, Laur. S. Marco 223 (s. XI ex., France? = F), the *Nux* appears together with the *Medicamina faciei femineae* (q.v.). This combination recurs in many *recentiores*[4] and may in fact be archetypal; if so, the absence of *Med. fac.* from the Oxford manuscript may be a result of that work's unsuitability for scholastic use. Neither O_1 nor F seems directly responsible for any of the other surviving manuscripts.[5] The *Nux* appears next in the collections of *Ovidiana* put together mainly in northern and central France from the late twelfth century onwards.[6]

As in the case of the *Ibis*, all extant manuscripts derive from a lost archetype (perhaps as late as s. X) in which a spurious couplet had been added in the margin: some manuscripts incorporated the lines after 178, others after 176.[7] As with the *Medicamina*, F and the consensus of other manuscripts are independent witnesses to the text of the archetype; it

The Paravia edition by F. W. Lenz (2nd edn., 1956) contains much information on the manuscripts (pp. 75–125) and an apparatus in which the readings of forty-three manuscripts and early editions are reported with undiscriminating zeal.

[1] Cf. A. G. Lee in *Ovidiana*, ed. N. Herescu (Paris, 1958), 457–71.

[2] See *Survival* 66–7, with plate of f. 11^r, no XX(a). Lenz cites O_1 in only a handful of places, even though he had been informed of its early date and given some account of its readings by R. W. Hunt and R. A. B. Mynors. The textual information about O_1 given here derives from a collation very kindly made by M. D. R.

[3] Ed. R. B. C. Huyghens (Brussels, 1955), 51.

[4] For example, in all the manuscripts listed above for *Med. fac.* except Ce and N_b (not mentioned by Lenz), and also in Vat. Chigi H. VI.205 (s. XV), Pal. lat. 910, Urb. lat. 347, Florence, Laur. 36.2, Bibl. Naz. Magl. VII.966, and B. L. Sloane 777 (all s. XV).

[5] The *Nux*, though, figures in the twelfth-century catalogues of Durham and Canterbury without the *Med. fac.*, a fact which might suggest a link with O_1.

[6] The excerpts from *Nux* in Douai 749 (s. XII^2, perhaps Cambrai) may be slightly earlier than all full texts except for O_1 and F; cf. B. Munk Olsen, *RHT* 9 (1979), 91–2.

[7] Other permutations also occur; only Venice, Marc. Lat. XII. 85 (4169) (s. XV) has removed the lines, cf. Oxford, Bodl. Canon. Class. Lat. 20 in *Ibis* (q. v.).

seems possible, though not certain, that the manuscripts other than F all derive from a single copy.[8] From among these manuscripts the following seem to merit notice (besides those listed for the *Medicamina*):

A   Antwerp 68 (s. XII/XIII, northern France/Belgium?), a corpus of Ovidian elegy.

A₁   Milan, Ambros. H. 225 inf. (s. XV), the 'Ambrosianus' of Heinsius. It is noteworthy for several agreements with F in error against all or nearly all other codices (36 *conspiciantur* (*percutiantur*), 75 *a tribus* (*quattuor*), 130 *nam* (*non*)).[9]

D   Dresden A 167ᵃ (s. XII?), destroyed in 1945.

F₂   Frankfurt, Univ. Barth. 110 (s. XV, probably a replacement copy of part of a s. XIII¹ French text).

V   Vatican lat. 9991 (s. XII², France).

The manuscripts of the *Nux* are unusually fertile in variants, and the process of proliferation is already far advanced at the earliest visible stage of the tradition. For example, lines 30–1 are found in the form *audiat hoc cerasus, bacas exire vetabit:/audiat hoc ficus, stipes inanis erit* only in F and one other manuscript (A₁), and several other versions of the couplet turn up in the *recentiores*; the most varied assortment (five hexameters and two pentameters), however, appears in the text and margins of O₁, the oldest manuscript of all. It is also noteworthy that several manuscripts of more than average interest (A₁, O₁, V) contain numerous nonsensical and unmetrical readings; the progenitor of the manuscripts other than F might have been unusually corrupt.

R. J. T.

---

[8] Errors of F from which others are free: e.g. 60 *poena* (*paene*), 74 *petat* (*-it*), 77 *iuvet ... optet* (*iubet .. . optat*), 95 *tenet os in* (*tenero est in/tenero de*), 106 *fraudis* (*fraudi/causa*), 176 *sed non metus* (*sed metus*), 181 *urar est nec* (*urar nec*). Errors common to all (or virtually all) manuscripts other than F: 45 *soli* (*solam*), 152 *manet/sedet* (*sua*).

[9] A₁ also shows significant agreements with B. L. Sloane 777 (Rome, *c.*1470, written by Pomponio Leto) and with the 1471 Rome edition.

PALLADIUS

Known to Cassiodorus and Isidore of Seville, the work of Palladius seems to have survived into the early Middle Ages in only one copy. From this was derived, possibly in the closing years of the eighth century, ω, the lost archetype of all our manuscripts, containing the complete work, that is to say the fourteen prose books and the *Carmen de insitione*. For unknown reasons, the earliest surviving manuscripts contain only Books 1–13, all deriving from one lost copy (α) which probably had its origin in north-eastern France. The most valuable members of this class are:

D   Cambridge, University Library Kk. 5.13, s. $IX^2/4$, written at Saint-Denis, formerly in the collection of Bishop Moore.

P   Paris lat. 6842B, s. IX^1, probably coming from the Loire valley, and textually close to D.

K   Montpellier 305, s. IX med., probably from southern France.

J   Paris n. a. lat. 1730, s. IX^2, written in north-east France.

L   Laon 426 bis, s. $IX^4/4$, written in north-east France.

A different tradition is to be found in two other manuscripts:

M   Milan, Ambros. C.212 inf., s. XIII/XIV, written in the north of Italy (school of Bologna). This book was almost certainly copied directly from a lost ninth-century text (β), and has the distinction of containing all fourteen prose books and the *Carmen de insitione*, thus suggesting that its text goes back to the complete ω.

V   Vienna 148, s. X med., probably written in southern Germany, and containing only Books 1–13. Its basic text presents routine α readings; but its interest lies in the numerous corrections (known by the siglum V^2, also s. X) inserted throughout. These readings derive from a source close to M's ninth-century ancestor β.

Somewhat more difficult to place, but none the less valuable are:

G   Leiden, B.P.L. 102, s. $IX^3/4$, written in western Germany or the Low Countries, and formerly in the library of the abbey at Egmond.

S   Paris lat. 6830E, s. XI, carrying the *ex libris* of the Abbaye-de-la-Sainte-Trinité at Vendôme.

While both G and S show evidence of much contamination, some good readings suggest that at some stage G and S bypass both the

---

The standard edition is the Teubner text of R. H. Rodgers (1975), which must be consulted in conjunction with his study *An Introduction to Palladius*, *BICS* Suppl. 35 (1975), which contains plates of DPGSVMv. See also the article 'Palladius' by Rodgers in *CTC* iii (Washington, 1976), 195–9.

hyparchetypes α and β, and derive their qualities from the archetype ω itself.

For Book 14 the evidence is remarkably meagre; and indeed the *editio princeps* (by J. Svennung) did not come until 1926. Other than M (discussed above), the only full witness, containing only Book 14, is v (Leiden, Vulc. 90 B, XVI ex.). Further help is available from two sets of excerpts, possibly both derived from a twelfth-century model. These are:

b   Vatican, Barb. lat. 12, s. XIII, written in France.
      A text so far lacking a siglum,[1] in the library at Oscott College, Birmingham (MS 20). This was written in northern Italy, possibly at Milan, s. XV med.

For the *Carmen de insitione* the evidence is slightly more plentiful, but (other than M discussed above) no witness is earlier than the middle of the fifteenth century. There are strong indications that (apart from M) this poem first came to the attention of humanists in Florence in that century. Forming a close unit are:

H   Vatican lat. 5245.
A   Vienna 3198, part of a collection probably put together by Giorgio Antonio Vespucci. The Palladius is in the hand of Niccolò Fonzio.
m   Madrid 1482, copied at Florence for Marino Tomacelli by Sinibaldus.
P   Harvard College Library, lat. 124, written by Jacopo di Poggio.

Standing apart from the above four witnesses is a group represented[2] by:

U   Munich Clm 454.
q   Venice, Biblioteca Querini Stampalia IX.14.
k   Hannover, Niedersächsische Landesbibliothek 505.

Also of some interest is e, the *editio princeps* (Jenson, Venice, 1472).

The editor of Palladius must also pay great attention to his sources, particularly the work of Columella, whom Palladius frequently follows very closely.

P. K. M.

[1] A preliminary report on this unused witness is given in P. K. M.'s review of Rodgers, *CPh* 73 (1978), 76–7. Although the Oscott manuscript was unknown to him at the time, much of value can be found in P. P. Corsetti, 'A propos d'une édition récente de Palladius. Remarques sur la tradition manuscrite et le texte du livre XIV', *Latomus*, 37 (1978), 726–46. See now Corsetti, 'Le Manuscrit Birmingham, Oscott College 20 et la tradition du texte de Palladius (livre XIV)', *REL* 57 (1979), 42–8.

[2] To the manuscripts of this group known to Rodgers may be added: Rome, Bibl. Naz., Vitt. Eman. 1417, and Vatican lat. 5185.

PANEGYRICI LATINI

The *Panegyricus* of Pliny the Younger was well known in late Antiquity.
It was a primary model for a collection of later encomia of fourth-
century emperors, with which it is often associated in the manuscripts,
and even as late as the seventh century it was used by Isidore for his
mosaic-like *Institutionum Disciplinae.*[1] The earliest witness to Pliny's text
is, indeed, still earlier than Isidore: a Bobbio palimpsest, Milan,
Ambros. E.147 sup. (CLA I.29, III. p. 20), in half-uncials of the sixth
century (R), a fragment containing parts of chapters 7–8, 78–80, and
85–6. The Middle Ages, however, seem to have been unaware of the
work, and it was not rediscovered until 1433, when Giovanni Aurispa
found an apparently ancient manuscript of the whole collection at
Mainz. This Moguntinus (M) did not survive. But it left behind
sufficient progeny to enable us to reconstruct it. On the one hand, we
have nearly thirty Italian manuscripts (to which may be added another
twelve with Pliny's panegyric alone), falling into two groups X1 and
X2, whose consensus (X) would seem to give the readings of Aurispa's
transcript of M. On the other,[2] we have a small German family headed
by British Library, Harley 2480 (H), the exemplar of the once prized
Uppsala C.917 via Cluj-Napoca lat. 7 (*olim* 168).[3]

   A lost Bertinensis, apparently a twin of M, bequeathed some readings to Livineius's edition of 1599; and Cuspinianus's edition of 1513
also seems to have had access to truths independent[4] of the
Moguntinus.[5]

M. W.

---

[1] See P. Pascal, *Traditio*, 13 (1957), 424–31.

[2] That H descends from M is disputed by P. Fedeli in his edition (Rome, 1976), xxvii–xxviii;
but see my review in *CR* 29 (1979), 234–5.

[3] See the OCT edition of R. A. B. Mynors (1964), vii; confirmed by D. Lassandro, *Bollettino*, 15
(1967), 55–97. For description and photograph see S. Jakó, *Revista Arhivelor*, 10 (1967), 58–62.

[4] See further W. Schetter, *Gnomon*, 39 (1967), 502–4; Fedeli, xxix–xxxvi.

[5] My account is based on the preface of Mynors's model edition. Fedeli's edition gives
bibliography and lists more conjectures than Mynors's. The first edition is that of Puteolanus
(Milan, ?1482). Chatelain, CXLIV gives a plate of Paris lat. 7840.

JULIUS PARIS, *Epitome of Valerius Maximus*
POMPONIUS MELA, *De chorographia*
VIBIUS SEQUESTER, *De fluminibus*

These three texts, which survive in a large number of fifteenth-century manuscripts, descend from a sixth-century edition made in Ravenna; they are preserved in a single manuscript of the ninth century, Vatican lat. 4929, owned and annotated by Heiric of Auxerre, and are transmitted to the fifteenth century via a copy owned and annotated by Petrarch. The history of MS 4929 and that of the three texts have been examined extensively by C. W. Barlow and by G. Billanovich, who discovered the identity of the participants in this story.[1]

Vatican lat. 4929 (V), containing Censorinus, *De die natali*; a unique epitome of Augustine, *De musica*; four anonymous sermons; Ps.-Plautus, *Aulularia sive Querolus*; Julius Paris, *Epitome of Valerius Maximus*; *Septem mira*; Pomponius Mela, *De chorographia*; and Vibius Sequester, *De fluminibus*, was written in France in the middle of the ninth century, and belonged to Heiric of Auxerre, who was probably responsible for assembling the collection. Three of the works, those of Julius Paris, Pomponius Mela, and Vibius Sequester, bear subscriptions indicating that they had been 'edited' in the sixth century by Rusticius Helpidius Domnulus of Ravenna. It has been suggested that Heiric acquired a sixth-century manuscript of the edition from his master Lupus of Ferrières; Lupus used either the old manuscript or V to correct his own copy of Valerius Maximus. It has also been suggested that the annotations and corrections in Heiric's own hand indicate that he corrected V against its old exemplar.

How the old Ravenna collection came into Heiric's or Lupus's hands is not known.[2] Once the texts were in V, however, their history can be

---

[1] C. W. Barlow, 'Codex Vaticanus Latinus 4929', *MAAR* 15 (1939), 87–124; G. Billanovich, 'Dall'antica Ravenna alle biblioteche umanistiche', *Aevum*, 30 (1956), 319–62. For editions of some of these texts, see G. Ranstrand, *Pomponii Melae de chorographia libri tres* (Göteborg, 1971); R. Gelsomino, *Vibius Sequester* (Leipzig, 1967); C. Kempf, *Valerius Maximus* (Leipzig, 1888).

[2] 'Aethicus Ister', the pseudonymous (eighth-century?) author of a *Cosmographia*, borrowed much from Mela's *De chorographia* for his own work; almost certainly he was using the same sixth-century codex that later reached Lupus and Heiric. In addition, it is likely that the old collection was once in the hands of an Irishman, who added to Mela's characterization of the Irish as 'omnium virtutum ignari magis quam aliae gentes' (3.53) the corrective gloss, 'aliquatenus tamen gnari', which has dropped into the text of V. It has previously been accepted that 'Aethicus Ister' was the Irishman Virgil, Bishop of Salzburg (746–84), who might have acquired the old Ravenna manuscript in Italy on one of his trips south and who might, also, be responsible for the pro-Irish gloss. Recently, however, this identification has been disputed. Perhaps the promised edition of Aethicus Ister will fill some of the gaps in our knowledge of the whereabouts of the Ravenna collection.

followed closely. V's *De chorographia* was used in the second half of the ninth century by the anonymous author of the *De situ orbis* (Leiden, Voss. Lat. F.113), who worked in Auxerre.[3] By the tenth century V had been moved to Orléans, where it acquired extensive annotations in the early twelfth century. In the middle of that century the text of Julius Paris in V was excerpted at Orléans in Vatican, Pal. lat. 957. The continued presence of V at Orléans is attested in the thirteenth century, when the annotator of Berne 276 quoted two of its works (Censorinus, *De die natali*, and the *Querolus*). While nothing further is known of its physical movement until it appears in Italy in the possession of Serafino Nibia of Novara in the fifteenth century, V's influence can be traced in its offspring.

There are three pre-Renaissance descendants of V's *De chorographia*. The oldest of these is a single leaf, now Paris lat. 152, f. 32 (P), from a mid-twelfth-century manuscript. It contains *De chorographia*, 1.13–1.36, ending at the bottom of the verso with 'cog[nomen]'. A direct copy of P, and of the leaf (now missing) which preceded it, survives in Vendôme 189, ff. 65–8 (s. XIII med., Mont-Saint-Michel), which contains *De chorographia* from its beginning to 1.36, where it stops with the same incomplete 'cog-'; the remainder of the page and the rest of the quire (ff. 69–72) are blank. P is probably a fragment of a manuscript left by Philip of Bayeux to Bec in 1164 and recorded in the Bec catalogue: 'In alio Pomponius Mela de cosmographia et Tullius de fine boni et mali et de academicis et Timeus Platonis ab ipso Tullio translatus et Tullius de particione oratoria et liber Candidi Ariani ad Victorinum de generatione divina et Hilarius de sinodiis et eiusdem liber contra Valentem et Auxentium' (Becker, 86.64, p. 201); for the Vendôme manuscript contains *Ad Victorinum* and the works of Hilarius, as well as the Mela fragment. A number of Mont-Saint-Michel books were copied from Bec exemplars. Evidently when Vendôme 189 was written, Philip's manuscript had lost the first four works, save for the (loose?) initial leaves.

A third manuscript, Florence, Laur. S. Marco 341 (F), containing *De chorographia*, Apuleius, *De deo Socratis, Trismegistus Mercurii*, Apuleius, *De habitudine, doctrina, et nativitate Platonis*, was written in central France in the third quarter of the twelfth century and belonged to Niccolò Niccoli; however, neither its medieval home nor its origin is known. Two manuscripts of the *De chorographia* are recorded by Bernard Itier in the catalogue of Saint-Martial-de-Limoges: '48. Trogus Pompeius, Suetonius de gestis duodecim Caesarum, Gneus Florus, Valerius Maxmus, Pomponius Mela', and '126. Pomponius Mela'. The Florence manuscript is clearly not that described in no. 48, but it might be no.

[3] R. Quadri (ed.), *Anonymi Leidensis de situ orbis libri duo*, Thesaurus mundi, 13 (Padua, 1974), esp. xxxviii–xliii.

126 – since the Mela text forms the bulk of the Florence codex, and the Apuleius begins on a verso, without rubric.

Collation indicates that F and P have as a common ancestor a lost copy of V's Mela, α, doubtless written at Orléans. In addition, Paris, Arsenal 711 (s. XII ex., Saint-Victor), one of the earliest manuscripts of the *Florilegium Gallicum* (compiled at Orléans), once contained the *De chorographia*, according to the fifteenth-century catalogue of Saint-Victor; this portion of the manuscript is now missing.

From these manuscripts, excerpts, and catalogue notices of Mela's *De chorographia* one can see that although MS 4929 was, as Billanovich puts it, 'congelato in una vecchia biblioteca' – probably the chapter library of Orléans Cathedral – it was sufficiently accessible that portions of it were copied on occasion. A fragment of at least a partial copy, written in the second half of the twelfth century, is now Vatican, Reg. lat. 314, part VI, containing the end of the *Querolus* and the beginning of Julius Paris' *Epitome*. There is no published evidence that this is a descendant, rather than a *gemellus*, of the manuscript later copied by Petrarch, as Billanovich has suggested; and, for the present, one may assume that Reg. lat. 314. VI is derived directly from V. V's *De fluminibus* was copied once in the twelfth century, producing Vatican, Reg. lat. 1561, part I, containing Palladius (fragment), Vibius Sequester, *De fluminibus*, the *Septem mira*, Ps.-Seneca, *Monita*, *De moribus* (extract), and *Sententiae theologiae*. It belonged to Pierre Daniel in the sixteenth century.

Petrarch obtained at least a partial copy of Vat. lat. 4929 by the year 1335, probably at Avignon; another copy, perhaps Petrarch's exemplar, appears in the catalogues of the papal library in the late fourteenth and early fifteenth centuries. Petrarch's manuscript no longer survives; but, as the source of all the Renaissance Italian copies of these works, it can be reconstructed from its descendants, in particular Milan, Ambros. H. 14 inf., Paris lat. 4800, and Vat. lat. 4496, all of the fifteenth century. There is no published evidence for assuming, as Billanovich does, that Petrarch's manuscript dated from the twelfth century. It must remain questionable whether or not Petrarch's manuscript contained Julius Paris' *Epitome*, since none of its descendants has copied that text.

R. H. R.

PERSIUS

The oldest extant witness, Vatican lat. 5750 (s. VI[1] = *Bob.*),[1] probably Italian and at Bobbio in the seventh century, is written in splendid rustic capitals. Yet it is sadly unrewarding: it preserves only *Sat.* 1. 53–104, and offers an undistinguished text which does not tell us anything about its history.

Our main knowledge of Persius comes from two sources. The first is P (Montpellier 125), written at Lorsch,[2] s. IX[1] (Chatelain, plate CXXIII), formerly owned by Pierre Pithou, and also containing Juvenal. It has the strange title[3] *Thebaidorum Persi Satura.* The choliambics are missing in the first hand, and a later hand (s. X) puts them before the text. The only other witness close to P is *Sang.* (St. Gall 870), s. IX¾ or IX/X, a florilegium containing scattered verses from Persius and Juvenal.

The other stream of transmission is represented by two manuscripts which must be *gemelli*.[4] The first is A (Montpellier 212) (Chatelain, plate CXXII), s. X[1], France, which has the choliambics *after* the *Satires*. After the choliambics comes a subscription (in capitals) present in B also, which, when corrected, runs: 'Flavius Julius Tryfonianus Sabinus Vir Clarissimus Protector Domesticus Temptavi Emendare Sine Antigrapho Meum et Adnotavi Barcellone [i.e. at Barcelona] Consulibus Dominis Nostris Archadio et Honorio Quintum [AD 402].' At the beginning of the *Satires* in the left margin, a different hand (again in capitals) puts in A (but not in B): 'Iulius Tryfonianus Sabinus Protector Domesticus Legi Meum Dominis Nostris Arcadio et Honorio Quinquies Consulibus Prout Potui Sine Magistro Emendans Adnotavi Anno Aetatis XXXmo et Militiae Quarto in Civitate Tolosa [i.e. Toulouse]'.[5] B (Vatican, Arch. S. Pietro H. 36, s. IX ex., France) (Chatelain, plate

---

The only worthwhile editions are by W. V. Clausen: a separate text of Persius (Oxford, 1956) and the OCT of Persius and Juvenal (1959).

[1] *CLA.*I.30. See also S. Monti, 'Contenuto e struttura del fascicolo che comprese il foglio di Bobbio (Vat. 5750) di Giovenale e Persio', *Annali della Facoltà di Lettere e Filosofia della Università di Napoli*, 11 (1964–8), 57–68.

[2] For date and provenance see most recently Clausen (review of D. Bo's edition), *Gnomon*, 47 (1975), 142–5, who cites the authority of B. Bischoff. This review contains valuable supplements to Clausen's 1956 edition.

[3] For an ingenious attempt to explain the title see O. Seel, 'Zum Persius-Titel des codex Pithoeanus', *Hermes*, 88 (1960), 82–98.

[4] The history of A and B has been worked out with great ingenuity by Clausen, 'Sabinus' MS of Persius', *Hermes*, 91 (1963), 252–6. Of interest for the text as a whole is N. Scivoletto, 'I codici di Persio e la loro autorevolezza', *GIF* 9 (1956), 289–304. The fundamental principles for the constitution of the text were first evolved by Otto Jahn in his 1843, Leipzig edition.

[5] Given here is an expanded version of the text as emended by Clausen (based on Jahn), p. viii of his 1956 edition. As the margin in A has been closely trimmed, this cannot all be read now.

CXXI) likewise has the order *Satires* followed by choliambics. The immediate lost ancestor of A and B (known as α) was itself demonstrably a ninth-century book.

Close to the combined witness of *Bob.*, P, *Sang.*, α is V (Vat. Reg. lat. 1560, s. X, Fleury or Auxerre). It contains only a fragmentary text of the *Satires*, but has the *Vita* and part of the so-called *Commentum Cornuti*. Of value also is X (Vat. Pal. lat. 1710), s. IX med./IX¾ (area of Tours), containing the choliambics and *Satires*, 1.1–5.171.[6]

While the text can be largely based on the above witnesses, a great number of good, early manuscripts survive which are *not* derived from them, and thus have independent value of their own. The tradition is so mixed that no *stemma codicum* can be presented.[7] A list of the seven most important manuscripts (whose agreement is designated with the siglum *Φ* by Clausen) is:

C   Paris lat. 8055, s. X/XI (southern France) (Chatelain, plate CXXV); choliambics and *Satires*.

G   Berne 257, s. X[1], France; choliambics and *Satires*.

L   Leiden, B. P. L. 78, s XI;[8] *Vita*, choliambics, *Satires*, *Commentum Cornuti*.

M   Munich Clm 23577, s. XI; choliambics, *Satires* (omitting 4.49–5.163), *Vita*, *Commentum Cornuti*.

N   Munich Clm 14498, s. XI, written at the monastery of St. Emmeram in Regensburg; *Vita*, choliambics, *Satires*.

R   Florence, Laur. 37.19, s. X/XI; *Vita* (abridged), choliambics, *Satires*.

W   Munich Clm 330, s. X ex., Germany; choliambics, *Satires*.

As other manuscripts may carry authoritative readings, editors have also availed themselves of the occasional help of witnesses outside this list.[9]

Besides the manuscripts of the text itself, help must also be sought from the so-called *Commentum Cornuti*[10] and the *Vita*. In the *Commentum*, the lemmata (and to a lesser extent the interpretations) are occasionally

---

[6] X was promoted to this more important position by Clausen in his 1959 OCT edition. This manuscript contains yet another text of Persius (choliambics and *Satires*, 1.1–4.28), s. X, on which see V. M. Lagorio, 'The Second Persius Manuscript in Codex Vat. Pal. lat. 1710', *CB* 53 (1975), 10–12.

[7] Note the plea by O. Seel in his review of Clausen's edition, *Gnomon*, 32 (1960), 119–28.

[8] For the date of L see Bischoff quoted by Clausen, *Gnomon*, 47 (1975), 144.

[9] Most recently a claim has been made for the value of Perugia H.55 by M. C. Lungarotti, 'Su un manoscritto di Persio', *GIF* 27 (1975), 215–17.

[10] For the text of the scholia, one still has to go back to Jahn's 1843, Leipzig edition. A new Teubner text is in preparation by Clausen and J. E. G. Zetzel. See Zetzel, 'On the History of Latin Scholia II: The *Commentum Cornuti* in the Ninth Century', *Medievalia et Humanistica*, 10 (1981), 19–31. Of interest is S. Jannaccone, 'Rapporti di codici nella tradizione degli scolii a Persio', *GIF* 12 (1959), 198–213. In addition, an eleventh-century commentary from Liège is reported by Bischoff, 'Living with the Satirists', in *Classical Influences on European Culture A.D. 500–1500*, ed. R. R. Bolgar (1971), 83–94 (= *Mitt. Stud.* iii. 260–70); and twelfth-century notes are given by G. de Poerck, 'L'Horace, le Perse et la Glose sur le Cantique des cantiques du ms. Paris B. N. lat. 11312, du XII[c] siècle', *Scriptorium*, 14 (1960), 61–74. Of great interest is the article 'Persius' by D. M. Robathan, F. E. Kranz, P. O. Kristeller, and Bischoff in *CTC* iii (Washington, 1976), 201–312.

of use in restoring the text. Clausen uses L, M (see above), and U (Munich Clm 14482), s. XI/XII, from the monastery of St. Emmeram at Regensburg.

For the *Vita*, Clausen uses mainly LMNV (see above), T (Cambridge, Trinity College 1241 (O.4.10)), English, s. X[2], from St. Augustine's Canterbury,[11] and H (Wolfenbüttel, Gud. lat. 79, s. XI).

P. K. M.

[11] Ker[2], 42.

PETRONIUS

Three discoveries in successive centuries made the text of Petronius what it is today. The stemma below relates to the first; the second and third will be accommodated later.

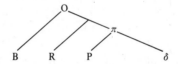

When Poggio in 1420 reported to Niccoli from England his discovery of Petronius, well might Niccoli ask what Petronius had to say. On receiving δ he found out, at least so far as the Carolingian scholar who excerpted O from a manuscript of *Satyrica* allowed him to find out. The many descendants of δ, itself lost, include the *editio princeps* (Milan, c.1482), which for almost a century provided all of Petronius that circulated in print. Oddly R, Paris lat. 6842D (s. XII[2]), seems to have arrived in Italy by s. XIV, and Fr. Barbaro (1390–1454) was one of its owners; but only its first part, Palladius, aroused interest.[1] B, Berne 357, ff. 34ᵛ–41ᵛ + Leiden, Voss. Lat. Q. 30, ff. 57–8 (s. IX[2]), and P, Paris lat. 8049 (s. XII[2]), are the Autissiodurensis and Bituricus used by P. Pithou in s. XVI[2]; his designations reveal that B had belonged to Saint-Germain-d'Auxerre, P to Jean Duc de Berry (1340–1416).[2] B is

[1] On R and the descendants of δ see A. C. de la Mare, 'The Return of Petronius to Italy', in *Medieval Learning*, 220–54.

[2] Both equations have been disputed, that of the Bituricus with P for trifling reasons. E. T. Sage, *CPh* 11 (1916), 21–3, argues against the other and in favour of assigning B to Fleury; but B. C. B.-B., 'The Manuscripts of Macrobius' Commentary on the *Somnium Scipionis*' (D. Phil. thesis, Oxford, 1975), ii. 337–68, after a thorough discussion of all the manuscripts that once made up a volume with B, concludes that the volume 'was probably written at and certainly belonged to the Abbey of St Germain at Auxerre'.

not only the oldest but the best member of the group. P contains amongst other things Calpurnius (1.1–4.12), so that when Poggio in 1423 asks Niccoli to return 'Bucolicam Calpurnii et particulam Petronii quas misi tibi ex Britannia' he is probably referring to a single manuscript.

The sixteenth century went outside O and more than doubled the text. By 1562 Cujas was quoting legal novelties, and by 1565 Pithou could be coy about 'meo libro, cuius ego procacitatem, petulantiam et lasciviam privato carcere ita damnavi ut tamen eius copiam viris optimis et amicissimis non negem', presumably the 'vetus Benedictinum exemplar' mentioned in his edition. Had one of the distinguished scholars who seized on the new material simply published it as it stood, modern editors would have fewer headaches and the history of the transmission would be far clearer. Instead, whether in preparing the first edition of the enlarged text (*editio Tornaesiana*, Lyon, 1575), or in writing out a personal copy as Scaliger for one did (Leiden, Scal. 61, *c*.1571), they started from the text already in print and came out with a conflation.[3] That they also consulted the *Florilegium Gallicum* is less of a nuisance, because their manuscripts survive.[4]

From France to Dalmatia. About 1650 Marino Statileo found at Trogir a descendant of δ augmented by the *Cena Trimalchionis* and headed 'Petronii Arbitri Satyri fragmenta ex libro quintodecimo et sextodecimo'. Its origin is not in doubt. On 28 May 1423 Poggio wrote to Niccoli from Rome, 'allatus est mihi ex Colonia XV liber Petronii Arbitri, quem curavi transcribendum modo cum illac iter feci'; and the Traguriensis, now Paris lat. 7989 (H), dates from late 1423 or soon after. Wherever written, most probably at Florence, it must have been whisked across the Adriatic, and Poggio's copy from Cologne left no other trace.[5] The full *Cena* was served up to the learned public in 1664; within two years Statileo had to undertake 'Petroniani fragmenti assertionem ac vindicias contra temerarios criticos vel potius calumniatores';[6] and in 1669 appeared the first edition to contain everything now known of *Satyrica*.[7]

Since Buecheler published his *editio maior* (Berlin, 1862) so much

---

[3] Besides the witnesses just named, the others concerned are Pithou's editions (Paris, 1577[1], 1587[2]) and three manuscripts derived from the Memmianus, H. de Mesme's copy of the Benedictinus. The editions all contain explicit statements about certain readings.

[4] Pithou used Paris lat. 17903 (s. XIII), Daniel Paris lat. 7647 (s. XII[2]). See B. L. Ullman, *CPh* 25 (1930), 144–5, 151–2.

[5] On the history of H see A. C. de la Mare (n. 1, above), 239–51; S. Gaselee published a complete facsimile of the *Cena* (Cambridge, 1915). For illustrations of other manuscripts, including BP, see G. Brugnoli, *Petronius* (Rome, 1961).

[6] *Marini Statilei Traguriensis i.c. responsio ad Ioh. Christoph. Wagenseilii et Hadriani Valesii dissertationes de Traguriensi Petronii fragmento* (Paris, 1666).

[7] For more information about editions or anything else published on Petronius, see G. L. Schmeling and Johanna H. Stuckey, *A Bibliography of Petronius, Mnem.* Suppl. 39 (1977).

work has been done on the tradition, especially by American scholars and by K. Müller, that no edition earlier than Müller's (Munich, 1961[1], 1965[2], 1978[3]) can safely be used, and even Müller's is in some respects out of date. In presentation and in critical penetration, however, it sets a high standard; furthermore, Müller's survey of the tradition ([1]Latin, [2]German) has no rival for lucidity and comprehensiveness,[8] and the different views taken by H. van Thiel and C. Pellegrino rest almost entirely on his material. The following exposition, which stays within bounds by not going into detail about the sixteenth-century witnesses, includes only one piece of new evidence and no new ideas beyond what this suggests.[9]

Müller depicts the relationship between O and the manuscripts of Cujas and Pithou as follows ([1]xxxv):

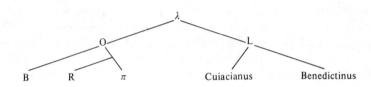

L, he supposes, reproduced the excerpts assembled in λ, while O cut them down further. Pellegrino, however, has pointed to firm evidence that the Cuiacianus omitted much of the *Bellum civile* (119–24); it must therefore be through conflation that its descendants in s. xvi give the longer text of O.[10] Elsewhere R. Merkelbach had already inferred such conflation, not necessarily in s. xvi, from errors of Lπ; and before that E. T. Sage and B. L. Ullman had inferred it from the curious fact that in *Cena*, 37.6–end L has nothing but the one excerpt in O and the seven in the *Florilegium Gallicum* (φ).[11] H. van Thiel, who proves not only L but also φ composite, puts both processes of conflation in s. xii and offers this stemma:[12]

[8] T. Wade Richardson, 'Problems in the Text-history of Petronius in Antiquity and the Middle Ages', *AJP* 96 (1975), 290–305, offers nothing fresh and misses the articles cited below in n. 10.

[9] A few manuscripts that present only the *Matrona Ephesia* or the *Bellum civile* haunt the literature; but Müller's remarks on Munich Clm 23713 ([1]210) dispose equally of Dresden Dc 141, Stockholm Va. 23a, and related editions of s. xvi¼, and the readings that have been cited from 'Ambros. 160', or more recently 'Ambros. 165', on the authority of Beck's collation (1863) show that it too (actually O.160 sup.) derives from δ. Paris, Mazar. 1261 (s. xii²) resembles P.

[10] *RCCM* 14 (1972), 155–64. His earlier articles too, ibid. 11 (1969), 203–13, and 10 (1968), 72–85, promise more than he achieves in his untidy edition (Rome, 1975).

[11] *AJP* 50 (1929), 36, *CPh* 25 (1930), 148–106, and J. Hamacher, *Florilegium Gallicum: Prolegomena und Edition der Exzerpte von Petron bis Cicero, De oratore* (Bern and Frankfurt, 1975), 122–38.

[12] *Maia*, 22 (1970), 238–60 = *Mnem.* Suppl. 20 (1971), 1–24 (where n. 1 of the *Einleitung* acknowledges Merkelbach's observation).

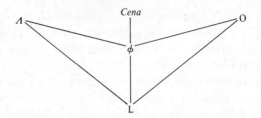

Like L, φ used π, from which it also took bits of Calpurnius; and as φ was compiled in s. XII²/₃ at Orléans,[13] both $\varLambda$ and π must have been thereabouts in s. XII.

It is here that new evidence comes in. The industrious annotator of Berne 276, who worked at and around Orléans in s. XIII¾, cites Petronius at least eight times, often from '(primo) libro satirarum', otherwise without qualification.[14] The first set of citations he must have taken from a source close to P, the only manuscript that garbles *Satiricon* in this way (and he also cites Calpurnius). Of the other set, however, two, picked up by Pierre Daniel ('ex glossario S. Dionysii'), constitute frr. XV–XVI in Müller's edition, and the third reads 'Petronius ponit depresentiarum impresentiarum' (58.3, 74.17, in H alone, though the word need not have been confined to the *Cena*).[15] In the neighbourhood of Orléans, therefore, it was still possible in s. XIII¾ to consult not only a manuscript like P but also one that contained passages of *Satyrica* absent from L.

What in fact had the Middle Ages received of *Satyrica*, and what did they do with it? Apart from OLφH and Berne 276, twelve pieces of evidence have accumulated.

1. Several writers in Antiquity, especially Fulgentius (s. VI), cite passages no longer attested.[16]

2. A French manuscript of miscellaneous verse, Leiden, Voss. Lat. Q. 86 (s. IX, Tours?[17]), contains frr. XXVII–XXVIII (not ascribed, but Fulgentius ascribes extracts from them to Petronius).

3. Two French manuscripts with Spanish connections, Leiden, Voss. Lat. F.111 (s. IX¹) and Berne 207 (s. IX), contain attested verses and others.[18]

[13] R. H. R., *Viator*, 10 (1979), 135–8.

[14] On Berne 276, whose importance first struck R. H. R., see M. D. R. and R. H. R., *Viator*, 9 (1978), 235–9, and R. H. R., op. cit. n. 13, above.

[15] I have failed to find in Berne 276 two passages cited by Daniel from his *glossarium S. Dionysii*, 2.3 *loqui debemus* and 11.2 *opertum*.

[16] See Müller's collection of fragments (¹185–94) and add V. Ciaffi, *Fulgenzio e Petronio* (Turin, 1963).   [17] See MARTIAL, n. 14.

[18] See Müller, ¹xvii–xviii and on 14.2 and frr. XXVIIII–XXX. The quotation in the Bernensis appears in a treatise closely connected with Julian, Bishop of Toledo from 680 to 690. On the Vossianus see AUSONIUS.

4. Fr. XXVI 'ex codice Isidori Bellovacensi deperdito edidit Claudius Binetus anno 1579' (Müller, [1]191, and cf. xlvii).

5. A French catalogue of s. XI includes Petronius, albeit in very devout company, among 'books of Wulfhad'.[19] Wulfhad, Archbishop of Bourges from 866, died in 876.

6. Heiric of Auxerre in his *Vita S. Germani* (a. 873) echoes 119.1–5, with 5 *fulvum quae* (L) and not *quae fulvum* (O), and 133.3.4, with *septifluus* (πL) and not *semper flavius* (B) or *semperfluus* (R).

7. Daniel spotted 'in vet. lexico S. Benedicti Floriacensis', now British Library, Harley 2735 (s. IX),[20] the following note on f. 43ʳ: 'Halosin quid sit Petronius Arbiter libro XV post multa de quodam agens manifestat: *sed video te totum* (O: *totum te* L) *in illa herere tabula que Troie halosin ostendit*' (89 init.).

8. An incorporated gloss in a manuscript of Fulgentius, Paris lat. 7975 (s. XI), cites 20.7 from Book 14.

9. Thierry of Chartres in s. XII²/4 quotes from 3.2 (OLφ).[21]

10. John of Salisbury in s. XII¾ cites passages preserved in OL, L, and H.

11. The author of some racy stories composed not before s. XI² and found in a manuscript from St. Augustine's Canterbury, Dublin, Trin. 602 (s. XIII¹), likewise echoes passages preserved in OL, L, and H.[22]

12. Someone at some date for some reason connected with Petronius a glossary found in fifteenth-century manuscripts.[23]

As there is no telling how early the verses mentioned in nos. 2–4 were culled from *Satyrica*, the medieval story begins in s. IX at Auxerre (B and no. 6) and Fleury (no. 7).[24] Book numbers survive only in H and nos. 7–8;[25] however they are to be reconciled, Fleury in s. IX must have possessed a manuscript equipped with at least one, and this manuscript may well have been the archetype of the extant tradition. Perhaps it survived long enough to be used in s. XII–XIII by John of Salisbury,[26] the compiler of the *Florilegium Gallicum*, and the annotator of Berne 276. Three other users were the creator of O (s. IX), the creator of Λ, and

---

[19] P. Lehmann, *Erforschung des Mittelalters,* ii (Stuttgart, 1959), 152–4.

[20] Müller, ²405. On the annotations see p. 129, n. 21, above.

[21] Manitius, *Geschichte,* iii. 199. Manitius's other references lead nowhere, except perhaps (iii.789) the use by Alexander Neckam in s. XIII¼ of *crotalistria* (55.6 OLH); Isidore has Tiberius and the unbreakable glass.

[22] M. L. Colker, 'A Collection of Stories and Sketches: Petronius Redivivus', *Analecta Dublinensia* (Cambridge, Mass., 1975), 179–257.

[23] E. Campanile edited it in *Stud. Urb.* 35 (1961), 118–34. For other manuscripts see M. L. Colker, *Scriptorium,* 24 (1970), 55–6, and M. Passalacqua, *I codici di Prisciano* (Rome, 1978), nos. 142, 364, and add Florence, Naz. Magl. I.43.

[24] That Harley 2735 had always been at Fleury is admittedly not certain.

[25] 'Book 1' in Berne 276 cannot have any authority and must reflect the annotator's use of two manuscripts.

[26] If John took a copy from France to Canterbury, that would account for the echoes in the Canterbury Tales (no. 11); see J. Martin, *Viator,* 10 (1979), 68–75. John read the *Matrona Ephesia* in a manuscript like B; see Müller, ¹xxxiii–xxxiv.

whoever carried off a copy of the *Cena* to Cologne. A descendant of O
available not far from Fleury, namely π, contributed to the *Florilegium
Gallicum* and the annotations in Berne 276. In s. XVI Pithou acquired a
descendant of $\varLambda$ from Fleury and Cujas another from somewhere unknown. But for Poggio and Statileo, then, the story continues and ends
where it began.

Little can be said about an archetype copied so selectively. Eduard
Fracnkel convinced Müller that a meddler had covered it with cross-
references and pedestrian explanations; controversy rages.[27] O, written
continuously, favours verse and dialogue and steers clear of homo-
sexuality. $\varLambda$ preferred narrative no matter how sordid; it is not clear
whether the archetype, $\varLambda$, or the descendants of $\varLambda$, should be blamed for
the jerkiness of the narrative, which in places dwindles to snippets.

What progress now? The discovery of editions used for collation by
Pithou and his contemporaries? More fruits of Daniel's example in
combing glossaries and annotated manuscripts? An identification of
Scaliger's 'autres traittez qui estoient avec' in the Cuiacianus,[28] which
might even lead to its recovery? More modestly, the sixteenth-century
witnesses may still have light to shed on whether the sixteenth century
or the twelfth played the larger part in creating L. Certainly in this
complex tradition there seems hope that *quod hodie non est cras erit* (45.2).

M. D. R.

[27] See most recently J. P. Sullivan, *PCPS* 202 (1976), 90–122.
[28] *Scaligeriana* (The Hague, 1666), 85.

PHAEDRUS

The main body of this text is preserved fairly simply. By far the most
important witness is P (New York, Pierpont Morgan Library MA.
906), probably written at Reims, s. IX[1], formerly owned by Pierre
Pithou,[1] and for a long time in private hands and inaccessible until its

The most recent text is that of A. Guaglianone (Turin, 1969). This is the only modern edition to
have had access to P and the *Schedae Dorvillianae*. However, it does not contain the prose
paraphrases, for which one still has to go to L. Hervieux, *Les Fabulistes Latins*,[2] ii (1894),
131–233, or Thiele (see nn. 7 and 8, below) for *Adem.* and *Rom.*

[1] A palaeographic edition of P was published in 1893 by U. Robert. More recently see O.
Zwierlein, 'Der Codex Pithoeanus des Phaedrus in der Pierpont Morgan Library', *RhM* 113
(1970), 91–3; C. E. Finch, 'The Morgan Manuscript of Phaedrus', *AJP* 92 (1971), 301–7. Finch
dates P to *c*.820.

acquisition by the Morgan Library in the 1960s. This manuscript contains the five books of Fables, to the front of which is now attached the paper manuscript, in Pithou's own hand, which he prepared for his 1596 edition. P (like R) writes the text as continuous 'prose' with no verse divisions.

A *gemellus* of P was R (the *codex Remensis*), a ninth-century book written at Reims[2] and destroyed by fire there in 1774. Our knowledge of R's readings is now very incomplete and rests on four sources: the collation of J. Sirmond to be found in the editions of N. Rigault (Paris, 1617 and 1630); the readings of M. Gude, published by P. Burman in his 1698 Amsterdam edition; the readings of D. Roche preserved on three sheets of paper inserted into a printed edition in Paris, Bibl. de l'Université, and published by É. Chatelain, *RPh* 11 (1887), 81–8; the readings of J. C. Vincent (formerly librarian at Reims) published in the 1830 edition of J. Berger de Xivrey.

To PR must be added D (Vatican, Reg. lat. 1616), written at Fleury and bearing the Fleury *ex libris*, s. IX/X (Chatelain, plate CLXV.1). This small fragment[3] (contained on ff. 17^r–18^r) has eight Fables from the fifth book (11–13 and 17–21) with the verses correctly separated.

Outside the 'mainstream' of PRD stands a tradition stemming from two fifteenth-century manuscripts: N (Naples IV.F.58) written by Niccolò Perotti,[4] Archbishop of Siponto, for his nephew; and V (Vatican, Urb. lat. 368), which would appear[5] to derive from N. Amongst much else, N preserves thirty-two Fables from Books 2–5, and thirty-two which do not appear in PRD, and which are thus often called the *Appendix Perottina*. As N is so affected by damp as to be largely illegible, it is fortunate that there recently came to light the so-called *Schedae Dorvillianae* (Oxford, Bodl. D'Orville 524), a copy of N made in 1727 by J. D'Orville.

Of some value and much interest are the medieval prose paraphrases[6] of Phaedrus. One (known as *Wiss.*, as the manuscript was formerly at the monastery of SS Peter and Paul, Weissenburg, as the fifteenth century *ex libris* shows) is contained in Wolfenbüttel, Gud. lat. 148, s. IX^4/4 (area of Reims). A second is in Leiden, Voss. Lat. O.15, ff.

---

[2] See the specimen of the hand given by Hervieux, 83. This *Remensis* also contained the *Querolus* (q.v.), a transcript of which was discovered in 1976 by M. D. R. (Hamburg 185 in scrinio).

[3] See E. K. Rand, 'A Vade mecum of Liberal Culture in a Manuscript of Fleury', *PhQ* 1 (1922), 258–77; 'Note on the Vossianus Q86 and the Reginenses 333 and 1616', *AJP* 44 (1923), 171–2; F. M. Carey, 'The Vatican Fragment of Phaedrus', *TAPA* 57 (1926), 96–106; C. E. Finch, 'Notes on the fragment of Phaedrus in Reg. Lat. 1616', *CPh* 66 (1971), 190–1.

[4] On Perotti (1430–80) see Cosenza, 2669–78.

[5] Despite A. Guaglianone, 'Il Codex Perottinus', *GIF* 1 (1948), 125–8; 243–9. The contents of the relevant section of this manuscript (ff. 100–46) all involve Perotti. According to G. Mercati, 'Per la cronologia della vita e degli scritti di Niccolò Perotti, Arcivescovo di Siponto', *Studi e testi*, 44 (1925), 107, V was copied by Federico Veterano. Mercati too did not think that V was a copy of N.

[6] See C. M. Zander, *Phaedrus Solutus* (Lund, 1921).

195–212, s. XI[1], known as *Adem.*, since it is in the hand of Adémar of Chabannes, a monk at Saint-Martial-de-Limoges.[7] A third is attributed to one Romulus[8] (hence *Rom.*), of which the oldest and best representative is B, British Library, Burney 59, s. XI[1].[9]

P. K. M.

[7] This manuscript is reproduced (with a text) in G. Thiele, *Der illustrierte Aesop in der Handschrift des Ademar* (Leiden, 1905). See also F. Bertini, *Il monaco Ademaro e la sua raccolta di favole Fedriane* (Genova, 1975); and 'Un perduto manoscritto di Fedro fonte delle favole medievali di Ademaro', *Helikon*, 15–16 (1975–6), 390–400.

[8] Critical edition by G. Thiele, *Der lateinische Aesop des Romulus und die Prosa-Fassungen des Phaedrus* (Heidelberg, 1910); this work contains a detailed description and evaluation of *Wiss.*, *Adem.*, and B, together with the later and less valuable manuscripts.

[9] See THE ELDER PLINY, n. 40.

PLAUTUS

The available evidence relating to the text of Plautus is fuller than for many classical authors, but it is also unusually complex and difficult to interpret. The problems of the tradition are perhaps best accounted for on the hypothesis that after Plautus' death his plays did not circulate immediately in stable published form, but were often performed in theatres instead, undergoing the usual changes introduced by producers and actors (removal of obscure or dated allusions, modernization of language, abridgement of scenes, and so on). The period of Plautine revivals coincided with the beginnings at Rome of serious philological and editorial activity on Alexandrian lines; the scholars responsible for the earliest texts of Plautus seem to have found good copies as well as the revised scripts used in later performances, and their

The basic study of the history of the text in Antiquity is in F. Leo's *Plautinische Forschungen*[2] (Berlin, 1912), 1–62; the survey in G. Pasquali's *Storia della tradizione e critica del testo*[2] (Florence, 1952), 331–54, is lucid and on the whole judicious. A convenient short account of the main manuscripts can be found in W. M. Lindsay's edition of *Captivi* (London, 1900), 1–12. *Editions: editio maior*, based on the work of F. Ritschl, by G. Loewe, G. Goetz, and F. Schoell (Teubner, 4 vols., 1879–1902); other important editions by F. Leo (Weidmann, 1895–6), W. M. Lindsay (OCT, 1904–5), and A. Ernout (Budé, 1932–6). Leo's edition is on the whole the most useful, Ernout's the least reliable. Plates of ABCDEJ in Chatelain, I–V.

practice of preserving whatever had been transmitted despite doubts of its genuineness ensured the survival of the original text in many places where it had ceased to be current. Questions of authenticity also began to be discussed, and critical scrutiny, although at times of a highly subjective kind, was directed at the great mass of plays to which Plautus' name had become attached (about 130 in the time of Aulus Gellius[1]). A canon of twenty-five plays was established by L. Aelius Stilo (*fl.* 100 BC), the teacher of Varro and leading philologist of his time; Varro himself designated twenty-one plays as indubitably Plautine. Varro did not think that this list included all the authentic plays, and other plays were still regarded as genuine in the Antonine period, but Varro's selection proved in the end decisive, since there can be no doubt that the twenty-one plays transmitted in our manuscripts are those singled out by Varro.

The direct tradition comprises two ancient recensions, of which the first is represented by a single ancient codex, the 'Ambrosian palimpsest' (Milan, Ambros. G. 82 sup. (S.P. 9/13–20) = A). This, the most extensive of all surviving palimpsests, contains the text of Plautus in rustic capitals (s. V, probably Italy, according to Lowe, *CLA* III.344a–45) over which an Irish hand (s. VI[2]) has written the Books of Kings in the Vulgate version; from repairs and additions made early in the seventh century it seems clear that the manuscript was then at the Abbey of Bobbio. When A's importance was recognized by Angelo Mai in 1815 an attempt was made to bring up the ancient script with chemical reagents; the results were disastrous, and Wilhelm Studemund's painstaking transcription of the text cost him his sight.[2] In its original form A contained all twenty-one 'Varronian' plays, but all or nearly all of *Amphitruo, Asinaria, Aulularia, Captivi, Curculio*, and *Vidularia* has been lost, and large parts of several other plays are now missing or illegible.

The other ancient recension is preserved in minuscule manuscripts of s. X or later; it is commonly called 'Palatine' because two of its most important representatives were once part of the library of the Elector of the Palatinate in Heidelberg. In this recension the alphabetical order of plays was disturbed by the placing of *Bacchides* after *Epidicus* (because of the reference to *Epidicus* in *Ba.* 214). The three oldest extant 'Palatine' codices are of German origin:

B Vatican, Pal. lat. 1615 (s. X ex.), containing twenty of the 'Varronian' canon (the manuscript breaks off with the *titulus* of the *Vidularia*); B contains important corrections in the early plays (B[3], see below), and B is also remarkable for having preserved much of the colometry of its ancient source. Often referred to as the *codex vetus*.

---

[1] 3.3.11; this chapter of Gellius is the basic source of information about Varro's editing of Plautine texts.　　　　　　　[2] *Codicis rescripti Ambrosiani apographum* (Weidmann, 1889).

C Heidelberg, Pal. lat. 1613 (s. XI, from Freising); contains twelve plays, 9–20 in the Palatine sequence, beginning with *Bacchides* followed by *Mercator* to *Truculentus*. Often called the *codex decurtatus* because of its incomplete state.[3]

D Vatican lat. 3870 (s. XI); contains the latter twelve plays as in C plus half of the first eight plays (*Amph., Asin., Aul., Capt.* 1–503). Later owned by Fulvio Orsini and hence called *Ursinianus*.

These twelve plays remained virtually unknown until D was brought from Germany to Italy in the fifteenth century. D contains notes in Poggio's hand and Poggio's apograph of it is now Vat. lat. 1629, but the copy made by Niccolò Niccoli was much more influential; a manuscript close to Niccoli's seems to have been the starting-point for the emended texts known as the 'Itala recensio'.[4]

Medieval copies of the first eight plays (*Amph., Asin., Aul., Capt., Cas., Cist., Curc., Epid.*), on the other hand, are not rare; in addition to BD editors have concentrated on the following:

E   Milan, Ambros. J. 257 inf. (s. XII[2], Italy).

V   Leiden, Voss. Lat. Q. 30 (s. XI, France?); lacking *Amph., Asin., Aul.* 1–189, *Epid.* 245–end.

J   British Library, Royal 15.C.XI (s. XII in., England).

O   Vatican, Ottob. lat. 687 (s. XI, France?), a fragment containing *Capt.* 400–555.

(One interesting, though fragmentary, medieval witness has not yet been used by editors: two conjoint leaves of a manuscript written in Italy (s. XI[1]?) and now at Duke University (no. 123) contain *Cas.* 226–88 and *Curc.* 372–433. See M. P. Harris, 'A Checklist of the Duke Latin Manuscript Collection', *Library Notes*, 47 (1977), 20, 31 (plate of *Curc.* 402b–433). The Duke fragment clearly merits close attention: in *Curculio* it offers a more correct text than BEVJ, the main Palatine witnesses there available; among other noteworthy readings it has *diligit* at 424 (so Nonius, against *dessicit* in the other manuscripts).)

The common ancestor of the 'Palatine' manuscripts was a Carolingian descendant (P) of an ancient codex, probably written in rustic capitals (P[A]).[5] The division of the plays into two groups, of eight (*Amph.–Epid.*) and twelve (*Bacch.–Truc.*), may have arisen when P was broken up for copying; the bulk of the text encourages simultaneous transcription, and both B and C are the work of a team of scribes. A copy of P containing only the last twelve plays (P[CD]) is the common source of CD, and in the first eight plays B and, for the first half of them, D similarly

---

[3] Complete facsimile ed. C. Zangemeister, Leiden, 1900 (*Codices graeci et latini photographice depicti*, 5).

[4] C. Questa, *Per la storia del testo di Plauto nel rinascimento: I, La recensione di Poggio Bracciolini* (Rome, 1968).   [5] Lindsay's sigla are used for these hypothetical sources.

derive from a copy of P (P^{BD}); it is even possible that P^{BD} and P^{CD} were the separated halves of the same manuscript.[6] In the last twelve plays, though, B is superior to CD and appears to be a copy of P itself; P could also be a source of B^3's important corrections in the first eight plays.[7] The later witnesses to the first eight plays (EVJO) stem from a copy of P^{BD} containing many attempts at emendation; a further stage of this process is visible in O, V^2, and above all in J, the work of a conscientious and sometimes acute scholar.[8]

The earliest and best representative of P^A is unfortunately lost. It belonged to the Benedictine monastery of Saint-Colombe at Sens, and was used by Turnebus in the sixteenth century; his collations of *Persa*, *Poenulus*, *Rudens* 1–*c.*790, *Pseudolus c.*730–end, and *Bacchides c.*35–80, 570–650, 810–900 were discovered by W. M. Lindsay in the Bodleian library.[9] The *codex Turnebi* (T) was probably a ninth- or tenth-century descendant of P^A, stemmatically equal to P and on occasion more faithful to the ancient source. The accession of T revealed that many errors thought characteristic of P^A had actually originated in P, and that P^A was not significantly inferior in quality to A.

The relationships of the major manuscripts may be depicted by a stemma (p. 306).

Behind the forms of the text represented by A and P^A stands an archetype, a copy (s. IV?) of a scholarly edition comprising the twenty-one 'Varronian' comedies. The existence of this archetype is shown by many corruptions common to AP^A which could hardly have arisen spontaneously in each, e.g. *Poen.* 670 *praesibi* (*praesidi*), *Pers.* 581 and 591 *est* (*es*), 386 *mala* (a gloss on *fama*) intruded into the text, ruining the metre.[10] Unless A and P^A derive from the same privately owned copy of the plays, which seems unlikely, these common errors point to a book-

---

[6] What is now the first quire in C was originally numbered xvii, showing that it was copied from an original containing at one point all twenty plays (D uses 8¾ quaternions to copy half of the first eight plays); Lindsay, 4.

[7] The original contents list on f. 9^v recorded only eight plays; the full list appears on f. 1 (a quaternion containing the *Querolus*, reckoned as the twenty-first play). Lindsay (p. 5) plausibly suggested that plays 1–8 were copied from a copy of P but that P itself later became available for plays 9–20 and was used to correct 1–8. The more recent study of B's correctors in *Bacchides* by Questa (*RCCM* 5 (1963), 227–39) confirms Lindsay's suggestion that in plays 9–20 B^3 and B^4 derive from inspection of the exemplar (P) rather than from a text related to CD.

[8] J's activity can be most easily surveyed in the edition of *Casina* by W. T. MacCary and M. M. Willcock (Cambridge, 1976); the editors think that 'a final judgement on J has not yet been made' (p. 234) and consequently report its readings in full. (It was largely ignored by Leo and Lindsay.) In the last act of *Casina*, for example, where P^A was obviously mutilated, J makes simple restorations like ⟨*cla*⟩*ndestinae* (946), but faced with *nia* (941) guesses *quia* (*omnia* Camerarius).

[9] *The Codex Turnebi of Plautus* (Oxford, 1898). Turnebus also cited readings from this manuscript in his *adversaria* on *Asin.*, *Capt.*, *Cas.*, *Curc.*, *Most.*, *Poen.*, *Pseud.*, *Rud.*, and *Stichus*.

[10] Leo, 6–13; Pasquali, 337–9. Lindsay vigorously propounded the view that A and P^A represented independent editions, A of the original text and P^A of the revival versions (*Ancient Editions of Plautus*, Oxford, 1904); the errors shared by AP^A are an embarrassment for this view, and led Lindsay into some very unfortunate editorial choices.

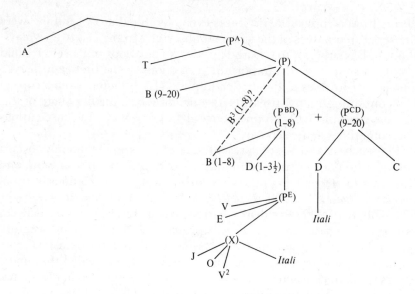

seller's exemplar (incidentally confirming the complaints of ancient authors about the poor quality of commercial copies).[11]

The edition of which the archetype was a copy was the work of a scholar employing Alexandrian critical methods. When more than one version of a line or passage had been preserved, the editor presented both versions, marking the one he thought spurious. These doublets were variously treated in the descendants of the archetype: at times both versions survive in the entire tradition, while in other places A or a predecessor (much less often P^A) has omitted the version stigmatized by the editor. The edition is presumably responsible for non-textual elements shared by A and P^A, such as colometry[12] and scene-divisions.[13] Where A and P^A diverge the picture is less clear. A, for example, but not P^A, contains *didascaliae* for some plays, and P^A offers acrostical summaries not found in A; this material could have been either omitted from or added to what was available in the archetype. A scholarly edition of this kind is not likely to have been produced later than the second century AD, but nothing else can be definitely stated about its origin. M. Valerius Probus is often invoked as its author or guiding spirit, but there is no evidence for this belief.[14] It is very plausible that Probus' interest in archaic Latin involved him in the study of Plautus,

[11] e.g. Cic., *Epist. ad Quint.* 3.4.5, Quint., *Inst.* 9.4.39. The presence of obvious blunders in a bookseller's exemplar has a medieval parallel: many of the exemplars licensed for copying in the universities, although in theory approved as correct by a committee of masters, contain blatant corruptions and lacunae; cf. L. J. Bataillon, *RPhL* 75 (1977), 243.

[12] C. Questa, *RFIC* 102 (1974), 58–79, 172–88.

[13] B. Bader, *Szenentitel und Szeneneinteilung bei Plautus* (diss. Tübingen, 1970). Many of the original scene-headings seem to have dropped out of P^A.

[14] Leo, 23 ff., Pasquali, 344–8.

but the extent of his responsibility for our tradition of the plays is beyond conjecture.

Citations in ancient writers are unusually important in the case of Plautus; for example, the quotations of Varro and the Augustan grammarian Verrius Flaccus (embedded in Festus) antedate the edition from which the archetype derives. On the whole the grammarians' citations attest the soundness of the direct tradition, but on occasion they preserve a true reading not otherwise on record. The Plautine text used by Nonius Marcellus has on occasion been regarded as belonging to a different strain of tradition circulating in fourth-century Africa, but his citations generally agree so well with the consensus of AP^A that the exceptions may instead be due to indirect (i.e. grammatical) sources.[15]

R. J. T.

[15] Lindsay (n. 10, above), 23–7.

THE ELDER PLINY

The thirty-seven books of Pliny's *Natural History* do not sit comfortably under one cover. Although there are some comparatively early manuscripts which do contain the bulk of the work, many have only part of it, and all the pre-Carolingian manuscripts are fragmentary. Consequently, with different manuscripts coming into play at different points in the work, it is impossible to build up a continuous and unified picture of the tradition. It has been customary to introduce some order into the

We owe our present text of the Elder Pliny largely to the German scholars of the nineteenth century, in particular J. Sillig, D. Detlefsen, L. von Jan, K. Rück, whose work lies behind the second Teubner edition by L. Jan–C. Mayhoff (5 vols., 1892–1906). Much of the fundamental work on the recension was done by Detlefsen: *RhM* 15 (1860), 265–88, 367–90; *Philologus*, 28 (1869), 284–337; *Hermes*, 32 (1897), 321–40; and his edition (5 vols., Berlin, 1866–73). All the present century has managed to produce is the Budé Pliny, a very uneven series of volumes launched by A. Ernout in 1950. There are now more than thirty volumes, and some of the introductions contain information (usually of a rather desultory nature, often out of date) about the manuscripts; the most useful are those of Ernout (Livre I, 1950, VIII, 1952), J. Desanges (Livre V. 1–46, 1980), R. Schilling (VII, 1977), E. de Saint-Denis (IX, 1955, X, 1961, XXXII, 1966, XXXVII, 1972), H. Le Bonniec (XVIII, 1972), J. André (XX, 1965, XXII, 1970). A good article on the manuscripts is that of J. Desanges, 'Le Manuscript (Ch) et la classe des *recentiores* perturbés de l'Histoire Naturelle de. Pline l'Ancien', *Latomus*, 25 (1966), 508–25, with its 'Note complémentaire sur trois manuscrits «recentiores» de l'«Histoire Naturelle» de Pline l'Ancien', ibid. 895–9. There is an interesting chapter on 'Pliny's *Natural History* in the Middle Ages' by Marjorie Chibnall, in *Empire and Aftermath: Silver Latin II* (ed. T. A. Dorey), London, 1975, 57–78.

manuscripts of the *Natural History* by dividing them into two groups, the *vetustiores* and *recentiores*. But the manuscripts have been so wildly mis-dated that some of the so-called *recentiores* are in fact older than some of the aspirants to the *ordo vetustiorum* and there appears to be some confusion between age and quality. Though this division of the manuscripts has held sway for over a century,[1] it cannot be strictly applied; but the general concepts of an older (and better) and a recent (and inferior) tradition do correspond to something real in the text of Pliny.

If we adopt a more flexible grouping of the manuscripts, the ancient codices must head the procession. Pliny was read, excerpted, and epitomized[2] throughout Antiquity, so that it is not surprising that fragments of five antique manuscripts survive. These are known respectively as M, N, O, P, Pal. Chat.[3] O is mutilated, often illegible, and has an unremarkable text; N and P and Pal. Chat. are good witnesses, but preserve such a tiny fraction of the total corpus that their contribution to the text is necessarily very small. The star performer among these early witnesses is the *codex Moneus*,[4] which is available for large stretches of Books 11–15. Written in the fifth century, presumably in Italy, it was rewritten *c.*700 with Jerome on Ecclesiastes. The upper script is Luxeuil minuscule, so that it must have been palimpsested in a house where that script was used, if not Luxeuil itself; it has a fifteenth-century Reichenau *ex libris*. It is an extremely valuable manuscript, often far superior to the other witnesses for these books, and a clear example of the general truth, that where no really good manuscript of Pliny is available we have a very indifferent text. Three of these ancient books found their way to France, but there they succumbed to other needs before they could generate, as far as we can tell, any north-European tradition.

Another uncial manuscript which remained isolated from the main

---

[1] Since Detlefsen, 1866. Cf. *Philologus*, 28 (1869), 287.

[2] C. Iulius Solinus, probably of third-century date, is Pliny's most noted epitomist; about three-quarters of his *Collectanea rerum memorabilium* is taken from the *Natural History*, so that he can be of some help in correcting the transmitted text of Pliny. His compendium, so brief when compared with Pliny and crammed with marvels, was very popular in the Middle Ages (see SOLINUS).

[3] M = codex Moneus, discovered by F. Mone in 1853 in the monastery of St. Paul in Carinthia, where it still is (Stiftsbibl.3.1 (25.2.36; xxv.a.3), *CLA* x.1455), s. v, uncial. N = Rome, Bibl. Naz., Sessor. 55 (*CLA* IV.421), s. v, uncial, containing a few sections of Books 23 and 25; most likely of Italian origin, it was rewritten s. VI[2] with patristic texts, most probably in northern Italy, and apparently restored at Nonantola in s. VIII/IX. O = Vienna 1a (*CLA* x.1470), s. v[1], uncial; written in Italy and probably in the south, it consists of fragments of seven leaves used for binding and contains parts of Books 33 and 34. P = Paris lat. 9378, f. 26 (*CLA* v.575), one folio, presumably of Italian origin, written s. VI ex. and containing a fragment of Book 18. It appears to have come from the binding of a Saint-Amand manuscript. Pal. Chat. = Autun 24 + Paris n.a.lat. 1629 (*CLA* VI.725), s. v, uncial, containing a few sections of Books 8 and 9. Presumably of Italian origin, it was rewritten in the late sixth century with Cassianus, *Institutiones*, in half-uncial, probably in southern France.

[4] A description and complete transcript of M by Mone constitute the bulk of vol. vi of Sillig's edition (Gotha, 1855).

stream of Pliny's transmission is Paris lat. 10318 (*CLA* v.593 = Q). This is the famous *codex Salmasianus* of the *Latin Anthology*, written in central Italy about the year 800.[5] Included in this remarkable anthology are medical excerpts from Books 19–20 of Pliny's *Natural History*. Though the text has been freely reworked to suit the needs of the excerptor and is consequently somewhat capricious, there is no doubt that it comes from a source infinitely superior to the other extant witnesses; like the *codex Moneus*, it is frequently right where other manuscripts are wrong, complete where they are lacunose.

Long before the *Salmasianus* was copied in Italy, another manuscript of Pliny had left the southern sun[6] to find a home in Britain; for it was in the north of England, in the first third of the eighth century, that its surviving descendant, Leiden, Voss. Lat. F.4 (*CLA* x. 1578 = A), was executed in a fine insular minuscule. This is by far the earliest surviving manuscript of Pliny to have been written north of the Alps. Although the English contribution to the history of Pliny's transmission has been overstated and in some respects misconceived, parts of the *Natural History* were clearly available in Northumbria in the eighth century. Apart from the tangible evidence of A itself, which contains (with large gaps) Books 2–6, these and possibly some other Books were known to Bede,[7] and Pliny is also among the authors listed by Alcuin as present in the library at York.[8] A is not in the same class as the *Moneus* or *Salmasianus*, but it belongs to a better tradition than that which constituted the main stream of the Continental text.

By the end of the eighth century a focal point for intellectual activity had come into being at the Carolingian court and it was in response to this cultural stimulus that the next and crucial stage in the history of Pliny's text began to unfold. The use of Pliny for astronomical and computistical purposes is one of the factors that make one sense the great figure of Charlemagne standing in the background. Two letters which Alcuin writes to him in response to his questions on astronomical matters cite Pliny as a standard authority,[9] as does an equally well-known letter by the Irish scholar Dungal.[10] While both excuse themselves from more detailed exposition because they do not have a copy of Pliny to hand – Alcuin is travelling about France, Dungal is probably at Saint-Denis – there is a fairly clear implication that Charlemagne can find a copy of the

[5] See *ANTHOLOGIA LATINA*.

[6] A has transmitted (f. 29) the subscription: 'Feliciter iunius laurentius relegi'.

[7] For Bede's knowledge of Pliny, see M. L. W. Laistner, *The Intellectual Heritage of the Early Middle Ages* (Ithaca, NY, 1957), 98 f., 124 f.; J. D. A. Ogilvy, *Books known to the English* (Cambridge, Mass., 1967), 222 f. Aldhelm also appears to have known Pliny, in particular Book 37: see the *index locorum* in R. Ehwald, *MGH, Auctores antiquissimi*, xv (Berlin, 1919).

[8] *MGH, Poetae latini aevi Carolini*, ed. E. Dümmler, i (Berlin, 1880–81), 204, line 1548.

[9] *Epist.* 155 (a. 789) and 170 (a. 799), *MGH, Epist.* iv (ed. E. Dümmler, Berlin, 1895), 250, 280.

[10] *Epist.* 1 (a. 811), *MGH, Epist.* iv. 577. On Dungal, see LUCRETIUS, n. 9.

Natural History at Aachen.[11] This must be the proper context for the so-called 'York excerpts', the *excerpta Eboracensia* (= m). These are astronomical excerpts drawn from Books 2 and 18 of the *Natural History* and derived from a manuscript better than any which have survived for these sections of the text.[12] Their supposed origin in Northumbria and the circle of Bede, which has loomed large in accounts of Pliny's transmission, rested on no real evidence and has now been effectively demolished by V. H. King.[13] The excerpts appear, as King has shown, in two separate forms of compilation, a Three-Book and a Seven-Book Computus. The Three-Book Computus is preserved in two sister manuscripts, Munich Clm 210 and Vienna 387; both were probably written at Salzburg in 818, but their exemplar may have come from Saint-Amand. The compilation itself goes back to 810. The Seven-Book Computus was compiled between 812 and 840, and the earliest manuscripts to transmit it point to the area Metz, Lobbes, Reims.[14] Behind both lies an earlier computus of 809, in which the Pliny excerpts would have been accompanied by illustrations, and this one would like to associate with Aachen and the Palace School.[15]

Those who want to build a bridge to the Venerable Bede are on somewhat firmer ground with a second set of excerpts, likewise published by Karl Rück,[16] which have received rather less attention. More varied in content but still having a strongly astronomical emphasis, this florilegium is drawn from Books 2,3,4,6 and transmitted in two extant manuscripts, Leiden, Voss. Lat. Q. 69 (= y)[17] and Paris lat. 4860 (= i). y was written at St. Gall about the year 800. i was copied at Reichenau in about the last quarter of the ninth century, but it tallies so closely with a manuscript written or owned by the monk Reginbert of Reichenau (d. 846) that it must be a copy of it.[18] So these excerpts go back at least to the early years of the ninth century and are firmly located at that time in the area of Constance. It was impossible to establish a firm connection between the so-called York excerpts and Northumbria, for they and our one Anglo-Saxon manuscript (A) never overlap, and it is in any case

---

[11] These letters do not imply, as has been argued by some, that there were no copies of Pliny in France.

[12] K. Rück, *Auszüge aus der Naturgeschichte des C. Plinius Secundus in einem astronomisch-komputistischen Sammelwerke des achten Jahrhunderts* (Munich, 1888).

[13] 'An Investigation of some Astronomical Excerpts from Pliny's Natural History found in Manuscripts of the earlier Middle Ages' (unpublished B. Litt. thesis, Oxford, 1969).

[14] Madrid 3307 (820–40), Monza F.9.176 (*c*.869), Vat. lat. 645 (s. IX²?). *Karl der Grosse, Werk und Wirkung* (Aachen, 1965) has descriptions of Madrid 3307 and Monza F.9.176 (nos. 479–80) and also of Vienna 387 (no. 455).

[15] King (n. 13, above), 61, 78.

[16] *SBAW* 1898, Band 1, 246–98.   [17] *CLA* x.1585.

[18] P. Lehmann, *Mittelalterliche Bibliothekskataloge Deutschlands und der Schweiz* i (Munich, 1918), 257 f. Cf also Th. Mommsen, *Abh. Kön. Sächs. Gesellschaft der Wissenschaften*, Phil.-hist. Kl. 3 (1861), 574 ff. Paris lat. 4860 was later at Mainz, but was not written there, as has hitherto been thought; I am grateful to Professor Bischoff for information on its date and origin.

plain that one Book which Bede did not know was 18.[19] But the y excerpts, on the other hand, do show a definite affinity with A. It is also significant that the one passage from Book 4 which caught the excerptor's eye (102–4) deals with Britain, Ireland, the Orkneys, and Thule. An Anglo-Saxon or Irish scholar[20] would appear to have taken a hand in the compilation, if only a *peregrinus*.

An abbreviated passage from Book 18, dealing with the seasons of the year and matters meteorological (309–65), is preserved in Lucca, Biblioteca Capitolare 490 (*CLA* III.303ᵉ = H). This manuscript was written in uncials at Lucca *c*.800. Less valuable as a witness than the other *excerpta*, it is none the less closer to the older than to the younger tradition and shows some textual affinity with m.[21]

The great misfortune for Pliny's text is that most of the good manuscripts are fragmentary or contain only excerpts. As A is a windfall for the early Books, so B is an even greater one for the latter part of the work. This manuscript of outstanding quality, which alone preserves the very end of the *Natural History* and must stand very close to the ancient exemplar whose *notae* it carefully reproduces, is Bamberg Class. 42 (M.v.10), containing Books 32–7. It is a pleasure to learn that this marvellous book was written in the first third of the ninth century in the palace scriptorium of Louis the Pious.[22]

These manuscripts all belong to what have been known as the *vetustiores*. But even when we put them all together, we are still far short of having a text of the Elder Pliny. For the bulk of the work we are dependent on a central tradition which, though inferior in quality and pitted with small lacunae, gives a largely continuous text. This is the so-called *ordo recentiorum*. The main manuscripts, which descend from a common parent, are:

D+G+V Vatican lat. 3861 + Paris lat. 6796, ff. 52–3 + Leiden, Voss. Lat. F. 61 (*CLA* X.1580 + Suppl., p. 28). This manuscript was written *c*.800 in north-east France; some affinity with the Maudramn type suggests the Corbie area. It contains, with some gaps, the bulk of the text.

Ch New York, Pierpont Morgan Library M.871 (formerly Phillipps 8297), s. IX¹, written apparently at Lorsch by a scribe using the style of St. Vaast.[23] Books 1–17.

F Leiden, Lipsius 7, written s. IX¹⁻²/₄ through the collaboration of a scribe from Luxeuil with at least one other from Murbach,[24] perhaps at Murbach. Books 1–37. Chatelain, plate CXLII.

[19] Otherwise, as has often been pointed out, he would surely have used it when writing his *De temporum ratione*.

[20] Already noted by Mommsen, 576.   [21] Rück, *SBAW* 1898, Band 1, 213–45.

[22] Bischoff, in *Medieval Learning*, 17, 19, plate II (= *Mitt. Stud.* iii. 182, 184, plate XII).

[23] Bischoff, *Lorsch*, 32–3, 34, Tafel 11.

[24] *Karl der Grosse*, 242 n. 67 (= Bischoff, *Mitt. Stud.* iii. 19 n. 67). I am grateful to Professor Bischoff for his help with the dating and provenance of FRE.

R   Florence, Bibl. Ricc. 488, s. IX² (Auxerre?). Books 1–34.
E   Paris lat. 6795, s. IX/X, France. Books 1–32. Chatelain, plate
      CXXXIX.

The dependence of these five manuscripts on a common hyparchetype is proved by a dislocation which they have all suffered in the
ordering of Books 2–6: two units of text (2.187b–4.67a and 4.67b–
5.34a) have been interchanged.[25] Further complications in D and E due
to attempts to correct the sequence do not obscure the nature of the
original disturbance. The precise interrelationship of these manuscripts,
which is not necessarily the same for all parts of the text, probably needs
re-examination, especially as Ch (clearly close to D) has been largely
neglected by editors.[26] F appears to have been copied from D+G+V
before the latter was corrected, though this has been disputed.[27]

It is interesting that this same dislocation in the sequence of the early
Books had clearly occurred in the text(s) of Pliny which the Irish
scholar Dicuil had used for his *De mensura orbis terrae*, written in 825.[28] It
is a pity that this fact fuelled the old obsession with the insular tradition
of Pliny, for there is no need to assume that Dicuil had found such a text
in his native Ireland; a man who was a prominent figure in Carolingian
circles and enjoyed close relations with the court had come to the right
place to find it. In general the curiously persistent belief[29] that Ireland
possessed texts of Pliny at a very early date, though not inherently
improbable given that country's computistical interests, appears to be
based on no firm evidence. Until evidence is found, it is perhaps safer to
regard early Irish Plinies as a species of early Irish leprechaun.

E and its ancestors were particularly prone to accident. In addition to
this dislocation and a botched attempt to remedy it, part of Book 24
(93b–100a) had been misplaced in an ancestor of E;[30] lacunae in Books
27 and 28 had likewise occurred in an ancestor, and the loss of leaves in
E itself caused a whole series of lacunae.[31] These disorders have left
their mark on the descendants of E, despite the great pains that were
taken to straighten out and patch up the family skeleton. It is becoming

[25] On the confused order of these Books, see Detlefsen, *RhM* 15 (1860), 270 ff., 368 ff., *Philologus*, 28 (1869), 287 ff.; Desanges, 'Le Manuscrit (Ch)', 511 ff.

[26] D. J. Campbell, 'Two Manuscripts of the Elder Pliny', *AJP* 57 (1936), 113–23; Desanges, 'Le Manuscrit (Ch)', 511 ff.

[27] Detlefsen, iv, praef. v–vii; Chatelain, ii. 14; Mayhoff, i, Appendix, 523–5.

[28] Edited by L. Bieler in *Scriptores Latini Hiberniae*, vi (Dublin, 1967). For his use of Pliny see Detlefsen, *Hermes*, 32 (1897), 325 ff. Dicuil implies (Prol. 2) that he had used more than one manuscript, and is aware of the disturbed sequence.

[29] e.g. K. Welzhoffer, 'Beda's Citate aus der Naturalis Historia des Plinius', *Abhandlungen aus dem Gebiet der klassischen Altertums-Wissenschaft, Wilhelm von Christ zum 60. Geburtstag* (Munich, 1891), 30; C. W. Jones, *Bedae opera de temporibus* (Cambridge, Mass., 1943), 111; Desanges, 'Le Manuscrit (Ch)', 509, 511; Chibnall, 61.

[30] E has the sequence 93a/100b–110a/93b–110b.   [31] Some were filled up by E².

clear that the E-text dominates the later tradition of Pliny and it is important to be able to detect its influence, though editors have been painfully slow to learn this lesson.

While there were no dramatic developments in Pliny's transmission between the ninth century and the twelfth, a recognizable process was at work. The *ordo recentiorum* provided the main stream of the text; but the old tradition[32] lived on as an undercurrent to provide an alternative and superior text which was repeatedly used to correct and supplement those more commonly in circulation. Hence the vital textual importance of the later hands in some of the *recentiores*, in particular $D^2F^2R^2E^2$, which found access to the superior tradition, at least for certain areas of the text, as their affinity with what remains of the early *vetustiores* clearly demonstrates. People also used their wits, and the process of correction, accompanied by the equally inevitable process of degeneration and corruption, eventually produced composite and contaminated texts of Pliny which are not easily sorted out and are still only partially explored.

The prime object of editorial quest has obviously been to seek out such elements of the old tradition as survive in the later witnesses. England became a focus of attention, both as an early refuge for Pliny's text and because readings originating with the older and superior tradition had been detected in the excerpts from the *Natural History* made by Robert of Cricklade in the twelfth century.[33] Thus Robert's *Defloratio Historiae Naturalis Plinii Secundi*, dedicated to Henry II (1154– 89) though probably compiled earlier, has long been assigned a place, *honoris causa*, among the *vetustiores*. This is an interesting compilation, but it has been misjudged as a witness to the text; it must be counted, with due respect to the venerable Prior of St. Frideswide's, as something of a mare's nest. It has been known since the end of the last century[34] that two manuscripts written in England, British Library, Arundel 98 (s. XII = 1) and Oxford, New College 274 (s. XIII in., St. Albans = Ox),

---

[32] Though it is convenient to speak of the old tradition as if it were a unity, we may be dealing with several strains of text which are united only in differing from and being superior to the *ordo recentiorum*, as Detlefsen saw (*Philologus*, 28 (1869), 287).

[33] Parts of the *excerpta* (as far as *N. H.* 7.215) were published by Rück: *Das Exzerpt der Naturalis Historia des Plinius von Robert von Cricklade*, SBAW 1902, 195–285; *Die Geographie und Ethnographie der Naturalis Historia des Plinius im Auszuge des Robert von Cricklade* (Munich, 1903); *Die Anthropologie der Naturalis Historia des Plinius im Auszuge des Robert von Cricklade, aus der Wolfenbütteler und Londoner Handschrift* (Neuburg, 1905). None of the editors of the later Books of Pliny could be bothered to consult the manuscript sources for the bulk of the *Defloratio*, not published by Rück. One complete manuscript of the *Defloratio* has been known for a long time, B.L. Royal 15.C.XIV, s. XIII. But there are two others: Eton College 134 (s. XII), which from its early date and fine initial Sir Roger Mynors would gladly think was the dedication copy, and Hereford Cathedral P.v.10 (s. XIII, from the Franciscan convent). Sir Roger Mynors brought the Hereford manuscript to my attention.

[34] J. Grafton Milne, 'The Text of Pliny's *Natural History* preserved in English MSS', *CR* 7 (1893), 451 f.

are textually so close to Robert that they must represent the same tradition, uncomplicated by the omissions and caprice of the excerptor.[35] Editors have used them, but without really asking what they were using. For instance, both manuscripts omit 3.38–70, which is one of the lacunae caused by the loss of a leaf in E itself; both omit 6.148–52, which is precisely that part of a lacuna in E which E[2], through a *saut du même au même*, failed to fill up. These manuscripts are firmly attached to E itself and must ultimately derive from it. The same goes for Robert's *excerpta*, though their authority has been such that scholars have been reluctant to admit the truth.[36] It can hardly be a coincidence that Robert has taken no excerpts from these two passages. He has no excerpts either from 23.166–24.7, where E has also lost a leaf, and at 23.55 he has been observed[37] patching up a sentence which the loss of another leaf in E had rendered headless. He does indeed provide excerpts from some passages which are still missing in E, but there is no need to assume that the filling of these lacunae ceased with E[2]. Robert's very close agreement with E[2] was established by Rück, but, as with other late witnesses, it has been too readily assumed that such agreements denote a common source in the older tradition rather than the dependence of one witness upon another. I doubt if the twelfth-century English tradition (which includes Le Mans 263, mentioned below) can be of significant help to the editor of Pliny, and Robert of Cricklade, interesting though he is, is just a fragment of it.[38] It is high time that he was politely ushered out of the *ordo vetustiorum*, an élite club to which he was elected by mistake. In the ante-room, still waiting to be noticed, he will find his fellow-countryman Retinaldus, another twelfth-century excerptor of Pliny whose claims for recognition were no weaker than his. Retinaldus's excerpts are now known from two manuscripts,

---

[35] But both, presumably each part of a two-volume book, contain only the first half of the *N. H.*, Books 1–18 and 1–19 respectively. William of Malmesbury had a complete Pliny, which he excerpted in his *Polyhistor*; cf. R. M. T., *Rev. bén.* 85 (1975), 380. We know nothing more of the Pliny owned by King John: on 3 April 1208 he acknowledges the receipt of 'librum nostrum qui vocatur Plini' from Reading Abbey *(Rotuli Litterarum Clausarum*, ed. T. D. Hardy, i (London, 1833), 108 b).

[36] D. J. Campbell noticed that Robert, like the excerptor of Montpellier 473, had taken no extracts from 3.38–70 and 6.148–52, which he found 'disquieting': *AJP* 57 (1936), 118. Desanges seems to have seen the point (*Latomus*, 25 (1966), 898; cf. his introduction to Livre V, p. 38) but is unable to grasp it; Robert looms as large as ever in his edition, as do a number of manuscripts whose derivative nature he helped to demonstrate.

[37] Desanges, *Latomus*, 25 (1966), 898.

[38] At all events, it is vital to sift out and weigh any noteworthy readings in the *excerpta Crickladensia* which Robert could *not* have derived from EE[2]; they may have come from another good source, or they may have come from Robert's own head. For instance, he is the authority for the commonly accepted supplement at 8.115 (on the effect of burning stag's-horn): *odore ⟨et serpentes fugantur⟩ et comitiales morbi deprehenduntur*. There is no trace of the supplement in 1 and Ox. For Rück's view, see *SBAW* 1902, 260 f.

Wolfenbüttel, Extrav. 160. 1 (s. XII) and Oxford, Balliol College 146 A (s. XV in.), both written in England.[39]

Sadly, the text of Pliny which circulated in England in the twelfth century is not an outcrop of the rich vein mined by Bede. It came from France and follows the common pattern of transmission. The holdings of manuscripts which England possessed in the eighth century did not in general survive the disorders and sackings of the ninth; the Leiden manuscript apart, Pliny is no exception. A survived, either by luck or because it was taken at an early date to the Continent, but it did not ensure the continuity of the English tradition of Pliny; his text had to be reimported after the Conquest.

Strains of the older texts of Pliny are more likely to have survived on the Continent, and the spectacular improvements which $D^2F^2R^2E^2$ were able to make to the text of the *ordo recentiorum* make it clear that they did. It would be useful if all the scattered evidence for this superior tradition was brought together and more rigorously examined. The big question is whether anything of value escaped the net of the correcting hands to surface in the later manuscripts of Pliny. The twelfth-century manuscripts, some of them handsome and massive books, do not hold out prospects of a rich harvest from the later tradition. The E text grew so fat at the expense of its fellows that it dominated the late medieval text. Berlin (East), Hamilton 517 (s. XI^2 = h),[40] Luxembourg 138 (s. XII^2, Abbaye d'Orval = X), Leiden, Voss. Lat. Q. 43 (s. XII, Orléans?), Montpellier 473 (s. XII, Clairvaux, mainly medical excerpts = n), Copenhagen Gl.Kgl.S.212 2° (*c.*1200 = Co) are all derived from E.[41] Oxford, Bodl. Auct. T.1.27 + Paris lat. 6798 (s. XII med., Mosan region)[42] and Le Mans 263 (s. XII = C),[43] a beautiful book and apparently of English origin, are very close to E and may well be derivative. Paris lat. 6796A (s. XIII = e) is a faithful copy of E and as such has its uses. Vienna 234 (s. XII = a) does not derive from E but from a common parent, and though it is a poor thing, it is an independent witness of the

---

[39] For Retinaldus, see R. A. B. Mynors, *Catalogue of the Manuscripts of Balliol College, Oxford* (Oxford, 1963), 124. The Wolfenbüttel manuscript had not then come to light; it is described in vol. xv of the Wolfenbüttel catalogue (H. Butzmann, *Die Mittelalterlichen Handschriften der Gruppe Extravagantes, Novi und Novissimi* (Frankfurt, 1972)), 92 ff.

[40] From Dijon: cf. A. J. Dunston, 'The Romulus-Pliny from St. Bénigne's Abbey at Dijon, recovered in MSS Burney 59 and Hamilton 517', *Scriptorium*, 7 (1953), 210–18.

[41] On the Luxembourg, Montpellier, Berlin, Copenhagen manuscripts, see Desanges, *Latomus*, 25 (1966), 518 ff, 895 f.

[42] R. W. Hunt saw that these two manuscripts were parts of the same book: 'A Manuscript from the Library of Coluccio Salutati', *Calligraphy and Palaeography*. *Essays presented to Alfred Fairbank on his 70th birthday*, ed. A. S. Osley (London, 1965), 75–9, plate 29. Auct. T.1.27 contains Books 7–15, Paris lat. 6798 Books 16–37. The history of the book in the Renaissance is rich and fascinating.

[43] E. de Saint-Denis, 'Un manuscrit de Pline l'Ancien ignoré des philologues', *RPh* 34 (1960), 31–50 (with two plates). Textually, and probably by origin, it belongs to the English group. W. Oakeshott associates the illumination, which is in the style of the 'Entangled Figures Master', with St. Albans: *The Two Winchester Bibles* (Oxford, 1981), 103 and n. 3.

ordo recentiorum. But large reaches of the later tradition have not been explored and there are certainly some manuscripts, for instance Paris lat. 6797 (s. XII¾, northern France = d),[44] which contain a generous element of the older tradition and may repay further investigation.

L. D. R.

[44] Probably from Saint-Amand: Delisle, i. 317, 318 n. 2, ii. 456. For its worth, see G. Münch, *Wert und Stellung der Handschrift d in Plinius, Naturalis Historia* (Breslau, 1930); R. Schilling, preface to Livre VII of the Budé edition, xxiii f.

THE YOUNGER PLINY

Epistulae

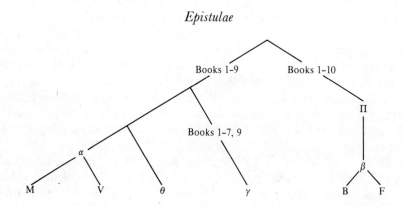

Pliny's extant correspondence consists of nine books of private letters, which he edited and published at intervals during his lifetime, and a tenth book containing his official correspondence with Trajan on the

The best account of the tradition of Pliny's *Letters* is the elegant and authoritative preface to Sir Roger Mynors's edition (Oxford, 1963), from which this vernacular account largely derives. Among his predecessors particular mention must be made of H. Keil, whose edition was a landmark in the editing of the text (Leipzig, 1870). Useful information can still be found in S. E. Stout, *Scribe and Critic at Work in Pliny's Letters* (Bloomington, Ind., 1954), though his enthusiastic and often important researches were sadly marred by misconceptions and illogicalities, and also in the series of articles in *Classical Philology* by E. T. Merrill, some of which are cited below. Stout's own edition (Bloomington, Ind., 1962) was something of a disaster, and the other editions in current use, the Budé by A.-M. Guillemin (Paris, 1927–47) and the Teubner by M. Schuster (Leipzig, 1958³), have been overtaken by the Oxford text. There is an excellent commentary by A. N. Sherwin-White, *The Letters of Pliny, A Historical and Social Commentary* (Oxford, 1966). For a list of manuscripts, see D. Johnson, 'The MSS of Pliny's Letters,' *CPh* 7 (1912), 66–75. Plates of BVM may be found in Chatelain, CXLIII–CXLV, of *Π*BF and Auct. L.4.3 in E. A. Lowe and E. K. Rand, *A Sixth-Century Fragment of the Letters of Pliny the Younger*, complete facsimile edition (Washington, 1922).

administration of Bithynia. The distinction in ancient times between *litterae privatae* and *publicae* was an important one, and the nine books could properly be considered a complete unit in themselves. The tenth book may well have circulated separately for a long time, but the chances are that eventually it would have been added to the other books. Pliny was read in later Antiquity[1] and interest in the *Letters* may well have revived in the late fourth century, when Silver Latin writers came back into fashion; it would be natural, especially at a time when rolls were being incorporated into the more capacious codex, to add the tenth book, when available, to the corpus. Pliny's imitator Sidonius Apollinaris, the fifth-century Bishop of Auvergne, chose to publish his own letters in nine books. This can hardly be regarded as conclusive evidence that he was unaware of Pliny's book of official correspondence, but it is possible that he did not know it. Symmachus' correspondence, on the other hand, follows that of Pliny in having nine books of private and one of official letters: this makes it clear that by the early fifth century[2] a ten-book corpus was known at least in some circles, and indeed a fragment of such a book from the end of the century survives. Pliny's text, well preserved even if at times difficult to recover, goes back ultimately to two antique sources, a nine-book corpus and a codex which contained all ten books.[3]

The manuscript tradition of Pliny is as complicated as it is fascinating. Pride of place must go to the Ten-Book family. In addition to preserving for us that unique dossier of an emperor's correspondence with his provincial legate, of particular interest for the light it throws on the early Christians, it has an extremely vigorous and interesting tradition which runs from the fifth to the sixteenth century. The head of the Ten-Book family still survives, though sadly reduced, in an age which should have known better, to a mere six leaves. This manuscript is now New York, Pierpont Morgan Library M.462, written in Italy towards the end of the fifth century;[4] known as Π, it now contains only *Letters* 2.20.13–3.5.4 and one of the indices (to Book 3) which are a special feature of the Ten-Book tradition. It probably reached France at a very early date, for its earliest descendants were written there, it seems itself to have been in the area of Meaux in the fourteenth century, and by the end of the Middle Ages it was in the library of Saint-Victor in Paris.[5]

[1] Alan Cameron, 'The Fate of Pliny's *Letters* in the Late Empire', *CQ* 15 (1965), 289–98, with an addendum in *CQ* 17 (1967), 421–2.

[2] Symmachus' letters were published after his death by his son, between 403 and 408.

[3] The split between the αθ and γ branches may itself have taken place at an early date. On the characteristics and comparative merits of the Nine-Book and Ten-Book traditions see G. Carlsson, 'Zur Textkritik der Pliniusbriefe', *Lunds Universitets Årsskrift*, 1922; K. Barwick, 'Zwei antike Ausgaben der Pliniusbriefe?', *Philologus*, 91 (1936), 423–48; Mynors, xxi–xxii.

[4] *CLA* XI. 1660; Lowe–Rand, op. cit.

[5] Where it was foliated and described by the librarian Claude de Grandrue.

From a copy of Π descend its two earliest offspring: Florence, Laur.
Ashburnham 98, s. IX^2 (= B), which was written in France, perhaps at
Auxerre,[6] and later belonged to Beauvais Cathedral; and Florence,
Laur. S. Marco 284, s. XI ex., France (= F). B originally contained all
ten books, plus the *Natural History* of the Elder Pliny. The *Natural History*
was detached and is now Florence, Bibl. Ricc. 488; the loss of the
gatherings containing the latter part of the *Letters* means that B now
stops in the middle of 5.6. By a coincidence F too does not go beyond 5.6,
but it has the whole letter and its stopping here seems to be deliberate.
It may not be an accident that F contains just 100 letters; the indices
have been dropped, it is interpolated and glossed, and looks the product
of a later age. In it the *Letters* are preceded by philosophical works of
Apuleius.

B seems to have fallen on stony ground, for it has no known descendants; it was left to F to carry the family flag, which it did with spectacular
success. Its precise place of origin is uncertain, but the way in which its
text circulated suggests the area of Orléans[7] and the pattern of its
distribution is typical of texts taken up by the literary revival of the late
eleventh and twelfth centuries. Descendants of F, or manuscripts with a
text very close to it, soon spread through central France and to the
monasteries of Normandy. Among these are Berne 136 (s. XII, Orléans?),
Rouen 1111 (s. XIII, from the monastery of Lyre, in Normandy), and
Leiden, B.P.L. 199 (s. XIII, northern France); the telling conjunction of
Apuleius and Pliny serves to identify the group and suggests that this
was the text of Pliny recorded in the twelfth-century catalogues of Bec
and Limoges and later attested at Mont-Saint-Michel.

The Ten-Book tradition was able to respond with uncanny speed to
the shifting currents of medieval and Renaissance culture. When the
first stirrings of humanism were reverberating in Italy and a point of
fruitful contact between north and south was established with the
translation of the papal curia to Avignon, the Ten-Book tradition was
quickly on its way to Italy. In 1338 Simon of Arezzo bequeathed a
manuscript containing Apuleius and Pliny to the Dominicans of his
home town.[8] His source for these texts may have been F itself, and it is a
plausible conjecture that he had acquired such a manuscript during his
stay at Avignon in the circle of Nicholas of Prato.[9] But the dominant
centre of Italian humanism was soon to be Florence, and there is no
doubt that F was there, in the library of its chancellor, Coluccio

---

[6] Information kindly supplied by Professor Bischoff.
[7] On the circulation of the F-text of Pliny, see Mynors, viii ff.; R. H. and M. A. Rouse, in
Medieval Learning, 74 ff., 80 n. 1, with particular reference to the *Florilegium Angelicum*.
[8] *Archivio storico italiano*, series 5, 4 (1889), 253. The manuscript in the bequest cannot have been
F itself, as has been suggested: see CICERO, *De oratore*, n. 20.
[9] Cf. R. J. Dean, *Studies in Philology*, 45 (1948), 562-4.

Salutati.[10] Salutati added, in what appears to be his own hand, an extra letter and a half from the Verona tradition (γ), stopping at 5.8.4 *curiosi* and thus leaving his mark on many of the host of fifteenth-century manuscripts which F went on to generate in Italy.[11]

F had been remarkably successful in establishing its 100 letters as the vulgate text of Pliny both north and south of the Alps, but it offered little more than half of its ancestral endowment. Scholars could in time make up much of this deficiency by adding letters from the other types of text coming into circulation, but these were all forms of the Nine-Book tradition and could not provide the correspondence with Trajan. It is therefore inevitable that the final stage of this particular story should be the reappearance in its complete form of the Ten-Book tradition. The main stages in the recovery of the complete text were these:

1. In 1502 Avantius published in Venice an edition (A) of the latter part of Book 10, letters 41–121. He tells us that they had been discovered in France by one Petrus Leander. The letters were numbered xvii–lxxiii, and so they appear in Avantius's edition. If their source, as seems likely, was Π, then someone must have been very careless to have so promptly mislaid forty letters.[12] His edition was reprinted by Beroaldus (Bologna, 1502/3) and Catanaeus (Milan, 1506/7).

2. During the years 1494–1506 Fra Giovanni Giocondo, the Veronese architect, epigraphist, and antiquarian, was in Paris applying one of his many talents to the building of a bridge over the Seine for Louis XII. There he discovered a complete manuscript of Pliny. This must have been Π, now in the library of Saint-Victor.

3. At this point the French scholar Guillaume Budé makes a decisive intervention in the history of Pliny's text. Anxious to have for his own use as complete and as good a text of Pliny as possible, and knowing of Giocondo's discovery, he caused to be bound together Beroaldus's 1498 edition of Pliny (which contained Books 1–9, with a gap in the middle of 8) and Avantius's 1502 edition of 10.41–121, fortunately of similar format. To this he added on inserted leaves, skilfully copied by a scribe to match the appearance of the printed page, the missing letters of Books 8 and 10, taken from Π. Then he added, in his own hand, letter 9.16 (missing in γ and hence in Beroaldus's edition) and a whole series of variants from Π. This remarkable confection, which became Budé's working copy of Pliny, survives in the Bodleian Library under the shelf-mark Auct. L.4.3, having been bought in 1708 by the English scholar and editor of Pliny, Thomas Hearne.[13] The sigla I and i are used

[10] Ullman, *Humanistic Script*, 16–19, plates 8–12; *Salutati*, 155.

[11] Mynors, viii f.

[12] On the mystery of Avantius's truncated copy, see E. T. Merrill, *CPh* 5 (1910), 451–3.

[13] For Budé's Pliny see Merrill, 'On a Bodleian Copy of Pliny's Letters', *CPh* 2 (1907), 129–56; Lowe–Rand, op. cit.

respectively to indicate the supplementary letters and the marginal variants in Budé's copy.

4. In the meantime Aldus was at work in Venice on the edition of Pliny which he completed in 1508. He was first able to procure from Giocondo a transcript of some letters; then, through the influence of the Venetian ambassador in Paris, the abbey of Saint-Victor was persuaded to part with its precious volume, so venerable that Aldus thought that it must date from Pliny's own time. In this way our uncial manuscript, which had survived all that had happened between late Antiquity and the beginning of the sixteenth century,[14] was dispatched to Venice to become a victim of the age of print. Aldus's text (a), put together from various sources and containing conjectures of his own, needs careful handling as a witness to the Ten-Book tradition.[15]

The Nine-Book tradition is less easy to follow. It comes to us in three forms, as can be seen from the stemma: γ, θ, and α.

1. (γ) The first of these actually contains only eight books (1–7, 9)[16] and is consequently known as the Eight-Book family. Its origin is known: it descends from a manuscript, now lost, which had been preserved, perhaps from ancient times,[17] in the Chapter Library of Verona. It was known to Rather of Verona in the tenth century, and was used at the beginning of the fourteenth century by such writers as Giovanni de Matocus, custodian of the cathedral,[18] and by the author of the Verona *Flores Moralium Auctoritatum*.[19] But it was really put into circulation about 1419 by Guarino of Verona and his circle.[20] No complete γ manuscript exists. Someone made a selection of 167 letters from the 218 which γ contained, and this survives in Holkham Hall 396, a useful witness for those letters which it has. But in general the γ text was used merely to supplement and improve the vulgate text of 100 letters which was in circulation. Where the F text was lacking and γ came to the rescue,[21] its readings can be elicited without much of a problem from the composite Fγ manuscripts of the fifteenth century.[22] But where the γ text has been superimposed on that of the 100 letters, teasing out its contribution is a more difficult and hazardous process.

---

[14] It had lost the last three leaves of Book 9.   [15] Mynors, xix ff.

[16] It also omits some individual letters: 1.8, 12, 23, 24, 9.16.

[17] On the antiquity of the Veronensis or its exemplar, see Mynors, x f.

[18] Author of the *Historia Imperialis* and the first in medieval times to distinguish, in his *Brevis adnotatio de duobus Pliniis*, the Elder and the Younger Pliny.

[19] Verona CLXVIII (155).

[20] Merrill, 'On the Eight-Book Tradition of Pliny's Letters in Verona', *CPh* 5 (1910), 175–88; Sabbadini, *Storia e critica*[2], 263 ff.

[21] 4.26 (missing in β), 5.7–7 *fin.*, 9 (except 9.16, missing in γ).

[22] Mynors uses Paris lat. 8621, 8622, Dresden Dc 166, and others of lesser note. Extracting the readings of γ (and indeed θ) is such a tedious task that Mynors is reluctant to take his readers into his counting-house; he prints in his apparatus what he judges on the evidence he has collected to be the γ (or θ) reading.

2. (θ) Most texts of Pliny had holes in them somewhere, but fortunately they tended to have their holes in different places. γ had been
very useful for supplementing the 100 letters of the F tradition, but γ
itself lacked Book 8, 9.16, and of course Book 10. It was not until the
latter half of the fifteenth century that the gaps in Books 1–9 could bè
filled and the text generally improved by conflation with other lines of
descent. The first to come to the rescue was θ.[23] This is a mysterious
source, of unknown date and origin; it is similar to γ in that no complete
θ manuscript exists, and it seems to have been mainly used to supplement and improve existing texts. It provided Pliny's readers with parts
of Book 8, but by a pretty blow of fate it itself had lost 8.8.3–18.1.
Among the manuscripts from which the θ text can be recovered are
Vatican lat. 11468, Turin D.II.24,[24] Paris lat. 8620,[25] and Vatican,
Chigi H. v. 154.

3. (α) Finally a good early Carolingian source for the Nine-Book
tradition, which had lurked in northern Europe for centuries, was
discovered and tapped by the Italian humanists. The first α manuscript
to arrive in Italy was Vatican lat. 3864, s. IX¾ (= V), the well-known
book written at Corbie in the time of Hadoard and containing, in
addition to Pliny 1–4, Caesar's *Gallic War* and the unique excerpts
from the *Histories* of Sallust.[26] Pomponius Laetus was able to borrow it
from the Vatican in 1475;[27] it had arrived in time to influence some of
the early printed editions. Then in 1508 it was joined by the most
complete[28] representative of the Nine-Book tradition, Florence, Laur.
47.36, s. IX (= M). M is written in the script of Fulda and its early
history is closely connected with that of the Mediceus of Tacitus' *Annals*
(Laur. 68.1), with which it had once formed one volume. This book had
been filched from the monastery of Corvey, as we know from the
testimony of such an impeccable source as Pope Leo x.[29] It was first
used by an editor in Cataneaus's edition of 1518.

The α text emanated from a group of monasteries which had connections with the Carolingian court,[30] and enjoyed a limited circulation.
Letters excerpted from a text of this type are found in three other
ninth-century manuscripts: Munich Clm 14641, formerly at St.
Emmeram, but written in a script of the Fulda type; Vatican, Reg. lat.

---

[23] On θ, see Stout, *Scribe and Critic*, 33–41, Mynors, xiv–xvi.
[24] Close to Turin D.II.24 is the edition printed in Rome in 1473 by Johannes Schurener de
Bopardia. The *editio princeps*, printed in Venice in 1471 by Valdarfer and edited by L. Carbo, had
been based entirely on a γ manuscript.
[25] Its text is related to that of the 1476 Naples edition by Iunianus Maius.
[26] See Bischoff, *Mitt. Stud.* ii. 55 ff.
[27] M. Bertòla, *I due primi Registri di prestito della Biblioteca Apostolica Vaticana* (Vatican, 1942), 3.
[28] In fact it lacks 9.26.9 to the end.
[29] P. Lehmann, 'Corveyer Studien', *ABAW* 30.5 (1919), 22, 38.
[30] Pliny, *Epist.* 2.1.10 is quoted by Einhard, *MGH, Epist.* vi, 10.6 f.

251, France?, which was at Saint-Bénigne in Dijon in s. XI; Leiden, Voss. Lat. Q.98, France. The manuscript recorded in the ninth-century Lorsch catalogue[31] may also have had an α text. Two later representatives of α, which descend from it via a common parent, are Prague 2425 (XIV A 12), written in Bohemia s. XIV/XV, and British Library, Harley 2497, s. XV, which belonged to Nicholas of Cues.

The history of Pliny's text is a tribute to the tenacity of humanism, the will to seek and to find. When the corpus of letters had become so fragmented and lacunose, it took a lot of time and patience and the work of many hands to put Pliny together again.

L. D. R.

[31] Manitius, *Handschriften*, 140.

PRIAPEA

All but lost to view after being quoted by the author of the *Cento Nuptialis*,[1] the eighty-one *Priapea* come to light again 1,000 years later in a manuscript written by the author of *Decameron*, Florence, Laur. 33.31 (A, 'copied at various dates, early to mid 1340s, to judge from the style of script, but the hand of the *Priapeia* . . . looks somewhat later'[2]). Within a century they had attained a wide circulation in Italy, though perhaps not as wide as the exchange of letters between Poggio and Panormita over the impropriety of a collection much indebted to these poems, the latter's *Hermaphroditus* (1425).

Panormita's defence might have cut less ice if the *Priapea* had not been accepted as a work of Virgil. This attribution, made in the original title and subscription of A and in most of the other manuscripts, doubtless arose because Donatus and Servius mention *Priapea* among the works of his youth. It was in the *editio princeps* of Virgil (Rome, 1469)

---

[1] *Priap.* 1.1 *carminis incompti lusus lecture procaces/conveniens Latio pone supercilium* ~ Auson. 25.3.1–2 (Schenkl) *carminis inculti* (Mk: *incompti* Tp) *tenuem lecture libellum/pone supercilium*; though the stemma of MkTp is uncertain, the innovation seems more likely to be *incompti*, which could easily have come into T and p (both of *c*.1470) from the *Priapea*. Vollmer on 5.3–4 in *PLM* ii.2 cites two *testimonia* from s. IX.

[2] A. C. de la Mare, *Handwriting*, 25–6. According to G. Cavallo, *Settimane*, 22.1 (1975), 411 n. 252, A. Campana has found a humanistic reference to a manuscript in Beneventan, which Boccaccio could well have unearthed like many another at Montecassino.

that the *Priapea* began their career in print, at any rate forty-one of them; the same editor's next edition (Rome, 1471) supplied all the rest but two (5, 63) and added an epigraphic *Priapeum* discovered near Padua in the 1450s (82)[3] and the *Priapeum* from the *Appendix Vergiliana*, *Quid hoc novi est?* (83), which many manuscripts had already appended to the collection. Two other editions of Virgil (Venice, 1471; Milan, 1472) printed 1–81 from manuscripts.

The younger Burman's edition, *Anthologia veterum latinorum epigrammatum et poematum*, ii (Amsterdam, 1773), 475–556, reports a dozen or so manuscripts, and H. Meyer's revision under the same title (Leipzig, 1835), ii, nos. 1616–94, adds a further seven; but Baehrens, *PLM* i (Leipzig, 1879), 54–87, limited himself to A, which he was the first to collate, and three others. The fullest modern apparatus is given by C. Pascal, *Carmina ludicra Romanorum* (Turin, 1918), who cites Baehrens's four manuscripts and eight besides. Vollmer, *PLM* ii.2 (Leipzig, 1923), 36–73, reverted to Baehrens's four despite drawing up a list of thirty-two,[4] and in Cazzaniga's purely derivative edition (Turin, 1959) these four are reduced to three. A full study of the tradition, together with text and commentary, is promised by V. Buchheit, whose review of Cazzaniga's edition, *Gnomon*, 35 (1963), 35–6, offers a provisional classification of the manuscripts into four groups. One of these, 'die Gruppe um Rehd. 60', looks suspiciously like the *ed. Rom.* 1471 and its numerous descendants (only descendants of this edition include 82 and 83), and that the *ed. Rom.* 1471 constitutes a group equipollent with the others is hard to believe. Of the others, 'die Gruppe um A' is clearly defined by omissions, but a verdict on the third and fourth must await Buchheit's exposition.

Commentaries of s. XV–XVI, published or unpublished, are surveyed by F.-R. Hausmann, 'Carmina Priapea', in *CTC* iv (Washington, 1980), 423–50.

M. D. R.

---

[3] 'Nomine Tibulli in antiquis Tibulli codicibus inveniri, et alii in editionibus suis admonuerunt [Achilles Statius, who found it in B. L. Burney 268, s. XV], et nos inter opera Tibulliana in optima scheda [the *vetus Cuiacianus*] reperimus': Scaliger, *Publii Virgilii Maronis Appendix* (Lyon, 1572), 473; but the coincidence is harder to swallow than a slip of Scaliger's in using his collations. According to a circumstantial note in B. L. Add. 12004 (s. XV⁴/₄), 'hoc epigramma a Nophrio Stroza Florentino repertum est in Euganeis montibus prope rus Arquati', a different story from those cited by Mommsen on *CIL* v.2803.

[4] For another thirty-odd see the list given on my authority by F.-R. Hausmann, *CTC* iv. 425 n. 9. Three unauthorized alterations to the list need correction: Oxford, Bodl. Lat. class. d.5, finished on 24 September 1421, was not 'precedenti (anno) inchoata', a mistake introduced by Hausmann from the catalogue, but 'precedenti (die) inchoata'; Padua, Univ. 527 does not contain the *Priapea*; and New York, Pierpont Morgan M.223 was not copied from an edition. Yet more manuscripts: Cambridge, U.L. Add. 6368, Florence, Bibl. Naz. Panciat. 146, Naples V.F.3, Paris Lat. 8257, Venice, Marc. Lat. XII.60 (4166), XIV.113 (4709), XIV.220 (4496).

PROPERTIUS

Propertius seems to have been virtually unknown from the end of Antiquity to the middle of the twelfth century.[1] Although the text achieved its greatest popularity in Italy during the fifteenth century, its circulation began in the north of France, perhaps in the valley of the Loire. The earliest references and imitations are in John of Salisbury[2] and the *Pamphilus*,[3] which suggests that a manuscript was available in the Loire region in the second half of the twelfth century. The earliest surviving manuscript, Wolfenbüttel, Gud. lat. 224 (previously Neapolitanus, hence N), was copied in northern France shortly before 1200;[4] the second oldest extant manuscript, Leiden, Voss. Lat. O.38 (A), was copied about fifty years later, probably near Orléans, for Richard of Fournival.[5] Two other thirteenth-century scholars, each working at or near Orléans, show knowledge of Propertius: the compiler of the florilegium in Vat. Reg. lat. 2120 (formerly part of the manuscript that is now Paris lat. 15155),[6] and the author of numerous marginal additions in a manuscript of Papias's *Vocabularium* (Berne 276).[7] Both sets of citations seem to be independent of N and A, and probably derive from their common source, which may be identified with the archetype.

The Italian manuscripts of the fourteenth and fifteenth centuries all derive from A and N (or, conceivably, a close relative of N).[8] After Fournival's death A went to the library of the Sorbonne,[9] where it was

This account is based on J. L. Butrica, *The Manuscript Tradition of Propertius* (diss. Toronto, 1978; a revised version is to appear in the *Phoenix* Supplementary Volumes series).

[1] The imitations in Alcuin, *c.*9.12 (*PLAC* I.229) and *c.*49,9 (I.262), and in Ermoldus Nigellus, *In Hon. Lud.* 1.78 (II.7) have no extant intermediate source, but could have come from a collection of *sententiae* or a glossary, rather than from direct access to a manuscript of Propertius.

[2] *De septem septenis* prologue (*Ioannis Saresberiensis postea Episcopi Carnotensis Opera Omnia*, ed. J. A. Giles (Oxford, 1848), 5.209).

[3] Ed. F. G. Becker (Ratingen, 1972); cf. lines 237 (1.12.5), 414 (2.15.30), 420 (2.32.2), 641 (1.5.30).

[4] M. R. James, *CR* 17 (1903), 462; complete facsimile, with introduction by T. Birt: *Codex Guelferbytanus Gudianus 224 olim Neapolitanus phototypice editus* (Leiden, 1911).

[5] R. H. R., *RHT* 1 (1971), 96 f. (with plate of f. 10ᵛ); *RHT* 3 (1973), 267; plate of f. 9ʳ, Chatelain, CII.2.

[6] D. M. Robathan, *CPh* 33 (1938), 188 ff.; É. Pellegrin, *BEC* 103 (1942), 74 ff.

[7] R. H. R., 'Florilegia and Latin Classical Authors in twelfth- and thirteenth-century Orléans', *Viator*, 10 (1979), 131–60; M. D. R. and R. H. R., 'New Light on the Transmission of Donatus's "Commentum Terentii" ', *Viator*, 9 (1978), 235–49.

[8] The claim that Propertius was known and imitated by the Paduan scholars Lovato Lovati and Albertino Mussato (cf. Guido Billanovich, *IMU* 1 (1958), 155 ff.) does not survive an examination of the alleged parallels; Butrica, 207–9.

[9] B. L. Ullman, *CPh* 6 (1911), 284.

seen and copied by Petrarch.[10] Petrarch's manuscript (now lost) was in its turn copied several times, and its direct and indirect offspring constitute the largest family of manuscripts. The earliest known copy, Florence, Laur. 38.49 (F), made about 1380 for Coluccio Salutati, was also the most influential single representative of the Petrarchan form of the text.[11] The other direct or close descendants of Petrarch's manuscript still extant are: Oxford, Bodl. Holkham misc. 36, formerly Holkham Hall 333 (L), copied, perhaps at Genoa, in 1421 by Giovanni Campofregoso;[12] Paris lat. 7989 (P), copied in 1423, the earliest surviving manuscript to combine Tibullus, Propertius, and Catullus, and the unique manuscript of the *Cena Trimalchionis*;[13] and Venice, Marc. Lat. Z. 443 (1912) (Z), copied at Padua in 1453.[14] Since A itself is extant only as far as 2.1.63 and Petrarch's copy of A is lost, the readings of A for most of the text must be reconstructed from FLPZ, with occasional help from the excerpts in Paris lat. 16708.[15] A was negligently copied (as were some other Fournival books), and its corruptions prompted valiant efforts at conjectural emendation in its descendants.

The other branch of the tradition, represented by N, had found its way to Italy by 1427, the probable date at which Vat. lat. 3273 was copied in Florence by Antonio Beccadelli (Panormita).[16] It is tempting to connect the copying of Panormita's manuscript with the fact that in May of 1427 Poggio agreed to send his copy of Propertius to Niccolò Niccoli in Florence; Poggio might have found N or a copy in France and brought it back to Italy.[17] Vat. lat. 3273 and five later manuscripts descended from the same N source[18] are of practical importance to the editor only in 4.11.17–76, where a leaf of N has been lost. They are of great interest for the history of the transmission, however, since some evidence suggests that their common source was not N itself but a manuscript of the same family. The common source has been identified with a manuscript that was in 1484 in the possession of Berardino Valla;

[10] The excerpts in Paris lat. 16708 (s. XV) seem to have been copied from A while it was at the Sorbonne; the existence of this florilegium was first noticed by P. Damon, *CPh* 48 (1953), 96 f.; complete list of Propertian contents in Butrica, 268 n. 7.

[11] For F see Ullman, *CPh* 6 (1911), 284 ff.; A. C. Ferguson, *The Manuscripts of Propertius* (diss. Chicago, 1934), 34–61.

[12] J. P. Postgate, *TCPhilS* 4 (1894), 1 ff.; the first gathering has been lost and the text begins at 2.21.3.

[13] O. L. Richmond, *JPh* 31 (1910), 162 ff.; A. C. de la Mare in *Medieval Learning*, 239 ff.

[14] C. Hosius, *RhM* 46 (1891), 577 ff.; it is a direct descendant of Petrarch's manuscript from 2.29 onwards.

[15] F and Z (from 2.29) are direct descendants of Petrarch's manuscript, but L and P derive from a lost intermediary copy; Butrica, 234–72.   [16] R. Sabbadini, *SIFC* 7 (1899), 106 ff.

[17] Butrica, 218 f., 231 n. 1. N itself may have been in Naples from the 1480s onward; Butrica, 166.

[18] Four are Florentine: Munich, Univ. Cim 22 (1460–70), Paris lat. 8233 (1465, signed by Gherardo del Ciriagio), Cologny-Geneva lat. 141 (formerly Abbey 5989, 1466), Vat. Urb. lat. 641 (1465–70); the last is Roman, Bibl. Casanatense 15 (1470–71, copied by Pomponio Leto and rubricated by Sanvito). On the relation of these manuscripts to N, see Butrica, 219–27.

readings cited by Poliziano in 1489 and Franciscus Puccius in 1502
establish the N-type character of Valla's manuscript, and Poliziano's
description of it as a 'codex vetustus' would seem to rule out the
possibility that it was a humanist copy.[19] The most striking indication
that Valla's manuscript was not N comes from Puccius's note that
Valla's manuscript did not begin a new poem at 2.27.1; this is true of
Vat. lat. 3273 and its five related manuscripts, but not true of N (or A).[20]
Further study of these six manuscripts may reveal whether a manuscript related to but independent of N circulated in fifteenth-century
Italy.

The other surviving manuscripts present various conflations of the N
and A texts, in most cases with some attempt at emendation.[21] One
group of three Paduan manuscripts of the 1460s collectively called Δ –
Deventer I.82 (1792) (D); Vat. Ottob. lat. 1514 (V); Leiden, Voss. Lat.
Q. 117 (Vo) – has been singled out by several editors and critics as
witnesses to a strain of text independent of N and A;[22] on close inspection Δ proves to be a carefully corrected descendant of Z and related
manuscripts, and its apparent superiority derives from the fact that it
exhibits in one recension readings that had originated in several sources
during the previous forty years.[23]

The *editio princeps* was probably that printed anonymously at Venice
in February 1472 (Hain Suppl. 4888); in the same year Vindelino de
Spira printed at Venice a text of Propertius together with Tibullus and
Catullus (Hain *4758), from which all other incunabular editions
derive. The edition most generally used has been for some time that of
E. A. Barber (OCT, 1960[2]); the Teubner text of R. Hanslik (Leipzig,
1979) offers much fuller information on manuscript variants, but the
reports lack discrimination and the text is marred by erratic judgement
in the choice of readings.[24]

R. J. T.

[19] S. Rizzo, *Il lessico filologico degli umanisti* (Rome, 1973), 149, accepting the identification of
Valla's manuscript with N.

[20] Butrica (224 f.) notes as well the presence in Vat. lat. 3273 and its fellows of nonsensical
glosses unlikely to be humanist in origin.

[21] For a classification cf. Butrica, 273–354.

[22] D and V were introduced by Baehrens in 1880, V misdated to c.1400 and D to 1410–20; these
false datings misled Housman and helped to vitiate his work on the Propertian transmission. The
value of Δ was most recently upheld by P. J. Enk in *Hommages à L. Herrmann* (Brussels, 1960), 339 ff.

[23] Butrica, 302–9.

[24] See A. La Penna, *Gnomon*, 54 (1982), 515–23.

PUBLILIUS

Why the mimes of the Syrian Publilius swept audiences of the late Republic off their feet might be easier to say if more had come down to us than two fragments quoted by grammarians and a collection of one-line maxims in *senarii* and *septenarii*. No doubt citizens too snooty to be caught enjoying light entertainment declared their admiration for the maxims, as in later generations the two Senecas and Gellius did. Already by the time of the Elder Seneca an alphabetical collection may have been made, and the *sententiae* that according to his son 'pueris ediscendas damus' (*Ep.* 33.7) may have included some of Publilius'; certainly Jerome learnt one of Publilius' at school (*Ep.* 107.8).

The medieval collections that survive show no sign of having been compiled from anything but one original collection larger than any of them.[1] Over 700 verses can be assembled from five sources:

1. Σ 265 vv. (159 peculiar to Σ) A-N; prose substitutes for O-V supplied from ps.-Seneca, *De moribus*,[2] whence the title 'proverbia Senecae'.

This collection had much the widest circulation. Lupus of Ferrières and Sedulius Scottus used it,[3] and several manuscripts survive from s. IX: Paris lat. 2676 (P^a, s. IX^2/$_4$, Loire valley) and 7641 (P^b, s. IX^1, France), Vienna 969 (A, s. IX^2/$_3$, Mainz), Berlin lat. 4° 404,[4] Valenciennes 411 (X, given to Saint-Amand by Hucbald[5]), and Zürich Rh. 95 (R, s. IX/X, south-west Germany[6]). Equally important is a manuscript of s. XI,

---

[1] Accretions from other authors might have been expected, but the versification and style are uniform and rival attributions do not occur. In that respect Publilius' *sententiae* differ from the Greek set ascribed to Menander, which includes lines from other authors; but the ascription may be a later curtailment of a fuller title. When these 'Menandri sententiae' were compiled is not known, but in their transmission they closely resemble Publilius'. See the edition of S. Jaekel (Teubner, Leipzig, 1964).

[2] On this see Manitius, *Geschichte*, i. 112–13.

[3] Lupus: *Correspondance*, ed. L. Levillain, i (Paris, 1927), 144–5 (*Ep.* 31, *c.*843), 196–7 (*Ep.* 46, a. 845); Sedulius: L. Traube, *ABAW* 19 (1891), 370.

[4] Described by Mommsen, *RhM* 18 (1863), 594–5; missing since the war ('Kriegsverlust' according to Dr Ursula Winter of the Deutsche Staatsbibliothek in a letter of 21.6.81). It is an important witness to Cicero's *De amicitia*.

[5] F. Giancotti, *Ricerche sulla tradizione manoscritta delle Sentenze di Publilio Siro* (Messina, 1963), 57–80 with plate I. It is one of the three independent witnesses to Seneca's *Apocolocyntosis*; its brother there, B. L. Add. 11983 (s. XII^1), also contains Publilius and appears to be its brother again (Giancotti missed it).

[6] Professor Bernhard Bischoff has kindly communicated the date and origin of P^{a}P^{b}AR.

Vendôme 127 (Iᵃ),[7] and true readings crop up from time to time in manuscripts even later.[8]

2. *Π* another 384 vv. A-V; A-I preserved pure in one manuscript, A-V used to supplement a lost descendant of *Σ*; overlap with *Σ* therefore uncertain between I and N.

The manuscript that preserves A-I (with no title) may be the oldest manuscript of Publilius: Vatican, Pal. lat. 239 (H, s. IX[1]), written in the neighbourhood of Mainz and already at Lorsch by s. X.[9] The text ends in mid-page. A descendant of *Σ* similar to X was collated against the full text of *Π* to produce *Ψ*, of which the only complete descendant is the well-known anthology from Freising, Munich Clm 6292 (F, s. XI[1]).[10]

3. Z 134 vv. (48 peculiar to Z) A-V, often rephrased.

The only complete descendant of Z is Vendôme 127 (I[b], s. XI);[11] Zürich C 78 (T, s. IX/X,[12] from St. Gall) covers C-V, Munich Clm 6369 (M, s. XI, south Germany) A-D with the title 'Sententiae philosophorum'. No other manuscripts are known.

4. O 60 vv. (16 peculiar to O) A-V, apparently from an exemplar with the title 'Publii Syri mimi sententiae'.

These sixty verses occur only in the Verona *Flores* of 1329, represented by Verona CLXVIII (155) of a decade or so later.[13] The *Flores* combine everyday material from older anthologies, such as the *Florilegium Gallicum*, with excerpts from rare texts available at Verona, such as Catullus and the *Historia Augusta*. Publilius was evidently one of those rare texts. No other collection preserves the author's name.[14]

---

[7] Giancotti, 81–94 with plates II–III.

[8] O. Skutsch, *P.-W.* 23.2 (1959), 1925, noticing that the Verona *Flores* of 1329 (about which more in a moment) ascribe to Seneca a verse absent from *Σ* (N 40), surmised that they took it from a manuscript slightly fuller than *Σ*; but Giancotti, 46 n. 9, has now shown that several *recentiores* import it from Gellius or Macrobius.

[9] Bischoff, *Lorsch*, 49, 108–9. W. Meyer, *Die Sammlungen der Spruchverse des Publilius Syrus* (Leipzig, 1877), 57–61, transcribes its text.

[10] See most recently B. Munk Olsen, *RHT* 9 (1979), 119–20. It is an important witness to Tibullus and Martial.

[11] Giancotti, 153–68 with plate IV. The whole manuscript is I, and I[b] follows Iᵃ without a break. [12] Bischoff, *Mitt. Stud.* iii. 210.

[13] G. Turrini, *Atti e Mem. dell'Accad. di Agr. Sc. e Lett. di Verona*, ser. VI, 11 (1959–60, publ. 1961), 49–65.

[14] 'Syrus' is surely not part of it but an adjective of origin. Cicero, both Senecas, Petronius, the Elder Pliny, Gellius, Nonius, and Priscian all call him plain Publilius; Jerome and Macrobius describe him as 'natione Syrus'; and the line of Caesar quoted by Macrobius is more pointed if 'a Syro' means 'by a Syrian' (all these *testimonia*, except Petron. 55.5, are set out in Meyer's edition (Leipzig, 1880), 2–4). Skutsch (n. 8, above), 1920, takes the opposite view.

. 5. *Φ*, *φ* two versions of an anthology that includes sixteen verses in garbled form and may include others not elsewhere attested.

The shorter version was known to Sedulius Scottus, Heiric of Auxerre, and Hincmar of Reims,[15] but first came to the notice of modern editors in manuscripts that took parts of it from John of Salisbury and ascribed them to the mysterious Caecilius Balbus of *Policraticus*, 3.14.[16] The longer version is peculiar to F of Publilius (see no. 2, above).

None of these five sources includes the fourth of the fourteen lines quoted by Gellius (C 46), and anonymous *senarii* quoted by the Younger Seneca and Porphyrio probably belong to Publilius as well (A 55–6, N 61, Q 74).

The *editio princeps*, a descendant of *Σ*, accepted the attribution to Seneca (Naples, 1475, Flodr, *Seneca* 1), but Erasmus (Louvain, 1514[17]) saw that the author of A-N must be Gellius' 'Publius' and removed the adventitious prose of ps.-Seneca. At the end of the sixteenth century someone used F for a much fuller edition (Ingolstadt, 1600, in *Orationes Mureti*[18]). T was brought in by Orelli (Zürich, 1832), 'Caecilius Balbus' by Wölfflin, and M and O by W. Meyer,[19] whose edition has not been superseded (Leipzig, 1880). F. Giancotti, who discovered I ($I^a + I^b$) and has collated many of the 150 manuscripts that he lists, promises a Teubner to supersede it.[20]

M. D. R.

[15] Traube (n. 3, above), 369–71; R. Quadri, *I collectanea di Eirico di Auxerre* (Fribourg, 1966), 62–4; S. Hellmann, *Quellen und Unters. zur lat. Philol. des Mittelatters* (Munich, 1906), 98 n. 3.

[16] A. Reifferscheid, *RhM* 16 (1861), 12–26, disentangled the truth after E. Wölfflin had edited 'Caecilius Balbus' (Basle, 1855). Meyer, *Die Sammlungen*, 45–6, held that the collection was a translation of a Greek anthology augmented by lines from Publilius. I have not seen J. Scheibmaier, *De sententiis quas dicunt Caecilii Balbi* (Munich, 1879).

[17] W. Nijhoff & M. E. Kronenberg, *Nederlandsche Bibliographie van 1500 tot 1540* (The Hague, 1923), 199–200, no. 534; copy in the Bodleian (Douce C 259). No other statement about the first printing of Erasmus's edition should be believed.

[18] I cannot verify the existence of this edition, but another of the same description appeared in 1603.   [19] He transcribes the relevant passages of O on pp. 61–6 of *Die Sammlungen*.

[20] In *RFIC* 94 (1966), 162–80, he supplements his *Ricerche*.

Addendum: Bruce Barker-Benfield kindly refers me to his thesis, 'The Manuscripts of Macrobius' Commentary on the *Somnium Scipionis*' (Oxford D.Phil. thesis, 1975), i.67–8, ii.386–7, where he points out that another witness to Z (no. 3, above) occurs on ff. 224ᵛ–225ʳ of Hadoard's anthology in Vatican Reg. lat. 1762; it includes A, B, part of C, and the opening of D and F. He gives other evidence of connections with Corbie in the ancestry of Munich Clm 6369.

QUEROLUS

The anonymous late-antique comedy known as the *Querolus* or *Aulularia* was written in Gaul around the year AD 400 and dedicated to a Rutilius, probably Rutilius Namatianus. It was first edited in 1564 by Pierre Daniel, who owned not a few of the manuscripts which figure in the story below. While the text of the comedy has been examined in some detail by G. Ranstrand,[1] the history of this transmission would probably reward further study.

The *Querolus* is one of the few texts for which the archetype survived the Middle Ages. It was an early ninth-century manuscript which contained in addition Phaedrus (q.v.), and which belonged to St. Remigius in Reims. In 1774 the archetype was burned. Before that date, one page of the *Querolus* in this manuscript was traced, and a photograph of the tracing was published in 1897 by A. von Premerstein. In 1976 M. D. Reeve discovered a transcript of the whole of the Reims *Querolus*, now Hamburg 185 in scrinio (H), copied in 1660 by Samuel Sciassius, patron of M. Gudius.[2] The view of the *Remensis* afforded by H puts no obstacle in the way of supposing that the *Remensis* was the archetype, and that Ranstrand's grouping of the surviving manuscripts is suspect.

Two groups can be discerned among the surviving manuscripts of the *Querolus*. The first of these includes the oldest extant manuscript of the *Querolus*, Vatican lat. 4929 (V), written for and annotated by Heiric of Auxerre in the first half of the ninth century.[3] V contains Censorinus, *De die natali*, an epitome of Augustine *De musica*, four anonymous sermons, the *Querolus*, Julius Paris (q.v.), *Epitome of Valerius Maximus*, the *Septem mira*, Pomponius Mela, *De chorographia*, and Vibius Sequester, *De fluminibus*. For the present text V is a sister of Leiden, Voss. Lat. Q.83 (L), containing the *Querolus* alone; L belonged to, and was probably written at, Fleury in the middle of the ninth century. While L remained largely unnoticed at Fleury, V apparently was at Orléans, where its text of the *Querolus* acquired a literal commentary in the eleventh or early twelfth century. In the middle of the twelfth century V was drawn on by

---

[1] *Querolus sive Aulularia*, *Acta Universitatis Gothoburgensis*, 57 (Göteborg, 1951); *Querolusstudien* (Stockholm, 1951). See also S. Cavallin, *Eranos*, 49 (1951), 149.

[2] M. D. R., 'Tricipitinus's Son', *Zeitschrift für Papyrologie und Epigraphik*, 22 (1976), 21–31.

[3] C. W. Barlow, 'Codex Vaticanus latinus 4929', *MAAR* 15 (Rome, 1938), 87–124; G. Billanovich, 'Dall' antica Ravenna alle biblioteche umanistiche', *Aevum*, 30 (1956), 319–54. Extracts from the *Querolus*, quite probably by Heiric, are added in the margins of B. L. Harley 2735, an early ninth-century *liber glossarum*.

the compilers of the *Florilegium Gallicum* and the *Florilegium Angelicum*.[4] The two *Florilegia*, which exist wholly or in part in numerous manuscripts, account to a large degree for the medieval circulation and knowledge of the *Querolus*. V or a copy of it came into Petrarch's hands; and Petrarch's own copy acquired his annotations, which still survive in the margins of a fifteenth-century descendant, Milan, Ambros. H.14 inf. (A) (see CENSORINUS). A hitherto unnoticed descendant of V is British Library, Sloane 1777, ff. 72^r–86^V, a small composite manuscript of the late twelfth century.[5] A fragment of a medieval descendant of V, containing the end of the *Querolus* and the beginning of Julius Paris' epitome, is now Vatican, Reg. lat. 314, ff. 112–116^v (S). The latter was written in France in the second half of the twelfth century. In the sixteenth century S belonged to Pierre Daniel, supporting the suggestion of a Loire circulation for this group of manuscripts. The thirteenth-century annotator of Berne 276 also knew V and left extracts from the *Querolus* in Berne 276.[6]

The second group consists of two closely related manuscripts which may descend from a common parent. The older of these, Paris lat. 8121A (P), containing the chronicle of Dudo of St. Quentin and the *Querolus* (with glosses and scholia), was written in France in the late eleventh or early twelfth century and belonged to Pierre Pithou in the sixteenth. The more recent of the two, Brussels 5328–9 (B), is a composite manuscript made up of the *Querolus* (with glosses and scholia) and a Terence, both of the mid-twelfth century. On f. 1 in majuscules stands 'WILELMUS ME FECIT'.[7] The volume was given to Francis Busleiden by Master John Isembart, canon and scholasticus of Brussels, in 1498. This pair of manuscripts has not yet been localized.

The last manuscript, Vatican, Pal. lat. 1615 (Chatelain, plate II) (R), originally contained Plautus, plays 1–8. A copy of the *Querolus* in one quire was added to the front, and a copy of plays 9–20 was added on the end. The text of the *Querolus* was written in an east-Frankish or Rhineland hand, and dates from the tenth or early eleventh century. In the sixteenth century the manuscript belonged to Joachim and Philip Camerarius. Ranstrand judged R to be a sister of the parent of PB; but Reeve has demonstrated that this is questionable. Further careful study of this text is needed.

The *Querolus* exerted whatever medieval influence it had in the literary schools of the Loire, particularly Orléans, and among twelfth-

---

[4] A. Gagnér, *Florilegium Gallicum, Skrifter utgivna av Vetenskaps-Societeten i Lund*, 18 (Lund, 1936); R. H. and M. A. Rouse, 'The *Florilegium Angelicum*: Its Origin, Content and Influence', in *Medieval Learning*, 66–114.

[5] Kindly brought to my attention by M. D. R.

[6] See M. D. R. and R. H. R., *Viator*, 9 (1978), 235–49.

[7] This does not appear to be the same twelfth-century William who signed the Gellius in Vatican. Reg. lat. 1646 and the Valerius Maximus in Paris lat. 9688.

century imitators of ancient comedy, in particular Vitalis of Blois.[8] It would be interesting to determine if the scholia in any of these manuscripts have left traces in Vitalis's works or those of his contemporaries; for among the Loire manuscripts described above were probably the ones they used.

R. H. R.

[8] Regarding the influence of the *Querolus* see K. Gaiser, *Menanders 'Hydria': Eine hellenistische Komödie und ihr Weg ins lateinische Mittelalter, AHAW*, Phil.-hist. Kl. (Heidelberg, 1977).

QUINTILIAN

Institutio oratoria

Quintilian's *Institutio oratoria* presents a striking example of a transmission[1] where extant Carolingian manuscripts can be shown to have generated the host of later codices that remain to us.

Considering Quintilian's later popularity, he was drawn upon surprisingly little by the authors of late Antiquity;[2] the use made of him in a single letter of Jerome (107 = Quint. 1.1.5–34) is exceptional in detail. In the age of the epitome, however, the *Institutio*, too large for use as a whole, was quarried by men like Fortunatianus and Julius Victor for their rhetorical handbooks; and it was drawn upon too by the notable eighth-century rhetorical collection Paris lat. 7530, from Montecassino (see *RHETORES LATINI MINORES*), while a few fragments attached themselves to the tradition of Cassiodorus' *Institutiones*.[3] In these circumstances, it is perhaps unsurprising that only two ancient manuscripts seem to have survived the Dark Ages.

One, preserved in France or conceivably obtained from York, was already gravely mutilated when it gave rise to Berne 351 (B) in the ninth

[1] A sketch (in Latin) in my OCT of 1970, i. v–xv. More detail, and argument for controversial details, in *Problems in Quintilian* (*BICS* Suppl. 25 (1970), 3–32) for the early manuscripts, and for the Renaissance texts *CQ* 17 (1967), 339–69. J. Cousin, *Recherches sur Quintilien* (Paris, 1975), adds information on ownership of the manuscripts, but does nothing to add to or alter the general picture (see *Gnomon*, 49 (1977), 574–9).

[2] Thus Servius cites the *Major Declamations*, but not the *Institutio*. See generally F. H. Colson's edition of Book 1 (Cambridge, 1924), xliii ff. Since then, see especially H. Hagendahl, *Latin Fathers and the Classics* (Göteborg, 1958), 197 ff.

[3] More use was made of the *Institutio* in Cassiodorus' commentary on the Psalms than is noted in my Oxford text; see U. Schindel, *Glotta*, 52 (1974), 100.

century: a Fleury book, almost certainly connected with Servatus Lupus.[4] B's most important descendant, the older part of Bamberg Class. 45 (M.IV.14), s. X, is very similar in format and will come from the same area; while the ninth-century Milan, Ambros. F. 111 sup., another copy of B, may well come from the same scriptorium. Both these manuscripts were to play important roles. Two other descendants of B, Paris lat. 18527, s. X, and Montpellier 336, s. XI were less fertile. But another copy of B, now lost to us, was vital for the knowledge of Quintilian in twelfth-century France, for it generated, by one branch, the lost Beccensis, known to us from a copy, Paris lat. 7719, s. XIII, and an epitome by Stephen of Rouen (in Paris lat. 14146, s. XII), and, by another, Cambridge, St. John's College 91 (D.16) and what is probably a descendant of that, Leiden Voss. Lat. Q. 77, both s. XII.

We have so far seen the French medieval tradition. Early Italian humanism, despite the efforts of Petrarch, had to go to France for its knowledge of Quintilian; in the fourteenth century, descendants of Ambrosianus F. 111 sup. – like Petrarch's own book, Paris lat. 7720 – abounded in Italy. And when Poggio eventually discovered a complete text in 1416,[5] it was neither in France nor in Italy, but at St. Gall. For unknown to the French, a tenuous tradition of the complete text had been progressing in Germany. The vital text here was our remaining ninth-century manuscript, Ambrosianus E. 153 sup. (A), now itself mutilated but originally complete. The book is thought to have been written in Italy, and in Italy it reappeared later in the fifteenth century; in Italy too may have been performed the crucial wedding of a relation of A[6] with the Bambergensis, whereby the latter became a complete text. So supplemented, the book doubtless reposed from very early on in southern Germany, where it had a small progeny: first the tenth-century British Library Harley 2664, from Cologne, then copies of that, Florence, Laur. 46.7 of the tenth century, domiciled at Strasbourg, and the St. Gall manuscript, now Zürich C 74a, of the eleventh.

If the St. Gall book was fortunate to receive the corrections of Ekkehard the Fourth in the eleventh century, it was even more honoured to be discovered by Poggio in 1416. Poggio's copy, now lost, but easily reconstructed from early descendants, especially Vienna 3135 dated 1416, was vital to almost the entire fifteenth-century tradition of the *Institutio*. Not only did it have descendants as a whole, including,

---

[4] I argue in *CQ* 12 (1962), 172–3, that the extracts of 10.1.46–131 and 12.10.10–15 which circulated from the eleventh century on independently of the main text were originally taken from a close relation of B, probably its exemplar when less damaged.

[5] I may note here that Vatican, Pal. lat. 1557, dated in *Problems*, 20, to the early fourteenth century, has been dated by Dr A. C. de la Mare to the early fifteenth; this awkward exception can now be disregarded. Dr de la Mare (*Handwriting*, 65 n. 7 with Addenda xvi) has found what she thinks is Poggio's hand in Laur. 46.7 (see below), which may thus have been Poggio's (controversial) second find.

[6] See most recently C. E. Murgia, *CPh* 75 (1980), 312–20.

remotely, the *editio princeps* of 1470: it was also widely used to supplement the *mutili* texts that the humanists inherited from the fourteenth century, most of them descended from Ambrosianus F. 111 sup. Humanist manuscripts cannot, in these circumstances, help us with more than conjectures. Many of the best emendations appear as early as 1418 in Florence, Laur. 46.9 ('Vespasianus domini Manni de Tuderto mihi scripsi'), others again in the class of Harley 2662 ('per manus Gasparis Cyrri': 1434), and especially in Paris lat. 7723, where to an already acutely corrected text Lorenzo Valla ('Laurentius Valla hunc codicem sibi emendavit ipse 1444') and other scholars added their suggestions.

The best witnesses to the text of the *Institutio* were not known, or not much employed, in the fifteenth and indeed subsequent centuries. It was left to Karl Halm's splendid text of 1868/9 to recognize the pre-eminent virtues of Bernensis, Bambergensis, and Ambrosianus, and to exploit the excerpts in Julius Victor. More recent work has done nothing to invalidate his conclusions.

M. W.

[QUINTILIAN]

Declamationes maiores

It is nowadays generally agreed that the attribution in the manuscripts (and in late Antiquity) of the *Declamationes maiores* to Quintilian is false: quite apart from the fact that the world of ideas and the method of argumentation reflected in these speeches have little Quintilianic about them, style and language indicate a later time of origin (at least for the majority) and also clearly show that the corpus consists of the works of

In 1475 *Declamationes* 8, 9, 10, edited by Domitius Calderinus, were printed by Johannes Schurener in Rome. The first complete edition is that of Georgius Merula, printed by Lucas Venetus (Venice, 1481). The latest standard editions are: P. Burman, *M. Fabii Quinctiliani, ut ferunt, Declamationes XIX majores* (Leiden, 1720); G. Lehnert, *Quintiliani quae feruntur Declamationes XIX maiores* (Teubner, Leipzig, 1905); L. Håkanson, *Declamationes XIX maiores Quintiliano falso ascriptae* (Teubner, Stuttgart, 1982). Works wholly or partly dealing with the manuscript tradition: H. Dessauer, *Die handschriftliche Grundlage der neunzehn grösseren pseudo-quintilianischen Declamationen* (Leipzig, 1898); R. Reitzenstein, *Studien zu Quintilians grösseren Deklamationen* (Schriften der Wissenschaftlichen Gesellschaft in Strassburg, 5), Strasbourg, 1909; R. Helm, review of Reitzenstein's *Studien, Göttingische gelehrte Anzeigen*, 173 (1911), 337 ff. L. Hakanson, *Textkritische Studien zu den grösseren pseudoquintilianischen Deklamationen* (Lund, 1974).

several authors.[1] Whatever the truth, the attribution to Quintilian was
probably of great importance for the survival of the declamations: the
Decl. mai. have been preserved in at least sixty manuscripts,[2] the
majority of which date from the Renaissance onwards and are of little or
no importance for an editor. The manuscripts all ultimately descend
from a recension made, it seems, in late Antiquity by two men otherwise
unknown, Domitius Dracontius and Hierius. This fact emerges from
two subscriptions surviving in parts of the tradition; in the so-called α
and β classes and in at least one branch of the γ class of the extant
manuscripts we read after *Decl.* 18: 'Descripsi et emendavi Domitius
Dracontius de codice fratris hieri feliciter mihi et usibus meis et † dis
omnibus.' The following subscription is found only in β, after *Decl.* 10:
'Legi et emendavi ego dracontius cum fratre ierio (Krio Par. lat. 16230)
incomparabili † arrico urbis rome in scola fori traiani feliciter.'[3] In the
absence of certain identification of the redactors, it is not possible to
date these subscriptions exactly; but we can hardly be much mistaken, I
think, if we suppose that the archetype of our manuscripts dates from
the fifth century.

H. Dessauer was the first scholar to make a thorough examination of
the tradition;[4] he recognized four different classes of manuscripts, since
Lehnert's edition called α, β, γ, δ. α is the most reliable class and
contains the two oldest and best manuscripts, Bamberg Class. 44
(M.IV.13) (s. X, Italy, = B), and Leiden, Voss. Lat. Q. 111 (s. XIII[1],
France, = V). Only two other members of α deserve to be mentioned
here, Montpellier 226 (s. XII[2], France = M) and Paris lat. 1618 (s.
XII = π). In both these manuscripts, as well as in the other classes of
manuscripts (especially in γ), the activity of interpolators and con-
taminators has played a considerable part. The text of β is reconstructed by means of two manuscripts, Paris lat. 16230 (P), s. XIV, and
Paris, Bibl. de l'Université 629 (S), s. XV. β has undergone a thorough
revision, which appears *inter alia* from the fact that it places the nineteen declamations in quite a different order from the majority of the
manuscripts.[5] The γ class comprises a great number of manuscripts,
divided by Dessauer into γ^1, γ^2, γ^3. The least interpolated and most
reliable witness for the recension is actually one of the younger manu-

[1] Cf. *inter alia* C. Ritter, *Die quintilianischen Declamationen, Untersuchung über Art und Herkunft derselben* (Freiburg and Tübingen, 1881); G. Golz, *Der rhythmische Satzschluss in den grösseren pseudoquintilianischen Declamationen* (Kiel, 1913).

[2] Dessauer, 5 ff., lists fifty-eight manuscripts, of which thirteen are preserved in the Bibliothèque Nationale at Paris, thirteen in the Vatican.

[3] For attempts to emend the corrupt 'dis' and 'arrico' and to identify the authors of the
subscriptions, see, e.g., E. Rohde (in Ritter, 205–9); C. Hammer, *Beiträge zu den 19 grösseren
quintilianischen Deklamationen* (Munich, 1893), 26 f., and *BPhW* 19 (1899), 521 ff.; Dessauer, 9, 81 n.;
Lehnert, 'Zur Textgeschichte der grösseren Pseudo-Quintilianischen Declamationen', *RhM* 60
(1905), 154–8; L. Herrmann, *Latomus*, 13 (1954), 37–9.

[4] Lehnert's edition makes use of Dessauer's collations.   [5] Cf. Dessauer, 21.

scripts, the Audomarensis, Saint-Omer 663, s. XIV. Another γ manuscript of some distinction (it contains a number of good emendations) is Paris lat. 7800, s. XII[1], France, once in the possession of Colbert. As to δ, only two manuscripts are worth considering here, Leiden, Periz. O.4. A, s. XIII, and Vatican, Ottob. lat. 1207, s. XIII, Italy.

The contamination in $\beta\gamma\delta$ and in parts of α, which cannot always be traced and explained in all details, makes the setting-up of a stemma a rather difficult task. During my work on a new edition, I have, mainly relying on omissions in the text, formed an opinion rather different from that of Dessauer and Lehnert. Dessauer thought that α and β are the only independent sources for the recension; δ simply forms a subgroup of α, and γ is the result of contamination of α and β and has no independent value. This opinion is reflected in Lehnert's text and apparatus. As I see it, the tradition is divided into α on the one hand, and, on the other, $\beta\gamma\delta$, descending from one and the same hyparchetype. Of these, δ was separated from $\beta\gamma$ at a rather early stage, which accounts for its sometimes obvious connection with α; still, it has a number of omissions in common with $\beta\gamma$. An ancestor of $\beta\gamma$ appears to have been contaminated with a large number of readings imported from a manuscript related to M in the α group; contamination and interpolation have gone further in γ than in β.

This activity clearly reflects the great interest taken in this genre from the Renaissance onwards. Not that the *Decl. mai.* were neglected in earlier times: we have some significant quotations and *testimonia* from late Antiquity,[6] the most interesting examples being Firmicus Maternus' imitation of a passage of *Decl.* 4 (cf. Lehnert, 80 f.), and Ennodius' *Dictio* 21 (Hartel's edition, 483 ff.), which is a reply to *Decl.* 5. The so-called *Decl.* 3[b] (Lehnert, 58–67) is an answer to *Decl.* 3, dating from very late Antiquity, or, as is commonly supposed, from medieval times. But the fourteenth century brought with it an increased interest in what was thought to be Quintilian's own work. The text was emended and interpreted by men such as Lorenzo Valla (who composed a new *thema* for *Decl.* 1, the original being lost), Guarnerio d'Artegna, Gasparino Barzizza, Janus Parrhasius, and others.[7] During these times the *Decl. mai.* were frequently copied; and there also exist a number of manuscripts containing Italian translations from the fourteenth and fifteenth centuries. The extant medieval excerpts (Lehnert, 357–431) are of no importance whatsoever for the text.

L. H.

---

[6] Cf. Lehnert's edition, 5, 54, 77, 80 f., 246, 248, 352 f.
[7] Cf. Dessauer, 1–3, 42 ff.

QUINTILIAN (?)

Declamationes minores

The Montpellier manuscript 126, s. IX¾, French[1] (see also THE ELDER SENECA), is our most complete witness (A) to the text of the so-called[2] *Minor Declamations*, containing as it does the declamations numbered 244 to 388.[3] This manuscript was unknown in the fifteenth century, but around 1470 a very similar[4] book, containing 136[5] declamations, was sent from Germany to Francesco Todeschini, the future Pope Pius III. It seems likely that this was the lost archetype (β) of the three known Renaissance manuscripts, all of which contain the last part of *Declamation* 252 and then 253–388. The three are: Munich Clm 309 (before 1494:[6] B), Vatican, Chigi H.VIII.261 (C), and Vatican, Pal. lat. 1558 (D); they are independent of each other.[7]

Dr Michael McCormick will shortly publish details of a quite new discovery, two mutilated fragments of a manuscript thought by Bischoff to belong to western Germany and to the second quarter of the ninth century, and containing parts of *Declamations* 354–7 and 377–81. The indications are that this new text is closely related to β.

M. W.

[1] 'ca IX¾, z.T. von deutlich Reimser Händen' (Bischoff).

[2] The terms *Minor* and *Major Declamations* perhaps do not go back beyond the eighteenth century. The manuscripts ascribe both collections to Quintilian, and C. Ritter, *Die quintilianischen Declamationen* (Freiburg and Tübingen, 1881), and an unpublished Tübingen thesis of J. Dingel (1972) vindicate the *Minor* for him. Ritter's text, published under the title *M. Fabii Quintiliani declamationes quae supersunt CXLV* (Leipzig, 1884), remains standard, but I have completed a new one, with commentary (De Gruyter, Berlin,).

[3] 244 and part of 245 survive only in a transcript by P. Pithoeus (published in his edition of 1580) of all that he could read of the first page, now totally illegible. A Leiden manuscript, Voss. Misc. 7, s. XVII, contains a copy of A up to where β starts (pp. 4, 9–32, 20 Ritter).

[4] Like A, it also contained THE ELDER SENECA (doubtless again in excerpt; late witnesses to this version of the Elder Seneca might therefore repay investigation) and Calpurnius Flaccus (now much mutilated in A; the author is found also in B and C; recent text by L. Håkanson, Stuttgart, 1978).

[5] i.e. from 253 (the first number to appear) to 388. For the details see Ritter's edition, xii–xiii.

[6] Because this manuscript is an ancestor of the *editio princeps* of that year (Taddeo Ugoleto, Parma): see Ritter, xv–xvi.

[7] Ritter used B and to some extent C. D contains conjectures of merit in the first hand as well as later corrections.

In 1421 Traversari wrote to Niccoli: 'Rutilium Lupum cum figuris graecis ad te mitto.'[1] The *figurae graecae* are doubtless those of Aquila Romanus, whose little book is in part the translation of the Greek of Alexander Numenius. Rutilius and Aquila, connected by subject-matter, continued to be connected in their transmission. Eight of the ten[2] fifteenth-century manuscripts of Aquila of which full details are available contain Rutilius also, and the two authors shared their first edition, published by Nicolaus Roscius Ferrariensis (Zopinus) at Venice in 1519. Two years later, a far more important edition, that of J. Frobenius, appeared at Basle. It prints, with apparent fidelity, the text of Aquila and Rutilius from a codex owed to the exertions of Beatus Rhenanus, who 'brought it back to life as though from the underworld', or, less romantically, from the library of Speyer. So close is this text of Aquila to that long ago presented in Florence, Laur. 37.25 (A)[3] that the identity of the Speyer book with that discovered by Traversari is highly probable. How all these witnesses relate to a much earlier extant manuscript in Beneventan script, Rome, Bibl. Casanatense 1086, s. IX, Benevento,[4] has yet to be determined. But this book contains only the *figurae elocutionis*, together with an introduction cobbled together from pp. 23, 5–7 and 27, 9–11 Halm, and cannot therefore be the parent of our other texts, though it shares the omission in 37.3 (see n. 3, below).

Other of the *Rhetores Latini Minores*[5] come to us by the slenderest of transmissions. Julius Rufinianus[6] and Sulpicius Victor emerge only in the Basle edition of 1521. Julius Victor is transmitted in full only, it would seem, in Vatican, Ottob. lat. 1968, s. XII, France. Less perilously preserved are Fortunatianus and Augustine's *De rhetorica*, often linked

---

[1] For details of this joint transmission see M. Welsh, *C & M* 28 (1969), 286–313, *Gnomon*, 44 (1972), 776–80.

[2] Welsh, *Gnomon*, 44 (1972), 776 n. 2, mentions an eleventh, identified by G. Ballaira, *SIFC* 49 (1977), 275, as Washington, DC, W. Hay-Adams House 1054. Ballaira adds three more Renaissance books, while M. D. R. has found yet another (Genoa, Univ. E.III.28).

[3] For which see A. C. de la Mare in *Medieval Learning*, 236–9. A and the Basle edition are marked off from the rest, which have succumbed to a juicy haplography at 37.3 (Welsh, *C & M* 28 (1969), 291).

[4] Along with Paris lat. 7530 one of the oldest grammatical books from the Beneventan area: E. A. Lowe, *Scriptura Beneventana* (2 vols., Oxford, 1929), pl. XVI. Scholars were reminded of its existence by Ballaira, 275–82 . It also contains the *Carmen de figuris vel schematibus*: for whose transmission see Ballaira, *RhM* 122 (1979), 326–37 (with photographs).

[5] Last edited under that title by the excellent Karl Halm (Leipzig, 1863) with full introduction.

[6] Welsh, *C & M*, 28 (1969), 288–9, is sceptical about Rufinianus' presence in the Spirensis; but both he and Sulpicius must have come from somewhere, and most probably thence.

in their tradition; no less than five manuscripts of the former pre-date the tenth century, most notably Paris lat. 7530, copied between 779 and 797 at Montecassino (*CLA* v. 569: further bibliography given by H. D. Jocelyn in *CQ* 30 (1980), 387 n. 2), and Cologne 166, s. VIII[2] (*CLA* VIII.1160; see above on CENSORINUS). Only slightly less grandly, the manuscripts of Julius Severianus[7] are headed by Würzburg Mp. misc. f. 5a, s. VIII/IX, from Germany (*CLA* IX.1402).

All these texts, apart from Fortunatianus and Julius Victor, would benefit from new editions.[8]

M. W.

[7] Far more numerous than Halm knew. C. E. Finch, *TAPA* 105 (1975), 73, summarizes earlier work, and adds a new ninth-century witness.

[8] For Edward Brooks, Jr.'s Rutilius (Leiden, 1970) see Welsh, *Gnomon*, 44 (1972), 776–80. For Fortunatianus, we now have Lucia Calboli Montefusco's excellent edition (Bologna, 1979). It would be unwise to trust her stemma, however; the affiliations of the manuscripts are not constant throughout the work. For Julius Victor there is a new Teubner, edited by R. Giomini and M. S. Celentano (Leipzig, 1980).

RUTILIUS NAMATIANUS

Rutilius was one of the authors discovered at Bobbio in 1493 by Merula's secretary Giorgio Galbiato. Nothing has been heard of the manuscript since a French general removed it from Bobbio in 1706. A fragment used before the discovery for repairing Turin F.IV.25 was recently brought to light by Mirella Ferrari, whose articles 'Le scoperte a Bobbio nel 1493', *IMU* 13 (1970), 139–80, and 'Spigolature Bobbiesi', *IMU* 16 (1973), 1–41, supersede not only previous accounts of the discoveries at Bobbio but also much that has been said about the tradition of Rutilius.

The fragment, which preserves the ends of thirty-nine lines, was written in s. VII/VIII, no doubt at Bobbio; for photographs see pl. IV of the later article. The manuscript when Galbiato discovered it probably contained Rutilius (docked at beginning and end) and the *Epigrammata Bobiensia* (including Sulpicia), but as none of the three appears in the extant catalogues, one of s. IX and the other of 1461, they presumably followed something else – on palaeographical grounds Ferrari suggests

Turin A.II.2, Julius Valerius, *Res gestae divi Alexandri (CLA* IV.439, burnt in 1904).

Who took copies of Rutilius in the twenty or thirty years after the discovery is a matter for speculation. Tommaso Inghirami, who had access to texts from Bobbio in 1496–7, is said to have brought many to Rome, and Rutilius may have been one; but beyond that the only evidence is the surviving witnesses, of which three alone present the whole text:

V   Vienna 277, written at or near Milan in 1501 by Jacopo Sannazaro, Filippino Bononi, and someone else; much corrected; first used in Zumpt's edition (Berlin, 1840).

R   Rome, Bibl. Cors., Caetani 158, written by Ioannes Andreas Crucianus; first collated by C. Hosius, *RhM* 51 (1896), 197–210.

B   the *editio princeps* (Bologna, 1520).[1]

V suffers from neither the inaccuracy of R nor the emendacity of B. RB agree in minor error at 2.62, VB at 1.211, 552; if V were right at 1.461 (*viam*), the error in RB (*algam*) would suffice to unite them.[2] Otherwise the variants are too small to permit any conclusions. The remaining witnesses are: the edition of O. Panvinius in *Reipublicae Romanae commentariorum libri tres* (Venice, 1558), towards which G. Faernus lent him a copy of B corrected in at least one place from a manuscript (1.575–8 *om.* B, *hab.* Panvinius); L. G. Gyraldus, who cites 2.41–4 and 49–56 in *Historiae poetarum tam Graecorum quam Latinorum dialogi decem* (Basle, 1545), 923–4; and Copenhagen Gl. Kgl. S. 429, f. 52^v (reported by Ferrari in the earlier article, 170–1), which cites 2.17–30. Gyraldus and Panvinius give the truth against VRB at 2.42 (*qui* for *quod*), and the other witness, probably written at Rome, has an interesting variant at 1.17 (*stringere* for *cingere*). Add that the two scholars who reproduce Merula's list of discoveries at Bobbio call the poet Rutilius Naumatianus (Namat- V, Numat- B Gyr. Cop., Numant- R).

Since the discovery of R far too many editions have appeared, the latest and fullest by E. Doblhofer (Heidelberg, i, 1972, ii, 1977).

M. D. R.

---

[1] For photographs of VRB see R. Merkelbach and H. van Thiel, *Lateinisches Leseheft* (Göttingen, 1969), no. 21.

[2] J. B. Hall, *PACA* 13 (1975), 13–14, defends *algam* (with *prohibente* . . . *symplegmate* for *praebente* . . . *symplegade*).

SALLUST

Catilina and *Jugurtha*

The manuscripts of Sallust's *Catilina* and *Jugurtha* are traditionally divided into two classes, *mutili* and *integri*; the former are so called because they have a large lacuna (103.2 *quinque delegit* – 112.3 *et ratam*) in the *Jugurtha*. This is a useful distinction, but it has caused a great deal of misunderstanding. It does not seem to be generally appreciated that *mutilus* and *integer* should be treated as purely descriptive terms: they do not denote manuscripts which belong to two different genealogical families.[1] It would have been clearer if the triple classification into *mutili*, *suppleti*, *integri* had been more widely used. When a later hand adds the missing passage to a *mutilus*, it becomes a *suppletus*; one more stage of copying may produce a perfectly good *integer*. There is a common assumption that these upstarts are not real *integri* at all, but merely *mutili* who have covered their shame with borrowed plumes. This assumption would be warranted if one could produce, from the large host of complete manuscripts of Sallust, something that looked like an original and genuine *integer*; but such a manuscript has proved as elusive as the Holy Grail. *Integri* appear to be nothing more than patched-up *mutili*. They do for all that have a certain character of their own:[2] they are in general later than the *mutili*, they have a less reliable text, and they are so thoroughly contaminated that their vertical lines of descent have in most cases been obscured. As there are no early *integri*, so there are no late *mutili*, and the *integri* function as a *recentior* tradition.

The abolition of the *integri* as a separate recension brings into sharper focus the problem of the origin of the missing passage. To judge from the dates of the manuscripts which first fill the gap, the missing chapters began to circulate in the late tenth or early eleventh century. It is just possible, I suppose, that the lost leaves of the archetype had turned up,

---

A. D. Leeman, *A Systematical Bibliography of Sallust (1879–1964)* (Leiden, 1965) removes the need for extensive bibliography. In fact, as far as the recension of the *Catilina* and *Jugurtha* is concerned, little of moment has appeared since the admirable study of A. W. Ahlberg, *Prolegomena in Sallustium* (Göteborg, 1911). The editions to which one normally has recourse are those of R. Dietsch (Leipzig, 1876⁴), H. Jordan (Berlin, 1887³), Ahlberg (Leipzig, 1919, preceded by separate editions of the *Catilina* and *Jugurtha*, Göteborg–Leipzig, 1911, 1915), A. Ernout (Paris, 1958³), A. Kurfess (*post* A. W. Ahlberg, Leipzig, 1957³).

[1] Ahlberg, *Prolegomena*, 68 ff.
[2] Which explains why Ahlberg should devote himself (pp. 96–103) to the apparently unreal question of whether those manuscripts which do not contain the latter part of the *Jugurtha*, and so cannot reveal whether they had a lacuna or not, were in fact *mutili* or *integri*.

that the missing passage had been copied from them and gradually infused into the *mutilus* tradition. If this is not the case, then we must assume that at least one complete text – an *Urinteger* as it were – was discovered. Such a manuscript would have been independent of the archetype of the *mutili* (Ω), but need not have had a very different or much superior text. At all events it is not clear, from our present knowledge of the tradition, whether those who exploited this new source to fill the lacuna in the *Jugurtha* also took the opportunity to use it to improve the other parts of the text. More investigation is needed, but it may still be useful to make some preliminary points about the sources for the text which exist outside the main tradition.

1. The lacuna passage (*J.* 103.2–112.3), whatever its precise origin, has a different tradition from the rest of the text and must be treated as an independent unit. Manuscripts which are good witnesses for these chapters are not necessarily so for the main text, and vice versa.

2. Variants and short supplements appear in the tradition at a somewhat later stage than the introduction of the missing part of the *Jugurtha*. The variants are a mixed bag,[3] often mere banalizations of the true text, and they provide no firm basis for discussion. But the existence of short passages of text,[4] apparently genuine, which are absent from all the earlier manuscripts of Sallust, *mutili* and *integri* alike, suggests a source outside the main tradition, though not necessarily the same as that which preserved the missing part of the *Jugurtha*. This external source, however conceived, is normally designated as Z. Since these supplements did not appear in the earlier *integri*, a new star appeared in the sky, the *integri recentiores* (ζ).[5]

3. Although the title *integri recentiores* gives these manuscripts a touch of class, it is difficult to see how they are more than plain *recentiores* – not that they are necessarily any the worse for that. What is disconcerting is that they have not emerged as a constant and coherent group. It could well be a mistake to assume, on present evidence, that these supplements (and variants) necessarily confer any distinction or identity on the manuscripts which carry them. They float at large in the tradition, rather more widely distributed than is generally supposed, and may be no more an intrinsic part of the manuscripts on which they have settled

---

[3] They can be most easily sampled in J. M. Pabón, *Emerita*, 1 (1933), 78–101, 2 (1934), 1–14.

[4] *C.* 5.9 *atque optima*; 6.2 *ita brevi multitudo divorsa atque vaga concordia civitas facta erat*; *J.* 21.4 *de controversiis iure potius quam bello disceptare*; 44.5 *neque muniebatur*. These are the crucial supplements, though others have been given the same status. Their origin can be explained in various ways, but no single explanation other than a source outside the older tradition will account for them all. For a vigorous statement of the problem they pose, see G. Perl, 'Probleme der Sallust-Überlieferung', *Forschungen und Fortschritte*, 33 (1959), 56–60.

[5] They are an important element in the tradition for R. Zimmermann, *Der Sallusttext im Altertum* (Munich, 1929) and Pabón (see n. 3, above; also *Emerita*, 2 (1934), 257–62, and his edition of Sallust (Barcelona, 1954, 1956).

than birds are of the trees in which they build their homes. Their ultimate source remains obscure.

While Z may have vanished from the scene like the Cheshire Cat, leaving little more than a grin and the tip of its tail, one source for Sallust's text quite independent of Ω does survive in the flesh. At some time in Antiquity somebody put together a collection of speeches and letters excerpted from the *Bella* and the *Historiae* of Sallust. This ancient florilegium, which was accompanied on its travels by the *Epistulae ad Caesarem*, found its own route to the Middle Ages. It first appears about 790 in the palace library of Charlemagne, being one of the texts listed in Berlin (West), Diez. B Sant. 66.[6] A copy of the book once at the palace, now lost, survives in Vatican lat. 3864 (= V), written in the third quarter of the ninth century at Corbie.[7] Some of the speeches and letters from the *Bella* were also copied, to fill a vacant space, into Berne 357, which is part of the great corpus[8] of largely grammatical works put together in France towards the end of the ninth century, probably at Auxerre. The compiler's lack of interest in the excerpts from the *Historiae* and in the *Epistulae ad Caesarem* suggests that he gave priority to works he knew. The text of Berne 357 is uncommonly close to that of V and could well be derived from it. Where V and Ω overlap we have two separate recensions, and their rival merits have been one of the most debated questions of Sallustian scholarship. Sallust was so popular in Antiquity that the abundance of *testimonia* and quotations in ancient authors[9] provides a further check on the medieval tradition, as do the five papyrus fragments,[10] unfortunately very short.

To come to the main core of Sallust's text, the *mutilus* tradition can be represented in stemmatic form if confined to the earlier and less contaminated witnesses. Although the exchange of variants between the different branches limits its value as an editorial instrument, the stemma depicted below, constructed by Ahlberg, draws the main shape of the early medieval tradition.

The manuscripts used in the construction of the stemma are as follows:

P   Paris lat. 16024, s. IX[2], written in the region of Soissons.[11]

---

[6] Now available in facsimile, with an introduction by B. Bischoff: *Sammelhandschrift Diez. B Sant. 66. Grammatici latini et catalogus librorum* (Codices selecti phototypice impressi, 42), Graz, 1973. For the Sallust entry, see pp. 39, 219.   [7] Bischoff, *Mitt. Stud.* i. 60.

[8] Berne 347 + 357 + 330 + Paris lat. 7665 + Leiden, Voss. Lat. Q.30 (ff. 57–8). The excerpts from Sallust occupy ff. 28ᵛ–32ᵛ of Berne 357.

[9] Examined by Zimmermann (cf. n. 5, above) and E. Höhne, *Die Geschichte des Sallusttextes im Altertum* (Diss. Munich, 1927).

[10] Florence, Laur. P.S.I. 110 (*CLA* III.288) s. v; London, Egypt Exploration Society, P. Ant. 154 (*CLA* Suppl. 1712), s. IV/V; Manchester John Rylands Pap. 42 (*CLA* II. 223), s. III; Oxford, Bodl. Lat. class. e.20 (P) (*CLA* II.246), s. v; Berlin (East) lat. 4° 914 (*CLA* VIII.1054), s. IV.

[11] I am grateful to Professor Bischoff for this information.

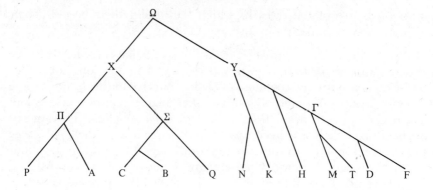

A   Paris lat. 16025, written in the middle or third quarter of the ninth
        century, probably at Auxerre.[12]
C   Paris lat. 6085, s. XI in., France.
B   Basle AN IV 11, s. XI[1], southern Germany.
Q   Paris lat. 5748, s. XI, France (?).[13]
N   Vatican, Pal. lat. 889, s. X[2], written at Lorsch.[14]
K   Vatican, Pal. lat. 887, s. XI, of unknown origin but also perhaps to be
        associated with Lorsch.[15]
H   Berlin (East), Phillipps 1902, s. XI, southern Germany.
M   Munich Clm 4559, s. XI/XII, southern Germany, belonged to
        Benedictbeuern.
T   Zürich Car. C 143a, s. XI/XII, Germany.
D   Paris lat. 10195, s. XI, probably written at Echternach.[16]
F   Copenhagen, Fabricius 25 2°, s. XI ex., Belgium or north-eastern
        France.[17]

The *integri* are so contaminated that they are best regarded as having
an open tradition, though their affiliation to one or more of the known
stemmatic groups is usually discernible.[18] As *integri* their obvious and
proper function is to fill the lacuna in the *Jugurtha*, but the better of them
have something to contribute to the rest of the text and it has been
customary to cite them alongside the *mutili*. From those known to him
Ahlberg selected four as the best witnesses:

1   Leiden, Voss. Lat. O.73, s. XII[1], France (?).
s   Leipzig Rep. I. 2° 4, s. XI, from Magdeburg.

[12] Bischoff, *Settimane*, 22.1, 77 n. 48 (= *Mitt. Stud.* iii. 66. n. 47).
[13] Of unknown origin, but its later (and very distinguished) history is French; its first recorded
possessor is Guillaume de Boisratier, Archbishop of Bourges (†1421).
[14] Bischoff, *Lorsch*, 114–15.
[15] Ibid. Its link with Lorsch is that it later belonged to Mathias Kemnat.
[16] It has an almost contemporary *ex libris*.
[17] P. Lehmann, *Nordisk Tidskrift för Bok- och Biblioteksväsen*, 22 (1935), 24.
[18] Ahlberg, *Prolegomena*, 73 ff.

n   Paris lat. 6086, s. XI, Rebais (diocese of Meaux).[19]
m   Munich Clm 14477, s. XI, from St. Emmeram, Regensburg.

The lacuna passage (*J*.103.2–112.3) has its own tradition, and the text of these chapters is usually reconstructed from two sets of manuscripts, the *integri* (lsnm) and the *suppleti* (CQKHMTDF).[20] Again, these are descriptive terms, which tell us nothing about the colour of the text. The first real attempt to study the manuscript tradition of this passage was made by Bertold Maurenbrecher, who devoted a whole monograph to the problem.[21] This is a thorough and meticulous piece of work, but it largely misfires: his information was not always accurate, some of the manuscripts he used were poor and late, and his approach was more elaborate than the nature of the problem allows. Ahlberg in the main accepted his findings, but in practice used a more restricted and better selection of manuscripts, and there the matter has rested. Our apparatus criticus of Sallust, normally a rather chaste affair, bellies out in this part of the text to accommodate a great deal of rubbish. It could easily be trimmed if the witnesses were more carefully selected.[22]

It is not possible to write the full story of Sallust's text in the Middle Ages until more work has been done on the manuscripts; but a start can be made by putting a little flesh on Ahlberg's stemma, and then the main lines of the earlier tradition begin to emerge. Despite contamination, an original division into two families (*X* and *Y*) is clear enough; and Ahlberg's view that *X* originated in France and *Y* in Germany,[23] though apparently based on little more than the shelf-marks of the manuscripts, proves to be right.

Although Sallust became one of the most popular prose writers of the Middle Ages and Renaissance,[24] the tradition got off to a comparatively slow start in the Carolingian period. It did not begin to swell out until the eleventh century. At first it was the French family (*X*) which held the field. Only two complete manuscripts and one set of snippets survive from the ninth century, and all are French. By the time that the text became common it was rapidly degenerating, and the two ninth-century manuscripts P and A are well ahead of the field in quality. P was written in the area of Soissons, A in all probability at Auxerre. Paris lat.

---

[19] 'liber sancti petri resbaci' (f. 72ʳ, in a thirteenth-century (?) hand), i.e. Saint-Pierre, Rebais. Cf. Delisle, ii (Paris, 1874), 397.

[20] Manuscripts which have earned their place in the apparatus as *mutili* tend to retain it as *suppleti*, though the quality and date of the supplementary text does not in every case justify this.

[21] *Sallustiana I. Heft: Die Überlieferung der Jugurthalücke* (Halle, 1903).

[22] The lacuna passage seems to be in good order, though it has been rather casually edited in comparison with the rest of the text. One wonders why modern editions should read *sic rex incipit* at 109.4, for instance, when the manuscript evidence indicates that Sallust wrote *rex sic incipit*.

[23] *Prolegomena*, 67.

[24] The manuscript tradition is vast; I know of more than 500 manuscripts, and there must be many more.

6256,[25] which contains some glosses and short excerpts from Sallust, was written in western France in the second quarter of the ninth century. It is therefore slightly earlier than P and A, but the brief passages in it tell us little about their source. A second hand in A links it with the school of Lupus of Ferrières, and we know from other evidence that Lupus had an interest in Sallust's text. In one letter[26] he asks his correspondent, unfortunately unidentified, to send him a copy of the *Catilina* and *Jugurtha*. It is not clear from his words whether he has no copy of Sallust or whether the copy he has is unsatisfactory, but some acquaintance with Sallust is in any case apparent from an earlier letter.[27] A was corrected against a manuscript of the Σ group, so that Σ too may have had its home near by. The corrections were taken from a manuscript close to C, and C, written in the early eleventh century, comes from some part of that area which stretches from Orléans to Paris.[28] The one X manuscript to survive from the tenth century is also connected with A. This is Montpellier 360,[29] which I shall call L. L was written in a French hand of the tenth century, but a number of leaves which had presumably become worn or damaged were neatly replaced in the twelfth century by other leaves made to match them; these had taken their text, not from the leaves which they replaced, but from a different manuscript. The tenth-century leaves have a rather indifferent text of the Σ type; the twelfth-century supplements are clearly derived from A. L found its way to Pontigny and it may well have been at Pontigny that it was repaired.

The Carolingian scholars had to make do with *mutili*, and it is possible that an *integer* is precisely what Lupus was looking for. The missing part of the *Jugurtha* did not circulate for a century or more, but a partial remedy was at hand: the speeches which had been excerpted from Sallust in Antiquity and preserved in V were available in at least two French centres, Corbie and Auxerre, and one of these speeches, that of Bocchus, king of Mauretenia (*J.* 110), was missing in the *mutili* because it happened to fall within the lacuna. Bocchus was thus in demand, and his speech was appropriated by the *mutilus* tradition at a

[25] E. Hedicke, 'Scholia in Caesarem et Sallustium', *Programm des Gymnasiums in Quedlinburg* (Quedlinburg, 1879), 9–18; B. Munk Olsen, *RHT* 9 (1979), 111. This is an interesting manuscript which contains glosses and extracts from a number of historical texts (Caesar, Sallust, Justinus, the Latin Josephus).

[26] *Epist.* 104 (Dümmler, *MGH, Epist.* II, p. 91), to Reginb[ertus?]: 'Catilinarium et Iugurthinum Sallustii librosque Verrinarum et si quos alios vel corruptos nos habere vel penitus non habere cognoscitis nobis afferre dignemini, ut vestro beneficio et vitiosi corrigantur et non habiti hoc gratius quo insperatius adquirantur.' The letter is dated by L. Levillain to 856–8 (*Loup de Ferrières. Correspondance*, ii (Paris, 1935), 124–5).

[27] He shows a knowledge of Sallust, for instance, in the letter which he sent to Abbot Bun and the monks of Hersfeld in 836 to accompany his *Vita S. Wigberti* (*MGH, Epist.* II, p. 108).

[28] I am grateful to Dr François Avril for an opinion on the origin of this manuscript.

[29] M. Bonnet, 'Die Handschriften von Montpellier H. 360 und Paris lat. 10195 [D]', *Hermes*, 14 (1879), 157–9.

much earlier date than has been thought. The text of P does not break off at *J.* 113.3, or even become illegible, as editors report; it merely became obscured when some clumsy hand glued the last verso to the flyleaf. Still in part legible, f. 46ᵛ contains the end of the *Jugurtha* and, more unexpectedly, the *Oratio Bocchi*, appended in the same or a contemporary hand. This confluence of the *mutilus* and V traditions at this early date is not really surprising. It would have been possible at Corbie, for instance, to add Bocchus' speech to a manuscript of the *mutilus* tradition. V was written at Corbie during the time that Hadoard was librarian, and Hadoard must have had a manuscript of the *Catiline* and *Jugurtha* to hand because he excerpted them for his own *Collectaneum*.[30] At a much later date the *Oratio Bocchi* was added in a similar way in C and B; and the agreement of PCB in one reading not shared by V and Berne 357[31] indicates either that there was a third ninth-century copy of these excerpts circulating in France, or that the *Oratio Bocchi* had broken away from V and formed its own tiny tradition as an appendix to the *mutili*. It became redundant when the whole of the lacuna passage became available, and we can see this process at work in C, where another hand has added the rest of the missing passage. B is written in a German hand, possibly from the area of Metz, but here the *Oratio Bocchi* is no late addition and may well have travelled with the text for some time. The texts which B carries are ultimately of French origin, and in B we have an early example of the diffusion of the *X* text to Germany.

There is no knowing whether the Sallusts recorded in the ninth-century catalogues of Reichenau and Murbach were early copies of the *Y* text, but it is a not unreasonable assumption. The doyen of the extant manuscripts of the *Y* family is N, written at Lorsch in the second half of the tenth century. K is of unknown origin, but its coming into the possession of Mathias Kemnat makes it not unlikely that it too was at one time at Lorsch. To judge by its script, H could well have come from the area of Metz, as did many other Clermont books. D is firmly attached to Echternach, M belonged to Benedictbeuern, T is clearly German, and F was written in Belgium or north-eastern France. Our rather restricted selection of manuscripts has made the *Y* family look more exclusively Germanic than in fact it is, but its location at this stage of the tradition to the south and west of the Germanic area is beyond doubt.

Historiae

What remains of Sallust's *Historiae* has come down to us through diverse

---

[30] Vatican, Reg. lat. 1762. See the transcription by P. Schwenke, *Philologus, Suppl.* 5.3 (1886), 445, 500. It is interesting to discover that Hadoard had drawn his excerpts from a manuscript of the *Y* family: at *Cat.* 10.5 he reads *et ambitio* with NK.   [31] 110.4 *vivis.*

channels. Apart from the indirect tradition, formed by the unusually large number of fragments quoted by ancient writers and grammarians,[32] there are three different types of direct transmission.

(i) Two sets of fragments have been preserved in the sands of Egypt. The first consists of fragments of a papyrus roll, written in expert rustic capital, s. II/III: Manchester, John Rylands Pap. 473 + London, Egypt Exploration Society, P.Oxy. S. N. (*CLA* Suppl. 1721). The high quality of the book suggests an importation. Secondly, a recent and remarkable discovery has recovered two more fragments of the *Historiae*; these are preserved in Vienna, P. Vindob. L 117, part of the bifolium of a parchment codex written in rustic capitals of the fourth century. Though this scrap has been known for some time (*CLA* X.1537), the fragments were first identified in 1963, when Professor Bischoff deciphered enough to see that they actually overlapped with Mauren-brecher, I.107 and I.136.[33] Found in Egypt, but probably imported from Italy.

(ii) The *Codex Floriacensis*, Orléans 192, ff. 15–18, 20 + Vatican, Reg. lat. 1283B + Berlin (East) lat. 4° 364 (*CLA* VI.809; also I, p. 34, VIII, p. 10). This fifth-century codex of the *Historiae* survived at least in part until the late seventh or early eighth century, when it was taken to pieces, apparently at Fleury, and used partly for bindings, partly to copy Jerome's *Commentary on Isaiah*. It is tragic that such a handsome copy of one of the most popular texts in Antiquity should have survived so long only to perish in this way. Parts of eight leaves survive,[34] of which three are non-palimpsest.

(iii) Finally we have the four speeches and two letters excerpted from the *Historiae* in ancient times and transmitted in V and its descendants. They are found, along with the *Epistulae ad Caesarem*, in a number of fifteenth-century manuscripts, all derived from early printed editions.[35] V or copies of it must have arrived in Italy much earlier, for it seems that the excerpts were known to Guglielmo da Pastrengo.[36] Pier Candido Decembrio copied the speeches of Lepidus and Philippus into his scrap-book (Milan, Ambros. R. 88 sup., ff. 98ʳ–99ᵛ), not later than 1455, but more interesting is his earlier discovery of the *Epistula Pompei ad senatum*.[37] Sometime between 1435 and 1439 he wrote an excited letter to Luigi Crotti enclosing what he took to be a genuine letter written by

---

[32] B. Maurenbrecher, *C. Sallusti Crispi Historiarum reliquiae*, Fasc. I–II (Leipzig, 1891–3).

[33] B. Bischoff, H. Bloch, 'Das Wiener Fragment der "Historiae" des Sallust (P. Vindob. L 117)', *WS* N.F. 13 (1979), 116–29.

[34] On the number and arrangement of the leaves, see the important article by Bloch, 'The Structure of Sallust's *Historiae*: the Evidence of the Fleury Manuscript', in *Didascaliae. Studies in Honor of Anselm M. Albareda*, ed. S. Prete (New York, 1961), 61–7, figs. 1–2.

[35] See *APPENDIX SALLUSTIANA* 1. Paris lat. 6093 does not contain the excerpts.

[36] Sabbadini, *Scoperte*, i. 16–17.

[37] Sabbadini, *Museo italiano di antichità classica*, 3 (1888), cols. 69–74; *SIFC* 11 (1903), 267–9.

Pompey himself, and this, it appears from a later letter, he had found in a manuscript belonging to Francesco Pizzolpasso, Archbishop of Milan: 'cum vetustissimum codicem nuperrime nactus studiose lectitarem et eo maxime quod plurima a Livio sumpta animadverteram, ex his potissimum libris qui iampridem periere.' Decembrio's own copy of the letter is found earlier in his scrap-book (f. 60ᵛ), separated from the two orations and without any ascription to Sallust. Pizzolpasso's *vetustissimus codex* with its excerpts from Sallust and Livy is a mystery. Sabbadini and Paladini[38] treat Decembrio's autograph seriously as an independent witness to the text of the *Epistula Pompei*, but it is clearly worthless for this purpose, having nothing to add to the text but error.

L. D. R.

[38] V. Paladini, *Sallustius, Orationes et Epistulae de Historiarum libris excerptae* (Bari, 1956).

APPENDIX SALLUSTIANA

1: *Epistulae ad Caesarem senem de re publica*

These two *suasoriae*[1] of disputed authorship are preserved in Vatican lat. 3864 (V.), along with the speeches and letters excerpted from Sallust's *Catilina, Jugurtha,* and *Historiae* (q.v.). V had arrived in the Vatican by 1475[2] and the first printed editions took their text from it.

The *Epistulae* are also found in a number of late fifteenth-century manuscripts. There are at least six of these,[3] but none has any independent authority. They were not copied from V but from one or other of the early printed editions. Vatican lat. 3415, written in 1484 by pupils of Pomponio Leto, derives from the *editio princeps* of the *Epistulae* printed at

[1] The standard text is that of A. Kurfess (Leipzig, 1970[7]). Recent texts with commentary are those of V. Paladini (Rome, 1952), K. Vretska (Heidelberg, 1961), P. Cugusi (Cagliari, 1968).

[2] See THE YOUNGER PLINY, n. 27.

[3] The only two known to editors of Sallust are Vatican lat. 3415 and Urb. lat. 411, whose dependence on the *ed. Rom.* and *ed. Mant.* respectively was demonstrated by E. Hauler, 'Junge Handschriften und alte Ausgaben zu Sallust', *WS* 17 (1895), 104–21. Kurfess (by inadvertently interchanging the sigla V² and V³) and Cugusi (by following Kurfess) make them dependent on ·the wrong editions.

Rome in 1475 by Arnold Pannartz. Urb. lat. 411, written between 1478 and 1482 for Federico da Montefeltro by Federico Veterani, is a copy of the edition printed at Mantua by Johann Schallus (1476–8). Ottob. lat. 2989, in the hand of Giacomo Aurelio Questenberg, is the dedicatory manuscript copy of Leto's first edition of Sallust (Rome, 1490) which he sent to Agostino Maffei. The three other manuscripts are Paris lat. 6093, written in 1496 for Robert Gaguin; Chantilly 762, richly decorated for Antonio Altieri; and Göteborg lat. 24. These all contain Leto's *Vita* of Sallust and so betray their dependence on one or another of his editions.

L. D. R.

2: [*Sallusti*] *in Ciceronem et invicem Invectivae*

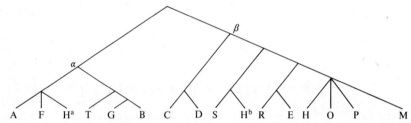

These mildly scurrilous and undemanding pieces of literary forgery enjoyed considerable popularity in the Middle Ages and Renaissance.[1] They are usually found in manuscripts of Sallust or Cicero, in the latter case commonly appearing in the company of the *In Catilinam*, the Caesarian orations, the *De amicitia*, and *De senectute*; but the diversity of the company they keep and their absence from the earliest manuscripts of Cicero and Sallust suggest that they did not originally travel with either. All recent editions depend on Kurfess,[2] but he gives no stemma and was unaware of the existence of some of the earlier manuscripts. The stemma depicted above, larger than it need be for editorial purposes, is based on a fresh collation of what appear to be the earlier and better manuscripts.[3]

---

[1] There are 200 or more extant manuscripts; climbing aboard the traditions of both Cicero and Sallust must have considerably enhanced the circulation of the text.

[2] A. Kurfess, *Appendix Sallustiana*, fasc. 2 (Leipzig, 1914[1], 1970[5]); his account of the manuscripts is not repeated after the first edition. There is a Budé text by A. Ernout (Paris, 1962) and an edition with commentary by K. Vretska (Heidelberg, 1961). The basic division into two families of manuscripts goes back to H. Jordan, *Hermes*, 11 (1876), 305–11. The *Invectivae* were put into print very early, at Cologne *c.*1471, by the Printer of the Dictys.

[3] I have used all the manuscripts employed by Kurfess except one (Vatican lat. 1746 = V) and retained his sigla. V is late and shows signs of contamination; it is not written in Beneventan script (as he says, [1]vi) nor does any part of it appear to be palimpsest.

The manuscripts used are, from left to right:

A Wolfenbüttel, Gud. lat. 335, s. X/XI, written in south-west Germany.

F Florence, Laur. 50. 45, s. XI, German (?).

Hᵃ British Library, Harley 2682, s. XI², later in Cologne Cathedral and probably written not far from there.

T Munich Clm 19472, s. XI, from Tegernsee.

G Vatican lat. 3251, s. XI/XII, from northern Italy.[4]

B Munich Clm 4611, s. XII ex., from Benedictbeuern.

C Paris lat. 11127, c.1000, from Echternach.[5]

D Oxford, Bodl. D'Orville 77, s. X, written in southern Germany.[6]

S Edinburgh, Adv. 18.7.8, s. XI/XII, English, from Thorney Abbey.[7]

Hᵇ British Library, Harley 3859, s. XII¹.[8]

R Reims 1329, s. XI², from the Chapter Library.

E Munich Clm 14714, s. XII, from St. Emmeram, Regensburg.

H British Library, Harley 2716, s. X ex., acquired by Graevius at Cologne and probably written in that area of the Rhineland.

O Oxford, Bodl. Rawl. G. 43, s. XI, written in south-east France.[9]

P Admont 363, s. XII, apparently a local product.

M Munich Clm 19474, s. XII/XIII, from Tegernsee.

The *Invectivae* appear to have surfaced in the tenth century. The geographical distribution of the earlier manuscripts suggests that the text re-emerged somewhere in south-west Germany, and that it remained a predominantly German text for some time. In the tenth century Froumund of Tegernsee borrowed the *Invectivae* from the episcopal library at Augsburg,[10] presumably to copy them or have them copied, and two of the extant manuscripts (T and M) did belong to Tegernsee. In general the Bavarian monasteries did much to disseminate these two works, for there were also copies at St. Emmeram, Benedictbeuern, and Admont. The text was soon on the move. It

[4] Written in a monastery between Lodi and Novara, according to M. Passalacqua, *I codici di Prisciano* (Rome, 1978), 341.

[5] J. Schroeder, *Bibliothek und Schule der Abtei Echternach um die Jahrtausendwende* (Luxembourg, 1977), 57–9. [6] B. C. B.-B., in *Medieval Learning*, 160–1.

[7] N. Ker, *Edinburgh Bibliographical Society Transactions*, 3 (1957), 169–78 and plates III–IV; *CLA* Suppl. 1689, 1690, 1691.

[8] If Harley 3859 is the Blandinianus which Fra Giocondo used for his edition of Vitruvius (Venice, 1511), it was at St. Peter's Ghent in the sixteenth century; see F. Granger, *The Times Literary Supplement*, 21 March 1929, p. 241. Like St. Peter's, it has strong associations with England, exemplified by its position in the tradition of Vitruvius and its connection here with S. Closer to Harley 3859 than S is another twelfth-century English (?) manuscript, Cambridge, Trinity College 1381 (O.8.6).

[9] O has Provençal glosses, written in the original hand (f. 56ʳ); and cf. B. Smalley, in *Classical Influences in European Culture A.D. 500–1500*, ed. R. R. Bolgar (Cambridge, 1971), 169.

[10] *MGH, Epistulae selectae*, 3, ed. K. Strecker (Berlin, 1925), *epist.* 17, p. 18. For Froumund see now C. E. Eder, 'Die Schule des Klosters Tegernsee im frühen Mittelalter im Spiegel der Tegernseer Handschriften', *Studien und Mitteilungen zur Geschichte des Benediktiner-Ordens*, 83 (1972), 6–155, particularly 36–51. She does not deal with M and T.

spread quickly into France: R was written at Reims,[11] O in the south-east of France, though, as with the genuine works of Sallust which it contains, its closest relations are Germanic.[12] In the late eleventh century the *Invectivae* crossed the Alps: G was written in northern Italy, while Florence, Laur. Strozzi 49 (s. XI/XII) was copied in a Beneventan hand of the Bari type. About the same time, as we can see from the evidence of S, they reached England and, with a helping hand from other classical authors, actually displaced works of Gregory and Augustine written in Anglo-Saxon hands of the eighth century. It is a fairly common text from the twelfth century onwards.

L. D. R.

[11] A manuscript of the *Invectivae* formerly at Metz (St. Arnulf) also belonged to the group RE, to judge from the few readings recorded from it (by Kurfess, *Jahresbericht über die Fortschritte der klassischen Altertumswissenschaft*, 269 (1940), 52–5). This was Metz 500, s. XI, destroyed during the Second World War.

[12] For the *Bella*, O is close to H (Berlin (East), Phillipps 1902), written somewhere in the Germanic area.

SCRIBONIUS LARGUS

Scribonius' medical *Compositiones* are dated between AD 43 and 48 by an observation made 'when I went to Britain with the emperor' (ch. 163) and the titbit 'Messalina's favourite toothpaste is . . .' (ch. 60). Galen used the work, and shortly after 400 Marcellus drew so heavily on it for his *De medicamentis liber* as to be an important witness.

Until recently Scribonius belonged to that select band of authors who survive in no manuscript. When Ruellius published the *editio princeps* (Paris, 1529), his printer called him 'vere et egregie medicus' for ministering to texts as well as people, but his ministrations did not include a description of his manuscript.[1] It was not, however, the one whose discovery S. Sconocchia announced in 1976,[2] a manuscript recorded by Haenel in 1830 but left unregarded in a place that has now sprung two medical surprises: the library of Toledo Cathedral. Shortly before Sconocchia found Scribonius in Toledo 98.12 (T), two other

[1] The printer continues: 'Scribonius ipse huius fidem facit, cuius codicis quum index pleraque contineret quae in ipso opere prorsum desiderabantur, et magni interim viri id putarent malum non posse ad integritatem converti, unus tu ea sic restituisti ut nihil reliqui factum sit cui industria humana mederi posset.' This refers to Ruellius's supplements from Galen in 167–70. About the manuscript, nothing more.   [2] *RFIC* 104 (1976), 257–69.

scholars found a missing passage of Celsus' *De medicina* in 97.12. Written *c*.1510–20 on French paper by a French hand,[3] T was apparently carried off before long to Italy, where it remained until 1797. It improves the text, confirms conjectures, often supports Marcellus against Ruellius's edition, and in general amply justifies Sconocchia's promised replacement of G. Helmreich's edition (Teubner, Leipzig, 1887).

The *editio princeps* of Marcellus was published by the eminent physician Cornarius even later than that of Scribonius (Basle, 1536), but its source survives: Paris lat. 6880 (P, s. IX²/4)[4], recorded at Fulda between 1415 and 1431 by the Italian explorers[5] and again in 1519 by Ulrich von Hutten.[6] Quires are missing from the other manuscript extant, Laon 420 (L, s. IX¹/4), written in north-eastern France and glossed at Laon by Martin the Irishman († 875).[7] The batch of letters that PL prefix to the text, which includes Scribonius' preface, also occurs in British Library, Arundel 166 (A, s. X¹, French[8]), a relative of L; as PLA attribute to Celsus both Scribonius' preface and someone else's, these may have been what Panormita in 1430 meant by 'Celsi epistolae'.[9]

M. Niedermann's edition of Marcellus, *Corpus medicorum latinorum*, v (1916), reported P for the first time, and in that respect Helmreich's Scribonius was already out of date before the discovery of T.[10] K. Deichgräber took account of Niedermann's Marcellus in his edition of the preface (*Abh. Akad. Mainz* (1950), 870–9). All these scholars doff their hats to Johannes Rhodius, who furnished Scribonius with a learned commentary (Padua, 1655); his introductory remarks on the causes of corruption in manuscripts deserve wider currency than an edition of Scribonius is likely to give them.

M. D. R.

---

[3] Sconocchia, *Per una nuova edizione di Scribonio Largo* (Brescia, 1981), 13–14. It is a great pity that he provides no photograph of the hand.

[4] E. Wickersheimer, *Les Manuscrits latins de médecine du haut Moyen Age dans les bibliothèques de France* (Paris, 1966), 70.

[5] Sabbadini, *Storia e critica*², 5–9; R. P. Robinson, *CPh* 16 (1921), 253.

[6] P. Lehmann, *Johannes Sichardus und die von ihm benutzten Bibliotheken und Handschriften* (Munich, 1911), 94.

[7] J. J. Contreni, *The Cathedral School of Laon from 850 to 930* (*Münchener Beiträge zur Mediävistik und Renaissance-Forschung*, 29, Munich, 1978), 123.

[8] A. Beccaria, *I codici di medicina del periodo presalernitano* (*secoli IX, X e XI*) (Rome, 1956), 265.

[9] Sabbadini, *Scoperte*, i. 99, 103.

[10] He also omitted the table of contents without explaining why, even though Ruellius's manuscript obviously had it (cf. n. 1, above).

SCRIPTORES HISTORIAE AUGUSTAE

Compiled at the very end of the fourth century,[1] and used in the early sixth century by Aurelius Memmius Symmachus, the so-called *Historia Augusta*[2] survives in Vatican, Pal. lat. 899, s. IX[1], written in Caroline minuscule (northern Italy). This manuscript, known as P, is possibly the only independent source for the text.[3] Over a period of some six centuries this book was worked upon by a succession of scholars, making it a splendid example of cumulative editorial acumen. At least seven different stages of correction can be determined:

1. The corrections of the original scribe himself.[4]
2. The improvements of a hand dating from s. X/XI, which betray no access to any witness other than P itself. Before this stage, B (Bamberg Class. 54 (E. III. 19), s. IX[2]/4, written at Fulda in Anglo-Saxon minuscule[5]) was copied directly from P – a useful aid, therefore, wherever the original reading of P is in doubt. Possibly contemporaneous with B was a text (also apparently copied from P) housed in the abbey at Murbach, where a copy is listed in the ninth century. Formerly thought entirely lost, the Murbach manuscript was used by Erasmus for his 1518 edition of the *SHA*.[6]
3. After a gap of several centuries, some corrections (involving the

The only reliable texts are the Teubner editions of H. Peter (2nd edn., 1884) and E. Hohl (1971, a reissue of the 1965 edition, which had been revised by Ch. Samberger and W. Seyfarth). Hohl's work is not careful enough, however, and does not give the reader the information he requires, especially about the various hands in P. A new text is badly needed. There is a Loeb Classical Library edition by D. Magie (3 vols., 1922–32). Of great value is the index by C. Lessing, *Scriptorum Historiae Augustae Lexicon* (Leipzig, 1901–6), although this too is not altogether reliable, because of the author's incomplete understanding of the history of P. Of considerable interest is A. Bellezza, *Historia Augusta. Parte prima: Le edizioni* (Istituto di storia antica dell' Università di Genova, 1959).

[1] R. Syme, *Emperors and Biography: Studies in the Historia Augusta* (Oxford, 1971). For its use by Symmachus, see Jordanes, *De rebus Geticis*, 83.

[2] This conventional title has no manuscript authority.

[3] Fundamental to the history of the text is S. H. Ballou, *The Manuscript Tradition of the Historia Augusta* (Teubner, Leipzig and Berlin, 1914). P is commonly said to have been written at Lorsch, an opinion denied by B. Bischoff (*Lorsch*, 66, 77, 81), who also questions any association with Lorsch.

[4] It should be observed that, in the writing of the text, the scribal hand changes in the third line from the bottom of f. 210[r].

[5] See B. B. Boyer, 'Insular Contributions to Medieval Literary Tradition', *CPh* 43 (1948), 31–9.

[6] Boyer, 36 n. 96. A fragment has now been discovered in a Nuremberg binding; see P. Zahn, *Bibliotheksforum Bayern*, 1 (1973), 121.

reordering of several lives) are found in the hand of the early fourteenth-century Veronese scholar Giovanni Mansionario.[7]

4. Next is discernible the hand of Petrarch. It is possible[8] that Petrarch acquired P from the Biblioteca Capitolare at Verona; in 1356 he had a copy made at Verona of the now much corrected P (Paris lat. 5816, in which his hand is likewise to be found).[9]

5. From the fifteenth century can be seen the hand of Poggio.[10]

6. The corrections of the Florentine scholar Giannozzo Manetti (d. 1459), whose *ex libris* is to be seen in P.

7. The hand of Agnolo Manetti (in two styles).

Much controversy has surrounded a group of fifteenth-century manuscripts designated as Σ. The representatives of this family that are normally used are: A (Admont 297, written in 1439); Ch (Vatican, Chigi H. VII. 239, Italian, probably Florence); R (Paris lat. 5807); V[11] (Vat. lat. 1897) and the unnamed Vat. lat. 1898. Hohl and others[12] have maintained that the improvements in the text (ranging from individual readings to large-scale transpositions) betray access to a source independent of P, a source first discernible in the fourteenth century. This question still remains to be answered definitively. Recent decades have seen such refinement in our understanding of the methods and abilities of the early Italian humanists that it seems possible that Ballou's verdict (with suitable modifications) may yet be maintained: that the Σ manuscripts nowhere provide readings which are beyond the powers of the humanists active at the time.

Tantalizing are three different[13] sets of excerpts:

[7] Identified by A. Campana. See R. Avesani, 'Il Preumanesimo Veronese', in *Storia della cultura Veneta: Le origini*, ed. G. Folena (Vicenza, 1976), ii. 120 n. 36.

[8] As suggested by Sabbadini (*Scoperte*, i. 15), who gives further information on the use made of P in Verona in the fourteenth century (ii. 228–9). See also E. Hohl, 'Petrarca und der Palatinus 899 der Historia Augusta', *Hermes*, 51 (1916), 154–9.

[9] The notion that Petrarch's annotations in P *precede* the copying of Paris lat. 5816 has been exploded by Billanovich. See de la Mare (*Handwriting*, 15–16 (item 42)), who confirms that the script of Petrarch in P 'has the look of the early 1360s'.

[10] The support for most of these identifications can be found in the stimulating analysis of L. Banti, 'Annotatori del manoscritto Vaticano Palatino Latino 899 della *Historia Augusta*', in *Studi in onore di Ugo Enrico Paoli*, Florence [1956], 59–70, with three plates. Ballou claimed, in addition, the hands of Coluccio Salutati and Bernardo Bembo, but these identifications are no longer accepted. For a specific denial for Salutati, see Ullman, *Salutati*, 207.

[11] V is wrongly dated to s. XIV by Hohl in his Teubner text.

[12] Hohl in his edition, and 'Beiträge zur Textgeschichte der Historia Augusta', *Klio*, 13 (1913), 258–88, 387–423; 'Textkritisches zur Historia Augusta', *RhM* 70 (1915), 474–79; 'Zur Textgeschichte der Historia Augusta. Ein kritisches Nachwort', *Klio*, 15 (1918), 78–98; 'Grundsätzliches zur Textgestaltung der Historia Augusta', *PhW* 48 (1928), 1115–18; A. Klotz, 'Beiträge zur Textgeschichte und Textkritik der Scriptores Historiae Augustae', *RhM* 78 (1929), 268–314. On wild attempts to find fragments of a lost manuscript embedded in Renaissance writers, see the trenchant refutation of Ch. Huelsen, 'Neue Fragmente der Scriptores Historiae Augustae?', *Rh M* 83 (1934), 176–80.

[13] On which see the brief, but penetrating, remarks of Boyer, 35–6; for the Lorsch origin of Π, Boyer (p. 39), who rightly observes the significance of the insular centres Fulda, Lorsch, and Murbach in the transmission.

1. *Π* (Vatican, Pal. lat. 886, s. IX[1]), written at Lorsch.
2. Vatican lat. 5114, s. XIV.
3. A series of excerpts contained in two manuscripts, Cues, Nikolaus Hospitalbibliothek 52, s. XII, and Paris lat. 1750 (ff. 127ᵛ – 129ᵛ), s. X/XI (eastern France).

The series of excerpts may be attributed[14] to the Irish scholar Sedulius Scottus, active at Liège in the middle of the ninth century. Unfortunately, none of these three sources can be pinned down with sufficient precision to allow a secure judgement on their relationship to P.

The *editio princeps* was issued at Milan in 1475, and displays an undistinguished text clearly based upon a fifteenth-century manuscript.[15]

P. K. M.

---

[14] So Mommsen, *Hermes*, 13 (1878), 298–301. For the slightness of the evidence for Sedulius's association with Liège, see F. Brunhölzl, *Geschichte der lateinischen Literatur des Mittelalters* (Munich, 1975), i. 450. On the Cues manuscript see Sabbadini, *Scoperte*, ii. 25. Note that Hohl incorrectly assigns Paris lat. 1750 to the twelfth century.

[15] Usually said to be Vatican lat. 5301. Ballou produces strong arguments, however, to show that the source was Paris lat. 5816, together with another witness from the *Σ* group.

THE ELDER SENECA

The (incomplete) *Controversiae* and *Suasoriae* (to give them abbreviated but convenient titles) of the Elder Seneca are transmitted in two overlapping ways. One group of manuscripts gives Books 1, 2, 7, 9, and 10 of the *Controversiae*, together with the prefaces to Books 7, 9, and 10, plus the two books of the *Suasoriae*; the other excerpts from all the books of the *Controversiae* together with the prefaces to Books 1–4, 7, and 10.

In the former class, it has been accepted since H. J. Müller's (still standard) edition[1] that three manuscripts are of importance. Antwerp 411, s. IX/X or X[1], eastern France (A),[2] and Brussels 9594, s. IX³/₄, north-eastern France (B), both somewhat damaged, give a basically sound but superficially corrupted text; Vatican lat. 3872 (V), s. IX³/₄ and from Corbie, while apparently independent of them, is perhaps more the result of medieval or late-antique correction than has been

---

[1] Vienna, 1887, with full preface. There has been no critical edition since, but one is promised by L. Håkanson.   [2] See H. D. L. Vervliet, *Scriptorium*, 13 (1959), 80–1.

realized.[3] Whatever the truth of this, the interpolator, as so often, reaped his reward, and the later manuscripts, only six of which are known, all derive from V.[4]

In the 'excerpted' class, the result, it is probable, of editorial activity in the fifth century or thereabouts,[5] we have the pre-eminent witness of Montpellier 126, s. IX³/₄, partly written by distinctively Reims hands (M: the best manuscript for the *Declamationes minores* of Quintilian (?), q.v.).[6] Numerous manuscripts of a later date exist, but nothing of the little that is known of them suggests that they can offer anything of inherited truth that is not available in M.[7]

M. W.

[3] *BICS* 21 (1974), 21–4. Plate in Chatelain, CLXVI.

[4] I owe this information to the kind help of Dr Vervliet, whose thesis on this topic (going beyond Müller's discussion, xiii–xxii) regrettably remains unpublished. He did, however, discuss three of the manuscripts in *AC* 33 (1964), 431–41. His article in *Gulden Passer*, 35 (1957), 179–222, gives valuable information on the printed texts (first Venice, 1490; see also Müller, xxxv–xxxviiii). For the corrector of the Toletanus (Brussels 2025), see Müller, xvii–xxi; H. Hagendahl, *Apophoreta Gotoburgensia Vilelmo Lundström oblata* (Göteborg, 1936), 313–22. For use of Seneca in the Middle Ages and later see J. E. G. Whitehorne, *Prudentia*, 1 (1969), 25–6.

[5] For good remarks on the excerpta see Hagendahl, 299–313. I discuss their use further in *BICS* (n. 3, above), 24–5.

[6] A text very close to that of M is provided by Bamberg Msc. Class. 45ᵐ, written *c*.800 in north-eastern France (Bischoff, *Mitt. Stud.* iii. 14, 158 n. 43); but this much earlier witness (information on which I owe to L. D. R.) now consists of only four leaves.

[7] See Müller, xxv–xxviiii; *BICS* (n. 3, above), 24–5. M is elaborately described by Schenkl in Müller, xxiiii n. 1; plate in Chatelain, CLXVI.

THE YOUNGER SENECA

Introduction

Apocolocyntosis
De beneficiis and *De clementia*
Dialogues
Letters
Natural Questions
Tragedies

Introduction

Although Seneca inevitably found detractors in all ages, the spiritual emphasis of his writing and the brilliance of his rhetoric were likely to win him as favourable a passage through Antiquity and the Middle Ages as most pagan authors.[1] A considerable number of his works did go astray; but given that Sallust's *Historiae* were lost and that Cicero was far from unscathed, Seneca did not fare too badly. Since the readers of Antiquity seem to have had a singular predilection for those works of Seneca which did perish, chance must have played a greater part in determining what survived than popularity. Lactantius has preserved fragments of three of Seneca's lost works, the *Exhortationes, De immatura morte,* and *Moralis philosophiae libri*; Jerome quotes at length from his *De matrimonio,* Augustine from the *De superstitione*.[2] Seneca was read down to the threshold of the Dark Ages. Cassiodorus quotes from the lost *De forma mundi* and donated his copy of the treatise to his foundation at Vivarium.[3] Spain rewarded its son by plagiarizing his work. Martin of Braga's *Formula honestae vitae,* written between 570 and 590, which enjoyed immense popularity in the Middle Ages, was adapted from another lost work, probably the *De officiis,*[4] and the same bishop's *De ira* is nothing more than a mosaic of passages lifted from Seneca's treatise of that name.[5] Only one ancient manuscript of Seneca's prose works survives, even in fragmentary form, and this contains bits of two other lost works, *Quomodo amicitia continenda sit* and *De vita patris*.[6] This manuscript, written in an early half-uncial, s. III/IV,[7] was palimpsested to form part of Vatican, Pal. lat. 24, that graveyard of so many fine classical books.[8] On f. 43ᵛ it bears the subscription 'Incipit eiusdem Annaei Senecae de vita patris feliciter scribente me Niciano die et lo(co) s(upra) s(criptis)'.

The large body of Seneca's work which did survive has come down to us in six main units, though two of these are dependent on more than one tradition going back to Antiquity. Four of these conform to a

[1] There is a considerable literature on Seneca's *Fortleben*. In addition to the works cited below in the accounts of the individual traditions, see W. Trillitzsch, *Seneca im literarischen Urteil der Antike* (Amsterdam, 1971); P. Faider, *Études sur Sénèque* (Gand, 1921); K.-D. Nothdurft, *Studien zum Einfluss Senecas auf die Philosophie und Theologie des zwölften Jahrhunderts* (Leiden–Cologne, 1963); G. M. Ross, 'Seneca's Philosophical Influence', in *Seneca,* ed. C. D. N. Costa (London, 1974), 116–65.

[2] For a complete edition of the fragments we still depend on the first Teubner text by F. Haase (Leipzig, 1853), iii. 418–45; but for an excellent study of the fragments, with a new edition of those from Lactantius and Augustine, see M. Lausberg, *Untersuchungen zu Senecas Fragmenten* (Berlin, 1970).   [3] *Inst.* 2. 6. 4.   [4] E. Bickel, *RhM* 60 (1905), 505–51.

[5] For Martin's works, see C. W. Barlow, *Martini episcopi Bracarensis opera omnia* (New Haven, Conn., 1950).

[6] The best edition is that of G. Studemund, in O. Rossbach, *De Senecae philosophi librorum recensione et emendatione* (Breslauer Philologische Abhandlungen, 2. 3, Breslau, 1888), i-xxxii. They were first published by B. G. Niebuhr, in *M. Tulli Ciceronis orationum pro M. Fonteio et pro C. Rabirio fragmenta* (Rome, 1820), 13–15, 99–104. For an antique manuscript of the *Tragedies,* see below.

[7] *CLA* I. 69; for the revised date, see E. A. Lowe, 'Codices rescripti', *Mélanges Eugène Tisserant,* v (*Studi e testi,* 235, Vatican, 1964), no. 187 (= *Pal. Papers,* ii. 514).

[8] The Seneca fragments occupy ff. 10, 15, 39–40, 43–4; for further details, see J. Fohlen, 'Recherches sur le manuscrit palimpseste Vatican, Pal. lat. 24', *Scrittura e civiltà,* 3 (1979), 195–222, and particularly 211–12.

common pattern; the text makes an appearance, in some cases very brief, in the ninth century and then fades away until the great blaze of Seneca's popularity in the twelfth and thirteenth centuries. The first texts to emerge after the Dark Ages appear to have been the *De beneficiis* and *De clementia*. They had travelled together and were copied in northern Italy about the year 800, to produce the archetype of our medieval tradition. The text had moved to northern Europe by the middle of the ninth century, but it remained dormant until the late eleventh and only blossomed in the twelfth. The earliest copies of both traditions of the *Letters* (one containing letters 1–88, the other 89–124) date from the first third of the ninth century and are both associated with the scriptorium of Louis the Pious. This is very much a Carolingian text, and letters 1–88 enjoyed some degree of continuous copying; but it was not until the twelfth century that manuscripts began to circulate on any scale, and then the two parts of the text, which had usually remained separate, begin to be more commonly found together. There was a copy of the *Natural Questions* at Reichenau in the ninth century but we have no means of knowing whether this was connected with the later tradition, which did not get off the ground until the twelfth century and then spread from northern France. The *Apocolocyntosis* was known to Radbert of Corbie about 846, but the earliest extant manuscripts date from the end of the century and then there is complete silence until the early twelfth; it must have been rare until the thirteenth century, and remained the least popular of Seneca's works.

The *Dialogues* and the *Tragedies* were in hiding during the Carolingian age. The *Dialogues* did not see the light of day until they were copied at Montecassino late in the eleventh century, and did not begin to be generally available in northern Europe until the second half of the thirteenth century. The earliest manuscript of the *Tragedies* was likewise written in Italy in the late eleventh century; it is probably the manuscript listed in the Pomposa catalogue of 1093, and Montecassino is a possible source for its exemplar. But the majority of the manuscripts of the plays belong to quite a different tradition; this emerged from some centre in northern France in the latter part of the twelfth century.

It will be clear from this summary of the salient facts of each tradition that they largely went their own way until the twelfth century,[9] when the demand for one work would help to promote the demand for others. From this time onwards, as texts became more readily available, they gradually join together to form a corpus. There is often a fair admixture of spurious works,[10] some of them abbreviated and reworked from

---

[9] A conjunction of texts remarkable for its date (not later than s. XII in.) is found in British Library, Add. 11983: see below, pp. 361, 364–5, 367–8.

[10] For the apocryphal works see G. G. Meersseman, 'Seneca maestro di spiritualità nei suoi opuscoli apocrifi dal XII al XV secolo', *IMU* 16 (1973), 34–135.

Seneca himself, and these did much to enhance his reputation in the Middle Ages; the apocryphal *Correspondence with St. Paul*[11] had been a frequent companion of the *Letters* from the early Middle Ages, and the chapter on Seneca in Jerome's *De viris illustribus*[12] does service as a sort of *accessus*. The *Suasoriae* and *Controversiae* of the Elder Seneca are some-times added to the corpus. Seneca was a gift for the florilegist,[13] and excerpta and various forms of abbreviated text become common, some-times appearing alongside complete versions of the same text. The *Letters* appear at an early stage in the company of the *De beneficiis* and *De clementia*; in due course one or both may be joined by the *Natural Questions* or the *Apocolocyntosis*. The *Tragedies* and the *Dialogues* begin to attach themselves to other texts in the thirteenth century, and in the fourteenth it was possible, for the first time, to find all Seneca's major works under one cover.

Seneca's popularity continued unabated in the Renaissance. The bulk of his prose writing had appeared in print by the end of 1475.[14] The *Tragedies* were first printed at Ferrara in 1484, by Andreas Belfortis; the *Natural Questions* had to wait until 1490, when they were incorporated with the other prose works in the edition produced at Venice by Bernardinus de Cremona and Simon de Luere;[15] the *Apocolocyntosis* did not appear in print until 1513.[16] The first editions of critical importance were those of Erasmus, printed at Basle by Froben in 1515 and 1529, of which the second was much superior to the first.

L. D. R.

---

[11] Edited by C. W. Barlow, *Epistulae Senecae ad Paulum et Pauli ad Senecam ⟨ quae vocantur ⟩* (American Academy in Rome, 1938).   [12] *Vir. ill.* 12.

[13] The texts most commonly excerpted are *Letters*, 1–88, the *De beneficiis*, and *De clementia*. Some of the main florilegia to contain Seneca are mentioned in the articles below; for these and others see B. Munk Olsen, 'Les Classiques latins dans les florilèges médiévaux antérieurs au XIIIe siècle', *RHT* 9 (1979), 47–121.

[14] No less than four editions of the *Letters* appeared in or about 1475 (Flodr, 1, 9–11): at Paris, 1475, *Sub signo follis viridis* (letters 1–88 only); at Rome, 1475, by Arnold Pannartz; at Naples, 1475, as part of the handsome *opera omnia* printed by Mathias Moravus; at Strasbourg, c. 1475, by the R-Printer, probably Adolf Rusch. The Naples edition is the *editio princeps* of the *Dialogues*, *De beneficiis*, and *De clementia*.

[15] Flodr, 4; the description of the contents of the Naples edition of 1475 given by Flodr, which among other things credits it with the *NQ*, does not fit the book.

[16] See below, *Apocolocyntosis*.

Apocolocyntosis

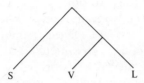

Though there are more than forty extant manuscripts of the *Apocolocyntosis*, it is the oldest three that provide the proper basis for the text. These are S = St. Gall 569, s. ix/x, of German origin, perhaps Fulda[1]; V = Valenciennes 411 (*olim* 393), s. ix ex., which, written in eastern France in the Reims area, was one of the books which Hucbald (840–930) owned and donated to his monastery of Saint-Amand;[2] L = British Library, Add. 11983, probably of the early twelfth rather than the late eleventh century.

The first indication that Seneca's malicious little satire had survived the Dark Ages is found in Radbert of Corbie, who quotes from it in his *Epitaphium Arsenii*, written shortly after 846.[3] V and S testify to its availability at the turn of the century, but then it falls from sight until the Norman revival. L is an interesting little book,[4] almost certainly of French origin, though it may have been imported into England at some time in the Middle Ages; in the fifteenth century it belonged to the English bibliophile Robert Aiscough, before becoming part of the Butler collection. Our satire was certainly known to William of Malmesbury (*c*.1090–*c*.1143)[5] and must therefore have reached England by the early twelfth century, but there is no indication that L had come to England in time to be his source; the first manuscript of English origin to survive is Princeton, Garrett 114, s. xiii in., probably written at Waltham

The standard text of the *Apocolocyntosis* for reference purposes is still that of F. Bücheler and W. Heraeus (Berlin, 1958[7]), the standard modern edition that of C. F. Russo (Florence, 1965[5]), who gives an account of the manuscript tradition and was the first to make full use of L. Mr P. T. Eden, whose own edition is forthcoming, has fully and rigorously re-examined the tradition in 'The Manuscript Tradition of Seneca's *Apocolocyntosis*', *CQ* 29 (1979), 149–61; he confirms the pre-eminence of SVL, gives a full list of manuscripts, and classifies them. The four manuscripts which he had not originally examined should be classified, he kindly informs me, as follows: Vatican, Arch. S. Pietro C. 121 (ff. 248ᵛ–250ᵛ, s. xiv, parchment), Chigi H. viii. 259 (ff. 245ᵛ–249ᵛ, s. xv, parchment), Rossi 604 (ff. 298ᵛ–299ᵛ, ending at *vocis incerto sonas* (7. 2), s. xv, parchment) belong to the L tradition; Holkham Hall 390 (ff. 259ᵛ–262ᵛ, s. xiv, parchment) is an S manuscript.

[1] For the dating and provenance of SV, supplied by Professor Bernhard Bischoff, see M. Coffey, *Roman Satire* (London, 1976), 176.
[2] Delisle, i. 312 f., ii. 454 no. 190.
[3] E. Dümmler, *Phil. u. hist. Abh. der kön. Akad. der Wiss. zu Berlin*, 1900, ii. 20, 21, 27 (citing *Apoc.* 1. 2–3).   [4] Cf. pp. 359, 364–5, 367–8.
[5] See R. M. T., 'The reading of William of Malmesbury', *Rev. bén.* 85 (1975), 362–402, in particular 377.

Abbey; Exeter 3549 B, s. XIII med., is also likely to be an English book.[6]

V proved to be a dead end,[7] and all the *recentiores* descend either from the L or the S branch of the tradition, with remarkably little horizontal interaction. Thanks to the Norman revival, it was the French tradition represented by L that first got off the ground. The majority of the pre-1300 manuscripts of this stream (Paris lat. 6630, 8501A, 8542, 8624) are of French origin: 8501A is probably from the area of Metz; 6630 has a thirteenth-century *ex libris* of the Celestines of Saint-Pierre-au-Mont-de-Châtre, in the diocese of Soissons; 8624, ff. 73–4, contains all that remains of the text of the *Apocolocyntosis* once in the library of Richard of Fournival.[8] But the Waltham Abbey book shows that this strain of the text had reached England by the beginning of the thirteenth century; Exeter 3549 B too belongs to the L stream and it is presumably this type of text that was known to William of Malmesbury. By the end of the fourteenth century it was widespread. The wave of S manuscripts, smaller in number, began somewhat later. Vatican lat. 2216 (s. XIV[1]), which must be among the earliest of them, is of French origin, though it had reached Siena by the fifteenth century; but the later S manuscripts are predominantly Italian.

The *editio princeps* (Rome, 1513) was a disaster. It was the work of a German dilettante who styled himself Caius Sylvanus. He had one poor manuscript which, in addition to other deficiencies, omitted the passages in Greek. This he eked out with interpolations of his own which were still infesting the text in the nineteenth century.[9] The next editor, Beatus Rhenanus (Basle, 1515[10]), had no manuscript at all and was content to reprint Sylvanus's text with minor modifications until 1529, when the second Froben edition of Seneca, Erasmus's great work (Basle, 1529), was at an advanced stage of printing; then, with the aid of a manuscript he had just managed to acquire, the lost *codex Wissenburgensis*,[11] he was able to make a real start on editing the text. This manuscript, which had an L-type text, seems to have been the only new source of evidence for the text until 1557, when Adrianus Junius made use of V.

L. D. R.

[6] Mr N. R. Ker thinks that the Exeter manuscript is 'probably English' and that the fourteenth-century additions on ff. 1–23[v], 169[r-v] are certainly English. The *Registrum Anglie*, compiled between 1230 and 1306, reports a copy of the *Ludus* at Margam Abbey.

[7] Eden, 157, correcting Russo.

[8] Where it was still part of his copy of the *Tragedies*: cf. Delisle, ii, 532 (item XI. 129); R. H. R., *RHT* 1 (1971), 95–6.

[9] R. Sabbadini, 'Il testo interpolato del Ludus di Seneca', *RFIC* 47 (1919), 338–45.

[10] His edition, printed by Froben, appeared in March and again, later in the year, as part of Erasmus's complete Seneca; it was often reprinted.

[11] From the Benedictine Abbey of St. Peter and St. Paul at Wissembourg. For an interesting account of this lost manuscript and Rhenanus's editing of the *Ludus*, see F. Spaltenstein and P. Petitmengin, 'Beatus Rhenanus éditeur de l'*Apocoloquintose* et le *codex Wissenburgensis*', *RHT* 9 (1979), 315–27.

De beneficiis and *De clementia*

The manuscript tradition of the *De beneficiis* and *De clementia* descends from an extant archetype.[1] This is Vatican, Pal. lat. 1547 (N), written in northern Italy about the year 800, possibly at Milan.[2] Few texts can boast of such an early Carolingian witness. It was taken north and had reached the monastery of Lorsch by about 850, where it remained until the latter part of the fifteenth century; hence its designation as the *codex Sancti Nazarii* or *Nazarianus*. Erasmus had access to readings from it for his second edition of Seneca (Basle, 1529); it was used by Gruter and others but not made the basis for the text until Gertz's edition of 1876. The *De clementia* is incomplete, and may never have been finished by the author.[3]

The fertile member of the tradition was not N but an early and possibly direct copy of it, Vatican, Reg. lat. 1529, known as R. R too was written in Italy, in the second quarter of the ninth century, and like N it seems to have quickly succumbed to the pull from the north: the marginal hands in R have been recognized as belonging to the circle of Lupus and Heiric,[4] and they indicate that by the second half of the century it had found its way to the monasteries of the Loire, perhaps

[1] The view that all the other manuscripts are derived from N 'aut ex codice plane gemino' was first put by M. C. Gertz (*L. Annaei Senecae libri De beneficiis et De clementia* (Berlin, 1876), vi f.), though he was ignorant of the existence of R. Subsequent discussion and the publication of R by O. Rossbach (*De Senecae philosophi librorum recensione et emendatione* (Breslauer Philologische Abhandlungen, 2.3), Breslau, 1888, 13–25) provoked a reaction against this view. But the dependence of the other manuscripts on N has been established beyond any reasonable doubt: see in particular J. Buck, *Seneca De beneficiis und De clementia in der Ueberlieferung* (Tübingen, 1908), 1–38; F. Préchac, *Sénèque De la clémence* (Paris, 1921), vi–xlii, *Des bienfaits*, vol. 1 (Paris, 1926), xlii–liv. It is a pity that C. Hosius still stuck to his guns in his second Teubner edition (Leipzig, 1914), with the result that the apparatus is cluttered with a mass of derivative matter.

[2] For the history and origin of N see *Karl der Grosse*, 251 (= Bischoff, *Mitt. Stud.* iii. 32); Bischoff, *Lorsch*, 21, 52, 63, 116–17; *Settimane*, 22.1, 80 f. (= *Mitt. Stud.* iii. 68 ff.); M. Ferrari, *Settimane*, 22.1, 308 f. Specimen pages of N are reproduced in Chatelain, plate CLXVIII, and in Préchac's edition of the *De clementia*.

[3] Hosius appends to the end of the *De clementia* (p. 252 of his edition) a passage from Hildebert of Le Mans (*Epist.* 1.3., *PL* 171.145A-B, written c.1101) which, it has been claimed, paraphrases part of the missing portion of the dialogue. Hildebert is of interest as one of the earliest medieval writers to have made use of these two works, but the chances that he had access to lost material (which the author may never have written) are slim indeed. For discussion of this hypothesis and for Hildebert's use of Seneca, see M. Adler, *WS* 27 (1905), 242–50; Préchac, xliv–xlix; P. von Moos, *Hildebert von Lavardin* (Stuttgart, 1965), 57 ff., 317 ff.

[4] Bischoff, *Settimane*, 77 n. 48, 81 f. (= *Mitt. Stud.* iii. 66 n. 47, 69); for a possible French origin, Pellegrin, *Manuscrits*, ii.1,252.

Fleury or Auxerre. It is R that generates the whole of the later tradition.[5]

The history of the text is a study in degeneration as the primitive text of N recedes behind successive layers of corruption. N[2] and R mark significant stages in this process; and in the skeletal stemma suggested above I have postulated a copy of R (ψ) to account for the new and thick layer of interpolation[6] which hangs like a pall over the bulk of the later manuscripts. There was such an explosion of interest in the text in the twelfth century that the *recentior* tradition is very large, amounting to nearly three hundred manuscripts, if one includes epitomes and *excerpta*; for in addition to being excerpted and pillaged for florilegia,[7] both works circulated in a variety of abbreviated versions. Corrupt and often reduced to variously mutilated forms, the later tradition is not a pretty sight. Some relief is afforded by a small number of manuscripts which appear to have descended from R via a different and less polluted channel, and this group I have called φ.

After the limited activity of the Carolingian period the tradition appears to have lain dormant until the quickening of interest in such texts which began in the late eleventh century. The first signs of an awakening all belong to the last decade of that century: then the *De clementia* is recorded in the library catalogue of Egmond (1090), both works appear in the Pomposa catalogue (1093), and the first quotation from either work to appear since Antiquity is found in the *Chronicle* of Hugo of Flavigny,[8] largely written between *c*.1090 and 1096. The earliest extant manuscript is British Library, Add. 11983, not easily

---

[5] In a recent article G. Mazzoli has sought to demonstrate that Munich Clm 2544 (s. XII = M) is derived directly from N, which he sees as the head of a German group of manuscripts: see *Bollettino*, 26 (1978), 98–109. But it is perfectly plain that M derives from N via R, as does every other manuscript I have seen. It so happens that M is the only non-abbreviated φ text which had come to light, so that it stands out in Hosius's apparatus as being closer to N than the other manuscripts. The handful of places where it agrees with N against R are probably the result of correction.

[6] A few examples taken from hundreds will show what I mean: *Ben.* 1.3.8 *reddendi*] *reddendique* ψ; 1.15.1 *non obicio moras*] *moras non obicio* ψ; 2.18.3 *dedissemus. Videamus*] *dedisse videamur* ψ; 5.6.6 *procederet* N: *procedere* R: *procedere solitus erat* ψ; 6.4.3 *ac si nihil* N: om. R: *licet* ψ; 7.15.1 *periculorum* N: *periculum* R: *periculi* ψ; *Clem.* 1.1.7 *aleam* N: *aliam* R: *albam* ψ; 1.11.4 *tutiores*] *totiores* NR: *potiores* ψ; 1.14.1 *simul deploratum est*] *postquam omnia simul deplorata sunt* ψ; 1.26.4 *horum ne* N: *morum ne* R: *morum. Apud homines autem ne* ψ; 2.4.3–4 *convenit. Ad rem pertinent quaerere*] *convenire ad rem certum est. Pertinent quaerere* ψ; 2.7.2 *vis honestiore tibi via* (*honestiore* ex *honestior et*) N: *vis honesto et tibi viam* R: *iustum est et tibi vitam* ψ.

[7] Excerpts are common in the twelfth-century florilegia; they occur, for instance, in the *Florilegium Gallicum*, the *Florilegium Angelicum*, the *Florilegium Morale Oxoniense*, the *Moralium dogma philosophorum*, the *Polyhistor* of William of Malmesbury.

[8] Hugo's use of the *De beneficiis* has been fully studied by Mazzoli (n. 5, above), 92–7. He was using a φ (or at least a non-ψ) manuscript, reading *Ben.* 2.1.2 *dantis manus* (so NRφ: *manus dantis* ψ), 3.17.2 *rei optimae* (so NRφ: *optimae rei* ψ). I agree with Mazzoli that the apparent echo of *Ben.* 1.3.8 (*Chrysippus quoque penes quem subtile illud acumen est*) in Radbert of Corbie (*Epitaphium Arsenii*, p. 20 Dümmler, *Crisippi acumine*) should be discounted, but not for the reason he gives. I do not see how *Chrysippi acumine* could have come from the Fulgentius passages which he quotes, where the phrase does not occur; but it could have come from Jerome, *Epist.* 57.14.4 (*Chrysippi acumina*).

dated or placed;[9] it may be as early as the late eleventh century, is not later than the early twelfth, and is conjecturally of French origin. It has a vulgate text of the *De clementia*, and a poor one at that, which shows how swift the downward path could be.

One would assume from the earlier presence of R in the region of the Loire that these texts were disseminated from central or north-west France and on the whole the later tradition bears this out, but the text was already on the move in the late eleventh century and is widespread by the end of the twelfth. There are about a dozen twelfth-century manuscripts with complete texts and more than double that number of abbreviated versions and excerpts. Many of these are of French origin, but others testify to the penetration of England and Germany. Leiden, Lipsius 49 was certainly in England in the twelfth century[10] and may well have been written there. Erfurt, Amplon. Q. 3 is certainly of German origin[11] and Admont 221 takes us as far as Austria. Most of these have the corrupt ψ text; the only twelfth-century φ manuscripts which I have come across,[12] apart from abbreviated texts, are Munich Clm 2544, from the Bavarian monastery of Aldersbach, Paris lat. 6331, s. XII², Pontigny, and Paris lat. 15085, written towards the end of the century at Saint-Victor.

L. D. R.

---

[9] Cf. pp. 359, 361, 367–8.

[10] L. D. R., *The Medieval Tradition of Seneca's Letters* (Oxford, 1965), 109. Both texts were known in England in the twelfth century, and there is a well-known story in Giraldus Cambrensis that Henry II always had the *De clementia* at his elbow: *Topographia Hibernica*, 48 (*Giraldi Cambrensis Opera*, Rolls Series, v (ed. J. F. Dimock, London, 1867), 191).

[11] Not English, as I once assumed (*The Medieval Tradition*, 109–10). The curious inscription on f. 1ᵛ (*H. Dei gracia rex Angliae, dominus Hyberniae, dux Normandiae et Aquitaniae, comes Andegavensis dilecto in Christo fratri Ulrico*), which obviously refers to Henry I, is in a hand more of the time of Henry III and the manuscript proves on inspection to be clearly of German origin.

[12] The φ text seems to have remained scarce. The only examples I have so far noticed among the later manuscripts are Leiden, B. P. L. 43A (s. XIV, *Clem.*), Paris lat. 8544 (s. XIV, both works), B. L. Burney 248 (s. XV, *Ben*).

Dialogues

Seneca's *Dialogues*[1] belong to the small number of classical texts which owe their survival to the Benedictine foundation of Montecassino. It was in this monastery towards the end of the eleventh century that the manuscript on which our text mainly depends was copied. This is Milan, Ambros. C. 90 inf., written in a Beneventan hand and known to editors as A. The Montecassino Chronicle provides a long list of texts copied on the instruction of Abbot Desiderius (1058–87), and this includes[2] an unspecified work by Seneca. It seems certain that this was a text of the *Dialogues* and that A is one of the fruits of the Desiderian revival: the script is Cassinese, the date fits,[3] and the *Dialogues*, which had lurked unknown since the sixth century, were used at this time by Guaiferius of Salerno, a local poet and hagiographer, who became a monk at Montecassino during the abbacy of Desiderius.

A has been corrected by a number of later hands and it is significant that three of these (a, A[2], A[3]), all at work in the twelfth century, were able to fill omissions in the original text of A by reference to another manuscript; there must have been at least two copies of the *Dialogues* still available at the monastery, A and either its exemplar (the archetype) or an independent copy of it. One of the fourteenth-century correctors (A[6]) has been identified as Pietro Piccolo da Monteforte, a Neapolitan jurist and friend of Boccaccio.[4]

A is the oldest and by far the best of the manuscripts, but there are over a hundred *recentiores* dating from the thirteenth century onwards. These fall into two main groups: β, which comprises the bulk of the later manuscripts, and γ. The β manuscripts are all ultimately derived from

---

For a fuller account of the manuscript tradition than is given here see L. D. R., 'The Medieval Tradition of Seneca's *Dialogues*', *CQ* 18 (1968), 355–72; *L. Annaei Senecae Dialogorum libri duodecim* (OCT, 1977), v–xix. More on Montecassino and its part in Seneca's transmission may be found in F. Brunhölzl, *Zum Problem der Casinenser Klassikerüberlieferung* (Abhandlungen der Marburger Gelehrten Gesellschaft, 1971.3); G. Cavallo, 'La trasmissione dei testi nell' area Beneventano-Cassinese', *Settimane*, 22 (1975), 357–424, particularly 392; D. Nardo, 'I Dialoghi di Seneca a Montecassino', *Atti e mem. Accad. Patav. di sc. lett. e arti*, 86 (1973–4), Parte III, 207–24; G. Mazzoli, 'Da Pietro Diacono al catalogo Becker 119: Seneca a Montecassino nel sec. XII (e oltre)', *RAL* 31 (1976), 297–326.

[1] The term 'Dialogues' is commonly used to designate that selection of Seneca's treatises which is preserved in the *codex Ambrosianus* under the title *Dialogi*, namely *De providentia, De constantia sapientis, De ira*, 1–3, *Consolatio ad Marciam, De vita beata, De otio, De tranquillitate animi, De brevitate vitae, Consolatio ad Polybium, Consolatio ad Helviam*. Other works which are as much 'dialogues' as these have been transmitted separately. 　　　　　[2] *MGH, Script.* VII, pp. 746–7.

[3] *Beneventan Script*[2], i. 71, ii. 56. Facsimiles in Chatelain, pl. CLXVII; F. Steffens, *Lateinische Paläographie*[2] (Berlin–Leipzig, 1929), Tav. 75; Lowe, *Pal. Papers*, ii. 586, pl. 141.

[4] Gius. Billanovich, 'Pietro Piccolo da Monteforte: Tra il Petrarcha e il Boccaccio', *Medioevo e Rinascimento: Studi in onore di Bruno Nardi*, i (Florence, 1955), 3–76. I owe the identification of the hand to Dr A. C. de la Mare.

A; the way in which they omit small blocks of text which coincide to the nearest word and letter with lines of A provides a classic demonstration of the usefulness of line-omission in establishing descent. The manuscripts are consequently of use only where A is lacking or has become illegible subsequent to the copying of β; in particular, the loss of a gathering means that A is not available for most of the *Consolatio ad Polybium*. The earliest and most serviceable of the β manuscripts are Vatican, Chigi H. v. 153, its copy Berlin (West) lat. 2° 47, Paris lat. 15086 and 6379. These span the thirteenth century; the first three are Italian, the last French.

The γ manuscripts are more problematic. None of them is earlier than the fourteenth century and they carry a heavily corrected and interpolated text. They are not infrequently right where A is wrong, usually as a result of conjecture; but the quality of some readings suggests that they go back to a manuscript close to A but independent of it, and there is good reason to believe that this manuscript too was of Cassinese origin. The earliest and best of the γ manuscripts are Vatican lat. 2215 and 2214, of the early and later fourteenth century respectively and both written in Italy.

Nothing is known about the history of the text between the sixth century, when Martin, Bishop of Braga, quarried his own *De ira* from Seneca's treatise, and its emergence at Montecassino in the late eleventh century. A probably descends at few removes from an ancient book which had survived in southern Italy into late Antiquity.[5]

The evidence of the extant manuscripts and the use of the *Dialogues* made by the writers of the period indicate that the text began to achieve a wider circulation in the thirteenth century, in both Italy and France. Of particular interest is the arrival of the *Dialogues* in northern Europe, where they had hitherto been unknown. Evidence for their availability north of the Alps continues to accumulate,[6] and a brief résumé of what has so far come to light may be useful.

1. A series of *sententiae* culled from *Dial.* 1–4[7] has until recently[8] lurked undetected under the title *Proverbia Lucii Annaei Senecae* in a well-known manuscript, British Library, Add. 11983, an important witness for the *Apocolocyntosis* (q.v.). The excerpts from the *Dialogues* occupy ff. 40r–43r; on ff. 28v–36v we have the common collection of *Proverbia Senecae per ordinem alphabeti disposita*.[9] The manuscript is certainly north-European, probably French, and not later than s. XII[1]; it is therefore, after A, the earliest witness to the text of the *Dialogues*.

[5] Brunhölzl, 136 ff. The handsomely written list of contents in A has a very antique appearance.
[6] The information in nos. 1, 3, 5 of the following account is comparatively new and will not be found in the works cited above.   [7] i.e. *De providentia, De constantia sapientis, De ira,* 1–2.
[8] I noticed them in 1977, Carlotta Dionisotti about the same time; I know of no earlier report.
[9] See PUBLILIUS.

This little florilegium is not unknown, but it has previously been found only in manuscripts of the thirteenth century and later.[10] The excerpts appear to derive from A and are of no textual value, but they serve to demonstrate that the *Dialogues*, at least in excerpt form, had reached the north with much greater alacrity than has been suspected. They were presumably compiled as a companion piece to the other collections of Senecan and pseudo-Senecan *flores* which had long been in vogue, particularly in the north, so that one cannot necessarily assume that the extracting of the excerpts from a complete text took place in Italy. At all events, the existence of a florilegium compiled from the *Dialogues* in northern Europe at this early date does explain at least one puzzling fact, the inclusion of a snippet from *De ira* in the *Moralium dogma philosophorum*, written about the middle of the twelfth century.[11]

2. John of Garland quotes from *Const.* 8.2 in his *Epithalamium B. Marie Virginis*, written in 1220–1 at the University of Paris.[12] He clearly knows the dialogue, so our text may already by then have reached the schools of Paris.

3. The *Dialogues* are among the texts quoted by the annotator of Berne 276, who worked in the area of Orléans about the middle of the thirteenth century.[13]

4. Roger Bacon dramatically claimed to have rediscovered the *Dialogues* in 1266, when he transcribed large portions of them for inclusion in his *Moralis philosophia*. He is in fact one of three, all Friars and all resident in Paris in the third quarter of the century, who reveal a knowledge of the text; the others are Guibert of Tournai and John of Wales.[14]

5. Roger Bacon did his best to introduce a dash of drama and panache into the history of our text; the element of romance we owe to

---

[10] It appears in various forms. Meersseman, on pp. 68–77 of the article cited above (p. 359, n. 10), gives an account of three manuscripts which contain the same or similar excerpts: Glasgow, Hunter U.3.4 (231), s. XIV, English; Vienna 3134, s. XV, German; Trier, Bibliothek des Priester-seminars R.II.11 (44), s. XV, Flemish. In the Trier florilegium, of which he provides an edition (pp. 72–7), some *sententiae* have been omitted and the rest put into alphabetical order. There are in fact earlier copies of this version, such as Paris lat. 6631, s. XIII (French, a Fournival book: cf. Meersseman, 68 n. 1, R. H. R., *RHT* 3 (1973), 265–6). For these and similar collections in a number of Paris manuscripts of s. XIV–XV, see E. Woelfflin, *Publilii Syri Sententiae* (Leipzig, 1869), 37–8.

[11] *De ira*, 2.34.1 *cum pare contendere anceps est, cum superiore furiosum, cum inferiore sordidum*, one of the excerpts in this florilegium, appears in the *Moralium dogma philosophorum* (ed. J. Holmberg (Uppsala, 1929). p. 50. 1–3) as *summopere autem fuge iurgia: nam contra parem contendere anceps est. . . .* For a discussion of this, see 'The Medieval Tradition', 360.

[12] 'The Medieval Tradition', 361; for the date of the *Epithalamium*, see E. Faye Wilson, *Speculum*, 23 (1948), 48 n. 68.

[13] Cf. R. H. R., 'Florilegia and Latin Classical Authors in Twelfth- and Thirteenth-Century Orléans', *Viator*, 10 (1979), 131–60; for further references to Berne 276 in this volume see the *Index of Manuscripts*. For a possible connection between the annotator's use of the *Dialogues* and their availability at Paris in the latter half of the century, see R. H. R., 148–50.

[14] 'The Medieval Tradition', 360 ff.

Amaury de Montfort, younger son of Simon, Earl of Leicester. While he was sailing on a French ship from Normandy to Wales with his sister Eleanor, who was to marry Llewelyn ap Gruffydd, the rebellious Welsh prince, their boat was seized off the Cornish coast and forced into Bristol harbour; there the two outlawed cousins of Edward I were handed over to the agents of the king. Amaury was imprisoned in Corfe Castle, in Dorset, and it was there, in 1276, while he was turning his enforced leisure to good use by writing a treatise on theology, that an apt passage from Seneca came to mind: 'numquam usque eo interclusa sunt omnia ut nulli actioni locus honestae sit' (*Tranq.* 4.8).[15] Since, as he tells us, he had no books to hand but the Bible, he must be quoting from memory. Amaury appears to have been in France from 1265 to 1268,[16] during the critical years when Bacon rediscovered the text, and he was acquainted with the *doctor mirabilis* himself.[17] But he then spent three or four years at the University of Padua, and it may also be significant that in 1272, his studies finished, he returned three books (on medicine) which he had borrowed from the library of Montecassino.[18] He had more opportunities than most to lay his hands on a copy of the *Dialogues*.

The text became comparatively common in the fourteenth and fifteenth centuries and was first printed by Mathias Moravus at Naples in 1475.

L. D. R.

[15] Amaury de Montfort, *De composicione, divisione, et ordine tabularum*, 125; an edition of part of this work, edited from Amaury's own autograph, together with a full account of the circumstances of its composition, is provided by L. E. Boyle, OP, '*E cathena et carcere*: The Imprisonment of Amaury de Montfort, 1267', in *Medieval Learning*, 379–97.

[16] For what is known of his life see also *Dictionary of National Biography*, xiii. 729; C. Bémont, *Simon de Montfort, Comte de Leicester* (Paris, 1884).

[17] *Opus tertium*, ed. J. S. Brewer, Rolls Series (London, 1859), p. 35, written in 1267.

[18] Bémont, 367.

Letters

The extant *Epistulae Morales ad Lucilium* number 124 and are divided into twenty books. This large corpus was split in Antiquity into two

This account is based on my earlier study, *The Medieval Tradition of Seneca's Letters* (Oxford, 1965), where more information may be found, and I have taken the opportunity to revise it in the light of facts which have become known since its publication. Professor Bischoff's precise placing of L, B, and Q has modified and sharpened our view of the early medieval transmission, and I am once again grateful to him for advice about other manuscripts. And there have been other significant contributions to the subject, in particular C. Villa, 'La tradizione delle «Ad Lucilium» e la cultura di Brescia dall' età carolingia ad Albertano', *IMU* 12 (1969), 10–51; J. Fohlen, 'Trois manuscrits parisiens des *Epistulae ad Lucilium* de Sénèque', *RHT* 1 (1971), 73–92; 'Manuscrits démembrés des *Epistulae ad Lucilium* de Sénèque', 3 (1973), 241–52.

volumes, containing respectively letters 1–88 and 89–124, so that we
have two distinct manuscript traditions. The citation by Aulus Gellius[1]
of excerpts from Book 22 shows that there was at least a third volume
which has not survived. Letters 1–88 enjoyed a much wider circulation
in the Middle Ages than 89–124, particularly in the early period. The
two parts of the corpus made an isolated appearance together in a
manuscript of the late ninth or early tenth century, but not again until
the twelfth, and from then on with gradually increasing frequency.

  There are also traces of an inner division between letters 1–52 and
53–88, so that the manuscript tradition of letters 1–88 is best
represented by two stemmata:

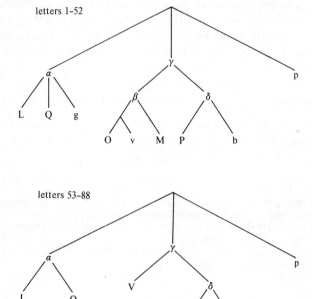

The manuscripts used to reconstruct the text of letters 1–88 are:

p   Paris lat. 8540, s. IX³/₄. This is a remarkable manuscript with a very
     primitive text, sometimes right where all the other witnesses are
     wrong. It stands alone and has no issue. It was written in central
     France and was later (s. XIII/XIV) at Auxerre. It contains 1–71.7.
     Chatelain, plate CLXXI.1.

L   Florence, Laur. 76.40, s. IX¹/₃. A very handsome book and the earliest
     extant manuscript of the first half of the text; it contains 1–65.
     Professor Bischoff now thinks that it is of west-German rather than of
     French provenance and groups it with a number of manuscripts

possibly to be associated with the scriptorium of Louis the Pious.[2] Chatelain, plate CLXX.3.

Q   Brescia B.II.6, s. IX ex./X in., written in Brescia and formerly at the Cathedral.[3] It contains 1–120.12 (the last gathering has been lost). The manuscript was used and annotated in the thirteenth century by Albertano of Brescia.[4] It is by far the earliest manuscript to contain both parts of the correspondence; its importance was first signalled by A. Beltrami in 1913.[5]

g   Wolfenbüttel, Gud. lat. 335, s. X ex./XI in., south-west Germany. An interesting anthology of texts,[6] containing *inter alia* twelve letters selected from 1–88, one of them abbreviated and all comparatively short.

O   Leiden, Voss. Lat. F.70.I, ff. 67–73 + Oxford, Bodl. Canon. Class. Lat. 279. This book was written about 900, almost certainly at Auxerre.[7] It contains 7.2–88.26, with many omissions and lacunae. Chatelain, plate CLXXII.

v   Vatican lat. 366, ff. 165–237, s. XII, north-east France or south-west Germany. A good manuscript despite its comparatively late date, it contains 1–52 only.

M   Metz 300, s. XI ex./XII in. 1–52 and 53–88 have been written by different hands. The second hand is certainly French and the book bears the *ex libris* of St. Arnulf Metz.

V   Venice, Biblioteca Marciana Lat. Z. 270 (1573), s. IX. This beautiful book, at one time at Reims, was written shortly after the middle of the century in north-east France, in or close to the German-speaking area. It contains 53–88 only. *The Medieval Tradition*, plate II.

P   Paris lat. 8658A, s. IX[2], possibly written in the area of the Loire. Chatelain, plate CLXXI.2.

b   Paris lat. 8539, s. X ex./XI in. It carries the type of text which formed the medieval vulgate and has many descendants of its own. It was certainly written in northern France; it has possible connections with the Loire, but its earliest descendants and the centre of the b text are located in Normandy. It stops short at 88.45 *si Protagorae credo*. Chatelain, plate CLXXI.2.

When we come to the tradition of letters 89–124, there are fewer early witnesses and more use has to be made of later manuscripts.

The manuscripts used to construct this part of the text are:

B   Bamberg Class. 46 (M.V.14). A splendid book, written in the court scriptorium of Louis the Pious.[8] It was probably copied from an

---

[2] See his article, 'Die Hofbibliothek unter Ludwig dem Frommen', in *Medieval Learning*, 3–22, particularly 20 (= *Mitt. Stud.* iii. 170–86, 185).

[3] C. Villa, 'La tradizione', has an admirably documented discussion of the provenance and history of Q, with numerous plates.

[4] *The Medieval Tradition*, 100 and n. 8, corroborated and fully worked out by Villa, 24 ff.

[5] *RFIC* 41 (1913), 549–78; 42 (1914), 1–32, 455–6.

[6] Cf. pp. 66, 123, 351.   [7] *Survival*, 53.

[8] Bischoff, *Medieval Learning*, 15 and plate I (= *Mitt. Stud.* 180–1, plate XI). There is another plate in Chatelain, CLXXIII.1.

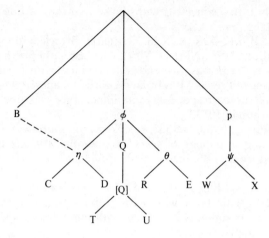

antique original written in uncials and is by far the best witness to the
text of 89–124.

Q   Brescia B.II.6, described above. The last and lost gathering of Q has
to be reconstructed from the two surviving copies of Q which have
come to light. These are Vat. lat. 2212 (s. XIV² = T), which belonged
to Giovanni Capitani Crespi,[9] and Vat. Urb. lat. 219, ff. 1–66
(s. XV = U).

C   Vatican, Pal. lat. 869, ff. 31–45 + Paris lat. 3385, ff. 121–36 +
Vatican, Pal. lat. 869, ff. 46–61, s. XII, written in France and probably
Normandy.[10]

D   Princeton, Garrett 114, s. XIII in. It was at Waltham Abbey early in
the thirteenth century and was probably written and illuminated
there. An initial, depicting Nero enthroned and Seneca in his bath-tub
having his veins opened, is reproduced in *The Medieval Tradition*,
frontispiece.

R   Rouen 931, s. XII, from the Abbey of Jumièges.

E   Avranches 239, s. XII, from Mont-Saint-Michel.

p   Paris lat. 8540, ff. 31–2. These two leaves of later date (s. X in.) were
inserted into p from another manuscript. They contain 121.12–122
fin. and have a good text, though heavily corrected by a second hand.
For the bulk of 89–124 we have to make do with the descendants of
p, infected from the start by the corrections and interpolations of p².
The best of these are Vienna 123 (s. XII = W), which has the *ex libris* of
the monastery of the Himmerod, in the Eifel, and Florence, Laur.
45.24 (s. XII = X), of French origin.

The tradition of 89–124 provides a firmer starting-point for a survey
of the medieval transmission of the *Letters* than that of 1–88, since we
can be more precise about where and when it emerged after the Dark

---

[9] Villa, 21 f.

[10] The missing leaves of Pal. lat. 869 were found in Paris lat. 3385 by Fohlen, who rightly argues
for a Norman provenance: *RHT* 1 (1971), 208–9; 3 (1973), 245–8 (with plates).

Ages. B not only offers by far the earliest and best text of these letters, it has a good claim to be a direct copy of the uncial codex which is the archetype of this part of the tradition.[11] The firm attribution of B to the court scriptorium of Louis the Pious gives this fine book the home it deserves and fits the other known facts. For it was probably during his stay at Aachen, when acting as tutor to the son of the imperial house, the future Charles the Bald, that Walahfrid Strabo copied an extract from letter 120, textually very close to B, into his personal scrap-book.[12] The direct copy of B formerly extant in Strasbourg C.vi.5 might possibly be the book listed in the ninth-century Lorsch catalogue, but its destruction in 1870 has robbed us of the chance of fitting this piece of evidence securely into the puzzle.[13] There were copies of the *Letters* in the ninth century at Reichenau and Murbach too, though these may not have been texts of 89–124.[14]

Q is unique in that it has succeeded in combining both halves of the text at a very early date. It has long been clear that the most likely source for its text of 89–124 (φ) was southern Germany, probably the monasteries of the Rhineland or Lake Constance, with which Brescia had close links.[15] Now that the α text can be located in the same area, likewise emanating in all probability from the Carolingian court, there can be little doubt that Q obtained its unique combination of $\alpha\varphi$ texts from the German side of the Alps. We know nothing of the origin of p, the progenitor of the third branch of the tradition, but its earliest extant copy (W) points in the same general direction; W was written at the Cistercian monastery of the Himmerod, in the Eifel to the north-east of Trier. The early medieval tradition of 89–124 is essentially a German affair.

The transmission of 1–88 is more complex. Although the tradition still appears to be predominantly French, the α branch at least has a German origin. The placing of L in west Germany rather than France, and the likelihood that it was executed, like B, at the court of Louis the Pious, allows one to explain in a convincing way the peculiar character of the one Italian witness, Q. The manuscript g comes from south-west Germany. Moreover, the discovery of an echo of letter 87.38 in Einhard[16] confirms the existence of a text of letters 1–88 in Germany. But letters 1–88 were also well established in France at an early date.

---

[11] *The Medieval Tradition*, ch. 4.

[12] Ibid. 92 ff.; *CR* 7 (1957), 5–8. For Walahfrid Strabo's scrap-book, see Bischoff, 'Eine Sammelhandschrift Walahfrid Strabos (Cod. Sangall. 878)', *Mitt. Stud.* ii. 34–51 (an enlarged version of his earlier article). There is a facsimile of the Seneca excerpt in *The Medieval Tradition*, pl. i.   [13] Bischoff (n. 2, above), 15 n. 2. Cf. *Lorsch*, 90. 102–3.

[14] Villa rightly argues (46 ff.) that the Reichenau manuscript probably contained 1–88.

[15] For Brescian links with the north, see ibid.

[16] In his *De adoranda cruce*, ed. K. Hampe, *MGH, Epist.* v (Berlin, 1899), p. 147.39 f., pointed out by S. Hellmann, *Historische Vierteljahrschrift*, 27 (1932), 93 n. = *Ausgewählte Abhandlungen* (Darmstadt, 1961), 212 n.

They were known to Radbert of Corbie in the second quarter of the ninth century,[17] and the three Paris manuscripts (pPb) were all written in central or northern France. While the influential δ text may well have originated somewhere between Normandy and the Loire, where it was well placed to benefit from the intellectual expansion of the Norman period, the other group of γ manuscripts (OvMV̇) point in the direction of north-east France, towards Alsace and the German-speaking area. V is probably the source from which O and M derived their texts of letters 53–88,[18] and the existence in V of an Old High German gloss[19] indicates a provenance closer to the German-speaking area than Reims, where V found its home. M has the *ex libris* of St. Arnulf Metz, and probably originated, like v, in the area of Alsace. O and M both succeeded in combining 1–52 and 53–88. O itself was almost certainly written at Auxerre, but the text it carried had probably come from Alsace: this was the home of its closest relatives and it was here that M had managed to combine the same texts of 1–52 and 53–88.

The tremendous surge in Seneca's popularity from the beginning of the twelfth century, and a predilection for the *Letters* in particular, created a large and rich tradition which soon carried them to all parts of western Europe. Their circulation in the later Middle Ages and Renaissance is too big and complex a subject to be treated here, and much work still remains to be done on the detailed ramification of the later tradition,[20] but some of the main points may be mentioned.

Copies of letters 1–88 were common, usually carrying a δ or mixed β-δ text, and by the end of the twelfth century their range extended from the west of England to Austria and Italy.[21] p had no issue, and α texts were rare; but L or a manuscript very like it must have passed through north-west France, for a couple of twelfth-century α texts have come to light, one of them probably written at Corbie.[22] Letters 89–124 began to circulate, but remained for some time in comparatively short supply. B and Q appear to have produced no offspring until very late in the day, and ψ texts do not begin to appear until the later reaches of the twelfth century; it was φ (in both its η and θ form) that joined with γ to provide the vulgate text. φ must have had a German origin, and traces of contamination between η and the B text may be a relic of this; but Normandy was clearly the centre of its diffusion in the twelfth century.

----

[17] To the quotation from letter 10.2 in his *De fide* (cf. *The Medieval Tradition*, 87) may be added a second: he quotes from letter 63.4–7 in his *Epitaphium Arsenii*, ed. E. Dümmler, *Phil. u. hist. Abh. der kön. Akad. der Wiss. zu Berlin*, 1900, II. 27.

[18] *The Medieval Tradition*, 30 ff.   [19] Ibid. 96.

[20] This work is currently being done by Mme Jeannine Fohlen.

[21] Fohlen has identified Paris lat. 13948 (s. XII) as an Italian book, and there may be others of similar date; cf. *RHT* 1 (1971), 77 ff.

[22] Paris lat. 12325; ibid. 73 ff. Oxford, Bodl. Rawl. G.29 has an α, L-type text for letters 1–65, though it has been contaminated with, and supplemented from, a δ source: *The Medieval Tradition*, 69 f. It was written c.1200 in north-west France, perhaps Normandy.

The two θ manuscripts, R and E, come respectively from the Abbey of Jumièges and Mont-Saint-Michel, and they have English cousins.[23] The η branch is similarly placed: C comes from Normandy,[24] D from the English side of the Channel, from Waltham Abbey.

Texts of both halves of the *Letters* must have crossed the Channel hard on the heels of the Norman conquerors. Both were available in Normandy in the twelfth century. In R letters 89–124 have been added by a later hand; in E there is no change of hand and the process of combining the two parts of the text is complete. A similar process had been taking place in the west of England. Since 1–88 were comparatively common, the determining factor was the availability of 89–124. New evidence suggests that these had reached England as early as 1082–3, when they were quoted by Goscelin of Saint-Bertin in his *Liber confortatorius*.[25] He had come from France as a young man in 1058 and had been for many years at Wilton Abbey, near Salisbury, when he wrote this work. About 1138 Robert of Cricklade was able to quote verbatim from the later letters,[26] but was clearly ignorant of the first half of the text. Consequently it is his fellow-countryman and near-contemporary William of Malmesbury who has the distinction of being the first person since Antiquity to quote from the whole range of letters.[27] William may have succeeded, characteristically, in bringing both parts of the text together at Malmesbury.

L. D. R.

[23] British Library, Harley 2659, from St. Peter's Gloucester, and Leiden, Lipsius 49. The latter was certainly in England in the twelfth century (*The Medieval Tradition*, 109) and, as Mr N. R. Ker informs me, could well have been written there. It has only two letters from the second half of the corpus (96 and part of 103), added in a slightly later hand and with a text close to that of the Harley manuscript.   [24] See above, n. 10.

[25] Ed. C. H. Talbot. *Analectica Monastica*, iii (Studia Anselmiana, 37, Rome, 1955), 1–117; see pp. 78 (letter 89.21), 79 (letter 123.2). It was the late Richard Hunt who drew my attention to the *Liber confortatorius*.

[26] He quotes from letters 90, 102, 108, 123; *The Medieval Tradition*, 117.

[27] Ibid. 123 ff. For 1–88 William used a text like that of Harley 2659, from Gloucester, and Oxford, Magdalen College Lat. 22, from Evesham. The Harley manuscript succeeded in adding 89–124 from another source; this is very close to the source used by William for these letters, and may well be the one on which Goscelin of Saint-Bertin and Robert of Cricklade also drew.

Natural Questions

The *Natural Questions* has fared worse than Seneca's other philosophical works, for no manuscript is earlier than the twelfth century, and the archetype was mutilated, lacking the end of Book 4a and the start of 4b.[1] At Constantinople in the sixth century John the Lydian possessed a more complete text, for in his *De mensibus* he gives a Greek paraphrase of surviving and lost portions of Book 4a.[2] In the ninth century there was a copy of the *Natural Questions* at Reichenau,[3] and that manuscript, or one closely related to it, was probably read by the unknown author of the ninth-century treatise *De mundi coelestis terrestrisque constitutione*.[4] The Reichenau manuscript may have no connection with the twelfth-century tradition, which, as we shall see, emanates from northern France.

A. Gercke divided the surviving manuscripts into two groups, Δ and Φ, relying heavily on the order in which they place the books; for while Δ follows the order found in our printed editions, Φ has the order 4b–7, 1–4a (conveniently called the *Grandinem* order, after the first word of Book 4b).[5] This division is still generally accepted, despite H. W. Garrod's just criticism of the status Gercke assigns to Δ, and despite P. Oltramare's demonstration of the independence and importance of Geneva lat. 77, known as Z (s. XII med., northern France; Chatelain, plate CLXX).[6] Oltramare thought Z belonged to the same branch as Φ; D. Vottero has recently suggested that Z maybe represents a third branch alongside Δ and Φ;[7] but in fact $\Delta\Phi$ share errors which make it plain that we are dealing with a bifid stemma, where Z represents the one hyparchetype, ζ, and practically everything else derives from the other hyparchetype, Ψ. It can be shown that the

The standard editions are A. Gercke's Teubner (Leipzig, 1907; repr. Stuttgart, 1970) and P. Oltramare's Budé (Paris, 1929; repr. 1961). Gercke's preface refers to, and summarizes the conclusions of, his earlier work on the manuscript tradition. The above account is based in part on H. M. Hine, 'The Manuscript Tradition of Seneca's *Natural Questions*', *CQ* 30 (1980), 183–217; *An Edition with Commentary of Seneca, Natural Questions, Book Two* (New York, 1981), 4–23.

[1] Until the nineteenth century it was not noticed that the so-called Book 4 is composed of fragments of two separate books.
[2] The relevant sections of John's text are printed in Gercke's edition.
[3] See P. Lehmann, *Mittelalterliche Bibliothekskataloge Deutschlands und der Schweiz*, i (Munich, 1918), 266.
[4] C. W. Jones, *Bedae Pseudepigrapha: Scientific Writings Falsely Attributed to Bede* (Ithaca, 1939), 83–5, gives reasons for thinking that this work, which is printed among the doubtful works of Bede in *PL* 90.881–910, and is generally assigned to the ninth century, was written in the region of St. Gall or Reichenau in the second half of the century. I intend to show elsewhere that the author was probably acquainted with the *Natural Questions*.   [5] Gercke, v–xlii.
[6] Garrod, *CQ* 8 (1914), 273–4; Oltramare, 'Le codex Genevensis des Questions Naturelles de Sénèque', *RPh* 45 (1921), 5–44, and his edition *passim*.   [7] *AAT* 107 (1973), 264–7.

archetype had the *Grandinem* book order, with the books numbered consecutively from 3–10. This anomaly is readily explained: internal evidence indicates that the true book order is 3–7, 1–2, so at some stage a copy must have broken in two near the end of Book 4a, with the loss of some folios containing the end of Book 4a and the start of 4b; when the two pieces were put together in the wrong order, and the numeration of Books 3–4a was altered to suit their new position, the result was a copy just like the archetype.

All we can safely say about the dates of the hyparchetypes, ζ and Ψ, is that they were pre-twelfth century. ζ had a perilous survival: apart from Z, it has left traces only in: Escorial O.III.2 (s. XIII, French), a composite manuscript which derives parts of Books 1–2 from ζ; some brief excerpts in a twelfth-century northern French florilegium;[8] and sparse corrections in Leiden, Voss. Lat. F. 69 (s. XII; Chatelain, plate CLXIX; L).[9] By contrast, Ψ has over eighty descendants, which fall into three groups, α, θ, and π. α is mainly represented by δ (Gercke's Δ; see below for individual manuscripts), which has a highly corrupt text and the deviant book order now established in our editions; but Escorial O.III.2 preserves a purer form of the α text in parts of Books 1, 2–3, 7. θ is best represented by Oxford, Merton College 250 (s. XII; F) and Paris lat. 8624 (s. XII², French; H), π by Paris lat. 6628 (s. XII², French; P).

Citations in contemporary writers and manuscript provenances[10] indicate that the *Natural Questions* was rediscovered in northern France not later than the early twelfth century; its spread perhaps owed something to the general renaissance of scientific and philosophical studies at that time. There is a tantalizing possibility – no more – that Anselm was acquainted with the work,[11] but the first writer who definitely used it was William of Conches[12] (who had a manuscript of the α group). Philip Bishop of Bayeux, 1142–64, and John of Salisbury also possessed copies, which they left respectively to Bec and Chartres. Twelfth-century manuscripts of the ζ, θ, and π groups whose script can

---

[8] Contained in Douai 285 (s. XII), 533 (s. XII/XIII), Troyes 215 (s. XII/XIII), Vatican, Reg. lat. 1707 (s. XIII), British Library, Add. 16608 (s. XIV). For this 'Florilegium Duacense', see now B. Munk Olsen, *RHT* 9 (1979), 84–9.

[9] See Hine, 'Escorial MS. O III 2 and related manuscripts of Seneca's *Natural Questions*', *CQ* 28 (1978), 296–311; 'The Manuscript Tradition of Seneca's *Natural Questions*: Some Manuscripts Related to Z', *Prometheus*, 5 (1979), 63–72.

[10] I am greatly indebted to the late Dr R. W. Hunt for his help in determining dates and provenances of manuscripts.

[11] Cf. R. W. Southern, *Saint Anselm and his biographer; a Study of Monastic Life and Thought, 1059– c.1130* (Cambridge, 1963), 59; G. M. Ross, in *Seneca*, ed. C. D. N. Costa (London, 1974), 134–5. On this and other aspects of the influence of the *Natural Questions* on the writers of the Middle Ages see K. -D. Nothdurft, *Studien zum Einfluss Senecas auf die Philosophie und Theologie des zwölften Jahrhunderts* (Leiden, 1963), 161–81, to be used with caution.

[12] See C. Picard-Parra, 'Une utilisation des Quaestiones naturales au milieu du XIIe siècle', *Revue du moyen âge latin*, 5 (1949), 115–26; Nothdurft, 162–75. Both these writers overlook indications that William used the *Natural Questions* in his *Philosophia mundi*, as well as in his later *Dragmaticon*.

be placed come from northern France; P belonged to the Abbey of Saint-Victor at Paris, Cambrai 555 (s. XII/XIII; K) to Cambrai Cathedral.

But already in the twelfth century some δ manuscripts were being copied in Germanic lands: Vatican, Pal. lat. 1579 (s. XII²; V) was written in north or east France, but Leiden, Voss. Lat. O. 55 (s. XII¹;A) was perhaps written in the Low Countries,[13] while Bamberg Class. 1 (M.IV.16) (s. XII, B; Chatelain, plate CLXVIII) and Heiligenkreuz 213 (s. XII²; C) were certainly written in Germany. By the thirteenth century the work was available in England, for Robert Grosseteste knew it; and it was becoming widespread in northern Europe, being used, for example, by Vincent of Beauvais, Roger Bacon, and Albertus Magnus. By the end of the thirteenth century it had reached Italy, where one of the earliest copies made was Vatican, Chigi E.VIII.252 (s. XIII²). In Italy copies proliferated in the fourteenth and fifteenth centuries, δ's erroneous book order became firmly established, and a singularly corrupt exemplar, with text compounded from δ and θ, formed the basis of the *editio princeps*, in the 1490 Venice edition of Seneca's works.

H. M. H.

[13] Dr J. J. G. Alexander has suggested this provenance, on the basis of a decorated initial in A.

Tragedies

Although nearly four hundred manuscripts of the tragedies survive, for several centuries the text had a remarkably limited circulation. Citations and direct references in late Antiquity and the early Middle Ages are rare.[1] Nor were the tragedies rediscovered by the Carolingians, although extracts from *Troades*, *Medea*, and *Oedipus* figure (together with several other rare texts) in a miscellany written in central or northern France (perhaps at Fleury) in the second half of the ninth century (Paris

This account is based (with some corrections) on that in R. J. T. (ed.), *Seneca: Agamemnon* (Cambridge, 1976), 23–94. The most useful critical edition now available is that of G. C. Giardina (2 vols., Bologna, 1966); an OCT edition by O. Zwierlein is in preparation. A handlist of manuscripts by A. P. MacGregor is forthcoming in *ANRW*.

[1] E. Franceschini, 'Glosse e commenti medievali a Seneca tragico', (*Pubblicazioni dell' Università Cattolica del Sacro Cuore*, ser. 4, vol. 30, Milan, 1938), 3 ff.; W. Woesler, *Senecas Tragödien. Die Überlieferung der a-Klasse dargestellt am Beispeil der Phaedra* (Münster–Neuwied, 1965), 106 n. 3; H. Hagendahl, *VChr* 28 (1974), 218. Seneca's *Agamemnon* is a main source of Dracontius' *Orestis tragoedia*; many of the *metra* in Boethius' *Consolatio philosophiae* have obvious Senecan models. A wide range of imitation in late-antique writers is alleged by H. Jürgens, *Pompa Diaboli. Die lateinischen Kirchenväter und das antike Theater* (*Tübinger Beiträge*, 46, 1972), 56–65, but many of the parallels adduced are insubstantial.

lat. 8071, owned by Jacques de Thou and hence called the *florilegium Thuaneum*).[2]

The earliest complete manuscript (Florence, Laur. 37. 13; tradition-ally called 'codex Etruscus' or E) was written in Italy in the late eleventh century; it is probably the manuscript of the plays registered in the 1093 catalogue of the monastery of Pomposa, and it may derive from a copy borrowed from Montecassino.[3] E has given its name to one of the two main classes of manuscripts, and it is the only complete representa-tive of its class with independent value. Three other manuscripts, Paris lat. 11855 (F), Milan, Ambros. D. 276 inf. (M), and Vatican lat. 1769 (N), all Italian of the early to middle fourteenth century, are derived from an apograph of E called Σ, which had been contaminated with a text belonging to the other branch of the tradition (= A).[4] The Σ manuscripts therefore have value only when the original reading of E has been erased after Σ was copied from it; the few good readings in the Σ group and not in E or the best A manuscripts are to be treated as successful conjectures. The extracts in the *florilegium Thuaneum* also belong to the E class, and help to distinguish some errors of the Etruscus from those of its ancestors; their value is reduced, however, by the high level of superficial corruption they exhibit.[5]

The E-class text in its pure form was not widely known in the later Middle Ages; E itself was owned by Niccolò Niccoli and was later consulted in the Medici library by Poliziano, but it seems not to have exerted a strong direct influence on the fifteenth-century tradition.

The dominant branch of the transmission throughout the Middle Ages was that now called A, to which almost all other extant manuscripts belong. The earliest surviving A manuscripts were written in northern France and England in the first half of the thirteenth century; it seems likely that the origin of A was a manuscript discovered in a monastic centre of central or northern France in the second half of the twelfth century.[6]

The A class is itself divided into two subgroups, δ and β; the β manuscripts often contain interpolated readings where δ agrees with E (and thus, presumably, with the archetype).[7] The δ group, clearly French in origin, consists of two complete manuscripts: Paris lat. 8260 (s. XIII[1], copied in northern France for Richard of Fournival = P) and 8031 (s. XV[1], northern France or Flanders = T);[8] one manuscript containing only the *Octavia*, Exeter 3549 B (s. XIII[1], probably England

---

[2] See above, pp. 10, 45, 181.   [3] On E cf. R. J. T., 24–8.
[4] Zwierlein, *Gnomon*, 41 (1969), 760, *Hermes*, 103 (1975), 253 n. 6; R. J. T., 63–71.
[5] Woesler, 105 n. 1; R. H. Philp, *CQ* 18 (1968), 170 f.
[6] R. H. R., *RHT* 1 (1971), 98–121; *JWI* 40 (1977), 283–6.
[7] C. E. Stuart, *CQ* 6 (1912), 1–20.
[8] T is a discovery of A. P. MacGregor; its independence of P (doubted by R. J. T., 401) was vindicated by Zwierlein, *Gnomon*, 49 (1977), 568–70.

= G);[9] and several sets of excerpts.[10] All other manuscripts whose text has been investigated belong to the β group, of possible English origin, the purest complete specimens of which are Cambridge, Corpus Christi College 406 (s. XIII[1], ? England = C) and Escorial T.III.11 (s. XIII ex., Italy = S).[11] The testimony of PT CS (with the addition of G for *Octavia*) seems adequate for the reconstruction of the A hyparchetype; in isolated cases of doubt reference may be made to the manuscripts closest to them in purity, Vatican lat. 2829 (s. XIV[1], ? Italy = V)[12] and Naples IV.E.1 (s. XIV, Italy = d).[13] Several other A manuscripts have been used by editors, but those readings in them which are not in PT CS are probably the result of contamination from the E class or independent conjecture, rather than traces of another strain of tradition derived from A.[14] The great mass of *recentiores* is still very imperfectly known, and manuscripts of value may therefore lie unrecognized, but in the present state of knowledge no A manuscript deserves to be placed on the same level as PT (G) CS.

At the beginning of the fourteenth century several developments contributed to a rapid growth in the popularity of the tragedies. The work of the Paduan scholars Lovato Lovati and Albertino Mussato showed a deeper understanding of Senecan dramatic form than had been achieved previously (and also, in the case of Lovati, a familiarity with the rare E-class text).[15] Interest in the tragedies emerged shortly thereafter at the papal court in Avignon; to help readers in coping with this difficult and unfamiliar text, a commentary was commissioned from Nicholas Trevet, a Dominican of Blackfriars Oxford. The commentary was based on a manuscript of the β group very much like C, and enjoyed a wide circulation in Italy during the next two centuries.[16] It is plausible, though it cannot now be shown, that Petrarch became familiar with the tragedies during his years at Avignon. Petrarch may even have played a part in the spread of the text; his hand has been recognized in the margins of S,[17] the earliest surviving specimen of the strain of β which, contaminated to varying degrees by readings of the E class, remained the vulgate until the end of the Middle Ages.[18]

The differences between E and A involve more than textual variants.

---

[9] C. J. Herington, *RhM* 101 (1958), 353–77; 103 (1960), 96; p. 362 n. 6, above.

[10] Details in R. J. T., 46 ff.   [11] Stuart *passim*.

[12] A. P. MacGregor, *TAPA* 102 (1971), 327–56; R. J. T., 35 f.

[13] Philp, 160 ff.; R. J. T., 36, 80.   [14] R. J. T., 35–9, 72–86.

[15] Gius. Billanovich, *I primi umanisti e le tradizioni dei classici latini* (Fribourg, 1953), 18 ff., 40 ff.; *Storia della cultura veneta: Il Trecento* (Vicenza, 1976), esp. 56–62 (with the suggestion that Vat. lat. 1769 was copied by Rolando da Piazzola and contains marginalia in the hand of Mussato). The link between the Paduans and Σ is also discussed by R. J. T., 64 f.

[16] Franceschini, 29 f.; R. J. T., 81–4; M. Palma, *IMU* 16 (1973), 317 ff.

[17] A. C. de la Mare, *JWI* 40 (1977), 286–90.

[18] This form of A was also the basis of the first printed editions (*editio princeps* Ferrara, 1484 (A. Belfortis), Hain 14662); the pure E text was first used by Gronovius (Leiden, 1661).

The E class transmits nine plays with the following order and titles: *Hercules, Troades, Phoenissae, Medea, Phaedra, Oedipus, Agamemnon, Thyestes, Hercules*. The A class contains in addition the pseudo-Senecan *Octavia*, and presents the plays with the following order and titles: *Hercules Furens, Thyestes, Thebais* (= *Phoenissae*), *Hippolytus* (= *Phaedra*), *Oedipus, Troas* (= *Troades*), *Medea, Agamemnon, Octavia, Hercules Oetaeuo*. The A class is also characterized by many interpolated readings and by a number of lacunae. Common errors show that E and A descend from an archetype; the absence of shared minuscule errors, among other factors, suggests that the archetype may have been of late-antique date. (The oldest extant manuscript evidence does, in fact, come from this period: five leaves of a manuscript in rustic capitals (s. V, probably Italy) survive in a seventh-century Bobbio palimpsest.[19])

Although the tradition is bipartite, the subdivision of A into δ and β offers some scope for the elimination of isolated variants: the agreement of δ or β with E against the other will normally yield both the reading of A and that of the archetype. When PT CS (A) agree against E, the recension is open and choice must be based on the quality of the readings themselves. Only when the transmitted variants are of roughly equal merit should any weight be accorded to E's status as the 'better' (i.e. less often interpolated) class.[20]

R. J. T.

[19] Milan, Ambros. G. 82 sup. (now S. P. 9/13–20), pp. 375–6, 385–6, 449–50, 471–4; *CLA* III. 346; cf. E. A. Lowe, 'Codices Rescripti', no. 83 (*Pal. Papers*, ii. 502). The place of this palimpsest (called R) in relation to E and A is disputed, cf. R. J. T., 55 f.
[20] G. Carlsson, *Die Überlieferung der Seneca-Tragödien* (Lunds Universitets Årsskrift, N. F. avd. 1 bd. 21), Lund, 1926.

Q. SERENUS

The *Liber medicinalis*, a verse treatise in sixty-four chapters, was written by a not firmly identified Quintus Serenus perhaps as early as the late second century AD, perhaps as late as the fourth. Its only known early use is by Marcellus Empiricus (*c.*AD 400), who borrowed from it for his *De medicamentis*. Given the lack of enthusiasm for Serenus' work in Antiquity and the early Middle Ages, it must owe its remarkable ninth- and tenth-century popularity, as well as its survival to modern times, to

its having been copied at the command of the emperor Charlemagne.[1]
To judge from the works with which it travelled, the *Liber medicinalis* was
not prized for its medical knowledge, but rather became part of that
body of late-antique and early Christian verse read by ninth-century
scholars. It provides a classic demonstration of the role of the Carolingian court in the history of textual transmission, and in the building of
libraries.

Manuscripts of Quintus Serenus are divided into two families, descended from the Carolingian archetype.[2] The first, and better, family
consists of one surviving manuscript and a ninth-century catalogue
description. The manuscript, Zurich C 78, part IV, ff. 57^v–82^v (A), s. IX
ex., belonged to St. Gall. In addition to Serenus' ten-verse preface, the
text in A is uniquely preceded by twenty verses which praise the book
and state that Jacobus made it at the order of Charlemagne ('. . . hec
fieri Karlus rex namque modestus/ mandat, ut in seclis rutilet sophisma
futuris:/ legit enim famulus stilo animoque Iacobus'). This Jacobus is
probably to be identified with a court notary known 787–792.[3] The
sixty-four chapters in A have been misnumbered as sixty-two; but A's
text is both more accurate and fuller than that of the B family, and it
lacks as well the interpolations characteristic of B.

A is doubtless either a sister or a copy of the earlier manuscript, now
lost, recorded in the catalogue at Reichenau (a. 842): 'In XXXI libello de
arte medicinae metris versibus Iacobus nomine ad Karolum regem
scribebat, comprehendens capitula LXII . . .'. The presence of Jacobus's
verse prologue, as well as the miscounting of the chapters, demonstrates
the close relationship of the lost Reichenau manuscript with A, at
nearby St. Gall. Walahfrid Strabo used the Reichenau text at that
abbey in AD 833. Perhaps the 'Metrum Quinti Sereni de medicina' in
the catalogue of Murbach (s. IX med.) is also a text of this tradition,
since Murbach seems to have copied a number of Reichenau books.
And the brief extracts from Quintus Serenus in the verse florilegium
written at St. Gall (St. Gall 870, s. IX ex.) come from A's branch of the
family, according to Vollmer. This family, as represented by A, preserves at least seven verses not found in any of the other manuscripts
(vv. 136, 250, 457, 502, 665, 944, 1049).[4]

---

[1] The *Medicinalis liber* that draws on Quintus Serenus, which A. Mai attributed to Benedictus
Crispus, Bishop of Milan (681–725), has been shown by F. Brunhölzl to be instead a late medieval
creation; see *Aevum*, 33 (1959), 25–67.

[2] The standard editions are those of E. Baehrens, *Poetae latini minores*, iii (Leipzig, 1881),
103–58, and F. Vollmer, *Corpus medicorum latinorum*, ii. 3 (Leipzig, 1916); but see also those of
R. Pépin (Paris, 1950) and I. F. Shuts'tsa (Moscow, 1961), and the useful review of Baehrens by
J. Schmidt, *Hermes*, 17 (1882), 239–50. Manuscripts are listed by A. Beccaria, *I codici di medicina del
periodo presalernitano* (Rome, 1956).

[3] *Karl der Grosse*, 45 (= Bischoff, *Mitt. Stud.* iii. 154).

[4] The number is probably as high as eleven. The four disputed *loci* are vv. 183, 216–17, found in
Siena F. V. 8, and v. 894, found in b (this part of the text is lacking in the Siena manuscript).

The second family, comprising all the remaining manuscripts, descends from a lost exemplar called B, which editors have reconstructed from some (not all) of its early descendants. Schmidt attempted in 1882 to show the filiation of B's progeny; Vollmer, in his edition of 1916, persuasively discounts Schmidt's interpretation of the evidence, but proffers no stemma of his own. Moreover, a number of ninth-century manuscripts have received either slight attention or none at all from the editors. Thus, the grouping of the manuscripts in the subsequent discussion is based on probabilities and on the need for coherent exposition, rather than on collation.

Although the lost B, and hence its progeny, lack Jacobus's verse prologue, the date at which this tradition suddenly bursts upon the scene suggests that it, too, must derive from Charlemagne's copy. Of the twenty or more manuscripts dated before 1200, over three-quarters were written in the ninth and tenth centuries, with the eleventh and twelfth centuries accounting for less than one-quarter between them. The earliest fairly sure evidence for a manuscript of the B family occurs in the catalogue (AD 831) of Saint-Riquier, 'Quintus Serenus de medicamentis'. Mico, deacon of Saint-Riquier in the first half of the ninth century, cites in his florilegium ten verses of Serenus which clearly derive from a B text.[5] In the Saint-Riquier catalogue the entries just prior to Quintus Serenus read 'Prosper, Arator, Sedulius, Iuvencus, epigrammata Prosperi, versus Probae, et medietas Fortunati I vol.'. Paris lat. 9347, ff. 49–57 (c), written at Reims (probably at St. Remigius, to which it belonged) in the first half of the ninth century,[6] may be related to the Saint-Riquier text since it contains the same body of works, from Prosper to Fortunatus.[7] Six other manuscripts of the later ninth century may also belong to this group, either because of their places of origin or because they contain elements of this collection of texts: Paris lat. 2773, part I, ff. 68–83, s. IX^2, St. Remigius of Reims; Paris lat. 2772, ff. 28–50 (e), s. $IX^3/4$, written probably at Lyon, belonged to Paray-le-Monial, a daughter house of Cluny, in the fifteenth century;[8] Vatican, Pal. lat. 1088, s. IX^2, also written in the area of Lyon; Vatican, Reg. lat. 215, f. 129, s. $IX^3/3$, written in Tours minuscule; Paris n. a. lat. 1613, f. 12, s. $IX^2/3$, thought by Rand to have originated at

According to Schmidt, these could be genuine. According to Vollmer (xv–xvi), these are contaminations from A, the more likely explanation.

---

[5] The single verse of Serenus quoted in the anonymous *Ecbasis captivi*, c. 940, seems to be taken from Mico's florilegium.

[6] Professor Bischoff has helped with the dating and placing of the early Serenus manuscripts.

[7] The same group of Christian poets, without Quintus Serenus, is mentioned in Alcuin's verses on the library at York (*MGH, Poetae latini aevi Carolini*, i. 20 ff.) and in Theodulph of Orléans's *De libris quos legere solebam* (ibid. 543). For a fuller discussion of the group see G. Glauche, *Schullektüre im Mittelalter, Münchener Beiträge*, 5 (Munich, 1970), esp. 27 f., 32 f., 36.

[8] The *Liber medicinalis* was also known at Cluny and appears in the catalogue of 1158–61; Delisle, ii. 478 no. 503, 'Virgilius cum commento Servii habens in principio Quintum Serenum'.

Tours, but perhaps written in Brittany; and Vatican lat. 10816, f. 1, s.
IX ex., western France. Two later manuscripts, of unknown pro-
venance, are Paris lat. 8048, ff. 56–62, s. X (g), and 7099, ff. 25–39, s.
XI/XII.

The manuscripts which contain the *Liber medicinalis* by itself or with
other *medica* are primarily German in origin or background. These
include Leiden, Voss. Lat. Q. 33, part III, ff. 145^v–155^v (b), s. IX^3/$_4$,
France. This is the B manuscript most heavily relied upon by editors; it
is probable, however, that many of b's 'good' readings are borrowed
from an A text. The exemplar of b was mutilated in places; corresponding lacunae allow one to identify as b's sister Brussels 5658, ff. 122–51
(f), s. X/XI, which probably belonged to the abbey of Gembloux. The
common parent of b and f must have been located somewhere in the
Carolingian heartland. Other manuscripts in this group are Vatican,
Reg. lat. 598, part IV, ff. 28^v–33^r, s. IX^2/$_4$, western Germany, once with
Paris lat. 8319, ff. 1–34 and lat. 8320, ff. 1–6; Bonn S 218, ff. 72^r–81^v, s.
XI, written possibly at St. Maximinus of Trier and later owned by
Maria Laach; Herten 192, ff. 77^r–83^v, s. XI/XII, destroyed in the Second
World War; and Brussels 2424, unfoliated, s. XII, owned by Val-Saint-
Lambert. Ten verses appear in the Florentino-Erlangense florilegium of
late twelfth-century German origin, preserved in Laur. 16. 5 and
Erlangen 395. One leaf of the tenth century, now Berne A. 92, part 15, is
still of undetermined origin.[9]

The *Liber medicinalis* appeared in Italy in the late ninth century and
enjoyed a reasonable circulation. Among the manuscripts of Italian
origin is St. Gall 44, part II, pp. 304–24, s. IX^2, written in northern Italy.
A long extract from Serenus, in a tenth-century hand which Campana
suggested was that of Rather of Verona,[10] appears in a ninth-century
Italian manuscript of Isidore's *Etymologiae* which belonged to the chapter library of Verona (now Cesena S. XXI.5). Others are Siena F.V.8, ff.
167–73, s. X with corrections of s. XI, which belonged to S. Justina of
Padua in the fifteenth century; Vatican, Barb. lat. 160 ff. 266–74^v (h),
written in the eleventh century in the area of Bari, in part in Beneventan
minuscule; and Modena Lat. 580 (α.O.9.19), s. XII–XV. The *Liber
medicinalis* reached Saxon England by the late tenth or early eleventh
century, as witness Paris lat. 4839, ff. 26–48 (d), and the work is
reported in three post-Conquest catalogues: Rochester, AD 1202;
Peterborough, s. XIV; and St. Augustine's Canterbury, s. XV (now
British Library, Royal 12. E. XXIII, s. XIV). In the same period a copy of
the *Liber medicinalis* went south-west along the pilgrimage route, to
produce Barcelona, Archivo de la Corona de Aragón, Ripoll 59, s. XI.[11]

---

[9] The *Liber medicinalis* is reported in the eleventh-century inventory of Weihenstephan in
Bavaria, and in a mid-twelfth-century gift to Göttweig in Austria; Manitius, *Handschriften*, 157.
[10] See Gius. Billanovich, *IMU* 2 (1959), 123 n. 1.
[11] Kindly brought to my attention by B. Munk Olsen.

With the twelfth century Quintus Serenus dropped out of favour, to re-emerge with a mild surge of interest in the fifteenth and sixteenth centuries. A dozen or so later manuscripts, of mixed tradition, survive.

R. H. R.

SERVIUS

The vast commentary on the works of Virgil was composed by Servius[1] in the fourth century, and quickly became standard fare for the scholarly world. In the sixth century it is quoted several times by Priscian; in the seventh century it is so extensively quarried by Isidore in his *Etymologiae* that in several passages Isidore may be regarded as having the authority of a very early manuscript of Servius; later in that same century, the English scholar Aldhelm[2] used Servius when writing his *De metris*. In the eighth century Alcuin mentions Servius as being in the library at York. Indeed, to the first half of the eighth century belongs the earliest manuscript of Servius, a fragment containing extracts, in the Pfarrbibliothek at Spangenberg (MS. S.N.), apparently written in south-west England (*CLA* Suppl. 1806).[3]

The only critical text of the whole of Servius that is available is *Servii Grammatici Qui Feruntur in Vergilii Carmina Commentarii*, G. Thilo and H. Hagen (3 vols., Leipzig, 1881–7, repr. 1961). The shortcomings of this edition are many, as pointed out, for example, by E. Fraenkel, *JRS* 38 (1948), 131. Still in progress is the Harvard Servius (*Servianorum in Vergilii Carmina Commentariorum Editio Harvardiana*), of which volumes ii (1946, covering *Aen.* 1–2) and iii (1965, *Aen.* 3–5) have so far appeared. Volume ii was the subject of E. Fraenkel's celebrated demolition in his review, *JRS* 38 (1948), 131–43. Of the more important studies of Servius, the following may be singled out: É. Thomas, *Essai sur Servius et son commentaire sur Virgile* (Paris, 1880); J. J. Savage, 'The Manuscripts of the Commentary of Servius Danielis on Virgil', *HSCP* 43 (1932), 77–121 (= Savage[1]); 'The Manuscripts of Servius's Commentary on Virgil', *HSCP* 45 (1934), 157–204 (= Savage[2]); C. Murgia, 'On Relations of the Manuscripts of Servius's Commentary on the *Aeneid*' (unpublished dissertation, Harvard University, 1966; abstract in *HSCP* 71 (1966), 331–3); 'Critical Notes on the Text of Servius's Commentary on Aeneid III–V', *HSCP* 72 (1968), 311–50 (= Murgia[1]); *Prolegomena to Servius 5: the Manuscripts* (University of California Publications: Classical Studies, 11, 1975; with sixteen plates, all of them lamentably reduced) (= Murgia[2]); G. P. Goold, 'Servius and the Helen Episode', *HSCP* 74 (1970), 101–68.

[1] Servius is charmingly introduced by Macrobius, *Sat.* 1, 2, 15 as 'terram intuens et uelut latenti similis', and is treated with great respect. For a less adulatory view of his work, see Goold, esp. 134–140.

[2] References for Aldhelm and Alcuin in J. D. A. Ogilvy, *Books known to the English, 597–1066* (Cambridge, Mass., 1967), 241–2.

[3] As this manuscript seems to have associations with Fulda (not far from Spangenberg), it is tempting, with *CLA*, to see some connection here with Boniface.

At some point in the seventh or eighth century, an unknown compiler grafted on to his text of Servius extensive additional material from another ancient commentary, now generally believed to have been that of the fourth-century scholar Aelius Donatus.[4] It is conjectured that this fusion was produced in Ireland, and from there spread to the Continent. This fuller version of Servius was first published by Pierre Daniel (Paris, 1600), and is therefore conveniently referred to as [DS] to distinguish it from the pure Servius [S], with the non-Servian material being called [D]. It is abundantly clear that our anonymous compiler made what he felt to be the necessary changes in order to harmonize the two commentaries.[5] Of great importance in unravelling these various strands is the fact that, whereas [S] has the order *Aeneid, Eclogues, Georgics*, [D] clearly arranged them *Eclogues, Georgics, Aeneid*. The resulting [DS] stitching is often plain to see.

It is totally impossible to give anything approaching a comprehensive stemma[6] for the manuscripts. Not merely are the various families within the [S] tradition contaminated amongst themselves, but in addition the [DS] tradition clearly contaminates [S]. So fluctuating is the allegiance of any manuscript from passage to passage, that what follows must be regarded as accurate in only the most general terms. Until the full evidence is available with the completion of the Harvard Servius, extreme caution is in order.

The [DS] tradition

From the comparatively small number of manuscripts representing [DS],[7] the following may be selected as most valuable:

L   Leiden, Voss, Lat. O. 80, s. IX[1], containing *Ecl.* 4–8 and *Geo.* 1.1–278. Daniel refers to this as the *Lemovicensis*, presumably meaning that he got it from the monastery of Saint-Martial at Limoges (although the book now bears no mark to confirm this attribution). This is the unique witness for [DS] on the *Eclogues*.

V   Vatican lat. 3317, s. X ex., southern Italy (E. A. Lowe, *Scriptura Beneventana* (2 vols., Oxford, 1929), pl. XLIX); contains [DS] for the *Georgics*. It was certainly in Montecassino by the end of the eleventh century.

---

[4] See, for example, E. K. Rand, 'Is Donatus's Commentary on Virgil lost?', *CQ* 10 (1916), 158–164. Further references in Goold, 104–5. The situation is made all the more complicated by the fact that Servius himself had used the commentary of Donatus.

[5] An excellent analysis of his method is to be found in Goold, 105–17. The [DS] material is often called *Scholia Danielis* or *Servius Auctus*. Daniel himself was under the misapprehension that [DS] represented the 'original' Servius, with [S] an abbreviated form thereof.

[6] A very general, but still helpful, diagram of the [S] and [DS] traditions is given by Goold, 141. A fuller (but equally hesitant) attempt is made by Murgia[2], 5.

[7] A complete list of all known manuscripts is given by Savage[1], 79–121. Helpful is the appendix 'Sigla' in Murgia[2], 186–92.

C   Kassel Poet. 2° 6, s. IX med. (c.840), written at Fulda; contains the [DS] text for *Aen.* 1–2, and a mixed text for *Aen.* 3–6. Several quaternions are now missing. This is apparently not identical[8] with the *Fuldensis* used by Daniel, a manuscript of great value where C fails. The *Fuldensis* is to be reconstructed largely from an appendix (based on notes supplied by Schoppe) to Daniel's 1600 edition, and from a series of notes in Daniel's hand put into his copy of the 1586 Fabricius edition of Virgil (now Berne O. 51).

P   Paris lat. 1750 + Leiden, Voss. Lat. F. 79, s. IX ex. (Fleury), containing a shortened form of [DS] for *Aen.* 1–5. 69. P was used (and separated) by Daniel.

F   Berne 172 + Paris lat. 7929, s. IX (Fleury), containing [DS] for *Aen.* 3–12. Savage[1] (p. 102) conjectured that F's immediate exemplar was Irish and acquired from Corbie or Fulda. It is of interest that G (Berne 167, s. IX[2]), a partial copy of F, is Daniel's *Autissiodorensis*, which he thus acquired from Auxerre.

T   Berne 165, s. IX (c.820), from Tours (Chatelain, pl. LXVII);[9] given to St. Martin's by Berno (f. 1ᵛ); contains excerpts from [DS] on *Aen.* 3–12.

The [S] *tradition*

The text of Servius himself is transmitted in two main families,[10] Δ and Γ. For Δ there are three principal witnesses, all of which descend from a lost manuscript, δ. These are:

L   Leiden, B. P . L. 52, written at Corbie[11] c.800. This was demonstrably a quaternion-by-quaternion copy of δ, made after δ had already lost ten quaternions. These missing quaternions were supplied in L by scribes writing c.850 (also at Corbie), but only two of these later quaternions survive, and they are derived from a different tradition from the original L material. This original L survives only for *Aen.* 5. 93–573; 6. 39–8. 664; 10. 775–11. 262.

K   Karlsruhe Aug. CLXXXVI, s. IX[1] (in Reichenau certainly by s. XII); contains *Geo.* 1. 21–4. 193; *Aen.* 1. 4–338.

---

[8] A point established by J. P. Elder, 'De Servii commentariis Danielinis, ut aiunt, in Aeneidos libros primum et secundum confectis' (unpublished dissertation, Harvard University, 1940; abstract in *HSCP* 51 (1940), 315–18).

[9] Description in E. K. Rand, *A Survey of the Manuscripts of Tours* (The Mediaeval Academy of America (Cambridge, Mass.), publ. no. 3, 1929), i. 127; ii, pls. LXXVI, LXXVII. A thorough examination of the scholia is to be found in J. J. Savage, 'The Scholia in the Virgil of Tours, Bernensis 165', *HSCP* 36 (1925), 91–164, 3 plates.

[10] Full accounts of the manuscripts are given in Savage[2], to which must be joined the highly important additions and corrections of Murgia in his various studies. The sigla used here are those of Murgia, which are somewhat different from those of Thilo or of either volume of the Harvard Servius.

[11] *CLA* x. 1573. A complete facsimile is given by G. I. Lieftinck, *Umbrae codicum occidentalium*, i (Amsterdam, 1960); the valuable chart in Murgia[2], 75–6, shows where Δ is now extant, and where the editor must turn to other sources to construct the [S] text.

J   Metz 292,[12] s. IX[2] (northern France); contains *Geo.* 1. 21–4. 193 and most of *Aen.*

For the *Γ* family, most important are the subdivisions *γ* and *σ*. For *γ* the most reliable witnesses are:

B   Berne 363, s. IX[3]/4, written in an Irish script;[13] contains *Ecl.*, *Geo.*, *Aen.* 1–7. 16.
Pb   Paris lat. 16236, s. X/XI, complete.
M   Munich Clm 6394, s. X/XI (at Freising by s. XII); complete.

For *σ* the representatives are:[14]

V   (see above on [DS]), which in addition to [DS] material contains [S] for *Aen.* 1. 1–35.
W   Wolfenbüttel, Aug. 2° 7. 10, s. XIII ex., a direct copy of V, made before V had suffered its extensive losses; contains *Ecl.*, *Geo.*, *Aen.* 1–12. 164 (Murgia[2], pl. 13).
N   Naples, Bibl. Naz. lat. 5 (formerly Vindob. 27), s. X[1] (southern Italy);[15] contains *Ecl.* 8. 21–end, and *Aen.* 1–11. 82.

Other groups of manuscripts show a bewildering amount of contamination. As the most influential we may single out the so-called 'Tours group',[16] of which the two most important representatives are:

Pa   Paris lat. 7959,[17] s. IX med. (Tours), complete.
Ta   Trier 1086,[18] s. IX[2]/4 (Tours connections); contains *Geo.* and *Aen.*

The editor of Servius has an unenviable task. First he must separate out the three different components, namely [S], [D], and the 'stitching' of the compiler of [DS]. Then he must face the enormously complicated problem of evaluating the variant readings within the [S] texts. Where descendants of *δ* are available, the general superiority of this tradition is helpful. Where *δ* fails, the editor walks on quicksand.

P. K. M.

[12] Destroyed by fire in 1943; a facsimile (unfortunately incomplete) survives in the extensive collection of Servius photographs in Harvard University. Two leaves are shown by Murgia[2], pls. 6 and 14.

[13] A facsimile may be seen in H. Hagen, *Codex Bernensis phototypice editus* (Leiden, 1897). For the dating and the Irish connections, see J. J. Contreni, *The Cathedral School of Laon from 850–930. Its Manuscripts and Masters* (*Münchener Beiträge*, 29, Munich, 1978), 91–2.

[14] This highly contaminated class has been greatly overvalued, as by A. F. Stocker, 'A New Source for the Text of Servius', *HSCP* 52 (1941), 65–97, and the editors of vol. ii of the Harvard Servius. The stemma in Murgia[2] (p. 5) puts *σ* in its correct place.

[15] E. A. Lowe, *Scriptura Beneventana*, pl. XXXI.

[16] Given the siglum *β*[2] by Savage and the Harvard editors; *τ* by Murgia. It was from a text of this type that the supplements were composed for L.

[17] Rand, i. 141 (no. 86); ii, pl. CVI; also Murgia[2], pl. 8.

[18] Rand, *The Earliest Book of Tours* (The Mediaeval Academy of America (Cambridge, Mass.), publ. no. 20, 1934), 106 (no 92A) and pl. LII. Rand conjectured that Ta might have been copied from a Tours book, but 'at some scriptorium in or near Trèves'.

SILIUS ITALICUS

After his contemporaries Pliny and Martial, no one mentions Silius by name in the next 500 years except Sidonius. The ordinariness of his language makes the detection of echoes more than usually difficult, and it does not take much scepticism to infer from E. L. Bassett's survey[1] that after s. VI there are only three traces of his *Punica* before Poggio discovered a manuscript in 1417:[2] a reference to 'Silus Italicus XV lib. de bellis Punicis' among the annotations in Berne 363 (s. IX),[3] 13.663 added by Wolferad, a priest at Constance in s. XI[2], to a manuscript of Bede (Stuttgart HB. VII. 38),[4] and the entry 'Ovidii Metamorfoseon Sili et Stacii volumen I' in a catalogue of s. X[2] (though it includes no work later than *c*.850) that has been variously assigned to St. Gall, Reichenau, and Constance.[5]

It was in all probability the selfsame *volumen* that Poggio discovered during the Council of Constance. Francesco Barbaro congratulated him from Venice on 6 July 1417, and early the following year Poggio dispatched a copy written by a local scribe and emended by himself up to Book 13.[6] In 1429 he was still asking Niccoli to return it, but it is probably the 'Sirius Ytalicus in papirio' that his library included at his death in 1459.[7] P. Thielscher[8] showed that it originally formed part of Madrid 3678 (M. 31), and so despite its loss the script is known.[9]

According to Francesco Filelfo, a manuscript of Silius written 'manu Germani librarii' and brought to Italy by Bartolomeo da Montepulciano had passed to the father of Antonio Barbadori and from him to his son, who lent it to Carlo Marsuppini; Marsuppini died in 1453, and in 1464 Filelfo, who takes it to be the source of all the Italian manuscripts, writes to Antonio Barbadori for news of it. Though other

[1] *CTC* iii (Washington, 1976), 342–8.

[2] P. K. M. points out, however, that *caput a cervice recidit* in the twelfth-century *Chronicle of Morigny* (ed. L. Mirot (Paris, 1909), 2) resembles Sil. 11. 478 *caput a cervice recisum* more than *Georg.* 4. 523 *caput a cervice revulsum* or Lucan 8. 677 *caput ense recidis.*

[3] Th. Gottlieb, *WS* 9 (1887), 157.

[4] J. Autenrieth, *Die Domschule von Konstanz* (Stuttgart, 1956), 79, 148.

[5] See most recently ibid. 18–20, and for an illustration of the entry A. Holder, *Die Reichenauer Handschriften* ii (Leipzig and Berlin, 1914), pls. IX–X.

[6] A. C. Clark, *CR* 13 (1899), 124–6.

[7] E. Walser, *Poggius Florentinus: Leben und Werke* (Leipzig, 1914), 421 no. 57. There is a strong chance that not only the catalogue of s. X[2] and the reference in Berne 363 but also the scribe of Poggio's copy called the poet 'Silus', because two humanists who mention the discovery do the same; cf. Sabbadini, *Epistolario di Guarino Veronese* (Venice, 1915–19), i. 665 (Petrus Thomasius, ? 1419), ii. 224 (Guarino, 1435). Add 'Silus Italus de Cicerone' (8. 408–11) quoted by a later hand on f. 175[v] of Vatican, Rossi 559 (s. XV[1]/[4]) and in other fifteenth-century manuscripts of Cicero.

[8] *Philologus*, 66 (1907), 87–91.   [9] See STATIUS, *Silvae.*

manuscripts in Switzerland were copied both for Poggio and for Bartolomeo, the length of the *Punica* and the absence of any evidence for a second copy of the surviving texts in Madrid 3678, Manilius and *Silvae*, combine to suggest that Filelfo's story supplements what little is known about the wanderings of Poggio's copy.[10] It is true that after H. Blass had divided the manuscripts into two groups, A. C. Clark surmised that a copy of Bartolomeo's lay behind the first and Poggio's copy behind the second;[11] but as far as Blass's evidence goes (pp. 223–6), the second is a group only in time and place, not in community of error, and both groups could perfectly well derive from Poggio's copy: the first through a transcript made soon after its arrival in Italy, the separate members of the second directly, during his final residence in Florence.

In 1508 Jacobus Constantius published eighty-two lines missing from all the manuscripts, namely 8.144–223, 157a, 224a; Baptista Guarinus, he says, claimed to have received them from 'Gallia'. W. E. Heitland upheld their genuineness against earlier doubts,[12] and G. P. Goold explained how they might have been lost and found again.[13] Both derive them from the Swiss manuscript.

Carrio before 1576 and Modius before 1584 collated in the library of Cologne Cathedral a manuscript that ended with 16.555, and each committed some of its more impressive readings to print; a few other readings appear at second hand in Dausqueius's edition (Paris, 1618). When Nic. Heinsius looked for the manuscript in the 1650s, it had disappeared, but he copied a collation (Carrio's?) lent to him by the Jesuits of Antwerp. Like the collations, Heinsius's copy is lost, but Drakenborch used it towards his edition (Utrecht, 1717), which gives a much fuller report than the other three sources. Carrio declares the manuscript Carolingian, and Modius implies as much. After a circumspect discussion Blass concludes that it differed little from the Swiss manuscript (pp. 245–9), but Goold's conjecture that the Swiss manuscript had migrated to Cologne and lost leaves at the end (pp. 12–13) founders on five omissions reported from the Coloniensis (Blass, 173). Whether the Coloniensis had Constantius's eighty-two lines is by no means clear.[14]

Blass's study of the tradition, hailed by Pasquali for its method,[15] also stands as a model of thoroughness; indeed, 'it is hardly possible to speak too highly of this admirable treatise'.[16] Nevertheless it has now been superseded by J. Delz, 'Die Überlieferung des Silius Italicus' (diss.

---

[10] Cf. H. Blass, 'Die Textesquellen des Silius Italicus', *Jahrb. für class. Phil.* Suppl. 8 (1875–6), 168–72.   [11] *CR* 13 (1899), 127–8; 15 (1901), 166.

[12] *J. Phil.* 24 (1896), 188–211.   [13] *RhM* 99 (1956), 9–12.

[14] Cf. W. C. Summers, *CR* 16 (1902), 171–2.

[15] *Storia della tradizione e critica del testo* (Florence, 1934), 68–71.

[16] Heitland (n. 12, above), 188 n. 1.

Basle, 1966), unfortunately not yet published; Delz is also preparing an edition that will replace Bauer's (Leipzig, 1890–2). Meanwhile thirty-two manuscripts, twenty-five of them known to Blass, can be found listed in print.[17] The main members of the later and better 'group' are F and L, Florence, Laur. Edili 196 and Laur. 37. 16; both were written at Florence, the former by G. A. and A. Vespucci,[18] the latter in 1457 by Gherardo del Ciriagio. The main members of the earlier group are O, Oxford, The Queen's College 314; V, Vatican lat. 1652; and G, Florence, Laur. (Gaddi) 91 sup. 35, the last important for the diffusion of the text.[19] The first edition was one of the two printed at Rome in 1471, of which Pomponio Leto's drew at least in part on the later 'group'.

M. D. R.

[17] *CTC* iii, 364–5.   [18] De la Mare, *Handwriting*, 128 no. 37.
[19] Delz ap. P. L. Schmidt, *Die Überlieferung von Ciceros Schrift 'De legibus'* (Munich, 1974), 334 n. 17.

SOLINUS

The *Collectanea rerum memorabilium* of C. Iulius Solinus, largely drawn from the works of the Elder Pliny and Pomponius Mela, and probably of third-century date, was a popular compendium. Citations in Augustine, Isidore, Aldhelm, Bede, and others provide evidence of a wide circulation in the early Middle Ages which antedates the surviving manuscripts. Mommsen[1] distinguished three classes of manuscripts, each in existence by the ninth century; and by the next century the traditions had already begun to merge.

The first is characterized by a hiatus near the end of the text, resulting from a missing penultimate folio in the archetype of class I. Manuscripts of this class are further distinguished by their freedom from interpolation, which is extensive in manuscripts of the other classes. The surviving manuscripts of this class divide into two families, one northern, the other southern.

The earliest witness to a northern text of class I comprises a number of excerpts from Solinus inserted by the Irish monk Dicuil in his *De*

[1] *C. Iulii Solini Collectanea rerum memorabilium* (Berlin, 1895²). See also H. Walter, *Die 'Collectanea rerum memorabilium' des C. Iulius Solinus, ihre Entstehung und die Echtheit ihrer Zweitfassung* (*Hermes*, Einzelschriften, 22, Wiesbaden, 1969).

mensura orbis terrae, written in 825, probably at the Palace School.[2] Dicuil omits information which he certainly would have used had it been available, information lacking only in the manuscripts of class I. Just after mid-century (*c.*860–70), the so-called Anonymus Leidensis included a large portion of Solinus in his *De situ orbis*, which was compiled in the circle of Lupus of Ferrières/Heiric of Auxerre. The unique surviving manuscript of this text,[3] Leiden, Voss. Lat. F. 113, part II (whence the misnomer), s. IX³/₄, was written probably at Auxerre, possibly at the instigation of Heiric. While the exemplar from which the extracts were taken does not survive, there is a late tenth- or early eleventh-century copy or descendant of it, Heidelberg, Pal. lat. 1568 (H). The second surviving manuscript of the northern family is Copenhagen Gl. Kgl. S. 444 (N), s. XI, formerly at Gottorp in Schleswig-Holstein; N has been emended from a manuscript of the third class.

The oldest witness to the southern family of class I is Vatican lat. 3342 (R), s. X², written possibly at Montecassino; the script is similar to that of other books written there under Abbot Aligernus (949–96). Parts of R now missing can be reconstructed from a late fourteenth-century copy of it, Vatican, Reg. lat. 1875, part II, of French or Italian origin, owned by Jean Basire, apostolic secretary from 1396. A second manuscript descended from the ancestor of R is Montecassino 391 (*olim* 841) (C), s. XI ex., in Beneventan script. It is likely that this branch of the family derives from a single manuscript at Montecassino, which was probably brought there from the north.

Important readings of class I are also provided by two Swiss manuscripts of mixed tradition, Engelberg 67 (I.4.15) (A), s. X, and St. Gall 187 (S), s. X. No doubt S (and possibly A as well) is derived from the manuscript of Solinus recorded in three earlier St. Gall book-lists: 'Polihystorem Solini in vol. I', mentioned among the books written at St. Gall under Abbot Hartmotus (872–83); 'Solinus I', in a St. Gall catalogue (s. IX?); and 'Solini polihistor', cited in another near-contemporary list. S is the codex 'venerandae vetustatis' acquired from St. Gall by Joachim von Watt (1484–1551). The text in S derives from two sources: the first part of the text is similar to N, while the remainder is a contaminated text of the third class.

The second class is headed by the oldest surviving manuscript, Leiden, Voss. Lat. Q. 87 (L), *c.*850. L was early on at the monastery of St. Maximinus of Micy, and later came to Orléans; in 1481 an instrument was added to the codex naming 'Sanson Cormereau doctor universitatis Aurelianensis et canonicus eiusdem ecclesie . . . [erased]'. The manuscript was acquired at Orléans by Paul Petau. Similar to L,

---

[2] Ed. J. J. Tierney, *Scriptores Latini Hiberniae*, vi (Dublin, 1967).
[3] Ed. R. Quadri, *Thesaurus Mundi*, 13 (Padua, 1974).

but with sufficient variants to justify considering it a second branch of the class, is Paris lat. 7230 (M), s. x, written at Saint-Denis. Along with L and M, three other manuscripts representing varying degrees of contamination are used to reconstruct class II: Paris. lat. 7230A (Q), s. x, written by a Waldiaudus at Auxerre;[4] Wolfenbüttel, Gud. lat. 163 (G), s. x, from Saint-Laumer at Blois; and Paris lat. 6810 (P), s. x, also from Saint-Laumer. P is noteworthy in that it presents, one after the other, three different colophons or subscriptions: that common to manuscripts of class II, and thus proper to P; that found in H, a manuscript of class I; and that common to manuscripts of the interpolated tradition, thus presumably representing class III.

Class III is represented by readings found in A, S, and P. It is worth observing that A and S contain texts essentially belonging to class I, and both were located in Switzerland, while P was basically a manuscript of the second class, and was written in the Loire Valley. Readings characteristic of this class are quoted by Walahfrid Strabo in his *Life* of St. Gall (s. ix[1]).

Evidently, three recensions survived from Antiquity to reach the Carolingian north. Two of these, the progenitors of classes I and II, seem to have travelled about the Loire abbeys, with the Anonymus Leidensis at Ferrières/Auxerre (class I: s. ix med.), Q (class II: s. x) at Auxerre, L (class II: *c*.850) at Micy and Orléans, and G (class II: s. x) and P (classes II, III: s. x) at Blois. Class III did not survive as an independent text; but from its clear traces in Walahfrid Strabo and in A and S, one might suspect that the exemplar of this recension was located at St. Gall. The mixed contents of P, however, preclude any such simple explanation; rather, they suggest the possibility that, in the tenth century, manuscripts of the third class were available both in Switzerland and along the Loire.

Solinus continued to be copied widely in the later Middle Ages. Excluding epitomes and excerpts, Mommsen lists 153 surviving manuscripts.

R. H. R.

[4] Q has evidently been collated against a text visibly older, for it bears marginal observations (in tironian notes) of 'antiquus' and 'antiquus non habuit'; see Bischoff, *Settimane*, 22, 79 (= *Mitt. Stud.* iii. 68).

STATIUS

Thebaid
Achilleid
Silvae

Thebaid

'Codicum Thebaidos tanta est multitudo ut iure suspiceris pluris per mediam aetatem librarios quam per nostram lectores Statio contigisse';[1] over 160 manuscripts have been listed.[2] Yet unlike Lucan's epic, which it equalled in esteem from s. x on, the *Thebaid* seems to have had a narrow tradition in s. IX. Only one manuscript so old has survived (P), and the single source that all the others derive from (ω) cannot have been much older.

Alcuin knew a 'Statius' at York, and the *Thebaid* occurs in a catalogue perhaps drawn up at the court of Charlemagne (Berlin (West), Diez. B Sant. 66, *c.*790);[3] but nothing connects P or ω with either. P, Paris lat. 8051 (Puteaneus; Chatelain, plate CLXI), was written at Corbie; errors show that its ancestry included a manuscript in insular minuscule.[4] The subscription to Book 4 begins 'codex Iuliani v.c.', and identifications of Julianus have not been wanting.[5] Amongst other errors, ω omitted 10.100–5 and 112–17. Not to mention its later progeny, it has left a dozen or more descendants of s. X–XI. Some have errors due to insular or pre-Caroline minuscule, presumably the script of ω itself.[6] No stemma can be drawn up, but rough groups emerge, one largely of German manuscripts, another of English. Paris lat. 13046 (S, s. x; Chatelain, plate CLXI) comes from the same monastery as P, and this origin has also been suggested for Cologny-Geneva lat. 154 (N, *olim* Phillipps 16409, s. X/XI).[7] In short, the medieval tradition seems to have radiated from northern France.[8]

Descendants of ω sporadically desert it and offer the reading of P or one not so corrupt;[9] a few restore all or part of 10.100–5 and 112–17. Conversely, the exemplar of P evidently carried readings of ω as variants.[10] At what stage either process of contamination took place is

---

[1] H. W. Garrod, OCT (1906), p. v.

[2] J. Boussard, *REL* 30 (1952), 223–8; P. M. Clogan, *Manuscripta*, 11 (1967), 102–12.

[3] *Karl der Grosse*, 57–61 (= Bischoff, *Mitt. Stud.* iii. 163–7).

[4] A. Klotz, edn. of *Achilleid* (Leipzig, 1902), xii–xx.

[5] F. Vollmer, *RhM* 51 (1896), 27 n. 1; Klotz, *Philologus*, 63 (1904), 157–60.

[6] Klotz (edn., see below), lvii–lx, with the correction of S. Timpanaro in *La genesi del metodo del Lachmann* (new edn., Padua, 1981), 113 n. 2.

[7] R. J. Getty, *CQ* 27 (1933), 135–8.   [8] Klotz (edn.), lvi.

[9] See most recently D. E. Hill, *CQ* 60 (1966), 333–46, esp. 338.

[10] Klotz (edn), lxvii–lxviii.

not clear.[11] For all that, the division between P and ω remains sharp. O. Müller, who established it, did not live to complete his edition (Leipzig, 1870). The first editor who used his findings, Ph. Kohlmann (Leipzig, 1884), clung to P through thick and thin. Klotz's Teubner (Leipzig, 1908), still too deferential to P,[12] is nevertheless the only edition fit to use; the revision by Th. C. Klinnert (1973) takes inadequate account of work done since on manuscripts and text (pp. 582–630).[13] The *editio princeps* (*IGI* 9154, Rome c.1470) has not been studied, and a direct comparison with manuscripts reported by Klotz is unlikely to reveal much in so dense a tradition.

Jerome apparently knew no commentary on the *Thebaid*, but Servius and Priscian frequently cite it, and medieval manuscripts transmit under the name of Lactantius Placidus a commentary generally assigned in its original form to s. v^2 or s. VI, though a proper edition could well remove the obstacles to an earlier date.[14] It is often said that Priscian follows P and Lactantius Placidus ω, but Klotz (*Hermes*, 40 (1905), 341–4) reached the former conclusion by a fallacious argument,[15] and (*Arch. für lat. Lex.* 15 (1908), 485–525) maintained not only that Lactantius Placidus shares errors with ω (pp. 487–90) but also that he gives the right text in several places against P ω (pp. 495–8). The dull truth about Priscian is that he nowhere agrees in error with P or ω against the other. How Klotz reconciled his two contentions about Lactantius Placidus he did not say; one thing is beyond doubt, that Lactantius Placidus sometimes gives variants and these are sometimes the readings of P and ω (pp. 498–501).

Lines quoted by Priscian (4.716–17) present the most interesting puzzle in the tradition; Klotz discussed it in *Hermes*, 40 (1905), 346–53 and 369–72, but made nothing of it in his edition. After 716 P and a descendant of ω add a line that disrupts the sense; it also occurs as the third of seven lines added after 714 by another descendant of ω, and in that context it is entirely at home. Whether genuine or not (Leo persuaded Klotz that they were not), these seven lines are indubitably ancient. G. Jachmann justly compared them with the longer Oxford

---

[11] R. D. Sweeney, *Prolegomena to an Edition of the Scholia to Statius, Mnem.* Suppl. 8 (Leiden, 1969), 82–4. Pages 76–84 of this important work contest Klotz's view of the tradition.

[12] A. E. Housman, *CQ* 27 (1933), 1 = *The Classical Papers of A. E. Housman*, eds. J. Diggle and F. R. D. Goodyear (Cambridge, 1972), iii. 1197; L. Håkanson, *Statius' Thebaid: critical and exegetical remarks* (Lund, 1973), 5.

[13] Cf. H. M. Hine, *JRS* 67 (1977), 246. Besides SWr and the Turonensis, another manuscript unsatisfactorily reported by Klotz is D; Garrod's apparatus, from which he took his information, has six errors on one page alone (10.107–32).

[14] Klotz (*Arch. für lat. Lex.* 15 (1908), 504–8) drew attention to the clausulae, Ciceronian and not accentual. Clausulae, incidentally, have been overlooked in the textual criticism of other commentaries, notably Donatus on Terence.

[15] He discounts 'Schreibfehler' of P (p. 341) but makes no such allowance for errors of ω, even though he puts its exemplar well after s. VI. No better is P. Dierschke, *De fide Prisciani in versibus Vergilii Lucani Statii Iuvenalis examinata* (Greifswald, 1913), 78–85.

fragment of Juvenal, incorporated by a similar member of a similar tradition long after an excerpt from it had been put to mysterious service elsewhere (Σ 6.348).[16] Other lines unevenly attested are discussed by Klotz in the same article (pp. 353–69).

M. D. R.

[16] *NGG* 1943, 250–2, with a trenchant footnote on attempts at saving the text of P: 'Jede Gewaltsamkeit der Kritik, mit noch so mangelhaftem Ergebnis . . ., ist erlaubt, nur nicht die Athetese'.

Achilleid

After editing the *Achilleid* (Leipzig, 1902), A. Klotz pronounced the tradition 'noch nicht aufgeklärt',[1] and that remains true despite several more editions. The best, that of O. A. W. Dilke (Cambridge, 1954), concisely summarizes the conclusions of Klotz and Dilke himself (pp. 19–25).

The *Achilleid* follows the *Thebaid* in P, and here again P has true readings corrupted by all the other manuscripts.[2] Whether any of the other manuscripts derive from ω of the *Thebaid* is quite uncertain; not all of them contain the *Thebaid*, and some of those that do show signs of having copied the *Achilleid* from a different exemplar. Four of the earliest manuscripts, including Q and K of the *Thebaid*, omit 1.529–660, 881–2, 2.53; Dilke discovered the fourth, Paris lat. 8040 (U, s. XI, probably from Fleury), too late to use it.[3] In s. XIII the *Achilleid* was added for its mythological and moral content to the *Liber Catonis*, a set text in schools,[4] and copies proliferated.[5] Already by s. XI, however, it appears amid similar company in a Beneventan manuscript, Eton College 150 (E; *New Palaeographical Society* (Oxford, 1903–30), First Series, plate 110), perhaps written in the Abruzzi.[6] Munich Clm 14557

[1] *Arch. für lat. Lex.* 15 (1908), 492.

[2] N. Terzaghi, *Bollettino*, 4 (1956), 1–16, pleads for less prejudice in its favour.

[3] *Latomus*, 17 (1958), 708–11.

[4] M. Boas, 'De librorum Catonianorum historia atque compositione', *Mnem.* 42 (1914), 17–46, esp. 37–9; cf. G. Glauche, *Schullektüre im Mittelalter* (Munich, 1970), index s.v. Statius. Besides the *Achilleid* the fully fledged *Liber Catonis* included the *Disticha Catonis*, Theodulus, Avianus, Maximianus, and Claudian, *De raptu Proserpinae*; on the tradition of Maximianus see W. Schetter, *Studien zur Überlieferung und Kritik des Elegikers Maximian* (Wiesbaden, 1970).

[5] P. M. Clogan, *Manuscripta*, 8 (1964), 175–8, lists ninety-four manuscripts, but P. Petitmengin, *Moyen Âge*, 76 (1970), 574, estimates the total at about 200. This review of Petitmengin's puts paid to a figment called 'the medieval *Achilleid*' that Clogan has edited from eleven manuscripts of s. XIII–XIV (Leiden, 1968).

[6] Mrs Brooks Emmons Levy ap. R. D. Sweeney, *Prolegomena to an Edition of the Scholia to Statius*, *Mnem.* Suppl. 8 (1969), 41. E contains two of the texts listed in n. 4 above, Theodulus and Maximianus, and two other texts used in schools, Ovid, *Rem.*, and Arator.

(R, s. XIV) has much the same text, and another Beneventan manu-script, Vatican lat. 3281 (s. XII), occasionally agrees with them.[7] The later manuscripts mostly divide the poem into five books and round it off with a spurious line.

PER often agree against the other manuscripts, and the main stem-matic problem is whether they outweigh them.[8] As E *cett.* sometimes agree in error against PR and R *cett.* against PE, E or R must be hybrid; but the problem remains. Another, not mentioned by Dilke, is whether the manuscripts besides PER that contain 1.529–660, 881–2, 2.53 acquired them by contamination.

R should have taught editors a lesson. If, out of thirty-odd manu-scripts that people happen to have looked at, a fourteenth-century one from St. Emmeram, Regensburg can resemble a Beneventan one of the eleventh century, there is no excuse for ignoring the other 160-odd and publishing derivative editions like the Budé of J. Méheust (Paris, 1971) and the Teubner of A. Marastoni (Leipzig, 1974), neither of whom even troubled to collate U.[9] Someone enterprising might tackle the whole tradition.[10]

The *editio princeps* of the *Thebaid* is also the *editio princeps* of the *Achilleid*.

M. D. R.

---

[7] Sweeney (45, 78 n. 1) overrates it.

[8] Cf. Sweeney, *CW* 65 (1972), 237.

[9] Marastoni's verdict on it (xvi n. 2) is unfounded. He also says that Klotz and others regarded P as the archetype (xxiii, xxxiv); ascribes to Ullman the view that a catalogue of s. VIII mentions a manuscript of s. X (xli n. 1); and thinks *evadere* is the Latin for 'be' (passim).

[10] Violetta de Angelis is studying glossed manuscripts.

Silvae

Silvae were never as well known as the *Thebaid* and *Achilleid*. Only one trace has come to light in the 500 years after Charlemagne:[1] 2.7, the *Genethliacon Lucani*, occurs amongst heterogeneous matter in L, Florence, Laur. 29. 32 (s. IX[1], western Germany[2]), where Politian discovered it and Heinsius rediscovered it[3] before E. Baehrens finally reported its presence there.

Early in 1418, during the Council of Constance, Poggio sent to Italy a

---

[1] For a few citations and echoes up to the time of Charlemagne, including one in a work of Charlemagne himself, see F. Vollmer's edition (Leipzig, 1898), 31–4. Guido Billanovich (*IMU* 1 (1958), 239–43) somewhat hopefully finds echoes of *Silvae* in the works of the Paduan pre-humanists.

[2] I am obliged to Professor Bischoff for this attribution. C. Thulin (*Abh. der preuss. Akad.* 1911, Anhang II, 73–5) had assigned it to s. IX[2], others to s. X. For a photograph cf. n. 5 below, and see also *AGRIMENSORES*.   [3] Leiden, Burm. Q.31, f. 7[r] preserves his collation.

manuscript of Manilius, Silius, and *Silvae*, written for him by a scribe whom he calls 'ignorantissimus omnium viventium'. Less Silius, it survives: M, Madrid 3678 (M. 31), discovered by G. Loewe in 1879 and recognized for what it was by A. C. Clark.[4] A photograph appended to A. Klotz's edition (Leipzig, 1900[1], 1911[2]) shows marginalia in the hands of Poggio and Niccoli.[5]

Silius, at least, was discovered before 6 July 1417.[6] Silius and *Silvae* in M were written at one stretch, and common features not present in Manilius suggest that they were copied from the same source.[7] In all probability this was the 'Ovidii Metamorfoseon Sili et Stacii volumen I' catalogued in s. IX[2] (so people say, though the manuscript is of s. X[2]) at a library near Lake Constance, perhaps Reichenau.[8] L could easily derive from it too: LM share several errors, and where they differ, which they scarcely do, M is usually right. Especially in the preface to Book 1, M repeatedly mistakes *r* for *s*, the commonest sign of descent from an insular copy; it also mistakes *ct* for *st* and *y* for *r*.[9]

Despite the arrival of M in Italy, *Silvae* seem not to have circulated before 1453, when Poggio took up his final residence in Florence.[10] Thereafter M was copied at least five times, and its earliest dated descendant, written at Rome in 1463, already bears witness to thoughtful work on the text. Much of this is reflected in Puteolanus's edition (Parma, 1473), a great advance on the anonymous *editio princeps* (Venice, 1472), which was printed from a remote and corrupt descendant of M emended with breath-taking ineptitude. Politian's sharp reaction to Calderini's commentary (Rome, 1475) led to a collation of M and a commentary of his own.[11] To pronounce on the best edition now available would merely be provocative, because scholars will argue till doomsday about what Statius could and could not have written;[12]

---

[4] 'The Literary Discoveries of Poggio', *CR* 13 (1899), 119–30. The watermarks confirm both place of origin and date; cf. A. J. Dunston, *BICS* 14 (1967), 99 n. 2.

[5] For larger but not better photographs of less interesting pages, see Dunston, plate IX. R. Merkelbach and H. van Thiel (*Lateinisches Leseheft* (Göttingen, 1969), no. 18) publish photographs of the *Genethliacon Lucani* from both M and L.

[6] M. Pastore Stocchi, *Atti dell'Ist. Ven.* 125 (1966–7), 45 n. 11.

[7] See §4 of Klotz's preface, 'De Matritensis exemplari', and P. Thielscher, 'De Statii Silvarum Silii Manilii scripta memoria', *Philologus*, 66 (1907), 85–91, 106.

[8] Cf. A. Holder, *Die Reichenauer Handschriften*, ii (Leipzig and Berlin, 1914), plates IX–X, and J. Autenrieth, *Die Domschule von Konstanz* (Stuttgart, 1956), 18–20.

[9] Cf. Klotz, ix–x.

[10] M. D. R., 'Statius's *Silvae* in the Fifteenth Century', *CQ* 71 (1977), 202–25.

[11] L. Cesarini Martinelli, *Angelo Poliziano: commento inedito alle Selve di Stazio* (Florence, 1978). His collation has given rise to long and heated argument, but objections to identifying his manuscript with M have evaporated; see *SIFC* 49 (1977), 285–6, and R. Ribuoli, *La collazione polizianea del codice Bembino di Terenzio* (Rome, 1981), 17 n. 7.

[12] One thing that has been misused in the argument is Statius' professed *audacia* (3 *praef.*). D. W. T. C. Vessey (*CPh.* 66 (1971), 274) interprets it as the stylistic *audacia* of one who may have 'strained and tormented the normal usages of the Latin tongue for the sake of novel effects', but in fact, as not only the rest of the sentence but also 1 *praef.* shows, it is the *audacia* of extemporization.

but Klotz's preface gives much the most helpful and succinct account of the tradition since the rediscovery of M.[13]

M. D. R.

[13] For those who find less to agree with in Vessey than in J. A. Willis, 'The *Silvae* of Statius and their Editors', *Phoenix*, 20 (1966), 305–24, and L. Håkanson, *Statius' Silvae: critical and exegetical remarks* (Lund, 1969), Klotz's edition has the further advantage of allotting reasonable space in the apparatus to conjectures.

SUETONIUS

De vita Caesarum
De grammaticis et rhetoribus

De vita Caesarum

Although over 200 manuscripts are extant, Suetonius' *De vita Caesarum* seems to have survived into the ninth century in a single manuscript, since lost. As late as the sixth century, Johannes Laurentius Lydus had seen a copy complete with a prologue including a dedication to Septicius Clarus.[1] The archetype for the text we now have had lost its first quaternion, so that we lack not only the prologue but also the beginning of the first life, *Divus Iulius*. The surviving manuscripts are traditionally divided into two classes, usually designated X and Z, following the work of L. Preud' homme.[2]

The standard critical editions are those of C. L. Roth (Leipzig, 1858) and M. Ihm (Teubner, Leipzig, 1907). The following studies should also be consulted: L. Preud'homme, *Première, deuxième, troisième étude sur l'histoire du texte de Suétone* de Vita Caesarum (Brussels, 1902–4); C. L. Smith, 'A Preliminary Study of Certain Manuscripts of Suetonius' *Lives of the Caesars*', *HSCP* 12 (1901), 19–58, and 16 (1905), 1–14; E. K. Rand, 'On the History of the *De Vita Caesarum* of Suetonius in the Early Middle Ages', *HSCP* 37 (1926), 1–48; M. Ihm, 'Beiträge zur Textgeschichte des Sueton', *Hermes*, 36 (1901), 343–63; A. J. Dunston, 'Two Manuscripts of Suetonius' *De vita Caesarum*', *CQ* 46 (1952), 146–51; J. Bridge, 'De quibusdam libris Suetonianis qui ex fonte Z emanaverunt', *HSCP* 41 (1930), 183–6; A. Gagnér, *Florilegium Gallicum. Untersuchungen und Texte zur Geschichte der mittellateinischen Florilegienliteratur* (Lund, 1936); J. Hamacher, *Florilegium Gallicum: Prolegomena und Edition der Exzerpte von Petron bis Cicero* de oratore (Frankfurt, 1975).

[1] Roth, x–xi.
[2] Op. cit. *passim*. The studies of the manuscript tradition that have been published since Roth's 1858 edition disagree about the relationship between members of a given family and the dating of certain manuscripts. While there have been changes of position within the families and some rearrangement of the antecedents of extant manuscripts, no new manuscripts have been accepted as having superior readings. No attempt is made here to dispute these conclusions, only to collate

After Isidore's use of the *Lives* in his *Etymologiae* in the seventh century, Suetonius' work drops from sight for about two hundred years. Possible references by Aldhelm of Malmesbury and Bede are most likely through intermediate sources. There is no evidence of any insular influence in the manuscript tradition.[3]

From the early ninth century comes the oldest surviving manuscript, Paris lat. 6115, traditionally called the 'Memmianus' (M), from its sixteenth-century owner, Henri de Mesmes. M was written at Tours about 820 and is a member of the first, or X, family. M remained at Tours until the end of the Middle Ages, and it is questionable whether it had any direct descendants.[4] Accompanying it as witnesses to an interest in the *De vita Caesarum* in the Carolingian era are several literary references. The best known of these is the famous *imitatio* of the *Divus Augustus*, Einhard's *Vita Karoli Magni*. It has been suggested that not only Einhard knew the work, but also Charlemagne, who consciously modelled his life after that of Augustus.[5] Another witness to interest in Suetonius is Servatus Lupus, Abbot of Ferrières, who sought a copy of the work, which he knew was at Fulda. Neither the Fulda codex nor Lupus's copy has survived. The Fulda codex may well be one of the ancestors of the X family. The one confirmed direct descendant of the Fulda codex is a series of excerpts taken down by Lupus's pupil, Heiric of Auxerre. Heiric's *excerpta* enjoyed some popularity in the twelfth and thirteenth centuries, and the earliest survivors are considered to be of some worth in establishing the text because of their proximity to the lost archetype.[6]

During the tenth century the trail remains difficult to follow. There are possible references to the *De vita Caesarum* by Atto of Vercelli[7] and Rather of Verona,[8] but we remain unsure whether they had actually seen the text. Gerbert of Reims sought to have a copy sent to him from Rome,[9] but there is no proof that it ever arrived in France.

them and present them in a logical manner. Confusion has arisen regarding the sigla of the various manuscripts. Preud'homme and Smith chose to break with traditional designations and rename the manuscripts according to their own systems; Rand returned to the traditional designations. As a consequence some manuscripts have as many as four different sigla. The weight of numbers will prevail here, with the most common sigla being used. All manuscript information has been verified by examination in 1974 and 1977.

[3] On insular references see: P. Lehmann, *Erforschung des Mittelalters. Ausgewählte Abhandlungen und Aufsätze* (Stuttgart, 1959), iii. 160; J. D. A. Ogilvy, *Books Known to the English, 597–1066* (Cambridge, Mass., 1967), 246; W. Levison, *England and the Continent in the Eighth Century* (Oxford, 1946), 144 n. 3.

[4] The most closely related manuscript is Paris lat. 5804 of the late fourteenth or early fifteenth century. Preud'homme praises it highly, while Ihm finds it contaminated and useless.

[5] Rand, 40–8.

[6] For Lupus, see Rand, 20–37; Lehmann disagrees with his conclusions. For Heiric, Ihm, 'Beiträge zur Textgeschichte', *passim*.

[7] *PL* 134, col. 544C.   [8] *PL* 136, col. 374B.

[9] *Letters of Gerbert with his Papal Privileges as Sylvester II,* trans. with introduction by H. P. Lattin (New York, 1961), 87–9, 117.

The evidence from the eleventh century is much more tangible. While references to the existence of the work in Italy are restricted to possible knowledge of the *Lives* by the Lombard Papias in his *Elementarium doctrinae rudimentum*,[10] and by Peter Damian in his letters,[11] there is a larger body of material which originated in the north. Jotsald of Cluny and Andreas of Fleury both quote from the *Lives* in their writings,[12] and once again there is the physical evidence of surviving manuscripts, the first since M, the lone survivor from the ninth century. Two of these are cousins of M in the X family and important witnesses to the text. Unfortunately, we know little more. They are not directly related to one another, and such knowledge as we have of their origins and subsequent history is fairly recent. The first is Vatican lat. 1904 (V), written in France in the later eleventh century and considered the more trust-worthy; it is incomplete, however, ending in *Caligula* 3. The other is Wolfenbüttel, Gud. lat. 268 (G), written in a German hand. Although it is older than V, G is considered inferior because of interpolations. It seems to have remained in German lands, away from the mainstream of interest in the *De vita Caesarum*. Its one confirmed descendant is Munich Clm 5977, a mid-fifteenth-century German manuscript from the monastery of Ebersberg.

The third survivor of the eleventh century, from late in the century, is Durham C.III.18 (D), the oldest copy of the second, and inferior, Z family. It probably derives from an early eleventh-century manuscript from the Loire Valley. Within Z, a group of manuscripts can be distinguished by a transposition within *Galba*, called the 'Galba error'. D contains this error. It was written in Norman lands, probably England, and has been at Durham since an early date. D and Florence Laur. 68.7 (L), an early twelfth-century manuscript of the X family, are the first witnesses to the revival of interest in Suetonius during the twelfth century. Although this increase in interest seems impressive, with twelve surviving manuscripts, mention of the text in several ancient catalogues, and numerous literary references, it is centred in a relatively limited area.

The trace of a German tradition begun by G continues, centred in Bamberg. The catalogue of the monastery of Michelsberg, dated to 1112–23, lists Suetonius. And, in the next generation, Gottfried of Viterbo, who was schooled at Bamberg, mentions Suetonius as one of his sources.[13] But, besides Bamberg, it is the Loire valley that is the centre from which the knowledge of the *De vita Caesarum* spreads among those with an interest in classical texts.

Among the twelfth-century manuscripts, the X family never ventured far afield; all were written in northern France. Montpellier 117 was at

[10] Manitius, *Geschichte*, ii. 721.   [11] *PL* 144, cols. 270, 439.
[12] Manitius, *Geschichte*, ii. 144–5 (Jotsald), 333 (Andreas).   [13] Ibid. iii. 392–5.

Clairvaux in the thirteenth century, while its daughter,[14] British Library, Egerton 3055, was close by at Saint-Bénigne Dijon in the fourteenth century. Of the other three twelfth-century members of the family, Paris lat. 5801 (c.1120–30) was written in north-western France, L and Florence, Laur. 66.39 in the region of the Loire valley; they engendered no extant descendants until the fourteenth century. No thirteenth-century manuscript of the X family is known today.

It is the Z family that forms the bridge to the Norman lands. Paris lat. 5802 (Q), which belongs to the same subgroup as D, was probably written at Chartres and was given by Philip of Bayeux to the monastery of Bec in the mid-twelfth century.[15] The D manuscript is not the only witness to an interest in the *Lives* in England at the turn of the century; Herbert of Losinga, Bishop of Norwich, wrote to his friend Roger d'Argences, Abbot of Fécamp (1107–19), for a copy of Suetonius, which he had been unable to find in England.[16] Nothing more is known of Herbert's copy, if he ever received it; but it is a possible ancestor of those English Z manuscripts which do not contain the Galba error present in D. Two twelfth-century Z manuscripts without the transposition can be localized: British Library Royal 15.C.III was at the Cathedral church of St. Paul, London in the later Middle Ages; Oxford, Bodl. Lat. class. d. 39,[17] which bears a striking resemblance to a listing in the Christ Church Canterbury catalogue of 1284–1331, was in the library of the Dominicans of Northampton before 1486.[18] The one remaining English manuscript with the Galba error that can be localized is San Marino (California) H. M. 45717,[19] which was written at Bury St. Edmunds and remained there throughout the medieval period.[20]

Knowledge of Suetonius was also spread in two extensive sets of excerpts which were popular in the twelfth and thirteenth centuries. The oldest complete manuscript of Heiric's *excerpta*, Paris lat. 8818, dates from the late eleventh or early twelfth century. Three other twelfth-century manuscripts of the *excerpta* survive. It has been proved that John of Salisbury's knowledge of the *De vita Caesarum* was based on Heiric.[21] The other major set of *excerpta* brings us back to the Loire

---

[14] A. J. Dunston has proved this relationship.

[15] Q matches the description in the list of manuscripts given by Philip to Bec: Becker, 75.76, 147.

[16] *The Life, Letters, and Sermons of Herbert of Losinga*, ed. and trans. by E. M. Goulburn and H. Symonds (Oxford, 1878), i. 64.

[17] Formerly Sion College, ARC L.40.2/L.21.

[18] N. R. Ker, *Medieval Manuscripts in British Libraries*, I: *London* (Oxford, 1969), 278; M. R. James, *The Ancient Libraries of Canterbury and Dover* (Cambridge, 1903), 44.

[19] Formerly Sion College, ARC L.40.2/L.9.

[20] R. M. Thomson, 'The Library of Bury St. Edmunds Abbey in the Eleventh and Twelfth Centuries', *Speculum*, 47 (1972), 639.

[21] R. W. Hunt, 'The Deposit of Latin Classics in the Twelfth-Century Renaissance', in *Classical Influences on European Culture, AD 500–1500*, ed. R. R. Bolgar (Cambridge, 1971), 51–5.

valley. The *Florilegium Gallicum* was written at Orléans in mid-century. Two twelfth-century manuscripts survive, Paris, Arsenal 711 and B. N. lat. 7647.[22] Although several extensive studies of this florilegium have been published, there is no edition of the Suetonian section.[23]

The excerpts in the *Florilegium Gallicum* are the source used by Vincent of Beauvais and by the author of the *Moralium dogma philosophorum*.[24] This is symptomatic of the *De vita Caesarum*'s fortunes in the thirteenth century, a time of assimilating and using relevant parts of the text, not of copying and reading the complete work. An outstanding example of the use of Suetonius during this time is the vernacular *Li fait des Romains*, composed from Suetonius, Lucan, and Sallust in the time of Louis IX.[25] The composition of the surviving manuscripts from this period reinforces the impression of use, rather than transcription, of texts. Of the fifteen manuscripts dated to the thirteenth century containing all or part of the *De vita Caesarum*, only four are complete texts. Of the remaining eleven, three are small excerpts or marginal notations, four are copies of the *Florilegium Gallicum*, and the last four contain Heiric's *excerpta*. Moreover, this use of the *Lives* seems to be limited to the lands north of the Alps. There is no sign of the use or circulation of the *Lives* in Italy during the thirteenth century.

The pattern changes markedly during the following hundred and fifty years. The *Lives* continue to be popular in northern Europe. Indicative of this popularity in France is the anonymous translation of the *De vita Caesarum* into the vernacular in 1381.[26] While the *Lives* seem to have escaped the interests of the Paduan pre-humanists, this is not true of Petrarch. Suetonius is on his list of favourite books.[27] Not many fourteenth-century manuscripts survive (ten), but two of them belonged to Petrarch. Oxford, Exeter College 186 was written for him by an Italian scribe in 1351; he also owned Berlin (West) lat. 2° 337 (T), written in northern Italy in the first half of the fourteenth century. It is worth noting that Petrarch had a member of each of the textual families: Exeter is a Z text; T belongs to the X family. In his later life Petrarch also obtained Q, the twelfth-century Bec manuscript of the Z family, complete with the 'Galba error'.[28] The question whether his marginal notations in Exeter and T were attempts to establish a critical text remains unanswered. Following Petrarch in his discovery of Suetonius is his younger contemporary Boccaccio. That inveterate collector of

---

[22] Gagnér, *passim*; Hamacher, *passim*; R. H. R., 'Florilegia and Latin Classical Authors in Twelfth- and Thirteenth Century Orléans', *Viator*, 10 (1979), 135 ff.

[23] Hamacher has edited only a portion of the collection.   [24] Hunt, 54–5.

[25] P. Meyer, 'Les Premières compilations françaises d'histoire ancienne', *Romania*, 14 (1885), 1–81.   [26] Bolgar, *The Classical Heritage* (Cambridge, 1954), 536.

[27] B. L. Ullman, *Studies in the Italian Renaissance* (Rome, 1955), 36, 122.

[28] G. Billanovich, 'Nella biblioteca del Petrarca. II. Un altro Suetonio del Petrarca (Oxford, Exeter College. 186)', *IMU* 3 (1960), 28–58.

historical facts and biographies made extensive use of Suetonius. Florence, Bibl. Naz., Banco Rari 50, written in his own hand, contains lengthy excerpts from the *De vita Caesarum*.

After Petrarch and Boccaccio, the production of Suetonius codices exploded. Over half of the surviving manuscripts were written after 1375, most of these in Italianate hands. The *Lives* were a necessary part of the learned man's library, be he bishop, cardinal, humanist, or self-professed scholar of the ruling class. Salutati and Poggio referred to their copies and quoted from them.[29] Extant manuscripts were owned by Niccolò Niccoli and Giovanni Tortelli. Giannozzo Manetti's copy survived to the twentieth century only to be destoryed during the Second World War.[30] Among surviving manuscripts are copies once owned by members of the Visconti, Medici, Strozzi, and Piccolomini families. Among prominent churchmen whose codices survive are the Curialist Theodoro Lelli and the cardinals Bessarion, Jean Jouffroy, and Stephanus Nardinus.

Only late in the fifteenth century were the *Lives* finally supplemented with learned commentaries by Domitius Calderinus and Philippus Beroaldus, and with biographies of Suetonius by Beroaldus and Marcus Antonius Sabellicus.[31] (To this day there is still no complete commentary on the *De vita Caesarum*.) A final note on the great popularity of the *De vita Caesarum* in fifteenth-century Italy is the record of early printed editions. As early as 1470 two different editions appeared in Rome, with a third the next year in Venice. Before 1500 twelve other editions appeared, eleven of which were definitely printed in Italy.[32] Although we know that M was not used in a critical edition until 1564, no complete study has yet been done on which codices were used for these early editions. Given the great number of editions and the even greater number of codices available to the editors, this puzzle will take some time to piece together.

S. J. T.

[29] Ullman, *Studies in the Italian Renaissance*, 222; P. W. G. Gordan, *Two Renaissance Book Hunters, The Letters of Poggius Bracciolini to Nicolaus de Niccolis* (Columbia, 1974), *passim*.

[30] G. Cagni, 'I codici Vaticani Palatino-Latini appartenuti alla biblioteca di Giannozzo Manetti', *La Bibliofilia*, 62 (1960), 41.

[31] Manitius, *Handschriften*, 145.

[32] M. Gutiérrez Caño, *Catálogo de los manuscritos existentes en la Biblioteca Universitaria de Valencia* (Valencia, n.d.), iii. 219, lists all editions to 1860.

De grammaticis et rhetoribus

The transmission of the incomplete text of Suetonius' *De grammaticis et rhetoribus* is entangled with that of the Minor Works of Tacitus (q.v.), and among those the transmission most similar is that of the *Dialogus*. In Suetonius, too, we have a family led by Vatican, Ottob. lat. 1455 (now known as O), and backed up by Vienna ser. nov. 2960 (now W). Here too is Vatican lat. 1862 (V), with Leiden, Periz. Q. 21 (L) in close attendance. Here too is Vatican lat. 1518 (I), with its relation Naples IV.C.21 (N). Here too a horde of *deteriores* can be traced back to a single exemplar (γ: φ of the *Dialogus*).[1] Lasting work was done on this picture by R. P. Robinson,[2] and it remains now only to review his results in the light of later work on Tacitus. My own impression is that the evidence for the independence of L from V is no stronger here than elsewhere, and that there is sufficient evidence in Suetonius, combined with that in the *Dialogus*, to suppose that Iγ go back to a common hyparchetype. But it is true that the evidence for a bipartite stemma overall (OW/Vγ), as suggested by Robinson, is much stronger here than for *Dialogus* or *Germania*.

M. W.

[1] Only Vatican lat. 4498 seems to step right out of line.

[2] *De fragmenti Suetoniani de grammaticis et rhetoribus codicum nexu et fide* (University of Illinois, 1920), with descriptions and bibliography. Robinson later edited the text (Paris, 1925). G. Brugnoli's Teubner text (Leipzig, 1960) adds new, though worthless, manuscripts, and picks no quarrel with Robinson's results. The first edition was *c*.1471 (Venice). For illustrations of some of the manuscripts, see TACITUS, *Minor Works*.

SULPICIA

According to a contemporary, discoveries at Bobbio in 1493 included 'heroicum Sulpici carmen LXX epigrammata'.[1] Shortly afterwards, a poem in which someone who purports to be the Sulpicia of Martial 10.35 and 38 'queritur de statu reipublicae et temporibus Domitiani' was published in two editions, one of fifteenth-century works (Venice, 1498), the other of Ausonius (Parma, 1499). The same edition of Ausonius and two more (Venice, 1496, 1507) were augmented with a number of epigrams, though fewer than seventy.[2]

Before R. Peiper dismissed the epigrams as fifteenth-century

[1] Raph. Volaterranus, *Commentarii urbani* (Rome, 1506), f. 56^r.

[2] By a misleading coincidence this happens to be the number of lines in 'Sulpicia'.

products,[3] E. Baehrens had already rebutted a similar attack on 'Sulpicia' and dated the poem soon after Ausonius.[4]

In 1950, A. Campana discovered both 'Sulpicia' and the epigrams in Vatican lat. 2836 (*c.*1500) together with other epigrams, which make up a total of seventy (seventy-one with 'Sulpicia' as no. 37). F. Munari published the *editio princeps* of the full collection under the title *Epigrammata Bobiensia* (Rome, 1955); a plate of the Vaticanus faces page 51. W. Speyer's edition (Teubner, Leipzig, 1963) has plates of the whole text. Baehrens would have been gratified to see that the collection dates from s. V[1].

The Vaticanus is probably a direct copy of the lost Bobiensis (s. VII/VIII), on which see RUTILIUS NAMATIANUS; the editions all derive from another copy,[5] and from the *ed. Parm.* 1499 derives in turn Venice, Mus. Civ. Corr., Cicogna 858.[6]

M. D. R.

[3] *Jahrb. für class. Phil.* Suppl. 11 (1880), 226–56.
[4] *De Sulpiciae quae vocatur satira* (Jena, 1873).
[5] Sc. Mariotti, *Epigrammata Bobiensia*, *P.-W.* Suppl. 9 (1962), cols. 37–9 (I. *Überlieferung*), an excellent summary. He discusses the date of 'Sulpicia' in col. 62.
[6] M. Ferrari, *IMU* 16 (1973), 19 n. 3. Her important articles on the discoveries at Bobbio are cited in full under RUTILIUS NAMATIANUS.

TACITUS

Annales, 1–6
Annales, 11–16, *Historiae*
Minor Works

Annales, 1–6

The first six books of the *Annales*[1] survive in a single manuscript, now in the Biblioteca Laurenziana in Florence (plut. 68.1) and hence called

Facsimile of M with introduction by E. Rostagno, Leiden, 1902 (*Codices graeci et latini photographice depicti*, 7.1); editions C. D. Fisher (OCT, 1906), M. Lenchantin de Gubernatis (Rome, 1940), E. Koestermann (Teubner, 1960), F. R. D. Goodyear (with commentary; 2 vols., Cambridge, 1972 and 1981).

[1] The titles *Annales* and *Historiae* are not found in the paradosis and were first used in the sixteenth century. The manuscripts present both works under the heading *Ab excessu divi Augusti*; *Historiae* 1–5 appear as Books 17–21. See R. P. Oliver, *TAPA* 82 (1951), 232–61.

the Mediceus, or M. M was copied c.850 in Germany, probably at Fulda;[2] the *Annales* were originally bound with the letters of the Younger Pliny (now Laur. 47.36). Subsequently M went to the monastery of Corvey, where it remained, apparently uncopied, until the first years of the sixteenth century. In or about 1508 M was taken to Rome and came into the possession of Pope Leo X.[3] Leo gave the manuscript to Filippo Beroaldo the Younger, who used it to produce an impressive *editio princeps* in 1515 (leaving numerous corrections in its margins); the aggrieved monks of Corvey had to content themselves with an elegantly bound apograph of their lost treasure.

R. J. T.

[2] In addition to the evidence of script, a reference in the *Annales Fuldenses* for 852 to 'Cornelius Tacitus, scriptor rerum a Romanis in ea gente gestarum' seems to show knowledge of *Ann.* 2.9, which refers to the river Visurgis (Weser). Oliver argued that M was copied from an exemplar in insular script.

[3] P. Lehmann, 'Corveyer Studien', *ABAW* 30.5 (1919), 22, 38.

Annales, 11–16, Historiae

These works are preserved in a single medieval manuscript, Laurentianus 68.2 (called M or 'second Medicean', to distinguish it from the unique codex of *Annales* 1–6), written in Beneventan script at Montecassino in the mid-eleventh century, perhaps during the abbacy of Richer (1038–55).[1] M ultimately derives from a manuscript in rustic capitals, but measurement of displaced passages suggests at least one ancestor in minuscules.[2] When and how M left Montecassino is still unknown. It was used by Paulinus Venetus, Bishop of Pozzuoli, between 1331 and 1344, and was then probably still at the abbey.[3] The honour of liberating it has been claimed both for Boccaccio and, more recently, for

Editions: C. D. Fisher (OCT, 1906 *Ann.*; 1911 *Hist.*), C. Giarratano (Rome, 1939 *Hist.*), E. Koestermann (Teubner, 1960 *Ann.*; 1961 *Hist.*; 2nd edn., 1965), H. Heubner (Teubner, Stuttgart, 1978 *Hist.*). Individual books: *Annales*, 11–12, H. Weiskopf (Vienna, 1973); 15–16, F. Römer (Vienna, 1976); *Historiae* 2, I. Schinzel (Vienna, 1971); 3, K. Wellesley (Sydney, 1972). The fullest discussion of the tradition is given by Römer.

[1] Facsimile of M with introduction by E. Rostagno, Leiden, 1902 (*Codices graeci et latini photographice depicti*, 7.2). For the date cf. E. A. Lowe, *Casinensia* (Montecassino, 1929), 257–72 (= *Pal. Papers*, i. 289–302); M seems to belong to a stage of development later than that reached under Abbot Theobald (1022–35) but earlier than the 'Desiderian' period (1058–87). In Laur. 68.2 the Tacitus is now bound with the major works of Apuleius, another Montecassino product of slightly later origin.

[2] Rustic errors: cf. Lowe, *Pal. Papers*, i. 300–1; minuscule ancestor: cf. H. Quentin, *Essais de critique textuelle* (Paris, 1926), 176 f. The putative minuscule intermediary contained approximately as much text per folium as the Fulda manuscript of *Annales* 1–6, but this fact may be without significance; it certainly does not show that Montecassino acquired *Ann.* 11–16 and *Hist.* from Germany. The text of Laur. 68.2 is more seriously corrupt than that of 68.1 in ways that make descent from separate ancient exemplars seem likely.

[3] K. T. Heilig, *WS* 53 (1935), 95–110.

Zanobi da Strada;[4] Boccaccio certainly had seen a manuscript of this part of Tacitus by 1371, and a text of Tacitus was among the books given to the monastery of S. Spirito in Florence at his death.[5] When M next surfaces, in 1427, it is the property of the Florentine Niccolò Niccoli; that Niccoli's ownership was in some way questionable transpires from a letter of Poggio asking to see the manuscript: 'Cornelium Tacitum, cum venerit, observabo penes me occulte. Scio enim omnem illam cantilenam, et unde exierit, et per quem, et quis eum sibi vindicet, sed nil dubites: non exibit a me ne verbo quidem.'[6] Poggio was, unfortunately, as good as his word, and so the mystery may never be entirely resolved, but the facts are accounted for if Boccaccio did in fact remove M from Montecassino and Niccoli in turn acquired it from Boccaccio's library.[7] Niccoli saw to the proper housing of Boccaccio's books at S. Spirito, and would then have had the opportunity to recognize the importance of M and to appropriate it for his own use. This would explain Poggio's elaborate secrecy as well as the slow diffusion of the text among the humanists. Poggio is also responsible for another enigma in the transmission of this text: returning M to Niccoli in disgust at its barbarous script, he wrote, 'legi olim quemdam apud vos manens litteris antiquis, nescio Coluciine esset an alterius'.[8] Poggio was probably referring to a humanist copy of M made after his departure for Rome in 1403,[9] but his words add another loose end to an already tangled episode.[10]

M passed to S. Marco at Niccoli's death in 1437, a date which roughly coincides with the beginnings of the humanist tradition of these works. For a long time it was generally agreed that the thirty-odd surviving *recentiores* all derive from M or a direct descendant (before the loss of the bifolium containing *Hist.* 1.69–75.2, 1.86–2.2.2), and little attention was paid to the fifteenth-century witnesses. This situation changed dramatically when C. W. Mendell identified Leiden, B.P.L. 16B as the manuscript written by Rudolphus Agricola (= Roelof

---

[4] Gius. Billanovich, *I primi umanisti e le tradizioni dei classici latini* (Fribourg, 1953), 23 ff. Zanobi's annotations appear in the text of Apuleius now bound in Laur. 68.2.

[5] On Boccaccio and Tacitus see most recently R. P. Oliver, *ICS* 1 (1976), 190–225 (esp. 198–210), and Römer–Heubner, *WS* 91 (1978), 159–67. Both studies reject the view that Boccaccio removed M from Montecassino.   [6] *Epist.* 3. 14, cf. Oliver, 192.

[7] One must suppose in addition that Boccaccio made a copy of M and that this copy, bound with Vitruvius, remained at S. Spirito until the inventory of 1451. It would then have been this copy of M from which a quire was carried off by Niccolò da Montefalcone, prompting Boccaccio to write 'quaternum quem asportasti Cornelii Taciti quaeso saltem mittas, ne laborem meum frustraveris et libro deformitatem ampliorem addideris' (Oliver, 205–6). The incomplete condition of Boccaccio's copy might explain why Niccoli chose the Beneventan M in preference to it.

[8] *Epist.* 3. 15, cf. Oliver, 194.

[9] So too Römer (n. 5, above), 160–1; for *litterae antiquae* to describe humanist script, cf. S. Rizzo, *Il lessico filologico degli umanisti* (Rome, 1973), 114–22. The term also designated Caroline minuscule, and Oliver (194–7) favours this interpretation of Poggio's remark.

[10] The knowledge of Tacitus shown by Leonardo Bruni in 1403 (Oliver, 196) is a further complication.

Huysman, 1444–85) and cited as the source of many unique good readings by Ryckius.[11] Mendell's contention that the Leidensis represented a strain of tradition independent of M won some support[12] but provoked forceful opposition.[13] It was argued that none of the manuscript's good readings was beyond the capacity of a scholar like Agricola,` and it was noticed that a copy of the *editio princeps* (de Spira, Venice, 1472–3) with corrections in Agricola's hand preserves an earlier phase of his work on the text.[14] The Leidensis therefore seems to be basically a corrected copy of the *editio princeps*, and its unique readings of value the work of Agricola himself.

The debate over the Leidensis prompted further investigation of the *recentiores* as a whole. These studies, instigated by R. Hanslik, have revealed a threefold division of the manuscripts.[15] The first and most important class contains the full text as in M, i.e. to *Hist.* 5.26.3 *Flavianus in Pannonia*. It comprises two subgroups: a small group, including Laur. 68.5 and Holkham Hall 359, whose text is closest to that of M; and a larger group, dominated by a closely related family of nine manuscripts, called 'Genoese' (the earliest dated member, Vatican lat. 1958, was copied at Genoa in 1449 by Giovanni Andrea de' Bussi).[16] The second class stops at *Hist.* 5.23.2 *magnitudine potiorem*, omitting about one folio's worth of text; it includes the source of the *editio princeps* (and therefore of the Leidensis as well). The third class ends at *Hist.* 5.13.1 *evenerant*, and must therefore derive from a manuscript that had lost its final quire.[17] Complete collations of the *recentiores* have been made and in part published; the material so far available contains no clear evidence that any of these manuscripts preserves a tradition independent of M. In the latest edition of the *Historiae* they have accordingly reverted to the modest but useful role of *fontes correctionum*.[18]

R. J. T.

[11] Facsimile, with opposing prefaces by Mendell and E. Hulshoff Pol, Leiden, 1966 (*Codices graeci et latini photographice depicti*, 20); first announcement in *AJP* 72 (1951), 337–45.

[12] The most noteworthy convert was Koestermann, who elevated the Leidensis to near-parity with M in his Teubner editions of 1960/1; Koestermann later modified his views (1965 edn. of *Ann.*, pp. xx–xxii), but did not revise his text.

[13] Bibliography in Wellesley, 29–30, Heubner, vii n. 8. The most forceful opponent of the claims of the Leidensis was F. R. D. Goodyear, *CQ* 15 (1965), 299–322; 20 (1970), 365–70.

[14] Hulshoff Pol (n. 11, above), Heubner, viii–ix. Supporters of the Leidensis argue that Agricola transferred the readings in question from the Leidensis to the copy of the *editio princeps*; cf. Wellesley, *AJP* 89 (1968), 302–20; W. Allen Jr., *TAPA* 101 (1970), 26–8, suspends judgement.

[15] Brief exposition in Wellesley 28–9; fuller treatment in Römer.

[16] The manuscripts of this group also share a marginal comment at *Hist.* 3.30.1 referring to the 'other' Genua, i.e. *Genua Allobrogum* (Geneva). The group is consequently called 'Genevese' by Wellesley and 'Genevan' by Oliver (215 n. 69), but all the manuscripts are undoubtedly of Italian origin, cf. Römer (n. 5, above), 163 n. 18.

[17] It is tempting to speculate that this was Boccaccio's own copy of M, lacking the quire taken by Niccolò da Montefalcone; cf. Oliver, 212–16.

[18] Heubner, v–vii; cf. also R. H. Martin, *CR* 24 (1974), 209–11; M. Winterbottom, *CPh* 70 (1975), 283–4.

Minor Works

The three Minor Works of Tacitus[1] were little known before their rediscovery in the Renaissance. The *Dialogus*, after a possible allusion in the Younger Pliny (*Ep.* 9.10.2), was lost to view. The *Agricola* and *Germania* were apparently available to Cassiodorus; later, *Germania* was quarried by Rudolf of Fulda in the ninth century, and Adam of Bremen (before 1075) and Peter the Deacon[2] (about 1135) seem to have known *Agricola*. The only manuscript to survive from the Middle Ages is, or was, Jesi lat. 8, primary text s. $IX^2/4$, perhaps written at Fulda, and containing: Dictys Cretensis, *Bellum Troianum* (partly in a fifteenth-century hand, identified with that of Stefano Guarnieri); *Agricola* (E: supplemented by Guarnieri = e); *Germania* (E: in Guarnieri's hand).[3]

In November 1425 Poggio wrote to Niccolò Niccoli of the discovery in a German monastery of 'aliqua volumina' including 'Iulius Frontinus et aliqua opera Cornelii Taciti nobis ignota'. By 1431 Niccoli was able to catalogue as at Hersfeld a book consisting of *Germania*, *Agricola*, *Dialogus*, Suetonius, *De grammaticis et rhetoribus*. A manuscript answering this description was seen by Pier Candido Decembrio at Rome in 1455, and it seems to have been brought from Germany by Enoch of Ascoli in that year. Everything points to this book as being the origin of the related traditions of *Germania*, *Dialogus*, and the libellus of Suetonius (q.v.).[4]

For *Germania* and *Dialogus* the same three hyparchetypes can be reconstructed, though by different means:

ζ   For *Germ.* from Vienna ser. nov. 2960 (1466: the work of Hugo Haemste; W) and Munich Clm 5307 (m).
For *Dial.* from the same Vienna manuscript (now known as V) and from Vatican, Ottob. lat. 1455 (E).

β   For *Dial.* this is represented by one manuscript alone, Vatican lat. 1862 (B).[5]

---

[1] I largely summarize my (Latin) preface to *Cornelii Taciti Opera Minora*, rec. M. Winterbottom and R. M. Ogilvie (Oxford, 1975): itself a summary of Ogilvie's remarks in *Cornelii Taciti de Vita Agricolae*, ed. R. M. Ogilvie, I. Richmond (Oxford, 1967), 80–90, and my own articles on *Dial.* in *Philologus*, 116 (1972), 114–28, and on *Germ.* in *CPh* 70 (1975), 1–7. Besides the editions mentioned, E. Koestermann's Teubner (Leipzig, 1970³) is standard for the Minor Works. First editions: *Germ.*, *Dial. c.*1470 (Venice); *Agr. c.*1485 (Milan).

[2] Peter was responsible for the oldest manuscript of Frontinus, *De aquis* (q.v.), also available at Hersfeld in the fifteenth century (see below).

[3] The manuscript has disappeared again, but a facsimile is available in R. Till, *Handschriftliche Untersuchungen zu Tacitus Agricola und Germania* (Berlin–Dahlem, 1943). B. C. B.-B. suggests that the ninth-century corrector of E belonged to the circle of Heiric of Auxerre.

[4] For the much disputed details of the discovery of the Minor Works, see references in D. Schaps, *CPh* 74 (1979), 28–42, together with F. della Corte, *Stud. Urb.* 53 (1979), 13–45.

[5] I regard the famous Leiden, Periz. Q.21, the work of Iovianus Pontanus (b), as a descendant of B, though it remains notable for its excellent corrections in the first and later hands. Facsimile in *Codices Graeci et Latini*, Suppl. iv (Leiden, 1907). Other illustrations in Chatelain, pl. CXLVIII (Vatican lat. 1862 and 3429).

For *Germ.* we have both this book and a group of manuscripts that includes E.

Γ A key witness for both works is Vatican lat. 1518 (C). As more sincere aids than the much employed Naples IV.C.21 (c) and its relation Vatican lat. 4498, which are heavily contaminated from the ζ stream, I have used for *Germ.* Venice, Marc. Lat. XIV.1 (4266) (1464, from Bologna: Q), and a *gemellus*, Paris n.a. lat. 1180 (p); for *Dial.* the Venice manuscript and a class of *deteriores* ψ (the agreement of Qψ I call φ).

The foundation of this view of the traditions was laid by R. P. Robinson in his work on the *Germania*[6] and on Suetonius. Robinson's great service was to have demonstrated the independent value of the ζ manuscripts, which had hitherto been largely disregarded in the enthusiasm for B, b, C and c. And it may well be that he was right to posit a bifurcal stemma (ζ/BΓ) rather than a trifurcal one.[7]

There remains the *Agricola*. D. Schaps[8] has recently made a strong case against the orthodox view that the Aesinas is a fragment of the Hersfeldensis; their contents indeed seem incompatible. Now editors tell us that, of our three fifteenth-century manuscripts of *Agricola*, one (Toledo 49.2, dated 1474) is an apograph of E, while two (Vatican lat. 3429 = A, in the hand of Pomponio Leto, and lat. 4498 = B) are descended somehow[9] from E: so that all three are commonly disregarded where E is extant. Hence a paradox:[10] our *Agricola* texts descend from the Jesi manuscript, but our *Germania, Dialogus,* and Suetonius texts from the Hersfeldensis: even though the Hersfeldensis contained the *Agricola*, at least when it first arrived in Italy.

M. W.

[6] *The Germania of Tacitus* (Middletown, Conn., 1935). M. D. R. draws my attention to a manuscript of the *Germania* unknown to Robinson and myself: Florence, Società Colombaria 238.

[7] This is the view of C. E. Murgia, *CPh.* 72 (1977), 323–43 (at 326–38). See also my remarks on Suetonius, *De grammaticis et rhetoribus.*

[8] In the article cited in n. 4, above.

[9] Murgia argues (323–6) that B descends from A, and that A descends from E *as supplemented.*

[10] If a three-pronged stemma is correct, one might resolve the paradox by supposing that the three families descended from (1) a lost German manuscript = ζ; (2) the Aesinas = β; (3) the Hersfeldensis = Γ. (B. C. B.-B. remarks that 'the 15th-century parts of E look like careful copies . . . of lost leaves of the 9th-century original', so that Guarnieri's *Germania* might be a direct copy of β. That might, however, run into difficulties with the fact that E of the *Germania* is part of a *family* of manuscripts as against B.) If the stemma is bifid, ζ might still be a lost German manuscript, and the Hersfeldensis the common parent of β and Γ; the Jesi manuscript would then be relevant only to *Agricola*: our original paradox.

TERENCE

Few Latin texts come into view before AD 800. Terence, almost always read where Latin has been read, can boast a commentary of s. IV, one manuscript of s. IV/V and fragments of three more, and numerous quotations in grammarians. Had chance denied us these, 650 manuscripts written after AD 800 would still remain to encourage or discourage study of the transmission.[1]

Most of our information about performances comes from the brief and austere introductions with which an ancient editor furnished the six plays:[2] the last performance supervised by the playwright himself took place in 160 BC, the last datable performance in 141 BC.[3] Varro, however, could not have learnt from the text of *Hautontimorumenos* that the farmer Menedemus wore a leather jacket; Horace speaks of packed houses for Terence amongst others; a passage of *Eunuchus* serves to make Quintilian's point about the difference between theatrical and oratorical delivery; and a mask carved on a theatre of s. II/III in Algeria perhaps represents the eunuch of *Eunuchus*.[4] Directions for *gestus* and *pronuntiatio* in Donatus' commentary concern recitation in schools,[5] which gave Terence a home when he left the theatres.[6] Whether or not for the benefit of schools, three or four commentators had already been at work before Donatus, to say nothing of Probus' edition in the time of Nero or the Flavians.[7]

[1] Published estimates stop at 450. I owe the new figure to Claudia Villa (cf. n. 59, below).

[2] They are conventionally known as *didascaliae*. None is preserved for *Andria*, but Donatus fills the gap.

[3] K. Dziatzko, *RhM* 20 (1865), 570–98; 21 (1866), 64–92. The source of the information is uncertain, and its value has been doubted; a particular difficulty arises over *Eun.* and *Haut.*, the former produced in 161 BC but 'facta II' and the latter in 163 BC but 'facta III'. D. Klose, *Die Didaskalien und Prologe des Terenz* (Freiburg diss., Bamberg, 1966), 5–41, takes 'facta' to mean 'composed' and maintains that only Terence himself could have given such information currency.

[4] *R.R.* 2.11.11; *Ep.* 2.1.55–61; *Inst. orat.* 11.3.181–2; S. Gsell, *Khamissa, Mdaourouch, Announa*, I: *Khamissa* (Algiers and Paris, 1914), 111–12 (sceptical). H. D. Jocelyn also draws my attention to the mysterious *Menedemerumenus* scrawled on several walls at Pompeii (*CIL* IV.1211, 1212, 1616, 1637, 1870, 4555, 5417).

[5] Cf. F. Leo, *RhM* 38 (1883), 330–2. On *Andr.* 716 Donatus speaks of female parts in his day taken by women, but does he mean female parts in Terence?

[6] The earliest express evidence seems to be Auson. *Protrept.* 56–65, where grandad imagines reliving his schooldays as he watches his grandson's progress through Horace, Virgil, Terence, and Sallust. H. Marti, 'Zeugnisse zur Nachwirkung des Dichters Terenz im Altertum', in *Musa iocosa: Festschrift A. Thierfelder* (Hildesheim, 1974), 158–78, surveys the reasons why Terence continued to be read.

[7] P. Wessner, *Aemilius Asper* (Halle, 1905), 12–33, discusses the evidence for an edition by Probus, a commentary on *Phormio* by Arruntius Celsus, commentaries on *Eunuchus* and *Adelphi* by Helenius Acro, a complete commentary by Aemilius Asper, and at least an introduction by Euanthius. Probus evidently marked up a text and commented on it. Whether his work counts as an edition is purely a matter of terms; the real questions are how and in what form it became public, and how much it affected later copies.

A firm place on the syllabus in late Antiquity did not assure an author of survival, but Terence escaped the sad fate of Sallust's *Historiae* by more than the skin of his teeth. Precisely how many copies reached the Carolingian renaissance is a simple question to ask, but it leads to a host of others and has not yet been answered.

All the extant manuscripts owe to a lost archetype a number of errors, including one absent from a papyrus of s. IV,[8] and broadly the same scene-divisions and scene-headings. The oldest, the Bembinus (s. IV/ V), has further errors and interpolations, but fewer than those handed down to all other manuscripts by a lost hyparchetype, Σ.[9] Two errors of Σ occur in a fragment of s. IV/V (eleven lines only),[10] and the presence in Σ of so many unmetrical lines need not suggest a later date.[11] Subscriptions in its descendants attest a *recensio* by one Calliopius, but there is no way of determining whether he worked on Σ itself.

From Σ sprang Δ and Γ; manuscripts that do not go back in direct line to either are regarded as mixed. Someone soon after AD 400, to judge from the style of the illustrations,[12] illustrated the text in accordance with the scene-headings of his manuscript, and these illustrations survive in descendants of Γ. Neither Δ nor Γ anywhere seems to preserve the truth significantly against the agreement of the other with the Bembinus,[13] but one descendant of Δ, namely p, quite often agrees with the Bembinus against Γ and the others, and sometimes has the truth on its own; whether these readings of p derive from Δ or were imported from elsewhere is a serious problem, and the traditional view that Δ outclasses Γ may need revising if they were imported from elsewhere.[14] The question of agreements between certain manuscripts and the indirect tradition is bedevilled by the possibility of contamination in

---

[8] *Andr.* 928 *tibi* del. Bentley and om. Π^b (on which see below).

[9] P. Fehl, *Die interpolierte Recension des Terenztextes* (Berlin, 1938), classifies the interpolations in Σ.   [10] Sa (see below).

[11] P. Wessner, *Gnomon*, 3 (1927), 344, inferred a later date from the fact that scholars did not feel any need to assert *mensuram esse in fabulis Terentii* until s. V/VI. Five points tell against this inference. (1) In *Andria* and *Eun.* John Grant (cf. n. 14, below) counts over seventy unmetrical lines in Σ; in *Eun.* alone I count over fifty in the Bembinus (s. IV/V). (2) Π^b (s. IV) divides the lines erratically, and Π^a (s. IV/V) does no better with trochaic *septenarii*. (3) Even if corruption accounts for some departures from Terentian practice in the 212 *senarii* of Ausonius' *Ludus septem sapientum*, H. Marti (n. 6, above), 169, may nevertheless be right to see in v. 206 a metrical misunderstanding of *Andr.* 758. (4) Of Quintilian's two remarks on Terentian metre one is curiously blinkered (10.1.99) and the other provokes the Oxford editor to the comment 'mira doctrina' (9.4.140–1). (5) The signs of editorial activity in Σ do not show that Σ itself was a scholarly product, and unmetrical lines could presumably occur in a poor copy of any period.

[12] A. W. Byvanck, *Mnem.* 7 (1939), 115–35. The matter is far from closed, however: C. R. Dodwell of Manchester University has argued in public but not yet in print for a provenance of third-century Africa.

[13] G. Jachmann, *Die Geschichte des Terenztextes im Altertum* (Basle, 1924), 127 n. 78.

[14] J. N. Grant has kindly shown me an unpublished article on Δ in which he corrects the reports of p given by R. Kauer and W. M. Lindsay in the OCT (1926) and examines its behaviour in detail. He tells me that if p is excluded from the reconstruction of Δ unmetrical corruptions occur in *Eunuchus* at least twice as often in Δ as in Γ.

either direction;[15] the question of disagreements, by the grammarians'
habit of taking over quotations from earlier treatises.

Readings that bypassed the archetype crop up occasionally in the
later manuscripts. The true version of *Phorm.* 689, for instance, appears
only in the margin of two 'mixed' manuscripts,[16] and the *alter exitus* of
Andria, well attested in s. IV and probably composed centuries earlier for
the stage, in no manuscript older than s. XI.[17]

This colourless summary of textual facts conceals both the progress
made and the problems aired in the latest studies of the tradition,
Jachmann's *Geschichte des Terenztextes im Altertum* (Basle, 1924) and two
articles by J. N. Grant, '*Γ* and the Miniatures of Terence', *CQ* 67 (1973),
88–103, and 'Contamination in the Mixed Manuscripts of Terence: a
Partial Solution?', *TAPA* 105 (1975), 123–53. Jachmann made progress
by establishing the literary nature of the illustrations, which had previously been thought to represent moments on the stage and therefore
to antedate the last performances. His chronological framework, however, has been shown to rest on two hazardous assumptions: that the
archetype descended from Probus' edition, and that $Σ$ antedated the
Bembinus.[18] Furthermore, Grant has now challenged his contention
that the illustrations were designed for $Γ$ or a descendant. None of this,
it must be admitted, will ever help an editor to find his way among the
extant manuscripts. Grant's second article will. In it he takes further M.
Warren's use of colometry for associating manuscripts;[19] two of his
conclusions are that manuscripts often switch from one exemplar to
another, and that the order of plays usually held to characterize $Δ$ may
be a late innovation in some of its descendants.

Other details will best be set out in a discursive treatment of the more
important manuscripts.

Pride of place goes to:

A   Vatican lat. 3226 (Bembinus, s. IV/V, rustic capitals, probably

---

[15] Three examples: *Ad.* 60 *clamitans quid agis* codd. omnes contra metrum = Cic. *De inv.* 1.27;
Phorm. 249 *usque Γ* et Lact. *Div. inst.* 7.27.3; *Andr.* 720 *dolorem Δ* et Don. (sed 'vel *laborem* secundum
Donatum' schol. D). For testimonia in general, see F. Umpfenbach's edition (Berlin, 1870),
xlvi–lxvii, and P. J. H. Mueller, *De veterum grammaticorum in Terentio studiis criticis* (Münster diss.,
Aachen, 1926); J. D. Craig's study of the testimonia in a series of publications, *Jovialis and the
Calliopian Text of Terence* (London, 1927), *Ancient Editions of Terence* (St. Andrews, 1929), *CQ* 24
(1930), 65–73, 183–7; 25 (1931), 151–5, takes scepticism to the point of tendentiousness.

[16] Cf. Jachmann, *Geschichte*, 80–1.

[17] O. Skutsch, *RhM* 100 (1957), 53–68. Donatus frowns on it, and *Π*[b] plainly continued with it.

[18] Wessner (n. 11, above), 339–47 (339– 43 give a good summary of Jachmann's argument); see
also G. Pasquali, *Storia della tradizione e critica del testo* (Florence, 1934), 354–73, essentially a review
of Jachmann's book. Wessner remarks that the presence in all the manuscripts of metrical *Periochae*
by Gellius' teacher C. Sulpicius Apollinaris supports a date *c.*AD 150 for the archetype; but such an
embellishment would be apt to spread. That Arruntius Celsus read *Phorm.* 643 without the
interpolation *libuit* (Jachmann, 79–80) proves at most that he used a copy in some respects better
than the archetype, and his date is uncertain anyway; cf. Pasquali, 360–1.

[19] *AJA* 4 (1900), 92–125.

Italian; Chatelain, plate VI, *CLA* I.12, published in facsimile[20]; *Andr.*
(1–786 lost, 787–924 fragments only), *Eun., Haut., Phorm., Hec. (Prol.*
1–37 lost), *Ad.* (915–end a few letters only); corrected by the scribe, a
corrector antiquus, one Joviales (s. VI), the scholiast (s. VI), and a *corrector
recens* (s. VII);[21] owned in roughly its present state not before 1452 by
Porcelius, and then by Bernardo Bembo and his son Pietro, who put it
at Politian's disposal in 1491.[22]

Scraps survive of three manuscripts not far removed in date from A:

*Π*ᵇ P. Oxy. 2401 (s. IV; 'in the hand elements derived from rustic capital,
Greek, and cursive can be detected'[23]); fragments of *Andr.* 602–68,
924–79a.

*Π*ᵃ P. Vindob. inv. L 103 (s. IV/V, early half-uncial; *CLA* X. 1537);
fragments of *Andr.* 489–582.

Sa St. Gall 912, pp. 299–300, 313–14 (s. IV/V, rustic capitals, probably
Italian; *CLA* VII.974); fragments of *Haut.* 857–78.[24]

Then the Dark Ages intervene before the family of *Σ* proliferates.
From *Δ* descend:

D Florence, Laur. 38.24 (Victorianus, s. X/XI, St. Gall;[25] Chatelain,
plate X).

p Paris lat. 10304 (s. X, once at Beauvais[26]).

[20] S. Prete, *Il codice di Terenzio Vaticano Latino 3226 (Studi e Testi,* 262, Vatican, 1970); he misguidedly omits the notes of ownership *et sim.* on ff. I–VI. A. Pratesi, *Palaeographica diplomatica et archivistica: studi in onore di Giulio Battelli* (Rome, 1979), i.71–84, prefers a date considerably later (s. V·²/Vɪ¹), and it must be admitted that footholds hereabouts are in short supply.

[21] These at any rate are the distinctions drawn by Prete, 25–48; but cf. Pratesi, 84 n. 24.

[22] R. Ribuoli, *RFIC* 109 (1981), 163–77, shows that Politian's collation includes readings now missing from the outer edge of f. 4 (*Andr.* 925–71) but does not include v. 88, for which Politian cites A in *Misc.* II.43.1–3, or vv. 346–8, for which P. Bembo cites A in *De Virgilii Culice et Terentii fabulis* (Venice, 1530), f. d viᵛ. Faerno, in a letter of 29 April 1558 to Vettori, mentions the latter passage and asks him to check Politian's collation of *Andr.,* the end of *Ad.,* and the beginning of *Hec.,* because it was made sixty years before and 'il libro all'hora dovesse essere piu intiero che non è hora' (British Library, Add. 10266, ff. 119ᵛ–120ʳ). More recent editors have been less conscientious.

[23] C. H. Roberts and O. Skutsch, *The Oxyrhynchus Papyri,* xxiv (London, 1957), 110.

[24] P. Lehmann, 'Eine Palimpseststudie (St. Gallen 912)', *SBAW* 1931.1; the last plate in A. Dold and A. Allgeier, *Der Palimpsestpsalter im codex Sangallensis 912* (Beuron, 1933), is better than Lehmann's or Lowe's. No discussion of the fragment rivals Pasquali's (367–8).

[25] Io. Metellus (1545) ap. A. Hobson in *Studies in the Book Trade in Honour of Graham Pollard* (Oxford, 1975), 57 n. 65 (unless he meant San Gallo in Florence: cf. ibid. 50). L. D. R., *CR* 71 (1957), 5–8, demonstrated that D owes its text of Sen. *Ep.* 120 to Walahfrid Strabo's notebook, St. Gall 878; B. Bischoff, 'Eine unbekannte Konstitution Kaiser Julians', *ABAW* N.F. 58 (1963), 11, considers the script entirely compatible 'mit deutschem oder lothringischem Schriftwesen der spätottonischen Zeit'. In an article that contains even stranger things than the ascription of D to Corbie and s. IX¼, E. Gutjahr, *Ber. der sächs. Akad.* 43 (1891), 281–2, drew attention to corrections taken from an Irish text of Priscian such as St. Gall 904 (s. VIII, probably not at St. Gall before s. X); as R. Klotz observed in *Grundzüge altrömischer Metrik* (Leipzig, 1890), 563–4, these point not to Corbie but rather to St. Gall or Reichenau. On the more recent parts of D see F. Schlee, *RhM* 46 (1891), 147–50.

[26] A. Fritsch, *Philologus,* 32 (1873), 446; Professor B. Munk Olsen would assign it to s. XI. The best manuscript of Eugraphius' commentary, Leiden, Voss. Lat. Q.34 (s. XI), was also once at Beauvais; see K. A. de Meyier, *Codices Vossiani Latini II: codices in quarto* (Leiden, 1975), 95.

G   Vatican lat. 1640 (s. X/XI; Chatelain, plate XI).

L   Leipzig, Rep. 1.4°.37 (s. X; photograph in *Phormio*, ed. K. Dziatzko and E. Hauler (Leipzig, 1913), plate I).

V   Vienna 263 (s. X, German;[27] photographs in S. Prete's edition, Heidelberg, 1954).

These five manuscripts, variously incomplete, have the order *Andr. Ad. Eun. Phorm. Haut. Hec.*, which was thought to define the family until Grant found affinities with DpGLV in:

Vb   Vienna 85 (s. XI[1], south-west Germany[28]).

N   Leiden, Voss. Lat. Q.38 (s. XI[1], Fleury?[29]).

Pb   Paris lat. 9345 (*c.*1000, Echternach[30]).

Pc   Paris lat. 7900A (s. IX/X, Milan[31]).

Except that Vb lacks *Hec.*, these manuscripts all have the order *Andr. Eun. Haut. Ad. Hec. Phorm.*, which characterizes Γ.[32] The purest descendants of Γ are said to be the oldest illustrated manuscripts and a fragment:

C   Vatican lat. 3868 (*c.*820–30, Corvey;[33] written by Hrodgarius, illustrated by Adelricus; Chatelain, plate IX, published in facsimile[34]).

P   Paris lat. 7899 (s. IX[2], from the neighbourhood of Reims,[35] at Saint-Denis in s. XIII; Chatelain, plate VII, illustrations published[36]).

[27] E. Steinmeyer and E. Sievers, *Die althochdeutschen Glossen,* iv (Berlin, 1898), 633; fullest account in E. Hauler, *WS* 18 (1896), 84–90.

[28] 'St. Gallener und Reichenauer Arbeiten verwandt' according to H. J. Hermann, *Beschreibendes Verzeichnis der illuminierten Handschriften in Österreich*, VIII.ii (Leipzig, 1926), 1–2 (with plate); fullest account in Steinmeyer-Sievers, 626–7. Close to Vb in its strange assortment of brevities preceding Terence is a bifolium of s. XI[1] transcribed by U. Winter, *Philologus*, 123 (1979), 174–81, namely Bibl. des obersten Gerichts der D.D.R. 14 (at present deposited in the Deutsche Staatsbibliothek, East Berlin).

[29] J. Vezin, *Les* scriptoria *d'Angers au XIe siècle* (Paris, 1974), 43 n. 24.

[30] J. Schroeder, *Bibliothek und Schule der Abtei Echternach um die Jahrtausendwende* (diss. Freiburg, 1975, publ. Luxembourg, 1977), 45–9, 174, plate 6.

[31] Bischoff cited by G. Glauche, *Schullektüre im Mittelalter* (Munich, 1970), 36, and by H. C. Gotoff, *The Transmission of the Text of Lucan in the Ninth Century* (Cambridge, Mass., 1971), 19. On this manuscript, no less important a witness to the text of Horace, Lucan, and Juvenal, see also Grant, *Manuscripta*, 22 (1978), 83–90, and C. Villa, *IMU* 22 (1979), 35–41.

[32] Grant, *Γ and the Miniatures*, 102–3, ingeniously suggests that the plays in the order of A were divided between two volumes and alphabetically rearranged in the second as they happened to fall out in the first. It would be surprising if the Terence in Charlemagne's library really put *Hec.* before *Haut.*; cf. B. L. Ullman, *Scriptorium*, 8 (1954), 32–3, and Bischoff, *Karl der Grosse*, 59 (= *Mitt. Stud.* iii. 165) and *Sammelhandschrift Diez. B Sant. 66* (Graz, 1973), 38, 218. A mnemonic preserved in Munich Clm 14420 (s. X[2], Brescia) and in descendants of a lost Bononiensis brought to light in s. XIV[2] has the first four plays in the order of Γ but reverses *Hec.* and *Phorm.*; cf. Gius. Billanovich, *IMU* 17 (1974), 38–9, and see also nn. 56, 59, below. This order has been reported only from manuscripts of s. XV; see R. H. Webb, 'An Attempt to Restore the γ Archetype of Terence Manuscripts', *HSCP* 22 (1911), 55–110, at 65 n. 5.

[33] Bischoff, *Mitt. Stud.* i. 60 n. 34.   [34] *Praef.* Jachmann (Leipzig, 1929).

[35] Bischoff ap. Glauche (cf. n. 31, above), 63.   [36] *Praef.* H. Omont (Paris, 1909).

Y   Paris lat. 7900 (s. $IX^{3/4}$, Corbie;[37] some illustrations published[38]).

λ   Lyon 788 (s. $IX^2/4$, probably from the neighbourhood of Paris[39]); *Haut.* 522–904 only.[40]

As CPY originally omitted *Andr.* 804–53, either they do not suffice for the reconstruction of *Γ* or else manuscripts that have the passage are hybrid. Bentley's Dunelmensis, now Oxford, Bodl. Auct. F.2.13 (O, s. XII, at St. Albans in s. XIII), includes in the passage two illustrations not obviously made up in the Middle Ages.[41] Some editors regard as descendants of *Γ*, others as mixed, the two manuscripts whose correctors provide the true version of *Phorm.* 689:

E   Florence, Ricc. 528 (s. XI; photograph in Prete's edition, Heidelberg, 1954).

F   Milan, Ambros. H. 75 inf. (s. IX/X, probably from the neighbourhood of Reims;[42] Chatelain, plate VIII, published in facsimile[43]); the illustrated manuscript next in importance to C and P.

Older perhaps than all these descendants of *Σ* is the text of *Haut.* 1–15 written in rustic capitals, apparently as a *probatio pennae*, on f. 1 of Paris lat. 2109, produced at Saint-Amand not later than AD 828.[44] No editor has used it.

A indicates speakers within scenes by Greek letters unrelated to their names, and gives the key in the scene-headings. This convention, attested from s. III BC, survives in D, p, and a part of Vb apparently derived from *Γ*; it was not universal in manuscripts contemporary with A, because *Π*[b] and *Π*[a] both abbreviate the speakers' names.[45] A divides the text accurately and distinguishes the longer metres from the *senarii*[46] – altogether an eye-opener to Politian, who in other manuscripts must have encountered everything from fair semblances of metre to prose,

---

[37] Bischoff, *Mitt. Stud.* i. 59. The date and attribution bear out the assessment of Y offered by Webb (n. 32, above), 56–64, who himself favoured s. X and Fleury.

[38] L. W. Jones and C. R. Morey, *The Miniatures of the Manuscripts of Terence* (Princeton, 1931), the fullest treatment of illustrated manuscripts.

[39] I am grateful to Professor Bischoff for this information.

[40] R. Kauer, *WS* 28 (1906), 111–34. The two fragments at Lyon distinguished by J. Marouzeau in his edition of Terence, vol. i (Paris, 1942), 79, are actually the same.

[41] C. Hoeing, *AJA* 4 (1900), 310–38; Webb (n. 32, above), 92–6; Jachmann, *Geschichte*, 132 n. 81, 143 n. 14. *Survival*, 71, says that O 'is probably a direct copy' of P, 'though with some changes introduced from another source'; but unless the authors had evidence beyond what has been published, so close a relationship seems unlikely.

[42] Information kindly supplied by Professor Bischoff.

[43] *Praef.* E. Bethe (Leiden, 1903). On non-Calliopian readings preserved by F in *Phorm.* 748–832, see L. Havet, *Manuel de critique verbale* (Paris, 1911), § 1613A.

[44] Delisle, i. 313; E. K. Rand, *Studies in the script of Tours*, ii (Cambridge, Mass., 1934), 68–70. Claudia Villa kindly brought the manuscript to my attention.

[45] E. J. Jory, ' "Algebraic" notation in dramatic texts', *BICS* 10 (1963), 65–78; K.-U. Wahl, *Sprecherbezeichnungen mit griechischen Buchstaben in den Handschriften des Plautus und Terenz* (diss. Tübingen, 1974), 74–134. Some corruptions in *Σ* seem to betray misunderstanding of such letters; cf. Havet, §§ 1558, 1565, Jachmann, *Geschichte*, 82–3, Grant, *AJP* 97 (1976), 239–40.

[46] Cf. Warren (n. 19, above), 94–7, 100–4.

just as modern editors do in the manuscripts listed above: P, for instance, is written quite accurately in verse, C and p almost entirely in prose, D partly in verse and partly in prose, and G and L in prose but with capitals in more or less appropriate places. Neither Π^b nor Π^a matches A, which seems to have been one of the better texts available in its time.[47]

In the investigation of Δ, Γ, and the 'mixed' manuscripts, two avenues of progress suggest themselves: competent palaeographers might pronounce on the date and origin of the earliest manuscripts, and the 'mixed' manuscripts might be sorted into those produced by contamination and those copied from more than one exemplar.[48]

Meanwhile, it appears that the tradition of Terence in s. IX was largely French, however many ancient manuscripts it drew on and wherever they came from; Corbie may have been an important centre.[49] In England before the Conquest knowledge of Terence is not securely established.[50] In Italy, Bobbio had 'libros Terentii II' in s. IX[2] and Montecassino 'Terentium' in s. XI.[51] In Germany, Freising lamented the lack of a copy in s. IX,[52] but in s. X[2] Hrotsvitha of Gandersheim, 'Deutschlands erste Dichterin', set about edifying those 'qui, licet alia gentilium spernant, Terrentii tamen fingmenta frequentius lectitant' by imitating him 'quo eodem dictationis genere quo turpia lascivarum incesta feminarum recitabantur laudabilis sacrarum castimonia virginum . . . celebraretur'.[53]

Germany also put into circulation the *alter exitus* of *Andria*, which never entered the French tradition:

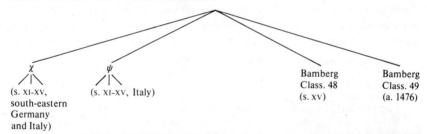

χ
(s. XI–XV, south-eastern Germany and Italy)

ψ
(s. XI–XV, Italy)

Bamberg Class. 48 (s. XV)

Bamberg Class. 49 (a. 1476)

[47] C. Questa, *RFIC* 101 (1973), 484–7, *Maia*, 26 (1974), 313–14; R. Raffaelli, 'Sulla presentazione metrica del testo nel Terenzio Bembino', in *La critica testuale greco-latina, oggi: metodi e problemi*, ed. E. Flores (Rome, 1981), 185–222.

[48] F, for instance, may be mixed in the latter sense; cf. Havet, § 1613.

[49] P. von Winterfeld, *Hrotsvithae opera* (Berlin, 1902), xx, suspected that the remonstration with Terence in Paris lat. 8069 (s. X) was composed in s. IX at Corbie; and see above on Y and below on Hildemar.

[50] J. D. A. Ogilvy, *Books Known to the English, 597–1066* (Cambridge, Mass., 1967), 248–50.

[51] Manitius, *Handschriften*, 15; for the date of the catalogue from Bobbio see G. Mercati, *M. Tulli Ciceronis De re publica libri e codice rescripto Vaticano Latino 5757 phototypice expressi*, i (Vatican, 1934), 26–7. According to A. Lentini, *Aevum*, 27 (1953), 248, Hilderic used Terence at Montecassino in s. IX, but without details it is impossible to tell whether he was quoting directly.

[52] Manitius, *Handschriften*, 12.

[53] p. 106 in Winterfeld's edition (see n. 49, above). She did not write her six plays for performance; cf. H. Homeyer, *Hrotsvithae opera* (Paderborn, 1970), 20 n. 48.

The archetype probably belonged from s. XI at the latest to a library in Bamberg.[54] The most important witness, despite its date, is Bamberg Class. 49, which repeats 977–81 in a different version after the *alter exitus*; from the Michelsberg at Bamberg comes Erlangen 391 (s. XII), which contains a third ending inspired by the other two.[55] The earliest manuscript of the *alter exitus*, Oxford, Bodl. Auct. F.6.27 (s. XI, south-eastern Germany), descends from χ, which also supplied the text added by a later hand to an old manuscript that could be seen during s. XIV–XV 'in catenis apud Sanctum Dominicum Bononie'.[56] A descendant of ψ, Milan, Ambros. G.130 inf. (s. XI²), is written in Beneventan; whether ψ, like the addition to the Bononiensis, migrated from Germany depends on the provenance and movements of the archetype. The relationship of all these manuscripts in the remainder of the text has not been explored.

So much for the *alter exitus* and the circulation of Terence in Germany. By the time that Aimeric, in his *Ars lectoria* (1086), put Terence among his *aurei auctores*,[57] no library in Europe would have had any difficulty in obtaining a copy. In the Renaissance the event of most note apart from the recovery of the Bembinus is a production of *Andria* at Florence in 1476, the first since Antiquity of any play by Terence.[58]

Commentaries and scholia complicate rather than illuminate the tradition. For a sample of the difficulties see AELIUS DONATUS, *Commentary on Terence*. Eugraphius' commentary (s. V/VI), one recension of which incorporates material from another commentary, was edited by P. Wessner (Leipzig, 1908); the scholia in the Bembinus by J. F. Mountford (Liverpool, 1934); and scholia from DGCE and Munich Clm 14420 (M) by F. Schlee, *Scholia Terentiana* (Leipzig, 1893). The whole body of scholia in M, now known as the *Commentum Monacense*, combines elements from extant commentaries, among them the Carolingian *Commentum Brunsianum*; M went to Regensburg from

---

[54] Skutsch's article (see n. 17, above) groups the manuscripts without offering a stemma or geographical inferences.

[55] F. Falbrecht, 'De tertio Andriae exitu', *Diss. Philol. Vindob.* 4 (1893), 1–38, esp. 36; H. Fischer, *Katalog der Handschriften der Universitätsbibliothek Erlangen*, i (Erlangen, 1928), 464. 'Terentii III' are recorded at the Michelsberg in 1120; see Manitius, *Handschriften*, 12. K. Pivec, *Mitt. des öst. Inst. für Geschichtsforschung*, 45 (1931), 452–67, establishes the importance of Terence in the Bamberg of Meinhard (s. X²), 'eine der bedeutungsvollsten lateinischen Sprachschulen jener Zeit in Deutschland'.

[56] Skutsch divides χ into two groups, χ¹ and χ². The former seems inadequately defined, but the latter is surely the progeny of the Bononiensis. Billanovich, *IMU* 17 (1974), 15–42, makes Pietro da Moglio responsible for bringing the Bononiensis to light; yet another descendant, besides Reggio Emilia, Bibl. Mun. Turri C.17, is Rome, Cors. 43.G.13 (s. XV¾), on which see M. D. R., *CPh* 74 (1979), 320 n. 36.

[57] Manitius, *Geschichte*, iii. 12, 180–2.

[58] P. Cennini in a letter of 29 Feb. 1476 quoted from Florence, Bibl. Naz. II.IX.14, f. 175 by V. R. Giustiniani, *Alamanno Rinuccini 1426–1499: zur Geschichte des florentinischen Humanismus* (Cologne and Graz, 1965), 236. If the oddly named *comoediae* of twelfth-century France were written for performance, which seems most unlikely, the pattern was not set by performances of Terence, who scarcely even influenced their text; for recent contributions on these issues see S. Rizzo, *GIF* 31 (1979), 97–103. Cf. also n. 53, above.

Brescia, where it was copied in s. x^2 from material taken there over a century before by Hildemar of Corbie.[59]

The first edition of Terence had appeared by 1470 at Strasbourg (Flodr, 1). G. Faerno was the first editor to use the Bembinus (Florence, 1565), though the 'Terentius in sua metra restitutus' of Benedictus Philologus (Florence, 1505) had profited indirectly from it.[60] The shrewdest judge in recent years, Jachmann, declares Bentley's edition (Cambridge, 1726) epoch-making, which no one would dispute, and Dziatzko's (Leipzig, 1884) relatively the best;[61] but as this has no apparatus worthy of the name, its place must be taken by the OCT of Kauer and Lindsay (1926, 'supplementum apparatus curavit O. Skutsch' 1958) or the Budé of Marouzeau (Paris, 1942–9), neither of which supersedes F. Umpfenbach's edition (Berlin, 1870) as a source of information. A new edition, properly constituted and more critical than the OCT, is badly needed.

This sketch of the tradition has perforce omitted a great deal. Anyone who wants to dig deeper should consult the excellent survey of H. Marti, 'Terenz 1909–1959', Lustrum, 6 (1961), 117–57; 8 (1963), 5–101, 244–7. Let Marti have the last word: 'Viel Material bedeutet auch viel Arbeit'.

M. D. R.

[59] Rand, 'Early Mediaeval Commentaries on Terence', CPh 4 (1909), 359–89; on the Commentum Brunsianum, Y.-F. Riou, RHT 3 (1973), 79–113, Hommages à André Boutemy (Coll. Latomus, 145, Brussels, 1976), 315–23; on the Commentum Monacense, G. Ballaira, BPEC 16 (1968), 13–24, Atene e Roma, 21 (1976), 203–4, Billanovich (n. 56, above), 43–60 (with plates between pp. 36 and 37), Grant, Manuscripta, 22 (1978), 83–90, Villa, IMU 22 (1979), 1–44, Billanovich, IMU 22 (1979), 367–95; on another Carolingian commentary, the Expositio, R. Sabbadini, SIFC 5 (1897), 322–7. Claudia Villa and Giancarlo Alessio have embarked on a thorough investigation of exegetical matter in the medieval manuscripts.

[60] J. N. Grant, to whom I owe this information, points out that his preface acknowledges a debt to Politian's collations.

[61] P.-W. VA (1934), 649.

TIBULLUS

All surviving whole manuscripts of Tibullus go back to a lost manuscript of which Coluccio Salutati obtained a copy. The text rests on the reconstruction of that manuscript, and on extracts in three important medieval florilegia. The primary question about the history of the text is where it was before it came into Salutati's hands.

A manuscript of Tibullus was brought to the Carolingian court and is among the books described in the late eighth-century book-list in Berlin (West), Diez. B Sant. 66, apparently a list of books at the Carolingian court at Aachen: 'Albi Tibulli lib. II. Horatii Flacchi Ars poetica explicit. Incipit Glaudiani De raptu Proserpinae lib. III. Sic incipit: Inferni raptoris equos adflataque curru. Ad Rufinum lib. II. Claudii In Eutropium lib. III. De bello Gothico. De bello Gildonico.'[1] At least two descendants of this codex can be identified. The first appears in the newly discovered twelfth-century catalogue of Lobbes: '239. Claudiani in Rufinum lib. II. Eiusdem in Aegyptium lib. II. Eiusdem de bello gothico lib. I. De bello gildonico lib. I. Albini Tibulli lib. III. Persius cum Cornuto super ipsum Persium. Vol. I.'[2] It is natural to expect texts from the court to reappear in monasteries around Liège; the Claudian, for example, the order of which is unique, reappears in a manuscript probably commissioned for Gembloux by Abbot Olbert (d. 1048), now Brussels 5380–4. However, the Tibullus and Horace in this instance were apparently not copied with the Claudian. In the second descendant of the court-library codex, an eleventh-century florilegium from Freising, now Munich Clm 6292, the whole codex appears to have been excerpted, reflecting again the unique order of the Claudian.[3]

Beyond these two, it becomes more difficult to trace the lines which connect the court-library codex with the later appearance of Tibullus; but there is no indication among the witnesses to the text that there was ever a second old manuscript of Tibullus. At some point the court-library Tibullus or a copy of it was taken to the Loire, most likely to Fleury, perhaps as early as the time of Theodulf. From there the text migrated to Orléans, where it leaves numerous traces. Tibullus is cited in a volume known to have been at Orléans in the late eleventh and twelfth centuries, Vatican lat. 4929. The master of the eleventh or early twelfth century who annotated the text of *Querolus* (q.v.) in this manuscript added, at the word *Ligerem*, a gloss indicating that Tibullus knew of the Loire: 'Ligerem dicit a nominativo Liger, quem ponit Albius Tibullus: Carnutis et flavi cerula limpha Liger' (1.7.12).[4] The same codex must have been the source of the extensive extracts from Tibullus included in the *Florilegium Gallicum*, which was compiled at Orléans in the middle years of the twelfth century.[5] The *Florilegium Gallicum*,

---

[1] B. Bischoff, *Sammelhandschrift Diez. B Sant. 66* (Graz, 1973), 39.

[2] F. Dolbeau, 'Un nouveau catalogue des manuscrits de Lobbes aux XIᵉ et XIIᵉ siècles', *Recherches Augustiniennes*, 13 (1978), 32; 14 (1979), 226.

[3] Identified by F. Newton, 'Tibullus in Two Grammatical *florilegia* in the Middle Ages', *TAPA* 93 (1962), 253–86. Heriger of Lobbes knew the same texts: Manitius, *Geschichte* ii.224.

[4] C. Barlow, 'Codex Vaticanus latinus 4929', *MAAR* 15 (1938), 106, 109.

[5] A. Gagnér, *Florilegium Gallicum* (Lund, 1936); J. Hamacher, *Das Florilegium Gallicum* (Frankfurt, 1975); R. H. R., '*Florilegia* and Latin Classical Authors in Twelfth- and Thirteenth-Century Orléans', *Viator*, 10 (1979), 131–60.

known in at least six manuscripts, was the main vehicle through which
Tibullus was read in the Middle Ages, not only because it contributed
to some of the smaller florilegia noted below, but also because it was
extensively used by Vincent of Beauvais in compiling the *Speculum
historiale*; Vincent's knowledge of Tibullus comes wholly from the
Florilegium Gallicum.[6] A lexicographer who worked at Orléans in the
third quarter of the thirteenth century, the annotator of Berne 276,
reproduces in the margins of that manuscript two lines of Tibullus
which were not available in the *Florilegium Gallicum* and which, hence,
appear to represent a knowledge of the whole text.[7]

   The manuscript of Tibullus which surfaced in the library of Richard
de Fournival, chancellor of Amiens Cathedral 1240–60, was in all
probability a copy of the Orléans codex. It is described in the
Biblionomia or catalogue of Fournival's library: 'Albii Tibullii liber
epygrammaton'.[8] Besides being an ecclesiastical administrator,
Fournival was also an accomplished poet, author of the *Bestiaire d'amours*
and probably of the pseudo-Ovidian *De vetula*, as well as of a body of
minor verse. He doubtless spent some years in the schools at Orléans
being trained in the *auctores*. Tibullus is only one of a number of ancient
works appearing in the *Biblionomia* which come straight from an Orléans
background, in particular Cicero's Verrine and Philippic orations, his
Epistulae ad familiares, Aulus Gellius, and Propertius. While Fournival
did own older manuscripts, the majority of his manuscripts that are
known appear to be copies made for him; and it is most probable that
his Tibullus, like his Propertius (now Leiden, Voss. Lat. O. 38), was
copied for him. After Fournival's death in 1260 this volume passed with
his other books to the recently founded Collège de Sorbonne.[9] While
Fournival's Tibullus is no longer known, brief extracts from it, as yet
unreported, survive in a collection of extracts, now Paris lat. 16708,
compiled at the Sorbonne largely from Fournival's manuscripts in the
first quarter of the fifteenth century.[10]

   In addition to the *Florilegium Gallicum* there are numerous smaller
florilegia containing brief extracts from Tibullus.[11] These manuscripts
are, to judge from their content and origin, manuals of examples from

---

   [6] B. L. Ullman, 'Tibullus in the Mediaeval *florilegia*', *CPh* 23 (1928), 128–74; on Vincent, pp.
154–6.   [7] R. H. R., 146–7.   [8] Delisle, ii. 531 no. 15.
   [9] R. H. R., 'Manuscripts Belonging to Richard de Fournival', *RHT* 3 (1973), 253–69.
   [10] Extracts from Propertius and Tibullus occupy ff. 24ᵛ–26ᵛ. Those from Tibullus (collated
against L. Mueller's Teubner edition of 1885, the only one to hand at the time) are 1.3.64 (*nescit*),
1.4.59–60 (59 *iam tu*, 60 *es* om.), 1.5.37–8 (37 *temptabam*, 38 *hic dolor*), 1.8.9–13 (9 *puellas*, 12
subticuisse), 17–18 (17 *pallentibus*, 18 *tacite . . . amor*; interpreted as *tacitae* the second variant deserves
consideration), 28 (*prosequitur peius*), 41–2 (41 *iuventus*, 42 *dum*), 47–8 (47 *ac* ut vid., *floreat*), 2.4.15
(*miseri*), 12 (*iam* om.), 2.5.105–6 (105 *pereatque*, 106 *in* om.), 3.4.73–6, 3.6.5–6 (6 *Salerna*), 35 (*non*),
43–8 (44 *discis . . . vitare*, 45 *non* ut vid., 46 *sordida . . . fide*, 47 *iuravit*). Not enlightening.
   [11] Hamacher, 92–100. Their contents are given in tabular form in F. W. Lenz's edition
(Leipzig, 1927, 1937; Leiden, 1959, 1964; rev. G. C. Galinsky, Leiden, 1971).

the *auctores*, used in the teaching of metrical composition in the schools at Orléans. The Tibullus excerpts derive from a single set of extracts compiled in the early thirteenth century, not entirely but perhaps in part taken from the *Florilegium Gallicum*.

There is only one body of medieval extracts from Tibullus that cannot be clearly explained in terms of the court library or Orléans; these appear in the florilegium (now Venice, Marc. Lat. Z. 497 (1811)) compiled at Montecassino in the eleventh century by Lawrence of Amalfi, tutor of the future pope Gregory VII.[12] The florilegium is the source of many quotations from ancient authors in Lawrence's writings. How Tibullus came to Montecassino is not known. Perhaps it came directly from the Carolingian court; or perhaps it came from Fleury, to which the Montecassino monks had fled with the bones of St. Benedict. In any case, the florilegium contains a number of northern authors, among them Bede, Alcuin, Hrabanus, and Remigius. One of the rarer items in it was known at Fleury; this is the *Poema ad coniugem*, extracts from which accompany two of the three sets of extracts from Tibullus in the florilegium.

What remains to be accounted for is the appearance of Tibullus in Renaissance Italy. Petrarch's friend at Verona, Guilelmo da Pastrengo, was once believed to have been familiar with the complete Tibullus; but, though he was not using verses from the Verona *Flores* of 1329, he may have been drawing from another florilegium, possibly the source of the Verona *Flores*.[13] Petrarch himself, the most likely agent to have brought a full text to Italy after his trip to France in 1333, provides no evidence of an acquaintance with more than a florilegium;[14] but the oldest manuscript of the full text, Milan, Ambros. R. 26 sup. (A) (Chatelain, plate CIV), s. XIV[2], has in the margin of f. 9[v] a 'nota' sign characteristic of Petrarch, which if not autograph seems likely to have been copied with the text from a manuscript that he had annotated.[15] The earliest owner of A, Salutati,[16] also owned the oldest surviving descendant of Petrarch's lost Propertius; and his Catullus too, again one of the oldest, may have been copied from a manuscript of Petrarch's.

Not for another generation after Salutati did Tibullus catch on; but two dated manuscripts survive from the 1420s, Paris lat. 7989 (a. 1423, Florence, connected with Poggio) and Vatican, Ottob. lat. 1202 (a. 1426, Florence, with additions in the hand of Giovanni Aurispa),[17] and

---

[12] Newton (n. 3, above).   [13] Ullman (n. 6, above), 172.   [14] Ibid. 173–4.

[15] We thank Dr A. C. de la Mare for this observation.

[16] Cf. Ullman, *Salutati*, 178. E. Baehrens, *Tibullische Blätter* (Jena, 1876), 60, surmised from letters that Salutati wrote in 1374 about Catullus and Propertius (quoted in his edition of Catullus (Leipzig, 1876), x–xi) that A was written about 1375; the date 1374 has hardened into a fact in some recent works.

[17] Lenz (n. 11, above) uses only the first, on which see now A. C. de la Mare in *Medieval Learning*, 239–51. On the second see R. Sabbadini, *Carteggio di Giovanni Aurispa* (Rome, 1931), 183–4.

by the third quarter of the century copies come thick and fast, so that it is no surprise when three editions of 1472 or thereabouts have to compete for the title of *editio princeps* (Flodr, *Tibullus* 1 and 12, *Catullus* 1). Altogether, like Catullus, Propertius, and the Ovidian *Epistula Sapphus*, one or more of which he frequently accompanies, Tibullus has come down from the Italian Renaissance in well over 100 manuscripts. Unlike them, however, he still awaits an investigator undaunted by the number. Since Baehrens first used A in an edition (Leipzig, 1878), its primacy has seldom been challenged; but no one yet knows whether none, some, or all of the other manuscripts are independent of it. The analogy of Salutati's Propertius and Catullus would suggest that some should be, but it may not hold.[18]

Independence of A has never been denied to a fragment that Scaliger collated towards his edition (Paris, 1577). He first cites it in *Publii Virgilii Maronis appendix* (Lyon, 1572), 474–9, for good readings in *Quid hoc novi est ?*, a *Priapeum* usually printed with Virgil but ascribed to Tibullus (or not to anyone else?) 'in veteri membrana Tibulliana, quae est penes te Iacobe Cuiaci, vir eruditissime'.[19] His collation of the *Priapeum* is lost, but his collation of Tibullus survives in Leiden 755 H 23 (ed. Plantin, 1569). The *fragmentum Cuiacianum*, known as F, appears to have contained roughly 3.4.65–end, conveniently as fragments go, because the Italian tradition either omits 3.4.65 or fills the gap with inventions; F included the brief epitaph 'Te quoque Vergilio comitem' and ascribed it to Domitius Marsus. Readings from F also appear in the margin of an anonymous Tibullus earlier than Scaliger's (Lyon, 1573).[20] A tantalizing glimpse of its previous history is afforded by the ascription of the *Priapeum* to Tibullus in a rare Virgil, edited by Antonius Goveanus with the help of collations made by Antonius

[18] Now that for a century editors of various texts have been availing themselves of manuscripts first discovered by Baehrens, it is easy to overlook the impact of his editions when they appeared. His Tibullus, by shattering the foundations of Lachmann's (Berlin, 1829), caused an outbreak of dissertations and articles. None of these added new material, however, except J. Bergman, *De Tibulli codice Upsaliensi* (Uppsala, 1889); the most sane and unprejudiced is Ph. Illmann, *De Tibulli codicis Ambrosiani auctoritate* (Halle, 1886). Far from resolving the disputes of the 1880s, Lenz's edition (n. 11, above) reports in pointless detail both Lachmann's five manuscripts and Baehrens's three, together with two used by Calonghi, two of his own, and a few others consulted sporadically. The best text of Books 1–2, A. G. Lee's (Cambridge, 1975, with verse translation), follows Baehrens in principle but rests on a fresh collation of A. Though Ullman embarked on a study of the tradition, his results, if any, lie unpublished among his papers in North Carolina. Anyone minded to chart the whole terrain might seek access to these papers; failing that, he should begin from the editions of Heyne-Wunderlich (Leipzig, 1817) and Huschke (Leipzig, 1819), proceed to the recent works cited under CATULLUS, PROPERTIUS, and OVID (p. 272 n. 19) (J. L. Butrica's dissertation on Propertius, for instance, describes fifty-three manuscripts that include Tibullus), and then strike out on his own.

[19] See also his letter of 13 Feb. 1572 to Pithou, published by P. Tamizey de Larroque, *Lettres françaises inédites de Joseph Scaliger* (Agen and Paris, 1881), 17.

[20] Cf. Huschke, i.lxxv–lxxviii; in the commentary (ii.676) he impugns the date, but without sufficient reason.

Molinius (Lyon, 1543).[21] Goveanus, a Portuguese born about 1513, studied at Toulouse in 1538 before moving to Lyon;[22] Molinius, born at Mâcon about 1510, also studied at Toulouse, but not later than 1535, and so he must have met Goveanus when his travels in royal service brought him to Lyon in 1538;[23] Cujas, born in 1522, studied and taught at Toulouse until 1554 and lived at Valence when Scaliger first saw F in 1571–2.[24] Though the mobility of Molinius multiplies possibilities, F seems to have entered circulation conceivably at Toulouse but more probably on the Rhône.[25]

The story has begun and ended in France; but from there, like his patron Messalla, Tibullus returned in triumph to Italy, and it is Italian manuscripts that editors must thank for having a text to edit.

R. H. R.

M. D. R.

[21] Copy dated 1543 in the British Library, copies dated 1544 in Lisbon and Nantes, copy without frontispiece in Strasbourg (kindly reported by Carlotta Griffiths). E. Hiller, *Hermes*, 18 (1883), 343–8, found no evidence of the ascription to Tibullus earlier than Muretus's reference in 1558 (*Epp.* (Paris, 1580), f. 11ᵛ) to Priapean iambics 'quae ab omnibus tribuuntur Tibullo'. From Goveanus's edition both the ascription and the readings *ligneo* in 17 and *annuo* in 29 passed through various edd. Gryph. and Plant., at least one of which Muretus had presumably seen.

[22] L. de Matos, *Sobre António de Gouveia e a sua obra* (Libson, 1966), 8.

[23] A. Cartier and A. Chenevière, *Rev. d'hist. litt. de la France*, 2 (1895), 471, 476.

[24] The letter of Scaliger's cited above (n. 19) was sent from Valence.

[25] Hiller, *Jahrb. für class. Phil.* 29 (1883), 273–4, maintained that readings of F occur so often in Italian manuscripts that it must have circulated in Italy; but his evidence came from old editions and would need checking before anything could be made of it. For instance, as Hiller admitted in his edition (Leipzig, 1885), xix–xx, Lachmann's note on 3.6.6 casts grave doubt on whether the *excerpta* of Antonius Petreius (1498–1570) in Berlin (East), Diez 8° 2474 (ed. Ald. 1515) show agreements with F. The matter needs pursuing, because if the suspicion endures that very little is peculiar to F, someone will eventually stand Hiller's argument on its head and declare that F was not a medieval remnant from a French library but an Italian manuscript less honest than most.

VALERIUS FLACCUS

The scholars who transcribed a text of Valerius 1.1–4.317 at St. Gall in the summer of 1416 could not know that within thirteen years Niccoli would be putting into circulation a text more than twice as long, 1.1–8.467. Not surprisingly, descendants of the Sangallensis (S), among which Madrid 8514 is Poggio's direct copy, number only six against nearly thirty of Niccoli's manuscript, Florence, Laur. 39.38 (L, undated but already in service as an exemplar by 1429). Not until Pius's edition (Bologna, 1519) does use seem to have been made of the one medieval manuscript still extant, Vatican lat. 3277 (V, s. IX²/4; Chatelain, plate CLXV), which goes as far as L but has five lines fewer on the way (and at some date lost five leaves); Pius says that 'Iacobus Orodryinus scriptor apostolicus' brought it 'ex Germania',[1] and certainly it was written at Fulda. Meanwhile, by courtesy of Taddeo Ugoleto, Politian had seen a manuscript 'e quo fluxisse opinor et caeteros qui sunt in manibus', which at 2.572 read *durica* with L and not *turica* with VS.

The latest editor but one, E. Courtney (Leipzig, 1970), is not the first to mistrust Politian and to see in V not only Ugoleto's manuscript but also the source of both S and L. He will be the last, however, because the discovery of the second *Miscellaneorum centuria* has vindicated Politian and with him W.-W. Ehlers, who defended the additional lines in L and offered other evidence for this stemma:[2]

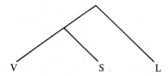

VL transpose 8.136–85 after 385, and the second *Centuria* now reveals that Ugoleto's manuscript presented the passage at the same point on a single misplaced leaf – conclusive proof, as Politian recognized, that it was the archetype.[3] With the aid of the transpositions and omissions in its descendants, Ehlers has reconstructed its pagination and shown that the curtailment of the poem cannot be blamed on damage to it.[4]

What became of Ugoleto's manuscript after Politian saw it is any-one's guess.[5] So too is the route by which it reached Niccoli, who not only copied L from it but according to Politian also wrote in its margins.

[1] He also calls it 'codex Dacicus' in the manner of the time.
[2] *Untersuchungen zur handschriftlichen Überlieferung der Argonautica des C. Valerius Flaccus* (Zetemata, 52, Munich, 1970).
[3] In the tradition of Cicero's *Ad familiares*, too, Politian drew the right inference from an observation of this kind.
[4] See P. L. Schmidt, *IMU* 19 (1976), 249–50; a diagram on p. 248 illustrates how an error in binding could have brought about the transposition of 8.136–85. It has generally been assumed that Valerius did not live to finish the poem, and its unfinished state has been held to explain some difficulties in the text; for energetic opposition on both counts see G. Jachmann, *RhM* 84 (1935), 228–40.
[5] Another Florentine scholar, Bart. Fonzio, also saw it. His copy of the *editio princeps* (Bologna, 1474), now Florence, Ricc. ed. rar. 431, contains his commentary on Valerius in the form of copious marginalia accumulated over at least twenty-eight years (1476–1504); he there cites three manuscripts, 'Nic.' throughout (L), 'Pog.' to the beginning of Book 4 (Madrid 8514), and 'vetus(tus)' in Books 1–2 (Ugoleto's manuscript). Cf. S. Caroti and S. Zamponi, *Lo scrittoio di Bartolomeo Fonzio* (Milan, 1974), 72 + plate XXV; V. Fera, *GIF* 31 (1979), 230–54.

Schmidt identifies it with a manuscript catalogued at Bobbio in s. IX[6] and tentatively takes it back to s. V/VI, the date of three Bobienses that have twenty-five lines to the page.[7]

Over seventy lines occur in the *Florilegium Gallicum* (s. XII, Orléans or thereabouts), and the Belgian scholar Carrio in his editions of 1565 and 1566 attributes to a manuscript 'ante sexcentos annos conscriptum' four lines absent from VSL; both the *Florilegium* and Carrio's manuscript give *polumque* at 1.331 for the bizarre *cretamque* of VSL. Ehlers sees no need to postulate a French tradition independent of VSL, but Schmidt is not convinced.[8] The presence of Valerius in a newly discovered catalogue of c.1049–1160 from Lobbes, near Liège, puts a fresh complexion on the matter.[9]

Like most descendants of L, the *editio princeps* (Bologna, 1474) owes some readings to S. C. Giarratano provides the fullest apparatus (Milan, 1904). Courtney's apparatus is unsatisfactory in other respects besides the exclusion of L,[10] but no one helps the reader more in *emendatio*. Ehlers's edition (Stuttgart, 1980) is the first to give L its due; after his thorough study of the tradition,[11] his apparatus also brings Courtney's 'Itali' into sharper focus.[12] G. Cambier has undertaken an edition for Budé.

M. D. R.

[6] This would also account for the echoes detected by Guido Billanovich (*IMU* 1 (1958), 178 n. 1) in the works of Pauan pre-humanists; but they do not amount to much.

[7] *IMU* 19 (1976), 251 n. 3. For knowledge of the poem from Quintilian to the Middle Ages see W. C. Summers, *A Study of the* Argonautica *of Valerius Flaccus* (Cambridge, 1894), 1, 8–14.

[8] Ehlers (n. 2, above), 112, Schmidt, 251 n. 1 and more fully in his review of Ehlers's book, *Gymnasium*, 81 (1974), 263.

[9] F. Dolbeau, *Recherches Augustiniennes*, 13 (1978), 10–11, 33 no. 303; 14 (1979), 227 n. 303.

[10] See Ehlers's review, *Gnomon*, 48 (1976), 255–60.

[11] For other manuscripts see ibid. 257, and add Messina XIII.C.7, 1048 ('C. Septimuleius infoelix exscripsit'). The *codex Burmanni* is Lisbon 49.III.40.

[12] Add that Munich Clm 802 contains emendations in the hand of Pontano and that Pomponio Leto, with whom Ehlers associates a group of emended manuscripts, actually wrote one of them, Naples IV.E.40.

VALERIUS MAXIMUS

Written[1] under Tiberius and much used in Antiquity itself, the *Factorum et dictorum memorabilium libri* survived into the Carolingian period in but one exemplar.[2] From this were copied three manuscripts, two of which are extant, while the third can be reconstructed:

1. L Florence, Laur. Ashburnham 1899, s. IX, northern Europe (Chatelain, plate CLXXX), containing (in a s. XII/XIII hand) the *ex libris* of Stavelot: 'Liber ecclesie sancti remacli in Stabulaus'. It may be significant that in the ninth century Sedulius Scottus of Liège (only twenty-five miles from Stavelot) knew Valerius, while it was presumably from L that Wibald[3] gained his knowledge of this author in the middle of the twelfth century. Despite its fundamental importance for the text, L appears to have left no progeny and to have made no impression on the very large number of extant manuscripts.

2. A Berne 366, s. IX²/₄, northern France (Chatelain, plate CLXXXI). This text was early in the possession of Servatus Lupus,[4] and shows much editorial work in his hand. Around the year 860 Lupus acquired a text of the Paris epitome (see below), and from this[5] he inserted a large number of readings into A. The numerous descendants of A thus fall into two categories: (i) those copied from the 'pre-Paris' state of A; (ii) the 'post-Paris' texts.

The only text worth considering is that of C. Kempf (2nd edn., Teubner, Leipzig, 1888). This edition is frequently wrong in the reports on L and A, and fails to understand the importance of the third family of manuscripts. A new text is badly needed.

[1] I am deeply indebted to Dr C. J. Carter, who generously allowed me to use his unpublished Ph.D. thesis 'The Manuscript Tradition of Valerius Maximus' (Cambridge, 1968). As Dr Carter has demonstrated the unreliability of Kempf's 1888 Teubner text, much of the subsequent published work on Valerius (of necessity dependent on Kempf) may safely be ignored. Of great value is D. M. Schullian, 'A Revised List of Manuscripts of Valerius Maximus', in *Miscellanea Augusto Campana* (*Medioevo e Umanesimo*, 44–5, Padua, 1981), 695–728. The commentaries are studied by Schullian in vol. v. of *CTC* (forthcoming).
[2] Various unconvincing attempts have been made to reconstruct 'the archetype', e.g. W. M. Lindsay, 'The Archetype Codex of Valerius Maximus', *CPh* 4 (1909), 113–17; J. Schnetz, 'Zu Valerius Maximus', *Philologus*, 78 (1923), 421–3.
[3] L. Traube, *Vorlesungen und Abhandlungen*, iii (Munich, 1920), 11.
[4] Carter suggests that it was written for Lupus after he became Abbot of Ferrières (840) and before he quotes Valerius in a letter dated 843/4 (*ep*. 93, p. 83 Dümmler). In the sixteenth century A came into the hands of Pierre Daniel (whose signature it bears), after which it went to Jacques Bongars.
[5] At Ferrières Lupus lectured on Valerius, and among his pupils was Heiric, whose *Excerpts* (*Collectanea*) have survived (ed. Schullian, *MAAR* 12 (1935), 155–84 with plates; most recently R. Quadri, *I Collectanea di Eirico di Auxerre* (*Spicilegium Friburgense*, 11), 1966). These *Excerpts* show no influence from the post-Paris text. Heiric left Ferrières in 859, and Lupus died *c*.862.

(i) Pre-Paris copies. The closest descendant seems to be Δ (Avranches 157), s. XII, France (?Bec). Of great importance also is K (Cambridge, University Library Kk. 3. 23), s. XII ex., which made its influence felt[6] on all the other pre-Paris texts (with the exception of Δ). This tradition was widespread in England: note, for example, Cambridge, Pembroke College 105, s. XIII, from Bury St. Edmunds.

(ii) Post-Paris copies. These split into two families. The leading representatives of the first are: Montpellier 131, s. XII, France,[7] and Troyes 513, s. XII, France (Clairvaux). The earliest member of the second family is: The Hague 128.E.19, s. XII/XIII (?France or the Low Countries).

3. From the common archetype of the *gemelli* L and A there derives also a number of manuscripts, which thus attest to a (lost, presumably ninth-century) brother to LA. Of this third family, the most important representative is G (Brussels 5336), s. XI, northern Europe, bearing the *ex libris* of Gembloux: 'Cenobium gemblacense me habet'. G was probably given to or commissioned for Gembloux by Abbot Olbert (who was educated at Lobbes and Abbot of St. James in Liège). This whole family seems to have been situated in the region of the Low Countries and the Rhineland.

It is thus possible for the editor usually to arrive with reasonable certainty at the common archetype of LAG. Additional help, however, is available from two epitomes, which come from late Antiquity. One is attributed to Nepotianus,[8] the other to Julius Paris.[9]

The popularity of Valerius was immense. In the eleventh century Rodolfus Tortarius, a monk at Fleury, wrote his *De memorabilibus*, a poem in nine books based on Valerius.[10] Excerpts, at least, of Valerius were in southern Germany by the end of the eleventh century,[11] and the full text had returned to Italy by the thirteenth century.[12] The

---

[6] Carter suggests that K may have been John of Salisbury's copy. In 1180 John bequeathed his text of Valerius to Chartres (see Manitius, *Handschriften*, 87). Valerius was also known to William of Malmesbury.

[7] This may be the text attested at Pontigny in the thirteenth century (ibid.). Significant may be the geographical proximity of Auxerre (later domicile of Heiric), Clairvaux, and Pontigny.

[8] J. Schnetz, *Neue Untersuchungen zu Valerius Maximus, seinen Epitomatoren und zum Fragmentum De Praenominibus* (diss. Würzburg, 1904).

[9] See JULIUS PARIS with the bibliography cited there.

[10] *Rodulfi Tortarii Carmina*, ed. M. B. Ogle and D. M. Schullian (American Academy in Rome, 1933). Carter does not 'exclude the theoretical possibility that Tortarius was versifying the archetype itself'.

[11] e.g. Munich Clm 22004, s. XI/XII, southern Germany.

[12] e.g. Florence, Laur. 63.25 and 63.28, both s. XIII, Italian.

fourteenth century saw commentaries[13] by Dionigi da Borgo S. Sepolcro, the Neapolitan jurist Luca de Penna, the versatile Benvenuto da Imola, the Frenchmen Simon de Hesdin and Nicolas de Gonesse (with a translation), and the German Heinrich von Mügeln. Translations also came in Catalan (by Antoni Canals), Castilian, Italian, and Sicilian.

P. K. M.

[13] G. di Stefano, 'Per la fortuna di Valerio Massimo nel Trecento', *Accademia delle scienze di Torino, Classe di scienze morali, storiche e filologiche. Atti*, 96 (1961–2), 777–90. M. T. Casella, 'Il Valerio Massimo in volgare, dal Lancia al Boccaccio', *IMU* 6 (1963), 49–136. M. A. Berlincourt, 'The Relationship of some Fourteenth Century Commentaries on Valerius Maximus', *Mediaeval Studies*, 34 (1972), 361–87. Valuable also are the lists in Schullian (n. 1, above).

VARRO

De lingua latina

The manuscript tradition of the surviving portion of Varro's *De lingua latina* descends from an extant archetype, Florence, Laur. 51. 10 = F, written in a Beneventan hand at Montecassino in the later reaches of the eleventh century.[1] This manuscript also contains Cicero's *Pro Cluentio*, and the *Ad Herennium*. An excerpt from Varro (5.41–6) in a manuscript still at Montecassino, the famous Casinensis 361 of the *De aquis* of Frontinus, was copied from F in the twelfth century by Peter the Deacon.

Boccaccio apparently visited the monastery of Montecassino in 1355 and may there have made or obtained a copy or both the Varro and the Cicero in Laur. 51. 10; for later in the same year he was able to send Petrarch a copy of these works written in his own hand.[2] This manuscript does not survive. Of the numerous copies which do survive,[3] made in the fifteenth and sixteenth centuries, the best is considered to be Laur. 51. 5 (= f), written in 1427. The second quire of F, containing

A full account of the manuscripts of Varro can be found in G. Goetz and F. Schoell, *M. Terenti Varronis De Lingua Latina quae supersunt* (Leipzig, 1910); J. Collart, *Varron, De Lingua Latina Livre V* (Paris, 1954).

[1] For further information see *Beneventan Script*[2], i. 70, ii. 42.
[2] G. Billanovich, *Petrarca letterato. I. Lo scrittoio del Petrarca* (Rome, 1947), 203–7; de la Mare, *Handwriting*, 18.
[3] Goetz and Schoell list forty-seven (pp. xxx–xxxv); cf. Collart, xxx–xxxviii.

5.118–6.61, was lost subsequent to 1521,[4] and here the *descripti* still have a part to play.

It has been attractively conjectured[5] that local pride may have contributed to the preservation of Varro's work at this particular monastery; for it was at Casinum that Varro owned the villa in which Antony is said to have behaved so disgustingly.[6]

L. D. R.

[4] When Petrus Victorius and Jacobus Diacetius transcribed variants from F into a copy of the *editio princeps* (by Pomponio Leto, Rome, 1471), which is now at Munich (4° Inc. s.a. 1908ᵃ).

[5] F. Brunhölzl, *Zum Problem der Casinenser Klassikerüberlieferung* (Munich, 1971, *Abhandlungen der Marburger Gelehrten Gesellschaft*, 1971. 3), 138 f.

[6] Cic. *Phil.* 2. 103 ff. It is worth noting that in the Montecassino manuscript of the *Philippics* (Vatican lat. 3227, f. 24ʳ) this very passage is marked with the contemporary marginal heading 'CASINVM' (see CICERO, *Speeches*, §4).

VELLEIUS PATERCULUS

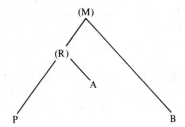

In 1515 Beatus Rhenanus discovered the archetype of our text of Velleius Paterculus in the Benedictine Abbey of Murbach.[1] This manuscript, known as (M) and now lost, appears to have survived into the eighteenth century.[2] Reports indicate that it was written in an early Caroline minuscule,[3] was difficult to read, and very corrupt. A copy (R),

This account of the textual tradition of Velleius is based on the recent and authoritative treatment of A. J. Woodman, *Velleius Paterculus: The Tiberian Narrative (2. 94–131)* (Cambridge, 1977), 3–27. A Budé edition by J. Hellegouarc'h is due to appear in 1982.

[1] On the date, see R. Sabbadini, *RFIC* 47 (1919), 346–7; G. von der Gönna, 'Beatus Rhenanus und die Editio Princeps des Velleius Paterculus', *Würzb. Jahrb. Altertumsw.* N.F. 3 (1977), 231, who shows that the discovery must be put a few months later than Sabbadini had thought.

[2] A letter of Marschall Baron Zurlauben dated 10 August 1786 refers to a sale of Murbach manuscripts which includes 'une collection des Épîtres de St. Jérôme de VIII siècle, un Velleius Paterculus du même temps et l'unique qui existe': cf. A. Allgeier, *Miscellanea Mercati*, vi (*Studi e testi*, 126, 1946), 457–8.

[3] The reported writing of *a* as *cc* suggests a date not later than the early ninth century, while the lack of punctuation and word-division and the description given above (n. 2) point to the eighth.

which has likewise perished, was hastily made for Rhenanus by an 'amicus quidam'.

Owing the the corrupt and lacunose state of (M), Rhenanus postponed the publication of the new text for a few years in the hope that a better manuscript might be found.[4] But in 1518 or 1519 he began to prepare an edition of Velleius to be published by J. Froben of Basle, basing his text not upon (M) but upon (R), though he sent both manuscripts to the printers and asked them to do the necessary collation, a delegation of responsibility no more unusual in this period than the subsequent recrimination. When the text itself had been put into print – this part of the book was completed by November 1520 – one of Rhenanus's scribes, J. A. Burer, noticed an error in the text, retrieved the Murbach codex from Froben, and proceeded to collate it against the *editio princeps*. His collation was added as a ten-page appendix (signature G), and the book was published in the first quarter of 1521.[5] Thus the *editio princeps* consists of two elements: Rhenanus's text = P, and Burer's collation = B.[6]

A new witness emerged in 1835 when J. C. Orelli published an edition based on a manuscript which he had discovered at Basle. This was a copy of Velleius made for his personal use by Bonifacius Amerbach, a young friend of Rhenanus, and completed on 11 August 1516. This manuscript, designated A, is now Basle AN II 38. After much controversy, it seems clear that A is a copy not of (M), but of (R).[7]

Thus we have three witnesses to the text of Velleius: APB. The reconstruction of the archetype is no easy matter, and not least because of the partial character of B. But Burer's collation appears to be such a meticulous piece of work that one is reasonably safe in assuming from B's silence that P = (M). Thus P, controlled by B, provides the main

---

[4] He had heard that there was a manuscript of Velleius in the Visconti library at Milan which had been discovered by G. Merula: cf. *ed. princ.* sig. A2^b, and his letter to Georg Spalatin, *Briefwechsel des Beatus Rhenanus* (ed. A. Horawitz and K. Hartfelder, Leipzig, 1886, repr. Hildesheim, 1966), no. 197, p. 269. His informant, who proved to have been mistaken, was probably the Pavia bookseller Francesco Giulio Calvo, and the cause of the confusion is likely to have been the *De orthographia* of Velius Longus discovered at Bobbio in 1493: see von der Gönna, 232 f.

[5] Dr Woodman has pointed out that his statement (p. 7) that the *editio princeps* was published in December 1520 was based on an incorrect dating (p. 4 n. 1) of Rhenanus's letter to Georg Spalatin. This letter (see previous note) should be dated 11 March 1521, and it provides the *terminus ante quem* for publication. The latest date printed in the book is 13 December 1520 (at the end of the *Vita*, sig. A3^b), but von der Gönna has shown (p. 238) from a letter written by Froben to Amerbach on 13 Jan. 1521 that the book had still not been published by that date: A. Hartmann, *Die Amerbachkorrespondenz*, ii (Basle, 1943), no. 764, p. 278.

[6] Further correction led to a handful of discrepancies between the texts of earlier and later copies of P. Rhenanus's own copy of the *editio princeps*, with his marginal corrections, is still extant at Sélestat: von der Gönna, 238 ff.

[7] This view, first put forward by D. A. Fechter (*Die Amerbachische Abschrift des Velleius Paterculus und ihr Verhältniss zum Murbacher codex und zur Editio princeps*, Basle, 1844), is cogently argued by Woodman, 11 ff.

basis for the reconstruction of the archetype. A is a hasty and careless copy of (R), but it occasionally preserves a reading of (M) which has been omitted, or is not explicit, in P and B.

L. D. R.

VIRGIL

It is not surprising that such a poet as Virgil should be in many ways a law unto himself. Greatness of that order has its own destiny and this has affected in some respects the very manner in which his poems were handed down to posterity. No poet became the pastime of grammarians and commentators as soon or to such a degree; no other text, whether by accident or design, has reached us in manuscripts written in the lapidary script more appropriate to monuments of stone; no other author with a full-blooded medieval transmission has a text which is so largely built on surviving ancient codices, as imposing as the monuments and ruins of Antiquity itself.

'Itur in antiquam silvam'[1] were the words with which Sir Roger Mynors aptly began the preface to his Oxford Classical Text,[2] and any account of Virgil's transmission must begin with the impressive parade of the ancient books, written in their capital scripts,[3] which are the main witnesses to his text. First come three manuscripts which, though they have all lost some leaves, preserve the bulk of the poems and are the editor's mainstay:

M   Florence, Laur. 39. 1 + Vatican lat. 3225, f. 76, known as the 'codex Mediceus'.[4] Written in Italy in the fifth century in rustic capitals, it

---

[1] *Aen.* 6. 179.

[2] Oxford, 1969 (reprinted with corrections, 1972). The most recent critical edition is that of M. Geymonat (Turin, 1973). Based on R. Sabbadini[2] (Rome, 1930–1) and drawing on Castiglioni (Turin, 1945) and Mynors, it has a larger apparatus than is necessary or even convenient for normal purposes, but where extra information may be found. Editors still lean on O. Ribbeck's great edition (Leipzig, 1859–66 and 1894–5). Where the dates assigned to the manuscripts are not those given in *CLA* I have relied on Bischoff (*Mitt. Stud.* ii. 316, *Paläographie des römischen Altertums und des abendländischen Mittelalters* (Berlin, 1979), 77 n. 35) and Seider (see n. 14, below).

[3] Known in the early Middle Ages as *litterae Virgilianae*: Bischoff, *Mitt. Stud.* i. 4–5.

[4] *CLA* I, p. 5, III. 296; Chatelain, plate LXVI. A complete facsimile was published by E. Rostagno (Rome, 1931).

bears a subscription[5] recording that it was corrected at Rome by Turcius Rufius Apronianus Asterius, consul in 494. It found its way to Bobbio, and was still there in 1467. Shortly after this it was taken to Rome and was in the hands of Pomponio Leto by 1471.[6]

P   Vatican, Pal. lat. 1631, the 'codex Palatinus'.[7] Written in Italy in s. V/VI, it was at Lorsch by the ninth century. Rustic capitals.

R   Vatican lat. 3867, the 'codex Romanus'.[8] Written in Italy in s. V/VI, it was in the thirteenth century, and probably from the early Middle Ages, at Saint-Denis. There, or possibly while sojourning at Fleury, it was used by Heiric of Auxerre.[9] When at the Vatican, it was consulted by Politian. It is written in rustic capitals and contains a number of miniatures, including a portrait of the author.

The four other ancient codices are in a more fragmentary state:

F   Vatican lat. 3225, known as the 'schedae Vaticanae'.[10] A magnificent book written in Italy in rustic capitals towards the end of the fourth century; it has fine illustrations and looks like a product of the professional booktrade. It later belonged to Gioviano Pontano, Pietro Bembo, and Fulvio Orsini. Seventy-five leaves survive.

V   Verona XL (38), s. V, rustic capitals.[11] It was in Gaul about 700, when it was rewritten, in Luxeuil minuscule, with Gregory's *Moralia*. By the ninth century it had reached Verona. Forty-nine leaves survive.

A   Vatican lat. 3256 + Berlin (West) lat. 2° 416, the 'codex Augusteus'.[12] A highly calligraphic and de luxe edition which, with its imposing square capitals and an estimated weight (when complete) of nine kilograms, well deserves its name. Written in the late fifth or early sixth century, it is the oldest extant manuscript with decorated initials. Of Italian origin, it probably spent the Middle Ages, like R, at Saint-Denis. Only seven leaves remain.

G   St. Gall 1394, s. V, likewise written in square capitals and of Italian origin.[13] In the fifteenth century it was taken to pieces at St. Gall and used for binding and repairing books. Twelve leaves and a number of fragments have been recovered.

---

[5] Though superimposed upon the manuscript, it is not clear that the subscription is an autograph: see, e.g., O. Ribbeck, *Prolegomena critica ad P. Vergili Maronis opera maiora* (Leipzig, 1866), 223.

[6] For Pomponio Leto's work on Virgil see *Survival*, nos. 26–8 (pp. 11–17).

[7] *CLA* I. 99; Chatelain, plate LXIV. A facsimile was published by Sabbadini (Paris, 1929).

[8] *CLA* I. 19; Chatelain, plate LXV; partial facsimile published by F. Ehrle (Rome, 1902).

[9] L. Traube, *Vorlesungen und Abhandlungen*, iii (Munich, 1920), 220.

[10] *CLA* I. 11; Chatelain, plate LXIII; facsimile by F. Ehrle (Rome, 1899). A new colour facsimile has been published, *Codices selecti* 71 (*Codices e Vaticanis selecti*, 40), Graz, 1980.

[11] *CLA* IV. 498; Chatelain, plate LXI. Lowe tentatively assigned it to Gaul, Seider regards it as being of Italian origin.

[12] *CLA* I. 13, VIII, p. 9; Chatelain, plate LXI. The facsimile published by Sabbadini (Turin, 1926) has been superseded by that of C. Nordenfalk (Graz, 1976).

[13] *CLA* VII. 977; Chatelain, plate LXII.

To these ancient witnesses must be added a number of papyri,[14] of less textual value than usual because of the abundance of the other ancient testimony, and the tangled mass of the indirect tradition, furnished by the writers, grammarians, and scholiasts of Antiquity.

Behind the ancient codices, but just ahead of the legions of later manuscripts, come two manuscripts which predate the great revival of the ninth century. The first is Munich Clm 29216 (7 (*olim* 29005 (18)), a fragment of the late eighth century, written in northern Italy in pre-Caroline minuscule and later at Tegernsee.[15] This is our oldest medieval manuscript of the *Aeneid*. The other is Paris lat. 7906, written in early Caroline minuscule in western Germany, s. VIII/IX.[16]

When we reach the ninth century, the 'antiqua silva' becomes the 'silva immensa' in which even Virgil's stout hero needed divine assistance to pluck the lurking gold. We have a clearer idea of what this forest is like, at least in parts, than we did before, for Mynors picked out thirteen ninth-century manuscripts, which he cites alongside the older witnesses. Largely from French centres, they allow one to form an impression of the Carolingian tradition. It is striking how many of the early manuscripts of Virgil had been drawn to northern Europe in the early Middle Ages, and it must be true that others, now lost, made similar journeys and survived long enough to contribute something to the medieval vulgate text. But the Carolingian scholars made such a thorough job of editing their texts of Virgil, correcting them, comparing one manuscript with another, drawing, as we do, on scholia and ancient learning, that there can be little hope in that mêlée of identifying and tracking down strains of text not otherwise attested. It is difficult enough to see the relationship between the medieval text and the ancient codices which have survived, but here Mynors was able to isolate some interesting and useful lines of descent. One of the ninth-century manuscripts, Berne 172 + Paris lat. 7929, from Fleury (= a), so faithfully follows R in the *Eclogues* and the latter part of the *Aeneid* that it can stand in for R in places where R is now missing. Wolfenbüttel, Gud. lat. 70 (s. IX, written at Lyon, =γ) mirrors the text of P so closely in the *Aeneid* that it must have descended from it and thus becomes a useful, if makeshift, witness when P is defective. P had certainly reached Lorsch

[14] R. A. Pack, *The Greek and Latin Literary Texts from Greco-Roman Egypt* (Ann Arbor, Mich., 1965), nos. 2935–52; R. Seider, 'Beiträge zur Geschichte und Paläographie der antiken Vergilhandschriften', in *Studien zum antiken Epos*, ed. H. Görgemanns and E. A. Schmidt (Meisenheim am Glan, 1976), 129–72, plates IV–XVI. Notable among the papyri are fragments of a magnificent fourth-century papyrus codex (Oxford, Ashmolean Museum P. Ant. 29; *CLA* Suppl. 1708); a third manuscript in square capitals (Cairo, Museum of Egyptian Antiquities, P. Oxy. 1098; *CLA* X 1569; s. IV); P. Strasb. Lat. 2, assigned to s. IV by Lowe (*CLA* VI. 833), but which Seider would put as early as s. I/II, making it our oldest Virgil manuscript. Milan, Ambros. Cimelio 3, ff. 113–20 (*CLA* III. 306; s. V/VI), has a bilingual Latin–Greek text, a format which crops up more often than not among the papyri.

[15] *CLA* IX. 1327.   [16] *CLA* Suppl. 1744; Chatelain, plate LXVI.

by the ninth century. If, as has been suggested,[17] it can be identified with the *Liber Vergili* which came to the monastery from the library of its former monk Gerward, it may, like its owner, have spent some time at the Carolingian court, well placed to exercise an influence on the medieval tradition and making an early bid for its title of Palatinus. If more discoveries of this sort can be made, there are obvious gains for Virgil's text. But Mynors has covered more of the ground than he modestly maintains, and his thirteen manuscripts must be a small selection of those he had examined. It is important to know what the medieval text of Virgil was like, but it has an almost negligible part to play when it comes to deciding what our poet wrote; it is so thoroughly conflated, so full of shifting alliances, that it must be wistful to hope that more gold can be disentangled from that thicket. Further study of Virgil's manuscripts will doubtless yield a rich, if at times hard-won, harvest for those who wish to illuminate specific aspects of medieval and Renaissance culture, and indeed the wider *Fortleben* of Virgil himself, but such problems as his text still presents[18] are as old as Antiquity and their solution, if there is a solution, lies in the ancient evidence and a critical understanding of his poetry. Q. Caecilius Epirota, who founded his school at Rome about 26 BC, put Virgil into the curriculum; he became a classic during his own lifetime, and his text the subject of scholarly discussion as soon as it could be questioned without fear of authoritative rebuttal. Virgilian scholarship was soon a thriving industry, and the problems lie in judging how much weight should be given to scholars with their own axes to grind – like Hyginus and Probus,[19] who supported their dubious emendations with even more dubious manuscripts 'ex domo atque familia Vergilii' or 'manu ipsius correctus' – and in sorting the grain from the chaff in scholiasts who preserve much of value but blankly misunderstood what great poetry is about.

L. D. R.

[17] Bischoff, *Lorsch*, 56. For another book which may have come from Gerward's library, see JUSTINUS.

[18] For a recent and stimulating discussion of some of these problems see E. Courtney, 'The Formation of the Text of Vergil', *BICS* 28 (1981), 13–29.

[19] For a refreshingly sceptical view, see G. P. Goold, *HSCP* 74 (1970), 161–2; J. E. G. Zetzel, ibid. 77 (1973), 233 ff.; on Probus in particular, Courtney, 24 ff.

APPENDIX VERGILIANA

An *Appendix Vergiliana* that included only the minor poems attributed to Virgil within a century or so of his death would be much slimmer than any modern edition under that title; one that included all the other poems ever attributed to him, much fatter. Modern editions owe their fairly stable content partly to the lists of juvenile works given by Donatus and Servius in their *Vitae*, partly to the conjunction of these works with others in the medieval tradition, and partly to a manuscript described in a ninth-century catalogue from Murbach.

The Murbacensis contained nine works: 1 *Dire*, 2 *Culicis*, 3 *Ethne*, 4 *Copa*, 5 *Mecenas*, 6 *Ciris*, 7 *Catalepion*, 8 *Priapeya*, 9 *Moretum*. Donatus lists *In Ballistam* + 78 + *Epigrammata* + 162 + ('de qua ambigitur') 3, Servius *In Ballistam* + 63287 + *Epigrammata* + 41; both, that is, ignore 5 and 9, Donatus ignores 4 (unless *et Copam* has dropped out), and both add *In Ballistam* and *Epigrammata*. The *Epigrammata* cannot be identified. In extant manuscripts *Priapea* refers inappropriately to the single *Priapeum Quid hoc novi est?*;[1] originally it may have referred to this together with the three *Priapea* that the manuscripts present as *Catal.* 1–3.[2] Otherwise no title poses any problem of identification. The main problem is how long the poems had been associated with one another; the suggestion that most of them were published together by Varius rests on a conviction of their genuineness, and scholars who do not share this conviction even speak of 'late Antiquity'.[3] The only ones attributed to Virgil before the time of Suetonius are *Culex* (Lucan, Statius, Martial) and *Catal.* 2 (Quintilian).

Since only two manuscripts contain as many as three works in the same order as the Murbacensis and only two late manuscripts contain in any order more than five, it is by no means clear that the Murbacensis or indeed any single manuscript gave rise to the extant tradition.[4] Nevertheless, as E. Courtney has shown in *BICS* 15 (1968), 133–41, a comprehensive stemma can be constructed with less difficulty than the absence of an archetype might have been expected to create. The main lines of his stemma will serve as a framework for the ensuing exposition.

---

[1] Some fifteenth-century manuscripts call it *minor Priapea* to distinguish it from the eighty-one *Priapea Carminis incompti . . . Priape fave*, which at that time were also attributed to Virgil.
[2] E. Gaar, *Anz. der öst. Akad.* 90 (1953), 226–7; cf. J. A. Richmond, *Hermes*, 102 (1974), 300–4.
[3] F. Vollmer, *SBAW* 1907, 337–50; R. O. A. M. Lyne, *CQ* 65 (1971), 233–8.
[4] Richmond, *RFIC* 104 (1976), 26–30, prefers to regard the Murbacensis as a fusion of what other manuscripts continued to transmit apart.

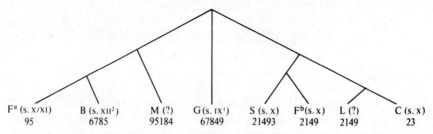

Fᵃ (s. x/xi)	B (s. xii²)	M (?)	G (s. ix¹)	S (s. x)	Fᵇ(s. x)	L (?)	C (s. x)
95	6785	95184	67849	21493	2149	2149	23

G, Graz 1814, is one of the oldest manuscripts but the newest arrival on the scene: it consists of four leaves disengaged in 1953 from an eighteenth-century register of bakers and millers. It shows signs of having been copied from a manuscript in capitals, and the hand strikes Bischoff as German.[5]

SFᵇLC almost certainly derive from a manuscript of 214936 attested in an old catalogue of St. Eucharius Trier. B, Brussels 10675–6, begins with *Ciris*, 454 and has on 459 the note 'quod in Virgilio S. Eucharii deest in libro Cirris hic est';[6] it does not look like an accident that between them B and the Eucharianus make up the contents of the Murbacensis. For the diffusion of the text much the most important of these manuscripts is L, the lost *iuvenalis ludi libellus*, represented by several witnesses of s. ix-xi and s. xv but curiously few in between; it was designed to precede the major works in a Carolingian edition.[7] C, Cambridge, University Library Kk. 5. 34, was at New Minster Winchester *c.*1000. S, a fragment in Paris lat. 17177, comes from Stavelot. F, Melk 2 (Chatelain, plate lxxiva), is a composite witness and interesting for that very reason: wherever it was written two texts of 9 were available. In 1 Fᵇ has a late relative in Escorial T.ii.9 (s. xv).

M is reconstructed from several south-German manuscripts, the oldest of which, Munich Clm 18059 (s. xi²/4), comes from Tegernsee.[8] The text of 5 that Enoch of Ascoli brought back from 'Dacia' in the 1450s derived from M.

The stemma has five other witnesses to accommodate:

(1) Independent texts of 35678 occurred in a lost manuscript, Z, copied more than once in s. xv³/4, probably at Padua, and best represented by Wolfenbüttel, Helmst. 332 (H, a. 1454).

(2) Λ, a lost manuscript similar to Z, supplied Pomponio Leto with 367, all three of which appear in the *ed. Rom.* 1471 of Virgil and the first in its less interpolated relatives Vatican lat. 3272 and British Library, Sloane 777.

---

[5] *Archival. Zeitschr.* 48 (1953), 206. For a photograph see *Anz. der öst. Akad.* 90 (1953), opposite p. 188.

[6] The view that it was actually written at St. Eucharius Trier, rather than at Liège, has gained ground: see K. Manitius, *Forschungen und Fortschritte*, 29 (1955), 317–19.

[7] See Vollmer, *SBAW* 1908. 11, a fundamental investigation of the whole tradition.

[8] See J. J. H. Savage, *HSCP* 45 (1934), 198–200.

(3) Vatican lat. 2759 (V, s. XII/XIII) offers independent texts of 2 and 8; in 8 it has several relatives of s. XIII and s. XV, in 2 only one of importance,[9] namely

(4) Rome, Cors. 43. F. 5 (Γ, c.1425), which also contains the first 5½ lines of *Aetna* in an erroneous order shared with ZΛ.

(5) The *Florilegium Gallicum* (φ, s. XII) quotes from 236 and preserves a title inexplicable unless its source contained 7 and the *Laus Pisonis* besides; such a manuscript seems to have been found at Lorsch in the 1520s by Sichardus.[10]

The stemmatic position of these witnesses, especially φ, is uncertain, but only one needs to be composite for them all to fit into place.

Work by work, then, the witnesses on which an edition must rest are these: 1 M///S/F Esc.//L; 2 ΓV//SF/CL; 3 CS/ZΛ and also the Gyraldinus, a lost manuscript of Claudian that contained a widely divergent text of vv. 138–286;[11] 4 M//G//SF/L; 5 BF/M//Z; 67 G/B/ZΛ; 8 G/BM/V/Z and also the lost *fragmentum Cuiacianum* of Tibullus, which did not derive from the archetype of GBMVZ; 9 G//FM//SF²/L.

The medieval circulation will remain obscure in detail unless more manuscripts are placed. L no doubt accounts for the quotations from 249 in Mico and Engelmodus (s. IX).[12] In Italy scarcely anyone knew 35678 until s. XV³/₄. At all dates 9, *Moretum*, tended to circulate on its own in miscellanies, and fifteenth-century copies abound.

The *ed. Rom.* 1469 of Virgil printed 2149 from a descendant of L and 5 from a descendant of Enoch's manuscript; the *ed. Rom.* 1471 added 367 from a descendant of Λ and 8 from a relative of V. For *emendatio* the best edition is the Oxford text of W. V. Clausen, F. R. D. Goodyear, E. J. Kenney, and J. A. Richmond (1966), whose symbols have been adopted above with the addition of Λ. In *recensio*, however, it has serious shortcomings, on which see M. D. R., *Maia*, 27 (1975), 231–47, and 28 (1976), 233–54.[13] For readings of the *recentiores* see R. Giomini's edition

[9] A descendant of L, Trier 1086 (W, s. IX²/₄), shows the influence of a similar text; the same interest therefore attaches to W as to F. According to Savage, 173–7, W was written either at Tours or by a scribe trained there; see also Bischoff cited by C. Murgia, *Prolegomena to Servius 5– the manuscripts* (Univ. of Cal. Publ.: Classical Studies, 11, Berkeley, 1975), 37.

[10] See B. L. Ullman, *CPh* 24 (1929), 109–11, and for the text of φ, J. Hamacher, *Florilegium Gallicum: Prolegomena und Edition der Exzerpte von Petron bis Cicero, De oratore* (Frankfurt, 1975), 139–46.

[11] See F. R. D. Goodyear, *Incerti auctoris Aetna* (Cambridge, 1965), 6–10, 29–52, and M. D. R., *Maia*, 27 (1975), 242 n. 53. A. Vilhar, *PhW* 47 (1927), 600–1, reported seeing at Rome in 1923 'bei einem Antiquar auf dem Petrusplatze' an early edition with the note 'cod. nuper legi veterr. Mon. Cass. Aen. Cir. Aet. Cul. Mor. Romae Ficinus'; more information either about this or about Vilhar would be welcome.

[12] Vollmer, *SBAW* 1907, 349–50.

[13] Add that the editor of *Est et non*, an Ausonian poem taken up in the Eucharianus, unduly subordinates V of Ausonius, Leiden, Voss. Lat. F. 111, by not realizing that ABDR further corrupt corruptions of PQ (vv. 8, 23).

(Florence, 1962²) and M. D. R.'s articles cited above, the second of which also discusses Courtney's stemma.

M. D. R.

VITRUVIUS

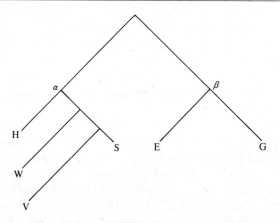

Very few of the students and admirers of the great literary legacy of the Augustan age could put their hands on their hearts and thank their lucky stars that they had been granted the opportunity to read the ten books of Vitruvius on architecture. Not so the Carolingian reader who at the end of our earliest manuscript of Vitruvius appended the comment 'compos voti factus sum qui cognoverim quae sint in structuris et aedificiis adservanda'.[1] Technological information was not so plentiful in the early years of the ninth century that Vitruvius could be taken for granted.

Of the eighty or so extant manuscripts of the *De architectura* of Vitruvius Pollio,[2] the great majority are descended from British

---

[1] Oxford, Bodl. Rawlinson D. 893, f. 136ᵛ. The last two leaves of British Library, Harley 2767 (see below) were cut out and are now part of this miscellaneous Rawlinson manuscript; for their identification, see B. Bischoff, 'Die wiedergefundene Schlussblätter des Vitruvius Harleianus', *PhW* 5 (1942), 504.

[2] A list of the surviving manuscripts is provided by C. H. Krinsky, 'Seventy-eight Vitruvius Manuscripts', *JWI* 30 (1967), 36–70. The information given there needs frequent correction, and in the case of some important manuscripts has been superseded by later publications. There is a brief but invaluable account of the tradition in Bischoff, 'Die Überlieferung der technischen Literatur', *Settimane*, 18 (1971), 267–96, plates 1–3, in particular 272–4; this is reprinted in *Mitt. Stud.* iii. 277–97, plates XIX-XXI, to which the notes below refer.

Library, Harley 2767 (H), written on the border between east and west Francia[3] about the year 800. Its splendid calligraphy and its dominant influence on the later tradition suggest that it might well have been written at the palace scriptorium of Charlemagne.[4] This is supported by the fact that the first two men to show any knowledge of Vitruvius after the Dark Ages are Alcuin, in a letter written to Charlemagne between 801 and 804,[5] and Einhard,[6] who in addition to his close association with the court had a practical interest in building. The whole tradition shows signs of a derivation from an archetype in Anglo-Saxon script,[7] and it has been suggested that Alcuin had imported a text from England.[8]

Among the descendants of H are a number of early manuscripts, all dating from before the twelfth century, which show that by then this form of the text had spread over a wide area ranging from north-west Germany through the Low Countries and France to England. The oldest of these is Paris lat. 10277, written at Corbie in the third quarter of the ninth century.[9] It may have migrated from Corbie at an early date;[10] a copy, Vatican, Reg. lat. 1504, s. x/xi, was written at Saint-Thierry Reims.[11] This is one of the branches of the prolific H family.[12] The others which can be traced are represented by (a) Escorial F. iii. 19 (s. ix, Soissons) and Leiden, Voss. Lat. F. 88 (s. x, north-west Germany); (b) Leeuwarden 51 and its copy Paris lat. 7227, both s. x/xi (the latter certainly of French origin) and bearing illustrations of the Archimedian water-screw; and (c) Leiden, Voss. Lat. F. 107 (s. x^2, west Germany or Belgium), Brussels 5353 (s. xi, written at St. Peter's Cologne), and British Library, Cotton Cleo. D. i (s. xi, English?).

It was not until 1879 that there appeared an independent witness to the α branch of the tradition, when A. Giry discovered a tenth-century manuscript at Sélestat, now Bibliothèque et Archives Municipales 17 (S), written in the first half of the century and almost certainly at St. Gall.[13] The two other independent witnesses to α are of considerably

---

[3] Bischoff, *PhW* 5 (1942), 504. Scant attention was paid to his denial that H could possibly have been written at Cologne, as proposed by L. W. Jones, *The Script of Cologne from Hildebald to Hermann* (Cambridge, Mass., 1932), 65 f., plate 89.   [4] *Mitt. Stud.* iii. 282.

[5] *MGH, Epist.* iv (Berlin, 1895), p. 472. 1–13.

[6] Ibid. v (Berlin, 1899), p. 138. 18–26 (Einhard to Vussin, between 823 and 840).

[7] Rose (1899 edn.), vi.

[8] *Mitt. Stud.* iii. 281; cf. T. J. Brown, *Settimane*, 22.1 (1975), 276, 286. There is no evidence for Vitruvius in England at this date.   [9] Bischoff, *Mitt. Stud.* i. 59.

[10] It is not listed in the twelfth-century Corbie catalogue and seems to have been later at Laon.

[11] Bischoff, cited in Pellegrin, *Manuscrits*, ii. 1, 247 n. 2.

[12] For the H family see P. Ruffel and J. Soubiran, 'Recherches sur la tradition manuscrite de Vitruve', *Pallas*, 9 (1960), 113–44.

[13] A. Giry, 'Notes sur un manuscrit de la Bibliothèque de Schlestadt', *RPh* 3 (1879), 16–18. For its date and provenance, see *Mitt. Stud.* iii. 282 n. 20. More information in K. A. Wirth, 'Bemerkungen zum Nachleben Vitruvs im 9. und 10. Jahrhundert und zu dem Schlettstädter Vitruv-Codex', *Kunstchronik*, 20 (1967), 281–91, with four plates of S.

later date and both French books: Vatican, Reg. lat. 2079 (s. XII ex., at one time at Rouen = W) and Reg. lat. 1328 (s. XV in. = V).[14]

The β family is a valuable complement to α, especially as it presents in places whole groups of words which the latter omits. But β manuscripts are rare, and only two independent witnesses survive. The older is Wolfenbüttel, Gud. lat. 132 (E), written in the mid- or late ninth century at Corvey;[15] unfortunately it contains only excerpts from Vitruvius inserted as explanatory material into Faventinus' epitome of the *De architectura*. The other, Gud. lat. 69 (G), s. XI, is complete; it was at the abbey of St. Pantaleon Cologne in the fifteenth century and was probably written there.[16] The only other pre-humanist manuscript of the β family is Vatican, Urb. lat. 293, s. XI. It is a direct copy of G. It is of German origin[17] and bears (f. 1^r) the *ex libris* of an unspecified St. Martin's abbey; under the circumstances this is likely to be St. Martin's Cologne.[18] Urb. lat. 293 reached Italy in time to become part of the library of Federico Duke of Urbino (d. 1482).

Germany obviously dominates the vital phase of Vitruvius' transmission, and we know that there were copies, too, in the ninth century at Reichenau[19] and its daughter house Murbach.[20] It is difficult not to see such figures as Einhard lurking in the background, men equally at home in the workshop as in the library and scriptorium. An interest in technology has fused at an early stage the α tradition of Vitruvius with that of a series of technical recipes known as the *Mappae clavicula*.[21] This remarkable collection tells one how to gild metals and distil alcohol, how to make various compounds, from pigments and varnish to incendiary bombs. It has a particular bearing on the making of stained glass and the illumination of manuscripts. These recipes appear in various degrees and combinations in H (and some of its descendants), in S, and W; and it is noteworthy that in the Reichenau catalogue of 821–2 Vitruvius is followed by 'Mappae clavicula de efficiendo auro volumen I'.[22] It is significant that S has derived one group of recipes from H, where they appear as an appendix to Vitruvius

---

[14] On the Reginenses, cf. Pellegrin, *Manuscrits*, ii. 1, 167 f., 504 f.

[15] Bischoff, cited by C. Leonardi, *Aevum*, 34 (1960), 493.

[16] H. Degering, 'Theophilus Presbiter, qui et Rugerus', *Westfälische Studien. Beiträge zur Geschichte der Wissenschaft, Kunst und Literatur in Westfalen Alois Bömer zum 60. Geburtstag gewidmet* (Leipzig, 1928), 252.

[17] It has glosses in High German on f. 1^r: R. Bergmann, *Verzeichnis der althochdeutschen Glossenhandschriften* (Berlin, 1973), no. 830. For further information see Pellegrin, *Manuscrits*, ii. 2, 533–4; *CLA* I. 116.   [18] Degering, 258.

[19] P. Lehmann, *Mittelalterliche Bibliothekskataloge Deutschlands und der Schweiz*, i (Munich, 1918), 247, 255.

[20] W. Milde, *Der Bibliothekskatalog des Klosters Murbach aus dem 9. Jahrhundert* (Beihefte zum Euphorion, 4, Heidelberg, 1968), 48 no. 320.

[21] For an account of the *Mappae clavicula* see, e.g., C. S. Smith and J. G. Hawthorne, *Mappae clavicula. A little Key to the World of Medieval Techniques*, *Trans. Am. Philos. Soc.* 64.4 (Philadelphia, 1974).   [22] Lehmann, 247.

and consist of original entries by several hands;[23] it has also incorporated with them the comment 'compos voti factus sum . . .' quoted above.

The more interesting aspects of the later tradition[24] are the diffusion of the text to England and its arrival in Italy. It has long been recognized that the mainspring of the English tradition is Cotton Cleo. D. I. This manuscript was certainly at St. Augustine's Canterbury in the fifteenth century,[25] and probably much earlier; it was in England by the twelfth century and may well be of English origin. It seems likely that Vitruvius was one of the texts brought over the Channel in the tenth century. Cleo. D. I is the head of a large family which numbers among its earlier representatives British Library, Harley 3859 (s. XII[1]),[26] Add. 38818 (s. XII, ? Durham), Berlin (West) lat. 2° 601 (s. XII), and Leiden, Voss. Lat. F. 93 (s. XIII, Winchester). A manuscript of this type was excerpted for his *Polyhistor* by William of Malmesbury.[27]

For our knowledge of the circulation of Vitruvius in the Italian Renaissance we are indebted to the researches of Lucia Ciapponi, who demonstrated[28] that Petrarch was the original author of the annotations transmitted in an Italian manuscript now in the Bodleian Library, Auct. F. 5. 7 (s. XIV[2]). Auct. F. 5. 7 is thus a descendant of Petrarch's own annotated Vitruvius. It has a text of the G type and Ciapponi suggests that Petrarch had acquired such a manuscript in France between 1350 and 1355.[29] The Vitruvius which Boccaccio is known to have possessed had a text very close to that of Petrarch's manuscript; Petrarch emerges once again as the source of an Italian tradition which in this case can be traced to Boccaccio, and beyond him to Giovanni Dondi dall' Orologio and possibly Nicola Acciaiuoli.[30] This cannot of course have been the first reappearance of Vitruvius in Italy. There must have been a manuscript at Montecassino in the earlier part of the twelfth century, for

---

[23] *Mitt. Stud.* iii. 281 n. 12. Bischoff points out that the stemmata currently proposed for Vitruvius do not take account of the fact that L (Leiden, Voss. Lat. F. 88), e (Escorial F. III. 19), and S have derived this group of recipes from H. This is not surprising in the case of L and e, which are derived from H for Vitruvius as well, but their appearance in S is more remarkable and deserves further investigation. It would seem that one of the compilers of S, presumably at St. Gall, had access to H or to a copy of it. The independence of SWV for the text of Vitruvius depends basically on their having a group of words (1.1 *cuius iudicio probantur omnia*) omitted in H.

[24] For such evidence as we have for the wider diffusion of Vitruvius in France and Germany, see Manitius, *Handschriften*, 82 f.; Krinsky, 36 ff.

[25] M. R. James, *The Ancient Libraries of Canterbury and Dover* (Cambridge, 1903), 320, 519. Oxford, St. John's College 66B was copied at St. Augustine's in 1316.

[26] See *APPENDIX SALLUSTIANA* 2, n. 8.

[27] H. Testroet, *HSCP* 76 (1972), 308; R. M. T., *Rev. bén.* 85 (1975), 380.

[28] L. A. Ciapponi, 'Il "De Architectura" di Vitruvio nel primo umanesimo (dal ms. Bodl. Auct. F. 5. 7)', *IMU* 3 (1960), 59–99.

[29] Ibid. 96 f. Vincent of Beauvais used a non-H text, but there is no evidence at present for the existence of the G strain of text in France.

[30] Ibid. 83 ff. We know nothing of Acciaiuoli's manuscript, listed in an inventory of 1359.

Peter the Deacon records[31] that he had copied one; but there is no evidence at present that this was more than an isolated phenomenon. Another early Italian Vitruvius which Ciapponi mentions, and about which one would like to know more, is Paris lat. 7228, written about the middle of the fourteenth century and of Bolognese origin.[32]

The *editio princeps* was printed in Rome between 1483 and 1490 by Eucharius Silber and edited by Johannes Sulpitius, but it was the illustrated edition first published in 1511 by Fra Giocondo (the fourth edition to appear) that had the most influence. The first critical edition, by V. Rose and H. Müller-Strübing (Teubner, 1867), is still the most useful, as much for its critical qualities and display of manuscript readings as for its pagination and lineation, to which the *Index Verborum* of H. Nohl (Leipzig, 1876; repr. Darmstadt, 1965) and succeeding scholarly literature refers. The second Teubner edition by V. Rose alone (1899) took S into account for the first time, but it is marred by needless emendation, as is the subsequent Teubner by F. Krohn (1912). Both considered S to be a descendant of H, and neither took into account W or V. P. Ruffel and J. Soubiran[33] were the first to collate W and V systematically in preparation for the Budé edition, but their stemma requires five independent witnesses to the archetype, and this can be shown to be mistaken.[34] Currently in progress is the Budé edition, of which two volumes have appeared so far, Livre VIII by L. Callebat (1973) and Livre IX by J. Soubiran (1969).

Faventinus

Vitruvius' cognomen is known only from the opening words of the epitome of the *De architectura* made by Faventinus in the late third or early fourth century AD. Faventinus himself had no name at all when he first appeared in print in 1540 in an edition published at Paris by Guillaume Postel and edited by Michael Vascosanus. He remained anonymous until 1871, when a manuscript in Vienna was discovered which gives both his name, M. Cetius Faventinus, and what appears to be the correct title of the epitome, *Artis architectonicae privatis usibus adbreviatus liber.*[35] This manuscript, Vienna 15411, was written in the first half of the ninth century at Salzburg.[36] About the same time

---

[31] *De vir. ill.* 47: *Vitruvium de architectura mundi emendans breviavit.* By *breviavit* he apparently means 'copied': cf. E. Caspar, *Petrus Diaconus und die Monte Cassineser Fälschungen* (Berlin, 1909), 129 n. 8.

[32] É. Pellegrin, *La Bibliothèque des Visconti et des Sforza ducs de Milan, au XVe siècle* (Paris, 1955), 130 no. 254. We are grateful to Dr François Avril for his opinion on the date and origin of this manuscript.

[33] In the article cited above (n. 12), 3–154.

[34] J. P. Chausserie-Laprée, 'Un nouveau stemma Vitruvien', *REL* 47 (1969), 347–77, returning to the bifid stemma first postulated by Rose and Müller-Strübing.

[35] H. Plommer, *Vitruvius and Later Roman Building Manuals* (Cambridge, 1973), 1 n. 1, 86.

[36] *Mitt. Stud.* iii. 282. Only one leaf survives.

Reginbert of Reichenau, a monk who died in 846, owned or copied 'libri duo de architectura Faventini'.[37]

The one other manuscript to give the author's name and the title in this form is the Sélestat manuscript of Vitruvius, in which the first thirteen chapters of the epitome precede the *De architectura*. Thus this tradition of Faventinus was known at Reichenau and Salzburg in the first half of the ninth century, and a century later at St. Gall.

The other extant manuscripts, which do not name the author and have a different title,[38] clearly constitute a separate branch of the tradition. They include three of the manuscripts of Vitruvius already mentioned, Paris lat. 10277 (Corbie), its copy Vatican, Reg. lat. 1504 (Reims), and Wolfenbüttel, Gud. lat. 132 (Corvey). These are joined by a pair which do not include Vitruvius: Berne 722, which contains a single leaf of Faventinus (s. IX³/₄, Fulda),[39] and Valenciennes 337 (s. IX, at Saint-Amand in the twelfth century).[40] In all later manuscripts the epitome has been interpolated with other technical matter.

The Teubner edition of Vitruvius by V. Rose (1899) included Faventinus and incorporated the readings of S for the first time. The most recent text is that of F. Krohn (1912); a commentary and translation was published in 1973 by H. Plommer.[41]

S. F. W.

L. D. R.

[37] Lehmann, 258.

[38] *De diversis fabricis architectonicae*, or something similar.

[39] Information supplied by Professor Bischoff. For references to the epitome in the Fulda catalogue, see K. Christ, 'Die Bibliothek des Klosters Fulda im 16. Jahrhundert', *ZBB*, Beiheft 64 (1933), 133, 215, 309.

[40] Delisle, ii. 454, no. 201.

[41] See n. 35 above, and Plommer's further remarks in *PCPS* 24 (1978), 116 f.

Monastic and other centres of Medieval Europe.

INDEX OF MANUSCRIPTS

INDEX OF NAMES AND
SELECTED SUBJECTS